Standard of Power

By the same author

The Grand Scuttle
The Last Corsair
The Ship that Changed the World
The Atlantic Campaign
The Pacific Campaign
Freedom was Never like This
Stealth at Sea
The Riddle of the Titanic (with Robin Gardiner)
The Good Nazi: the Life and Lies of Albert Speer

Standard of Power

The Royal Navy in the Twentieth Century

Dan van der Vat

HUTCHINSON
LONDON

First published in the United Kingdom in 2000 by Hutchinson

The Random House Group Limited
20 Vauxhall Bridge Road, London SW1V 2SA

Random House Australia (Pty) Limited
20 Alfred Street, Milsons Point, Sydney,
New South Wales 2061, Australia

Random House New Zealand Limited
18 Poland Road, Glenfield,
Auckland 10, New Zealand

Random House (Pty) Limited
Endulini, 5a Jubilee Road, Parktown 2193, South Africa

Random House Group Limited Reg. No. 954009
www.randomhouse.co.uk

A CIP catalogue record for this book
is available from the British Library

Papers used by Random House are natural, recyclable products made from wood grown in sustainable forests. The manufacturing processes conform to the environmental regulations of the country of origin.

ISBN 0 09 180121 4

Typeset by MATS, Southend-on-Sea, Essex
Printed and bound in Great Britain by
Biddles Ltd, Guildford and King's Lynn

It is on the Navy under the Providence of God
that the safety, honour and welfare of this realm
do chiefly attend.

King Charles II, *Preamble to the Articles of War*

A ship, like a shell, is merely a weapon to be
expended profitably.

B. H. Liddell Hart, *History of the First World
War*

If blood be the price of Admiralty,
Lord God, we ha' paid it in full!

Rudyard Kipling, *The Song of the Dead*

Contents

Illustrations

First section

Grand Admiral Alfred von Tirpitz (*AKG*)
Admiral of the Fleet Lord Fisher (*IWM* Q22155)
HMS Dreadnought, 1907 (*IWM* Q21182)
Royal Review of the Fleet at Spithead, 1914 (*IWM* Q22094)
Cruiser messdeck in the First World War (*IWM* Q18676)
The *Lusitania* (*Hulton Getty*)
HMS Invincible, sinking at Jutland (*IWM* SP2470)
Admiral Sir John Jellicoe (*IWM* Q55499)
Admiral Reinhard Scheer (*IWM* Q20348)
Admiral Sir David Beatty (*IWM* Q19571)
Vice-Admiral Franz von Hipper (*AKG*)
U-Boats at Kiel (*IWM* HU3280)
Admiral Graf Spee in flames off Montevideo (*IWM* A3)
Admiral of the Fleet Sir Dudley Pound (*IWM* A16717)
Admiral of the Fleet Sir Andrew Cunningham (*IWM* A15702)
Admiral Sir Bertram Ramsay (*IWM* A23440)
Grand Admiral Erich Raeder (*Hulton Getty*)
Admiral Doenitz (*IWM* A26643)
Troops evacuated from Dunkirk (*IWM* C1741)
Surrender of Singapore (*Topham*)

Second section

Western Approaches Command during the Battle of the Atlantic
  (*IWM* A4527)
The corvette *HMS Pentstemon* (*IWM* A5448)
Convoy with naval escort (*IWM* A964)
Fairey Swordfish (*IWM* A3532)
Liberator (*IWM* CH2978)

HMS Hood (*IWM* A111)
The *Bismarck* (*IWM* HU7927)
Landing troops at Suez (Royal Naval Museum)
HMS Devonshire with *HMS Ark Royal* (*IWM* A34744)
HMS Dreadnought, 1962 (*IWM* A34690)
HMS Invincible (*IWM* FL2422)
Admiral Sir John Fieldhouse (*IWM* MH30655)
Ian McDonald (*PA*)
Major-General Jeremy Moore with Admiral John (Sandy)
    Woodward (*IWM* FKD2608)
HMS Sheffield struck by an Exocet (*IWM* FKD66)
The Royal Navy in the Gulf Armilla Patrol (*IWM* GLF830)
Tomahawk missile loaded on to *HMS Splendid* © Crown
    copyright 2000
Vanguard class Trident-missile nuclear submarine © Crown
    copyright MOD
Admiral Sir Michael Boyce, First Sea Lord © Crown copyright
    MOD

AKG – © AKG London
IWM – © Imperial War Museum
Hulton Getty – © Hulton Getty Picture Collection
Topham – © Topham Picturepoint Collection
PA – © 'PA' Photos Ltd

Preface

A wayward course which began accidentally in 1978 in the Orkney Islands, principal haven of the British fleet in two world wars, culminates here twenty-two years later. This volume is intended, like all my previous books on the maritime past, for the general reader and is the product of more than two decades of reading, research and writing about the naval history of the century just ended. A journalistic assignment all those years ago which did not work out as planned left me with a day or two to explore the shores of Scapa Flow. In the little town of Stromness I found in the local museum a display on the mass scuttling of the German Imperial High Seas Fleet by its own crews in the anchorage on 21 June 1919. Shortly after my visit *The Times*, for which I then worked, was shut down for a year by its own management in a bungled clash with the old-style print unions over 'new' technology. I used the unexpected free time to research my first book, on the scuttling, which duly appeared after many vicissitudes in 1982 and even won a literary prize. One thing led to another, more precisely five others – further forays into modern naval history before this one.

I have written books as long as this dealing with the history of just one type of vessel (the submarine) or a single campaign (the Battle of the Atlantic, the war in the Pacific). In seeking to encompass the most important century in the history of the Royal Navy within the confines of a book of this size, therefore, what to leave out has been at least as problematical as what to include. It is not for me to describe this volume as a 'miracle of compression', but I have tried to include as much as possible. Inevitably I have been forced to leave some things out, which means that I shall not have satisfied everyone with the breadth of my coverage.

The focus is operational, which means that the ten years of conflict in two world wars command the lion's share of the space. But I have also attempted to provide a fair measure of context to help the reader understand what happened, and what went wrong, before, during and after those protracted struggles. Diplomacy, politics, finance, technology, strategy and tactics all receive attention in the background to events at sea. So do the conditions in which officers and sailors had to serve in peace and war.

The story of the British Navy over the past hundred years is rich in ironies. The most arresting one concerns a fleet obsessed with the 'big-gun' battleship which was brought to the brink of defeat twice in twenty-six years by the frail, pre-nuclear submarine. And when the double lesson of the vital importance of submarines and of anti-submarine warfare (ASW) had at last been thoroughly absorbed, the ASW fleet built up in the 1970s was faced with the unlikely challenge of mounting a vintage colonial expedition to the south Atlantic, in order to recover unwanted British possessions seized by a Latin American dictatorship.

There are many subsidiary ironies, such as a fleet which historically neglected naval aviation producing a whole series of radical advances in carrier equipment and construction, from the steam catapult to the Harrier aircraft, eagerly adopted by the postwar world's leading fleet, the US Navy's; or a Labour Party which, when in power in the 1960s, 'abolished' the British fleet aircraft carrier, only to reintroduce it when it was in office once more at the very end of the century. The submarine, dismissed by the admirals as 'damned un-English' in 1900, dominated the defence budget and the British fleet in 2000 as the custodian of a British 'independent' deterrent that would not have been possible without detailed technological cooperation from the United States. There were constant cuts in the surface fleet from 1945, but Britain was left with far more destructive power at sea, in the shape of its four 'Trident' nuclear ballistic-missile submarines (the most modern of their kind in the world) and a dozen 'fleet' or hunter-killer boats, 'the new capital ships', than it had ever possessed in all its earlier fleets combined. And a surface fleet always strapped for cash somehow managed to parade a long series of major technical advances, such as the first fibreglass warship, the gas-turbine engine and the world's quietest submarines. Personal ironies also abound, starting with Churchill, political chief of the Navy at the beginning of both world wars, forced to resign in the First for bungling and damned as a 'danger to the empire', only to be hailed in the Second by the jubilant signal that went round the fleet: 'Winston is back'.

Since as a non-naval person I have so often been asked to explain my interest in nautical history – whether it derives from service at sea (no), jingoism (no) or aggressiveness (likewise no) – I may permit myself to make the attempt on paper here. What fascinates me above all is how commanders and sailors coped when a mistake at any level could have such fateful, possibly fatal, results, such as the First Sea Lord whose order to scatter led to the disaster of convoy PQ 17 or the man who painted over a tiny hole in a torpedo-tube indicator and unwittingly doomed a submarine. There is also the fact that war at sea, much more often than overland or from the air, can be fought without what is nowadays euphemistically called 'collateral damage', i.e. massive destruction of civilian lives and property. The biggest naval campaign in world history since 1945, the Falklands conflict, is a case in point. So are Jutland and Matapan. This is not to ignore the non-military but undoubtedly special status (in every sense) of those brave volunteers in the Merchant Marine who crewed the commercial vessels that have always been a principal target, known in advance, for surface warships and latterly submarines in wartime; and the number of casualties were a Trident missile ever to be fired in anger does not bear thinking about.

From the very beginning of the twentieth century, modern communications made it possible for political and naval leaders to move warships round the globe in 'real time' like pieces on a chessboard. Navies were and remain the principal, often the only, instrument whereby military force can be applied far from home. Already by 1907 wireless was well-nigh universal in navies. Detailed records of these signals survive, helping the historian, provided he is suitably wary of hindsight, to analyse how, when, where and why something went wrong – or right. It is an incontrovertible fact that a great deal went wrong, whether in battle or in preparing for it. Inadequate ships and equipment, panicky politicians, over-promoted admirals and incompetents at every level all helped to ensure that the record of the Royal Navy over the past hundred years is riddled with error, complacency, inertia and inability to learn the lessons of history. This is not a story of glory, but rather a 'warts and all' account of a service which, more than any other British institution, can fairly be said to have saved the nation itself twice over, just as it was always intended to do. It did so not by flashes of glory, although there were plenty of those, but by dogged, unglamorous determination and hard work, often in gruelling circumstances where bravery and dedication beyond the call of duty became unrecorded routine.

The Royal Navy began the century as the pride of the nation and ended it not only smaller in numbers of ships and personnel alike than for a century and a half but also further away from the heart of national consciousness than at any time since Nelson's strategic victory at the Battle of Trafalgar in 1805. Most of the naval bases and shore establishments all over the country which constantly reminded local people of the Navy's existence have been closed. All the same, service in today's Navy is more likely to involve working ashore than at sea, and the complexity of even the lowliest jobs is awe-inspiring. The Navy has almost always had a recruiting problem; but there were signs at the turn of the century that this was becoming more and more intractable as an island nation appeared to be turning its back upon, and losing interest in, the sea which had so often preserved its independence, its freedom and its power. Britain all but stopped building ships, flagged out its merchant fleet and seldom thought of the Royal Navy, especially after it ceased to have an identifiable potential enemy for its monstrous firepower. Even Britain's status as an island-nation was compromised by the Channel Tunnel which had once been a gleam in the eye of Napoleon. Deference was out of style, women went down to the sea in warships, and homosexuality, never absent if we are honest, officially emerged from the locker by order of the European Court of Human Rights. Times they were a-changing and the Royal Navy changed with them.

I am most grateful for the support and encouragement of my literary agent, Michael Shaw at Curtis Brown, my editor and publisher, Tony Whittome, Editorial Director at Random House, and Nicholas Blake, copy editor with an eagle eye. My thanks also to the staffs of the London Library, the libraries of the London Borough of Richmond upon Thames and the archives mentioned above. I should further like to place on record my profound gratitude for the advice, moral support and other kindnesses freely dispensed over many years by Richard Hough, erstwhile doyen of British naval historians and in many ways my informal mentor in this field, who sadly died in 1999. None of these is responsible for any error or omission in what follows.

Introduction – The Finest Hour

Towards the end of April 1943, forty-two battered merchant ships, mostly unladen, mostly British, assembled in the estuary of the River Mersey, off the north-west coast of England. The freighters were assigned to Convoy ONS 5, outward bound to New York and slow. Most were destined for New York itself, where they would load food and munitions to help sustain the United Kingdom's resistance to Nazi Germany and prepare for the planned invasion of Hitler's 'Fortress Europe'. In charge of the merchantmen as convoy commodore was Captain Brook of the Royal Naval Reserve. Assigned as their close escort for the slow progress across the north Atlantic at seven to nine knots was the Royal Navy's Support Group B7, led by Commander Peter Gretton, RN, Senior Officer, Escort (SOE). His destroyer, HMS *Duncan*, was accompanied by another destroyer, a frigate, four corvettes and two armed trawlers. The group was controlled by Headquarters, Western Approaches Command, in a bunker beneath the streets of Liverpool, nerve-centre of the defence against Germany's second attempt in a generation to besiege Britain by submarine and starve it into submission.

As usual, the formation's sailing was detected by the German naval decryption service, which routinely deciphered the departure message listing the final composition of a convoy. The U-boat Command in occupied France mustered by radio a 'wolf pack' of (initially) sixteen submarines in a patrol-line south of Iceland to attack ONS 5. There were at least thirty more U-boats available in the area. The pack was gathered on the customary ad hoc basis and was given the codename 'Star'.

One of the pack, *U650* (Lieutenant von Witzendorff), duly sighted the convoy on 28 April and reported it to headquarters. Almost immediately it was forced to dive by Catalina flying boats of the United States Army Air Force, patrolling from Iceland. During the night the British surface escort detected several U-boats by ASDIC echo-sounder and damaged three in depth-charge attacks. At 0730 on the 29th, *U258* (Lieutenant-Commander von Mässenhausen) sank the Germans' first victim, the American steamer *McKeesport*, even as a Catalina damaged another member of the pack.

In Liverpool, Admiral Sir Max Horton, Commander-in-Chief, Western Approaches, decided to send reinforcements. One destroyer was detached from slow convoy SC 127, sailing in the opposite direction, and four destroyers of the 3rd Escort Group, a tactical reinforcement unit commanded by Captain J. A. McCoy, RN, were dispatched eastward from St John's, Newfoundland. On the 30th the weather turned foul, grounding air patrols but also causing the Germans temporarily to lose contact with ONS 5. On the escorts the characteristic 'pinging' of the ASDIC submarine detectors was barely audible above the roar of wind and waves. The convoy was forced to heave to in the storm but eleven of its ships fell out, left to make their own way as 'stragglers'. Meanwhile many U-boats had been diverted to attack the eastbound SC 128, located by German signals intelligence; but the Admiralty, warned by the no less accomplished British eavesdroppers constantly sifting through the German traffic, had ordered the convoy to divert out of danger. Meanwhile a Royal Canadian Air Force (RCAF) patrol destroyed *U209* by depth charges; *U630* vanished by unknown cause at the same time.

By 4 May the U-boat command had assembled some forty submarines into the 'Fink' (finch) pack from other groups, including 'Star' – the largest concentration of U-boats against a single convoy of the entire war. The target was still SC 128; but that evening ONS 5, now consisting of thirty-one ships, unwittingly sailed into the midst of the pack, just as Commander Gretton was forced to withdraw his own ship and three of McCoy's to Iceland to refuel after five days struggling against the appalling weather. The Germans, having gained some relief from the turbulence by submerging as much as possible, set about picking off six freighters and one straggler from ONS 5. Another five were torpedoed and sunk the next day, although several U-boats were damaged. A late afternoon mist seduced the Germans into a fatal charge on the surface; their radar technology was backward and their presumed 'invisibility' was pierced by the escorts' latest sets, in the greatest coup thus far achieved by this new technology. The 1st Escort Group of five ships (Commander G. N. Brewer, RN), called out by Horton from St John's as further reinforcement, joined the ensuing melee in its final stage, when four U-boats were sunk and several others damaged.

On 7 May the Germans ordered all U-boats involved in the action to withdraw. The final score in the battle for ONS 5 was eight convoyed ships and five stragglers sunk, nearly all of them sailing in ballast, against seven U-boats lost (five to Royal Navy surface escorts, one to aircraft and one to unknown cause, probably air attack) and five badly damaged. Of the nineteen surface escorts engaged, none was hit.

Thirty-six U-boats were, however, still on hand to attack convoys HX 237 (fast from Halifax and New York) and SC 129, in the week beginning 7 May. The former's protection included HMS *Biter*, the Royal Navy's first escort aircraft carrier, which sank one U-boat. Shore-based Very Long Range (VLR) Liberator anti-submarine aircraft sank a second, and helped the surface escorts sink a third, in the fighting around HX 237; the Germans sank three merchant ships from it. But they managed to destroy only two from SC 129, for two U-boats lost and a few damaged.

Even so there were still thirty U-boats on hand to attack the thirty-eight ships of SC 130 in mid-May. Captain Forsythe, RNR, was commodore and Commander Gretton was once again SOE with Support Group B7, backed by the 5th Escort Group (Captain E. M. C. Abel Smith, RN) including *Biter*. At their conference before departure, Gretton told Forsythe that he was particularly anxious not to be delayed on this voyage as he had a very important appointment on arrival – his wedding. Promising to do his best, Forsythe said he had an engagement of his own to which he attached considerable weight – a round of golf.

The homeward-bound voyage of SC 130 from Canada proved to be an unprecedented triumphal progress. Sighted on the night of 18 to 19 May by *U304* (Lieutenant Koch), the convoy evaded an attack from three submarines by a sharp change of course on the morning of the 19th. A single VLR Liberator deterred no fewer than six U-boats by dropping depth charges to force them under while calling up surface escorts to hunt them. One boat was damaged and another sunk. Around noon, Brewer's group caught up with the convoy, sighting and damaging two more boats and sinking *U954*; among those lost on this submarine was

Sub-Lieutenant Peter Dönitz, aged twenty, younger son of Grand-Admiral Karl Dönitz, Commander-in-Chief of the German Navy and still personally heading the U-boat arm as he had been since before the war.

Three more Liberators from 120 Squadron, RAF Coastal Command, arrived in time to force a dozen submarines underwater in the afternoon. During the night the plethora of escorts managed to force all remaining U-boats to disperse and lose touch with SC 130, sinking one in the process. The last attack, by the lone *U92* (Lieutenant-Commander Oelrich), failed completely. As the Germans broke off on the morning of 20 May, a patrolling Liberator sank *U258*. The Germans had lost five boats without damaging a single merchantman or escort. The convoy reached Londonderry, Northern Ireland, ahead of schedule. Commander Gretton was thus comfortably on time for his wedding to Judy Du Vivier, a 'Wren' officer – and Captain Forsythe teed off as arranged.

The roughly one-for-one exchange rate between attacking submarines and defending escorts in the clashes over ONS 5, HX 237 and SC 129 was already unsustainable for a German U-boat force of some 400, of which barely a third was operational at any one time, the rest being on the way out, on the way home, training or refitting. But to lose five submarines in a single action with nothing at all to show for them was catastrophic.

Yet only two months earlier, in March 1943, the Admiralty had been reduced to despair by a gigantic double battle involving four large eastbound, fully laden convoys and forty U-boats which shifted in and out of half a dozen packs. In the first part of the engagement, convoys SC 121 and HX 228 lost a combined total of seventeen merchantmen out of 113, and one destroyer, against only two U-boats sunk. In the even fiercer combined clash over SC 122 and HX 229, spread over hundreds of square miles of gale-lashed ocean, twenty-two merchantmen out of ninety were lost, a total of 146,000 tons of shipping and an all-time record for a single convoy action. One destroyer was sunk by torpedo attack and one trawler foundered in a squall. Only one U-boat was destroyed.

There were so many convoys, and so many U-boats, at sea in the north Atlantic at this stage of the war that the Admiralty's Operational Intelligence Centre with its Submarine Tracking Room, directly linked to Western Approaches, found it ever harder to steer shipping out of danger through analysis of enemy radio traffic and penetration of signals by the Government Code and Cipher School at Bletchley Park in Buckinghamshire. Further, the weather in March 1943 was so bad that air cover was unsustainable for most of the month. The first escort carrier to take part in the 'Battle of the Atlantic', USS *Bogue*, sailed with HX 228 – but was unable to fly her aircraft in the storms and had to take refuge in the middle of the convoy she was meant to be protecting.

Most importantly, at the end of the month, President Franklin D. Roosevelt ordered the US Navy to transfer sixty Liberators from the Pacific to anti-submarine patrol over the north Atlantic, and the US Army Air Force to reassign seventy-five from Europe and North Africa for the same purpose. Churchill ordered RAF Bomber Command to hand over 120 Liberators to Coastal Command, which was under the operational control of the Admiralty. These aircraft, and the first handful of British and American escort carriers, at last extended air power all over the ocean – the strategic keystone of the triumphal transatlantic arch.

Admiral Horton immediately recognized the fight for ONS 5 as the turning point in the long and gruelling Atlantic campaign. SC 130 was incontrovertible proof of the victory for which tens of thousands of seamen from the Royal, Merchant and Allied navies had been dying, suffering and praying since they went to war against Germany in September 1939. The transatlantic lifeline, which they fought so hard to keep open and which the German U-boat service, by far the most cost-effective arm of the Wehrmacht, came so close to cutting, was the main artery of Britain's survival and of ultimate victory against Hitler, the most dangerous enemy the country ever faced.

On 24 May 1943, Admiral Dönitz ordered his U-boats to withdraw from the north Atlantic. The Royal Navy had won the most important victory in all the centuries of its existence. Admiral Horton signalled to all escorts:

> In the last two months the Battle of the Atlantic has undergone a decisive change in our favour . . . All escort groups, support groups, escort carriers and their machines as well as the aircraft from the various air commands have contributed to this great success . . . The climax of the battle has been surmounted.

The Royal Air Force and its airborne allies, the United States and (especially) Royal Canadian navies, together with ships and aircraft from a dozen other countries as far apart as Australia and Norway, had all played their part, but it was overwhelmingly a British, and specifically a Royal Navy, triumph. The war for Europe still had two hard years to run before final and total victory; but by May 1943 the Navy had already made the most important strategic contribution to the defeat of an expansionist Germany – for the second time in twenty-five years.

It was the finest hour of British seapower in a uniquely turbulent century – which for the Royal Navy really began in 1898. In that year, the Navy was enjoying a revival in public interest after decades of inertia and neglect, during which Britannia's claim to rule the waves was based largely on a bluff that had never been called. The Navy League was founded in 1895 to foster the renewed interest, and little boys of all classes were commonly attired in sailor-suits. A near-flood of books and magazines fed a healthy public appetite for naval news, and the lay press, especially the *Daily Mail*, founded in 1896 (as was the Navy Records Society), displayed a generally positive interest in the fleet and its well-being. Once again the Navy was admired as an institution, part of the fabric of the nation and supreme guarantor of its empire and place in the world. All this was providential, because the complacency which had settled on the Navy after the most glorious victory in its history, at Trafalgar in 1805, was about to be dispelled altogether by the simultaneous rise of a new enemy and a new presiding genius.

PART I

The Central Powers

1

The Two-Power Standard

Her Britannic Majesty's Government, on introducing supplementary naval estimates in 1898, announced its determination to maintain a fleet 'superior in power and equal in numbers to the fleets of any other two countries' – a rare official reaffirmation of a two-power standard already more than a century old. The dying days of the nineteenth century, which had encompassed the heyday of the Pax Britannica as symbolized above all by the Royal Navy, bequeathed three issues to an overburdened Admiralty for the twentieth. One was for the short term, one for the medium and one for the long: a colonial war, an urgent need for renewal and a deadly new rival.

The conflict that broke out in South Africa in October 1899 between a gold-hungry British Empire and the independent Boer republics of the Transvaal and the Orange Free State was overwhelmingly fought on land but could not have been won, or even begun, without the Navy. By the time it ended in May 1902, nearly half a million British and Imperial troops had been deployed against far fewer Afrikaners, white settlers of mainly Dutch descent whose stubborn mounted commandos enjoyed the tactical initiative for much of the war at home and the sympathy of the leading powers, especially Germany, abroad. The landlocked republics had no fleet, but the British Navy had much to do during a war which only intensified a British sense of isolation that had ceased to feel splendid and was turning uncomfortable, if not positively alarming. There were troop and supply convoys from Britain and other parts of a worldwide empire to organize and escort to Britain's Cape Colony and Natal, as well as the time-honoured British strategy of coastal blockade to enforce.

It had become commonplace in the preceding two decades to put Royal Navy men, sailors as well as Royal Marines, ashore in scratch naval 'brigades' (usually consisting of a few hundred men, not to be compared numerically with Army brigades) to fight alongside the Army in colonial police actions. Officers and ratings often found these shore adventures a relief from stifling shipboard routine and many distinguished themselves in such forays.

The Boer War was Britain's largest and longest expansionist conflict and the Navy played a central landward part in one of its most famous incidents, the siege of Ladysmith. As the Boers closed in on the town, a hundred miles north-west of Durban, at the beginning of the war, the heavy cruisers *Terrible* and *Powerful* hastily disembarked an ad hoc brigade of about 300 sailors and marines under Captain Hedworth Lambton, RN. With their small arms and two 4.7-inch guns borrowed, with a modest quantity of ammunition, from HMS *Terrible*, the bluejackets marched to join the defence and helped to hold the formidable Boer field artillery in check with accurate counter-fire. The Fleet Paymaster had the foresight to buy up the town's entire stock of beer for the naval canteen on arrival; and when the besiegers cut off the water supply, naval engineers improvised a coal-fired still from a locomotive's boiler pipes, enabling the garrison to live off muddy river water without major infection. General Sir Redvers Buller raised the siege on 28 February 1900 after four months, and when the sailors got home six weeks later, they marched in triumph through London to be reviewed by Queen Victoria herself. The Navy also lent the Army in the latter days of the war five of its first experimental seagoing wireless sets which, though not intended for land use and thus of limited application, proved extremely useful. There was no seaborne engagement as such, apart from one harmlessly amusing incident. Two scouts from General Jan Smuts's Commando were riding along the beach at Lambert's Bay, 125 miles north of Cape Town on the west coast, in the dying months of the war when they saw a cruiser just offshore and promptly fired at it with their rifles. The bullets bounced off the side of the unnamed ship but it returned fire with its secondary armament. The riders fled into the dunes, but on rejoining their unit they proudly claimed to have fought the sole naval action of the war.

As the sailors sweated it out on and offshore, their colleagues out to sea provoked a crisis with Germany. A Royal Navy boarding party stopped and searched a German mail steamer on her way to South Africa. A report that the vessel was carrying volunteers and contraband for the Boer cause, which had won the strong sympathy of Kaiser Wilhelm II and German public opinion alike, proved groundless and the Germans were furious. A major dispute laced with stiff diplomatic Notes ensued, inflaming already mutually hostile sentiment on both sides of the North Sea. The British eventually conceded they had been in the wrong and paid compensation. But the incident played into the hands of the burgeoning German naval lobby just as plans for a massive expansion of the navy were going ahead.

What the Germans wanted was a modern battlefleet, the ultimate strategic weapon and symbol of world-power status of the day. Only the strongest and richest nations could afford the great battleships around which such a fleet was built: Britain, France, Russia, Italy, Austria-Hungary, the United States and Japan. The line-of-battle ship had been built of wood in the time of Vice-Admiral Lord Nelson, whose victory over the combined French and Spanish fleets at Trafalgar in October 1805 brought Britain a good century of world supremacy at sea. But that century was also a time of headlong and accelerating technical development. First the wooden ships were clad in iron and then steam propulsion was added to sail, leading to HMS *Warrior*, 9,210 tons, Britain's hasty but heavier response in 1860 to the French ironclad frigate *Gloire* of 1859. Advances in steam technology enabled designers to dispense with sails and produce the first 'mastless' ship, HMS *Devastation*, 9,300 tons, designed in 1869 and the first recognizably modern battleship. At the same time the breech-loading naval gun with rifled barrel displaced the Nelsonian muzzle-loader, cordite was overtaken by high explosive, and iron replaced wood altogether, only to be superseded by steel.

The last three decades of the nineteenth century brought bewildering progress in all naval technologies – armour, propulsion, guns and explosives, optics, mines, torpedoes – such that HMS *Majestic* displaced some 15,000 tons when she was completed in 1896. By then battleship design seemed settled. The lumbering ship of the line had mighty coal-fired, triple-expansion steam engines, a thick belt of armour round its vitals, four long-barrelled guns in even more heavily armoured turrets with magazines directly below, about twelve lesser cannon in casemates along the sides – and smaller, rapid-firing guns to deal with a new menace, the fast torpedo boat. The first self-propelled underwater missile, future nemesis of the battleship and very nearly of Britain itself, had been produced by the Briton Robert Whitehead in 1867 and was developing at a similar pace. To protect its capital ships the battlefleet deployed torpedo boat destroyers, larger than torpedo boats but similarly armed (the two types soon merged into the destroyer, with its dual role of escort and high-speed, hit-and-run attacker). Battleships were so greatly valued that they never sailed alone, an ironic comment on their much-vaunted might as well as an often unheeded reminder of the importance of escorting precious maritime assets. Light cruisers also had a dual role in the battlefleet of the turn of the century, as scouts for the battle squadrons and leaders of destroyer flotillas.

The steam-and-steel battleship had been extolled as mistress of the seas by the American naval historian and strategist Rear-Admiral Alfred Thayer Mahan, who published his cardinal work on the importance of the battlefleet, *The Influence of Seapower on History*, in 1890. Readers directly affected by his thesis included naval officers round the world, the future President Theodore Roosevelt – and the new Emperor of Germany, Wilhelm II. His admiration for the book ensured that a certain under-employed staff officer in the Baltic Fleet, Captain Alfred von Tirpitz, was pushing at an open door when he submitted his most obedient memorandum to Germany's All-Highest in 1894, advocating the acquisition of a battlefleet worthy of the nation's much enhanced place in the world.

The more their fossilized routine was challenged before 1914 by one technical great leap forward after another, the more Britain's admirals, their ignorance, if not downright dismissal, of science masked by their upper-class background and manners, clung to the immortal (and conveniently distorted) memory of Horatio Nelson. And one of the other short-sighted and long-enduring characteristics of the Admiralty, the only government department that was also an operational headquarters, in running the service that was Britain's first and last line of defence and guarantor of its Empire, was its mean treatment of the volunteers on whom the Royal Navy totally relied. Another not unimportant event in the cardinal naval year of 1898, when Germany initiated her arms race with Britain, was Petty Officer James Wood's decision to purchase his discharge after nineteen years' service, whereupon he changed his name to Lionel Yexley and began publishing *The Bluejacket* magazine, the start of a remarkable quarter-century of campaigning for better conditions for ratings. It is hardly surprising that officers, even those commanding capital ships, though rather better treated than their lower-deck 'people', having been denied freedom of action or thought on their way up, made lacklustre (and all too often stupid) admirals; fortunately there were a few extraordinary exceptions. Captains concentrated on mastering new machinery, weapons and equipment, and training their professional crews to use them properly; little or no thought was given to the implications of such headlong technical progress for formation tactics, let alone fleet strategy.

The performance of individual ships in the Royal Navy at the end of the century of the Pax Britannica was therefore as good as the deployment of squadrons and fleets was bad. How bad was shown in 1893 by the Navy's most embarrassing disaster, when the flagship of the commander-in-chief of the Mediterranean Fleet, the battleship HMS *Victoria*, was rammed and sunk by another, the *Camperdown*. The C-in-C, Vice-Admiral Sir George Tryon, had ordered the two parallel divisions in which his fleet was then sailing to reverse course by column, turning inward. Rear-Admiral A. H. Markham on the *Camperdown*, his staff and Tryon's staff soon realized that the distance between the leading ships was less than the combined diameters of their turning circles, which meant that a collision was inevitable unless the fancy turn were abandoned. But nobody on either bridge, from Markham down, dared say a word. The *Camperdown* therefore sliced into the side of the *Victoria*, sinking the flagship and killing the innumerate Tryon, twenty-one other officers and 339 ratings. At the court of inquiry Tryon's order was blamed; but those who failed to question it were not. The golden rule remained the same: follow the senior officer's motions and if in doubt request instructions. It was not only the admirals' calibre that was at fault: the stricken ship's main armament, two 16.25-inch guns (the largest ever fitted to a British man-of-war) were so heavy at 111 tons each that the muzzles drooped under their own weight and an order had been given never to fire them with a full charge of explosive. Small wonder that such crass errors occurred: the Navy, unlike the Army, had no war staff to co-ordinate intelligence, strategy, tactics, propulsion, ship construction, armament, supply, personnel and training in an age of bewildering technical complexity, dangerous international rivalry and conflict.

In the same year as the gratuitous catastrophe Rear-Admiral John Arbuthnot Fisher, Third Sea Lord and, as Controller of the

Navy, responsible for ship construction, started a five-year battle-ship building programme for completion by 1898. He also introduced the destroyer and the water-tube boiler during his five-year term (1892–7), a first taste of the technical and organizational revolution whose full realization would follow his elevation to First Sea Lord in 1904. The impending upheaval was long overdue because the British fleet, despite such fitful flirtations with modernity as HMS *Warspite*, had been sailing perilously close to obsolescence for decades, as observers noted at Queen Victoria's Golden Jubilee review of the fleet at Spithead in 1887. The press had been exposing the state of the Navy and government complacency on the subject since 1884.

Five years later came the belated response: the first Naval Defence Act, with provision for seventy new warships and a renewed commitment to British naval supremacy. The government even spoke of a ratio of five British battleships to three in any possible hostile combination of foreign navies – a two-power standard with a generous margin to allow Britain to protect its worldwide empire at the same time. Modernization, restoration of efficiency, increased recruitment and faster construction over a five-year programme were promised. The main threat was seen as an alliance between France and Russia, both of which had substantial fleets. Neither Germany nor the United States were considered likely enemies at this time. The controversy in the press and a hugely popular Naval Exhibition in London in 1891 revived public interest in the neglected service.

Germany in 1898 was already the world's leading military power, boasting its strongest and most modern, best-led army. It had ousted France as the foremost Continental power in 1870, when Bismarck's Prussia routed the armies of Napoleon III, successfully laid siege to Paris, seized Alsace-Lorraine and in January 1871 turned itself into the second German Reich by means of a ceremony of unbridled tactlessness in the Hall of Mirrors at Versailles. The new Reich had emerged as a world power of the first rank with worldwide colonial and trading interests. Prussia, the locomotive of German unification, had brought this off with only a small fleet, a point conveniently suppressed by Germany's own Navy League, a powerful lobby which began agitating for a world-class fleet before the end of the nineteenth century. It was supported by industry, by the new German nationalism and by the

Kaiser himself, a man who, as Crown Prince, had briefly dabbled in designing battleships and had been deeply impressed by the Jubilee review. An important component of the motivation behind his inchoate programme to secure Germany's 'place in the sun' was jealousy of the majestic British fleet. Wilhelm wanted a battlefleet too, a dangerous ambition that was bound eventually to bring his Reich into conflict with his grandmother's Empire.

Asked by the Kaiser to clear up some loose ends in his 1894 paper, the future Grand-Admiral Tirpitz produced a supplementary one in the following year, consolidating his argument for the High Seas Fleet. One of its most pertinent elements was his 'risk theory', a foretaste of the idea of deterrence which was to become so important in the nuclear age half a century later. Germany, he wrote, should be strong enough at sea to be able to damage seriously the world's most powerful fleet (Britain's, though not referred to by name) – even in a losing battle. The unnamed leading naval power would be deterred by such a prospect from opposing Germany's will or attacking its fleet, because it could not afford thus to put at risk the world maritime supremacy on which its power and empire depended.

The Kaiser may have been Victoria's grandson and nephew of her heir apparent, the future King Edward VII, but none of this prevented a serious deterioration in Anglo-German relations over South Africa at the turn of the century, prior to which Britain had benevolently looked upon Germany as a likely ally (much more likely than the 'old enemy', France) rather than as an actual rival and a potential foe. It was the first major rift. When President Paul Kruger of the Transvaal repulsed the Jameson Raid (a botched, semi-official British attempt to intervene in the Boer republics) in January 1896, Wilhelm, whose colonial possessions included neighbouring South-West Africa, dispatched an effusive telegram of congratulation. He even considered sending German troops but thought better of it, not least because he lacked adequate maritime resources to deliver and support them – a fact which lodged in his mind as another point in favour of a strong navy. When Tirpitz took over as State Secretary (minister) at the Navy Office in June 1897 he quickly started work on his grand project of creating a German battlefleet. The result was the first Fleet Law, presented to the Reichstag for enactment in March 1898.

After a two-day debate, in which no mention was made of Britain as the target of the proposals, 139 deputies voted against and 212 in favour of a radical expansion of the German fleet. The German Navy League was founded at the same time, three years after its British model, to raise interest in the Imperial Navy among the public. Its main early source of funding was the Krupp steel, arms and shipbuilding conglomerate based in the German industrial heartland of the Ruhr, one of the companies that stood to gain most from the impending expansion. The League attracted nearly 250,000 members in three years, proving that the idea of a strong navy enjoyed widespread public support amid the new nationalism. Its patron, inevitably, was the Kaiser, and an important by-product of its mission to generate enthusiasm for a big fleet was the arousal of anti-British feeling, based on envy of the Royal Navy and the empire it sustained. Another straw in the wind was the seizure by the Germans in 1897 of the northerly Chinese enclave of Kiaochow, including the port of Tsingtao, an asset of no value except as an exploitative colony (one of many nineteenth-century European intrusions in China) and strategic naval base. It became the headquarters of the Asiatic Squadron of heavy and light cruisers, then Germany's sole 'blue-water' naval formation, which Tirpitz had briefly commanded until recalled to Berlin in 1897.

In 1898 the British fleet fielded twenty-nine modern battleships with twelve more on the stocks, compared with thirteen and five respectively in Germany, all about a third smaller than their British counterparts. The Fleet Law required the construction of seven more battleships and two heavy cruisers. The net result, after decommissioning older warships, would leave Germany with nineteen battleships, twelve heavy and thirty light cruisers by 1903, the end of the five-year period covered by the law.

But three years before that, as the new century dawned, Tirpitz was already hard at work on his second Fleet Law, the point of no return in relations with Britain. His new objective was to double the High Seas Fleet in sixteen years by building three capital ships a year. He told the Reichstag that by 1920 it would have two flagships (North Sea and Baltic), four squadrons of eight battleships apiece, eight heavy and twenty-four light cruisers plus swarms of destroyers. The admiral's openly avowed aim (unstated in 1898, but that was before the Boer War damaged both Britain's reputation and its relations with Germany) was to enable Germany to challenge the Royal Navy in the North Sea, known in those days (even in Britain) as the German Ocean. Supporting the draft, the

Foreign Secretary, Bernhard Prince von Bülow, rashly declared that Germany needed a large fleet to deal with Britain, and the High Seas Fleet would expand with a close eye to British naval policy. As a challenge to a 'friendly' foreign power such sentiments could hardly be less diplomatic. How would the British react?

The Kaiser's impatience was only exacerbated by the outbreak of the Boer War in 1899. Wilhelm tried but failed to assemble a Continental League against further British imperial expansion. Germany had no choice but to maintain neutrality, however benevolent towards the Boers, watching enviously as the mighty Royal Navy sealed off the war zone from outside interference. The German Navy League seized with both hands the opportunity to promote its cause. Given Britain's worldwide commitments, the anticipated size of the High Seas Fleet in 1920 would enable the Germans to concentrate as many capital ships in the German Ocean as the British, or possibly more.

But only if the British took no countervailing action. Their reaction to the new and growing German hostility was at first and in general one of genuine puzzlement. The alarm bells had failed to sound when the first Fleet Law was enacted in 1898. Feeling towards Germany was hazy but generally friendly, much more so than towards France, against which naval strategy was still vaguely directed: all the main British naval bases were in the south of the country, facing France, as they had been for centuries. Anglo-French cooperation in the abysmally conducted Crimean War in mid-century had not erased the folk-memory of the great struggle at its beginning against Napoleon I, final victory in which heralded the era when the Royal Navy acted as lone world policeman. The British monarchy had been German for nearly 200 years, and the Kaiser's aged grandmother still mourned her long-dead German consort, Prince Albert. Not a few in high places regarded united Germany as a natural ally for Britain, despite the latter's traditional policy of 'splendid isolation', which meant intervening in Europe only to maintain or restore the balance of power, without entering into formal alliances there or anywhere else.

Tirpitz intended to give Germany a fleet strong enough to deter Britain from confronting it, for fear of losing the mastery of the seas on which its empire and maritime pre-eminence depended. He was realistic enough to acknowledge that there was one great weakness in his design, a weakness he himself defined as a 'danger zone'. This was the period between the adoption of his expansion programme and its completion. The new High Seas Fleet would only deter the British if they sat back and allowed it to grow, without counter-building in order to maintain their margin of superiority. Against this possibility the naval lobby could only offer a gamble on the continuation of British inertia, of the kind shown when the first Fleet Law went through and began to be implemented. Besides, the expansionists argued, British commitments were diffuse and worldwide, so that they would never be able to concentrate all, or even the bulk, of their naval strength in the North Sea: this meant that Germany did not need a fleet anything like as large as the British in order to be able to deter them. They would not be able to take on the enlarged German battlefleet because they might then sustain enough damage to prevent them from defeating a coalition of hostile naval powers thereafter. The coalition in question was France and Russia, linked by an entente since 1891, the former a traditional rival and the latter engaged in a stealthy struggle with Britain and British India for domination in central Asia, the 'Great Game'.

Yet even the very absence of a coherent naval policy in Britain worked against the German expansionists. Throughout the nineteenth century, ever since defeating the combined and numerically superior French and Spanish battle fleets at Trafalgar, the Royal Navy had rested on its admittedly dazzling accumulation of laurels. There was no coordinated building programme and no global strategy – except to keep an eye on what other powers were doing and react accordingly. One example of this has already been mentioned: when the French built the revolutionary *Gloire*, the first ironclad, as a frigate, the British built the ironclad *Warrior* – as a battleship, if not better then at least bigger and more heavily armed. The guiding principle behind this policy of wait and see, of reaction rather than action, was the two-power standard.

In 1817 Castlereagh, then Foreign Secretary, first identified a combination of France and Russia as the greatest potential threat to the post-Napoleonic peace settlement in Europe and successfully argued that the Royal Navy should adopt a two-power standard, to match the combined strength of the second and third naval powers in the world. But the standard already existed de facto, if not formally stated, in the last quarter of the eighteenth century, when first the American and then the French revolutions presented major threats to British interests, not least at sea. At that time it meant France – always France – as number two, plus one other.

In 1889 it was calculated that the British fleet needed not only to surpass the combined naval strength of France and Russia in capital ships by 5:3 but also to maintain a force of 106 cruisers for the worldwide defence of trade and imperial sea lanes. This conclusion was drawn from a fleet exercise in which faster cruisers readily evaded battleship squadrons patrolling the Channel to deliver 'attacks' on shipping with impunity. The solution to this, enshrined in the Naval Defence Act, which introduced a five-year supplementary construction programme worth £21.5m, was seen to be more cruisers to patrol designated shipping lanes. That ancient naval standby, convoy, compulsory in the Napoleonic Wars, was dismissed as irrelevant in the age of steam, a miscalculation that was to prove catastrophic. All this added up to a strength probably sufficient to make a three-power alliance think twice. In 1898 the government modified this impossibly high, peak standard to aim for a fleet 'superior in power and equal in numbers to the fleets of any two other countries', in response to a Russian naval expansion programme recently announced.

The self-elected role of Wilhelm's Germany as cuckoo in the European nest was bound to erode British security, as some Britons began to realize even before the first Fleet Law was passed. An anonymous article in the *Saturday Review* in September 1897 argued that a trade war between Britain and Germany was 'inevitable'. Tirpitz seized on this and for a decade quoted it in support of his expansionist policy. In fact, some thirty years after German unification, the British had woken up to the new commercial competition and were holding their own in world trade: Germany was actually their biggest customer after India. On hearing of the Tirpitz 'danger zone' Royal Navy officers realized by 1899 at the latest that Britain could prolong this zone indefinitely by using her much greater construction resources to outbuild the Germans – if she so chose.

Open concern was expressed in Parliament in 1900 after the second Fleet Law was enacted. For the moment the British did nothing, not without noting the Kaiser's remark in 1901 that Germany's 'future is on the water' and his production of a chart in the Reichstag in 1902, showing the comparative strengths of the British and German navies as two converging lines. But the British naval estimates had risen from £15m in 1890 to £26m in 1900. The first visible British countermeasure to German naval expansionism

came in March 1903, near the end of the five-year programme
initiated by the first Fleet Law. It was neither aggressive nor
dramatic, but it delivered a clear message at minimal cost. It took
the form of an announcement that the Royal Navy was to have a
new base at Rosyth, in the Firth of Forth on Scotland's east coast,
400 miles or so north of all other important naval bases. The port
faced north-east – towards Germany. The Admiralty stated, disingenuously perhaps, that the Navy's greater numbers of modern
warships needed the extra space offered by the sheltered Firth of
Forth. In Germany the 1898 programme was completed in
September 1903, enabling Tirpitz to assemble one of the two battle
fleets (North Sea and Baltic) envisaged for German waters in the
1900 plan. The Kaiser Wilhelm (Kiel) Canal allowed it to operate
at will in either or both seas.

Britain's naval supremacy and geographical advantage as an
island state meant that it needed only a small standing army,
mainly to deal with colonial problems. After the Boer War the
British Army was overhauled in the light of the many shortcomings
revealed by the campaign against a sophisticated and resourceful
enemy with modern European weapons – but it remained small,
with no conscription and half its strength scattered across the
Empire. It could muster six infantry divisions at home – compared
with the seventy-two Germany could put in the field in a fortnight's
mobilization. Britain thus depended entirely on its fleet to protect
it from invasion, and had not been subjected to an occupying
enemy since the Norman Conquest in 1066. Now it contemplated a
Germany which, having acquired the world's strongest army, was
building a navy out of all proportion to its short coastline,
merchant fleet and collection of small, commercially insignificant
colonies, a navy now expressly directed against Britain. The
consequence was a seismic shift in British foreign policy, away from
isolation.

It was always open to the British to eliminate the risk of facing a
Franco-Russian alliance after or at the same time as the enlarged
German Navy. The Germans feared that the British might
'Copenhagen' them during the danger zone period (the inelegant
verb refers to Nelson's attack on the Danish fleet in 1801 to prevent
it joining Napoleon). There was no shortage of demands in Britain
for such a pre-emptive strike, including a public one from Admiral
Sir John Fisher, who was to become First Sea Lord (and Britain's

answer to Tirpitz) in 1904. The government preferred a rapprochement with Russia and/or France, possibilities discounted in Berlin because of the former's rivalry with Britain in central Asia and the latter's in Africa, as well as the French understanding with the Tsar. In so thinking the Germans underestimated such weighty factors as French ambition to recover Alsace-Lorraine and Russian rivalry with Austria-Hungary, Germany's ally, in the Balkans, a region which also included part of the crumbling empire of Ottoman Turkey, cynosure of the acquisitive eyes of all five powers. The British meanwhile still showed no sign of a response to German expansion at the start of the new century, and the Germans were confident that the bloated Royal Navy would soon run into manpower problems if it tried. These three issues, however – Alsace, the Balkans and capital ships – became the terrible ABC that led to the First World War.

The second Fleet Law in the very first months of the new century was the hinge of fate for Anglo-German relations, making the German Navy the overriding concern of British maritime strategy until 1945. Just as the Germans underestimated Britain's will to defend its interests by all available means when it awoke, at last, to the danger, so the British underestimated German legalism. Tirpitz needed a law to justify and underpin the massive expansion of industry required for his new fleet. German shipbuilding capacity was far smaller than Britain's, which meant new yards had to be opened. Given the money, this was an advantage for the Germans, because they could build wide new docks for capital ships, enabling them to turn out vessels rather broader in the beam, and thus more stable as gun platforms, than their British contemporaries.

By the same token the main British advantage lay in vastly superior shipbuilding resources and experience; yet it is much cheaper and easier to lengthen a dock than to broaden it, which meant that the latest British battleships were longer and narrower than German, and were also less strong and technologically advanced, thanks to older construction facilities. The Germans built mainly for the North Sea (the High Seas Fleet was constructed with the nearest waters in mind), which entailed smaller coal bunkers and less crew accommodation. German sailors lived ashore and manned their ships for battle. The British built for long periods at sea, which meant higher fuel capacity and larger compartments for messing. German metallurgy, optics and electrical and mechanical engineering were also generally superior to British.

Tirpitz needed a law to guarantee continuity for his shipbuilders and to provide funds for the largest warships ever built in Germany and their expensive maintenance, as well as for the even larger ships expected to follow as marine technology advanced. The British never quite understood that in Germany a law, once passed, was as if cast in stone. If urged to stop building warships for the sake of peace, a German official would have shrugged and said he was merely obeying the law. The only admissible responses to the fleet laws were either to adhere to the programme laid down or to expand it; there could be no question of repeal, which would have implied an admission of error as well as a climbdown. This legalism made it all but impossible for the Kaiser's Germany to indulge in the British art of compromise.

This did not mean that there was no opposition in Germany to the headlong rush to build up the Navy. The most persistent and vocal opponents were the Social Democrats (SPD), who complained of the cost and the risk of conflict with Britain. Tirpitz reduced his programme by ten cruisers and also cut the reserve fleet (neither affected the strength of the battlefleet), ensuring a respectable Reichstag majority of three to two in 1900. Anti-expansion rallies were far outweighed by the Navy League's favourable demonstrations; the expansion of the fleet was now a doubly established legal obligation.

Even so, in 1898, when the first law went through, Joseph Chamberlain, Britain's Secretary of State for the Colonies, had advocated an alliance with Germany regardless. The Kaiser rejected this, believing that difficulties with the Russians in Asia would force the British to plead for admission as fourth member of the Triple Alliance on his terms. This pact, at once cornerstone and millstone of German diplomacy, went back to 1882 and embraced Germany, Austria-Hungary and Italy. The latter, at odds with Austria over their shared border, was the weak link in the alliance, which required members to help each other only if attacked by France or any other power. Austria, the sclerotic, polyglot empire in eastern and southern Europe, had become more of a liability than an asset ever since Bismarck excluded it from his Reich. And because it was Germany that initiated hostilities in 1914, Anglophile Italy could not be called upon to help the other two, remaining neutral until it actually declared war on them.

Meanwhile, however, when it came to defending Western imperialism, the British and the Germans worked rather well together, along with other nations, on several occasions up to the very eve of war. These included the ruthless suppression of the Boxer Rebellion in China in 1901 and an intervention by gunboat in Venezuela, which had defaulted on overseas debts and mal-treated foreign traders.

A year before the first visible sign of British strategic precautions aimed specifically at Germany, the Rosyth base, His Majesty's Government (Victoria had died in 1901) tore up the policy of 'splendid isolation' and concluded a modest, three-year treaty with Japan. The Japanese, intent since 1868 on becoming a world power after emerging, under American pressure, from centuries of self-imposed isolation, adopted Western institutions, ideas and technologies wholesale before embarking on a programme of expansion which began with the seizure of Korea from China in 1895. The treaty with Britain, especially as it had been proposed by London, was a prized certificate of respectability for Tokyo. It required each power to show 'benevolent neutrality' to the other if attacked by a third, and to intervene actively if the other were attacked by a combination of powers. The treaty protected British interests in the Far East, leaving London free to withdraw naval units westward. In the same year the Royal Navy subsumed its Home Fleet into a greatly expanded Channel Fleet, the better to defend home waters.

The risk for the British in the unprecedented alliance lay in a (highly likely) Russian attack on Japan, whereupon the Russians might invoke their alliance with France, which could entitle the Japanese in turn to call for a British intervention against the French. The natural solution to that potential complication was for Britain to seek an understanding with France, based on a shared mistrust of Germany. The result was the Entente Cordiale of 1904, a rapprochement officially well short of an alliance but the foundation of a genuine convergence. The entente defined the two powers' spheres of influence outside Europe in order to eliminate a repetition of the Fashoda incident, another historic milestone passed in 1898, when the French first made a bid for control of the upper White Nile and then withdrew in the face of British threats, backed by the Royal Navy. France eventually recognized British hegemony in Egypt in return for Britain's acknowledgement of French primacy in Morocco. There was no specific provision for bilateral cooperation in Europe or for a military understanding;

but there was no bar to either. And before the ink was dry on the documents the Admiralty reinforced the newly expanded Channel Fleet with ships from the Atlantic Fleet based on Gibraltar, as well as from more distant regions such as the Far East. One implication of the new warmth was that a further reinforcement for squadrons in home waters from the Mediterranean Fleet, Britain's most important overseas command, became possible: the Mediterranean, always the French fleet's chief concern, was now primarily its responsibility as the British began to concentrate in home waters. The main artery of the French Empire was the north–south axis to Africa across the western basin while that of the British Empire ran from Gibraltar in the west via Malta, Egypt and Suez in the east – the route to India. German diplomats in London did their duty by drawing attention to the new British naval dispositions, which they emphasized were due entirely to concern for naval primacy and not to trade fears. The Kaiser and Tirpitz took no notice and built on.

In February 1904 rivalry between an expanding Russian empire and an ambitious Japan over their conflicting ambitions in northern China led the Imperial Japanese Navy, trained and largely equipped by Britain, to launch a torpedo attack on the Russian squadron in its Port Arthur enclave on the north Chinese coast, without warning. The Japanese then imposed a blockade which lasted until August, when their army reached Port Arthur overland. The six undamaged Russian battleships thereupon came out to confront Admiral Marquis Togo Heihachiro's four. The Russians returned to port unscathed after an inconclusive exchange of gunfire, their honour apparently satisfied but their opportunity to break out irretrievably lost. Their withdrawal allowed Japanese Army artillery and Togo's big guns to crush the Russian Far East Fleet between them by the end of the year.

The Russians reacted to the siege of Port Arthur by sending the bulk of their Baltic Fleet, led by four battleships, from its main base at Kronstadt in the eastern Baltic on an enormous voyage to the rescue, round Europe, Africa and Asia. The badly led formation entered the North Sea on the night of 21 to 22 October. A shoal of trawlers from the eastern English port of Hull was mistaken for a hostile fleet and the Russians sank five off the Dogger Bank. The Channel Fleet put to sea; war seemed imminent between Japan's ally, Britain, and Russia – ally of France, Britain's new-found friend across the Channel. But the British let the doomed Russians straggle past, fouling the nets of the Dover fishing fleet as they went.

On reaching east Asian waters, Admiral Rozhdestvensky's force encountered Togo's fleet in the Strait of Tsushima on 27 May 1905 and was annihilated (quite literally: every Russian ship was either sunk or captured). Togo was able to 'cross the T' by sailing across the Russians' course and bringing his heavy broadsides to bear together on the Russian battleships one by one. For a while the Russians gave as good as they got, but when Rozhdestvensky tried to manoeuvre his slower ships behind the Japanese rearguard and back on course, the ensuing close-range action sealed his fate. A night attack by torpedo boats (like mines, Japanese torpedoes made an often overlooked but important contribution to the downfall of the Tsar's seapower) compounded the damage and a brief attack on the following morning completed the rout.

Observers from several major navies, including the British and German, were aboard Togo's flagship to watch the first fleet action involving armoured ships and modern heavy guns, the most important naval battle in the hundred years since Trafalgar. Their unanimous conclusion was that the battleship armed with the big gun was the unchallengeable mistress of the seas, just as Admiral Mahan had written fifteen years before. The torpedo, as carried by small, fast attack boats, had been checkmated by larger and faster destroyers, armed with guns as well as torpedoes from 1893, when the first of this new type was commissioned into the British Navy. In fleet actions destroyers could fight each other, leaving the battleships to slog it out with their heavy weapons. Although both sides possessed them, neither deployed their admittedly primitive and untried submarines, in effect submersible torpedo boats. There were thus no reservations in the expert consensus on Tsushima, which unfortunately led to an enduring ascendancy for the advocates of the big gun, in the Royal Navy in particular.

Always on the lookout for a chance to embarrass Britain, the Germans tried to exploit the Dogger Bank incident by suggesting a revival of their once friendly relations with Russia, neglected since Bismarck's time. The Russians were interested but, chastened by their defeat at the hands of Japan, the first time a European power had been crushed by a non-European one, they stuck with France and thus opted for an understanding with Britain in 1907 – the Triple Entente.

The Germans had already put the new Entente Cordiale to the test in March 1905 by demanding a say in the enclave of Tangier which, though an international zone from 1904, was geographically part of Morocco and thus in the French sphere of influence. When the French refused, the British supported them. In response to German demands an international conference on Morocco was held at the beginning of 1906, in the Spanish port of Algeçiras on the opposite side of the Strait of Gibraltar. Germany was isolated; even its nominal Italian ally as well as the neutral Americans sided with France and Britain. The Kaiser's attempt to bully the French therefore turned into a diplomatic fiasco for Germany, which nonetheless returned dangerously to the charge in 1911, as will be seen.

2

Germany Plus Sixty Per Cent

Admiral Sir John Fisher (later Admiral of the Fleet Lord Fisher of Kilverstone) was appointed First Sea Lord, the operational chief of the Admiralty, in October 1904, at the age of sixty-three, just when the Anglo-German naval arms race came to a head. Seldom in British history was the man so well suited to the hour and the appointment. John Arbuthnot Fisher joined the Navy at thirteen from a modest family, rising on merit in a service dominated by blue blood and snobbery. He rose to command the Navy's most powerful vessel of its time, the battleship *Inflexible*, in 1881. A series of land-based appointments followed, making Fisher one of the most knowledgeable officers in the service. After two years as captain of HMS *Excellent*, the gunnery school, he served for four and a half as Director of Naval Ordnance and Torpedoes. Following a brief stint as Admiral Superintendent, Portsmouth, Fisher became Third Sea Lord and Controller of the Navy in 1892, a key post he held for five years. His five-year capital-ship programme of 1893 was large enough for its time but would soon be spectacularly surpassed in the race with the Germans.

After sixteen years ashore Vice-Admiral Fisher went back to sea in 1897 for an uneventful two years in command of the North America and West Indies station. Recalled in 1899 as the naval delegate to the first Peace Conference at The Hague, Fisher proved that, whatever his remarkable qualities as seagoing commander and administrator alike, he was no diplomat. He was a tireless enthusiast, and his ruddy complexion, strong features and habit of peppering his correspondence with heavy underlinings, exuberant capital letters and furious exclamation marks were entirely in keeping with a blunt, even explosive manner of speaking. But he was also witty, charming and high-spirited as well as tenacious and exceptionally energetic. He shocked the courteous negotiators at The Hague when he advocated the preservation of peace by making war too horrible to contemplate, and by asserting that 'moderation in war is imbecility' and 'war is the essence of violence'. Indiscretions in the Dutch capital, however, had no effect on Fisher's rise to the pinnacle of his profession: soon after the conference he was appointed Commander-in-Chief of the Mediterranean Fleet, the plum overseas posting.

A year later Fisher, known as Jacky to the nickname-loving lower deck, was given a new second-in-command, Rear-Admiral Lord Charles Beresford, a sailor even more renowned than Fisher and a naval reformer whose background, however, earned him the cordial loathing of his chief, a feeling vigorously reciprocated. Beresford, known by ratings as Charlie B, was the younger man by five years, having likewise joined the Navy at thirteen in 1859. The second son of the fourth Marquess of Waterford, Beresford in Fisher's eyes represented almost all that was worst about the Royal Navy's officer class of the time – high birth and social cachet, personal wealth and the arrogance that went with such unearned privilege. For his part Beresford, a man of great personal courage and charm, average intelligence and indifferent professional achievement, looked down upon Fisher's lowly origins, managing to respect his ideas while simultaneously disparaging him as a bourgeois upstart. As a young man Beresford got involved in several escapades of the kind that would put a lower-class young man in prison but were tolerated from aristocratic sprogs as mere youthful indiscretions. He was also a personal friend of the Prince of Wales – until they quarrelled over a woman in 1891. Appointed Fourth Sea Lord in 1886, when he was a forty-year-old captain, Beresford saw the need for reform as clearly as Fisher and successfully proposed the creation of the Naval Intelligence Department at the Admiralty. But when the Board rejected his call for a naval staff, Beresford resigned and went back to sea as captain of a cruiser. His chagrin at having to serve under Fisher on promotion to flag rank can be imagined. Fisher too, surprisingly, opposed the idea of a naval staff – probably because it came from Beresford.

But in the Mediterranean Fisher made war on complacency, poor training and inefficiency in the fleet, castigating the type of captain who kept gunnery practice to a minimum to avoid soiling his ship's paintwork. The result was a dramatic improvement in readiness for war, competence and morale – and an accumulation of reformist experience which Fisher applied with gusto to the entire Navy when he became First Sea Lord in October 1904. His brief term as Second Sea Lord, the member of the Admiralty Board responsible for personnel (1902–3), enabled him to reorganize and standardize officer entry and training, with the accent on new technologies that were already transforming naval strategy and tactics (the 'Selborne Scheme', named after the contemporary First Lord of the Admiralty, the Navy's political chief).

Naval staff or no, Fisher as head of the Royal Navy launched an unmatched quinquennium of radical reform, prompted principally by the German threat. King Edward VII personally chided him soon after his appointment for publicly proposing to 'Copenhagen' the High Seas Fleet, a characteristically undiplomatic outburst which briefly caused panic in northern Germany. In some respects the peppery admiral (his rank since 1901) proved to be a visionary, recognizing before most of his contemporaries the potential of the torpedo, the new-fangled aircraft and even the despised, equally untried submarine.

The intensity of Anglo-German naval rivalry was vividly illustrated in November 1905, when Tirpitz introduced a supplementary Fleet Law, augmenting the 1900 programme. Within three weeks Earl Cawdor, then First Lord of the Admiralty, announced that British construction would henceforward be directly related to German year by year. There would in any case be four new battleships annually, but building would increase if necessary. At the Admiralty Fisher set up a committee on ship design.

But the most sensational innovation associated with Fisher had been initiated less than a year after he was promoted to First Sea Lord: the laying of the keel of a new battleship at Portsmouth naval dockyard on 2 October 1905. It was Fisher who forced the pace of construction to such a degree that the vessel was launched in less than four and a half months, ready for sea-trials a year later and completed in December 1906. He also took a close personal interest in all aspects of its design, especially its armament. The result was HMS *Dreadnought*, the world's first 'all big-gun' ship, which rendered all earlier capital ships obsolete. She carried ten 12-inch guns in five double turrets, three on the centre-line and two on either side amidships. This meant she could fire a broadside of eight 850-pound shells from either side as far as 18,500 yards, ten and a half statute miles, or of six shots over the bow. The latest 'pre-dreadnoughts' (as older battleships became known) had a broadside of only four and could fire a mere two shots ahead at a time.

The *Dreadnought*'s firepower was thus worth two old battleships broadside-on and three bow-on; the need for clear fields of fire all round gave the ship an uncluttered elegance. She also had eleven inches of Krupp armour in a belt round her vital parts and a design speed of twenty-one knots, two and a half quicker than her most modern predecessor and equal to most contemporary cruisers, thanks to her Parsons turbines and four screws. The turbines were a particularly radical innovation as this means of propulsion had been introduced in the much smaller destroyer only seven years before; it saved £100,000 in capital costs as well as 1,000 tons of displacement and gave better acceleration than traditional recipro-cating engines. *Dreadnought* displaced an unprecedented 17,900 tons (20,700 fully loaded) and measured 520 feet by 82, with a draught of 31. All ten big guns were controlled by a single officer with the latest rangefinder and sights in a 'control top' observation post halfway up the ship's tripod mast, another revolutionary advance (guns on older capital ships were fired individually).

All this was achieved within a displacement less than 10 per cent greater than a pre-dreadnought's, and for under 20 per cent more money (£1.75m). The new battleship's faults – insufficient armour below the waterline, inadequate secondary armament and one side-turret unavailable to each broadside – were eliminated in later designs. All major navies immediately made plans to follow this extraordinary example, but British building capacity enabled the Royal Navy to establish a massive lead in the new capital ships by 1914. The decision to build a faster, 25.5-knot variant with only six inches of armour and six, later eight, big guns, however – the battlecruiser as typified by HMS *Invincible*, launched in April 1907 – proved to be a major blunder. Conceived by Fisher as giant scouts capable not only of finding the enemy fleet but also of engaging it while awaiting the arrival of the main body, battle-cruisers proved, despite their superior speed and maximum-size guns, to be too thin-skinned to withstand incoming heavy shells, especially plunging shot. This lack of balance, sacrificing much armour and some guns for speed, was compounded by the tendency of naval commanders to classify them as full-blown capital ships and thus capable of serving in the line of battle.

Fisher also ruthlessly scrapped large numbers of ships too old to be of use in contemporary conditions while fundamentally reforming the manning of the reserve fleet, where each ship was allocated a 'nucleus crew' of two-fifths of wartime strength. Nevertheless events in the opening days of the coming war showed that even Fisher's ruthlessness was not ruthless enough. These maintenance crews, which included a cross-section of essential technicians, were to live aboard and sustain a level of readiness sufficient to ensure that the crew could be filled out by other reservists, trainees and shore-based personnel in a swift mobilization. The extra manpower was obtained from the discarded ships. Fisher imposed a far higher standard of gunnery while reorganizing the Royal Navy's major formations to produce a much stronger concentration of ships in or near home waters, considerably reducing the size of the Mediterranean Fleet. The hyperactive admiral also found the time to improve the conditions and terms of service of the lower deck, a concern for the ordinary men characteristic of great commanders. He opened the officer corps to talent by scrapping fees at the naval colleges at Dartmouth and Osborne.

The scale and pace of reform, however, split the officer corps. Although Beresford, a Conservative MP before he was thirty, had produced his own ideas for modernizing the Navy, orthodox elements gathered round the Irish aristocrat in what Fisher dismissed as a 'syndicate of discontent' (Fisher's enemies, of whom there were many, disparaged his own supporters and acolytes as 'the Fishpond'). Beresford had moved on from the Mediterranean under Fisher to command the Channel Squadron of battleships and then, in 1905, to be C-in-C in the Mediterranean in his turn. When he was given command of the Channel Fleet in 1907, however, Fisher had already decided, in October 1906, to hive off much of its strength into a new Home Fleet, which would not come under the C-in-C Channel except in wartime. Beresford was furious and launched a frontal attack on Fisher, his undoubtedly dictatorial and underhand methods in reshaping the Navy as well as his refusal to allow his rival a sight of the Admiralty's detailed war plans (this, however, was normal practice in Britain's government in general and its 'silent service' in particular, in both of which the principle of 'need to know' predominated and knowledge w' equated with power). Beresford was, as ever, the junior officer a had made himself guilty of persistent insubordination. He therefore ordered by the government to retire in March which left him free to devote more time to politics.

The Germans meanwhile had announced in 1907 th' would build three dreadnoughts a year to Britain's fo second Peace Conference at The Hague took place in year. Called on the initiative of President Theodore Roosevelt of the United States and chaired by Tsar Nicholas II of Russia, this was a renewed attempt by forty-four nations to limit the horrors of war in the same way as the Queensberry Rules imposed restraints on boxing. Although Germany refused even to discuss limitations on naval armament, the second round was less ineffectual than the first in 1899, producing clear procedures for the treatment of enemy or neutral shipping by naval vessels in wartime – Prize Rules. Under the Hague Convention passengers and crew had to be provided with the means of reaching safety before a ship carrying 'contraband' (goods that would help the enemy war effort) could be seized or sunk. The Japanese tradition of attack without warning, as at Port Arthur, was outlawed: states were required to give notice of belligerent intent by ultimatum. One backward step was the acceptance of the concept of the 'auxiliary cruiser' armed with naval guns to prey upon enemy commerce. It was not always obvious when a merchantman was armed, and whereas an unarmed ship was at least partly protected by Prize Rules, an armed one was fair game. Such considerations will be shown below to be particularly relevant for submariners.

In 1908, having completely failed to persuade the Germans to slow down, the British Liberal administration offered them a ratio of three to two in capital ships, a retreat to a one-and-a-half-power standard which the Kaiser dismissed out of hand, completely failing to grasp what an enormous sacrifice in prestige this meant. But if Wilhelm had been capable of seeing an opponent's point of view there would have been no 'German Question' and no war. His Navy had already begun to build dreadnoughts, and the Kiel Canal had to be widened, at huge expense, to take them. New bases and port facilities had to be provided, including the barracks in which crews spent most of their service. The Imperial Navy chose the 28-centimetre (11-inch) gun for its new generation of capital ships, a weapon which all but made up for its smaller calibre (compared with the British 12-inch) through better optics, propellant and steel: at some 200 shots a German barrel had twice the life expectancy of a British one. German armour was also stronger, although the British proved pragmatic enough to import Krupp steel. A further Fleet Law amendment in 1908 provided for four dreadnoughts a year until 1911 and two thereafter. Instead of the heavy cruisers of previous laws, battlecruisers would be built. The result would be a vast fighting fleet of thirty-eight battleships and twenty battlecruisers.

In 1908 the Royal Navy was four times larger than the Imperial in tonnage, with an advantage of five to two in dreadnoughts. But the Admiralty was worried when it learned that the Germans were also stepping up their gun-making capacity, because guns had been taking twice as long to make as hulls. At this rate the Germans could match the British in dreadnoughts in four years: the Admiralty asked for eight capital ships in 1909 instead of four. 'We want eight and we won't wait' was the cry of the jingoists in and out of Parliament. Anti-German feeling was now rampant, verging on panic in some quarters as the Imperial naval estimates for 1909 made their biggest annual jump, of 22 per cent. The German Navy League now boasted a membership of 900,000 and would soon pass the million.

On the geopolitical front the German threat, enhanced by the Kaiser's customary blunt-instrument diplomacy, had driven Britain and Russia together despite their Great Game in central Asia. Wilhelm had failed to separate Russia from France in 1905 and Britain from France shortly afterwards, but now positively drove the Russians to seek a rapprochement with Britain. Germany had antagonized both powers with its project for a Baghdad Railway from the Mediterranean to the Persian Gulf via the Euphrates valley, a threat as much to British as to Russian interests in the region (as well as in the Balkans, where Austria-Hungary, Germany's ally, and Turkey, assiduously wooed by the Germans, confronted each other). The Russians had been sending positive signals since 1905 and in August 1907 they and the British agreed to redefine their spheres of interest in Asia, thus completing the Triple Entente with France. The Germans were startled and resolved to build even more ships. The Kaiser wrote to Lord Tweedmouth, First Lord of the Admiralty, in February 1908, disingenuously denying that he wished to challenge the Royal Navy's supremacy. Even the most reluctant shipbuilders among British Liberals, in power since 1906, could not swallow this and held to the plan for four capital ships a year.

There was now a near-total consensus in Britain on the German threat. Even after a 'Copenhagen' against the Imperial fleet, Britain's little army could not hope successfully to invade Germany, protected as it was by a short coastline, a deep hinterland and the world's best military machine. But a single defeat of the Royal Navy could lay Britain open to invasion as it had never been since the days of the Armada in 1588. The Kaiser could not or

would not see this. The two-power standard had already been
redefined by David Lloyd George, Chancellor of the Exchequer,
extremely worried by escalating naval estimates, as Germany plus
any other power (by now the USA); the Admiralty's offer of three
dreadnoughts to two was, however, potentially dangerous for the
Empire. Sir Edward Grey, the Foreign Secretary, remarked: 'If the
German Navy ever becomes superior to ours, the German Army
can conquer the country.' But when King Edward VII visited
Germany in August 1908, his nephew refused to discuss naval
matters. Talks in 1909 got no further; the Germans proposed three
to four, in exchange for a free hand in Europe, while the British
pressed for a naval agreement both less generous to Germany and
in advance of a political one (the Germans wanted this order of
events reversed). France meanwhile began to modernize her fleet in
1909–10, while Britain recalled more ships from Australasia.

Even as the Kaiser refused to come to terms with Britain on naval
construction, he was seeking once again to bully France in
Morocco. The 1906 Algeçiras agreement broke down amid internal
unrest and the inability of the Sultan to cope. In February 1909
Germany prised from France a concession of equal commercial
and financial interests there while piously recognizing French
political primacy. At the beginning of 1911 an indigenous revolt
against the Sultan's new taxes prompted the French to send an
expedition to Fez in April to protect Europeans and their property.
The Germans took exception to this unilateral action and, with
sublime lack of logic, demanded the French Congo in west Africa
as 'compensation'. As if that were not enough, the Germans sent
the gunboat *Panther* to the Moroccan port of Agadir in July, 'to
protect German interests', a clear breach of French hegemony.

There was alarm all over Europe. On the London insurance
market marine rates doubled amid rumours of secret naval movements. The German press wallowed in Anglophobia as panic
overcame financial institutions in Berlin. The Royal Navy put its
home squadrons on standby in port and conducted an experiment
in shifting coal by rail from South Wales to Rosyth. The Kaiser
proposed yet more naval expenditure – but the Entente Cordiale
triumphantly survived the Agadir Incident, its second crisis in five
years. The British, fearing a German attempt to establish a naval
presence so close to Gibraltar, the key to the Mediterranean,
backed the French, who kept the Congo and conceded a strip of

territory in west Africa adjacent to the small German possessions in Togoland and Cameroon, in exchange for a new German acknowledgement of their political primacy in Morocco.

The Kaiser had risked a major war for a strip of jungle but the German naval lobby was unrepentant, encouraging Tirpitz to press for a ratio of two to three. Britain's 1911 naval estimates were relatively modest compared with 1910; and had the Admiralty not offered three to two as recently as 1908? It had, but Tirpitz ignored the objective of a guaranteed peace in Europe, regarded as inseparable by the British; without that, they would hardly allow him to complete the crossing of his 'danger zone' with impunity. For the first time the German navy lobby ceased to carry all before it. The Chancellor, Theobald von Bethmann-Hollweg, who had succeeded Bülow in 1909, was uneasy; so were the government's financial advisers and the Foreign Office. Most significant of all, the General Staff felt that quite enough had been spent on big ships, each of which cost the equivalent of two infantry divisions. In the Reichstag election the anti-expansionist SPD gained a million votes, capturing a third of the seats for the first time. The Kaiser retreated slightly in February, announcing the addition of just three battleships to the programme of twelve due by 1917. But in British eyes this was just another escalation – and the last straw.

In the background the Entente Cordiale was slowly but surely turning into a de facto alliance. French and British staff officers had been conducting military 'conversations' with each other and with Belgium since 1906. Meanwhile Admiral Fisher had fallen on his professional sword on his sixty-ninth birthday, 25 January 1910, in the backwash of the long and highly damaging feud with Beresford. An inquiry into the latter's complaints failed to substantiate them but revived hostility against the First Sea Lord, who was even blamed unofficially for being allegedly caught napping by renewed German naval expansion. Fisher, hurt by what he saw as half-hearted government support, had enough influence left to ensure he was succeeded by a supporter (Admiral Sir Arthur Wilson, VC) and wisely resigned with a peerage and the rank of admiral of the fleet. Nevertheless he would be heard from again, after the damaging rift in the Navy had been healed and a rudimentary naval staff set up in 1912. His legacy was a modernized, structurally streamlined and expanded fleet, capable of facing any likely threat to itself with renewed confidence and efficiency.

Winston Leonard Spencer Churchill had been appointed First Lord of the Admiralty on 23 October 1911. The Liberals, having won both the general elections of 1910, were still in power, with Herbert Henry Asquith as Prime Minister. At this time the Royal Navy enjoyed a lead in capital ships over Germany and America combined of 13 per cent – but the safety margin had fallen by a quarter in three years, and the lead in completed dreadnoughts was a mere 4 per cent. Taking rival building plans into account, to get back by 1915 to a strength of two powers (plus 10 per cent for the Empire) Britain would need to lay down seven dreadnoughts in 1912. In March of that year Churchill proposed a 'naval holiday', no construction for one year; failing that, he said, Britain would build four, resolving to add to this if German plans required it.

The Admiralty now officially revised the two-power standard downwards to a frank 'Germany plus sixty per cent' in dreadnoughts, a ratio of five to three rather than the three to two suggested in 1908. For the sake of the Empire, the 'two-powersplus' standard remained in force for cruisers and lesser ships. The US Navy effectively disappeared from British battlefleet calculations as Churchill and the admirals finally resolved to extend the Tirpitz danger zone for ever. If Germany adhered to two new ships a year for six years, Britain would achieve the new margin by building four and three in alternate years over the same period. If Germany were to add the threatened three, Britain would lay down six in 1912 and five in 1913; but if Germany reduced, so would Britain. In a typical rhetorical flourish, Churchill added to his challenge the remark that German restraint would reduce the Royal Navy by five dreadnoughts – more than she could hope to achieve in a brilliant naval action!

Four days later, Tirpitz announced that Germany would add three battleships to the programme resulting from the two fleet laws and their subsequent amendments, now due for completion in 1920. The Reichstag endorsed this supplement, itself supplemented by an expensive sop to the General Staff of extra funds for the Army. Churchill responded in May that Britain would start five new ships in the ensuing year and four in each of the four following, instead of three-four-three-four-three, thus adding four extra dreadnoughts by 1917; there would also be more non-capital ships and a recruitment drive. All the other major navies were now building or planning dreadnoughts.

By autumn 1912, therefore, the Tirpitz danger zone appeared to stretch ahead to infinity. Not only had the British assembled forty-nine capital ships in home waters compared with Germany's twenty-nine; they had also come to a naval accommodation whereby France took charge of the Mediterranean while the British covered the French Atlantic and Channel coasts. This sensible arrangement was formalized in the Anglo-French Naval Agreement of 10 February 1913. An immense strategic shift, it also destroyed the residual credibility of the Tirpitz risk theory, already fatally undermined by clear British determination to outbuild Germany at any cost. And the reduced British Mediterranean Fleet remained large enough to face the Austrian fleet unaided if need be.

None of this deterred the Kaiser from creating, on a whim in November 1912, a naval 'Mediterranean Division', consisting of his most modern capital ship, the battlecruiser *Goeben*, escorted by the fast light cruiser *Breslau*, and commanded from October 1913 by Rear-Admiral Wilhelm Souchon. The *Goeben* might be the finest warship in the Mediterranean, but her presence did not seem to affect the overwhelming superiority of the Franco-British over the Triple Alliance navies, even if Italy were to support Germany and Austria, a prospect for which it showed no taste. The post-Tsushima Russian Black Sea Fleet was old and weak and as yet had no dreadnoughts; the Turkish Navy, though under British tutelage just as the Turkish Army was under German, was in even worse case, albeit awaiting delivery of two British-made dreadnoughts. The 'Young Turks' of the Army-dominated Committee of Union and Progress (CUP) had taken power in 1908 and were committed to modernizing the Ottoman Empire before it disappeared altogether, having effectively lost control of Egypt and the Maghreb (North Africa) and the Balkan–Aegean region of Europe while retaining Arabia and the Levant. The Germans were pursuing more actively than any other power what seemed to be a golden opportunity for an understanding with the young officers of the CUP, especially Enver Pasha, hero of the Balkan Wars of 1912–13.

Anglo-German relations, and those among the other leading European powers, had not reached rock bottom; far from it. In October 1912 the world was reminded of Bismarck's long-standing prediction that if there was to be a general war in Europe, it would be triggered by 'some damned foolish thing in the Balkans'. War broke out there between Serbia, Montenegro, Bulgaria and Greece on the one hand and tottering Turkey on the other. An armistice was declared in December but in January the Bulgarians renewed hostilities. A crisis committee of the ambassadors to London of the leading European powers, chaired by Sir Edward Grey, the Foreign Secretary, harmoniously managed to impose a settlement by May 1913. Ships of the leading powers were also cooperating well in an international squadron stationed off the Albanian port of Durazzo (Durres) because of unrest inside the country (the century was to end in the irrepressible Balkans in similarly murderous chaos: anarchy in Albania, shooting in Sarajevo and tension in Turkey, with outside powers, including Britain and her Navy, reluctantly intervening or hovering anxiously on the sidelines).

Two months earlier Tirpitz, knowing Churchill was about to announce his naval estimates, told the Reichstag that he would accept a British margin of 'Germany plus sixty per cent' in battleships – a ratio of thirty-two to twenty, or eight squadrons to five. He now had no choice, because the Army, Germany's senior service, was to increase its standing strength by a quarter in three years and the country could not afford to continue the breakneck expansion of its Navy at the same time, especially as it was an open secret that the British were planning a third generation of dreadnoughts with 15-inch guns. Churchill noted that the Tirpitz 'offer' included no moratorium or cut in construction as such and thus took no account of his idea of a naval holiday. Britain would therefore go ahead with five dreadnoughts, eight light cruisers, sixteen destroyers and recruiting 7,000 extra men. The Admiralty settled for a lead of 50 per cent in home waters; the remaining 10 per cent of the margin was for training and missions further afield. When Canada jibbed at funding three dreadnoughts, Churchill resolved to add three to the British estimates for 1914, to preserve the crucial North Sea margin.

Tirpitz finally if reluctantly saw the light when the Kaiser and he considered their naval estimates for 1914. The grand-admiral for the first time urged restraint upon his sovereign, who wanted to bring forward the completion of the dreadnought programme and to build more 'blue-water' cruisers for distant operations. It would be 'a great political blunder' to step up the rate of construction, Tirpitz loftily told his naval attaché in London, as if the past sixteen years of headlong shipbuilding had never happened; Churchill would only seize upon it for another spurt of his own. Germany had now spent more than £200m on warships from 1900 to 1914 without getting anywhere near the exit from the danger zone, and the almighty General Staff had put its foot down, demanding absolute priority for strengthening the Army. British naval estimates rose from £45m for 1912 to £49m, over 25 per cent of the total budget and a peacetime record, in 1913; and in cross-Channel staff talks, London undertook to send a British Expeditionary Force of six divisions to France in the event of war with Germany, to stand between the left of the French line and the Channel. The belated 'U-turn', as we would now call it, by Tirpitz might have enhanced the promising Anglo-German detente which had begun in 1912 with their cooperation over the Balkans, but for the powder keg of rival nationalisms in Europe. This was duly ignited by an assassin's pistol in hapless Sarajevo in June 1914, when the heir to the Austrian throne, Archduke Franz Ferdinand, and his wife were shot dead by a boy fired up with Serbian nationalism.

During the period of frenetic diplomatic manoeuvring and naval competition described above, three momentous new additions were made to the inventory of technical advances since sail made way for steam at sea. Capital ships were the strategic weapons of their day, the yardstick by which the leading powers measured their might. The huge sums spent on them were further inflated, not only by the arms race of the time but also by the speed and variety of technological advance already noted, which even affected their colour: the Germans started to camouflage their warships with grey paint in 1902, an idea quickly adopted by the other navies. Each of these developments had arisen mainly in an evolutionary way, if also at startling speed; but at the beginning of the century three inventions initiated a multiple revolution in naval strategy.

Giuseppe Marconi invented radio in 1894 and brought it to a receptive England in 1897, when the Marconi Wireless Telegraph Company was founded in London. The Royal Navy ordered thirty-two sets as early as 1900, agreeing to pay an annual royalty of £100 on each set for ten years. The Admiralty was so impressed by early results that it secretly ordered the Ediswan company to make fifty pirate sets with no thought of royalties. The first military use of wireless was made, as we saw, in the Boer War, when the British Army 'borrowed' five Marconi mobile stations intended for shore-to-ship communication and used them for overland transmissions, where they proved very useful when they worked, but unreliable in a role for which they had not been designed.

Marconi next patented the breakthrough concept of tuning, to overcome interference between transmitters, and bought the rights to his admirer Thomas Edison's patent aerial; in December 1901 the first faint transatlantic transmission was achieved. The invention spread round the world with extraordinary speed, urged on its way by competition from rival companies, especially Telefunken of Germany. An Italian cruiser with a Marconi set was afforded a place next to the British Royal Yacht for the Coronation Review in August 1902 (Italy was Marconi's fatherland, Britain his motherland; he was befriended by the kings of both countries as he became the world's most famous person of the age).

In a few short years wireless telegraphy was standard equipment at sea, not only among men of war but also on merchant ships. Marconi was awarded the Nobel Prize for Physics in 1902 but had to share it with his arch-rival, Professor Ferdinand Braun of Telefunken. The significance of wireless for navies was immeasurable. Hitherto ships had been reachable only by visual signals (flags and latterly electric lamps) at a maximum range of about twenty miles. Admirals and the captains of detached ships had been able to communicate with the Admiralty by landline (telegraph, then telephone) for some years but had to go ashore to do so. At sea before Marconi they had perforce acted independently, sailing with orders whose detailed interpretation on the spot had to be left to them, perhaps with hair-raising results – and sometimes enabling history to be made by a mere lieutenant, the modest rank held by such captains as Bligh of the *Bounty* and Cook of the *Endeavour*. Now the Admiralty could reach flagships and individual vessels alike, directly or by relay, thousands of miles away, including the furthest reaches of the Mediterranean and the Atlantic.

The invention was a decidedly mixed blessing, with detailed interference by the Admiralty in minor operational, tactical and administrative detail largely offsetting the advantage of being able to transmit the latest intelligence (a facility used all too rarely and regarded with the deepest suspicion in instinctively furtive Whitehall). Exasperated seagoing commanders were wont to remark that if Nelson had been reachable by wireless, he would never have won at Trafalgar; true or not, he certainly interpreted his orders creatively to win that decisive victory (a point lost on most of his successors). Further, early wireless was decidedly temperamental; transmissions were in Morse code and often took hours, even days, to get through after countless repetitions.

Garbled and incomplete messages were commonplace, and sloppy drafting often increased rather than resolved confusion at sea, as would be dramatically demonstrated in the very opening hours of the coming war. But only a few years after wireless was invented, a ship's whereabouts could be detected by an enemy using radio direction-finding (RDF), a practical application which by 1911 also offered the positive advantage of navigation by wireless beacons.

The American Orville Wright made the first truly successful powered flight in December 1903. Only eight years later another American, Eugene Ely, made the first take-off and landing on a platform erected over the turrets and deck of a cruiser. Shortly afterwards the Briton Commander Samson, RN, flew a biplane off the long foredeck of the battleship HMS *Africa* (but landed ashore). By 1914 larger warships routinely carried one or more seaplanes, capable of taking off from a crosswise ramp, landing in the sea after their mission and being hoisted back aboard. The main maritime value of these fragile machines of wood and cloth held together by wire was for reconnaissance. Early models carried no weapons (or wireless), but by extending a warship's 'eyes' many miles over the horizon they soon earned their keep. Navies had also adopted airships for observational purposes before the war, especially over the North Sea. It was not until 1917 that operational aircraft would be able to land on a flight deck (HMS *Furious*); the first purpose-built aircraft carrier, HMS *Argus*, did not put to sea until 1918. But by then the war itself had forced aircraft development at such a pace that the fighter, the bomber and, most significantly for navies, the torpedo-bomber, had already proved themselves.

Marconi, always at the forefront of wireless development in his lifetime, was the first to try installing it in aircraft, experimenting as early as 1915. But voice transmission, the real breakthrough here, had yet to be developed. Pioneer pilots, especially if flying alone, already had more than enough to do with their hands without being required to tap out signals on a Morse key or scribble down incoming messages.

The submarine completes our trio of revolutionary inventions. Conceived as an 'equalizer', its main inspiration was the might of the Royal Navy. It came into service in its first, barely viable form as a despised underdog's weapon at the very beginning of the century – and ended it as the ultimate weapon, unless and until the human race takes its penchant for aggression into space. The history of the Royal Navy was dominated by the submarine for by far the greater part of the century. The first attempt by a submersible craft to sink a warship was made in 1776 by the American Sergeant Ezra Lee in an egg-shaped, hand-propelled, wooden vessel designed by David Bushnell and modestly named the *Turtle*. The target was HMS *Eagle*, the flagship of Vice-Admiral Earl Howe in the blockade of New York during the American War of Independence. The attempt failed because the drill with which Lee tried to attach a bomb to the hull broke. A century later, after several experiments elsewhere, a young Irish immigrant to the United States, John Philip Holland, inspired by Fenian anti-British sentiment, was at work on a submersible warship, but a plot to smuggle Holland's prototype, the *Fenian Ram*, to Britain collapsed when the conspirators ran it aground in 1882. The inventor's ninth design, the first production model, included a remarkable range of features which established J. P. Holland as the father of the submarine. 'Hollands' were ordered by several navies from 1900, including the American, Japanese, Russian – and the British.

The prototype 'Holland' on which the production model was based had been commissioned into the US Navy early in 1900. But it was not the first to go into service; the French Navy was the first to commision a submarine a year earlier, and it was this development that provoked a classic Admiralty kneejerk reaction. Admiral Sir Arthur Wilson, Fisher's successor as First Sea Lord in 1910, had said in 1901 that the submarine was 'underhand, unfair and damned un-English'. He wanted submariners caught in wartime hanged without trial as pirates. Two years earlier fears of the still embryonic submarine had led the British and other delegates at the first Peace Conference at The Hague to invite the twenty-six governments represented to outlaw not only the submarine but also the torpedo, which would truly come into its own when deployed by the underwater warship. Fisher was one of the first to recognize the potential of this deadly combination, saying soon after his appointment as First Sea Lord in 1904:

I don't think it is even faintly realised – the immense impending revolution which the submarines will effect as offensive weapons of war. [He went on to say, in January 1914:] There is nothing else the submarine can do except sink her capture . . . This submarine menace is a terrible one for British commerce and Great Britain alike, for no means can be suggested at present of meeting it except by reprisals.

But the idea of outlawing the submarine, which would recur after it had proved itself indispensable, was thrown into the same wastepaper-basket as all other major disarmament proposals. In March 1901, therefore, the Admiralty included £175,000 in the naval estimates of 1901–2, for five 'Hollands' to be built under licence at the Vickers Yard in Barrow-in-Furness, still the centre of British submarine construction at the end of the century. His Majesty's *Submarine Number One* (Lieutenant F. D. Arnold-Forster, RN) was commissioned early in 1902. The Inspecting Captain of submarines appointed at the same time was Captain (later Admiral Sir) Reginald Bacon, who made the periscope standard equipment and helped to design the second British class of thirteen larger 'A' boats from 1903. *Holland No. I* foundered under tow to the breaker's yard in 1913 but was detected by a minesweeper off Plymouth in 1981. She was restored as a prize exhibit at the Submarine Museum in Gosport, near Portsmouth. Visitors may squeeze into her hull and marvel how as many as nine men managed to go to sea in her and return sane and unharmed.

'Germany has no need of submarines,' Tirpitz told the Reichstag in 1901; but when the British began building their third batch in 1904 he minuted: 'I intend to have a submarine built by the Navy Office and authorize . . . the construction.' *Unterseeboot 1* (*U1*) was completed in September 1906. Unlike the 'Hollands' she had twin engines and a double hull, as all German submarines did until 1944; she used paraffin rather than petrol for propulsion. The Germans may have come a little late to submarine construction but they were soon introducing one innovation after another, such as diesel engines (1913). The last prewar class, starting with *U19*, displaced 650 tons surfaced (837 submerged) and was 210 feet long, a measure in the most literal sense of how rapidly the technology was advancing. By that time also, torpedoes had increased their range of about 2,000 yards at Tsushima in 1905 up to sixfold, as well as doubling their speed (up to 40 knots).

Viewed with disdain by orthodox naval strategists and tacticians, the submarine was not envisaged before the First World War as a predator on commerce, the role in which it has done the most actual damage so far. Its very name was a misnomer because it usually travelled on the surface, submerging only to avoid detection when escaping, reconnoitring or attacking an armed vessel. It was a submersible torpedo boat, its main asset being stealth, for which it paid a very high price in vulnerability. Seen as vaguely tasked auxiliaries to the battlefleet, submarines were at an immediate disadvantage because of their lack of speed, even on the surface. They might serve as scouts or sentries; minelaying was a natural role soon to be recognized by the rival navies on the North Sea. But in their early days the main effect was psychological – yet also profound. The attachment of submarines to the fleet was marked by their great successes against much bigger ships on manoeuvres.

On an exercise in spring 1904 HM Submarine *A1* scored four dummy hits on a battleship before submerging; shortly afterwards a borrowed liner duly reported a hit on herself – followed by a bumping under her bottom. *A1* did not return to the surface after being accidentally run over by the liner in shallow waters. After this first British submarine disaster all other boats in the service were fitted with a watertight hatch at the bottom as well as the top of the conning tower. Yet the high number of hits by submarines in exercises, and the inability of surface ships to destroy them except by ramming, or even to find them, were ignored or countered by restrictive rules of engagement (until 1910, submarines on exercise had to be escorted by a surface vessel flying a red flag, like a maritime version of the 'horseless carriage'!). The mere existence of the submarine inspired even more fear in commanders than the dreaded mine.

The most important strategic result was the decision by the Admiralty as late as July 1914 to abandon its traditional close blockade of enemy ports in favour of distant blockade. This led the Royal Navy to hold back its Grand Fleet (the newly unified home-waters formation) in readiness for a new Trafalgar while deploying cruisers and submarines to keep watch from forward positions. Vice-Admiral Sir John Jellicoe, the Grand Fleet's C-in-C, was so worried by the submarine threat that he resolved to keep his battle squadrons on the move once war began. The new principal wartime base, Scapa Flow in the Orkney Islands off the north coast of Scotland, had no defences against submarines. The name 'dreadnought' already seemed decidedly ironic before any such ship had fired a shot in anger.

The Navy that nervously deployed them after nearly a century of general peace in Europe was still embroiled in an organizational upheaval only partly due to the endless stream of technical innovations since the demise of sail. Manpower had passed 60,000 for the Crimean War (1854–6) and stayed at this level for nearly thirty-five years. In 1891, two years after the first Naval Defence Act, the reviving service reached 70,000. In the pivotal year of 1898 there were 103,000 sailors; when Victoria died in 1901 there were 117,000; when Edward VII died in 1910 there were 131,000; and on the outbreak of war 146,000. By the end of 1914 ranks would swell to 250,000 – still entirely made up of volunteers. Not only had numbers risen at an increasing rate; so had the number of specialist branches, from the appointment of the first engineer officer in 1835 (there were over 25,000 officers and men in the branch in 1900) via the first intelligence officer in 1887 and the first physical training instructor in 1900 to the arrival below decks of the first specialized telegraphists in 1908.

The basic pay of an able seaman was 1s 7d per day, perhaps augmented by one or more of a bewildering array of extra allowances until they were simplified in 1906. Stokers, a race apart aboard ship, got more because of the hellish nature of their work. By 1912 junior ratings got an extra 3d a day after six years' service (when aged about twenty-four) and senior rates 4d; the 'hard-lying' allowance (for arduous berths such as small ships) was 6d a day until Churchill made it 7½d, and there was no married man's allowance until after hostilities began.

These were not riches; and conditions in the service on which Britain's security rested were anything but extravagant, leading to a constant undercurrent of grievance that sometimes forced its way to the surface in the not always entirely silent service. Ratings slept (in hammocks) and ate in the same messdeck quarters, which were commonly damp, either too hot or too cold and always too crowded for privacy. Only two meals a day, morning and evening, were provided, and then only after a campaign by ex-Petty Officer Yexley's *Bluejacket* magazine for the second. The notorious daily tot of rum encouraged drunkenness, creating far more real problems than it was believed to solve. Venereal disease was common (sufferers had a separate mess) and so was homosexuality, a taboo subject covered, like many another commonplace breach of the Naval Discipline Act, by the 'eleventh commandment' (thou shalt not be found out). Bullying was rife, often anything but

discouraged by those in authority. So was 'bull', as a later generation of servicemen learned from the Americans to call the obsession
with spit and polish, whether applied to uniforms or a battleship's
huge decks and guns.

Among the many grievances taken up by Yexley were the poor
quality of food and the fact that sailors had to provide their own
cutlery; the cost to ratings of uniforms; the absence of a career
structure for such as stokers; and a general official indifference to
welfare matters. Both before and during his term as First Sea Lord
Fisher achieved enormous improvements in most such areas, and
from 1911 Churchill was responsible for further ameliorations.
Even so, crass orders by a martinet of a lieutenant to a parade at
Portsmouth Barracks in November 1906 led to a prolonged riot
(mutiny can occur only at sea) in which stokers, always chary of
discipline, featured prominently and for which a commodore and
two commanders were dismissed, while the stoker-ringleader got
three years' penal servitude (reduced from five after a press
outcry).

Fisher's changes were radical. Some 150 obsolete ships, mostly
on overseas stations, were paid off and whole fleets realigned as the
bulk of the Navy concentrated against Germany. The Third or
Reserve Fleet – in home waters, like the First (later Grand) and
Second (later Channel) fleets – underwent a transformation both in
efficiency and readiness, with ships permanently manned at 60 per
cent, capable both of turning out immediately in emergency and of
swift reinforcement to wartime strength. The Royal Naval Volunteer Reserve (RNVR) was founded in 1903 to support the Royal
Naval Reserve, the basis of rapid wartime expansion.

Nevertheless the brief panic caused by the Agadir Crisis in 1911
showed up the Navy as woefully unprepared for emergency
mobilization, with severe discipline problems on the capital ships
and in barracks ashore. The predominant grievances were the
traditionally harsh punishment regime, pay, pensions and lack of
promotion opportunities. Fisher's successor, Wilson, was invited
to retire as Churchill became First Lord with a brief to extend
reform. The harsh punishment regime was modernized sufficiently
to last through the Second World War and beyond, while
conditions on the larger ships became more humane. The old four
hours on, four off system, unworkable on a modern ship in wartime, was replaced by one of three watches (four on, eight off).
Petty officers were allowed to run their own messes as they saw fit,

and facilities such as laundries, libraries, chapels and even film projectors were introduced.

Officer recruitment and training, already shaken up by the self-made Fisher, were broadened and more were recruited from the ranks ('up the hawsepipe') from 1912, when the pay rates mentioned above were introduced, raising lower-deck morale just in time for the war. The service at last acquired a War Staff – though only in an advisory capacity, with no member on the Admiralty Board! The feverish pace of administrative reform in the new century had, however, begun too late to produce a crop of good admirals by the time it was needed. Ships' captains were sound and their crews of surprisingly high quality, better trained and better disposed to the service; but there were still too many donkeys in gold braid to lead them.

By August 1914 Britain had thirty-one dreadnoughts (including eight battlecruisers) in commission and thirteen building (all but one of them battleships). France had four battleships at sea and three on order while Russia had one battleship and two battle-cruisers at sea and six of the latter on order. Germany had thirteen dreadnought battleships and five battlecruisers at sea with five and two respectively on the stocks. Italy had three dreadnoughts and three more under construction; Austria had two afloat. Turkey had none, once the two dreadnought battleships ordered from Britain were brusquely seized by the Royal Navy.

Britain also had the world's largest submarine arm on the outbreak of war: seventy-five in commission and twenty-eight building. Of the former only twenty were ocean-going (with diesel engines, a deck gun and a displacement of 550 tons or more); the rest were suitable only for coastal work or training. None had yet been converted to carry mines. France had sixty-two in service and nine under construction. Russia had thirty-six and nineteen. Germany's U-boat arm was fourth in size but first in quality, with twenty-eight in service and seventeen on the stocks. Ten were ocean-going, 650-tonners with the longest range and highest performance in the world; Germany started building minelaying boats in 1915. Italy had twenty-one boats, mostly of poor quality, with seven being built. Austria had just six operational submarines and two building, but these incorporated the latest German technology and were to prove the most effective, boat for boat, deployed by any belligerent. But it was Britain's dreadnoughts that made the decisive opening move, several days before the country found itself at war.

The main fear of the High Seas Fleet command was, with every good reason, blockade, which was however expected to be at close range. The Germans planned to pick off blockading units with locally superior concentrations of force until attrition had reduced British strength sufficiently for them to stand a good chance of winning, or drawing (which would have been quite enough), a fleet action. All this was entirely secondary to the role of the German Army, which was to repeat its swift victory against France in 1870 by a massive swing round Paris before tackling the main enemy, Russia. Britain relied on its Navy for victory at sea while the French Army, reinforced by the six British divisions, held the Germans on land in the west and the Russians fought them in the east.

All concerned believed the issue would be decided by Christmas when Austria, Germany's ally, attacked Russia's client, Serbia, in the wake of the Sarajevo shootings. Russia mobilized; so did Germany, and when the Tsar ignored the Kaiser's ultimatum to stand down his troops, Germany declared war on Russia on 1 August 1914. Thereupon France mobilized, well behind its frontier to ensure the Germans struck the first blow. When they did so, violating Belgian neutrality with their swollen right wing, Britain had no option but to join the fight, at midnight on 4 August.

3

The Great War: Cruisers

The Grand Fleet had assembled for a royal review at Spithead, in the waters between the south coast of the English mainland and the Isle of Wight, on 17 July 1914. The reorganized Reserve Fleet had also been brought up to full strength on the 10th, for this purpose and for the first time, by a call-up of all 20,000 first-line reservists as a rehearsal for a full naval mobilization. But instead of dispersing this greatest array of firepower yet seen on the 29th as planned, the Admiralty issued the order which was to influence the outcome of the imminent war more than any other single factor, not excluding the slow Armageddon to come on land. Anticipating war at any moment, it turned the parade into a real mobilization by dispatching the fleet to Scapa Flow in the Orkney Islands, some 800 miles of steaming to the north; the ships of the reserve, having dispersed to their war stations, were still fully manned and were ordered to remain so. The line of grey steel eighteen miles long – over a hundred light cruisers, destroyers, battlecruisers, battleships and auxiliaries – took two days to reach its new principal wartime base under the flag of its Commander-in-Chief, Admiral Sir George Callaghan. But on arrival Callaghan, aged sixty-one, was abruptly superseded by his second-in-command, Admiral Sir John Jellicoe, aged fifty-four, who had the grace to protest vehemently to Churchill, the First Lord, and the First Sea Lord, Admiral Prince Louis of Battenberg.

The self-effacing but popular Jellicoe, slightly built and just five feet six inches tall, thus became leader of the bulk of the Royal Navy, the nation's bulwark – the man who, in Churchill's words, 'could lose the war in an afternoon' and could not afford to lose a single battle. He struck outsiders as a colourless figure but had been the beneficiary of accelerated promotion by Fisher, who admired his exceptional intellect and mastery of detail as well as his early prowess as a gunnery officer. The political and operational chiefs of the Royal Navy stuck to their joint decision, despite the shock to morale among the 60,000 men of the Grand Fleet, as it was now officially known. But Callaghan had been due to retire in two months. The Fleet's Battlecruiser Squadron, led by the impossibly vainglorious Rear-Admiral Sir David Beatty, fresh from his stint as Churchill's Naval Secretary, turned aside to its separate station in the Cromarty Firth on the north-east coast of Scotland.

'From that moment Germany's arteries were subjected to an invisible pressure which never relaxed,' wrote Sir Basil Liddell Hart of the early deployment of the Grand Fleet in his *History of the Great War*. Until 1912 the Admiralty had favoured a policy of close blockade as used against Napoleon a century before. Then it decided on an 'observational' blockade, a screen of cruisers in a 300-mile crescent from Norway to Holland, with the Grand Fleet lying in wait off Scotland. Fear of mines and submarines, however, caused the admirals to rethink their strategy a second time in the last days of peace. In July 1914 they adopted distant blockade, clear of minefields, U-boats and the fortress of Heligoland, the Germans' forward base in the North Sea. The new fear of submarines had not prompted anyone to provide practical defences at Scapa Flow, a huge deep-water anchorage accessible by several unobstructed channels. The Grand Fleet would still be lying in wait at Scapa, but secondary forces such as the Northern Patrol, including old cruisers and submarines, would watch for any German vessels, whether skirmishers such as minelayers and fast raiders, the High Seas Fleet in whole or in part, incoming merchant shipping or blockade-runners in the North Sea and in the 300-mile gap between the Orkneys and neutral Norway.

The pre-dreadnought Channel (Second) Fleet, under the ailing Vice-Admiral Sir Cecil Burney, was ordered to cover, from its bases on the south coast of England, the closure of the Strait of Dover, barely twenty miles wide, thus blocking Germany's southerly exit to the broad Atlantic. Burney's other early assignment was to superintend the transfer to north-west France of the first four divisions of the British Expeditionary Force (soon to muster six divisions and 150,000 men), smoothly accomplished by 20 August. The Strait itself was under the close protection of the Dover Patrol of two dozen destroyers and supporting ships, commanded by Vice-Admiral Reginald Bacon. Between the First and Second Fleets the Admiralty stationed a strong force of light cruisers and destroyers at Harwich on the coast of East Anglia under Commodore Reginald Tyrwhitt; Commodore Roger Keyes,

Inspecting Captain of Submarines, was also based there with many of his charges. Auxiliary forces were stationed at lesser bases along the British east coast.

Many witnesses ashore in the Solent area must have seen the battlefleet form up for departure, and someone standing on the white cliffs of Dover might well have espied it sailing past at fifteen knots a few miles offshore. On the following day, 30 July, many Germans certainly stood agog on the banks of the Kaiser Wilhelm Canal, only just broadened to accommodate the latest dread-noughts (in one-way single file), as the High Seas Fleet, com-manded by Admiral Friedrich von Ingenohl, took a whole day to pass from Kiel on the Baltic to Brunsbüttel on the Elbe estuary, en route to the North Sea bases; the great grey sides of the un-expectedly graceful battleships loomed over the flat green country of Schleswig-Holstein. Their main armament was lighter but their armour heavier and their engines more reliable than those of their British counterparts. The low profiles of twenty submarines modestly brought up the rear, led by their chief, Hermann Bauer, a mere commander, on their way to form a defensive screen in the Heligoland Bight, west of the island fortress, on 1 August.

But the Germans had no intention of dashing out to take on the British in the second Trafalgar which the Royal Navy and the British public expected or desired. The High Seas Fleet had indeed been built to fight the Grand Fleet – but only after the latter had been whittled down by attrition. The Imperial Navy's strategy remained as conceived by Tirpitz: to apply locally superior force against individual British ships and squadrons engaged in the traditional close blockade the Germans were expecting. Then, when the Grand Fleet was sufficiently reduced, the High Seas Fleet would engage it in a fleet action with a fair chance of victory, confident that a mere draw would suffice to neutralize the principal strategic asset of the British, laying them open to invasion, and thus to force them and their little army, dismissed by the Kaiser as 'contemptible', to negotiate from a position of weakness.

This was a sound strategy because Germany's narrow and treacherous North Sea coastline conferred virtual immunity from seaborne assault while offering protected accommodation for the battlefleet in Wilhelmshaven, the principal North Sea base, Cuxhaven and Bremerhaven, as well as a series of subsidiary harbours accessible only at high tide. The attenuated Russian

Baltic Fleet presented no major threat in the congested waters of Germany's 'Eastern Sea', which could quickly be reinforced via the Kiel Canal. The British could reach the Baltic only by sailing round neutral Denmark into narrow and shallow waters offering no sea-room for major warships. Fisher's prewar proposal to 'Copenhagen' the High Seas Fleet in its North Sea lair, to say nothing of Churchill's in August 1914 to send capital ships charging into the Baltic, looks less viable the more one studies the map. For the Germans with their favourable maritime defensive position the answer to the former threat was dispersal and to the latter concentration; neither materialized.

Nor was there a new Trafalgar as an early naval climax to a war everyone assumed would be 'over by Christmas'. The British were as anxious to conserve their fleet as the Germans were to wear it down piecemeal before a frontal attack. The opposing battle fleets prudently stayed out of reach of each other except for occasional hit-and-run raids, each side hoping to lure the other into an error that would allow it to pounce. This mutual wariness had all the makings of a mighty stalemate even if early events gave a different impression. And although the focus of attention, and of the main strength, of both sides in the maritime war was the North Sea, the first important clashes between the two leading navies, the Royal and the Imperial, took place in distant waters. The protagonists were not the mighty battle squadrons so swiftly and expensively constructed by the great rivals but cruisers – including battle-cruisers, in their originally conceived role as giant, free-ranging corsairs rather than pass-for-battleships.

Dramas come no higher than the great chase across the length of the Mediterranean which began frustratingly for the Royal Navy even before it was at war. As his Franco-British colleagues guessed, Rear-Admiral Souchon was under orders in the event of war to lead his battlecruiser, SMS *Goeben*, and her solitary escort, the light cruiser *Breslau*, to attack French North Africa and disrupt the transfer of colonial troops to their places in the line facing Germany. Then he surely had just two options: to reinforce his Austrian allies by taking refuge in the Adriatic, or else to carry on westward to run a British gauntlet at the Strait of Gibraltar and a worse one at the Dover Strait on the way home (sailing the long way round, west of the British Isles, would have left him without any reserves of coal; even the Channel route would have presented a fuel problem).

In the last days of July 1914 the *Goeben*, a 23,000-ton ship with a design speed of twenty-eight knots, was at Pola, the principal Austrian naval base in the north-eastern Adriatic, while the *Breslau* lay off Durrazzo (Durres), Albania. The 4,550-ton, 28-knot cruiser was the German member of the international squadron supporting the new, German-derived monarchy against a rebellious population, upon which it had been imposed by the Central Powers after the country gained independence from Turkey in 1912. Souchon on the *Goeben*, determined not to be trapped in the Adriatic, ordered his two ships to link up at Brindisi, on the eastern side of the Italian 'heel', on 1 August. From there they sailed round the Italian foot to Messina, the harbour on the Sicilian side of the strait of the same name, arriving at lunchtime on the 2nd. The short-range *Goeben* in particular needed coal, and Messina was the agreed wartime naval rendezvous for the Triple Alliance of Germany, Austria-Hungary and Italy. They were required to help each other if one or more was attacked by France or Russia. Since Germany initiated hostilities against Russia on the 1st and against France on the 3rd, there was no *casus foederis* and Italy was free to announce her neutrality.

The two cruisers, having taken what coal they could, sailed at midnight Greenwich Mean Time on the night of 2 to 3 August. They took an initially northerly course, which meant they were westward bound along the north coast of Sicily. Evading with ease the bulk of the French Fleet under Vice-Admiral Augustin Boué de Lapeyrère, the *Goeben* turned south to shell Philippeville while the *Breslau* bombarded Bône at dawn on the 3rd, disrupting as planned the transhipment of the French XIX Corps from North Africa. At 9.05 a.m. GMT on the 4th, however, as they sailed back to Sicily at economical cruising speed (fifteen knots), the Germans were sighted from due east – by a pair of westbound British battlecruisers, *Indomitable* and *Indefatigable*. Germans and British went to action stations amid high tension on both sides, but kept their big guns aligned fore and aft as they passed each other at a distance of some 10,000 yards, well within optimum big-gun range; the customary exchange of salutes did not take place. The British pair, which together decisively outgunned the *Goeben* but lacked her speed, put about to follow the Germans, who piled on steam and raced back to Messina for more coal. By 3 p.m. the British battlecruisers had fallen back over the horizon; only the light cruiser *Dublin*, which had joined the chase by lunchtime, was fast enough to maintain contact at a respectful distance.

This extraordinary drama, during which several German stokers were worked to death feeding the *Goeben*'s voracious furnaces, developed without a shot, although the ether was thick with frantic wireless messages between the twin battlecruisers and an electrified Admiralty. By a supreme irony Britain would not be at war until midnight on the night of 4 to 5 August; the Royal Navy was thus unable to snatch an early victory. The two battlecruisers were on temporary detachment, under Captain Francis Kennedy of *Indomitable*, from the British Mediterranean Fleet, led by Admiral Sir Berkeley Milne and based at Malta. Their mission was to trap the Germans at or east of Gibraltar with their superior firepower, the assumption being that Admiral Souchon must, sooner rather than later, attempt to run for home. Milne retained a third battlecruiser, his flagship *Inflexible*, at Malta, together with a light cruiser and four destroyers. Other light cruisers, including *Dublin* and *Gloucester*, were on the alert and patrolling in adjacent areas.

Sir Archibald Berkeley Milne was known to the lower deck as 'Arky Barky', but his appointment in April 1912 to what was still the plum command in the Admiralty's gift, the Mediterranean Fleet, prompted the retired Fisher to write to Churchill: 'I consider you have betrayed the Navy . . . *You are aware that Sir Berkeley Milne is unfitted to be the senior admiral afloat* . . . I can't believe that you foresee all the consequences! The results would be IRREPARABLE, IRREMEDIABLE, ETERNAL!' All the emphasis was the explosive Fisher's. Well-connected son of an admiral of the fleet, Milne was Commodore of the Royal Yacht Squadron in 1903 and a close confidant of Alexandra, hapless consort of the womanizing King Edward VII; by now she was the Queen Mother of George V.

Milne's second-in-command, Rear-Admiral Ernest Charles Thomas Troubridge of the First Cruiser Squadron, came from a background no less privileged. Descended from a long line of distinguished admirals and soldiers who came to the fore in the Napoleonic and Crimean wars, Troubridge was nicknamed 'the Silver King' by sailors for his great mane of hair, over a ruddy face which went well with a bluff and cheery manner. Although he too had served on royal yachts, he was no mere social sailor. He was much cleverer than he appeared and also physically brave, winning a medal from the Royal Humane Society as a young officer by diving into the sea at night from a speeding torpedo boat to save a rating who had fallen overboard. He served as naval attaché in Tokyo during the Russo-Japanese War, writing astute and valuable analyses. A natural sailor, Troubridge was also a natural staff officer, having proved himself as Naval Secretary to Churchill's predecessor as First Lord, Reginald McKenna. Later he became the Royal Navy's first Chief of Staff when a rudimentary War Staff was set up on the basis of an expanded Naval Intelligence Department in 1912. He also enjoyed the approbation of Fisher.

Troubridge's squadron consisted of four superannuated 'heavy' or armoured cruisers with 9.2-inch guns, a design speed of 22–23 knots and six inches of side-armour. No such ships had been built since 1905, the type having been rendered superfluous to the battlefleet by the greater armament and speed of battlecruisers, of which Milne had three in his Second Battlecruiser Squadron, and by light cruisers (Milne had four), nimbler and faster scouts which could also lead destroyers. The Mediterranean Fleet included sixteen destroyers and three submarines. Since the Italians began the war as neutrals, the main threat would come from the small but high-quality Austrian fleet of three dreadnoughts, thirteen heavy cruisers, three modern light cruisers, thirty-six destroyers and six coastal submarines.

The Admiralty's war orders, wirelessed to Milne at Malta on 30 July, had been personally vetted and partly written or rewritten by Churchill himself and said, inter alia:

> Your first task should be to aid the French in the trans-
> portation of their African Army by covering, and, if possible,
> bringing to action individual fast German ships, particularly
> *Goeben* . . . Do not at this stage be brought to action against
> superior forces.

The verbose order, which took no account of the time needed by a wireless operator to tap out every letter in Morse, also told Milne not to get involved with the Austrians until Italy's attitude was known, and to 'husband your forces at the outset'. Milne passed on the gist to Troubridge, including the words: 'In the earlier stages, I am to avoid being brought to action against superior force. You are to be guided by this.' There was a protocol problem because under the Anglo-French naval agreement Vice-Admiral Boué de

Lapeyrère as French C-in-C became responsible for all allied naval forces in the Mediterranean in time of war: he was outranked by Milne, who would thus have to be relieved by a British vice-admiral. 'You will be notified by telegraph when you may consult with the French admiral,' Churchill told Milne in the 30 July order, the opening shot in a bombardment of signals from London made possible by wireless. Milne had been in possession of his general (written) War Orders since 1 May 1913, which reached him along with various enclosures, including the sealed 'Secret Package A', containing a signal book for use with the French Fleet in time of war. A telegram would tell him when to open it.

On 2 August, the Admiralty told Milne he could contact Lapeyrère. The sapping effect of constant wireless interference (or Milne's cautious character) was revealed by his reply, which took nearly twelve hours to get through: 'At present I have no cipher in which to communicate with French admiral; can contents of Secret Package A be used as cipher?' – a question to which he already knew the answer. This did not prevent Milne from wasting another twelve hours awaiting the affirmative reply. Milne therefore signalled his offer of cooperation to Lapeyrère only on the afternoon of the 3rd; when he picked up no reply (it never reached the French), the British admiral dispatched the light cruiser *Dublin* (Captain John Kelly, RN) to the French North African base at Bizerta repeating his offer – by letter.

Sensibly, however, Milne had sent the light cruiser *Chatham* to the southern end of the Strait of Messina on the evening of the 2nd, when he also ordered Troubridge to take his own heavy cruisers, the light cruiser *Gloucester* and eight destroyers, plus two of Milne's battlecruisers, to cover the mouth of the Adriatic against an Austrian and/or German foray. By that time the two German ships were in Messina. The *Chatham* passed through the Strait (two miles wide at its narrowest, and therefore entirely in Italian territorial waters) on the morning of the 3rd, six hours after the Germans had sailed north and then westward along the Sicilian coast for their hit-and-run raids on French North Africa. Milne ordered the *Chatham* to head west also, and wirelessed Troubridge, by this time off the south-east of Sicily, to take his cruisers plus *Indomitable* and *Indefatigable* westward after the *Goeben*, by now repeatedly identified as the prime objective of the Mediterranean Fleet in orders to Milne and Troubridge. *Gloucester* and the destroyers were left to watch the Adriatic. On the evening of the 3rd the Admiralty ordered the two battlecruisers to proceed at high speed to Gibraltar.

This placed them due north of Bône just after 9.30 a.m. on the 4th, when lookouts on the *Indomitable* spotted the Germans. At 9.46 Captain Kennedy signalled to Milne (intercepted at an enthralled Admiralty): 'Enemy in sight in latitude 37 degrees 44 minutes north, 7 degrees 56 minutes east, steering east, consisting of *Goeben* and *Breslau*.' But, as we know, the word 'enemy' did not yet apply, and the sixteen 12-inch guns of the two battlecruisers remained silent as the Goeben with her ten 11-inchers sailed past. At 2.05 p.m. on Cabinet orders the Admiralty alerted all ships worldwide that Britain's ultimatum to Germany (over the violation of Belgian neutrality) would expire at midnight and 'no act of war should be committed before that'. In a postscript to the Mediterranean, the signal ordered hands off the *Goeben*, even if she attacked French transports before that moment. 'At the Admiralty we suffered the tortures of Tantalus,' Churchill wrote. The Admiralty meanwhile ordered Milne to respect Italy's neutrality 'rigidly' and not to go within six miles of her coast.

So when the Germans returned to Messina, Milne felt unable to probe up the Strait on the example of the *Chatham* because this would have meant passing into Italian waters. He recalled the chasing battlecruisers and the watchkeeping *Dublin* to the western end of Sicily, the largest island in the Mediterranean. From there they sailed the short distance southward to rejoin Milne off Pantelleria Island. He ordered Troubridge, who had returned to the Adriatic, to detach the *Gloucester* (Captain Howard Kelly, RN, brother of the *Dublin*'s commander) to watch the southern end of the Strait. Kelly had to take up station ten miles away from the harbour to stay out of Italian waters; the Germans, however, paid no attention to Italian neutrality. Ten hours after her arrival, at 2 p.m. on the 5th, the *Gloucester* intercepted powerful signals betraying their presence. Reassembling his main force after various ships had been detached to Malta and Bizerta to refuel, Milne began a slow eastward sweep along the northern coast of Sicily on the morning of 6 August, anticipating a German run for home after a northerly exit from Messina. He was in a position to divide his ships in such a way that superior firepower could have been assembled at each end of the Strait, even without reinforcement from Troubridge. But neither Milne nor his controllers at the Admiralty could envisage anything except a westward breakout by the Germans.

At 5.10 p.m. on the 6th, *Gloucester* signalled that *Goeben* and *Breslau* had emerged southward from the Strait – 'steering east'. This must surely mean that Souchon was going into the Adriatic cul-de-sac to join his Austrian allies. Despite being on paper three knots slower than either of her quarries, the *Gloucester* began a bold and superbly handled exercise in keeping contact. Her supremely competent chief wireless operator, Petty Officer Telegraphist Theodore Perrow, provided a running commentary in a long series of crisp and clear signals, none of which took more than a quarter of an hour to get through.

His first alert reached the eastbound Milne about one-third of the way along Sicily's northern shore; he promptly turned west to take the long way round the island because the short route through the Strait of Messina would have entailed violating Italian waters. Milne still believed the Germans must come west in the end, regardless of their race north-east for the mouth of the Adriatic. So, mindful of the *Goeben*'s purported three-knot advantage over his battlecruisers, he took his ships to Malta at a leisurely speed of fifteen knots, to coal before resuming the chase. En route, at about 10 p.m. on 6 August, he received a three-hour-old signal from London saying, 'If *Goeben* goes south from Messina you should follow through the straits, irrespective of territorial waters'! What Milne did not know was that the *Goeben* had a long history of boiler trouble and could barely attain, let alone sustain, her maximum design speed. Meanwhile the *Gloucester* had worked herself up to twenty-six knots, one more than she was designed to deliver.

Milne sent Captain John Kelly with the *Dublin* and two destroyers to support his brother – who however signalled at 9.46 p.m. on the 6th: 'Urgent. *Goeben* altering course to southward.' Souchon was not bound for Pola after all; and if he kept to his new course long enough, John Kelly realized he would be able to intercept the Germans shortly after midnight for a night torpedo attack. He, at least, ordered full steam ahead, encouraged by the steady stream of reports from the dogged *Gloucester*. John Kelly did sight the *Breslau*, and later the *Goeben* (or it might have been the *Gloucester*'s smoke), but the Germans kept their distance and he was denied his chance of a death-or-glory attack. Instead, he slowed down and made for Troubridge's squadron as originally planned.

*

The second-in-command of His Majesty's Mediterranean Fleet had also been following PO Telegraphist Perrow's messages. On learning that the Germans had gone back to Messina on the 5th, he patrolled south and east of Italy in case the Germans came east. When they did, he set up a screen of ships across the narrowest point of the mouth of the Adriatic, east of Cape Santa Maria di Leuca, hoping to sight and engage Souchon in due course. But Troubridge was now racked by doubt. He had four heavy cruisers, but they were all slower and less protected than the *Goeben*, which heavily outgunned them – and would therefore, he calculated, constitute a superior force unless caught in narrow waters in bad light. When he realized the Germans were not going to enter the Adriatic but had settled on a south-easterly course, meaning they were, inexplicably, bound for the eastern Mediterranean, he planned to cross Souchon's path from the north at about 3 a.m. on the 7th. But, at about the same time as the *Dublin* gave up the chase, Troubridge turned aside at 2.55 a.m. and sought shelter off the island of Zante. He had concluded that he would not sight Souchon's ships until 6 a.m., well after daylight, in maximum visibility and in open water, giving the *Goeben* the chance of picking off the four old cruisers one by one from well outside the range of their inferior guns. That made her a superior force, which his orders forbade him to engage.

On the open bridge of the *Gloucester*, Captain Howard Kelly decided to interpret his own orders rather more creatively. Told by Admiral Milne early on the 7th to fall back and avoid capture, Kelly worked out that the *Breslau*, which he could not see, must be ahead of the *Goeben*, which he could, indicating he would not be caught between them. Therefore, as he delicately put it in his report, 'It was considered permissible to continue shadowing.' Kelly was the man on the spot and decided that he knew best. When the *Breslau* indeed fell back behind the *Goeben* and towards him, in a bid to let the bigger ship get clear of the pestilential contact-keeper, the *Gloucester* boldly opened fire, provoking a reply from the lighter German cruiser. Only when the *Goeben* menacingly reversed course did *Gloucester* slow down. But with the two enemy ships now so close to each other, it was all the easier to keep in visual touch, if from a greater distance. The British ship was unscathed; *Breslau* took a harmless dent in her side from one shell. Only when the Germans passed the southern extremity of Greece did Howard Kelly obey Milne and abandon the chase, after two and a half gruelling but exciting days, to rejoin Troubridge. This was wise as the Germans had planned a trap for him if he persisted. Troubridge's flagship, HMS *Defence* (Captain Fawcet Wray, RN), signalled, not without envy, perhaps: 'Congratulate you on your splendid feat.' Kelly replied: 'Yes, they are very large.'

Nobody on the British side had the remotest inkling of what was driving Souchon ever eastward instead of trying for home. But on 2 August 1914 the Kaiser's wooing of the Young Turks had paid off: the German Ambassador to Constantinople signed a secret treaty of alliance with the Grand Vizier (chief minister) of Turkey. The pact was aimed at Russia, the Germans' main enemy and the Turks' main rival for influence in the Balkans. The Turks controlled the Dardanelles, the strait between the Black Sea and the Mediterranean which carried 98 per cent of Russia's exports and 95 per cent of its imports. Russian ambition to gain a gateway to the Mediterranean had led to war with Turkey and others, including Britain and France in the Crimea, several times in the nineteenth century. The British and French had all but left Turkey out of their prewar calculations, having between them taken control of the rotting Ottoman Empire's African possessions. On the eve of war the Admiralty contemptuously seized two all but complete dreadnoughts ordered by Turkey from British yards, renaming them HMSs *Agincourt* and *Erin*. The two ships had been funded mainly by public subscription and ordinary Turks felt humiliated and angry.

The Germans were fully aware that the Turkish government was at sixes and sevens, with War Minister Enver Pasha's pro-German hawks in the minority. In a short-lived dash for modernity, the Turks had invited Western advisers to reform national institutions in the later nineteenth century. After the CUP takeover in 1908–9 this invitation was renewed: Italian engineers, French financiers, educationists and communications experts moved in as the British took over the Navy and the Germans the Army. But whereas Rear-Admiral Arthur Limpus was making heavy weather of reviving the moribund fleet (while selling the Turks British warships), the future Field-Marshal Otto Liman von Sanders was taking tight control of the tough but as yet ill-equipped Turkish soldiery. Having brought off the alliance, the Kaiser's one great diplomatic coup in preparing for war, the Germans felt the need to prove that it would make a real difference. Hence the order to Souchon on 3 August: 'Alliance concluded with Turkey . . . Proceed immediately to

Constantinople.' He arrived at the entrance to the Dardanelles on 10 August; a Turkish torpedo boat emerged, flying the 'follow me' flag signal, and the Germans dropped anchor off the Asian shore of the Narrows, some 140 miles short of Constantinople.

The first British ship to arrive off the Dardanelles was the light cruiser HMS *Weymouth*, on the afternoon of 11 August, twenty-four hours behind the Germans. Captain W. D. Church's request for a pilot, however, met with the brusque reply, 'Not practicable.' Two blank warning shots from the Turkish forts at the mouth of the straits reminded him to stay outside the three-mile limit; and an officer on a visiting Turkish dispatch boat informed Church that the two German ships had joined the Turkish fleet under new names. Three of Milne's ships – *Indomitable*, *Indefatigable* and the gallant *Gloucester* – took up station outside the stable door, now firmly bolted with the runaway safely on the inside. Milne went home via Malta, his career at an end after his lacklustre 'chase' of the Germans, in which he was almost as much sinned against (by the Admiralty) as sinning. He had been told first to avoid, and then belatedly to break through, the Strait of Messina; he was told that war had broken out with Austria, a signal that had to be cancelled as it was some days premature; and when he reached the Dardanelles, he was told to 'blockade' the Strait, an act of war under international law! When he not unreasonably queried this order, 'blockade' was amended to 'carefully watch' . . . Nothing could more clearly illustrate the disadvantages of wireless than this display of inept interference in an operation being run by a lacklustre admiral over-endowed with caution – just as the superbly handled *Gloucester* showed its advantages under a captain never at a loss in an ever-shifting operation.

Having acquired the choice between breaking into the Black Sea or breaking back to the Adriatic by a suicidal dash through the British Mediterranean Fleet, Souchon naturally chose the former, although it took him eleven weeks to overcome Turkish dithering, shown by a prolonged refusal to allow the Germans to anchor in or near the Golden Horn, the inner harbour of Constantinople. He ended the impasse by taking the law into his own hands, as ordered by Berlin. Having donned the fez and become Commander-in-Chief of the Turkish Fleet while remaining head of the Imperial Navy's Mediterranean Division, Souchon gathered every sailable Turkish ship, proceeded into the Black Sea and shelled the Russian ports of Sevastopol and Novorossiysk at dawn on 29 October 1914. He did it without consulting his Turkish allies and nominal masters. The result, as intended, was a declaration of war against Turkey by Russia on 4 November. We shall return to the awesome consequences; meanwhile the British needed a scapegoat.

His name was Ernest Troubridge, who was court-martialled on the charge that he 'from negligence or through other default, [did] forbear to pursue the chase of . . . *Goeben*, being an enemy then flying'. Majority opinion in the Admiralty would have preferred 'cowardice' to negligence, making it a capital charge. Even so, the trial, which began on 5 November 1914 on a pre-dreadnought battleship at Portland, was the first such action against a flag officer in wartime in over a century. A key early witness was of course Milne, now nicknamed by a disgusted Fisher 'Sir Berkeley Goeben'. He took great care to cast his former deputy's conduct (both admirals had been relieved) in the worst possible light while glossing over his glaring failure either to block each end of the Strait of Messina with a force superior to the Germans or to show any initiative or sense of urgency. Mr Leslie Scott, KC, Troubridge's brilliant advocate, concentrated on the issue of 'superior force', arguing that the *Goeben* decisively outclassed his client's four elderly cruisers on grounds of superior speed and armament alone. Troubridge's flag captain, Fawcet Wray, who had urged him not to attack, argued that the *Goeben* was in mathematical terms 'infinitely' superior to the First Cruiser Squadron, as she could hit them at her own optimum range with her heavier guns while using her decisive speed advantage to stay comfortably outside theirs.

Scott won the argument, even though no reference was made to the *Goeben*'s third area of superiority, armour, off which the shells of Troubridge's old guns would probably have bounced harmlessly had he managed to get within range. Also omitted from the somewhat half-hearted proceedings was any hint that the *Goeben*, faced with four cruisers well spread out, might have run out of 11-inch shells before sinking all of them and would then have been open to a fast torpedo attack by the light cruisers and destroyers. All Troubridge needed to do was to 'wing' or lame the German battlecruiser so that the slower British ones could come up and finish her off. Neither Milne nor Troubridge had shown a trace of the 'Nelsonian spirit' upon which the Royal Navy's reputation was built. Unfortunately there was to be many another British admiral who would fail to grasp the principle cited by Liddell Hart in his *History of the First World War*: 'A ship, like a shell, is a weapon to be expended profitably.' Troubridge was acquitted on 9 November; but it is hard not to conclude that he should have attacked his 'main objective'. He got no other seagoing command and, like Milne, never recovered from the '*Goeben* affair'.

Much space has been given to this debacle for three reasons. It earns its place as a tantalizing saga of 'might have beens' at the very opening of the Great War. Secondly, the consequences radically altered its course, at sea as well as on land, and helped to change world history, not only by bringing Turkey into the conflict but also by severing Russia's main supply line inward and outward. The possibility was now excluded of using a short, easily protected Mediterranean route to exchange Anglo-French munitions for grain, which would now have to come to Britain across the north Atlantic, soon to be infested with U-boats. The Russian collapse and revolution in 1917 also went back, at least indirectly, to the profitably expended *Goeben*.

But in the third place, the most relevant for this history, the affair highlighted most of the command weaknesses then prevalent in the Royal Navy, a fact recognizable not only by hindsight but also to the far-sighted minority in the contemporary service. In charge of Britain's most important overseas naval formation were two of many inadequate admirals, the one an effete, unimaginative bureaucrat with friends in high places, the other cautious and indecisive, both badgered to distraction by Admiralty interference. It was a German (Clausewitz) who said that 'war is the province of chance', a factor for which the British Mediterranean command and its French Navy colleagues alike made little or no allowance (the French also missed two opportunities to confront Souchon).

Troubridge hesitated because of what the Germans could have done to him in conditions ideal for themselves, which, however, might not, and surely not all, have materialized; in the worst case, he could have saved most of his ships by dispersing them had an action started to go against him. He should have given more weight to the Germans' known disadvantages, such as limited access to coal and a finite quantity of effectively irreplaceable ammunition. He certainly could not have known at the time that the *Goeben* had chronic boiler trouble; but the only way he would have discovered the enemy's weaknesses and strengths was by attacking him. The conclusion that he should have tried is irresistible. Both the gifted captains Kelly duly became senior admirals; had either of them been C-in-C or his deputy in the Mediterranean Fleet by 1914, it seems well nigh certain that Souchon would never have reached the Dardanelles – or any other refuge.

The Great War at sea was fought, broadly speaking, in three phases, overlapping in time and space as well as definition. The first centred upon cruisers and was worldwide, involving above all attacks on merchant shipping but also hit-and-run raids and coastal bombardments, minelaying, cable-cutting and chases such as the *Goeben* saga. This warfare on the open sea was styled *guerre de course* by French naval strategists looking for a way to circumvent or counter the world supremacy won by the Royal Navy at the beginning of the nineteenth century, chiefly at French expense. The main contenders in this 'blue-water' phase were a handful of German commerce-raiding warships, supplemented by auxiliary cruisers converted from fast merchant ships ('armed merchant cruisers' in Second World War parlance), and the much larger, principally British, forces, including battlecruisers, assigned to clear them from the seas. Supported by a worldwide *Etappendienst* (staging service) to make up for their shortage of colonial or allied bases, the German raiders started the war with the initiative, free to attack anywhere until the huge defensive effort gained the upper hand by sheer weight of numbers.

The second phase was the fitful skirmishing of the capital ships, willing to wound but afraid to strike across the narrow North Sea and culminating in just one great fleet action, off Jutland. This *guerre d'escadre*, or squadron warfare, including the battlecruisers in their other, tactically dubious role as pretend-battleships, was nevertheless decisive for the outcome of the war. The third phase would have decided the war had it gone the other way, as it very nearly did: the German submarine campaign against merchant shipping, a new and deadlier form of *guerre de course* which began almost by accident in the war's third month and grew exponentially into a catastrophic threat to Britain's survival by its third year. The U-boats sought to counter-blockade Britain as it blockaded Germany with its surface fleet. Each phase has its own chapter here, each presented chronologically from 1914. Underlying themes such as strategy, intelligence, diplomacy and technology provide continuous threads throughout. The Mediterranean theatre saw events in all three phases and will therefore be visited in each of the next two chapters as it has been in this one.

The Imperial German Navy possessed two 'blue-water' flag-commands based beyond the North Sea – Souchon's Mediterranean Division, whose strategically profound contribution has been described, and the East Asiatic Squadron of heavy and light cruisers, commanded by Vice-Admiral Maximilian Graf (Count) von Spee. His formation's main base was at Tsingtao in Germany's Chinese coastal enclave of Kiaochow, but the Danish-born admiral was free to deploy his cruisers against British and French shipping and territories anywhere outside European waters, including the south and central Atlantic, the Pacific and the Indian Ocean. His command included the twin armoured cruisers *Scharnhorst* (flag) and *Gneisenau*, completed in 1907 and the most formidable non-capital ships afloat, plus half a dozen light cruisers, five of which he detached on the eve of war: the *Dresden* and *Karlsruhe* to the Atlantic, the *Leipzig* to the north-eastern Pacific, the *Königsberg* to the western and the *Emden* to the eastern Indian Ocean, all to attack commerce and cause disruption. He led the core of his squadron, the two heavy cruisers plus the light *Nürnberg*, at a stately speed to conserve the fuel carried by the accompanying colliers, via the German Caroline Islands to the trade routes round South America, eluding British and Japanese cruisers already searching for him in the vast waters of the Pacific.

The *Königsberg* left Dar es Salaam in what was until 1918 German East Africa, which she had been visiting, on 31 July, to be ready to attack British trade when the war started. Although shadowed for a while by three elderly British cruisers, the German raider sidestepped them comfortably and began a spectacular odyssey by capturing and scuttling the British steamer *City of Winchester* 280 miles east of Aden in the Indian Ocean on 6 August. Two days later the old cruiser HMS *Astraea* bombarded Dar, destroying the radio station and crippling two merchant ships; *Astraea* returned to the charge accompanied by another old cruiser, *Pegasus*, on the 13th. The latter moved on to the East African port of Tanga on the 17th, disabling a German ship. The solitary German light cruiser managed to surprise the *Pegasus* at Zanzibar on 20 September, sinking her in a short, sharp engagement. She evaded her many pursuers and took refuge in the delta of the Rufiji River, where she was located by the British light cruiser *Chatham* (detached from the Mediterranean via the Suez Canal) only on 31 October. British ships came as far upriver as they could and tried to destroy the *Königsberg* by shelling, which failed. The Royal Naval Air Service pinpointed the enemy twelve miles upriver, but the extraordinarily protracted siege by water, air and land continued until 11 July 1915, when British monitors (small bombardment ships with disproportionately heavy guns) shelled the cruiser for ninety minutes, their shooting guided by circling RNAS aircraft. The Germans scuttled their ship.

The *Emden* was the last warship to leave Tsingtao before the Imperial Japanese Navy arrived to blockade it. Her captain, Karl von Müller, hurriedly converted two modern merchantmen into auxiliary cruisers, *Cormoran* and *Prinz Eitel Friedrich*, before his last rendezvous with Spee in the German Marianas Islands north of Guam in the Pacific. On 13 August the admiral detached Müller with a collier to attack British shipping in the Indian Ocean, which he reached early in September after stealing through the neutral Dutch East Indies (two of Spee's four colliers were captured by the French cruiser *Dupleix* in the mid-Pacific on 21 August). On 8 September the *Emden* captured her first victim out of twenty-two, a Greek steamer carrying coal for the British and therefore a legitimate prize for Müller, who now began to acquire a reputation unique in the German Navy for punctilious and chivalrous attention to Prize Rules. He led more than seventy British and allied warships a merry dance, disrupting troop movements yet seldom firing a shot. Müller bombarded Madras in India (on 22 September, the same day as Spee shelled Papeete in the French Pacific colony of Tahiti) and also raided the Malayan harbour of Penang.

Twelve days later, on 9 November, the *Emden* was at last caught in the Cocos Islands north of Australia by HMAS *Sydney*, an Australian light cruiser with a British commander, Captain John Glossop, RN, and superior firepower. In the Australian Navy's first gun action the 6-inch cruiser proceeded to batter the *Emden*, with her now useless 4.1-inch guns, until she grounded herself on a reef and ran up the white flag. Müller was as highly regarded by his enemies by the time he went into captivity as by his own side for his gentlemanly conduct, always ensuring that his victims got away safely after he sunk or seized their ships. Tsingtao fell to the Japanese early in November; the *Cormoran* gave up her unsuccessful role as a privateer and went into internment at Guam in December; the converted liner *Prinz Eitel Friedrich* had a spectacular career as a commerce raider, mainly in the Atlantic, going into internment at Newport News in Virginia in March 1915.

The *Karlsruhe* went marauding in mid-Atlantic and engaged the British light cruiser HMS *Bristol* in an inconclusive exchange of gunfire on the night of 6 August in the Caribbean. On the same day the *Dresden* captured three British merchant ships, sinking two, 180 miles north-east of Pernambuco in north-east Brazil, and the *Königsberg* sank her first victim. The British could be forgiven for thinking that the German cruisers were 'everywhere at once' in the opening weeks of the war: the handful of raiders proved their value as a distracting force and real threat to hundreds of British and allied naval and mercantile vessels beyond the north-east Atlantic and the Mediterranean. The *Karlsruhe* went on to capture a total of fifteen merchant ships before succumbing to a mysterious explosion of her own ammunition on 4 November, some 200 miles north-east of Trinidad, a fact of which the Royal Navy did not become aware until January 1915. That year was not much older before the British and their naval allies, at the cost of a considerable tally of merchant shipping destroyed and a massive deployment of warships in the great oceans, had swept nearly all the Kaiser's cruisers and auxiliary raiders from the seas and captured all the Pacific islands of the German Empire, which could otherwise have served them as bases. The Imperial Navy's ingenious *Etappendienst* which had tried to mitigate this inevitable development in advance by making supply arrangements in far-flung, neutral ports was forced out of business, obliging such raiders as *Emden* to take coal from her own captures. The Japanese besieged and, on 7 November, occupied Kiaochow with Tsingtao, and they and the British Empire shared the large scattering of German island colonies in the Pacific (which would play a disproportionate part in Japanese hands in the Second World War).

It remains to record the brief but awesome history of the bulk of Spee's Cruiser Squadron, consisting as we have seen of Germany's two sole armoured or heavy cruisers, *Scharnhorst* and *Gneisenau*, plus up to six light cruisers, several of which, in war as in peacetime, were likely to be on detached duty at any given time. Each category of German cruiser was inferior to its contemporary British counterpart in weight of broadside, armour and speed but superior in quality of construction and steel, reliability, gunnery control equipment and optics. Spee and his captains and crews had begun serious preparations by the end of June 1914 for what they, like so many others in faraway Europe, expected would be a short war (they could not hope to survive a long one). A few gunboats were recalled to Tsingtao, merchant ships sent home or to neutral ports and colliers positioned in strategic places in Far Eastern waters.

The forces ranged against the German cruisers included the Imperial Japanese Navy, a strong, modern, British-nurtured fleet, confident after its earthshaking triumph at Tsushima, and two French and two Russian cruisers plus supporting ships. The Royal Navy controlled Vice-Admiral Sir Thomas Jerram's China Squadron of two heavy cruisers, one old battleship, two light cruisers and eight destroyers; and the Australian Squadron, commanded by the British Vice-Admiral Patey and led by the modern battlecruiser HMAS *Australia*, the most powerful ship in the southern hemisphere, plus light cruisers and destroyers.

Covering the other side of the southern Pacific was the Falkland Islands Squadron, a scratch force of mostly elderly ships based on Port Stanley. It consisted of two twelve-year-old armoured cruisers, *Good Hope* (flag) and *Monmouth*, the 1897 battleship *Canopus* and the light cruiser *Glasgow*, the only modern ship under the flag of Rear-Admiral Sir Christopher Cradock, commanding the South America station from 30 September. Troubridge's flagship, the heavy cruiser *Defence*, was earmarked as a reinforcement but took part in a Franco-British sweep up the Adriatic against the Austrians on 15 August, which cost the Habsburg empire one small cruiser.

On 7 September Graf Spee called at Christmas Island, briefly detaching *Nürnberg* to cut telegraphic cables in the area; five weeks later, on 12 October, he reached Easter Island, where he was rejoined by *Dresden* and *Leipzig*. The two heavy and three light cruisers completed with coal from German colliers were ordered to rendezvous with Spee at the tiny island of Mas-a-Fuera, halfway to Chile, and sailed on in company at economical speed towards the long western coast of South America to look for Allied commerce.

Cradock meanwhile, charged with covering the eastern coast as far as the River Plate estuary between Uruguay and Argentina, and the whole of the Chilean coast on the west, was in no doubt after one of Churchill's long and verbose telegrams that it was his job to destroy Spee: 'Concentrate a squadron strong enough to meet *Scharnhorst* and *Gneisenau*' once he had received his promised reinforcements, the refitted but desperately slow, superannuated

Canopus, and *Defence*, which would have been the only member of his squadron suited to a slogging match on the open sea with one of Spee's heavy ships. Cradock searched the treacherous waters round Cape Horn in vain early in October. *Glasgow* (Captain John Luce, RN) searched southward from Valparaiso and joined Cradock at the small Chilean port of Coronel. On leaving Stanley for Chilean waters the admiral had buried his medals in the garden of the Governor's residence. Fully aware of Troubridge's failure to tackle Souchon, Cradock was determined to fight Spee, even if *Canopus* could make only twelve knots rather than her official seventeen. Spee, advised by the *Etappendienst* at Valparaiso, which had been monitoring wireless traffic, of a multiple British presence off Chile, was more than ready to oblige, confident that his force was superior to anything he was likely to meet. Cradock decided to dispense with the *Canopus*, which he thought would only slow him down, so detached her to protect British colliers in the area, signalling the *Defence*, on passage in the south Atlantic, to join him. Churchill, however, overruled this order, telling the heavy cruiser to stay in the waters off Argentina in case Spee made for the east coast – another dubious example of the First Lord's readiness to interfere unilaterally in operational and tactical matters by wireless. Even so, Cradock ordered his hotch-potch squadron into an east–west line of ships twenty miles apart (the limit of visibility) to sail north from Coronel on 1 November in search of the enemy. The *Glasgow* called briefly at Coronel to send what amounted to Cradock's suicide note – his signal stating his intention to seek out Spee – by secure landline and cable.

Canopus was now some 300 miles to the south, well out of harm's way – just as Engineer-Commander William Denbow had planned. Unbeknown to his captain, and therefore to Cradock, there was nothing wrong, antiquity apart, with her engines, which were capable of seventeen knots after all, rather than the twelve which the acutely battle-shy Denbow had reported. If the admiral had known this, it is doubtful whether he would have sent her away. Her four old 12-inch guns would have been hard put, even when new, to match the range of Spee's sixteen modern 8.2-inch main armament; her armour was only as thick as that of the German 'heavies' but inferior by reason of age; and she was six knots slower than they were – but six, not eleven. She could at the very least have drawn the German fire and withstood a battering for longer than any other of Cradock's ships – and Spee had even more reason than his Mediterranean colleague Souchon to fear the consequences of even minor damage, should it slow him down with no friendly modern repair yard within reach. Spee noted immediately after the battle that the day might have gone rather differently had the *Canopus* been on hand.

Rejoining the line of search on 1 November, *Glasgow* signalled by lamp to Cradock on the *Good Hope* that she had heard loud wireless traffic from the *Leipzig*, Spee's slowest ship. Cradock hoped to pick her off; but at 4.30 p.m., fifty miles west of Coronel, the British to the south-west and the Germans, nearer the coast to the north-east, sighted each other's smoke and formed up for battle. The setting sun, and an almost full moon also to the west, gave Spee the advantage in visibility, clearly outlining the neat British column – *Good Hope*, *Monmouth*, *Glasgow* and *Otranto* in line ahead – as the Germans opened fire six miles off. They hit the outranged British flagship with their third broadside in heavy swell before she could start shooting. Three minutes later *Monmouth* was also on fire. Both armoured cruisers probably had difficulty in the prevailing rough sea with shooting from guns housed in old-fashioned casemates close to the waterline. Cradock sent the hopelessly outclassed *Otranto* out of harm's way, leaving only the light *Glasgow* to shoot back at the Germans as they pounded the old British heavy cruisers to pieces, closing to three miles and then to point-blank range. Neither hauled down her flag and each sank with the loss of all hands, totalling some 1,400 men, including Cradock. The *Glasgow*, initially targeted by two enemy light cruisers and finally *Gneisenau*, was able to escape at full speed despite five hits at close range, Captain Luce warning *Canopus* by wireless as he fled. Three German sailors were wounded by six hits from British shells.

Ironically *Canopus*'s dash to the south reduced her engines to the very condition Denbow had falsely diagnosed to ensure she was excused; even so she would get a chance to show her mettle before long. Denbow was already on his way home, on the orders of three doctors, in a supply steamer before battle was joined off Coronel and was duly discharged on health grounds soon after his arrival. Another irony was the Admiralty decision on 3 November, before the totality of the Coronel defeat was known, to send HMS *Defence* to the dead Cradock after all 'with all possible dispatch'.

The last occasion on which the Royal Navy had been defeated in a squadron action was almost exactly a century earlier at Lake

Champlain in New England, during the war of 1812 with the United States. Spee's crushing victory was therefore a mighty shock for the British at every level, from Buckingham Palace to the ordinary people, still nurturing the illusion of a ceasefire by Christmas. Apart from a few destroyer victories and the spectacular and successful raid on the Heligoland Bight at the end of August 1914 (see Chapter 4), the Navy had not performed well in the first three months of hostilities. Before Coronel there had been the *Goeben* fiasco. Five old cruisers – three within an hour – had been sunk in the North Sea by U-boat attack, with massive losses of life. In the week before Coronel the battleship *Audacious* was sunk by a mine, the first dreadnought ever lost, a fact which the Admiralty was prevented from hushing up by passengers on the liner *Olympic*, who took photographs as she tried to save the warship. On 30 October a U-boat sank the seaplane carrier *Hermes* in the North Sea. Clearly a new scapegoat was needed; fortunately for Churchill, who bore the political responsibility for the Navy, one such had more or less selected himself two days before Cradock succumbed to his doom – the First Sea Lord himself.

Churchill's own position as First Lord of the Admiralty had been considerably undermined, not only by the indifferent performance of the Navy but also by his own foibles, which included an inability to resist meddling in operational matters and a taste for harebrained schemes from which his admirals were not always able to divert him. An example of the latter was Churchill's proposal to send capital ships into the shallow Baltic which, as noted above, could only be reached by circumnavigating Jutland and sailing into narrow waters monitored by the Germans. He put up this idea, also advocated by Fisher (shades of 'Copenhagen') long before the war and still favoured by several gung-ho admirals, on 17 September 1914 at a conference with the Grand Fleet attended by Jellicoe, its C-in-C, Beatty, his battlecruiser commander, and others. An alternative proposal was to seize the island of Heligoland, defended as it was by heavy coastal artillery, minefields and U-boats. The Grand Fleet could doubtless have taken the bristling outpost, though at some cost; but keeping and supplying it would have required an unsustainable and disproportionate effort. Churchill reluctantly accepted instead a suggestion by Commodore Roger Keyes to send a few British submarines into the Baltic to help the Russians. It should be noted that this conference took place at Loch Ewe because mines and U-boats had made the inadequately defended Scapa Flow, north-east of the Scottish mainland and the Grand Fleet's designated main base, all but unusable, forcing Jellicoe to divide his time in harbour between Loch Ewe on the north-west coast of Scotland and the even more remote Lough Swilly on the north coast of Ireland.

Worries about Churchill at the Admiralty were hardly eased by his decision early in October to take personal command of the new Royal Naval Division, hurriedly formed from the Royal Marine Brigade and two brigades of naval reservists turned infantry, to defend Antwerp (threatened and soon to be taken by the German Army). Asquith, the Prime Minister, and the Cabinet laughed but were not really amused and brusquely ordered the impulsive First Lord back to his desk in Whitehall. The raw division was decimated but was rebuilt to fight again in another Churchillian diversion, his last in this war.

The First Lord's hide was saved this time by the First Sea Lord, who had the misfortune to be a German with a noticeable accent – Admiral Prince Louis of Battenberg. Although there was nobody in the Navy with more of the aristocratic attributes so loathed by the self-made Fisher, the latter admired his royal colleague's professionalism (and became his friend for life when the hated Beresford took against Battenberg). The powerful jingoistic element in the British press attacked Battenberg for being German and openly blamed the Navy's failures on him, whipping up a nervous public opinion against the hapless brother-in-law of the Kaiser's younger brother, Admiral Prince Heinrich, German C-in-C in the Baltic. The hostile editorials reaped a harvest of readers' letters which in turn generated even more hostile comment, in an atmosphere where shops and even individuals with German-sounding names were liable to attack. Battenberg was broken-hearted, and when the *Audacious* sank he resigned after less than two years in office. Promoted Admiral of the Fleet, he was to die in obscurity in 1921. The family changed its name to Mountbatten to appease the xenophobes, and Battenberg's son, also called Louis, acquired an all-consuming ambition to rise even higher than his father and restore the family's honour. Battenberg's contribution to the outcome of the war, however, was decisive: the order to the Fleet not to disperse in July 1914 but rather to go to its war stations.

On 30 October, for better or worse and against the wishes of King George V, Admiral of the Fleet Lord Fisher of Kilverstone, aged seventy-three, was reappointed First Sea Lord, ten years after his first term in that office had begun. Not all admirals welcomed his return: there was still a Beresford faction, and a few younger commanders thought Fisher too old and temperamental for wartime supreme command. But he knew rather more than Churchill about naval strategy and tactics, and Churchill respected his professional judgement. Those who thirsted for decisive leadership were not about to be disappointed. Fisher laid about him, calling meetings and issuing an endless stream of orders aimed at a radical reorganization of the service. He demanded hundreds of submarines and inaugurated a new shipbuilding programme; and when the scale of Cradock's defeat at Coronel became clear, he went into conclave with Churchill to plan a fitting and total revenge.

Where Churchill proposed sending a squadron of heavy cruisers, including *Defence*, Fisher called for an annihilatingly superior force of three battlecruisers, one to cover the central Atlantic and the other two to blast Spee out of the waters of the southern hemisphere, supported by four heavy and two light cruisers, plus *Canopus*. The man chosen as Cradock's avenger was the Chief of Naval Staff (CNS), Vice-Admiral Sir Doveton Sturdee, aged fifty-five. Fisher sacked him on his own reappointment, blaming Sturdee for the Admiralty decisions that had let Cradock down (and recalling, like the good hater he was, Sturdee's support for Beresford in the 1909 imbroglio that led to Fisher's departure). But, as we saw above, the new staff was viewed with suspicion by many admirals, and it was not until the post of CNS was subsumed into that of First Sea Lord later in the war that the naval staff and its chief ceased to be peripheral. We also saw how it was Churchill's interference, rather than Sturdee's impotence, that compromised Cradock. Sturdee, a fighting admiral, was clearly unsuited for the cerebral task of leadership, let alone asserting the authority, of a war staff. Churchill's solution was therefore to accept Fisher's decision to remove Sturdee and send him to the south Atlantic. Sturdee was delighted; Jellicoe and Beatty complained in vain about having to lend him three precious battlecruisers.

HMSs *Invincible*, Milne's erstwhile Mediterranean flagship and now Sturdee's, and *Inflexible*, each with six 12-inch guns, and the new *Princess Royal*, with 13.5-inchers, were detached from Beatty's command (the last-named to guard the central Atlantic). Sturdee's pair reached Devonport on 8 November; Fisher gave the yard three days to turn them round. Sturdee, however, took his time, reaching the rendezvous with the rest of his squadron off the Brazilian coast in the 'waist' of the Atlantic. It was only when Captain Luce of the *Glasgow*, with his unique knowledge of the enemy, injected a sense of urgency into Sturdee's stately progress that events began to gather pace.

Glasgow and *Canopus* (Captain Heathcoat Grant, RN) had reached Stanley in the Falklands on the 8th, Grant beaching his ship as a battery to defend the harbour. Spee had gone to Valparaiso after the battle to revictual and receive the plaudits of the large German expatriate community. Presented with a bouquet of flowers, the German admiral said, 'They will do for my funeral.' He foresaw his own fate as clearly as his vanquished enemy had done, and over a rather longer period, going back to well before the war. 'Fair to see and yet bound to die' was Churchill's postwar description of the German Cruiser Squadron. The only question was when: the British were bound to assemble a force as superior to his as his own had been to Cradock's. Spee worked his way slowly southwards towards Cape Horn, capturing on the way the Scottish barque *Drummuir* and seizing her providential cargo of 2,800 tons of coal, thankfully transhipped in the Beagle Channel on 2 December.

Sturdee's powerful squadron – the two Invincibles, three heavy cruisers, *Carnarvon*, *Cornwall* and *Kent* (the *Defence* stayed further north in the Atlantic), and two light cruisers, the battle-scarred *Glasgow* and *Bristol* – were detected by their smoke on the morning of 7 December from several of the observation posts set up on the hills round Port Stanley by Captain Grant. Once in port the unhurried Sturdee, lacking precise information of his objective's whereabouts, called a captains' conference.

At his own last staff conference on 6 December Spee overrode the opinion of his subordinates that they should run up the east coast to the Plate, attacking any British merchantmen they came across, and then on to the north Atlantic and home, aided by a diversionary sortie of the High Seas Fleet. Any amount of coal was available from the *Etappendienst* posts at Pernambuco, Brazil, and in equally neutral New York. Spee, however, insisted on raiding the Falkland Islands as a further blow to British morale, rendering the base facilities there useless to the enemy. He brushed aside reminders that they had already expended half their irreplaceable ammunition. German intelligence knew the size of the force now looking for Spee but all attempts by the *Etappendienst* at Valparaiso to get an acknowledgement of its warnings failed. Spee may have been keeping wireless silence or, more likely, simply did not pick up the distant signals.

Gneisenau and *Nürnberg* were detached northward to bombard Stanley at 5 a.m. on the 8th. On their arrival they were confronted by accurate 12-inch salvos from *Canopus*, which had been practising. At the same time German lookouts spotted the unexpected tripod masts of the two battlecruisers. Otherwise the British were anything but ready, with most of Sturdee's ships busy coaling amid an enormous pall of coal dust, hampering the visual warning signals from *Canopus*, which had no landline to *Invincible*.

There had not been such excitement at the Admiralty since the tantalizing sighting of the *Goeben* on the eve of war when, at 5 p.m. GMT on 8 December, Sturdee's ill-thought-out signal reported that Spee had arrived while he was coaling and they were now in action. Churchill was present and feared that Sturdee had been taken by surprise. But instead of rushing up to attack the harbour with all his ships, Spee had waited for the detached bombardment pair to rejoin him. This gave the British squadron the minimum two hours it needed to belay coaling and get up steam to leave harbour at 10 a.m. local time. *Glasgow* had already gone out to scout when *Carnarvon* led *Invincible*, *Inflexible* and *Cornwall* in line ahead on to the unusually calm, sunlit battlefield, where Spee's ships were sailing north in line abreast, the two detached cruisers in the last stages of catching up. *Glasgow* joined up for the chase as the recently serviced British engines gained on the tired German machinery; the British battlecruisers at last opened fire at under nine miles. Their shooting was very poor as Spee boldly dispersed his three light cruisers and turned the *Scharnhorst* and *Gneisenau* to face the much heavier British guns, which outranged the German by a mile or so. But a following wind blew the thick smoke from maximum revolutions over the bows of the battlecruisers, clouding the view of the gunnery directors in their posts on the tripod masts. Even so their salvos were shamefully inaccurate as Spee violently and evasively manoeuvred his two heavy ships.

The Germans' shooting was first class as they bracketed and then hit home with their lighter main armament, remaining unscathed themselves while they tried to escape to the south. But Sturdee closed the range so that the Germans began to score hits, albeit ineffectual, with their secondary, 5.9-inch guns. The battlecruisers at last got their eyes in and began to register crushing blows on the thin deck-armour, and finally the sides, of the Germans. The *Scharnhorst* started to burn and list under more than forty shellbursts; Spee's last signal to *Gneisenau*'s captain, who had opposed the Falklands diversion, was, 'You were right all along.' At this fateful moment in the fight a large sailing ship passed between the smoke-covered battle lines, her massed white sails gleaming in the sun like a heavenly vision and engendering a brief ceasefire. After she had silently cleared the scene, the blazing *Scharnhorst* rolled over to port and went down by the bow, her screws still turning. The *Gneisenau* fought on and on, down to her last operable gun, as she in her turn was battered by the Invincibles. She sank only when her seacocks were opened and scuttling charges were fired; 215 Germans were plucked from the water by the victorious British, who had expended 1,174 12-inch shells (leaving only fifty-two) in their less than impressive, first director-controlled gunnery action. It was just after 6 p.m.

Glasgow and *Cornwall* chased, caught and sank the *Leipzig* while the *Kent* dispatched the *Nürnberg*. Only the light cruiser *Dresden* got away for the time being, eluding the *Carnarvon*; Spee's last ship eventually blew herself up under a white flag when trapped off Juan Fernandez, Robinson Crusoe's island due west of Santiago de Chile, by HMS *Glasgow* and two other British ships on 14 March 1915. About 2,200 German sailors including Spee were killed in the fierce and dramatic Battle of the Falkland Islands, which restored British naval morale and prestige, cheering the public as nothing had done since the raising of the siege of Mafeking during the Boer War. A surly Fisher criticized Sturdee for letting the *Dresden* deny him a clean sweep and meanly struck names off his list of recommendations for medals, yet could not prevent Cradock's uninspired but thorough avenger from receiving a baronetcy for his Falklands victory.

The destruction of Spee's squadron, whose fighting qualities were widely admired in the Royal Navy, and of the various detached German light cruisers and auxiliaries, cleared the seas for British commerce and such other strategic traffic as trooping convoys from the Dominions. When the armed liners *Prinz Eitel Friedrich* and *Kronprinz Wilhelm*, which had sunk five and nine British merchantmen respectively, sailed into Newport News, Virginia, by April 1915, their voluntary internment seemed to mark the end of Germany's remarkable campaign of classic *guerre de course.* A handful of cruisers had caused havoc out of all proportion to their numbers in all the great oceans of the world, tying down scores of ships from the British and half a dozen other navies, sinking scores of merchantmen and disrupting troop and supply movements. The last conventional warship in this buccaneering category, the *Königsberg*, may have been scuttled in July 1915, but her ten 4.1-inch guns fought on; divers recovered them from the wreck and gave them to the brilliantly led German Army in East Africa, which was still in the field and undefeated when the Armistice came in 1918. For nine months no British freighter was attacked by a German surface raider.

But the Imperial Navy had not lost its taste for privateering, although what follows is a mere postscript to the stark story of the Asiatic Cruiser Squadron. On 26 December 1915 the first and most formidable of a handful of highly effective disguised raiders quietly set sail from Bremen, eluding the British Northern Patrol between Shetland and Norway and heading south into the Atlantic. The *Möwe* ('Gull'), her modern naval guns concealed by false upper-works and her paint locker full of camouflage and disguise possibilities, sailed innocently into Norfolk, Virginia, on 1 February 1916; on the way she had captured a British liner with a cargo worth £2m and two colonial governors aboard. On returning safely to Bremen on 3 March, she had sunk fourteen cargo ships, eleven of them British. On 6 January one of the mines she laid near Cape Wrath, northern Scotland, on her way out sank the battleship *King Edward VII* before it had fired a shot in anger. Five days later the *Möwe* used her guns and boarding parties to sink the first of the eight British steamers she managed to catch in the eastern Atlantic by the 20th (three were destroyed on the 13th).

A new raider, the *Wolf*, started work in mid-January 1917, mining the waters off Cape Agulhas, the southernmost point of the African continent: two steamers were lost. A month later she laid more mines off Ceylon. The *Möwe* fought an epic action on 10 March with the New Zealand freighter SS *Otaki*, which boasted a single old 4.7-inch gun. With this her master, Captain A. Bisset Smith, a lieutenant, RNR, managed to hit the raider seven times before succumbing to thirty German shells and sinking; he was awarded a posthumous Victoria Cross. These depredations by daring lone raiders were hardly noticed amid the catastrophic losses being inflicted on Allied shipping in this period in the Atlantic, at the climax of the U-boat campaign described in Chapter 5.

On the 16th a new raider tried her luck: but the *Leopard*, converted from the captured British steamer *Yarrowdale*, was caught by the Northern Patrol and sunk by the cruiser HMS *Achilles*, assisted by the boarding vessel SS *Dundee*, 200 miles north-east of the Faroe Islands. Four days later the *Möwe* stole into Kiel harbour via the Kiel Canal. As late as August 1917 the seemingly innocuous sailing ship *Seeadler* ('Sea-eagle') was wrecked on the rocks of Lord Howe Island in the Pacific after a remarkable run in the age of steam, during which she sank sixteen vessels (six British) totalling 30,100 tons in the South Atlantic. In August the *Wolf* was still causing grief at a distance: one of her mines sank a British freighter off Cape Town. A month later the ship was sowing her final batch of 110 mines off the British Andaman Islands in the Indian Ocean. It was not until 24 February 1918 that this last of the Kaiser's privateers completed her final voyage, entering Pola in the Adriatic after sinking eleven merchantmen totalling 33,000 tons in the previous fifteen months.

The author of the two volumes of the official German naval history of the 1914–18 war dealing with the work of the cruisers in distant waters was a serving officer called Erich Raeder. He learned a great deal from what he wrote in the 1920s and put it to effective use as Commander-in-Chief of the German Navy when war broke out again in 1939.

After the first few months of the Great War the doings of the cruisers became a sideshow, provoking just enough activity to remind both sides how the advantage in this kind of wide-ranging naval warfare lay with the aggressor, at least until he ran out of places to hide; and how disproportionate the efforts of the defence had to be in protecting from a handful of cruisers a worldwide merchant fleet upon which the British seaborne empire's survival depended. And all this was as nothing to what happened when the campaign against Allied shipping went underwater. Before we consider that crucial campaign, however, we need to go back to the beginning of the war and the waters from which the decision at sea was expected by both sides: the North Sea – or, as the Kaiser and his admirals would have it, the German Ocean.

4

Battleships

Battenberg's masterstroke, endorsed in advance by Churchill, of sending the British line of battle to Scapa Flow instead of standing it down after the review of July 1914, and the almost simultaneous arrival of the German dreadnoughts at their North Sea bases, raised expectations on both sides of a decisive fleet action as the likely maritime highlight of a short war. The opposed governments and naval staffs on either side of the North Sea, however, did not envisage such a development, no matter how much junior officers and the public might relish the prospect. The Germans were intent on knocking out the French Army with a massively reinforced right-wing sweep through Belgium and northern France to seize Paris, force the French to sue for peace on the Kaiser's terms and then tackle 'the main enemy', Russia. Britain's 'contemptible little army' did not even figure in the calculations of the German General Staff, which may explain why the Imperial Navy made no serious attempt to interfere with its disembarkation. Russia would be held off until the German eastern front could be reinforced by rail with the victorious western divisions for a decisive battle. In the ensuing peace negotiations the High Seas Fleet would, if undamaged, represent a powerful bargaining chip to discourage the British from being too stubborn about the terms to be imposed on her partners in the Triple Entente.

Britain's army of 250,000 regulars was indeed tiny by German or French standards, though hardly contemptible, as it had learned a great deal from the Boer War. Only four of the planned six divisions of the British Expeditionary Force (BEF) were ready for immediate transshipment to the agreed position on the Channel coast and the French left. For the time being it was once again upon the Royal Navy that 'the safety, honour and welfare of the realm [did] chiefly attend', and the Grand Fleet was not about to be frittered away in penny packets. It was seen as Britain's highest card in any early peace-round as Admiral Jellicoe took up his appointment in command of the fleet on 4 August.

The circumspection of the two naval rivals was made clear to those in the know on 6 August 1914. The Kaiser ordered the High Seas Fleet to adopt a purely defensive posture, leaving it to U-boats and light forces to reconnoitre the North Sea. The British on the same day instituted the Northern Patrol between Shetland and Norway – Germany's northern exit to the Atlantic – consisting initially of eighteen auxiliary or armed merchant cruisers (AMCs). Meanwhile the Grand Fleet, having made one fruitless sweep towards Jutland in search of German raiders on the 4th, left its designated main base at Scapa Flow for the open sea, with orders to remain north of the Cromarty Firth and/or west of Orkney for fear of mines and U-boats. Other old British cruisers and auxiliaries, including trawlers and requisitioned boarding vessels with armed search parties, were assigned to patrol the waters south of the Northern Patrol line and north of the Dover Straits, to look out for contraband cargoes and enemy warship movements.

Thus the most powerful pieces on the North Sea chessboard, the two battle fleets, had to be covered by a screen of lesser, even expendable, pieces such as second- and third-rate cruisers, auxiliaries, minelayers and sweepers, destroyers and torpedo boats – and their submersible cousins, submarines. Prewar experiments and limited performance ruled out submarines as constituents of a battlefleet on the move, but they could make scouting sweeps, spy on harbours and lie in wait for an approaching enemy in order to attack it before battle was joined; or else they could be lookouts in a defensive screen. Submarines thus appear frequently in this chapter in their original role as outliers of the fleet and targeted upon the enemy's military assets; their other, ultimately much deadlier, role as submersible commerce raiders in the context of total war is the subject of the next chapter.

The Royal Navy's first sinking of an enemy vessel in the war took place on 5 August, one day after Britain became a belligerent and fifty miles east of the Suffolk coast, when two destroyers from Harwich caught the minelayer *Königin Luise*: HMS *Lance* had the honour of firing the Royal Navy's first live shot of the war and the German ship scuttled. But two of the enemy's 180 mines already sown sank the modern light cruiser HMS *Amphion* off the Thames estuary on the same day, with the loss of 151 men – plus the eighteen Germans she had saved from the *Luise*. On the same day also, British submarines from Harwich sailed to the Heligoland Bight to keep watch for German warships, while a British cable ship cut five international telegraphic cables off Germany's narrow North Sea coast. The latter stroke forced the Germans to rely on wireless for overseas communication, to the considerable advantage of the British intelligence effort, considered below.

On the other side, two flotillas of U-boats, twenty in all, had assembled off Heligoland on 1 August, the day Germany went to war against Russia, to form a defensive screen. On the 6th their chief, Commander Hermann Bauer, sent fourteen boats out scouting up to 350 miles into the North Sea, even as British patrols seized four German steamers in the north-east Atlantic. Two days later, while no fewer than 196 trawlers were requisitioned by the Admiralty to sweep mines in home waters, four U-boats failed to get near the Channel Fleet when seventy-nine warships covered the inaugural BEF crossing to France, completed without loss on the 23rd. Further to the north the dreadnought *Monarch* (1911) was attacked by *U15*, which got away after her torpedo missed. But on the way home the next day the German boat was forced to stop on the surface to repair her engines and was sighted, rammed and sunk by the cruiser *Birmingham* with the loss of all hands – the first submarine to be destroyed in action.

On 11 August the Harwich Force, at this stage consisting of two light cruisers and forty destroyers, was officially constituted under Commodore Reginald Tyrwhitt. It was to be kept considerably busier than the Grand Fleet it was formed to support. On the same day, three cross-Channel steamers were taken up for conversion to seaplane carriers. The nervous early probes continued as the 1912 light cruiser HMS *Fearless* drove off the identical-twin light cruisers *Strassburg* and *Stralsund* while scouting across the North Sea, where, three days later, a German light cruiser and destroyers sank eight British fishing boats. Even when the expected British close blockade did not materialize, German sea strategy remained broadly the same: to attack Grand Fleet units with superior force whenever possible so as to whittle down the Royal Navy until it could be comprehensively cut down to size by the High Seas Fleet: win, lose or draw, the British would then cease to dominate.

The stakes were raised on 27 August, when thirty-one British destroyers from two flotillas, the First and Third, led by light cruisers and with six more of the latter in support, crossed the North Sea from Harwich on a sweep led by Tyrwhitt. Commodore Keyes sent three of his submarines in support from the same base, sharing his colleague's view, widely held by naval and public opinion alike, that it was high time the British fleet took positive action. The Admiralty concurred but, in the misconceived priority given to wireless silence, failed to tell Tyrwhitt that it had also decided to send Beatty's five battlecruisers to back him up in what became the Battle of the Heligoland Bight – the first major engagement in Anglo-German waters. The raiders attacked at dawn on the 28th, sinking the fleet destroyer *V187*. When what was mistaken for a German heavy cruiser appeared, Beatty's Invincibles attacked, sinking three old light cruisers, *Mainz*, *Köln* and *Ariadne*.

First blood to the British it might have been, but the failure to pass vital intelligence to Tyrwhitt, and much confusion over signalling (never Beatty's strong suit), would dog the Royal Navy throughout the war. The British light forces were nonplussed by the unexpected appearance of the big ships and some commanders took them for German (which they might well have been, had the tide in the Jade estuary allowed the three German battlecruisers lurking there to come out in time over the sandbanks as ordered). Had the British not spent so much of their time chasing their own tail the damage inflicted on the enemy's light forces could well have been much greater. One British light cruiser and several destroyers were damaged; British casualties at seventy-two were a fraction of the German 1,162 (plus 381 taken prisoner, including the son of Admiral Tirpitz) in a clear if limited victory for the overwhelmingly superior British force.

The pinpricks and the probes continued for another five months. Otto Hersing's *U21* became the first submarine to sink a warship on the open sea, in the unfortunate shape of light cruiser HMS *Pathfinder*, which took 258 men down with her on 5 September; but when Harwich Force and the battlecruisers made another sweep into the Bight three days later they found it empty. Four days after that, on the 12th, Lieutenant-Commander Max Horton in HM Submarine *E9* torpedoed and sank the small German cruiser *Hela* just a few miles south-west of Heligoland (he would also sink the destroyer *S116* at the mouth of the Ems almost a month later). Horton started a British submarine tradition by returning to Harwich flying a home-made skull and crossbones to indicate an enemy victim. This exploit was enough to persuade the German Navy to ban all future fleet exercises in the North Sea and shift them to the protected Baltic. But the shocking possibilities of ruthlessly pursued submarine attack were made unmistakably clear on 22 September when *U9* (Lieutenant-Commander Otto Weddigen, Germany's first U-boat 'ace') exacted a terrible revenge for the three cruisers sunk in the Bight.

On patrol some twenty miles north-west of the Hook of Holland, Weddigen sighted three fourteen-year-old British cruisers dawdling along in line abreast at ten knots, in breach of an Admiralty standing order to cruise at a minimum fifteen – a speed they would have had trouble to maintain. Nicknamed in advance the 'live-bait squadron', the *Aboukir*, *Hogue* and *Cressy*, 12,000 tons each, had been classified as a liability by such as Commodore Keyes and First Sea Lord Battenberg; as recently as 17 September Churchill himself had recommended they be paid off. Weddigen fired one torpedo, hitting the *Aboukir*, which turned turtle and sank in twenty minutes. When her two sisters naively stopped to pick up survivors, he destroyed them in turn. The *Cressy* sank out of sight at 7.55 a.m., ninety-five minutes after his first shot. The neutral Dutch steamer *Titan* had viewed the massacre from a safe distance but gallantly moved in to lift 114 British sailors from the sea; 1,459 men, two-thirds of the three Reserve Fleet crews, died – more than had been killed in the Navy's greatest victory, at Trafalgar in 1805. When the primitive, paraffin-powered boat returned in triumph to Wilhelmshaven, Admiral Friedrich von Ingenohl, C-in-C of the High Seas Fleet, came down to the quayside to distribute decorations; and when Weddigen left for his next patrol the admiral could not resist signalling: 'After *E9* comes *U9*.' As if to prove the triple tragedy was no fluke, Weddigen got the even older cruiser *Hawke* in his sights on 15 October off Peterhead in north-east Scotland, coolly sinking her amid her destroyer escorts with the loss of 525 men; twenty-one survived. The Admiralty had already issued a standing order that ships in company should not stop to rescue survivors if a submarine might still be in the vicinity. After this 'postscript' Weddigen received the Kaiser's highest decoration, the order *Pour le mérite*. He wore it round his neck for barely five months: newly promoted commander and given a modern boat, the diesel-driven *U29*, Weddigen was rammed and sunk by HMS *Dreadnought* on 18 March 1915 off Beachy Head on England's south coast. The mother of all modern battleships and flagship of Vice-Admiral Sir Doveton Sturdee's Fourth Battle Squadron sighted *U29* on the surface and turned 'on a sixpence' to crush a boat one-thirtieth of her displacement, with the loss of all aboard. But this success was also a reminder that the ancient ram was still the only effective weapon against submarines, not one of which had been sunk or even hit by gunfire.

Unbeknown to the Germans, the *U9* had driven the Grand Fleet out of Scapa Flow to Lough Swilly while the battlecruisers took refuge at the Isle of Mull; but on 27 October the dreadnought *Audacious* hit a mine and sank, twenty-six miles north of the lough. The German loss of four destroyers in a fierce little action with a Harwich Force light cruiser and four destroyers off the Dutch island of Texel on the 17th was scant compensation for this shock. On that day also, *E1* (Lieutenant-Commander Noel Laurence, RN) and *E9* (Horton) stole into the Baltic to go to the aid of the Russians; *E11* (Lieutenant-Commander Martin Nasmith, RN) had to turn back with engine trouble after evading German pursuers. Commodore Keyes, as usual all gung-ho and no staffwork, had forgotten to inform the Russians of their impending arrival at Libau (now Liepaja, Latvia), proclaimed in each case by the unfurling of an outsize white ensign. Thus, however, did Keyes, after several false starts caused by mechanical breakdowns in his unreliable boats, make good his diversionary promise to Churchill to infiltrate the Baltic by submarine instead of risking a battle squadron. The U-boats for their part caused more alarm on the last day of October, when *U27* sank the seaplane carrier HMS *Hermes* only eight miles north-west of Calais. The Admiralty retaliated by declaring the whole of the North Sea a military free-fire zone and stepping up the blockade with more minefields.

The High Seas Fleet command trailed its coat on 3 November by sending Rear-Admiral Franz von Hipper and his squadron of three battlecruisers across to Norfolk to shell Great Yarmouth. It was the first time in more than a century that the British coast had come under attack, and a foretaste of the bombardment of civilians by high explosive that was to become such a feature of twentieth-century warfare. The damage this first time was minor, its purpose to cover a minelaying operation a little further to the south and also to test British defences, which were unable to strike back at the Germans before they turned for home. Jellicoe returned from his Lough Swilly refuge with the bulk of the Grand Fleet to Scapa Flow the same day. Fortunately the battlefleet was on the move again on the 23rd, when *U18* (Lieutenant-Commander Heinrich von Hennig) stole into Scapa Flow, only to find it empty of worthwhile targets. The boat was sighted by a minesweeper, which struck it a glancing blow, and again by the destroyer HMS *Garry*, which rammed it fair and square, forcing Hennig and his crew of twenty-five to surrender: one submariner died.

On 16 December Hipper was back, this time with five battle-cruisers and their light escort, to conduct a heavier bombardment of the ports of Hartlepool in County Durham and Whitby in North Yorkshire. Admiral Ingenohl led the bulk of the High Seas Fleet out to sea to lie in wait for a British counterstroke. There were nearly 700 civilian casualties and thirty-five soldiers were wounded; two fishing boats sank. Beatty duly came racing down from the Firth of Forth with five battlecruisers, backed by Vice-Admiral Sir George Warrender's squadron of six battleships, their efforts to close with the Germans frustrated once again by poor signalling. The visibility that day was also poor, saving the British from attack by a superior German force just as the Tirpitz strategy had envisaged.

On Christmas Day the British chanced their arm in a sortie across the North Sea when three seaplane carriers were sent against the Zeppelin sheds at Cuxhaven, the first ever carrier air raid. Although none of the seven attacking aircraft hit the target, one 'buzzed' the battlecruiser *Von der Tann* in the Schillig Roads, causing her to damage her hull severely as she sought to evade this unwelcome attention and collided with one of her own cruisers. The observer in the offending Short Seaplane number 135 was Erskine Childers, whose uniquely motivated thriller *The Riddle of the Sands* had set out in 1903 to warn Britain of the rapid expansion of the High Seas Fleet and its North Sea hideouts.

The New Year began gloomily for the Royal Navy: on its first day the unescorted pre-dreadnought HMS *Formidable* (1898) succumbed in the Channel to a torpedo attack by *U24* (Lieutenant-Commander Rudolf Schneider) which cost 547 British sailors their lives. The dreadful precedent of the *Aboukir* and her sisters ensured that they died alone; no Channel Fleet warship came rushing to the rescue, although eventually 201 men were picked up from the sea.

The long-awaited clash of the naval titans came at last on 24 January, when for the first time the dreadnoughts of the two North Sea rivals opened fire on each other. Vice-Admiral Beatty's Battlecruiser Force now consisted of two squadrons, the first with three newer ships each with six 13.5-inch guns (flagship HMS *Lion*), and the second with two older 12-inch ships, under the flag of Rear-Admiral Archibald Moore in the *New Zealand*. Hipper came out of the Jade estuary on the evening of the 23rd with his

First Reconnaissance Group of four battlecruisers; the damaged *Von der Tann* had been replaced by SMS *Blücher*, a hybrid design which, though Germany's heaviest cruiser, was no match for an Invincible with her twelve mere 8.2-inch guns. Also in company was the Second Reconnaissance Group of four light cruisers; there were some twenty destroyers with each group. To meet this considerable fragment of the High Seas Fleet the Admiralty sent Beatty's five ships from Rosyth in the Firth of Forth, supported by seven pre-dreadnoughts and a squadron of four heavy cruisers, while Tyrwhitt sent three light cruisers and thirty-five destroyers from Harwich. Keyes dispatched submarines to reconnoitre, and finally Jellicoe sailed after dark from Scapa to lie in wait for the High Seas Fleet with the bulk of the Grand Fleet, including three battleship and three cruiser squadrons plus one of light cruisers and twenty-eight destroyers. North of the Dogger Bank, which gave its name to the ensuing battle, the two sides made contact through the outermost light cruisers of their screens, which opened fire on each other at long range.

One firm sighting of Beatty's superior force was enough for Hipper, whose purpose in coming so far south remains unclear. The High Seas Fleet's battleships were not ordered to sea until after he began the run for home. The *Blücher* at the rear now became a liability as her maximum of just over twenty-three knots held the rest down to a speed which helped the pursuing British battlecruisers to close the range quite quickly: the heavier three opened fire at ten miles with their 13.5-inch guns as the slower *Indomitable* was left behind. They concentrated on the *Blücher*, which was soon seriously damaged. The three German battlecruisers returned fire in an orderly and accurate manner with their lighter guns (the flagship *Seydlitz* had 12-inch and the others 11-inch guns, better made and better directed than the British main armament). The *Lion* at the head of the British line was hit seventeen times and considerably damaged; the *Seydlitz* took three heavy hits and was badly affected by fires.

Once again Beatty was let down by the bane of his career, weak signalling. The wounded *Lion* had lost her wireless and was reduced to flag signals, which the uninspired Admiral Moore misread or missed. Instead of shifting his fire to other German ships Moore concentrated on the already crippled *Blücher*, as did the captains of at least two other British ships, sending her to the bottom but allowing the German battlecruisers to escape. A

German seaplane added to the carnage by firing bullets and grenades at the *Blücher*'s survivors as the British light forces tried to save them: 234 out of about 1,000 survived. Beatty's allocation of enemy targets was so vague that one German battlecruiser was left unshelled and free to shoot with deliberation at the *Lion*, which fell out under the fire of three Germans in all and had to be towed home after the battle for four months of repairs. An enraged Beatty transferred to the *Princess Royal* in order to give chase, but it was too late – especially after he suddenly ordered a ninety-degree turn away from the Germans to evade a feared but imaginary U-boat attack. 'Periscopitis' or false submarine sightings had already often reduced Royal Navy formations to chaos, leading on one notorious occasion to wild shelling inside Scapa Flow that made several dents in the Orkneys. Ironically the turn caused Hipper to cancel the destroyer torpedo attack he had just ordered to cover his retreat. By the time the British resumed the chase Hipper was well on his way to Heligoland and the bosom of the German battlefleet; Jellicoe was nowhere near enough to influence events.

It was undoubtedly a British victory, with the enemy's heaviest cruiser sunk and her most modern battlecruiser, *Seydlitz*, very badly damaged by fire, out of action for several months like the *Von der Tann*: the British thus retained a clear superiority in battlecruiser numbers. Later analysis revealed that the British had fired 958 heavy shells and scored seventy-three hits, while the Germans made twenty-five out of 1,276. But it was a clear victory – which could have been clearer still if only the British admirals had been able to control their ships' movements better. They had the potentially decisive advantages of numbers, squadron speed and weight plus range of guns, but dissipated them in a welter of inadequate signalling. Admiral Moore was scapegoated, ordered to transfer his flag to a cruiser squadron covering the Canary Islands in the Atlantic. In Germany Ingenohl was sacked on 2 February for not coming out to support Hipper; he was replaced by the Chief of Naval Staff, Admiral Hugo von Pohl. The jingoistic British press rejoiced over the defeat of 'baby-killer' Hipper, the man who had shelled the northern English towns. But the Germans made one important gain from this heaviest clash at sea thus far: they saw that the *Seydlitz* had almost been burned out thanks not only to three British heavy shell-hits but also to weaknesses in her construction, making her vulnerable to long-range, plunging shot and the consequent 'flash' effect below decks. She would have blown up had an officer not flooded her magazines. The entire High Seas Fleet was therefore given extra anti-flash protection. The Grand Fleet was not.

The two battlecruiser forces had been brought together for their extended skirmish by a burgeoning British naval intelligence initiative which was already showing enormous potential to the few who knew about it, even though the Admiralty proved overcautious, unimaginative and inflexible in exploiting it. But the new art of signals intelligence – 'sigint' as it became known in mid-century – was pioneered and rapidly developed by the Royal Navy. It consisted of systematic eavesdropping on the enemy's wireless transmissions, accompanied by a sustained assault on his codes and ciphers. As radio technology developed swiftly under the necessity of war, enemy signals even when undeciphered proved highly useful: traffic analysis revealed ship and formation movements; later the same signal from an individual vessel picked up by two separate listening posts could be used to detect its position by triangulation.

We saw how the British SS *Telconia* cut the main German overseas cables near Emden on the Dutch frontier on 5 August 1914 as one of the very first acts of war, forcing the enemy to fall back on wireless, much easier to intercept than landline traffic to this day. There followed a series of remarkable strokes of luck, intelligently exploited by the relatively new but highly alert Naval Intelligence Department at the Admiralty. The first windfall came all the way from Melbourne, where a Royal Australian Navy party in civilian clothes walked aboard a German steamer on 11 August for a purported medical inspection. Her master was observed preparing to destroy the ship's papers, which were taken from him at gunpoint. They included a copy of the codebook employed until March 1916 for communication between merchant ships and naval authorities. This valuable tome eventually got to the Admiralty by the end of October via various ships.

The greatest coup came on 26 August, when the modern light cruiser SMS *Magdeburg* ran aground in thick fog on the island of Odensholm off Estonia (then Russian) during an ill-advised armed reconnaissance, with another cruiser, off the Gulf of Finland. Two Russian cruisers came up as the fog faded and opened fire. Some Germans got away on a destroyer but attempts to dispose of the ship's papers were botched and the cruiser's copy of the naval codebook was recovered in pristine condition by the Russians. This main signal book of the Imperial Navy was accompanied by its current key and a coded grid-chart of the Baltic. In an all too rare but exemplary spirit of inter-allied cooperation, the Russians told their naval attaché in London to offer a copy to the Admiralty if a ship could be sent to collect it. The cruiser *Theseus* brought it back on 10 October after a number of misunderstandings with the Russians, who insisted on accompanying their gift all the way to the First Lord's office, where Churchill gratefully took delivery on 13 October. The Germans did not find out until 1918.

The treasure was immediately passed to Room 40 in the Admiralty's Old Building, where the Director of Naval Intelligence, Rear-Admiral Henry Oliver, had installed his friend and colleague on the Naval Staff, Rear-Admiral Sir Alfred Ewing, Director of Naval Education, to analyse intercepted German signals from 15 August 1914 (the first of fourteen 'Y-stations' was opened for this purpose on the English east coast on 1 September; more were soon set up in the Mediterranean). On 30 November a trawler fortuitously fished up another important codebook, used by the Imperial Navy for communicating with the German Army, from the wreck of one of the four German destroyers sunk off the Texel on 17 October. Room 40 now held a copy of each of the enemy's three principal naval codebooks, a priceless advantage. This astounding coup was unsurpassed in importance for the British in the Great War at sea and a decisive victory for the Royal Navy, helping it to overcome or offset its own shortcomings and weaknesses – some of which were potentially fatal – throughout the war. It is difficult, for example, to imagine how *Undaunted* and her four destroyers could have managed otherwise to trap and sink the four German destroyers off the Texel before they could even begin to lay their mines, just four days after the arrival of the main German naval cipher in London.

Room 40 was handed over to a seven-man team of mostly civilian cryptanalysts on 6 November 1914 (they had been using Ewing's office), after the highly gifted master-spy Captain Reginald Hall, RN, succeeded Oliver as Director of the Intelligence Department (DID) for the duration. At Churchill's suggestion Hall appointed a solitary officer – Commander Herbert Hope – to sift and analyse the decoded German messages so as to build up a picture of the enemy's thinking as well as actions. But it was only after the personal intervention of Fisher that Hope was allowed to see the whole of the traffic rather than the innocuous selection reluctantly fed to him in his isolated office by Ewing's hyper-retentive cryptanalysts in Room 40 itself. Otherwise, on Churchill's orders, decrypts were restricted to himself as First Lord, the First Sea Lord (Fisher), the Chief of Staff (now Oliver) and Hall as DID, a classic case of Churchillian interference in matters of detail and refusal to delegate. Even as Prime Minister in the Second World War Churchill showed the same appetite for seeing all decrypts produced by that other great British intelligence triumph, Bletchley Park. It was Hope who became the main 'brain' of Room 40 until he was posted to the Adriatic in 1917. But the Silent Service was also secretive, keeping its crucial source of intelligence so much to itself that even the War Office was not informed until spring 1917; with the exception of Hall, not even the Intelligence Department was in on the secret and Admiral Oliver was not sure after the war whether Downing Street knew. Had it been up to the admiral, the Prime Minister would clearly not have been told.

But Room 40 had the wit to warn Jellicoe on 14 December 1914 of the imminent appearance on the North Sea of the High Seas Fleet, heralded by Hipper's hit-and-run bombardment of Hartle-pool and Whitby; as we saw, both sides fluffed an opportunity for a fleet or a squadron action. Six weeks later the British eaves-droppers correctly warned of another probe by the High Seas Fleet, the tip that led to the Battle of the Dogger Bank and the first dreadnought duel.

It was fortunate for the Admiralty and the British war effort alike that William Reginald Hall, son of the Navy's first Director of Intelligence, suffered from poor health. Known as 'Blinker' because of a nervous tic of the eyelids, Hall joined the service at fourteen in 1884 and by the time war broke out thirty years later he was captain of the battlecruiser *Queen Mary* under Beatty, one of his greatest admirers. There was no better-run ship in the Grand Fleet and she was the Battlecruiser Squadron's gunnery champion; it was Captain Hall who first tried out the three-watch system of four hours on and eight off and improved conditions for the lower deck with such innovations as a book exchange, a chapel and a cinema. He stood down the hated 'ship's police' even though he was renowned for his firm but fair standards of discipline. But after two months of war his health broke down and he had to be found a post ashore. When Oliver was promoted to Chief of Staff, he nominated Hall as his successor in the post of DID (alternatively abbreviated to DNI), inspired by a plea from a worried Mrs Hall. Her husband may have lacked physical strength but those who met him always remarked on his piercing eyes, formidable mind and extremely powerful personality, ruthless, devious and charming by turns. Oliver's choice was a blessing for the Navy, the nation and Hall himself, but it was Oliver who for more than two years frustrated Hall's desire to make maximum use of the 'Miraculous Draught of Fishes', as Room 40 called the German codes culled from the sea.

Far away from the chill waters of the North Sea, the British and French naval commands in the Mediterranean were wondering in September 1914 what to do about the Dardanelles after Admiral Souchon had sailed his two cruisers into the strait upon which Russia, the third member of the Triple Entente, had relied for nearly all her imports and exports. On 26 September a Turkish torpedo boat emerged; the British naval force on guard boarded it and on finding German soldiers ordered the small warship to go back. On his own initiative the German general in command of the forts at the mouth of the waterway promptly closed it to all shipping. The entrance was mined, warning notices erected on shore and the lighthouses went dark. Russian grain ships piled up in one of the greatest maritime 'traffic jams' ever known; eventually they went back to the Black Sea, never to return. After the *Goeben* shelled the Russian Black Sea ports under the Turkish flag, Russia, France and Britain declared war on Turkey at the beginning of November.

Doubtless preoccupied by the rising carnage on the Western Front, the British War Council took its time in getting round to considering a proposal to force the straits by a simultaneous naval and military assault. Lord Kitchener at the War Office, dominant figure in the War Cabinet, however, vetoed diverting troops from France and in mid-January 1915 the British decided on a purely naval assault. There was a precedent: in 1807, in the heyday of sail, Admiral Duckworth had blasted his way to within eight miles of Constantinople, only to be beaten off in adverse winds. Even without landward support, he extricated all his ships with only a few casualties. The French were happy to go along with the British proposal, provided their troops were not required. Churchill sought the view of Vice-Admiral Sackville Carden, the former Admiral-Superintendent at Malta who had succeeded the disgraced Troubridge in command of the blockading squadron. Carden, old and not very well, reluctantly conceded that a careful, suitably massive bombardment might achieve the objective in a month if he could please have twelve battleships, three battle-cruisers, four light cruisers, sixteen destroyers, six submarines, twelve minesweepers, seaplanes and auxiliary vessels plus a mass of ammunition.

Churchill concurred. There was no shortage of pre-dreadnoughts for a task where their slow speed and fewer, shorter-range guns would not put them at undue or extra risk. The battlecruisers were included as insurance against an encounter with the *Goeben*. Churchill even threw in the latest battleship, the *Queen Elizabeth*, whose mighty 15-inch guns could usefully be worked up in bombarding the forts.

The services of Rear-Admiral Arthur Limpus, head until war broke out of the British naval mission to Constantinople, were not enlisted for fear of offending the Turks whose fortifications were about to be pounded by Britain's (and the world's) heaviest shells. This curious omission was only the first of a series of pulled punches that would undermine the whole operation. The Admiralty was confident that bombardment alone would achieve the desired result: if one capital ship (*Goeben*) had been enough to pitch Turkey into the war, surely an entire battlefleet would be enough to force her out. The threat to Constantinople once the ships had blasted their way within range of that vast and vulnerable metropolis was obvious. This was the first major instance of an error so often made in the twentieth century: the belief that bombardment alone could achieve a strategic objective without risking the potentially much higher casualties associated with the use of ground troops, still the only military instrument capable of seizing and holding a major land objective. Presidents Saddam Hussein of Iraq and Slobodan Milosevic of rump Yugoslavia were among those still exposing this error (with the Royal Navy in the offing in each case) as the century came to an end.

The far-sighted Fisher, who had almost alone foreseen the potential of submarines and aircraft before the ink was dry on the patents, had misgivings, and would have liked an invasion at the same time, but Kitchener's word was law. The old admiral was quite prepared to expend some superannuated ships but was worried by the likely loss of scarce trained manpower. At the confirmatory War Council on 28 January Fisher, finding himself in a minority of one, threatened to walk out but was reluctantly won over by Kitchener and Churchill. He added two more old battleships to the bombardment force; and the French sent a squadron of four more, plus supporting ships, to complete the largest concentration of firepower thus far assembled in the Mediterranean.

The besiegers faced some hundred cannon at the entrance and along the shores of the straits, distributed among eleven forts; seventy-two of the guns were in fixed emplacements, the heaviest at the entrance. The German Army and Navy had supplied two dozen more 5.9-inch mobile howitzers, plus naval guns of a similar calibre from the *Goeben*'s secondary armament, as well as hundreds of naval and military artillerymen and technicians. The defences also included shore-based as well as shipborne torpedo tubes, search-lights and (especially) minefields. The defenders were, however, short of shells, particularly armour-piercing.

Admiral Carden aboard his flagship, the awesome *Queen Elizabeth*, began a deliberate, long-distance bombardment on the morning of 19 February. After four hours he closed the range to three miles, within reach of the Turkish guns, which tried a few return shots but conserved their ammunition. The salvos ended at twilight and were not resumed for six days because of foul weather. The British second-in-command, Vice-Admiral John de Robeck, took the lead on the 25th with a much fiercer, close-range bom-bardment, forcing the Turks and Germans to abandon the entrance forts. Royal Marines and bluejackets went ashore to complete the destruction of the outer defence works, meeting no opposition. Then minesweepers came up to clear the way for an incursion into the straits, fighting the eternal current that flows from the Black Sea into the Mediterranean but finding few mines and suffering little damage from the artillery ashore. An unusually buoyant Carden wirelessed on 2 March that he hoped to be off Constantinople in fourteen days, weather permitting. World grain prices dropped in anticipation of a resumption of Russian exports.

But in a first demonstration of their fighting qualities, Turkish troops arrived to fend off landing parties and patch up the outer defences; the howitzers lobbed shells at the decks of the attacking force, constantly shifting their positions and sapping the nerve of the largely mercantile minesweeper crews. By 8 March the attackers were in a dilemma: the minesweepers could not clear a channel until the battleships silenced the forts, but the battleships could not silence the forts until the minesweepers had cleared a channel. Roger Keyes had left his submarine inspectorate at Harwich to be Carden's chief of staff, his aggressive spirit a useful counterpoint to his new chief's ingrained caution and anxiety. Keyes took charge of the faltering minesweepers and on 13 March led a fourth sweep with sailors replacing merchant seamen, clearing many mines despite a shore bombardment that put all but three of his vessels out of action. Meanwhile Churchill was urging the commanders on the spot to get on and finish the job, for once a justified intervention at long distance: Carden was ill and losing his nerve, despite having sustained few casualties and no noteworthy material loss. Churchill expressly told Carden that some losses, even of battleships, were acceptable in taking such an objective. Carden was hurriedly relieved of his command on medical advice and replaced by his deputy, de Robeck, who was in charge for the grand assault planned for 18 March.

He wanted a rolling attack on the model of an old-fashioned musketry engagement, with the first of three lines opening fire and then allowing the second to advance through its ranks to take over the lead, followed in turn by the third and then the first again. The first line consisted of the six heaviest British battleships, the second of the four French plus two more and the third of six older battleships. The *Queen Elizabeth* with her eight 15-inch guns, supported by the 12-inchers of her five companions, opened a cataclysmic broadside whose shattering noise was compounded by the echoes from the nearby shore. The French under the dashing Admiral Guépratte moved smartly through de Robeck's line and opened fire half a mile ahead, leaving a clear field of fire behind him and doubling the fall of shot. De Robeck next called up the third line of six to relieve the French, who began an orderly retirement. The defenders had scored major hits on two British battleships and one French but their armour enabled them to carry on firing.

As the French retired, however, their second in line, the *Bouvet*, took a plunging hit on one of her magazines, exploded and sank in two minutes with the loss of 640 men, a terrifying sight. Undeterred, the ships kept up the shelling through the afternoon. At dusk de Robeck sent in the minesweepers again to clear the way for the next move forward – but once more, and amid great confusion, the adapted trawlers were driven off by renewed and determined Turco-German fire. The mines unswept, the battlecruiser *Inflexible* ran on to at least one and was only saved by the superhuman damage-control efforts of her crew, who also managed to take her slowly to safety out of the firing line. But only five minutes later the 1898 battleship *Irresistible* was crippled by an underwater explosion and drew the enemy's main fire. She stayed afloat, most of her crew having been evacuated by destroyer.

Keyes stayed in the straits with two battleships, *Ocean* and *Swiftsure*, as the bombardment force withdrew for the night, preparing to tow the stricken ship away. Then the *Ocean* (also 1898) hit a mine and began to list and sail in circles, her steering gear immobilized. Keyes rescued her crew and ordered *Swiftsure* to withdraw; he now planned to return in the destroyer *Jed* after dark to torpedo the *Irresistible* and either salvage or sink the *Ocean*. As the little warship stole back into the straits, the silence after one of the most intense bombardments in history was itself almost deafening. In the meantime, to the perplexity of the searching British, their two stricken battleships had quietly sunk, though the vast majority of their crews were safe.

On the 19th large numbers of sailors volunteered to re-man the minesweepers as morale on the British and French ships held up very well despite the triple loss of the previous day. De Robeck was depressed by the removal from his fleet of the equivalent of a battle squadron; but Keyes, his staff colleagues and the captains remained confident that the straits would be forced by one more determined assault. The Admiralty took the same view, Churchill ordering de Robeck that very morning to try again. Replacements for the knocked-out British and French battleships were promised as a squadron of land-based naval aircraft began to arrive for reconnaissance work. By 20 March repairs were as complete as possible and de Robeck had sixty-two minesweepers, all manned by British and French naval volunteers, ready to start a new approach. The admiral announced that he would renew the attack in a day or two, after the gales died down.

But on 22 March, in circumstances never satisfactorily explained, de Robeck lost heart and changed his mind – or had it changed for him. To the amazement of the defenders, who were almost out of heavy ammunition and down to less than a dozen armour-piercing shells and a handful of mines, the fearsome floating artillery barrage never came back. Four weeks of effort, 700 lives, three lost battleships, many other damaged vessels and untold quantities of ammunition had been expended for no profit at all. In fact sentiment in London had begun to shift at least a month before the Navy gave up. Even Kitchener had come round by mid-February to the view that an attack across the Gallipoli Peninsula towards Constantinople was unavoidable; on the 16th he even offered the crack 29th Infantry Division. Only when his Western Front generals protested did he propose sending instead the two divisions of the Australia and New Zealand Army Corps (ANZAC), in Egypt at the time.

A General Staff representative reported to Kitchener from the Dardanelles on 5 March that he thought the Navy could not manage alone – only three days after the cagey Carden had said it could. On 10 March Kitchener decreed that the 29th, the Royal Naval, one French and the two ANZAC divisions would go, 75,000 men in all, under General Sir Ian Hamilton, who managed to be with the fleet at the great bombardment of 18 March. He came aboard the *Queen Elizabeth* at the British base on the island of Lemnos in the Aegean on the 22nd, for a meeting of which conflicting accounts survive: but it seems de Robeck went into it believing the Navy could finish the job and came out convinced that it could not be done without the Army. Keyes was outraged; so was Churchill, now isolated on the War Council.

The invasion fleet of 200 ships gathered off Lemnos. Conditions were chaotic as the concept of 'combat loading' of ships for modern warfare had yet to be invented (it had its beginnings in the Dardanelles campaign now starting), but somehow troops landed at five different points on Sunday 25 April 1915, establishing strong but restricted beachheads at Cape Helles on the tip of the peninsula and on its south-western edge at what became known as Anzac Cove. Colonel (later General) Mustafa Kemal, Turkey's modern national hero, was in charge of the defence and managed to confine the invaders to their two toeholds as he built up his forces inland, helped by German soldiers and sailors. A Western Front-style impasse soon developed, the tortuous terrain lending it a peculiarly savage character with some trenches only yards away from the enemy's. A new naval attack was planned for May but the loss to mines of another old battleship, HMS *Goliath*, was quite enough to put paid to it.

By the end of May both Fisher and Churchill had resigned over the Dardanelles fiasco, the one in a typically fiery gesture, the other at dictation speed, both casualties of an ever-strengthening perception that Britain's conduct of the war had fallen into incompetent hands. The Conservative politician Arthur Balfour succeeded Churchill as First Lord, while the old salt Admiral Sir Henry Jackson took over from Fisher as First Sea Lord. The service was hugely relieved: Sir David Beatty, one of Churchill's protégés, wrote at the time: 'The Navy breathes freer now that it is rid of the succubus Winston.' Another admiral wrote to King George V: 'He was, we all consider, a danger to the Empire.' Churchill rejoined the Army and went to France, to return only in 1917 as Lloyd George's Minister of Munitions. Fisher next headed the Admiralty's Board of Invention and Research, a short-lived body which nonetheless oversaw or initiated some useful work in naval technology, especially submarine detection.

The siege of the Dardanelles now involved all main arms of twentieth-century warfare, on land, in the air and at sea, including under it: British submarines were also at work in the Dardanelles. Lieutenant Norman Holbrook in the primitive B11 scored a double first when he sank the old Turkish *Messudieh* almost opposite Constantinople on 13 December 1914: for being the first submariner to sink a battleship he won the first Victoria Cross in 'the Trade', as the submarine service was known to its clannish members. In May 1915 Lieutenant-Commanders E. C. Boyle in *E14* and Martin Nasmith, still in *E11*, each also won the VC for his exploits, Boyle sinking a troopship with 6,000 Turkish soldiers aboard, all of whom drowned, and Nasmith blowing up an ammunition ship and many others. The Germans soon followed suit as Lieutenant-Commander Otto Hersing arrived from the North Sea in *U21* to sink two old British battleships, *Triumph* and *Majestic*, in quick succession.

On land the bloodletting continued; Hamilton's five divisions swelled to eight, and in August 1915 five more landed at Suvla Bay, north of Anzac Cove. Even this failed to turn the trick as casualties built up to more than 200,000 on each side and the outnumbered Turks hung grimly on; in September the French offered a whole army and the British earmarked two more divisions for yet another landing, postponed until November. When Bulgaria, Turkey's prewar enemy in the Balkan Wars, joined the Turco-German side, Hamilton was forced to divert two divisions to Salonika in northern Greece to protect Serbia, opening another wasteful front in the Mediterranean. Hamilton was dismissed for incompetence after Australian and British press campaigns and replaced by General Sir Charles Monro from France in October 1915. Keyes went to London to demand a new naval attack, even persuading

Kitchener to come out and see for himself in November. Monro argued for withdrawal; Kitchener was persuaded and made one of his typical, oracular pronouncements that not a single man would be lost. The British Cabinet concurred on 7 December; within a fortnight Suvla and Anzac were evacuated without casualties. Four divisions were left at Cape Helles, and the Cabinet resolved on 27 December to pull them out also. The French came next, embarking completely unharmed on New Year's Day. That left the gallant 29th, which pretended to be an entire army to such good effect that it drove off the final massed Turkish attack on 7 January. The last redoubt was evacuated – again without loss – on the night of the 8th to 9th, after 259 days.

The whole enterprise, the largest amphibious operation in history so far, had been a huge and sorry fiasco for the Army as much as the Navy, caused in the main by inept leadership; but the British showed an unexpected talent for superbly improvised seaborne evacuations in the teeth of the enemy which would stand them in good stead on many future occasions. Gallipoli was almost all they had to go on in 1940, and again in 1944. Keyes tried in vain for the rest of the war to persuade the Admiralty to try a second naval assault. But the Dardanelles remained firmly closed and Russia was all but cut off from her allies, a fact which Quartermaster-General Ludendorff of the German Army reckoned was worth two years of survival to a heavily outnumbered Germany – in a war that lasted little more than four. Britain could obtain grain only from North America, a fact that seriously increased her vulnerability to the counter-blockade by U-boat described in the next chapter. If Rear-Admiral Troubridge had managed just to wing SMS *Goeben* and slow her down none of this might have happened. For the want of a shot . . .

Back in the North Sea the stalemate continued. On 1 March 1915 the British government declared a total blockade of Germany, but fear of antagonizing the United States, increasingly important to Britain's material and financial survival, meant that cargoes bound for Germany could still reach it via Scandinavia and the Netherlands, neutrally prepared to sell to both sides. The High Seas Fleet came out on 21 April to deter a feared British attack on the Zeppelin sheds at Tondern, which did not materialize; Room 40 warned Jellicoe but fog foiled the Grand Fleet once again. In autumn 1915 the Harwich Force rounded up dozens of German trawlers fishing in the North Sea, converting some of them for service in the eastern Mediterranean.

The bleak and empty times experienced by the opposed battle fleets, still afraid to commit themselves, began to affect morale, more in Germany, where the sailors lived in barracks ashore, than in Britain: 'Our country needs to care for naught: / the Fleet is fast asleep in port,' the street urchins of Wilhelmshaven had been chanting ever since the Dogger Bank action. But in February 1916 the ailing Pohl was replaced as C-in-C of the High Seas Fleet by Admiral Reinhard Scheer, a much more gifted and aggressive officer. He wanted to go back, but rather more boldly, to the original German maritime strategy of attrition of the British fleet. Scheer took to making brief sorties: in February German destroyers sank a Harwich Force sloop near the Dogger Bank, and early in March the German battlefleet came out as far as the Texel, the furthest south yet, almost trapping a large segment of the Harwich force, which sailed out of sight in bad weather. But six days later the general disappointment over the small return from the great fleet which had been his brainchild drove Grand-Admiral Tirpitz to resign as Navy Minister. Even in autocratically ruled, Prussian-led Germany scapegoats had to be found for the lack of progress in the war.

Scheer chanced his arm again on 25 March, coming out as far as the Horns Reef in response to a probe by Harwich Force and Beatty's Battlecruiser Fleet (as it had been styled since February 1915). The Germans too were capable of making intelligence deductions from radio traffic. Massive storms caused Scheer to decline battle and return home. One calendar month later Rear-Admiral Boedicker, standing in for the sick Hipper of the German battlecruisers, led four of them into a second, twenty-minute bombardment of Great Yarmouth and also Lowestoft; there were twenty-three casualties and 200 houses were destroyed. The responding sally by the Harwich Force was enough to cause the Germans to abandon their pinprick. Jellicoe sent the Third Battle Squadron all the way south to Sheerness in Kent to help cover the east coast from the south. On May 23 ten U-boats laid mines off the east coast of Scotland as part of an attempt to draw out and damage the Grand Fleet. Room 40 warned Jellicoe not only of an impending High Seas Fleet sortie but also of the presence of sixteen U-boats in the area. Jellicoe once more sailed out of Scapa Flow and pulled his ships out of the supplementary base of Invergordon in the Cromarty Firth; Beatty left Rosyth the same evening. Both admirals wondered, as they had wondered before, whether this was the long-desired, long-anticipated and, secretly perhaps, long-feared confrontation between the two mightiest fleets ever assembled. Or would it be another false alarm, a missed chance, a futile, blind stroke in the fog of war that had set so fixedly upon the North Sea?

Admiral Scheer was still pursuing the basic German North Sea strategy of piecemeal attrition, trying to draw out a section of the Grand Fleet – battlecruisers preferred – so it could be engaged by the German battlecruisers and then overwhelmed by the High Seas Fleet before Jellicoe's battleships arrived from further north. Bolder than his predecessors, the new C-in-C planned to trail his coat by bombarding Sunderland, on the north-east coast of England, much closer to Beatty's base at Rosyth on the Firth of Forth in south-east Scotland than the coastal towns previously shelled by the Germans. Scheer hoped his submarines would inflict some preliminary damage and confusion on the British as they emerged from both Rosyth and Scapa, and planned also to put up Zeppelins to watch British movements. But the wounds of SMS *Seydlitz* from the Dogger Bank took a fortnight longer to heal than expected, which meant that most U-boats lying in wait reached the end of their endurance and had to return home before Hipper was ready to deploy his full strength.

Scheer therefore abandoned the Sunderland attack in favour of a run up the west coast of Danish Jutland by Hipper's battlecruisers – with the German battleships fifty miles, or just over two hours' hard steaming, behind. Once again the plan was to tempt Beatty to attack Hipper and to crush the British vanguard before Jellicoe arrived. At no time did Scheer intend to seek a fleet action, an often overlooked fact intimately related to the outcome of the impending battle. Jellicoe had his own plan, to lure the Germans into a fleet action by manoeuvring off the Skaggerak, the waters between northern Denmark and southern Norway, but postponed this on receiving Room 40's warning of a large German sortie.

Hipper put to sea at 0100 on 31 May 1916, Scheer came out at 0230. Room 40 did not pick up the orders to set sail, probably because the Germans had no need in port to use wireless for this purpose; but intelligence anticipation of a German move had ensured that both Beatty and Jellicoe began to deploy two hours before Hipper came out. The Germans were sailing northward in line ahead, the battlecruisers well clear of the battleships; the British were sailing east in two converging lines, the battleships well to the north of the battlecruisers. For the first time in the war the bulk of each of the great opposed fleets was committed to the open sea at the same time. But neither side knew of the scale of the other's deployment. Bad weather had grounded the Zeppelins; and the handful of U-boat scouts available were insufficient to detect the extent of the British sortie. Jellicoe on his flagship *Iron Duke* had received a misleading signal from the Admiralty that Scheer's, the *Friedrich der Grosse*, was still in harbour, based on the absence of her call-sign among wireless intercepts.

The converging forces were immense. Jellicoe had three squadrons of eight dreadnoughts (each in two divisions of four apiece), the Second, Fourth and First, plus one squadron of three of the oldest invincibles, the Third. Also in company were the First and Second Cruiser Squadrons, each of four slow armoured ships; the Fourth Light Cruiser Squadron of seven; and three flotillas of destroyers, the Twelfth (sixteen ships), the Eleventh (fifteen plus one light-cruiser leader) and the Fourth, of nineteen, plus two extra destroyers attached to the battlefleet. Beatty's fleet consisted of two squadrons of Invincibles, the First of three ships and the Second of two, plus HMS *Lion* as fleet flagship; and, standing in for the Third (temporarily with Jellicoe), the Fifth Battle Squadron of four 15-inch battleships. He also had the First, Second and Third squadrons of four light cruisers each; two destroyer flotillas, the First (nine plus a light cruiser) and the Thirteenth (ten plus leader), together with eight destroyers drawn from the Ninth and Tenth, plus a seaplane carrier with three aircraft.

Scheer led three squadrons of battleships, the Third of seven and the First of nine dreadnoughts, plus the Second of six pre-dreadnoughts. He had the Fourth Reconnaissance Squadron of five light cruisers, and one more led half of the First and the whole of the Third, Fifth and Seventh destroyer flotillas. Hipper's First Reconnaissance Group consisted of his five battlecruisers and the Second of six light cruisers. Another of the latter led the Second, Sixth and Ninth flotillas. The Germans were outnumbered by thirty-seven to twenty-seven in 'big-gun' ships; six of theirs were not dreadnoughts whereas all the British were dreadnoughts or their invincible cousins. Even if Beatty had stayed in port the

British would have had an advantage of six dreadnoughts or invincibles. The British guns had greater weight of shot and longer range but the German lighter main armament had greater accuracy, helped by superior optics, and endurance. The British generally had the advantage of speed but the Germans still had better armour, stronger hull design, more reliable engines and superior protection against 'flash' explosions, thanks to lessons learned at the Dogger Bank.

Vice-Admiral Beatty was due to turn north to join the eastward-bound Admiral Jellicoe at 1415 on 31 May when his lookouts spotted a neutral Danish steamer, some ten miles to the east. At about the same time Hipper's screening light forces sighted her – about ten miles to their west. Each battlecruiser force sent scouts to investigate. At 1420 the scouts made contact, opened fire and signalled, 'Enemy in sight.'

By 1550 the opposed battlecruiser forces were in action against each other at about eight miles. Hipper had high hopes of 'crossing the T' of the British, which would have enabled his line of ships to concentrate their fire on the head of Beatty's line. The British admiral now made the same mistake as he had at the Dogger Bank, failing to ensure by unmistakable signals that each of the five German ships was engaged by at least one of his own six. His first two, *Lion* and *Princess Royal*, however, correctly concentrated on Hipper's flagship, *Lützow*. Once again British gunnery proved markedly inferior to German at first, by a ratio of about one hit to four. HMS *Indefatigable* succumbed to a colossal explosion after five accurate salvos from the patched-up *Von der Tann*, firing at leisure like the *Derfflinger*, both untargeted. Beatty's flagship *Lion* almost suffered the same fate but for the gallantry of Major F. J. W. Harvey, RMLI, whose last act was to order the flooding and closure of the magazine doors in Q turret when it was pierced by a shell: he was awarded a posthumous VC.

Beatty meanwhile had sheered off northward to frustrate Hipper's T-crossing attempt, just as his Fifth Battle Squadron (Rear-Admiral Hugh Evan-Thomas) was catching up, having lost touch as a result of an earlier signalling failure (again) aboard the *Lion*: but the four battleships at last increased Beatty's numerical advantage to almost two to one, and their 15-inch guns had opened fire at the unprecedented range of almost 22,000 yards, well beyond the Germans' reach but well up to their standard of accuracy. Hipper was alarmed by this reinforcement of an enemy he thought he had already beaten.

But now the *Derfflinger* and the battered *Seydlitz* concentrated their fire on the battlecruiser *Queen Mary*, which rolled over and sank quickly by the bow after her magazines exploded, the second 'flash' victim of the day. When the *Princess Royal* disappeared behind a huge cloud of smoke Beatty (mistakenly) feared the worst and uttered the remark to his flag captain for which he is most often remembered: 'There's something wrong with our bloody ships today, Chatfield,' before ordering a change of course towards the Germans. But Hipper had also executed a turn, away from the British, to evade a torpedo attack by destroyers, and the two sides disengaged. The first phase, fought off the Skaggerak (the name given by the Germans to the entire battle) had ended with honours to Hipper's men, who had sunk two British Invincibles from a much superior force, though at considerable damage to themselves.

Two hours after the battle began Beatty's light cruisers sighted the head of Scheer's battleship line to the south-east. Now it was Beatty's turn to trail his coat, so as to lure Scheer north-westward on to the guns of Jellicoe, advancing, unbeknown to the Germans, south-eastward at top speed. The ruse succeeded and the screening light forces of the two main fleets became involved in furious fighting in the vicinity of their charges, several of which, especially the British, were damaged. Fortunately for the persistently under-informed Jellicoe, Beatty drew the Germans' attention while the Grand Fleet laboriously but impeccably manoeuvred from its cruising formation of six columns into a single line of battle. But the signalling silence from Beatty went on so long that Jellicoe felt obliged to send him the plaintive message, 'Where is enemy battlefleet?' This did not prevent him from telling an electrified Admiralty: 'Fleet action is imminent.'

HMS *Defence*, which had missed a fight with Souchon in the Mediterranean and again with Spee in the south Atlantic, blew up and sank under Scheer's heavy guns, lacking both the firepower and armour of a capital ship or the speed of a light cruiser: she should not have been there. Hipper had remained in touch, taking the lead in the German line of battle, and his *Derfflinger* and *Lützow*, though damaged, were allowed by the British to concentrate their fire on HMS *Invincible*, with the Third Squadron at the head of Jellicoe's line. She went the cataclysmic way of her two sisters earlier in the day, exploding, breaking up and sinking in halves, bow and stern up. But damage to *Lützow* led Hipper to transfer to the *Moltke*.

Scheer's battle-line was eight miles long and had sagged in the middle during the fighting, bending towards the east. The German commander coolly ordered a 180-degree fleet turn, not in a great long curve nor yet squadron by squadron, but ship by ship, on the model of the Japanese at Tsushima; the shattered *Lützow* which had led the line now brought up the rear as the Germans sailed west for a while. But Scheer repeated his ship-by-ship reversal of course about an hour before dusk, heading once more towards the Grand Fleet, which was still in good order but just as ill-informed of the enemy's position, course and speed. The German destroyer screen confused the British line by launching torpedo attacks, beaten off at the cost of some disruption. Scheer sent Hipper ahead in a last charge to help the destroyers extricate themselves: but he soon sent the little ships in again for the last time, to mask another reversal of course. By the time darkness fell the Germans had disengaged and were running for home at the end of the second stage of the battle.

After dark, Beatty's battlecruisers, again separated from the bulk of the British fleet, opened fire on the enemy battlecruisers, once more at the rear of their line, and on the six pre-dreadnoughts of the German Second Squadron ahead of them. His attack divided his targets from the rest of the German fleet, forcing them to turn westwards, away from safety. Next, the British Second Battle Squadron (Vice-Admiral Sir Martyn Jerram), now leading the bulk of the fleet, sighted the German main body – but mistook them for the ships led by Beatty, who had dashed off a message to the British battleships, urging them to follow him and help cut off the separated Germans. So Jerram did not open fire; nor did Scheer, who had not seen him, and the two lines diverged. Jellicoe had no idea at the time that this had happened because he was not told. Beatty was the principal culprit in a general failure to keep the C-in-C informed of his squadrons' and the enemy's movements in detail or at all, despite Jellicoe's standing order to the contrary. Both fleets were now heading south, the British east of the Germans and in a position to bar their way home. Jellicoe sent his light forces to the rear to oppose any attempt by Scheer to turn across the British wake for home, only ninety miles away – which he would duly do nevertheless.

Having abandoned the crippled *Lützow* to her fate, and transferred to a destroyer en route to the *Moltke*, Hipper managed to board her and ordered his four remaining battlecruisers, now at the rear, to resume their place at the head of the line. Only the

Seydlitz, badly damaged by twenty hits, listing and down at the bow, had the spirit to respond. But the Germans had the advantage of familiarity with working their ships at night, having trained with star-shell and searchlights, although the main fighting during the brief early summer night involved the light forces. The British blew up the light cruiser *Frauenlob* by gunfire and then the pre-dreadnought *Pommern* with a torpedo. Jellicoe did not know that the German main body had fallen back or that Scheer had ordered another ship-by-ship turn eastward behind the British, forcing a path through the British light forces and blowing up the armoured cruiser *Black Prince*. Jellicoe was not informed of Scheer's last turn until it was far too late to catch him.

Like the first, the last shots of the Battle of Jutland were fired by Beatty's battlecruisers, at 0320 on 1 June – at a Zeppelin which had managed to reach the otherwise silent battlefield. At 0415 the Admiralty forwarded to Jellicoe a Room 40 interception revealing that the High Seas Fleet was already threading its way through its own minefields off Horns Reef. The debate about who won the battle has continued ever after. It was and remained the heaviest big-gun sea action in all history, the dreadnought zenith of the line-of-battle era, even though, given the size of each fleet, it fell far short of fulfilling the British dream of a steam-powered Trafalgar. The Germans lost one battlecruiser and one old battleship, four light cruisers and five destroyers, 2,551 killed and 507 wounded, reducing the High Seas Fleet by 62,000 tons or 6.79 per cent. The Grand Fleet lost 111,000 tons or 8.84 per cent in the shape of three battlecruisers, three heavy cruisers and eight destroyers sunk, 6,197 men killed, 510 wounded and 177 captured.

What may seem like a victory for the German underdog takes no account of the much higher degree of general damage inflicted on the High Seas Fleet by the Grand Fleet, once its shooting steadied, than vice versa: Scheer with his numerically inferior force was unable to risk taking his fleet out for a good two months, whereas Jellicoe reported his squadrons ready for sea at four hours' notice the day after the battle. The British had twenty-four dreadnoughts without significant damage to the Germans' ten. Even so, the Imperial Navy had come from nowhere in under twenty years to deploy a fleet capable of fighting the Royal Navy with all its glorious tradition and giving as good as it got ship for ship. The 'man of the match' award would have gone to Hipper for his dash against a superior opposing force. Scheer deserves special mention for his skill in manoeuvre, enabling him to preserve the Kaiser's fleet by evading a superior one which for a while blocked his escape.

Beatty was impetuous and imperious as usual but showed flashes of brilliance in manoeuvre: he engaged the enemy vanguard and then drew the main body towards Jellicoe, shielding the battleships from discovery until they were in line of battle, which was what he was supposed to do. Jellicoe was as much sinned against as sinning because his Admiralty superiors and his subordinates in the battle both starved him of the information which might have enabled him to smash the German battlefleet. Where the British C-in-C erred was in the rigidity of his own over-detailed battle orders to the Grand Fleet, which robbed subordinate commanders of any chance to show initiative or adapt to quickly changing circumstance. Jellicoe was a master of detail but congenitally incapable of delegating, an abiding fault in British commanders, especially in the earlier part of the century, when 'good staffwork' was almost a contradiction in terms. His cunning plan to cut the Germans off and destroy them nearly worked all the same; more importantly, he had been presented with his chance to lose the war in an afternoon and had refrained from doing so. This left the British in command of the North Sea, so much so that the High Seas Fleet never came out again in anything like full strength after summer 1916. The indecisive twelve-hour battle was therefore decisive after all, because it entrenched the status quo ante, which was the most important precondition for the eventual Allied victory on land. The surface blockade of Germany continued, and bit ever harder.

Reinhard Scheer, however, was not the kind of man to give up after a setback. He was able to field nineteen dreadnoughts and two battlecruisers with supporting light cruisers and destroyers on 16 August, ten weeks after Jutland. The U-boats were deployed in force off the English east and Dutch west coasts, and ten Zeppelins were up in clear weather. Room 40 forewarned Jellicoe and Beatty, who were therefore already at sea with twenty-nine dreadnoughts and six battlecruisers respectively, plus the usual swarm of light escorts. The Harwich Force was called out, as well as twenty-five British submarines. When *U52* sank the light cruiser *Nottingham* off the Northumberland coast, however, Jellicoe, always afraid of a debacle at the hands of the U-boats, steamed north for two hours in the mistaken belief that he could return and catch the Germans (who were already much further west than he thought and had put about before he could come back; a signal from a German battleship which had fallen behind after being damaged by a British submarine torpedo misled Room 40 about the position of the main body of the enemy).

Scheer too was misled, by one of his Zeppelins, which mistook the Harwich Force for capital ships. He once again abandoned his original plan to bombard lucky Sunderland and turned south-east to meet them – thus unwittingly saving himself. Had he sailed on, he would have been cut off from home; as it was he turned back well to the east of the Humber minefields, shaking off the harriers from Harwich, which vainly tried to race ahead of him for a bow-on torpedo attack. U-boats sank the light cruiser *Falmouth* of Jellicoe's escort as he sailed back to base without seeing a German ship. Scheer came out again just once more, for a half-hearted sweep towards the Dogger Bank, abandoned in bad weather on 18 October 1916 after a British submarine damaged a light cruiser. From September the Grand Fleet confined itself to the area north of the River Tweed on the Anglo-Scottish border and west of longitude four degrees east unless in dire emergency – or unless Jellicoe, who suggested this caution, and Beatty, who supported it, could count on having no fewer than a hundred destroyers in support.

The need for these fast workhorses in the Channel, let alone the Mediterranean, precluded this possibility, so the fleet stayed in its Scottish lairs on 18 October, for fear of U-boats. Ironically, Scheer for his part was not seen on the open sea again for lack of them. He could no longer count on having enough submarine flotillas for scouting and torpedo attacks on the much more numerous British fleet. The U-boats were increasingly being diverted to assaults on merchant shipping in the north Atlantic and the Mediterranean. An anything but masterly inactivity, interrupted by occasional forays involving small vessels, settled on the North Sea for the rest of the war. The battleship was already checkmated by the torpedo even before that weapon could be launched from the air. The last Nelsonian, surface-only action between the broadsides of opposed lines of battle had been fought: it was another irony that the increasingly shy battleships were only brought out on to the open sea in the later stages of the war to cover submarines and other small warships as they left or entered harbour. In all some sixty-five dreadnoughts languished on the two sides of the North Sea, the Germans increasingly discontented in their barracks, the British bored stiff in Scapa Flow until they moved permanently to Rosyth in April 1918, whence at least the urban fleshpots of Edinburgh and Glasgow were within reach. The main burden of the war at sea now fell on those smallest vessels, the U-boats on the one side and the destroyers, sloops and trawlers mustered against them on the other.

5

Submarines

In his far from apologetic report to the Kaiser on the battle, Vice-Admiral Reinhard Scheer strongly advocated unrestricted submarine warfare on British trade as the best, probably the only, means of winning the war at sea for Germany – while the Germans were still claiming their victory at the Skaggerak. He sent two dozen smaller ships from the High Seas Fleet to Zeebrugge to support the U-boat, destroyer and torpedo boat campaign in the Channel. But Scheer was neither the first nor the only German military leader to think in such terms.

The first British merchantman lost to enemy action in the Great War sank out of sight off Cuxhaven in the North Sea even before Britain went to war. The SS *San Wilfrido*, 6,458 tons, had run on to a German defensive mine on 3 August 1914. She was but the first of 2,479 vessels totalling about 7,700,000 gross registered tons (GRT) that flew a British mercantile ensign until they sank as the result of shelling, scuttling at gunpoint, mining or torpedo attack. By far the greatest role in this extraordinary saga of destruction was played by German submarines, which also usurped surface ships as the principal layers of mines just as they usurped cruisers as the principal exponents of *guerre de course*.

Commander Hermann Bauer's First Flotilla of twenty boats ran on paraffin and emitted sparks, flames, steam and smoke on the surface. Hardly anyone in any navy took such delicate early submersibles seriously (with the notable exception of the prophetic Fisher), apart from their smelly, pale-faced, oil-stained officers and crews, who tended to live in a world of their own ashore as well as at sea. When Bauer took some of his boats for a first sweep across the North Sea on 6 August his target was military – the British warships at Scapa Flow. No submariner at war at this innocent stage of the history of the underwater torpedo boat would have thought of any other kind of target. Two boats broke down and had to limp home and one was lost to unknown cause. *U15*, commanded by *Kapitänleutnant* Pohle (lieutenant-commander, the usual rank of submarine skippers everywhere) strayed out of the line of advance and sighted three British battleships on gunnery practice off Fair Isle, halfway between Orkney and Shetland, on 10 August. He fired a torpedo at HMS *Monarch* but missed. Such was the origin of the 'periscopitis' which spread through the Royal Navy at the beginning of the war as indiscriminately as influenza did at its very end.

As we saw, the light cruiser *Birmingham* caught the boat on the surface with an engine breakdown and cut it in two by ramming the next day – the first of 192 German U-boats to be lost in the war. Revenge was exacted on the old cruiser *Pathfinder* on 5 September by Otto Hersing's *U21*, Germany's first diesel boat. Then Max Horton sank two small German warships and Otto Weddigen destroyed the three old British cruisers in a shocking bloodbath. Both battle fleets temporarily withdrew from the North Sea for fear of submarines.

But it was to the humble British tramp-steamer SS *Glitra*, all of 866 tons, that the dubious honour fell of being the first mercantile victim of a submarine. The little ship hove to when a shot was fired across her bow off southern Norway on 20 October 1914 by *U17* (Feldkirchner). German sailors came aboard, politely but firmly ordered the crew to take to their own lifeboats, made sure they had retired to a safe distance and opened the seacocks – all with impeccable respect for Prize Rules. But six days later Schneider in *U24* felt unable to afford such luxuries when he torpedoed the unarmed cross-Channel steamer *Amiral Ganteaume*, 4,500 tons, with 2,500 Belgian refugees aboard. Amazingly, only forty people died and the stricken ship managed to make harbour. Ominously, Schneider had fired from periscope depth without warning.

Angered and frustrated by the British blockade of Germany, Admiral Hugo von Pohl, Chief of Staff of the High Seas Fleet, sent a memorandum in the first week of November to Chancellor Theobald von Bethmann-Hollweg, advocating a counter-blockade of Britain by U-boat. The suggestion originated with Bauer, whose commanders had made many comments on the huge number of merchant ships in British waters. The Chancellor was the only real statesman in Germany and demurred, seeing at once the likely effect of such a campaign on neutral opinion. Tirpitz, still Navy minister, was in two minds but inclining towards the idea as the High Seas Fleet failed to alter the course of the war. He had seen a staff paper in spring 1914 suggesting that 221 U-boats would be enough to strangle Britain's trade by underwater blockade. That Germany had only a tenth of this number on the outbreak of war suggests such a blockade was not included in her war plans; but opinion in the Imperial Navy, egged on by the British surface blockade, was moving inexorably towards such a strategy.

By the end of 1914, the U-boats had sunk seven old warships, plus ten merchantmen totalling about 20,000 GRT – not much of a sign of things to come. Five U-boats had been lost and eighteen new ones commissioned, leaving Germany with a net total of thirty-three at the turn of the year. There was a naval stalemate on the North Sea and a military one on the already congealed Western Front; only in the east against Russia had the Germans scored massive victories. The British had managed to get two submarines into the Baltic, which caused disruption out of all proportion to their tiny presence: without further ado the German Baltic command put all merchant shipping into protected convoys, a prudent move not imitated by their hidebound British contemporaries for two and a half years. By the end of 1914 four British submarines had been lost, two to enemy action, two to unknown cause; like the enemy losses, all took place east of Britain.

When the Kaiser went to Wilhelmshaven for a review on 4 February 1915, the new C-in-C of his battlefleet, Admiral von Pohl, won his approval for deploying the U-boats against British commerce. The waters round the British Isles, as far north as Shetland and as far east as neutral Dutch territorial waters, were declared a war zone: any ship inside it from 18 February could be sunk without warning, regardless of flag. The threat to neutral shipping in the reference to flagging, which angered the Americans in particular, was prompted by, of all people, Captain William Turner, master of the fast and vast Cunarder *Lusitania*, who had hoisted the Stars and Stripes aboard his British-registered liner in the Irish Sea on 31 January. He excused himself by saying he had many American passengers aboard and that he had been alerted by the Admiralty that there was a U-boat in the area. The alarm was not false: Otto Hersing's *U21* had cheekily shelled Barrow-in-Furness on the north-west English coast on the 29th and sunk three freighters under Prize Rules on the 30th. U-boat skippers were not now under orders to sink neutrals on sight but rather to be absolutely certain a ship was neutral before sparing it, and not to accept a flag as absolute proof of neutrality.

By the time British waters became a free-fire zone for the U-boats they had sunk a dozen merchantmen and nine warships – for the loss of seven boats when their operational numbers averaged fewer than thirty, of which a maximum of one in three was on patrol on a given day (the rest being outward or homeward bound, in training or under repair). But they had already aroused fear out of all proportion to these modest numbers. We have met periscopitis, the new affliction to which even, or perhaps especially, the crews of mighty dreadnoughts were not immune. Panic broke out several times in Scapa Flow as heavy guns were brought to bear on wavelets in such incidents as the 'first battle of Scapa' or the unintended bombardment of Jemimaville in north-east Scotland. U-boat sinkings without warning were categorized by press and public in Britain as examples of German 'frightfulness', a word first applied to the serious excesses of the German Army in Belgium. But, apart from the specific threat to neutrals, a political decision, the conduct of the U-boats was almost always indistinguishable from that of Allied submarines in the Baltic, the Mediterranean and the Dardanelles. There were two other differences: the better quality of the German boats and the much greater quantity of targets available to them.

In the first ten weeks of the new dispensation the German submarines sank four times as many merchantmen as they had done in the first six months of the war. In January 1915 they had sunk 47,900 tons of Allied shipping and in February 65,000; in the first half of May they destroyed 120,000 tons. As numbers of sinkings rose, discrimination declined, so that on 28 March Freiherr (baron) von Forstner in U28 sank the British liner Falaba, killing fifty-seven civilian passengers (including one American) and forty-seven merchant seamen; a few days earlier the noble skipper had continued to fire at a ship he had mortally wounded as passengers and crew were scrambling over the side. In April the master of a US tanker was killed in an attack that failed to sink his ship. American opinion was further inflamed by the torpedo from the small coastal submarine UB4 that sank the British SS Harpalyce in the Channel, although she was flying a white flag and banners along her sides stating her mission of collecting American food for starving Belgians. As the 'frightfulness' mounted at sea, the Admiralty could not conceal its helplessness against the submarine threat, even though HMS Dreadnought made her dramatic contribution on 18 March by sinking U29, Weddigen's new boat.

But the incident that stands out, not only in this first period of unrestricted U-boat operations or even in the maritime record of the Great War but also in the entire history of submarine warfare, took place on 7 May 1915. Walter Schweiger in *U20* was looking for a target for his last three torpedoes, having sunk three ships in the past two days and being on his way home. As he stood in the lunchtime sunshine on top of the conning tower of his boat, sailing eastward along the south coast of Ireland, he sighted a great cloud of smoke, also eastward bound. He could soon make out the unmistakable black hull with white trim and four black-collared, scarlet funnels of a Cunard transatlantic liner, a huge ship of 31,550 tons, the Royal Mail Ship *Lusitania*, built in 1906 and winner of the Blue Riband for fastest transatlantic crossing in 1907.

Six days earlier there had been much excitement in New York, from which she was about to sail, when newspapers carried a reminder of the U-boats' rules of engagement, in the form of a warning from the German diplomatic mission to the US: 'Travellers sailing in the war-zone . . . do so at their own risk.' The threat was neatly positioned under Cunard's normal notice of that day's sailing to Liverpool by the *Lusitania*. The bluff Captain Turner, aged fifty-eight and nicknamed 'Bowler Bill' for his sartorial taste ashore, dismissed the threat as reporters roamed the great ship gathering copy for what the ghouls were already calling her 'last voyage'. Although he tended to describe his passengers (in private) as monkeys, he reassured them by saying they would be under the protection of the Royal Navy and that, if they were attacked, his twenty-six-knot ship was 'unsinkable' because she was much more strongly constructed than the *Titanic* (lost to an iceberg in 1912). Departure on May Day was delayed by two hours of lingering farewells to the 1,257 passengers, of whom 197 were Americans, including the transport magnate Alfred G. Vanderbilt. The crew totalled 721.

Also aboard were 173 tons of ammunition plus detonators for mines and torpedoes. The big Cunarders were fitted with decks strengthened for eight 6-inch guns and the British government had the right, in exchange for its construction subsidy, to requisition them for war service. But the ship had no guns or anything else aboard that would have enabled her to make use of the munitions in her hold; she was therefore unarmed, though German propagandists made much of her cargo manifest, a public document. But it seems cavalier on the part of the master and owners to have embarked such a dangerous mixture of war matériel and civilian passengers. Captain Turner also disdained naval advice to zigzag, maintain high speed and keep clear of coastal waters, even after two warnings of U-boat activity off south-west Ireland from the Admiralty on the evening of the 6th. Instead he slowed from twenty-one to eighteen knots to time his arrival off Liverpool at high tide, so as to be able to take his deep hull over the Mersey Bar without delay. But he doubled the lookouts, closed all but a few watertight doors, darkened ship and had the lifeboats swung out ready for a quick launch.

At lunchtime Turner fatefully slowed down and swung north towards the coast to take a navigational fix off the Old Head of Kinsale. This gave Schweiger the time, at full surface speed, to close up to the ship sufficiently for a shot at her starboard side at his torpedoes' optimum range of 700 metres, as soon as the *Lusitania* turned across his bow to resume her easterly course. The horrified lookouts watched the torpedo track take a full minute to reach the ship, leaving no time for evasive action. It struck home amidships, ten feet below the waterline, at 2.15 p.m. Eviscerated by a 'sympathetic explosion' of coal dust in her almost empty bunkers, or else the detonation of her hot boilers on sudden submersion in the cold water of the Atlantic, the ship rolled over and sank by the bow in eighteen minutes. The starboard lifeboats swung out of reach as she listed; the port-side boats swung inboard and slithered, full of screaming passengers, over others who had fallen on the tilted deck. Only 780 people (472 passengers, 308 crew) survived; 1,198 were drowned (785 passengers, including 94 children and 128 Americans; 413 crew). In the circumstances the survival rate of nearly 40 per cent, compared with 31 per cent on the *Titanic*, which took 160 minutes to sink, looks little short of miraculous.

A savage propaganda battle ensued. The Germans accused Churchill of failing to send the Navy to the liner's aid in order to draw the United States into the war. President Woodrow Wilson was reported to have wept on hearing the news of this worst-ever assault on civilians – and sent a telegram of protest to the Kaiser. Americans were called cowards in London's streets and places of entertainment for staying neutral. Germanophobia reached new heights. Schweiger claimed not to have recognized his target and his government pointed to the general warning of the war zone and the specific one before the ship sailed, as well as the munitions aboard. Under Prize Rules the *Lusitania* as an unarmed ship could only have been sunk legally once a boarding party had established the presence of contraband and given all aboard the chance to evacuate in safety. The U-boats eased off their marauding after the disaster, leading Churchill rashly to declare that they had failed and given up.

But as early as August, one year into the war, the monthly shipping loss rose to 185,000 (165,000 to U-boats) – a sinister statistic because for the first time sinkings surpassed Britain's monthly maximum shipbuilding rate. On the 19th of the month, the '*Lusitania* factor' as it became known reasserted itself when *U24* (Rudolf Schneider) torpedoed the White Star liner *Arabic*, 15,800 GRT. Although she sank in just ten minutes not far from where the *Lusitania* had gone down, only forty-four passengers and crew were drowned, a remarkable feat of rescue by the crew. Three of the dead being Americans, their President sent another telegram, more angry than the last.

The Admiralty and the Cabinet were deeply anxious about the rate of losses to U-boats and had no inkling either of what to do or of the deep divisions about the campaign in Germany. Chancellor Bethmann-Hollweg and the diplomats warned of American intervention with all that this implied in resources, industrial capacity and manpower. Admiral Henning von Holtzendorff, Chief of Naval Staff, promised that Britain would collapse in six months if unrestricted sinkings continued – not a boast but an accurate appraisal of how long it would take, other circumstances being equal, to reduce British shipping to a level at which it could no longer keep the country sufficiently supplied with food and raw materials to carry on fighting. The Chancellor prevailed and the vacillating Kaiser ordained that the U-boats should not sink passenger ships, unless under Prize Rules, after the end of August. As this was now far too dangerous in British waters, U-boat skippers would adopt a 'when in doubt, don't' policy rather than risk mistaking a liner for a cargo ship. But only one error was needed to revive the issue. Sinkings duly fell sharply in September, and on the 20th the U-boats withdrew from British waters except for strictly military purposes in the southern North Sea and Channel.

Yet a ship was a ship no matter where you sank it, and the tonnage war on the British Merchant Navy continued almost unabated – in the Mediterranean, where there was any amount of Allied shipping and virtually no Americans. By the end of 1915,

855,000 tons had been sunk, 748,000 of them British, in the war thus far. Mines, mostly laid by the new, small, purpose-built 'UC'-class boats, sank ninety-four ships in 1915.

These vessels were operating as part of the Flanders Flotilla from the Belgian ports, alongside the even smaller coastal 'UB' boats designed for shallow waters. One of these, *UB29* (Lieutenant Pustkuchen), resuscitated the *Lusitania* factor on 24 March 1916, when he torpedoed the French ferry *Sussex*, carrying 380 passengers to Folkestone from Dieppe in perfect weather. Twenty-five Americans were among the eighty killed; the vessel was towed into Boulogne and beached while a British destroyer and a French trawler picked up some 300 survivors. Pustkuchen claimed to have seen uniformed men on deck and taken it for a troopship. This time the German Ambassador to Washington, Count Johann von Bernstorff, was summoned to the State Department for a dressing-down. Washington then sent a Note on 20 April threatening to break off relations. The reply from Berlin, accusing the Americans of one-sidedness in not protesting to the British about their surface blockade, indirectly revealed how deeply it was biting.

But on 24 April the Chancellor prevailed once again over the admirals and all U-boats were ordered to observe Prize Rules at all times. A compliant Note was sent to Washington on 4 May – by which date, exactly twenty-one months at war, Britain alone had lost more than a million tons of shipping to all causes, including 131 vessels (442,000 tons) to direct U-boat attacks (the rest had been sunk by mines or surface ships). Lost with them was a whole mountain range of supplies. For this important result Germany had forfeited thirty-two U-boats and under 1,000 submariners, a high return on a small investment. Despite the welcome lull, much worse was to follow for Britain.

The Admiralty had no anti-submarine strategy or tactics, weapons or technology for anti-submarine warfare (ASW). The French were hard at work from 1914 on active underwater detection, one of only two realistic ways forward. Fishermen and others on coastal craft were offered substantial rewards for reporting U-boats or mines but as they lacked wireless their tips tended to be useless. A fishing boat spotted *U9* the day before it sank the 'Cressys' but did not report until it landed its catch – three days too late. On his resignation in May 1915 Fisher chaired the Board of Invention and Research (BIR, soon to be subsumed into the still extant Council on Scientific and Industrial Research – CSIR – started by the War Office in 1915). One of the Bureau's six sub-committees was concerned with submarines and wireless. The public submitted 38,000 suggestions on how to deal with submarines. Dowsers, sea lions and even birds were put forward as detectors. The Navy was recommended, on sighting a periscope, to put a paper bag over it and hit it with a hammer to blind the enemy, who would doubtless remain motionless.

British research on passive detection began at the Admiralty's Hawkscraig experimental station in Fife, under Commander C. P. Ryan, RN, recalled from the reserve and the Marconi company. He concentrated on the hydrophone listening device from late in 1914, aided by academics from Manchester University sent by Sir Ernest Rutherford, one of the greatest scientists of the century, a member of the sub-committee. In March 1916 Professor W. H. Bragg, another Nobel prize-winner for physics, was appointed director of the civilian staff at Hawkscraig, but irreconcilable differences between the theoreticians and Ryan's practical but instinctively secretive naval technicians lay behind the dissolution of the BIR before the end of the war. When Jellicoe became First Sea Lord in December 1916, he at last set up an Admiralty Anti-Submarine Division (ASD) under Rear-Admiral Alexander Duff. The ASD assumed control of Hawkscraig and a separate theoretical research station was set up at Harwich. Ryan meanwhile developed a shore-based system of listening for submarines along the coasts through hydrophones on the seabed at such key places as Dover and Scapa. These were supported by submerged mines, to be detonated by electric current from shore when a U-boat passed. Although this system scored a few successes, it was unreliable in rough weather or other noisy conditions – and by virtue of the fact that early hydrophones could not provide a bearing for the sound source, which could be misread by as much as 180 degrees: underwater acoustics was a new science, as yet little understood. But hydrophones soon improved and began to be fitted both to picket boats to listen for U-boats and to submarines to listen for enemy ships.

The Germans, driven by the needs of their U-boats, acquired a temporary technical lead in this new field, refining the range, discriminatory and directional capabilities of passive underwater detection. The British developed the 'depth charge', or underwater bomb, detonated by water pressure, in 1915, but this crucial weapon was not widely available until well into the following year, claiming its first victim in July 1916. More and more merchantmen were fitted with guns in the hope of engaging a U-boat on the surface, but this only encouraged the Germans to stay submerged and/or to attack without warning.

The 'Q' ship (probably named after Queenstown, now Cobh, in Ireland, where many were based) was the most famous or notorious anti-submarine device of the war: a disguised trawler or other small vessel acted as bait to lure a U-boat into an attack, which it would counter by unmasking its relatively heavy gun, running up the White Ensign and opening fire. This ruse soon collided with the law of diminishing returns as the German skippers became aware of it and once again inclined towards the safety-first philosophy of shooting first, especially if in doubt. The pioneer was the *Prince Charles* (Lieutenant W. P. Mark-Wardlaw, RN), which caught and sank *U36* on 24 July 1915. The most controversial Q-ship incident involved the *Baralong* (Lieutenant Godfrey Herbert, RN), a 4,200-ton tramp concealing three twelve-pounders on its deck. On 19 August 1915 Herbert was trailing his coat off the south of Ireland, hoping to lure the boat that had sunk the liner *Arabic*. Herbert did not bother to haul down the Stars and Stripes before attacking Wegener's *U27*, caught in the act of shelling the British SS *Nicosian* and sent to the bottom within a minute. Six unarmed Germans, including Wegener, swept off the conning tower as their boat disappeared under them, swam over to the abandoned *Nicosian*, scrambling up her side. Unconcerned with the niceties of war, a party from the *Baralong* then boarded the freighter and massacred them. The trend on both sides to give no quarter in this new form of warfare had already been shown by the Germans earlier in the summer. Sighting a U-boat off the Belgian coast, the British Captain Charles Fryatt, master of the unarmed SS *Brussels*, had bravely rammed it, though it did not sink. Three months later, on 23 June, a German torpedo boat stopped his ship in the Channel and took him prisoner. On 27 July he was shot as a franc-tireur or civilian guilty of an act of war after a brief court martial at Bruges. The star of the short-lived Q-ship campaign was Captain Gordon Campbell, RN, who won the DSO and the VC for his exploits in 1916 and 1917.

Submarines first took a hand in events in the Mediterranean in December 1914, when three tiny British 'B'-class boats began to probe the Dardanelles and then the Sea of Marmora within, Lieutenant Holbrook winning his VC in *B11* on the 13th by sinking an old Turkish battleship. As we saw, the Germans were not far behind. But in addition to the deployment of submarines against military targets as part of the struggle for the straits, a more general U-boat campaign against commerce developed in the broader Mediterranean. The enclosed ocean, 2,200 miles long, was mostly dominated by the British and the French. Between them they controlled the whole of the North African coast, Gibraltar at the western entrance and Cyprus and the Suez Canal in the east, Malta in the middle, the south of France and Corsica. Spain and Italy were neutral and Greece was torn between a pro-German king and a pro-Entente prime minister, which left the Anglo-French besiegers of the Dardanelles free to use the Greek islands in the Aegean as bases and to open a new front at Salonika. But there were two important areas under the control of the Central Powers and their allies: Turkey and the Levant or eastern Mediterranean coast, and the Adriatic outside Italian waters, dominated by the Austrian Fleet along the Balkan west coast as far south as Albania.

Under Anglo-French naval arrangements France was in command of the Mediterranean as a whole, even if the British were in charge of operations against Turkey. The French took the lead in the Adriatic, sending their fleet to sweep the enclosed sea; in December 1914 their fleet flagship, *Jean Bart*, a dreadnought, was damaged by an Austrian U-boat, the first stroke by the small but extremely deadly Austrian submarine service which soon proved to be the most effective, boat for boat, in the war. The Austrians were also the first to use aircraft systematically for ASW, sending up effective patrols which helped to find and sink five French submarines in the Adriatic in the opening months of the war.

In September 1915, four months after Italy had joined the Entente powers as a result of U-boat attacks on her ships, sometimes carried out by Germans illegally flying the Austrian flag, the Otranto Barrage was set up across the Adriatic at its narrowest. It ran forty-four miles from Italian Otranto to the Greek island of Fano (now Othonoi) and was intended to bottle up the Austrians while preventing German U-boats from joining them or using their ports. It began as a chain of sixty British drifters with nets hung between them, but seemed to consist mainly of gaps. More of a wide-mesh sieve than the intended lid, it seldom proved more than a minor inconvenience for the German and Austrian submariners, even when more nets, patrolled by more and more light craft from the British, French and Italian navies, were added, with heavier ships in the background to guard against the Austrian surface fleet, which seldom ventured out. In the last phase of hostilities the Americans sent thirty-six submarine-chasers, claiming a great success for them which postwar research disproved: they probably sank one U-boat. As in the Aegean, local command devolved on the British, but the real weakness of the barrage was the Allied failure to unify command in the Mediterranean for almost the entire war.

The leading Austrian ace, Lieutenant-Commander Georg von Trapp, sank a French heavy cruiser just before the barrage was installed. Given a larger, converted French boat shortly afterwards, Trapp passed to and fro under the barrier as if it had not been there. The Austrian U-boats were joined by German-built coastal submarines brought in sections by rail and assembled at Pola. The Austrians alone mounted a total of just seventy-nine torpedo attacks. On every one of these occasions they scored at least one hit while only one torpedo in ten was a wasted shot; they also did much effective minelaying off the Italian coast as well as using their guns against merchant ships, a uniquely efficient record.

The barrage caught one Austrian U-boat for certain and probably two, as well as one German, but several Italian and French warships were sunk by enemy submarines in its vicinity. So were sixteen of the British drifters, in a series of hit-and-run raids by Austrian light cruisers; three British cruisers were damaged by U-boats. The Admiralty stationed a flotilla of six small 'B'-class submarines under Commander Wilfrid Tomkinson, RN, at Venice; he reported to the Flag Officer, British Adriatic Force, Rear-Admiral Cecil Thursby (replaced by Rear-Admiral Mark Kerr in June 1916). The adventurous Austrians achieved the distinction of the first submarine 'kill' by aircraft when they raided Venice in August 1916 and sank *B9* in harbour; the crew escaped. Otherwise the 'Bs' achieved nothing and were replaced by three modern 'H' boats, equally unsuccessful except for *H4* (Oliver North), which sank the German *UB5* with two torpedoes near the barrage on 23 May 1918; *H1*, however, managed to sink *H5*, her sister-boat bought by the Italians. Even the trusty 'E'-class boats which performed more than adequately in the Dardanelles achieved nothing in the Adriatic while on their way to and from British bases further west.

Meanwhile the British naval forces in the eastern Mediterranean retained most of their strength, even after the final withdrawal from Gallipoli in January 1916. Bulgaria had entered the war in September 1915, helping the Germans and Austrians to overrun Serbia. Rear-Admiral Troubridge, who had failed to tackle the *Goeben*, was now head of the British Military Mission to Belgrade and proceeded to save the bulk of the Serbian Army by organizing its evacuation to Salonika, where it was joined by Anglo-French forces just after the Dardanelles withdrawal. British submarines and naval aircraft continued to operate against the Turks and Germans in the Dardanelles area, although all attempts to bomb the *Goeben* failed, except for very minor damage, even when she was stuck aground in January 1918. The seaplane carrier HMS *Ark Royal* flew torpedo-bearing aircraft for the first time at this juncture, a deadly combination which was not yet technically advanced enough to prove itself before the Armistice.

The British missed their second and last chance to catch the *Goeben* on Sunday 20 January 1918. The destroyer HMS *Lizard*, on patrol off the Dardanelles entrance, sounded the alarm 'GOBLO, GOBLO' (*Goeben* and *Breslau* out) at dawn. Admiral Souchon had gone back to Germany in September 1917 to command a High Seas Fleet battle squadron and was replaced by Vice-Admiral Hubert von Rebeur-Paschwitz, who decided after four months on a foray against the blockaders. The collapse of Russia meant he could turn his back on the Bosporus at the other end of the straits. Paschwitz planned a hit-and-run raid on the British ships anchored off the Aegean islands of Imbros, Lemnos and Tenedos, including two pre-dreadnoughts, two monitors, a French heavy cruiser, a British light one and a flotilla of destroyers. *UC23* would also steal out to sow mines off the main British base of Mudros on Lemnos and await developments. *Goeben*, now sporting the Turkish name *Yavuz*, and *Breslau*, renamed *Medilli*, ran into trouble almost at once. The battlecruiser hit a mine, shook herself and carried on. Both ships shelled and sank a British monitor, the *Raglan*; the light cruiser sank a smaller one, the *M28*. The *Lizard* (Lieutenant N. A. G. Ohlenschlager, RN) joined by her sister ship *Tigress* (Lieutenant-Commander J. B. Newill, RN), could not get within torpedo range. No other ship of the thirty-five in the Aegean Squadron joined the action, but Flight-Commander Edward Feeny, RN, led the Scout biplanes of C Squadron, RNAS, from Imbros into an ineffectual attack; his bombs caused only minor damage, although the Germans were forced to zigzag as they jammed his wireless. While 132 men out of a total of 310 were being rescued from the two wrecked monitors, the two destroyers lost touch as the Germans made for Mudros with intent to bombard. Of the rest of Rear-Admiral Arthur Hayes-Sadler's squadron there was no sign; he had arrived to take over only eight days earlier, yet another in the melancholy procession of feeble British flag-officers to appear in the Mediterranean. He had gone off to Salonika on the 16th in one of the two old battleships, the inappropriately named *Lord Nelson*, which meant the other would have been outgunned by the faster *Goeben*. The whole point of having two pre-dreadnoughts on hand was to avoid this possibility.

At 0731 the *Breslau* ran into a dense British minefield and set off no fewer than five under her hull. Captain Georg von Hippel abandoned his sinking ship with more than 500 men and awaited capture by the Royal Navy: only 140 survived the hours of waiting in chill water amid the bobbing mines. The pair of destroyers meanwhile chased four Turkish torpedo boats back into the Dardanelles. The *Goeben*, rocked by two more mines, returned as well, harried by British aircraft. Two further mines exploded under her, one on each side, near the entrance, and she just managed to zigzag northward up the strait at fourteen knots – only to run aground opposite Constantinople. Vice-Admiral Sir Arthur Gough-Calthorpe, then British C-in-C in the Mediterranean, was chagrined to learn that the Royal Navy had missed its chance to sink the *Goeben* after waiting for nearly three and a half years. The rest of the Aegean Squadron, in the absence of its commander (soon relieved), raised steam and crept through its own minefields, emerging from Mudros only at 9.30 a.m, by which time the Germans had vanished. Despite air-raids, long-range bombardment and submarine sorties, the *Goeben/Yavuz* was repaired and survived the war, serving for many years as the flagship of the Turkish Navy. She was broken up only in 1975. The new First Sea Lord, Vice-Admiral Sir Rosslyn Wemyss, noted:

The *Goeben* getting away is perfectly damnable and has considerably upset me, since we at the Admiralty were under the happy delusion that there were sufficient brains and sufficient means out there to prevent it: of the latter there were; of the former apparently not.

The complex Mediterranean theatre was the scene of three separate campaigns in 1914–1918, in the Aegean, in the Adriatic and against the U-boats. It cannot be said that the Royal Navy distinguished itself, individual heroism always excepted, in any of them. We may now consider the most important strategic conflict in the inland sea, the anti-submarine struggle which was really an adjunct of the German counter-blockade of Britain by U-boat in the north Atlantic.

The first German submarines reached the Mediterranean by land. Four coastal 'UBs' and three minelaying 'UCs' arrived in sections at Pola by rail from north Germany. Once assembled, they made their own way via the Dardanelles into the Black Sea to support Souchon in his 'private war' against the Russians there, a campaign in which the Royal Navy took no part. Later the Austrian submarine arm was reinforced by the same route. The first ocean-going U-boat to enter by the 'front door', the Straits of Gibraltar, was Hersing's *U21*, on its way to the Dardanelles. Otherwise there was no German submarine activity on the broad Mediterranean until August 1915, when the General Staff recognized its usefulness as an 'American-free' zone. On the 23rd *U35* entered the then Austrian harbour of Cattaro as forerunner of a German flotilla of initially five new boats. Its long-term skipper, Lothar von Arnauld de la Perière, became the highest-scoring submarine commander of all time (454,000 tons sunk, including 187 merchantmen, almost all by gunfire under Prize Rules, plus five troopships and two warships).

The fifth to arrive, early in November, was *U38*, commanded by Max Valentiner, Germany's third most successful ace but a different kind of man altogether, killing far more civilians than any other submariner in a series of bloodthirsty attacks on liners and troopships from the day of his arrival, even before he reported to Cattaro. On the 7th he surfaced on sighting the Italian liner *Ancona* and ran up the Austrian ensign (Italy had been fighting Austria-Hungary since May but was not yet at war with Germany, although the U-boats made sure she soon would be). He appeared to be observing Prize Rules as he ordered all aboard to disembark, but then he opened fire amid chaotic scenes in the water round the ship, later being accused of deliberately shooting at passengers. The Mediterranean may have been conveniently free of US ships, but individual American civilians were still travelling there and twenty of them died with the *Ancona*.

Valentiner, one of only eighteen war criminals (including seven U-boat men) on Britain's 'wanted' list at the Armistice, managed to kill a similar number of Americans when he chased a small Italian steamer on the surface while flying his Austrian flag, torpedoing her two days later. Valentiner, a natural Waffen-SS man ahead of his time, resuscitated single-handed the very *Lusitania* factor which the diversion of U-boats to the Mediterranean had been intended to evade. A four-cornered diplomatic row followed, involving Italy, Austria, Germany and the United States. Admiral Haus, the Austrian C-in-C, had entered *U38* on the books of his fleet, backdated to 21 October, and took the blame, paying compensation to the Americans in December – the month in which an unrepentant Valentiner killed 314 more civilians on the British liner *Persia* south of Crete without warning (although this victim had a single gun bigger than his).

In the last quarter of 1915, the Allies lost eighty ships (293,000 tons) to the handful of U-boats in the Mediterranean – 80 per cent of the total loss worldwide in that time. An Allied naval conference in Paris at the end of the year divided the ocean into eighteen ASW patrol zones distributed among their three main navies. This was an attempt to prevent the Germans from availing themselves of the secret shore bases they were wrongly assumed to possess: in fact the German boats were so much more reliable than their enemies' submarines that they could stay on patrol for weeks without needing to enter harbour. At another conference in Malta in March the zones were reduced to eleven, but because this was the wrong ASW strategy the adjustment made no more than a bureaucratic difference. The ununited Allied admirals insisted on patrolling shipping lanes instead of protecting the shipping itself. All the U-boats needed to do was to hide from the warships and attack the unescorted merchantmen: even troopships were left to their own devices, something that never happened in the Channel, or to dreadnoughts anywhere.

The renewed torrent of allegations of 'frightfulness' led the vacillating Kaiser and his high command to tinker repeatedly with the U-boats' rules of engagement throughout 1916. Once again the rate of sinkings fell back as skippers reverted to the rule of thumb, 'when in doubt, don't', rather than its opposite. The gallant and correct Arnauld, who only ever fired four torpedoes from *U35*, carried on as before, an increasingly rare demonstration that chivalry was still possible, even in submarine warfare on commerce.

He and his ilk forced the Admiralty to begin diverting as much shipping as possible – Far Eastern and Australasian traffic – round the Cape of Good Hope to avoid the Mediterranean, although traffic for India continued to sail via the Suez Canal, built for that purpose. This huge diversion increased the total need for shipping if the same rate of delivery of troops and supplies was to be maintained – just as the U-boats were increasing their sinking rate. The Allies had lost 1m tons in the Mediterranean alone by August 1916, the second anniversary of the war: yet it was only from this moment that the Germans were able to keep more than one boat on patrol at all times, thanks to the addition of ocean-going boats to the Cattaro flotilla. By autumn it included ten such, plus three coastal and nine minelaying boats. Italy declared war on Germany on 27 August, after finding incontrovertible evidence of duplicity on a sunken 'UC' minelayer in the form of Austrian flags and other deception material.

On 14 October 1916 Rear-Admiral George Ballard, who had just taken over from Admiral Limpus in command at Malta, made what amounted to a revolutionary suggestion. In a dispatch to the Admiralty he urged it to propose to the French, still in nominal supreme command in the Mediterranean, the establishment of a convoy system. The soon-to-be First Sea Lord, Vice-Admiral Rosslyn Wemyss, then C-in-C, East Indies and Egypt, made a similar suggestion in December. There was no reaction from London or Paris. The shipping stock continued to bleed away at a faster rate than transfusions of new tonnage could restore it.

In 1917 the losses to U-boats became a haemorrhage, especially after the Kaiser and his admirals finally decided that they might as well be hanged for the sheep of completely unrestricted U-boat warfare as the lamb of constantly changing, erratically observed restraints. After Jutland Admiral Scheer pressed for 350 U-boats; fortunately for Britain the German Army always came first and only forty-six extra boats could be budgeted for in the 1916–17 construction programme, over and above the current building rate of a dozen a month. But the newer boats showed an ominously increased capability; from boat number *U51* they had the capacity to cross the north Atlantic, and *U53* proceeded to sink five Allied merchant ships in a few days just outside American territorial waters – 'within sight of the Nantucket Lighthouse' as David Lloyd George indignantly noted in his memoirs. The unarmed submarine freighter *Deutschland* with her mercantile captain and crew easily evaded Vice-Admiral Sir George Patey's North American and West Indies Squadron without having to submerge (despite a Room 40 alert) to sail in triumph into Chesapeake Bay and unload 700 tons of cargo at Baltimore, Maryland, after passing Washington, DC. The boat 'joined the Navy' in February 1917 along with six similar to form a flotilla of long-range 'U-cruisers', armed with a pair of 5.9-inch guns as well as torpedo tubes.

The mounting shipping crisis helped Lloyd George, Secretary of State for War, to launch a successful bid for supreme power against the tired and depressed Liberal Prime Minister, H. H. Asquith. Lloyd George wanted to chair the three-man War Council, founded in 1915 and consisting of Asquith, himself and Balfour as First Lord. By the end of 1915 shipping losses passed 500 vessels or 1m tons; a year later they stood at more than 1,150 (2.6m tons). Germany had fifty-eight operational U-boats at the beginning but 140 at the end of 1916, after losing two dozen (only seven to Allied action). From October they were back in strength in British waters, though avoiding passenger ships and only firing without warning on armed vessels; they were also operating in mid-north Atlantic as well as in the 'wild south' of the Mediterranean. Britain was finding it harder and harder to persuade neutral shipowners to carry its cargoes. One lost ship in four was now a neutral, while the British loss rate was four times the replacement rate. The life expectancy of a freighter at the end of 1916 fell below ten ocean voyages.

The two North Sea rivals were in complete agreement on one thing. In Britain in November the President of the Board of Trade, Walter Runciman, warned the War Council that if sinkings carried on as in late 1916 there would be a complete breakdown in British shipping by the middle of 1917, if not sooner. In Germany in December, Admiral Holtzendorff forecast during the revived debate on unrestricted U-boat warfare that if Germany sank 600,000 tons per month it would deter 1.2m tons of neutral shipping from carrying British cargoes and force Britain, its imports shrunk by 40 per cent, to stop fighting in five months.

The facts on which these remarkably similar calculations were based were ineluctable. In the last full year of peace Britain imported 55m tons, roughly half in food and half in raw materials, and exported 100m tons in coal and manufactures. The ocean-going commercial fleet of ships over 1,600 tons amounted to 8,600 bottoms, 14m tons, or 43 per cent of world stock. In the war France and Russia, and then Italy, came to rely on British ships to deliver vital necessities from North America. Yet while the Admiralty had almost over-prepared for enemy cruisers, a threat that faded by spring 1915, it had, like everyone else including the Central Powers, woefully underestimated the potential of the submarine.

The Admiralty was under the impression, on the basis of 1914 shipping-movement figures from Customs and Excise, that there were about 5,000 arrivals and departures of vessels from Britain's ports and harbours every week. This, however, included not only ocean liners but also fishing cobles; not only oil tankers but also tramp steamers and even barges. If a 'dirty British coaster with her coal-stained smokestack' managed to call at ten ports in a week, twenty movements – ten in, ten out – were recorded. Commander R. G. H. Henderson, RN, in the new Trade Division of the Admiralty, was rare among naval staff officers in being numerate, and was moved to look at the figures more closely. When he had eliminated all movements except by ocean-going vessels of more than 1,600 tons, Henderson arrived at an average of around twenty movements in each direction, inward and outward, per day – *under 300 per week*.

In the first two-thirds of 1916 Britain lost some 600,000 tons; in the last, 632,000. Monthly building was 52,000, hardly one-third of the peacetime rate. At the end of the year Britain had lost 738 ocean-going ships in the war so far and Mr Runciman calculated that the Merchant Navy's tonnage had fallen below 50 per cent of what was needed to supply the country's 'irreducible needs'. The neutrals barely covered half the shortfall. There were not enough ships available to collect crops from India and Australia; 100 per month were needed but fewer than thirty could be found in Britain. There was just about enough sugar left for one week's consumption. Of the 10m tons-plus needed for all non-military purposes just over 7m had been available in Britain at the start of 1916. At the end of the year, of 3,731 ocean-going ships (British, Dominion and neutral; 16.6m tons), 2,231 were on war work, leaving 1,500, of 7,082,000 tons, for all other purposes.

At the same time the majority view in the Admiralty was that convoy – grouping merchant ships under the protection of a naval escort – was unworkable in the age of steam and wireless, the torpedo and the long-range gun. The column of smoke under which a ship sailed meant she could be seen an hour or two before she could sight a surfaced submarine. Convoy had been compulsory in the latter stages of the Napoleonic Wars, when swarms of more than 1,000 ships, slow and totally dependent on fickle wind power, had often sailed unharmed. The very naval officers who harked back so fondly to the Nelsonian tradition overlooked this, just as they ignored the fact that Nelson and his colleagues had fought many important actions arising out of escorting merchant ships. They also believed that merchant skippers would never be able to keep station and convoys would be held to the speed of their slowest member (solved by sailing separate convoys for slower vessels). More pervasive was the psychological factor, which led most naval officers to view convoy as defensive, passive and ultimately unmanly, an attitude which would surely have made Nelson laugh. Shipowners and masters commonly viewed convoy as a waste of fuel, time and therefore money (though surely the ship that arrived late but safe cost a lot less than the late ship seen from her lifeboats going down with a hole in her hull).

But if the Navy were to place its patrol ships with the vessels whose protection was one of its primary tasks, then no U-boat would be able to attack a target without having to contend with a warship. By the same token, a warship would be most likely to get a chance to attack a U-boat if she was accompanying a convoy. The rest of the open sea, devoid of unprotected shipping, could safely be left unguarded as of no interest to either side. In this context the best form of attack was defence. The proof of the value of convoy was staring the Admiralty in the face: not a single troopship had been lost in the thousands of sailings across the Channel between Britain and France. Millions of men passed back and forth without harm, despite the menacingly competent presence in the Flanders ports of Commodore Michelsen's flotillas of coastal and minelaying U-boats, of German destroyers and torpedo boats, all forced to concentrate their attentions on naval targets in the absence of unguarded shipping.

We saw how Jellicoe refused after Jutland to take the Grand Fleet to sea south of Scotland unless escorted by a hundred destroyers. Although several major warships fell victim to mines, usually laid by U-boats, very few were even attacked by U-boats and no dreadnought was sunk by one. At the meeting of the War Council on 2 November 1916 Lloyd George argued with his customary passion for the introduction of convoy, the first time the idea had reached the highest level of government in the war, although a few admirals, including Beatty and Wemyss but not Jellicoe or even Duff, the Director of ASW, were coming round to the idea. Fortunately press and public opinion was more than ever impatient of the 'incompetence in high places' for which heads first rolled in the wake of the Dardanelles failures, and on 7 December 1916 David Lloyd George displaced Asquith as Prime Minister, at the head of a coalition administration of Liberals, Conservatives and Unionists.

The French in particular were concerned as 1916 wore on about the high number of colliers being sunk in the Channel by enemy action, particularly as France had lost the coalfields of Lorraine to the Germans in 1870 and was dependent on British supplies. The complaint reached Lloyd George; the Admiralty detailed Commander Henderson to investigate. On 7 February 1917 he instituted 'controlled sailings' to the Normandy ports – groups of colliers sailing with armed trawlers, convoys by another name. After that, the collier loss rate did the sinking and only one vessel was lost in every 450 sailings. Henderson was transferred to the new Ministry of Shipping, where he made the statistical discovery described above. At the beginning of April 1917, Vice-Admiral Beatty, now C-in-C, Grand Fleet, took the view that he needed nobody's permission to institute what he carefully styled 'protected sailings' on the Norwegian route, vital for mineral supplies and dangerously close to Germany's North Sea bases. One ship in four was being sunk, giving vessels a life expectancy of just two round trips. From 21 April this plunged to one ship lost per 400 sailings, or 1 per cent of the disastrous rate that prompted Beatty to act.

As War Secretary, Lloyd George had notably failed to change the attritional thinking of the generals, who continued to immolate the British Army in the mud of the Western Front. As Prime Minister he was determined to shake up the Admiralty. Regrettably for him, Jellicoe took up his appointment as First Sea Lord in the week before he moved into 10 Downing Street, so there was nothing to be done there for the moment. Jellicoe had failed to lose the war in an afternoon in 1916 but was now exhausted and set fair to lose it in a few more weeks of the creeping shipping disaster. The new premier, master of patronage, depended on a very uneasy coalition. This meant, among many other things, that he felt obliged to find a Cabinet post for Sir Edward Carson, the leader of the Unionist faction which accounted for about half of the Conservative and Unionist Party, itself a coalition. Carson was a

Protestant Ulsterman and leader of the movement that totally opposed Home Rule for Ireland, whose implementation was imminent when the war supervened. His resistance was only hardened by events in spring 1916, when the British Army put down the Easter Rising centred on Dublin. Carson, who had promised that 'Ulster will fight and Ulster will be right', led the armed Ulster Volunteers, determined to keep the hapless province in the Union with Britain.

In other words Carson was a traitor and ready to sanction what the modern world calls terrorism. Lloyd George made him First Lord of the Admiralty. A brilliant advocate, KC and MP for Dublin University, Carson, briefly Attorney-General in 1915, had no experience of running a ministry, let alone the only one in London that was also an operational headquarters. The relief of the dominant hidebound faction at the Admiralty can be imagined when on his first day he told the assembled Board: 'My only great qualification for being put at the head of the Navy is that I am very much at sea.' He would leave the business of running the Navy to the admirals, he said. Needing a 'hands-on' figure to galvanize a depressed, not to say defeatist, department, Lloyd George had appointed an ignorant amateur who abdicated before he took office, and for that the 'Welsh Wizard' alone must carry the historical blame.

The ultimate crisis for Britain in the war at sea was fast approaching. From November 1916 to January 1917 the U-boats sank 961,000 tons, sustaining the average monthly rate achieved in October. On 17 January 1917 Room 40 intercepted and deciphered a telegram from Arthur Zimmermann, head of the German Foreign Office, to the head of the German Legation in Mexico City, which read in part as follows:

> We intend to begin unrestricted U-boat warfare on 1 February. The attempt will however be made to keep the US neutral. In the event that this should not succeed, we offer Mexico alliance [to reconquer Texas, New Mexico and Arizona] . . . Please inform the President [of Mexico] that ruthless deployment of our U-boats now offers the prospect of forcing England to [make] peace.

Post-revolutionary Mexico wisely decided to have nothing to do with this madcap scheme, but British Naval Intelligence assiduously leaked the telegram to the United States administration. Washington was no less angry on 31 January when the German government made it official, sending a Note warning of its plan to resort to totally unrestricted submarine warfare, as usual citing the British surface blockade. Chancellor Bethmann-Hollweg was still opposed to this last throw at sea but could no longer restrain the admirals or the General Staff, which had the final say in naval matters. They were banking on bringing Britain to her knees before a US intervention, now recognized as inevitable, could influence the outcome on the Western Front.

In the first week of unrestricted U-boat attacks from 1 February, the Germans sank thirty-five ships, an average of five a day, towards a worldwide total of 520,000 tons for the month. In February Britain alone lost 311,000 tons, twice as much as in January; in March this rose to 352,000. More than a million tons of shipping from all sources went down in the eight and a half weeks to the end of March. The enemy started the year with 105 operational boats. In April 1917, 881,000 tons of shipping were sent to the bottom worldwide, a monthly record which survived even the Second World War; Britain alone lost 564,000 tons (over 300 ocean-going ships, or 10 per cent of her stock, *in one month*). The forecasts by Holtzendorff and Runciman at the end of 1916 were beginning to look positively optimistic for Britain as the average life expectancy of all ocean-going vessels declined to four return voyages. On 6 April 1917 Congress declared war on Germany. Yet the U-boats might still throttle Britain before an American Expeditionary Force could reach the Western Front – always assuming enough ships could be found to deliver the troops and equipment in safety.

On 23 April Mr Lloyd George lost his patience. He, Carson and Sir Maurice Hankey, former Royal Marine colonel, Cabinet Secretary and far-sighted strategist long in favour of convoys, had participated in a working breakfast with Jellicoe and his ASW Director, Alexander Duff, on 13 February, at which the admirals had agreed to convoy if the impending trials with the French colliers and the Norwegian ore ships proved successful. Nothing had been done, and Lloyd George, having quietly sounded out go-ahead officers like Henderson, called a crisis meeting of the revamped War Council (now a War Cabinet of five, not including Carson) for the 25th. This inner circle approved the Prime Minister's proposal to send Carson a telegram announcing his intention to call at the Admiralty on 30 April – to hear its proposals for convoy and other ASW measures. It was an unmistakable threat as well as an unprecedented direct intervention in the operations of a department of state by a prime minister who was supposed to be first among equals in a Cabinet with shared responsibility for government.

By the time he got there he had already won his point. Jellicoe and Duff had understood the message; Jellicoe endorsed Duff's memorandum ('we must be ready to introduce a comprehensive scheme of convoy at any moment') on the 27th. The Board was ready when Lloyd George presented his six-point plan for frustrating the U-boats. Number one was convoy. All merchant ships were to be armed. Submarine detection and destruction would be priorities for research. More ships would be built in Britain and more ordered from the United States. Existing shipping was to be used with maximum efficiency. There would be an import-substitution campaign, especially in agriculture. Lloyd George had already appointed two key officials to run new ministries with vast powers over the economy: Sir Joseph Maclay as Shipping Controller and Lord Devonport as Food Controller.

Another key appointment on 2 May 1917 directly affecting the Admiralty was that of the energetic and youthful Sir Eric Geddes as Controller of the Navy. In theory this post on the Board placed him in charge of warship construction, but he was appointed as a catalyst for reform. Geddes (1875–1937) had made his name as Director-General of Military Railways from 1916, reorganizing transport on the Western Front. Lloyd George did not think it safe to shift Carson until July, whereupon Geddes was promoted to First Lord in his place. At the end of 1917 Geddes replaced Jellicoe with Wemyss, who was to see out the war as First Sea Lord and Chief of Naval Staff (the posts were at last combined, a service to logic as well as efficiency). Carson joined the War Cabinet without a portfolio; and in 1918 Geddes was co-opted to it. We shall meet him again.

There was relief at the Admiralty that worldwide shipping losses fell to 600,000 tons (345,000 of them British) in May; these terrible figures were a good third down on the worst-ever month of April. But in June sinkings rose again, to 685,000 (399,000 British) the second-worst month of the war; in July they fell again, to 550,000 (360,000). In August 1917 there was another easement, to just over 500,000 tons (330,000), the last time global losses exceeded half a

million. Thus the introduction of convoys was no miracle cure –
but only because they were inaugurated piecemeal. The first (apart
from the trailblazing French and Norwegian sailings) left Gibraltar
for England only on 10 May and arrived untouched. The first
transatlantic convoy of twelve ships set off from Hampton Roads
(off Long Island) on 24 May; two were sent back without escort to
Halifax, Nova Scotia; one of the two was torpedoed. The other ten,
protected by a single cruiser, were met by destroyers for a safe
passage through the Western Approaches. The first dozen escorted
sailings to Britain collectively lost one ship sunk and one damaged
but towed into port.

The admirals were still dragging their feet; Lloyd George made
another direct intervention in Admiralty operations in June when
he demanded a much larger allocation of the Navy's destroyer
strength of 279 than the miserly thirty so far diverted to convoy
duty. On 6 June Fleet Paymaster (later Rear-Admiral Sir) Eldon
Manisty was placed in charge of escorts as Organizing Manager,
Convoys; and in September Captain F. A. Whitehead, RN, was
appointed Director of Mercantile Movements under him, a post
last filled in the Napoleonic Wars. The Ministry of Shipping also
opened a parallel convoy section under Mr Norman Leslie, who
organized the merchantmen in close consultation with Manisty.
The convoy system grew in fits and starts: in August it spread to the
central Atlantic on the Dakar, Senegal, route; in September to the
south Atlantic; and only in November to the Mediterranean, where
the divided command led to a dangerous delay in U-boat infested
waters. American admirals took almost as much convincing of the
virtue of convoy as their British colleagues; fortunately the Anglophile Rear-Admiral William Sims, commanding US naval forces in
Europe, was able to convince them, and by the end of the war
almost eighty American destroyers were on escort duty. So were
two flotillas of Japanese destroyers in the Mediterranean. When the
new statistical department set up at the Admiralty by Geddes
observed that 10 per cent of sinkings in the waters round the British
Isles were within ten miles of shore, coastal convoys were added to
the system towards the end of 1917.

The anti-convoy lobby remained surprisingly strong among
innumerate naval officers. In October 1917 disaster struck a
convoy from Bergen, Norway, to Shetland, whose escort was led by
the destroyer HMS *Mary Rose*. The twelve ships were attacked, not
by U-boats but by two light cruisers. The Germans first sank the

two escorts, which gallantly but impotently interposed themselves, and then destroyed nine of the freighters, all within an hour. There was a lot of headshaking among the diehards over this loss of 10,250 tons of shipping, which was equivalent to just over one-third of the average *daily* loss six months earlier. As a result convoy tactics were reviewed; while it remained wisest for ships to stay together if attacked by submarine, it was best to scatter a convoy threatened by superior surface forces (no solution was found for simultaneous submarine and surface attacks, which fortunately did not occur in 1914–18).

Enemy submariners could be relied upon to find and exploit the gaps as the convoy system slowly became almost worldwide. They never ran out of targets because large numbers of ships were still allowed to sail independently on almost all routes. In the last eighteen months of the war to November 1918 there were 16,657 convoyed sailings of individual ships to and from Britain in which 154, or 0.92 per cent, were lost; of these thirty-six were stragglers, sailing alone when attacked, and sixteen were lost to accidents and storms, a true loss of 0.61 per cent in convoy. The worldwide loss rate was even lower: in 88,000 convoyed sailings just 436 ships were sunk, 257 of them British, or not quite 0.5 per cent. But in the same period almost 6 per cent of ships sailing independently were sunk; 85 per cent of British losses, some 1,500 ships, were unescorted. After May 1917 a solitary ship stood a 1:16 chance of being sunk, a life expectancy of eight return voyages – and twelve and a half times the odds of 1:200 against convoyed shipping. To their astonishment, naval escort officers found that most merchant skippers were able to keep station in their convoy columns as if born to it: they too were professionals.

The search for ASW systems failed to master the submarine threat before the end of the war, which left the submersible torpedo boat neither defeated nor even held in check tactically, and only temporarily frustrated in strategic terms. The Allies merely managed to reduce shipping losses to a level at which new shipping construction, thanks to American intervention, overtook the U-boats' construction and destruction rates. The Germans meanwhile rationalized their command structure by giving Commodore Micheloon in Flanders control of all their U-boats, including those previously administered by the High Seas Fleet. He promptly sent the new large, long-range U-cruisers into the north Atlantic, a new risk for the ocean link with the US.

The most successful innovation against the submarine was the maritime aircraft, even though the latter could not yet destroy one. Airborne torpedoes were very promising but of limited value so far against surface ships and no use at all against undamaged submarines. Contemporary bombs were too small and inaccurate. The depth charge had not yet been adapted for airborne use, not least because contemporary aircraft were too small. Wireless was still telegraphic rather than vocal, which meant that pilots on their own could not operate it (but sets were fitted in airships and some two-man aircraft in the latter part of the war).

Nonetheless it was soon discovered that aircraft by their mere presence drove submarines to dive, drastically reducing their speed and endurance, which was quite enough on most occasions to prevent them doing damage. Convoys with constant air cover, necessarily close to home, were hardly ever damaged by submarines, most notably on the short Anglo-Dutch route, even though this ran between the German and Belgian U-boat bases. By the end of 1917 the Royal Navy had over 400 aircraft on anti-submarine duty: nearly 100 airships, 291 seaplanes and 23 aeroplanes. By the end of the war it had 657, including 272 aeroplanes, 285 seaplanes and 100 airships. The U-boats gave up attacking on the surface by day, adopted the altiscope (upward-looking periscope) and moved westward into the Atlantic to avoid detection from the air.

But on All Fools' Day, 1 April 1918, there occurred an event which has been described, with the benefit of hindsight, as the worst defeat suffered by the Royal Navy in the twentieth century: the amalgamation of the Royal Naval Air Service and the Army's Royal Flying Corps into the Royal Air Force. It must have seemed logical at the time: the Navy fought on water, the Army fought on land, and now the Air Force would fight in the air. That this was dangerously simplistic is shown by the survival into a new millennium of the Fleet Air Arm and the Army Air Corps, as well as the deployment by all three services not only of fixed-wing aircraft and helicopters but also of ground troops (Royal Marines, RAF Regiment), artillery and missiles. The United States did not acquire an autonomous air force until 1947, by which time the aircraft carrier had won the Pacific campaign and the importance of mobile airbases at sea could not be gainsaid. Inevitably the RAF became a rival for power and influence in the Whitehall apparatus, competing with the other services for scarce resources and claiming a sometimes absurd, absolute monopoly of anything that flew. An early and portentous example of the consequent disadvantage to the Navy, which was to recur in even more dangerous circumstances less than a generation later, was the RAF's refusal in 1918 to spare a handful of the new, long-range bombers then coming into service for ASW patrols over the broad Atlantic. They were retained for such purposes as bombing the heavily protected Flanders U-boat pens, although not one of Michelsen's craft was sunk in the escalating and costly air raids of the last months of the war. The Navy chose not to bombard these bases for fear of retaliation in kind, although the inertia of the High Seas Fleet and the other preoccupations of the U-boats made this highly unlikely. Not for the first time the effect of aerial bombardment was ridiculously overestimated, just as it would be at the end of the century in Iraq and rump Yugoslavia.

Even so, Allied shipping losses fell by 50 per cent between August and September 1917, after which the rate generally rose and fell in alternate months, but on a downward trend. Yet it was only in August 1918, when the British alone lost a not inconsiderable 166,000 tons, that the rate at last dropped below the 1916 monthly average. British new construction doubled in 1917 to 1,229,000 tons (one-third of British losses that year); in 1918 Britain built 1,579,000 tons, still 52,000 tons below her losses in the same period. It was American output, especially of standardized freighters, that prevented Holtzendorff's and Runciman's predictions of a British defeat within six months from coming true. The contribution of US shipyards (and American money) was probably more important for the outcome of the war than the two million fresh young men of the American Expeditionary Force in France.

Only in the last six months of conflict did the German U-boat loss rate exceed the building rate, just when the Allies began to outbuild their own shipping losses. The U-boats alone destroyed 4,837 merchantmen, 11,135,000 tons of shipping, during the Great War, including 55 per cent of the prewar British Merchant Navy or 7,662,000 tons, 69 per cent of the total worldwide loss to German and Austrian submarines. Of the extra 2,000,000 tons sunk by other means, a high proportion was lost to mines laid by U-boats. Overall, the average monthly rate of shipping losses in the First World War surpassed (by over 2,000 tons) that in the Second – when Germany fielded more than twice as many operational U-boats – and brought Britain even closer to defeat in 1917 than she would come in 1942–3. The British lost 15,313 merchant seamen, a death rate of 5.5 per cent, to the first generation of U-boats; the Royal Navy lost 4 per cent of its total wartime manpower, 22,811 sailors, including almost 6,000 more merchant seamen seconded to it on requisitioned small vessels. One-third of naval fatalities occurred in the defence of trade, which had so unexpectedly claimed its rightful place as a central concern of the Royal Navy, and brought it within a hair's breadth of defeat.

Looking back on his youthful time in the Mediterranean late in 1917 in his memoirs many decades later, a submariner named Karl Dönitz recalled:

> The oceans at once became bare and empty; for long periods at a time the U-boats, operating individually, would see nothing at all; and then suddenly up would loom a huge concourse of ships, thirty or fifty or more of them, surrounded by an escort of warships of all types . . . The lone U-boat might well sink one or two of the ships, or even several, yet that was but a poor percentage of the whole.

The four British 'E'-class submarines supporting the lacklustre Russian Navy boats and surface ships in the Baltic were 'locked in' by the German guard on the Baltic entrance, but even so were joined by four 'C'-class coastal boats in September 1916: towed to Archangel in the far north, they were placed on barges and conveyed by canal to Petrograd (St Petersburg). During 1916 only five submarines were active against the Germans in the Baltic; three were British. In 1917, before Russia sank into chaos and revolution, they achieved little, and the four 'Es' and three 'Cs' left in the British flotilla were scuttled in Helsingfors (Helsinki) in April 1918.

The British at home were still interested in the 'fleet submarine', a concept that would not come into its own until the nuclear age. The Admiralty designed a new, large 'K' class in 1915 with a speed of twenty-four knots, but chose to power these exceptionally large and fast boats, displacing 1,883 tons surfaced and 2,565 submerged, by steam. Switching from surface to the usual battery propulsion for submerged movement was both complicated and very dangerous, as the loss of no fewer than eight K-boats to accidents out of the seventeen commissioned during the war tragically demonstrated. One, *K13*, sank off Faslane, the submarine base in south-west Scotland, with the loss of twenty-five men, but was raised and recommissioned as *K22*. Experiments continued into the 1920s but the 'K' class was then written off. The first hero of the British submarine service, Commander Max Horton, was the first skipper of the freakish submarine *M1*, a submersible monitor of 1,600 tons surfaced and 1,950 submerged, armed with a single 12-inch gun. Commissioned in August 1918, *M1* (and *M2*) saw no action and, converted to experimental seaplane carriers, were both lost to accidents years after the war. But the wartime 'R' class, with futuristic, hydrodynamically rounded hull, developed by the Admiralty as the first 'hunter-killer' or ASW submarine, proved robust and reliable as well as extremely fast underwater (fifteen knots, compared with nine and a half surfaced). Not only did this type come too late to influence events; its revolutionary potential was discounted because the Admiralty came to believe as the war ended that it would not be needed (see below). It was to be twenty-five years before the 'R' class was surpassed – by Germany.

An Allied Submarine Detection Conference was held in Washington in June 1917. The British and Americans decided to work with the French, whose leading scientist in the field, Paul Langevin, had been conducting promising experiments in active underwater detection. The apparatus developed as a result was built round the newly invented quartz transducer, capable with an amplifier of picking up the pinging echo of a pulsating ultrasonic radio beam reflected back by an underwater object: the closer the object, the more frequent the pings. The Royal Navy pursued the technology with the greatest dedication and the first vessel to deploy ASDIC (Allied Submarine Detection Investigation Committee) was His Majesty's Trawler *Ebro II* – five days after the Armistice on 11 November 1918. At that point the British took the lead in active submarine detection and regarded the submarine problem as solved. And a defeated Germany, required to surrender all U-boats, was forbidden to acquire or build any in future.

The last major surface action by the Royal Navy in the war was the brainchild of Vice-Admiral Roger Keyes, in command of the Dover Patrol from the beginning of 1918. He wanted to strike a blow at Michelsen's fifty U-boats based in Bruges (linked by canal to Zeebrugge on the coast) and using Ostend as a forward base. The ever-aggressive Keyes planned to close the Belgian ports by sinking blockships. It was entirely typical of the man that the day chosen for the 'Zeebrugge Raid' was the feast of St George, 23 April 1918. Three old cruisers were earmarked as blockships and a fourth, HMS *Vindictive*, would lead a pair of old ferries in landing Royal Marines to storm the German artillery battery covering the Zeebrugge Mole. Lieutenant R. D. Sandford, RN, was to take the small submarine *C3* into the canal and light the fuse to five tons of explosives aboard, once he had positioned and evacuated his eleven-year-old craft under the railway viaduct across the waterway, so that the wreckage would block the canal.

A second boat assigned to this task did not arrive in time to take part. The blockships could not be sunk in the right spots to cause the desired long-term obstruction. The Marines alone took over 300 casualties in very bloody fighting on the mole, won by the defenders. But *C3* blew up in spectacular fashion, bringing down the viaduct as planned. The crew of six, including the wounded Sandford, were picked up from their launches by the latter's elder brother, Lieutenant-Commander Francis Sandford of Keyes's staff, who had helped to plan the enterprise and requisitioned a launch for rescue purposes on his own initiative. The younger Sandford received the VC. The Germans needed only a few days to clear the canal and shore up the viaduct, resuming U-boat operations after only a short intermission. But the British public, the press, the Allied armies and a proud Admiralty rejoiced over the dashing and widely trumpeted raid, whose main and not unimportant effect was to raise morale after nearly four years of war and two years of apparent underachievement by the Navy. Keyes was knighted, twice over. The U-boats sank 214,000 tons of British shipping in April 1918, their highest score for four months.

The sailors of the Imperial German High Seas Fleet mutinied at the end of October 1918, putting paid to officers' plans for a last 'death or glory' sortie into the North Sea. Some large German Army units on the Western Front showed similar reluctance, signalling the end of Germany's will to fight, eroded by the silent British naval blockade, much less 'frightful' or visible than submarine sinkings but in the end just that bit more effective. In the last full month of the war the counter-blockade by the U-boats still managed to sink seventy-three ships of 116,000 tons, the lowest return since July

1916. The last charge of the phenomenally destructive and almost victorious U-boat arm was carried out by Lieutenant-Commander Kurt Emsmann and his crew of thirty-four men in *UB116*, late of the dispersed Flanders Flotilla, on 28 October 1918. The boat stole into Scapa Flow, last penetrated abortively by Hennig's *U18* on 23 November 1914, as far as Hoxa Sound. Its target, the Grand Fleet flagship *Queen Elizabeth*, was not in harbour. The intruder was detected by the chain of hydrophones on the seabed, and when it passed over a submerged minefield a switch was thrown by a seaman ashore: the boat exploded, killing every man aboard. Hennig and Emsmann were not forgotten (except by the Royal Navy).

It was only with enormous difficulty that Rear-Admiral Ludwig von Reuter assembled the seventy-four ships of the High Seas Fleet that were to be interned in Scapa Flow with German skeleton crews aboard, pending the signing of the Treaty of Versailles in June 1919. The ships were in a sorry state and their crews were mutinous, especially on the five battlecruisers and nine battleships, and elected Sailors' Councils on the all too recent Soviet model. They were met in a light mist off the Firth of Forth on 21 November by more than 250 vessels, including forty-four dreadnoughts, from the Grand Fleet plus representative ships of the US and other Allied navies, in the greatest assemblage of seapower yet seen. In his Order of the Day Beatty congratulated his men on:

> the victory which has been gained over the sea power of our enemy. The greatness of this achievement is in no way lessened by the fact that the final episode did not take the form of a fleet action. Although deprived of this opportunity which we had so long and eagerly awaited and of striking the final blow for the freedom of the world, we may derive satisfaction from the singular tribute which the enemy has accorded to the Grand Fleet. Without joining us in any action he has given testimony to the prestige and efficiency of the fleet without parallel in history, and it is to be remembered that this testimony has been accorded to us by those who were in the best position to judge.

Two days later the Admiralty signalled to all ships:

The Board of Admiralty desire to express to the officers and men of the Royal Navy and the Royal Marines on the completion of their great work their congratulations on a triumph to which history knows no parallel. The surrender of the German fleet, accomplished without shock of battle, will remain for all time the example of the wonderful silence and sureness with which sea power attains its ends. The world recognises that this consummation is due to the steadfastness with which the Navy has maintained its pressure on the enemy through more than four years of war, a pressure exerted no less insistently during the long monotony of waiting than in the rare opportunities of attack.

To the Germans on 21 November Beatty was more succinct:

The German flag will be hauled down at 3.57 in the afteroon (sunset) and is not to be rehoisted without permission.

This order was defied exactly seven months later when Reuter, believing that the German government would refuse to sign at Versailles and therefore that hostilities would recommence, decided to stop the Royal Navy seizing the rotting High Seas Fleet by ordering it to scuttle itself on 21 June 1919. Fifty-two ships went to the bottom of Scapa Flow; twenty-two were beached. The Treaty of Versailles was signed on 28 June.

On New Year's Eve, 31 December 1918, Admiral of the Fleet Sir John Arbuthnot Fisher, First Baron Fisher of Kilverstone, now aged seventy-seven, visited the new aircraft carrier HMS *Furious* at Rosyth. Addressing the crew, he predicted that the next war would break out in twenty years' time.

PART II

The Axis Powers

6

The One-Power Standard

The Royal Navy reached its maximum manpower in the Great War around the time of the climax of the U-boat crisis in 1917. Despite the hiving off of the Royal Naval Air Service (55,000 officers and men) into the RAF a year later, the Navy maintained, with considerable difficulty amid a manpower shortage, its peak strength of 448,000 for the rest of the war. When it ended there were, including the Royal Marines and the RN Division, 38,000 officers and 410,000 men, plus 7,000 women in the WRNS. On 24 June 1918 the United States government announced that the US Navy and Marine Corps had a combined strength of 450,093. The British had about twice as many dreadnoughts as the Americans (who commissioned no battlecruisers); but the Royal Navy, which had measured its strength against the French Navy at the beginning and the German from the end of the nineteenth century, had to gauge its power after 1918 against the Americans. The drastic economic changes caused by more than four years of war, which beggared the British and the other European belligerents while enriching the Japanese and (especially) the Americans, saw to it that the British fleet was soon found wanting by the new yardstick. At least Britain could be thankful, however, that this latest and sometimes quite bitter rivalry at sea, unlike its predecessors, would not foreshadow a war with the leading foreign maritime power.

The prewar naval arms race between Britain and Germany had been focused upon, and expressed in, battleships, a trend accelerated by the gunnery 'lesson' of Tsushima and again by the development of the dreadnought. But the German strategy of piecemeal attrition culminating in a North Sea battle on even terms which would end British maritime supremacy, win, lose or draw, had collapsed at Jutland. By the same token, the British strategy of outbuilding the German fleet before the war, and conserving the Royal Navy's superior strength for a distant blockade during it, had triumphed. But the unexpected success of the new-fangled submarine had left the Admiralty, less than halfway through the war, with an idle battlefleet and a catastrophic shortage of ASW vessels, weapons, technologies and ideas. Win or lose, the destruction of so many million tons of shipping (and so many seamen and cargoes) can only be viewed as a catastrophe. Once again outbuilding the enemy threat, this time in mercantile tonnage, proved to be the route to survival and victory, thanks to American shipyards and money (and the complementary fact that the Germans could not afford the 350 extra U-boats demanded by Admiral Scheer, or even enough to keep pace with their own submarine losses). Such was the outcome of the war of attrition at sea.

In 1914–18 the Admiralty had, if anything, overcompensated for enemy cruisers and taken the right measures against the enemy battlefleet, but had been completely caught out by the U-boats, which came closest of all to defeating Britain. Obsessed like all their foreign colleagues with the big-gun ships, British admirals only recognized when it was almost too late that while a 50 per cent margin in dreadnoughts was all very well, there was no such thing as enough destroyers, a whole flotilla of which could be built for the price of a single dreadnought. Small wonder that the submarine dominated the thoughts of British and Allied admirals as the war came to an end and the peace talks began at Versailles.

It being a truism that when preparing for the next war military leaders plan to refight the last, the victors retained their fixation on the big gun, discounting the torpedo and the aircraft, and tried to banish the problem of submarines by (a) forbidding the losers to own them, (b) pressing for a worldwide ban on them, and (c) relying on ASDIC to detect and the depth charge to destroy them if all else failed. Tragically for another generation of merchant seamen, the admirals ensured that the measure of naval power and prestige remained the dreadnought, a trait reinforced not only by the dominance of gunnery-specialist officers within the two leading navies, British and American, but also by the postwar rivalry between them. Even though Fisher, once again, had been the first to recognize the possibilities of maritime air power before it had even been invented, the admirals of 1918 could no more be condemned for failing to foresee the rise of the maritime torpedo-bomber than those of 1914 for not anticipating the destructive potential of the submarine, especially in Britain, where the Navy had the bumptious RAF and its political arm, the Air Ministry, to

The Anglo-German arms race personified: Grand Admiral Alfred von Tirpitz (LEFT), creator of the Imperial German High Seas Fleet; and Admiral of the Fleet Lord Fisher of Kilverstone (shown here as Vice-Admiral and C-in-C, Mediterranean Fleet)

Fisher's masterpiece, HMS Dreadnought, *which made all other battleships obsolete at a stroke in 1906; and a mighty display of firepower for the Royal Review of the Fleet at Spithead in July 1914, on the eve of war*

Where they ate and slept in the First World War: stokers dining on their cruiser's mess-deck. Note the lockers in the foreground and the bars above, from which hammocks were hung

Lost ships: a German propaganda picture of the Cunard liner Lusitania (ABOVE), *sunk by* U20 *on 7 May 1915 with heavy loss of life; and the bow and stern of the battlecruiser HMS* Invincible, *destroyed by ammunition explosions at the Battle of Jutland on 31 May 1916*

The admirals at the Battle of Jutland, 31 May–1 June 1916: Admiral Sir John Jellicoe (ABOVE LEFT), Commander-in-Chief, Grand Fleet; Admiral Reinhard Scheer (ABOVE RIGHT), Commander-in Chief, High Seas Fleet; Vice-Admiral Sir David Beatty (BELOW LEFT) of the British battlecruisers; Vice-Admiral Franz von Hipper (CENTRE, BELOW RIGHT) of the German battlecruisers

*The reborn German Navy: the First Flotilla of new U-boats at Kiel before the
Second World War; the 'pocket battleship'* Admiral Graf Spee, *on fire after
scuttling in the estuary of the River Plate, 17 December 1939*

The highest admirals: Admiral of the Fleet Sir Dudley Pound (ABOVE LEFT), *First Sea Lord and Chief of Naval Staff until his death in 1943; his successor, Admiral of the Fleet Sir Andrew Cunningham* (ABOVE CENTRE); *Admiral Sir Bertram Ramsay* (ABOVE RIGHT), *mastermind of Dunkirk and D-Day.* (BELOW), *Grand-Admiral Erich Raeder* (LEFT), *Commander-in-Chief of the German Navy until 1943; and his successor Grand-Admiral Karl Dönitz, who also personally commanded the U-boats throughout the war*

Desperate days for Britain: troops evacuated from Dunkirk arriving at Dover (ABOVE) *in June 1940; the surrender of Singapore on 15 February 1942*

contend with. The airmen soon developed a knack for public relations and a feel for the power-politics of Whitehall, neither of which had ever been the strong suit of the Silent Service.

The Germans meanwhile secretly resolved to retain their lead in underwater technology – and to build better commerce raiders. They were equally determined to ignore the ban on military aircraft imposed by Versailles.

The peace treaty limited the German Navy to 1,500 officers and 15,000 men, six armoured ships of a maximum 10,000 tons each, six cruisers of 6,000 tons, twelve destroyers up to 800 tons and twelve torpedo boats up to 200 tons. It was the French who blocked the British proposal at Versailles to outlaw submarines, arguing that they were a perfectly legitimate weapon for a weaker naval power provided they were operated within the laws of war. An Allied Control Commission supervised German observance of the Versailles treaty; its naval section felt its work was complete by 1924 and wound itself up in September. By then German naval officers and shipbuilders had been secretly advising foreign powers such as Japan and Italy, Argentina, Spain and Sweden on submarine construction for four years; they also founded a 'front' company in the Netherlands in 1922 to design, build, test and deliver submarines for foreign clients. Government funds were illicitly siphoned, through dummy companies set up by the Navy in Germany, to the yard in Rotterdam, while undermining Versailles became a national pastime for Germans at all levels and of all shades of opinion, left, right or centre.

The future shape and strength of the Royal Navy in an all but bankrupt Britain was tortuously considered by a series of committees in the early postwar years. The Committee of Imperial Defence spawned the Naval Shipbuilding or Bonar Law Committee, chaired by the Scots-Canadian Cabinet minister and future premier, Andrew Bonar Law, who had been Chancellor of the Exchequer in the latter half of the war. Beatty served on it, presenting the Admiralty's case for continuing to build capital ships. Skilled labour would disperse without new orders; contemporary aircraft presented no threat to battleships; Britain had only one modern capital ship (HMS *Hood*, a battlecruiser launched in August 1918, commissioned in 1920 and misguidedly often classed as a battleship, with ultimately fatal results), whereas the United States planned sixteen. Such a disparity would leave Britain in a weak bargaining position when it came to the general disarmament talks presaged by the Versailles treaty. Churchill, now Secretary of State for War and Air, was also on the Committee and argued for four new battleships a year for the next four to five years, just as he had proposed in 1912, when Germany, not America, was the key rival.

More decisive for the Navy's future was the Committee on National Expenditure, familiarly known as the Geddes Committee after its chairman, the former First Lord, who was the first Minister of Transport in 1919–1921. Sir Eric wielded what the press soon referred to as the 'Geddes Axe' with gusto. It was to this Committee, set up in August 1921, that the Admiralty presented its case for a One-Power Standard: 'The Navy should be maintained at sufficient strength to ensure the safety of the British Empire and its sea communications as against any other naval power.' Parity with foreign naval forces within reach of British home waters was not enough as it would imply a purely defensive strategy; but absolute equality with the US Navy, especially in modern capital ships, 'the gauge of a country's seapower', would be very hard to maintain. Fortunately for the impoverished British, there was a strong anti-naval lobby in Washington which fought against untrammelled expansion of the US fleet. But there was also a powerful and far-sighted lobby within the US Navy which was already swinging service opinion away from the big-gun ship towards the aircraft carrier. Prominent among the air power advocates was Admiral William Sims, who wrote to a senator in 1921: 'It is all a question as to whether the airplane carrier, equipped with eighty planes, is not the capital ship of the future.' The Japanese, bent on constructing twenty-seven capital ships by 1927, were even more enthusiastic.

For the twenty years from the Armistice to the Munich Crisis the Admiralty and the Air Ministry were locked in a power struggle over the control of maritime aviation which caused the Navy to fall at least a decade behind the Americans and Japanese in the development of naval aircraft and seriously impaired the fleet's effectiveness in the Second World War. At times it must have been difficult to regard the two departments as belonging to the same side. The amputation of the RNAS in 1918 had stripped the Navy not only of officers with knowledge and experience of aviation but also of enthusiasts for it. In December 1919 Churchill as responsible minister presented the RAF's charter to Parliament, providing 'a small part specially trained for work with the Navy' and another for the Army, each of which 'small portions' would eventually become an arm of the relevant older service. The Navy's small portion was RAF Coastal Area Command (the word 'area' was soon dropped), under Air Vice-Marshal A. V. Vyvyan. The Command's three shore-based groups were to 'cooperate' with the Navy and its chief was to advise the Admiralty and all home naval commands on air matters; but the Air Ministry retained responsibility for supply and maintenance. Vyvyan regarded ASW patrol and convoy escort as 'purely defensive' and was therefore opposed to devoting more than a minimum of aircraft to them. He preferred the 'offensive' policy of attacking enemy submarine bases.

The Admiralty Board's requests for air support were clear-sighted and on the same lines as those of the US Navy's General Board: carrier aircraft, including spotters and fighters, bombers with armour-piercing anti-ship bombs, torpedo-bombers, float-planes for short-range and flying boats for long-range recon-naissance. Beatty's flag captain at Jutland, now Rear-Admiral A. E. M. Chatfield, a future First Sea Lord, was the member of the Board responsible for aviation and fought his corner with conviction. But he could make no impression on the aggressive campaign for control of everything that flew led by the 'Father of the Royal Air Force', Sir Hugh, later Lord, Trenchard, Chief of the Air Staff from 1919 to 1929. In March 1921 he and the Air Staff presented a paper to the Committee of Imperial Defence paying lip-service to the need for air support of the older services but claiming primacy for the RAF in defending Britain against invasion, policing its colonies and protecting its coastline. His central aim was to make the RAF truly independent of the older services rather than auxiliary to them. In May Trenchard wrote another memorandum, baldly demanding the transfer to the Air Ministry of responsibility for the defence of Britain. Trenchard was also the father of the dangerously seductive 'strategic bombing' and independent air power concepts. Neither the naval nor the general staff seemed capable of standing up to the light-blue upstarts, let alone of working together to restrain them. The naval repre-sentatives on the Geddes Committee were the first to dig in against the airmen, but their resistance proved to be too little, too late against the lobbying and public-relations machinery of the Air Ministry, which got its way more often than not throughout the period between the wars. In Britain, when it came to air power at sea, the Navy proposed but the RAF disposed.

Aboard His Majesty's ships disaffection was growing in the aftermath of the war. Wartime inflation had by 1918 pushed prices two and a half times higher than they had been in 1914. Pay rates remained generally the same. Another committee, on naval pay, was set up in 1919 to tackle this widespread grievance. A separate committee looked at officers' pay, fossilized for half a century. The pay of an able seaman was more than doubled to 4s per day, and that of a petty officer from 3s to 7s. Allowances and pensions went up too, though also by less than inflation. Officers did less well in percentage terms; a lieutenant received 70 per cent while a commander got 100 per cent more. The officers' increases were index-linked but not those of the ratings, who, however, were given a married man's allowance from age twenty-five, something not extended to officers (who remained on half-pay between appointments).

The process of shrinking from record manpower levels to those required for an uncertain peace was even more painful than the wartime expansion which made it necessary. Demobilization began two months after the Armistice; priority was given to industrial workers, which often entailed a de facto last in, first out approach instead of first in, first out, which was widely seen as the only fair procedure for 'hostilities only' (HO) ratings and wartime volunteers – the vast majority. There was much unrest in the Army against last in, first out, and since the crews of most ships consisted of four HO men in every five, there were justified fears of mutiny in the Navy too. Even during the war there had been agitation over pay, leading to minor increases at the end of 1917, and Yexley, now editor of *The Fleet*, warned Geddes of massive discontent; the future axe-wielder was able to defer but not to resolve the problem, which could only be cured by money that could not be found.

The demobilization took place at high speed, alongside a radical reorganization of the Navy's main formations. The Grand Fleet ceased to exist on 7 April 1919, when Beatty became First Sea Lord and Admiral of the Fleet. At this stage some 40,000 HO ratings were still awaiting release. It was replaced by a considerably reduced, all-dreadnought Atlantic Fleet under Admiral Sir Charles Madden, previously Second-in-Command of the Grand Fleet. The smaller Home Fleet, also all-dreadnought in its main strength, replaced the Channel Fleet. The Mediterranean Fleet remained the principal overseas formation, while cruiser squadrons stayed on stations covering North America and West Indies, China, East Indies and Africa.

A new Baltic Squadron of cruisers, a seaplane carrier, destroyers, submarines and minesweepers was set up to protect the independence of the four Baltic states, hived off from the Tsarist empire after the 1917 Revolution, from the Bolsheviks. The Baltic ships offered dismal serving conditions in winter and almost no recreational facilities as the unit had no permanent base. When the seaplane carrier *Vindictive* called at Copenhagen on the way east there was a mutiny aboard; well over a hundred ratings deserted when given leave from the First Destroyer Flotilla; there was widespread insubordination on the minesweepers and even on the cruiser HMS *Delhi*, flagship of Rear-Admiral Sir Walter Cowan. The Soviet revolution had aroused anti-left hysteria in the higher reaches of the British Establishment, especially the Admiralty, which was terrified of the idea of trade-unionism on the lower deck. It set up a Welfare Committee, including ratings as well as officers, in an effort to defuse complaints; in the absence of unions the lower-deck benefit societies became a forum for discontent. Many 'agitators' were arrested by the Special Branch.

The first naval Welfare Conference was almost torpedoed in advance in 1922 when the Treasury made it clear that there would be no significant extra funds for improvements. This did nothing for morale in the service. There was to be such a conference every two years at each of the main home ports in turn (Chatham, Plymouth, Portsmouth, Rosyth). The Navy, Army and Air Force Institute (NAAFI) was allowed from 1922 to run canteens ashore; at sea each ship had its own Canteen Committee (more appropriately styled Welfare Committee in the Second World War) with the second-in-command – the commander or first lieutenant – presiding and all rates represented. It also looked after the ship's fund for recreational and charitable purposes, including ex gratia payments to relatives of the dead. The fund was financed by a rebate on items bought in the mess. The Royal Navy Benevolent Trust was set up to help serving or former ratings in difficulty or seeking work.

The officer corps had its problems too, starting with over-recruitment in the war and problems with redundancy. The intake at Osborne and Dartmouth training colleges was cut by 40 per cent under the Geddes Axe and parents were even paid a lump sum of £300 to withdraw cadets (Osborne closed altogether in May 1919); one captain in three was made to leave and 550 lieutenants. The Admiralty, however, showed rare imagination in sending some 700 sub-lieutenants promoted during the war to Cambridge University for two terms to broaden their education and training. Later this function was given to the Royal Naval College at Greenwich. Conditions for promising ratings to be sent for officer training were considerably eased in 1920, though in the teeth of abiding class prejudice on the Board.

Deflation succeeded a postwar boom in less than four years, as a result of which pay scales for junior officers and ratings were actually cut in 1923; cost-of-living allowances went down in 1924 (and again in 1927, 1930 and most significantly in the Slump in 1931). Perhaps the most fateful decision fell on 5 October 1925, when lower pay rates were applied to new entrants only: an able seaman received only 3s a day instead of 4s and a lieutenant 15s instead of 17s. Meanwhile those on the strength on the previous day were guaranteed the higher, 1919 scales until they left the service (unless there was to be a general cut in scales in the future, a small-print proviso unwisely ignored by many pre-1919 men). Here surely the Board of Admiralty was making a rod for its own back. Meanwhile manpower declined to 275,000 in mid-1919, 136,000 in 1920, 124,000 in 1921, 118,500 in 1922 and 100,000 in 1923, its lowest level since 1897, where it more or less stayed until the Depression in 1931. The Royal Marines' Artillery and Light Infantry arms were amalgamated in 1923, but the Admiralty was making no headway in its campaign to recover control of the Fleet Air Arm from the RAF.

Two new battleships, *Nelson* and *Rodney*, each of 35,000 tons with 16-inch guns, and eight 8-inch long-range heavy cruisers (10,000 tons) of the 'County' class were ordered in the early 1920s. Three white elephants left over from the war, the overblown cruisers *Furious*, *Courageous* and *Glorious*, each of about 19,000 tons and originally conceived in 1915 by Fisher with four 15-inch guns and shallow draft, were converted into aircraft carriers. To these was added the purpose-built *Hermes* (the first two American carriers were built on rather larger battlecruiser hulls, to the advantage of aviation in the rival navy). In 1924 the Admiralty opened HMS *Osprey* at Portland as an ASW school and experimental establishment where the top-secret ASDIC was fitted and training given – but only on selected, individual ships. Even so, the big gun still dominated naval thinking, despite the long-standing and repeated public warnings of Fisher and the Navy's leading gunnery expert, Admiral Sir Percy Scott, that the battleship had already been rendered obsolete by the torpedo, as carried by the submarine and (especially) the aircraft.

The desperate need for economy in Britain, combined with the strong opposition in Washington to a large fleet, gave a powerful impetus to naval disarmament and arms limitation alike on the part of the two naval powers on either side of the north Atlantic. The Americans took the initiative in what was to be a prolonged and fitful saga of international conferences on the relative strengths of navies and the size and armament of the principal classes of ship. The Americans called the first, the Washington Conference, attended by representatives of the five leading naval powers, the USA, Britain, France, Italy and Japan, in 1921. The US delegation was led by Charles Evans Hughes, Secretary of State, who made detailed proposals for discussion. The British delegation included Arthur Balfour, Lord President of the Council and former First Lord, Sir Auckland Geddes, the axeman's brother and Ambassador to Washington, and Admirals Beatty, First Sea Lord and Chief of Naval Staff, and Chatfield, Deputy CNS.

Among the key proposals put up by the Americans and adopted with some modifications were: a ten-year 'naval holiday' from the construction of major ships; a ratio of 5:5:3 for the Royal Navy and the US Navy on the one hand and the Japanese fleet on the other, with 1.65 each for France and Italy; and a limit of 35,000 tons on the displacement of capital ships. Numbers of smaller ships in each fleet were to be in proportion to the capital ships, which were used as the yardstick of naval strength. The 5:3:1.65 ratio roughly reflected existing relative strengths at the end of 1921, but the Americans, British and Japanese in particular would be called upon to scrap some existing ships and abandon plans for others, some of which were already on the stocks.

The Americans offered to scrap fifteen pre-dreadnoughts and a similar number of unfinished dreadnoughts, a total displacement of 846,000 tons, far exceeding the tonnage of the German Fleet interned and scuttled at Scapa Flow. To match the thus reduced US fleet, the Royal Navy would be called upon to scrap 583,000 tons – four super-battlecruisers, modelled on HMS *Hood* and only just ordered, plus nineteen older capital ships. This would leave Britain with twenty-two capital ships of 604,000 tons and the US with eighteen of 501,000 tons. This disparity was to allow for the fact that the British ships were mostly older than their American counterparts: eventually each would have a dreadnought fleet of 500,000 tons. Japan would be left with ten dreadnoughts of 300,000 tons, a sacrifice because the Empire had started a massive, ten-year naval expansion programme in 1917. No new capital ship would be built for ten years and none replaced until it was twenty years old.

Beatty was still concerned about losing shipyard skills and proposed a rolling replacement programme, plus a disproportionate number of cruisers for Britain to reflect her imperial requirements. The underlying British concern was that at the end of the ten-year holiday the British fleet would be decidedly older than the American on average, and therefore inferior. But the proposed ratios were in general acceptable. He also advocated total abolition of the submarine – provided all nations agreed. Considering the potential complexity of the issues involved, it is remarkable that the conference, which convened on 12 November 1921, led on 13 December to the signature of the first Washington Treaty. It included some adjustments to individual fleets, most notably in Britain's case allowing for the construction of the *Nelson* and *Rodney*. The British delegation had wanted a 43,000-ton limit on individual ships so as to be able to build two 'super-*Hood*s' but had to settle for 35,000. Each navy was allowed to build two 'experimental ships' of up to 33,000 tons (the uncoincidental displacement of the two US battlecruisers converted to carriers, all of which were classed as experimental and open to replacement at any time) within its overall fleet limit. The 5:3:1.65 ratio for capital ships was agreed, along with the ten-year pause in general construction. Carrier tonnage was limited to 135,000 in the two leading navies, 81,000 for Japan and 60,000 for Italy and France, a ratio of 10:6:4.5 and rather higher than the Americans had envisaged.

On cruisers, the Conference set an upper limit of 10,000 tons and 8-inch guns, but not on numbers. For most navies this amounted to a challenge to build *up* to these new, untried 'limitations'. Unwisely the delegates sanctioned the survival of the armed merchant cruiser, which was allowed to be prepared in peacetime for carrying guns of up to 6-inch calibre. A British proposal to outlaw submarines was opposed once again by the French, as it had been at Versailles. But the boats were subjected to Prize Rules in dealing with unarmed ships, although no limit of any kind was placed on numbers or size of submarines, any more than on destroyers and smaller vessels.

The Conference, which ended in February 1922, was responsible for a series of nine treaties and twelve resolutions, all of which affected not only the five participating powers but also other nations, which were encouraged to subscribe to them. The deadline for destruction of ships was set for three years later, February 1925. The French and Italian navies were hardly affected. Britain emerged with twenty-two capital ships, which would fall to twenty when the two 'Treaty' battleships, *Nelson* and *Rodney*, were completed and four older battleships were scrapped. Twenty old ships and four uncompleted ones were to be scrapped at once. After these adjustments British tonnage would fall to 500,000.

Since the British post-Treaty battlefleet would have a markedly higher average age than that of the US Navy, the day on which Britannia ceased to rule the waves, or at least to enjoy naval supremacy over any other single power, can be identified as 14 June 1922, when the Treaty of Washington Bills were laid before Parliament. They received the Royal Assent in 1923. The USA meanwhile adopted the watchword, 'a Navy second to none'.

The results of the Washington Naval Conference were a large step in the right direction but mixed nevertheless. The five leading battle fleets were limited and locked into a strict ratio with one another. But there were no limits of any kind on submarines, destroyers or smaller vessels, no limit on cruiser numbers, and plenty of scope for competition in building carriers, their aircraft and armament. Germany, her navy reduced to a rump by Versailles, was not involved or affected.

In Britain, no work had been done on the four 'super-*Hood*s' since October 1921; construction was abandoned in January 1922. The design of the pair of new 'Treaty' battleships was approved by the Board in February. Existing ships were allowed by the Treaty to have up to 3,000 tons of extra protection added to their displacement; most of this was taken up by the addition of 'bulges' along the waterlines of major ships to reduce the effect of torpedo and mine blast, a modification which had begun to be adopted before the end of the war (ships started from 1922 had this extra layer of protection internalized as a double hull). Work on the new 10,000-ton Treaty cruisers with their 8-inch guns and the carrier conversions also went ahead from 1923. The Controller of the Navy, in charge of construction, told designers to save every scrap of weight they could.

In Whitehall, committees continued to proliferate. A new Cabinet committee chaired by Churchill was set up in January 1922 to work out how to apply the cuts imposed by the Geddes Committee on the armed forces, as part of a slashing review of all government expenditure. Beatty was forced to spend much of his time fighting the consequent restrictions. But Churchill and other ministers were determined to uphold the new one-power standard down to the last rivet, which was a help to the embattled Board of Admiralty. Naval estimates for £65m were presented to Parliament on 10 March 1923, nearly £5m more than in the Geddes proposals. Only fifteen capital ships were to be kept in full commission; twelve were to be scrapped in the coming financial year. The Atlantic Fleet would lose some destroyers, twenty-seven submarines would be scrapped and the Treaty battleships would not be laid down until the following year. Manpower in the Navy was to be cut by 20,000 and in the naval dockyards by 10,000.

The prevailing economic stringency between the wars played into the hands of the RAF with its demand for a monopoly of aviation. Although the Admiralty did sanction aircraft for cruisers and upwards, launched by a catapult-ramp on top of a gun turret and recovered from the sea by crane, these were purely for reconnaissance and gunnery spotting (though extremely valuable as such) and not for protection against air attack. The Board put its faith in rapid-firing, 'pom-pom' anti-aircraft guns for defence against such attacks, but saved money by purchasing too few and by neglecting to develop heavier, dual-purpose, high-angle/low-angle guns or anti-aircraft gunnery control systems. All this added to the general culture of underestimation, if not outright dismissal, of the airborne threat to seapower prevalent in the Royal Navy from 1918. The Americans had a much greater appreciation of the potential of naval air power, not least after July 1921, when Brigadier-General 'Billy' Mitchell in an aerial experiment bombed a sequestered German dreadnought, which sank in twenty-five minutes.

The Geddes Committee wanted to reduce the seven squadrons of the Fleet Air Arm to two; when the Admiralty and its friends, such as Sir Reginald Hall, wartime Director of Naval Intelligence and now MP, protested, another committee was set up to study RN–RAF cooperation. It took the form of a special sub-committee of the Committee of Imperial Defence, chaired by Lord Salisbury, Lord President of the Council in the short-lived Conservative government of Andrew Bonar Law, who had ousted Lloyd George's tired Liberal-led coalition in October 1922. The Salisbury Committee in turn delegated the task of examining air cooperation with the fleet to its Balfour Sub-Committee. The result was an agreement between Admiral Keyes, Deputy CNS, and Trenchard, Chief of Air Staff, whereby the Admiralty would determine the numbers of aircraft it needed and their performance, while the Air Ministry would be responsible for specifications and construction; the Admiralty would lay down its training requirements for aircrew but the RAF would be responsible for instruction. Service and maintenance aboard carriers would pass from RAF technicians to naval ones, while up to 70 per cent of officers in the Fleet Air Arm could be drawn from the Navy and Marines. Airborne observers at sea would all be naval officers.

Keyes had done well to extract major concessions from the claws of Trenchard in time for the arrival of the carrier conversions; but the Fleet Air Arm was still embroiled in a bureaucratic jungle dominated by the RAF, of which it constitutionally remained a part, and the Navy, with much justice, never shed its belief that the FAA was always at the back of the queue when it came to development, construction and equipment of aircraft. The consequences became clear in 1940–1. Meanwhile the American and Japanese navies held on to their own separate air arms in the teeth of competition from their respective army air forces. France and Italy did not acquire carriers during or between the two world wars; Germany started two but has never sailed a carrier. Each of these leading Continental powers acquired an autonomous air force between the wars.

The relative cheapness of ASDIC, as operated by the small new ASW branch, only encouraged the admirals to proclaim the imminent demise of the submarine as a strategic threat. The British did enjoy a world lead in underwater detection and built up a vitally important cadre of trained personnel between the wars; yet not one convoy-protection or other group exercise with ASDIC was ever conducted in the period. The equipment, whose American version was called SONAR (SOund NAvigation and Ranging), could not detect a submarine on the surface or in the immediate vicinity of the searching ship – but could detect all too easily such diversionary objects as shoals of herring or submerged wrecks.

In fighting the swing of the Geddes Axe the Admiralty went out of its way to insist that the war had proved the importance of convoy and therefore of escorts, but too many staff officers were still inclined to discount escort work as defensive, not quite manly and therefore infra dig. The painful lessons learned at the cost of millions of tons of shipping and cargo and many thousands of lives were written up at the end of the war by Commander Rollo Appleyard, RNVR, in an Admiralty Confidential Book called *The Elements of Convoy Defence in Submarine Warfare*. One of his many important findings was that larger convoys were safer than small ones. But no attempt was made to produce a staff history of the almost lost U-boat war for the benefit of new generations of officers; and Appleyard's analysis, almost universally unread, was regarded as so tedious that it was scrapped – in 1939. There were very few peacetime exercises involving surface ships and submarines together, and the British submarine service once again became a world apart.

The Admiralty in November 1923 approved a shipbuilding programme including the eight Treaty cruisers, three fleet submarines, two depot ships (one for destroyers, the other for submarines), a minelayer, two destroyers and a new carrier at a combined cost of £23m, to be spread over five years. The Treasury agreed; but in January 1924 Britain acquired its first Labour government, under Ramsay MacDonald. Within weeks another committee was set up to look at long-term construction of non-capital ships over the ensuing ten years. The first Labour naval estimates in March sanctioned only five of the eight Treaty cruisers and two destroyers as new construction. In November 1924 Stanley Baldwin, who had briefly succeeded Bonar Law on his death a year earlier, became Prime Minister again in a period of political instability and uncertainty, which was of no help at all to the Admiralty in its efforts to secure a long-term programme for the refurbishment and maintenance of the fleet. The Board's objective was a settled, ten-year programme and it put forward an amended version in spring 1925: the eight heavy cruisers, five fleet submarines, a 23,000-ton carrier plus destroyers and 300 aircraft.

Germany was brought into the international diplomatic disarmament circuit in autumn 1924 at the Locarno Conference in northern Italy, also attended by Mussolini, Italy's new Fascist leader, and by Britain, France and Belgium. The resulting treaty was signed in London in December, its main provision being the agreed immutability of Germany's borders with Belgium and France. Acceptance of this entitled Germany to join the League of Nations with a seat on its Council, which duly took place in 1927. The treaty also reaffirmed the disarmament provisions of Versailles, which the uneasy German democracy of the Weimar Republic was already busy undermining with secret submarine development and plans for the rebirth of the Navy, a trend encouraged by the appointment in 1928 of Vice-Admiral Erich Raeder as head of the service.

Back in Britain, that staunch defender of the one-power standard, Winston Churchill, was now Chancellor of the Exchequer in the Baldwin government and took the view that the country could not afford extra naval expenditure, especially the ship replacement programme. Beatty, still First Sea Lord, did his best to defend it. Yet another committee, a Cabinet one under Lord Birkenhead, was set up in March to investigate. In July 1925 Baldwin announced the results: seven cruisers to be laid down in 1925–6, and one light cruiser with its flotilla of eight destroyers together with six submarines in 1927–8. Similar numbers of destroyers and submarines would be started annually until 1929–30, by which time a general election would be due. The total cost of this revised building programme would be £58m, spread over seven years.

The wrangle over air power was still going on between the Admiralty and the Air Ministry, to such an extent that even the supremely bland Baldwin was moved to remark that 'the liaison between them had not hitherto been as close as might be desired'. In July 1926 he reaffirmed the existing principles that the RAF should raise, train and maintain the Fleet Air Arm, which was under naval control at sea; and that naval officers would continue to supply 70 per cent of officers in the FAA, which, however, was not to run shore establishments. The Admiralty failed to acquire permanent operational control of Coastal Command, the RAF's shore-based maritime section; the Air Ministry would only concede temporary naval control over specific operations. Baldwin merely urged a spirit of 'cooperation rather than strict subordination' on the rival services. The Americans meanwhile in 1925 came down firmly against centralizing authority over aviation and determined that only naval officer-pilots should command carriers and naval air stations ashore (which produced some remarkably ancient candidates for 'wings' among ambitious senior officers, including the future fleet admirals King and Halsey). Small wonder that the disparity in both quantity and quality between the two leading navies in aviation grew exponentially, to the Americans' advantage.

Germany was present in June 1927 when the next attempt at naval and general disarmament opened at the League of Nations in Geneva. The principal naval question was cruisers. The Americans proposed a ceiling of 300,000 tons for each of the two leading navies, but Britain wanted a special exemption for policing her empire. The Japanese disingenuously proposed an indefinite naval holiday (having already built very powerful cruisers well in excess of the Washington 10,000-ton limit since 1924). The British now suggested a 7,500-ton limit on future cruisers, proposing seventy for themselves, forty-seven for the USA and twenty-one for Japan (10:7:3). The Americans stuck to the 10,000-ton limit and a tonnage ceiling of 300,000, which would have left Britain with little more than half the number she required. The conference broke up in August without agreement.

But the International Treaty for the Renunciation of War (the Kellogg–Briand Pact), signed in Paris a year later by fifteen nations including the three future Axis powers, and later by forty-seven others, improved the general diplomatic climate and raised hopes of progress on disarmament. The central undertaking was to outlaw aggressive war. The consequences of the Wall Street crash in October 1929 would also encourage arms limitation as government revenues sank amid high unemployment. Another incentive was the arrival in the White House of a Quaker President, Herbert Hoover, and the return to Downing Street of Ramsay MacDonald of the Labour Party with its idealistic dedication to disarmament.

The latter leader called the London Naval Conference in 1930, attended by the five leading maritime powers. For this occasion the British and Americans abandoned their rivalry and presented a united front on the vexed question of cruisers. Britain was ready to accept fifty instead of seventy, while the Americans went for eighteen Washington Treaty cruisers and nineteen in a lighter, 7,500 ton, 6-inch gun category, of which the British would have thirty-two to add to their eight 10,000-tonners. Japan almost sank the conference with its intransigent demand for a 10:10:7 cruiser ratio instead of the proposed 5:5:3 (the difference represented three heavy or four light cruisers and reflected actual or planned construction in Japan), but was prevailed upon to accept 5:5:3 in heavy while gaining 10:10:7 in light cruisers.

Destroyers were also limited in armament (5-inch guns) and individual tonnages (1,500, except 3,850 for flotilla-leaders) for the first time; the Anglo-Americans were restricted to 150 each and the Japanese to 100. The 'naval holiday' was extended for six years (except for replacement and modernization) and the three strongest fleets limited their dreadnoughts to fifteen each for RN and USN but ten for the IJN, a gain of one battleship over 5:5:3 for Japan. The big three accepted equality in submarine tonnage, if not in numbers, of 52,700 (no more than 2,000 tons for an individual boat) with a 130mm (5.1-inch) limit on their guns. This parity was another gain for Japan. France once again vetoed the third Anglo-American attempt to ban submarines, which were naively re-subjected to Prize Rules. Thanks to the general obsession with the big gun, nobody seems to have considered a more flexible, general tariff whereby a power might have been allowed to trade a capital ship or two for an agreed number of smaller warships, an idea which could have been of use to Britain with its unique imperial and commercial priorities. But for better or worse the London Naval Treaty was signed on 22 April 1930, to expire at the same time as the Washington pact, in 1936. Perhaps its most important result was the end of the sometimes sharp antagonism between the British and the Americans. The relative moderation and flexibility shown by the Japanese, however, did not long survive this last general success in naval arms limitation before 1939.

7

Rearmament

The General Disarmament Conference which was the long-delayed legacy of Versailles started at Geneva in February 1932. By the time it adjourned in June 1934, without agreement and never to reconvene, the world situation had changed drastically. The British and Americans put forward various proposals, inter alia, for naval arms reductions while the Germans demanded equal rights, which in this context meant the cancellation of the Versailles limitations. These had already been massively breached, not only by the Nazis who took power democratically in January 1933, but also by the last Weimar governments, which had been experimenting with tanks and aircraft in the Soviet Union from 1926.

Developments in Germany had been causing alarm at the Admiralty since no later than 1928, when Raeder took office as Chief of the Naval Command and was promoted to full admiral. The naval estimates for that year included money for *Panzerschiff A* (armoured ship), a cruiser nominally of 10,000 tons (actually 13,000) in deference to the Versailles limit, but classed as experimental to justify its six 11-inch guns in two triple turrets, fore and aft, truly massive main armament for a cruiser. This turned out to be the first of three in a class named 'pocket-battleships' by the British, who correctly assumed that they could only be intended as commerce raiders. The Royal Navy had only three ships that could both outgun and outrun them – the battlecruisers *Hood*, *Repulse* and *Renown* (now foolishly classed as fast battleships despite their relatively light armour).

The Japanese and the Italians were also engaged in heavy naval building programmes. In their calculations about Italy, with its expansionist designs in North and East Africa, the Admiralty now had no Austrian fleet to worry about and could still look to the entente with France and its own Mediterranean Fleet. But Japan, an ally in the war, was ruled by an ambitious and aggressive military junta with plans for regional expansion and domination which were soon recognized as a threat to European (British, French, Dutch) imperial possessions throughout the Far East and Pacific. American interests in the Philippines and the Pacific, sometimes indistinguishable from colonies but never to be described as such, were equally menaced by Japanese expansionism, as were Western stakes in China. The Americans controlled the Panama Canal and could concentrate their naval forces in the Pacific without abandoning the Atlantic; the British with their one-ocean, Atlantic Navy could not afford to station heavy naval forces so far from Europe, any more than they could before 1914.

Faced after the war with the choice between their brief understanding with Japan and their permanent need to be on good terms with an inexorably rising and powerful United States across the Atlantic, the British sensibly and inevitably chose the latter. But they still wanted to have their cake and eat it, which meant action had to be taken to protect the vast British Empire in Asia from Japan, something the Americans as professed anti-imperialists made it absolutely clear they would not do. The instrument eventually chosen was bluff, which was no more effective against the Japanese generals than it was against the Nazis or the Italian Fascists. At great expense (£60m) the British expanded and modernized their naval facilities, including the dockyards, at Singapore as a base – 'the Gibraltar of the Orient' – for a squadron of capital ships which was to be sent out to 'deter' the Japanese if necessary. This project was completed in 1938. The Imperial Japanese Navy, ship for ship the world's strongest and with the world's most formidable naval air arm, had been outbuilding the British and the Americans alike since 1917, and enjoyed the advantage of comparatively short lines of communication. Tokyo was as immune to bluster as Hitler when he turned his acquisitive eye on Germany's eastern neighbours. Bluff and the spirit of compromise shown by the war-weary European democracies were no answer to the absolute intransigence and insatiability of the totalitarian regimes, untrammelled appeasement still less so.

From the pivotal year of 1933, if no earlier, Britain with her one-ocean fleet was forced to contemplate the possibility of being dragged into a three-ocean war, and in that year abandoned the 'ten-year rule', invented by Churchill when Chancellor of the Exchequer (1924–9): the assumption had been annually renewed that there would be no war for a decade (a device not to be confused with the ten-year naval holiday agreed at Washington). The Germans had played no part at Geneva from September 1932; in May 1933, four months after Hitler took over, they gave two years' notice of renunciation of the Versailles armament restrictions; in October they officially departed from the Geneva Conference and shortly afterwards left the League of Nations itself. Japan had already walked out of the League in May, after being condemned as the aggressor in Manchuria which it had occupied, putting it in a strategic position to move against Soviet or Chinese territory. Having won the presidential election for the Democrats in November 1932, Franklin D. Roosevelt moved into the White House in March 1933 with plans for economic recovery that also foreshadowed a massive naval construction programme. More modestly, Britain stretched its cruiser ratio by building a new light category of 5,000-ton ship with 6-inch guns within the overall tonnage ceiling. From 1932 ASDIC was fitted to all destroyers and other relevant categories of ship (such as sloops, ideal for escort work and earmarked for it).

The burdens foisted on the Admiralty by political problems both diplomatic and domestic, involving grand strategy and petty squabbling with the Air Ministry alike, were matched by largely self-imposed internal stresses and strains. The parlous state of the economy played the leading role, exacerbated by short-sightedness, false economy and abysmal man-management. The postwar improvements in pay, allowances and conditions precipitated by widespread disaffection and sometimes unrest in the fleet were followed by the lower pay scales of 1925; in 1927 officers' pay went down by 6 per cent to reflect a fall in the cost of living. This was not altogether a clever move as the previous year had seen Britain's greatest civil upheaval of the century, the General Strike of 1926, which, among many other things, threw the antiquated class system into sharp relief and affected the national psyche. For the next two generations the British were obsessed with strikes, the great fear of the ruling class, especially in the armed forces, and the most effective if also blunt instrument of the lower orders for extracting economic and social improvements, particularly from Labour politicians, who first tasted power in the 1920s.

The enduring economic crisis triggered by Wall Street in 1929 sank into the Slump of the 1930s as unemployment in Britain approached the three million mark. Another swingeing review of government expenditure on the Geddes model was carried out in 1929 by the May Committee, which with dreary inevitability proposed large cuts in public-sector pay, including that of the services. On 1 September the Baldwin government accepted its recommendations. The main effect on the Navy was to impose a pay cut across the board, which meant that the 72 per cent of ratings on the 1919 scale were reduced to the 1925 one on October 1, despite that year's apparent guarantee that the differential would apply to them as long as they stayed in the service. Some 94 per cent of officers were affected by this and married men were particularly hard hit. The result was the worst unrest in the fleet for more than 130 years.

Admiral Sir Michael Hodges, C-in-C Atlantic Fleet, had fallen ill early in September, temporarily handing over to Rear-Admiral Wilfred Tomkinson, Flag Officer of the Battlecruiser Squadron. Tomkinson arrived in the Cromarty Firth on 11 September with HMS *Hood* (flag) and the *Repulse*, plus five battleships, three cruisers and a minelayer, to prepare for an exercise on the 15th. The ships anchored in two parallel lines off Invergordon on the 11th and the pay cuts were announced on Saturday the 12th. Although the general reduction was said to be 10 per cent overall, the Admiralty crudely reduced all rates by one shilling a day. This meant a 25 per cent cut for an able seaman, from 4s to 3s, but 10 per cent for a sub-lieutenant, from 10s to 9s. Pension entitlements were also cut and only short notice was given. The fact that seamen learned of the cuts from the press rather than the Admiralty compounded the sense of grievance.

Meetings were held on the lower decks and in canteens ashore. The widespread anger among the 8,000 men on the anchored ships was channelled and stoked up by 'agitators' from the lowest ranks – able seamen and a few leading seamen and marines, men with typically ten or more years' service. No outsiders were involved. The most prominent spokesman was Able Seaman Len Wincott, aged twenty-four, of the heavy cruiser HMS *Norfolk*; the fieriest speaker was A/B Bond from the new battleship *Rodney*. Tomkinson foolishly decided to carry on with the exercise, which collapsed in confusion when some ships were unable to sail, while others had to return shortly after leaving. On three ships the crews refused duty altogether. The Admiralty ordered all vessels to disperse to their home ports in the south of England on the afternoon of the 15th; local weekend leave was given on arrival, which helped to put an end to the Invergordon Mutiny.

The damage to the Royal Navy's reputation at home and abroad, and that of Britain as a whole, was incalculable. The role of sailors in the Russian and German revolutions only a few years earlier was recalled by a frightened establishment. Sterling's recent, disastrous return to the gold standard, masterminded by Churchill as Chancellor and a recipe for pricing British industry out of world markets in the middle of the Depression, was abandoned within a week of the Atlantic Fleet's revolt, and the pound fell almost 30 per cent against the dollar. The unrest was confined, as it had been in Germany in 1918, to the big ships; the destroyers and submarines at Rosyth and elsewhere were not affected because morale was higher and officers and ratings knew each other better (two intimately related facts). Nor were ships on foreign stations, where there was time for commanders to familiarize themselves with the reasoning behind the cuts and to explain them to crews out of reach of immediate news from home. The only overseas exception was the cruiser *Delhi*, now flagship of the North America and West Indies station, where a mutiny was faced down without injury.

Mr Baldwin told Parliament on 21 September that public sector pay cuts would be limited to 10 per cent in all individual cases. Naval men on the 1919 rate would lose this much but those on the 1925 scale would not be affected at all. A special fund was set up for the large number of married ratings under twenty-five who were especially hard hit. The Navy's battlefleet was restyled the Home Fleet (the Atlantic designation was abolished) and got a new C-in-C, the popular Admiral Sir John Kelly, who led it to sea on its delayed autumn cruise after offloading the ringleaders and paying a long, personal visit to each lower deck. All 124 identified Invergordon mutineers were amnestied, although twenty-four who rebelled later at Devonport were dismissed. A/B Wincott took up residence in Moscow.

The failure of leadership at Invergordon was reflected not so much by Kelly's relief of the genuinely sick Hodges but rather by the censure of Tomkinson, soon followed by his retirement, and the replacement of seven captains. The real culprits were to be found at the Admiralty, which had once again failed to put up a fight in Whitehall and had completely lost touch with, or simply ignored, lower-deck sentiment. There had been warnings of discontent over pay and conditions prior to the May Committee's proposals, most notably a mutiny on HMS *Lucia*, a submarine depot-ship at Devonport, eighteen months before Invergordon, against the bullying discipline aboard. The officers were reprimanded and a few ringleaders jailed while the ship was paid off and the crew dispersed.

Promotion for ratings and officers alike in a shrunken Navy had become inordinately slow and there were too many officers with too much time for creating rather than solving problems, as well as an excess of dead wood near the top. Bernard Collard, the lieutenant whose harshness had led to unrest at Portsmouth Barracks in 1906, had nevertheless managed by 1928 to rise to rear-admiral of the battle squadron in the Mediterranean Fleet. Even the captain and the commander of his flagship, HMS *Royal Oak*, could not stomach his bullying; the former complained to the C-in-C, Admiral Keyes, when Collard publicly called him incompetent, while the latter was merely amazed when the rear-admiral, at a ship's dance, lost his temper with the Royal Marine bandmaster, who rejoiced in the surname Barnacle. Keyes suspended Collard but his captain and commander were court-martialled for 'subversion' and dismissed their ship with severe reprimands. The hugely embarrassing affair provided the press at home and abroad with a rich feast and cost Keyes his chance of promotion to First Sea Lord.

Seven years after that officer had come to terms with Trenchard of the RAF about the Fleet Air Arm, inter-service differences over naval aviation were once again coming to a head in the Navy's nadir year of 1931, when Rear-Admiral Reginald Henderson of convoy fame was appointed the first Flag Officer, Aircraft Carriers. He was able to streamline the FAA and make some improvements on carriers but could not overcome the stifling restrictions placed by the RAF on naval aircraft development and supply, aware as he was of how far the British had already fallen behind the Americans and the Japanese. When the inflexible and ill First Sea Lord, Admiral Sir Frederick Field, made way for Admiral Ernle Chatfield in 1933, the struggle for control of naval aviation entered its final inter-war phase. Chatfield demanded an autonomous naval air force, arguing that flying had become very sophisticated and maritime operations required specialist skills. He threatened to resign if he did not get one, a card no senior admiral had dared to play hitherto in the destructive aeronautical tug-of-war. In July the Air Ministry was forced to retreat, surrendering the Fleet Air Arm in its entirety to the Navy from 1 January 1937, though keeping control of RAF Coastal Command, which was to 'cooperate' with the Navy as before.

But for the first time the FAA was allowed to open and operate five land-based naval air stations under the control of their own flag officer, and 1,500 RAF officers serving with the fleet volunteered to transfer to the Navy. Rear-Admiral J. H. D. Cunningham was given charge of naval aviation on the Admiralty Board as Director of Naval Air Services. A Naval Air Branch was set up in 1938 to recruit and train aircrew and the RN Volunteer Reserve got its own air branch. This was the Navy's most important Whitehall triumph since the separation of the Royal Air Force from the two older services twenty years earlier; but it did not open the way to a revolution because time did not permit one. The principal aircraft of the Fleet Air Arm by the time war broke out again was the Swordfish, a very reliable but obsolete and agonizingly slow (100-knot) biplane which had to serve in three main roles, torpedo-bombing, gunnery spotting and reconnaissance, and was known to all as the 'Stringbag'. As a fighter the Navy adopted the tiny Martlet. The most graphic measure of the disaster inflicted on the Navy by the Air Ministry is the fact that the FAA had 423 aircraft on the outbreak of war whereas the US Navy had 2,000, all more modern. What was worse, the Navy had no strategy and only the most rudimentary and patchy tactics for the use of its handful of undersized and obsolescent carriers.

From its numerical low point of 91,500 men in 1931–3 the Navy expanded to 99,000 in 1935 and 119,000 in 1936 (134,000 in 1938–9). In 1934 half the 1931 pay cut of 10 per cent was restored and in 1938 ratings' marriage allowances were raised: junior officers' pay was stingily cut by 2s a day to finance an unprecedented marriage allowance for officers over thirty; and the mean practice of keeping temporarily unemployed officers on a half-pay string was abolished at the same time. The WRNS was re-established too, with 3,000 women in service by late 1939.

From the end of 1929 to 1935 Ramsay MacDonald was Prime Minister again, first heading a Labour administration and then, after the 1931 general election, a crisis coalition, the National Government, in which the main element was Conservative. Growing international tensions led it to launch in 1934 the biggest naval construction programme since the war: a carrier (*Ark Royal*), four cruisers, nine destroyers, six sloops and three submarines. The

Americans made this look like small change with their 1934 New Deal programme of one carrier, seven battleships, seven cruisers, eighty-nine destroyers and thirty-seven submarines. While the Japanese all but took the year off (two carrier conversions, two destroyers and one submarine) after their huge, fifteen-year postwar naval expansion drive, the Italians ordered two battleships, two cruisers and four destroyers, compared with one battlecruiser and eleven destroyers for France. The resurgent Germans ordered two battleships (classed by their speed as battlecruisers in Britain), *Scharnhorst* and *Gneisenau*, one cruiser, nine destroyers and – unbeknown to the rest of the world – twelve submarines. Henceforward in the last years of peace Britain would outbuild every other major naval power, but without a hope of matching the triple threat from Germany, Italy and Japan.

Hitler's denunciation of Versailles took effect in May 1935. In the following month Britain fell for his 'offer' in the Reichstag of 21 May, during a speech in which he raucously proclaimed his eternally peaceful intent, to 'limit' the new German Navy to 35 per cent of the British. To attain this would have entailed a decade of profligacy but the disingenuous offer was enough to detach London from the united front hitherto preserved by the Versailles victors. The Anglo-German Naval Agreement was concluded in June and marked the demise of Versailles as a brake on Germany. The Germans were allowed five battleships (placing them in the third category of naval powers as defined by the 1930 ratio of 5:3:1.65), twenty-one cruisers and sixty-four destroyers (a total tonnage never attained even in wartime) but were permitted 45 per cent of British submarine strength, with one proviso: that in time of danger they would be entitled to parity! Thus in 1939 Germany had fifty-seven submarines to Britain's fifty-eight.

One more attempt was made at general naval disarmament, in 1935. With the expiry of the Washington and London treaties at the end of the following year in mind, the British invited the leading naval powers to London in November, by which time Baldwin was Prime Minister again. Deadlock was reached within days: Japan withdrew in January 1936, rejecting any new limits and reaffirming its intent to renounce the treaties at the end of the year, as notified in 1934. Germany was not invited because the French were furious about the Anglo-German agreement and the scuttling of Versailles, and would not negotiate with the Nazis, to the discomfiture of the hosts. Once again France vetoed a British proposal to outlaw submarines. But a copy of the draft treaty was sent to Berlin. In general the results of the ill-omened conference were slim. There were minor adjustments to carrier and cruiser ceilings; battleships, on Washington's initiative, were allowed 16-inch guns; the 2,000-ton limit on individual submarines was retained, as was the overall tonnage limit of 52,700, regardless of numbers of boats; and there was to be no new construction between 8,000 and 17,000 tons (to stop the spread of super-cruisers on the 'pocket-battleship' model).

But a promising special protocol, open to all nations, was added to the otherwise toothless London Naval Agreement accepted by America, Britain and France in 1936: a complete ban on unrestricted submarine warfare against merchant shipping from July 1937. Japan and Germany were among the forty nations that subscribed to this by the end of the year. But in September 1935, within three months of the Anglo-German agreement and in a spectacular publicity coup, the German Navy unveiled its new First Flotilla of three coastal U-boats under their freshly appointed commandant, Captain Karl Dönitz. Germany's first post-Versailles submarines had been built under cover and thus appeared to spring fully armed from the brow of Hitler. A dozen were in service by the end of 1936, and when war broke out no U-boat was more than four years old. Italy had 115 boats and France 77 by 1939; the US Navy had 112 when it went to war at the end of 1941, by which time Japan had 64.

After abandoning the disastrous 'K' class and expressing over-confidence in ASDIC by foolishly scrapping the 'R'-class ASW boats, the British built in three general categories in the 1930s: coastal, medium and ocean-going. The 'S' (*Swordfish*) class of medium boats meant for the North Sea proved sturdy and reliable at 715/1,000 tons and fifteen knots surfaced; thirteen were completed by 1938, with twenty-six still on order. The mainstay of the wartime flotillas was to be the 'T' (*Triton*) ocean-going class of twenty-four boats, of 1,320/1,523 tons; three of the latest 'U' (*Ursula*) class, cheap but reliable coastal boats of 540/730 tons, were commissioned in 1938 for the Mediterranean and twelve more were ordered in 1939.

The third member of the 'T' class to be completed was His Majesty's Submarine *Thetis*, which left the Cammell Laird yard at Birkenhead on Merseyside at lunchtime on 1 June 1939 for a second round of sea trials. The first, two months before, had revealed teething troubles with her diving and steering gear. Commander Guy Bolus, RN, had a crew of fifty-two aboard, plus fifty experts and technicians from the Navy and the yard. It was a highly unusual overload but the plan was to complete the reinspection within a day. Thirty-eight miles out of Liverpool along the North Wales coast Bolus signalled his intention to the accompanying tug *Grebecock* to submerge for three hours. The boat at first appeared reluctant to dive, her conning tower remaining above the surface for more than half an hour before her bow came up briefly in a large gout of air and the boat sank quickly out of sight. She was supposed to fire a signal flare when she reached sixty feet but failed to do so. Half an hour after she was due back on the surface the alarm was raised.

A small swarm of destroyers and other vessels with Coastal Command aircraft turned out, eventually sighting the stern of the *Thetis* protruding from the water fourteen miles offshore at breakfast time on the 2nd, just four miles from where she had last been seen. A destroyer dropped small charges to reveal her presence and two officers came to the surface from an escape hatch only twenty feet below the surface. They revealed that the submarine's eight forward torpedo tubes had been left empty instead of filled with water as extra ballast. A lieutenant had checked them one by one; when he came to the fifth, he concluded from an indicator dial that the tube's bow-cap was closed. But it was not. Therefore when he opened the inboard loading cap a great jet of water crashed into the compartment. Ratings could not close the watertight door because a nut jammed. Yet everyone was able to retreat behind the second watertight bulkhead and seal the door in it from inboard. But by then the boat had plunged bow first and embedded its prow in the mud 160 feet down, at an angle of forty degrees.

Each of the two escape compartments could be used by only two at a time, at half-hourly intervals and with high expenditure of much-needed air from within the hull. After the two officers had used the forward outer hatch to escape, residual water in the compartment fell back into the inclined boat when the inner hatch was opened, causing a short circuit and a small fire, quickly put out but not before it had consumed more priceless oxygen. Two more men got out via the escape hatch aft, but the remaining ninety-nine were asphyxiated amid incompetence, indecision and ignorance among the would-be rescuers, who lacked expert leadership, training and special equipment. A misguided attempt to lift the boat by the raised stern failed disastrously when a cable snapped and the *Thetis* sank out of sight. Those on the surface were reduced to hammering 'come out' in Morse code on the hull: answer came there none. Nobody seems to have thought of sending down a diver with an air hose. Hope was abandoned on 3 June amid massive media and public concern.

The four survivors told the inquiry what had gone wrong: the needles to show that bow-caps were closed pointed to the right for the starboard four tubes but leftward for port. The misreading had been made at the fifth tube. Further, the tiny hole that should have let water into the test-cock on that tube to show it was flooded had been blocked by paint and the indicator was stuck on 'dry'. *Thetis* had been lost to a designer's misplaced love of symmetry and a drop of gloss paint. The thirteenth British submarine sunk between the wars was salvaged and recommissioned as HMS *Thunderbolt* in April 1940. Sadly she sank again and for ever, with all hands, when depth-charged by an Italian destroyer near Malta in March 1943.

Technology continued to advance in the twenty-one years of tenuous and far from universal peace, but not with the breakneck pace or revolutionary manner of the period before 1914. The big gun and its dreadnought platform, the mine, the torpedo, the bomb and the depth charge, the submarine, the aircraft and its carrier had indeed improved, mightily in some cases, but none was new. The fixation on the big gun was as strong as ever, but even that had one positive effect, affording officers a period of calm and continuity rather than upheaval, whatever might have been going on below decks, ashore or outside the introverted world-unto-itself of a cash-strapped Senior Service. ASDIC was untried in battle but a cadre of specialists had enjoyed two decades of practice with the equipment.

No navy in 1939 had surface-scanning radar (the Germans used it for aiming guns). The sets were still too bulky for horizontal use on ships. Its first British application at sea, as on land, was to detect aircraft. If any single technical advance can be said to have 'won the war' – an untenable over-simplification – radar is the prime candidate, starting with the Battle of Britain and culminating in the Battle of the Atlantic. But it was only one of many factors. Some important lessons at least had been remembered from the Great War and did not have to be repeated: Admiral Manisty had been at work from 1936 on recreating the worldwide convoy organization he pioneered in 1917; a tiny core of naval cryptanalysts at the Government Code and Cipher School (GC & CS, parent of today's Government Communications Headquarters, GCHQ) had managed to continue attacking foreign ciphers throughout the postwar cuts and the Depression; and Whitehall had filed the names of tens of thousands of scientists and others with high technical qualifications to ensure they were not swept up in the coming mobilization as they had been in 1914–18.

On the outbreak of war the Royal Navy had 165 destroyers, thirty-five sloops and others plus twenty trawlers operational, a total of 220 vessels equipped with ASDIC and therefore suitable for ASW escort. But the destroyers were needed for all sorts of other work as well, such as protecting the twelve battleships, three battlecruisers, seven aircraft- and two seaplane carriers in the fleet, which also had sixty-two cruisers and nearly forty armed merchant cruisers on its books. Their first enemy, the Germans, apart from fifty-seven U-boats, started the war with two battlecruisers, three pocket-battleships and four heavy and four light cruisers, all capable of causing havoc among commerce, plus twenty-five destroyers and thirty-seven torpedo boats (small, high-speed destroyers mostly known as 'E-boats' to the British). Two super-battleships were building.

The vast majority of British capital ships – all but two – had been commissioned or at least ordered during the First World War, although they had all been modernized at least once (five more battleships were ordered in 1939). Something similar could be said of their admirals, who had been captains or lieutenants in 1914–18 and therefore had first-hand experience of wartime conditions, if not always of action, to a man – an advantage denied to the previous generation of naval commanders. The Navy was now run by a properly trained staff and its operational chief, the First Sea Lord, was ex-officio Chief of Naval Staff; the admirals of 1939 were generally superior in quality to those of 1914 (which did not mean that all deserved their gold braid; far from it).

Chatfield, having supervised the start of the naval rearmament programme from 1934, was succeeded as First Sea Lord in November 1938 by Admiral Sir Roger Backhouse, a most able gunnery specialist but an incorrigible centralizer of command incapable of delegating, who resigned due to ill-health, thought to have been brought on by overwork, in June 1939 (he died of a brain tumour a month later). Nonetheless he influenced the outcome of the war with Germany considerably by ensuring that Vice-Admiral Bertram Ramsay, a supremely efficient administrative specialist with long experience of staffwork, was earmarked for the post of Flag Officer at Dover in the event of hostilities. Ramsay, chief of staff to Backhouse when the latter was Home Fleet C-in-C, appeared to have committed professional suicide when he resigned his post in 1935, and ultimately left the service, because he was not given any real work to do.

The Navy lost another Fisher (unrelated) – Admiral Sir William Wordsworth Fisher – in 1937; this outstanding successor to Chatfield in the Mediterranean command from 1932–6, widely regarded as a tactical genius to compare with his namesake, had gone from there to Portsmouth as C-in-C. He had moved his fleet headquarters to Alexandria in Egypt in 1935 because Malta was in easy reach by air from Italy, which was aggressively seeking to acquire an empire in Abyssinia in defiance of international opinion. Fisher, variously nicknamed 'W. W. ' or 'the great Agrippa' after the Roman naval commander who twice defeated Pompey, was expected to succeed Backhouse in the top post until his sudden death at sixty-two. In the same year another outstanding admiral, the deputy C-in-C in the Mediterranean, Sir Geoffrey Blake, was invalided out of the Navy after an accident.

Fisher's successor in the Mediterranean, Sir Dudley Pound, was promoted Admiral of the Fleet and became First Sea Lord and Chief of Naval Staff by default on the premature departure of Backhouse. Not only was the new operational chief already sixty-two; he also had an arthritic hip which caused him to limp in constant pain. He had been a competent captain of a dreadnought at Jutland but resembled his then C-in-C, Jellicoe, in his capacity for anxiety and inability to delegate; he was also stubborn, narrow-minded and obsessed with detail. The man who relieved Pound in summer 1939 as C-in-C in the Mediterranean, on the other hand, was the right man in the right post at the right time: Admiral Sir Andrew Browne Cunningham, known from his initials as A.B.C. (not to be confused with his brother J. H. D., met above as chief of Naval Air Services). He returned at the age of fifty five the dash of the destroyer commander he had been in the First World War and was the most popular admiral in the service, despite being a hard taskmaster to his staff and his captains. The C-in-C of the Home

Fleet, the Royal Navy's principal formation in 1939, was Admiral Sir Charles Forbes, a gifted but reserved figure who lacked the rare inspirational quality of a Cunningham yet was of strong character, exuding taciturn calm in the almost constant crisis that was to be his lot in wartime.

Disarmament having failed by 1933, the deterioration of the international scene accelerated. Japan had installed a puppet regime in Manchuria in 1931 and set out to dominate neighbouring northern China thereafter. The objective of the generals in charge of the expansionist empire was autarky, or economic self-sufficiency, the absence of which in Germany in 1914 they, just like Hitler, selectively identified as the main reason for the fall of the Second Reich in 1918. The junta therefore wanted to acquire the vast natural resources which Japan lacked but which China, the Soviet Union and the West's colonies in east Asia, such as the Dutch East Indies with their oil, possessed in abundance. The irony in all this was that in order to achieve their goal by conquest the Japanese had to raise to unprecedented levels the very imports of strategic raw materials that the desired autarky was meant to render unnecessary. American economic sanctions, prompted by US jealousy of Japanese designs on China, led the junta to choose a southward, maritime expansion strategy, towards the Philippines, Indochina and the East Indies, rather than the northern, landward option against the Soviet Union.

In Europe two powers were bent on expansion: Italy invaded Abyssinia (Ethiopia) in October 1935, earning international condemnation. Mussolini later admitted that had the British closed the Suez Canal to his shipping, the entire adventure would have collapsed in a matter of days. Hitler meanwhile was bent on *Lebensraum*, recovering every metre of territory lost in 1918 plus a large swathe of Slav territory so as to make a Greater Germany self-sufficient and immune to blockade. But by this time appeasement of the Fascists and the Nazis was in full swing in Britain and France, whose leaders were generally and under-standably horrified by the prospect of another monstrous slaughter in Europe. Many of them were survivors of the mud and blood of the Western Front, since which such weapons as the tank and the bomber had achieved destructive capabilities scarcely imaginable in 1918. The desire to avoid a new European war by all means was popular and not at all dishonourable in itself. Unfortunately the dictators in Tokyo, Rome and Berlin were bullies, immune to bluster and appeals to the better nature they so totally lacked. The Axis powers were also much better at threats and bluff than the democracies. Appeasement reached its nadir in September 1938, when Czechoslovakia was thrown to the Nazi wolves by the British and French at Munich. The ensuing backlash in the Western democracies led to the Anglo-French offer of an unfulfillable guarantee to Poland, next on Hitler's list, making war inevitable when the Führer's last bluff was called a year later. In January 1939 Britain promised to send an expeditionary force to France on the 1914 model if Germany invaded.

The Royal Navy was placed on full alert in the tension that followed the Munich Agreement, a move which disrupted rearmament and reorganization but usefully revealed many flaws in mobilization procedures and the state of readiness of the fleet. A fortunate result was that many of these weaknesses were remedied or at least identified by the outbreak of war a year later. It was no less fortunate that determination to maintain the One-Power Standard led to an unprecedented postwar shipbuilding pro- gramme drawn up in 1934 and implemented from 1936, when the RAF also began to rearm seriously. Roosevelt's first massive peacetime naval programme was until 1938 almost certainly a stronger challenge and incentive for the British than Hitler's.

From 1936 the Spanish Civil War served as a laboratory for the Italian and German forces sent in to help their Fascist ally Franco overturn the legitimate leftist republican government in Madrid. The democracies denounced this intervention but failed to oppose it effectively. While the Royal Navy's patrols made no impression on the streams of troops and munitions flowing into Spain from Germany and Italy on the one hand and Russia on the other, the Home Fleet, watching the Atlantic coast, and the Mediterranean Fleet, on the far side of Spain, made an enormous humanitarian contribution to the alleviation of the immense civilian suffering caused by a very bloody conflict. British destroyers and other warships took untold thousands of refugees to safety in France over two and a half years – and got some useful practice evading bombs and torpedoes close inshore as well as listening for submarines on their ASDIC sets. The Admiralty's new Operational Intelligence Centre (OIC), inaugurated in June 1937 under Lieutenant-Commander Norman Denning, RN, kept track of foreign shipping off Spain and pressed for more 'Y' interception and direction-finding stations; the Naval Section at GC & CS under Commander Alastair Denniston, RN, a Room 40 veteran, profitably studied wireless traffic.

Britain had ordered two new battleships in 1936 and three more in 1937 (plus two carriers and seven cruisers in each year and a total of thirty-four destroyers, twelve sloops and fifteen submarines); the 1938 estimates included a carrier, seven cruisers and three each of cruisers and minelayers. The last peacetime estimates in 1939 added another carrier, two cruisers, a minelayer, sixteen destroyers – and seventy-eight escort vessels.

Hindsight enables us to conclude that the last item was the most important, reflecting a belated realization at the Admiralty that insurance should be taken out against the new U-boats, despite the general belief, as in 1914, that surface raiders were the main threat to Britain's uniquely vulnerable merchant fleet. However, all the construction during the naval rearmament period of the late thirties had caused a shortage of turbine blades in Britain, which meant that the Navy could not have anything like as many des-troyers as it might have wished, even with unlimited funds. The ideal convoy escort was the sloop, a smaller vessel (about 1,200 tons) which had already proved itself in this role in 1917–18. But this type too needed turbine blades for its engines. The last-minute rush for escorts included just two sloops and twenty vaguely described 'escort vessels' – the future 1,500-ton, twenty-six knot '*Hunt*'-class escort destroyer that was to prove invaluable. As sixteen fleet destroyers had been included in the 1939 programme on top of the thirty-four in the previous two years, the Admiralty did not wish to make unnecessary waves in Parliament by categorizing the new escort type as a destroyer, however small.

Shortage of time, funds – and turbine blades – led to a special order for a new category of escort, in the shape of fifty-six 'corvettes'. These were adapted from an 1895 whalecatcher design originated by Smith's Dock of Middlesbrough, a 925-ton vessel powered by old-fashioned coal-fired reciprocating engines capable of just sixteen knots – slower than a U-boat could travel on the surface. But they were simple, sturdy and safe in rough seas, even if they rolled uncomfortably and shipped water constantly in heavy weather (a fault eliminated in later batches by raising and lengthening the bow section). They were intended for coastal escort work, but the wartime destroyer shortage until 1943 forced the

Navy to fall back on these humble workhorses to escort ocean-going shipping. The Canadians and even the US Atlantic Fleet also deployed them for want of anything better. Britain's corvettes, like Great War sloops all bearing the names of sometimes outlandish flowers, saw to it that the coming maritime fight for survival was not lost for the want of a turbine blade.

8

War on One Front

The bulk of the Home Fleet left Scapa Flow on 31 August 1939 to search the waters between Scotland, Iceland and Norway for inbound German shipping, ordered by a worldwide radio appeal on the 27th to come home, or else to seek shelter in friendly or neutral ports, 'within the next four days'. Admiral Sir Charles Forbes had five battleships, *Nelson*, *Rodney*, *Ramillies*, *Royal Oak* and *Royal Sovereign*, two battlecruisers, *Hood* and *Repulse*, twelve cruisers and two flotillas of destroyers, sixteen in all, under his flag. His two carriers stayed at home, one at Scapa, the other at Rosyth. He was hoping in particular to catch the fast German transatlantic liner *Bremen* (51,731 tons), which as flagship of the enemy merchant fleet would have been a useful propaganda coup, but she got away to the then friendly Soviet Murmansk.

What Forbes lacked, unlike his 1914 predecessors, was first-class intelligence of the enemy's whereabouts, movements and plans. Airborne reconnaissance of German waters naturally started with hostilities, and traffic analysis of radio transmissions intercepted by the Y-stations had begun well beforehand; but the contents of the transmissions could only be guessed at. Like many other major powers, Germany had adopted electromechanical encipherment ('Enigma') in place of the age-old manual system based on secret books; unlike the other British services, the Royal Navy had stuck to a ledger system which had already been seriously penetrated by the Kriegsmarine, whereas the British side, as will be seen, would need well over a year in order to be able to reciprocate. But when the breakthrough came, it did so with a vengeance.

Forbes, having searched with meagre results for runners of the blockade imposed by Britain on 3 September, returned empty-handed in mid-month, leaving cruisers, backed by submarines and aircraft, to form the Northern Patrol covering the waters north of latitude 60 degrees between Iceland and southern Norway (Vice-Admiral Sir Max Horton with the eight cruisers of the 7th and 12th

Squadrons). By that time Britain and France had been at war with Germany for two weeks: Hitler had invaded Poland on the 1st and ignored an Anglo-French ultimatum to withdraw.

There was one other strategic formation in home waters on the outbreak of war – the Channel Force of two battleships, two carriers, three cruisers and nine destroyers, based at Portland, about midway along the English south coast. A flotilla of ten submarines was based at Dundee on the east coast of Scotland and another of six at Blyth on the north-east coast of England. The British coastline was divided among six naval home commands: Western Approaches, based at Plymouth and covering the Irish Sea and the entrance to the Channel; Portsmouth, covering the south coast; Dover, for the Channel; the Nore for the Thames Estuary and eastern England, based at Chatham; Rosyth for east and west Scotland; and Orkney and Shetland, covering northern Scotland from Scapa Flow. Western Approaches (Admiral Sir Martin Dunbar-Nasmith, who as plain Martin Nasmith had won the VC in *E11* at the Dardanelles) had special responsibility for ASW from the outset and controlled thirty-two destroyers, more than any other command.

The principal overseas command remained Cunningham's Mediterranean Fleet, with his flagship *Queen Elizabeth* and two other battleships plus a carrier and seven cruisers, based at Alexandria. Other commands included the North Atlantic (Gibraltar); South Atlantic (Freetown, Sierra Leone) including the South American Division of four cruisers; North America and West Indies (four cruisers); China (Vice-Admiral Sir Percy Noble at Hong Kong); and the East Indies (Singapore). The Royal Australian Navy had six cruisers and the Royal New Zealand Navy two; the Royal Canadian Navy had six modern destroyers. On the outbreak of hostilities Britain had one battleship in dock and five more building plus six carriers on the stocks; orders were immediately placed for six cruisers, fifty-eight destroyers and sixty more corvettes.

The Fleet Air Arm, having completed its transfer from the RAF to the Navy early in 1939, had just 232 first-line aircraft, mostly obsolescent, and 191 in reserve or for training, spread among six carriers and four naval air stations. RAF Coastal Command mustered three groups, a total of seventeen squadrons, several of which were under strength; it could not fully cover the Northern Patrol line between Shetland and Norway because the range of its mainstay, the adapted Anson bomber, fell sixty miles short and the gap had to be covered by submarines. The Command had no effective striking power (the airborne depth charge was not yet available); which meant that Bomber Command, without maritime experience, had to be called in to bomb major naval objectives, and Fighter Command had to protect ports and harbours (but not initially the coastal convoys which, ship for ship, were precisely as important as those on the open sea: four Trade Protection squadrons were announced in summer 1939 but were not in place for the first half-year of the war, when coastal shipping suffered badly).

The Dover Strait was heavily sown with mines and only one U-boat is known to have passed through in the Second World War, before the barrier was complete six days after fighting began. Three were then destroyed and one ran aground in the early weeks. The Germans thereafter took the long way round the British Isles. Vice-Admiral Ramsay had hoisted his flag at Dover Castle ten days before war broke out. During the Munich crisis he found no offices or wireless there but these elementary deficiencies were remedied in the intervening year: tunnels dug during the Napoleonic Wars were reopened and extended into the White Cliffs. Having swiftly planted minefields on either side of the Channel, Ramsay also had to deploy his minesweepers, covered by destroyers, constantly in order to keep passages free for his own side, including French shipping and naval units controlled by his opposite number at Dunkirk as well as the British Expeditionary Force. 'Vice-Admiral, Dover' was detached from the Nore command at the end of October, making Ramsay directly answerable to the Admiralty and simplifying what was already a crucial chain of command.

At its head as First Lord once again, a generation after leaving under the Dardanelles black cloud, was Winston Leonard Spencer Churchill. The relief of Beatty and others at his departure in 1915 was replaced by near-euphoria in the service when the man who had so resolutely opposed appeasement and warned against the Nazis came back from the political wilderness to lead the Navy for the second time in a quarter of a century: 'Winston is back' was the excited message that flashed round the fleet, as staff scoured the Admiralty for the furniture he had used in 1914. His first operational order was brief: 'Total Germany,' the instruction to all ships and commands to wage all-out war on Hitler. But the Conservative Neville Chamberlain, the man who had so hopefully proclaimed 'peace in our time' after the humiliation of Munich, was still Prime Minister amid the ruins of his policy, and showed little stomach for the coming fight. His reappointment of Churchill was less than enthusiastic, the product of political necessity rather than a will to win.

The first Allied convoy of the Second World War formed up in Gibraltar and set sail for Cape Town, South Africa, on 2 September, the day before Britain and France went to war. Any lingering doubts at the Admiralty about the need for convoy against U-boats as well as the clearly identified surface threat was dispelled the next day by Lieutenant Fritz-Julius Lemp, captain of *U30*. He was patrolling to and fro slowly on the surface at dusk, some 250 miles north-west of Ireland, not far from Rockall. His boat was one of thirty-nine deployed from 19 August onwards by Commodore Karl Dönitz, Chief of U-boats since 1 January 1936, in the waters round the British Isles and as far south as Gibraltar. Like all the others Lemp had picked up the anticipated message, 'Open hostilities with England at once' that morning, Sunday 3 September. Half a dozen hours later he was studying through his Zeiss binoculars a medium-sized liner zigzagging towards him from the east. He was conveniently able to submerge south of the ship's mean course for a shot from his bow tubes, and duly hit her just abaft of amidships on the port side.

The SS *Athenia*, 13,581 tons (Captain James Cook), a sixteen-year-old ship of the Donaldson Atlantic Line, had left Glasgow for Montreal on 2 September, calling at Liverpool and Belfast. Cook told his 1,103 passengers and 350 crew at noon on Sunday of Mr Chamberlain's war broadcast to the nation an hour earlier. Most of the passengers, including 300 Americans and many Canadians, were sailing away from Europe for that very reason. Cook said that the ship was entirely unarmed and was therefore immune from attack under international law. The explosion of the torpedo warhead, however, smashed the bulkhead between the ship's boiler-room and the engine-room, demolishing stairways from lower decks to the main deck and thus trapping most of the 118 people who died in the attack. They included twenty-eight Americans, more than enough to revive the *Lusitania* factor' twenty-four years on. The *Athenia*, though mortally wounded, was a stout old ship and stayed afloat for nearly twelve hours, enabling 1,335 survivors to abandon her in orderly fashion in the undamaged lifeboats, once the hulk had corrected her initial thirty-degree list to port and settled in the water. Before fleeing the scene, *U30* surfaced briefly to fire two shells over the ship, presumed to be aimed at her wireless aerial. They missed; the operator was already tapping out the 'SSS' signal signifying a submarine attack and giving the position.

Three British destroyers and three neutral merchant ships picked up all the survivors. The news reached a furious Churchill in his Admiralty office at 10.30 p.m. on the 3rd and his department immediately announced that the unarmed liner had been sunk by a U-boat. Because of the time difference the American press had plenty of scope to make the most of the announcement as American diplomats and reporters rushed to Ireland to interview survivors. Lemp observed wireless silence, so Dönitz was informed by the BBC on the morning of the 4th. He was angry that Lemp had exceeded his orders; even Hitler was embarrassed enough to issue an order that no passenger ship should be attacked, even if under escort. Propaganda Minister Goebbels launched a virulent offensive, claiming that the British destroyers on the scene had sunk the liner to enable the well-known Germanophobe Churchill to influence neutral opinion against Germany. Both sides referred to the *Lusitania* in their broadcasts and it was only a year later that the US government accepted the British account of the sinking. On their return on the 27th, Lemp and his men were sworn to secrecy and his log was altered to erase the entry about the liner.

The Admiralty concluded (wrongly as yet) that Germany was committed to unrestricted submarine warfare, despite her undertakings to the contrary in 1935 and 1936. The worldwide convoy system was therefore rapidly extended: the first eastbound transatlantic convoys sailed in mid-month, including HX 1, the first of a long series from Halifax, Nova Scotia, with an escort of two Canadian destroyers, and HXF 1 (fast) covered by another and two British cruisers. Churchill, however, having been out of the Admiralty for two years by the time the U-boat crisis came to a head in spring 1917, was no convoy enthusiast. He had fallen into the typically gung-ho error of ordering warships to hunt U-boats all over the ocean 'like cavalry' instead of staying with their charges and counter-attacking. Thus the prized carrier *Ark Royal*, the Navy's most modern (for what that was worth), was on detachment from the Home Fleet hunting U-boats west of the Scottish Hebridean islands with an escort of destroyers on 14 September when Lieutenant-Commander Gerhard Glattes in *U39* sighted her and fired four torpedoes. They missed narrowly but their tracks were spotted and the destroyers depth-charged the boat, the first German loss of the war.

But three days later the oldest British carrier at sea, HMS *Courageous*, 22,500 tons (Captain W. T. Makeig-Jones, RN), was leading a hunting group west of Ireland when she was sighted by Otto Schuhardt in *U29*, on his way home after sinking three freighters. He fired three torpedoes at the high side of the converted cruiser and watched through his periscope as two struck home at 2,500 metres, causing a massive sympathetic explosion. The carrier sank in fifteen minutes and 519 men including the captain were killed; astonishingly, a similar number survived. Schuhardt escaped a four-hour hunt by the two destroyers still with her (two had gone away to help an attacked merchant ship). Hitler went to Wilhelmshaven to decorate the victorious crew personally. The Admiralty excluded all other carriers from hunting groups. The loss of the *Courageous* was rightly seen as tragic by the British public and as a serious blow to morale by the Navy; but it was far from a strategic disaster because the ship and her aircraft were obsolete – and the Admiralty had no idea how best to use such maritime air power as it possessed against the obviously resurgent U-boat menace. It was, as yet, more anxious about the threat presented by the German surface raiders.

Against them the British and French navies organized eight groups of heavy ships, mostly cruisers, in the first week of October to cover the entire Atlantic and the Indian Ocean. They were prompted by the knowledge that one of the three formidable pocket-battleships, the *Admiral Graf Spee* (Captain Hans Langsdorff), was on the loose in the south Atlantic with her high speed, her phenomenal cruising range of 21,500 miles and her six big guns. Each force was known by a letter: Force G, the four cruisers of the British South American Division (Commodore Henry Harwood), covered the east coast of that continent; Force H patrolled off the Cape of Good Hope; Force I (a carrier and two cruisers) was based at Trincomalee, Ceylon; the strong Force K with *Ark Royal* and the battlecruiser *Renown*, off Pernambuco, Brazil, watched the 'waist' of the Atlantic; the French Force L operated from Brest with a battleship, a carrier and three cruisers; Force M at Dakar, Senegal, was also French with two cruisers; and Force N included a French battleship, a British carrier (*Hermes*) and cruiser.

*

Closer to home, the main warlike activity by both sides in the waters between Britain and Continental Europe in the opening weeks of the war was minelaying, which cost Britain a quarter of a million tons of shipping in the first three months. The Germans laid mines defensively, along their narrow North Sea coast and in the Heligoland Bight, as well as offensively along the east coast of England by surface minelayer, submarines and aircraft, including 1,500 of the new, highly dangerous magnetic mines (Germany's total stock). The entrance to the Baltic was effectively blocked by heavy mine barrages, although several Polish submarines and small surface ships managed to escape to Britain, where they would serve with distinction alongside the Royal Navy. The Luftwaffe made the mistake of dropping a precious magnetic mine on the mudflats at Shoeburyness on the Essex coast, enabling the intrepid Lieutenant-Commander J. G. D. Ouvery, RN, to dismantle it, find out how it worked and have it copied. British naval and merchant ships had to be 'degaussed' in an elaborate programme of installing cable circuits inside their hulls to carry an anti-magnetic electric current.

Early attempts by RAF Bomber Command to attack German naval units proved vain, as did Luftwaffe attacks on the British fleet. A total of fifty-four Blenheim and Wellington bombers was sent up on 3 September against enemy warships sighted in the North Sea, without result. The next day fifteen Blenheims tried their luck in the Heligoland Bight and ten sighted the pocket-battleship *Admiral Scheer*; five were shot down and none of the three bombs that hit the ship's deck exploded. One Blenheim caused minor casualties and damage on the elderly light cruiser *Emden*, in use as a training ship, by crashing into her side and blowing up. Five Blenheims turned back without finding a target. At the same time fourteen Wellingtons tried to attack the *Scharnhorst* and *Gneisenau* in port at Brunsbüttel but were driven off by Messerschmidt Me 109 fighters with the loss of two bombers. A month later the German Navy tried to give two of its pocket-battleships more room to manoeuvre – the *Deutschland* (soon renamed *Lützow*) in the north Atlantic and the *Graf Spee* in the south – by sending the *Gneisenau* into the North Sea with a light cruiser and nine fleet destroyers, in the hope of seducing the Home Fleet into crossing a U-boat line and sailing within range of 148 Luftwaffe aircraft. Two British battleships, two battlecruisers, a carrier, six cruisers and twelve destroyers, as well as a dozen

Wellington bombers, searched for the German ships but neither side's ships or aircraft proved able to catch or damage the other's.

Before the war was two weeks old the Allied cause received two extremely valuable boosts from the neutral United States, one open, the other secret. From 12 September the US Navy began patrolling a Neutrality Zone, declared on Washington's urging by the Organization of American States and consisting roughly of the western half of the Atlantic Ocean. Only the warships of nations with territory west of that line were allowed in the Zone, a restriction which affected Germany but not Britain and France with their territories in the Western hemisphere – or Canada, which loyally went to war alongside Britain and provided western bases and termini plus assembly ports for shipping on the main transatlantic convoy route. The US Navy set up a new Atlantic Squadron to enforce the Zone, with initially four battleships, a fleet carrier, four cruisers and destroyers. More ships were soon added.

At the same time President Roosevelt, who had been Assistant Secretary of the Navy in the 1920s, wrote to the First Lord of the Admiralty, Winston Churchill, with an offer of a direct line of communication with the White House. This personal, secret 'hot-line' as it would be styled today was of immense importance once Churchill became Prime Minister in May 1940, and soon became central to the entire Allied war effort. After a long and often dirty political struggle with the Isolationists, Roosevelt remained convinced that supporting Britain and France against Germany was in America's best interests; but he had strict neutrality laws, passed by Congress between the wars, to contend with and felt obliged to proceed with caution in circumventing them, especially in the early days of the war. Britain's gold and foreign currency reserves amounted to barely £1bn on the outbreak of war, and her desperate need for munitions of all kinds from ships and aircraft to rifles and bullets was soon to collide with one particularly irksome restriction: the 'cash and carry' rule for arms purchases, for which no credit was allowed by US law. Isolationist in origin, this rule was also reasonable, as neither Britain nor France had been able after the First World War to repay more than a fraction of what they had borrowed from the US to fight it; Washington in the end, with great generosity if not alacrity, wrote off these debts but was understandably moved to add the rider, 'never again'. Canada fell over itself to supply everything from wheat to warships and its contributions in these and other areas, including transit facilities for US goods, were of enormous value and importance; but the Dominion could not begin to stand in for the potential cornucopia of American industry, which Britain needed to tap as a matter of life or death.

The early stages of the Second World War bore a remarkable resemblance in many respects to the opening phase of the First. Most of the similarities were the opposite of coincidental. Hitler was bent on undoing the adverse results for Germany of 1918 by recovering lost territory and creating a self-sufficient Greater Germany that would dominate Europe. A British Expeditionary Force once again began in the first week of September to cross the Channel to fight alongside the French Army in northern France; 161,000 troops were landed under the protection of the Nore and Dover naval commands without loss. The main base of the main British fleet was once again Scapa Flow which, while not as defenceless as in 1914, was far from secure, causing Admiral Forbes to spend as much time as he could at sea. Commodore Dönitz remembered the abortive U-boat attempts on Scapa in 1914 and 1918 and was determined to try again.

Lieutenant-Commander Günther Prien, captain of the *U47*, was the first skipper in the second U-boat campaign to sink a British merchantman, the SS *Bosnia*, off northern Spain on 5 September. It was a chivalrous affair; Prien did open fire on an unarmed steamer, but only because she refused to stop when challenged and was signalling 'SSS' on her wireless. Prien allowed the crew to take to their boats and stood by as they were taken aboard a neutral Norwegian freighter which had come to investigate the burning ship; he then torpedoed the *Bosnia* before she attracted further interest. Nobody was hurt in the incident. On his return to Wilhelmshaven he was summoned by Dönitz on 1 October and asked whether he was interested in volunteering for a raid on the British fleet at Scapa Flow. The U-boat chief assured him it was a free choice but knew his man: Prien jumped at the chance (without affording his crew a similar choice).

U47 set off on 8 October. A fifty-foot gap in the defences of the Flow had been spotted by a reconnaissance aircraft. The northernmost entrance on the eastern side of the Flow, Kirk Sound, between the principal Orkney island of Mainland and the islet of Lamb Holm, now completely blocked by the Churchill Causeway built later in the war, was only half closed. Prien crept across the North Sea and lay on the bottom until the night of 13 to 14 October, when there was no moon. Ignoring a spectacular display of Northern Lights (aurora borealis), he entered the Flow on the surface – unaware that his naval colleagues had ensured it would be almost deserted by sending the *Gneisenau* and escort to sea to lure out the Home Fleet. But he sighted the old seaplane carrier *Pegasus* five miles away in the north-eastern corner of the Flow at Scapa Bay, and in front of her the elderly battleship *Royal Oak*, 29,150 tons, with her four double 15-inch turrets. One of his four bow tubes jammed, reducing his first salvo to three torpedoes, one of which blew a small hole in the bow of the battleship. Suspecting air attack, Captain W. G. Benn, RN, ordered his crew to take shelter under the ship's armoured deck, thus tragically ensuring massive casualties when Prien fired his second salvo of three just after 1 a.m. on the 14th. All three struck home amidships on the starboard side, causing sympathetic explosions among the full load of ammunition and tearing the heart out of the ship; 833 men were killed. The *U47* got away unscathed, returning to a heroes' welcome. Prien was awarded the Knight's Cross by Hitler personally; Dönitz was promoted rear-admiral; German propaganda was ecstatic. On 15 October an old steamer arrived in the Flow as the result of an Admiralty decision of 10 July 1939 – to be sunk as a blockship, completing the closure of Kirk Sound.

Once again the Navy was under attack in the press for its indifferent performance so far and the humiliation of losing a battleship at anchor in its principal harbour. The Home Fleet scattered to its alternative anchorages, including the Firth of Forth and Loch Ewe on the west coast of Scotland. Dönitz had thoughtfully provided for that possibility, sending U-boats to lay mines in the latter half of October. On 4 November the Home Fleet flagship HMS *Nelson* was badly damaged by a mine off Loch Ewe; on the 21st the brand-new cruiser HMS *Belfast* broke her back on another off the Firth of Forth. Both ships were out of action for many months. The Home Fleet stayed away from Scapa Flow until March 1940, by which time the defences of the base had at last been completed and reinforced; three squadrons of Hurricane fighters were now on call to deal with airborne intruders. What the Royal Navy did not know until after the war was that Lieutenant-Commander Wilhelm Zahn in *U56* had found the *Nelson*, the *Rodney* and the *Hood* (flagship of the British fleet) in Scottish waters and fired a salvo of three torpedoes from his little Type II coastal U-boat on 30 October. Two missiles hit the *Nelson* but failed to explode and were not even noticed by her crew as the core of the Home Fleet sailed serenely onward. The abortive attack was food for thought for the Germans, who soon began to realize that they had a torpedo crisis, of which the British were unaware.

On 23 November the Home Fleet was ordered to sea from Loch Ewe when Captain E. C. Kennedy, RN, of the AMC *Rawalpindi* sighted the two most powerful warships then in German service, *Scharnhorst* and *Gneisenau*, on the Northern Patrol line between Iceland and the Faroe Islands. The former opened fire on the converted liner which bravely fired back with her antiquated 6-inch guns, scoring one ineffectual hit before the Germans demolished the *Rawalpindi* in just fourteen minutes. *Scharnhorst* picked up twenty-one survivors. The next British ship in the line, the cruiser *Newcastle*, tried to keep in touch with the German pair as the Home Fleet mustered seven capital ships; but lacking surface radar, only just beginning to be issued to the fleet, she lost them in poor weather. No further contact was made.

Kennedy's first sighting report had correctly identified a battle-cruiser; he amended this to pocket-battleship and issued no recorrection before going down with his ship. For three weeks therefore confusion reigned at the Admiralty about the whereabouts of the *Deutschland*, which in fact had returned home from the north Atlantic on 8 November. But her sister, *Graf Spee*, was still at the other end of the ocean, as was her floating supply-depot-cum-prison-ship, the *Altmark*. The eight hunting groups were still on standby when the British freighter *Doric Star* sent out the 'RRR' alert, signifying she was under attack by a surface raider, from the central Atlantic north of Brazil on 2 December. Commodore Henry Harwood's Force G, consisting of two heavy cruisers, *Exeter* and *Cumberland* (replenishing in the Falklands), and two light, HMNZS *Achilles* and HMS *Ajax*, covered the great estuary of the River Plate between Uruguay and Argentina, anticipating a move by the *Graf Spee* against the rich pickings in the area. The raider had sunk ten ships, over 50,000 tons, by the 7th and refuelled on the 27th from *Altmark* off Tristan da Cunha, the British island in the central south Atlantic, and again on 6 December off Brazil.

Harwood flew his pennant on the *Ajax*, which sighted smoke to the north-west just after dawn on 13 December. Sent to investigate, the *Exeter*, with her 8-inch guns his strongest ship, reported a pocket-battleship. Harwood immediately ordered all three ships to attack, the *Exeter* from the south and the pair of 6-inch cruisers from the east. Although heavily outgunned by the *Graf Spee* with her six 11-inch and eight 5.9-inch guns, the British had three advantages: they had divided the enemy's attention, they could report the fall of each other's shot and they could outrun the enemy's twenty-eight knots. Not for Harwood the agonized calculations of a Troubridge about superior force and the possibility of having his ships picked off one by one from outside their own gun-range; the commodore decided to get within range regardless, by attacking at top speed.

Captain Langsdorff duly concentrated on *Exeter* (Captain F. S. Bell, RN) as his most heavily armed opponent. Bell took terrible punishment from 11-inch shells as he tried a torpedo attack at his maximum thirty-two knots; when reduced to only one turret of two 8-inch guns, *Exeter* withdrew, still firing occasionally as she began limping towards Port Stanley.

Meanwhile the Germans' secondary armament of eight 5.9-inch guns was engaged with the sixteen 6-inch of the two lighter British cruisers (7,000 tons each). *Achilles* lost her gunnery control system and *Ajax* two of her four gun turrets; the former was lightly and the latter more extensively damaged when Langsdorff briefly turned one of his main turrets on them. After ninety furious minutes Harwood made smoke and ordered the pair to withdraw out of range. The British had lost seventy-one men, sixty-four on the *Exeter*; the Germans thirty-six. The *Graf Spee* had taken twenty hits, leaving her with a six-foot hole in her side and a battered and scorched superstructure; all her guns and vital control systems, however, were still fully effective as she made for Montevideo in Uruguay for repairs. The ship was alone and a long way from safety, but she had seen off the *Exeter* and could at least have neutralized the two smaller British cruisers before disappearing into the broad Atlantic for another rendezvous with the *Altmark* (last seen on 6 December) or for a direct run home, eased by distractions organized by the German command. But under international law Langsdorff was allowed twenty-four hours in the neutral port. The German Embassy negotiated a seventy-two-hour extension.

HMS *Cumberland* was racing north from Stanley to replace *Exeter*. Other, distant hunting groups were sending reinforcements to the area, including a battleship, a carrier and cruisers. British merchant ships in Montevideo were sent to sea at daily intervals, which meant under international law that the Germans had to give each one twenty-four hours to get clear before leaving. The BBC carried news of the British naval build-up in the south Atlantic, which was much slower than the reports implied. Langsdorff contacted Grand-Admiral Raeder, the German C-in-C, for orders. He felt he could not fight his way across the Atlantic against the entire British fleet but he might well find a safe haven on the south bank of the Plate in friendly Argentina. Hitler was consulted and forbade internment.

On the evening of 17 December 1939 the *Admiral Graf Spee*, battle flag flying at the foretop, emerged slowly from Montevideo accompanied by the German steamer *Tacoma*. Downstream in international waters *Ajax*, *Achilles* and *Cumberland* waited with full steam up, their guns swinging towards the Germans. No other British ship was in sight. Thousands of spectators lined the shore. The pocket-battleship stopped on the three-mile territorial boundary and men were seen transferring to the steamer. The silence was then broken by a series of explosions inside the warship's hull, small at first, then shattering as the ammunition began to detonate after the scuttling charges. The *Graf Spee* settled on the bottom on an even keel, her upperworks still in flames which burned all night. The *Tacoma* took the crew across to Argentina. On 20 December Langsdorff wrapped himself in the old imperial war flag under which he had fought at Jutland and shot himself.

It was twenty-five years to the month since a dramatic victory in the south Atlantic had last lifted public spirits in a Britain desperate for good news from the Royal Navy. In December 1914 it had been the annihilation of Admiral Graf Spee's squadron off the Falklands in revenge for the defeat at Coronel; in December 1939 it was the elimination of the powerful pocket-battleship named after him, forced to scuttle by the elan of three outgunned but well-handled cruisers. No matter that she had sunk herself; it was the bold South American Division that drove her to it and thus inflicted on Hitler his first notable military and propaganda setback. Harwood was promoted rear-admiral and knighted.

In the same week Lieutenant-Commander E. O. B. Bickford, RN, in the submarine *Salmon*, sank *U36* while waiting for the German liner *Bremen*, homeward bound from her refuge in northern Russia, to enter the Heligoland Bight. A covering German aircraft forced him to submerge and thus saved the ship;

but on the next day Bickford fired a salvo of torpedoes from extreme range at a returning German minelaying force of three light cruisers and five destroyers, damaging two of the former (*Leipzig* and *Nürnberg*). Minelaying, submarine and aircraft probes over, on and under the North Sea and British waters continued into spring 1940 with considerable losses on both sides; German shipping was severely reduced by capture, or by scuttling to avoid it.

The saga of the *Graf Spee* was satisfyingly completed nine weeks later, when the *Altmark* was sighted in southern Norwegian waters. Her master, Captain Dahl of the merchant service, had managed to hide from British forces in the far south Atlantic before starting his epic voyage home on 24 January and reaching the Norwegian Sea, undetected as he crossed the busy main convoy route (if he could do it, Langsdorff might have managed it also). The 12,000-ton tanker pretended to be Norwegian as she sailed down the long coastline inside territorial waters, her 299 British prisoners (unbeknown to the Admiralty) secured below decks. Norwegian patrol boats discovered her true identity but turned a blind eye for fear of provoking Hitler.

Thanks to espionage in Norway, the *Altmark* was known by the Admiralty to be in Norwegian waters and the Home Fleet was alerted. Captain Philip Vian, RN, and his Fourth Destroyer Flotilla, led by HMS *Cossack* plus the light cruiser *Arethusa*, were on patrol in the area looking for iron-ore carriers bound for Germany. The *Arethusa* sighted the *Altmark* on the afternoon of 16 February; two Norwegian patrol boats were with her and they prevented men from two of Vian's destroyers from boarding. The ship went into the Jøssingfjord, an inlet in the coastal cliffs to the south of Stavanger. Vian, without consulting Forbes but directly urged on by Churchill, gambled on finding something incriminating on the *Altmark* to justify a blatant violation of neutrality. He sent over a strong boarding party after blocking the exit to the sea, ignoring protests from a Norwegian gunboat the while. A brisk small-arms battle between the British bluejackets and German sailors ensued.

The victorious British were amazed to find the prisoners, who were overjoyed; the *Altmark* was stripped of such weapons as remained aboard but otherwise left unharmed. Forbes was angry that Churchill had interfered directly in the operation but led the Home Fleet to sea to cover the triumphant return of HMS *Cossack* to Rosyth on the 17th after her classic destroyer exploit. Once again the British press and public had good news from the Navy to crow about as the survivors told their stories. The incident also served to concentrate the minds of both sides on neutral Norway, from or via which each was importing Swedish iron ore, and whose long coastline would give a great strategic advantage in the north Atlantic to the belligerent that decided to seize it.

Both sides decided to do so, the British hesitantly and the Germans with ruthless resolve. The first move was made by Britain and boasted the suitably unaggressive codename of Operation 'Wilfred', a half-hearted plan to mine the waters off south-west Norway through which ore-carriers bound for Germany had to pass. Three groups of ships set off on 5 April 1940. One was to act as decoy off Kristiansund (not to be confused with Kristiansand to the south), one was pulled back on the 8th before it could start work and the third, of eight destroyers distantly covered by the battlecruiser *Renown* and four more destroyers, laid mines off Bodø. The ingloriously named destroyer *Glowworm* (Lieutenant-Commander G. B. Roope, RN) lost contact with the latter group on the 6th when searching for a sailor fallen overboard in a storm. Instead, two days later, she sighted a large German ship, the heavy cruiser *Hipper* (14,000 tons), accompanied by four destroyers and north-eastward bound. To the incredulity of the Germans the *Glowworm* (1,345 tons) came on at full speed to ram the *Hipper*, tearing a 120-foot gash in her side. She was sunk in a hail of gunfire within minutes, with the loss of all hands, but the *Hipper* was out of action for several months. Commander Roope was awarded a posthumous VC when the facts became known.

The heavy cruiser was leading one of no fewer than eleven groups of German warships, almost everything the enemy navy possessed, on their way to seize Denmark and Norway – Operation 'Weserübung', the opening move of Hitler's Blitzkrieg in the west which would leave him master of Europe from the North Cape to the Pyrenees and from Brest to Breslau. Hipper's Group 2 was to capture Trondheim while other forces were launched against Narvik in the north, Bergen (Group 3 with light cruisers *Köln* and *Königsberg* plus eleven other ships), Egersund, Kristiansand, the Norwegian capital Oslo (Group 5 led by the heavy cruiser *Blücher* and the pocket-battleship *Lützow* plus fourteen others) and five objectives in Denmark, including the capital Copenhagen (Group

8). The *Scharnhorst* and *Gneisenau* were also at sea as a covering force in the waters south of Narvik and north of Trondheim.

The British meanwhile were working to 'Plan R4', to occupy four Norwegian Atlantic ports – Narvik, Trondheim, Bergen and Stavanger – but only in the event of a German military reaction to 'Wilfred'. Troops, transports and escorts for the first two were assembled in the Clyde while an expeditionary force of four heavy cruisers with troops and six destroyers to take the two southerly objectives gathered in the Firth of Forth. The Home Fleet put to sea on the 7th; Admiral Forbes had three capital ships, two cruisers and ten destroyers with him, and also sent the battlecruiser *Repulse*, a light cruiser and four destroyers to reinforce Vice-Admiral W. J. Whitworth on *Renown* when *Glowworm*'s last message came through on the 8th. On the same day, the Polish submarine *Orzel* sank a German troop transport; when survivors were saved by Norwegian ships they told their rescuers that they had been on their way to 'protect' Bergen against an Anglo-French attack. Both sides deployed large numbers of submarines in support of their respective moves against Norway; the U-boats contributed very little whereas their British and Allied counterparts caused considerable damage and disruption to the German invasion fleet. Their combined haul included twelve transports sunk and several more damaged, one light cruiser, one destroyer, one training ship, one U-boat and six minesweepers sunk by torpedo or mine and several other warships damaged, including the *Lützow*, hit and badly holed by a torpedo from HM Submarine *Spearfish* (Lieutenant-Commander Forbes, RN) on 11 April, on her return from Oslo. The renamed pocket-battleship was out of action for a year.

Norway, massively outgunned by the Wehrmacht, managed to strike a few blows in her own defence. Coastal artillery at Bergen damaged the training ship *Bremse* and the *Königsberg*, which was left dead in the water. Fifteen Fleet Air Arm Skua dive-bombers flew over on the 10th and finished her off, making the cruiser the first warship ever sunk in war by air attack. South of Oslo the coastal artillery (supplied many years earlier by Krupp, the German arms conglomerate), supported by shore-based torpedo tubes, gloriously sank Group 5 leader *Blücher*, the *Hipper*'s sister ship, carrying the Occupation government and its administrative paraphernalia. Command was transferred to the *Lützow* and the invaders withdrew temporarily, leaving it to Luftwaffe paratroops to land and march on Oslo from ten miles away. The twelve-hour delay in taking the capital enabled the Norwegian royal family, government and gold reserves to escape; the cruiser HMS *Glasgow* eventually picked them up to the north at Molde, near Andalsnes, on the 29th and took them to Britain.

But all six German objectives in Norway fell easily, local setbacks notwithstanding. Denmark was even easier. Admiral Whitworth sighted *Scharnhorst* and *Gneisenau* (sporting the flag of Vice-Admiral Günther Lütjens) heading north towards Narvik and promptly engaged them with his one capital ship on hand, *Renown*, slower but armed with six 15-inch guns against the eighteen 11-inchers of the Germans. The latter landed two superficial strikes on the old British battlecruiser but took three rather more damaging British hits: the *Gneisenau* lost her gunnery control system and one of her triple turrets. Whitworth could not keep up with the enemy in the bad weather and contact was lost after ten minutes.

Narvik, however, fell to the German naval Group 1's ten destroyers according to timetable. Captain B. A. W. Warburton-Lee, RN, led the five small 'H'-class destroyers of the Second Flotilla into the Vestfjord to attack the much superior Group 1, pestered by direct orders from the Admiralty over the heads of Forbes and Whitworth (who remained briefly in the offing with *Renown*). Achieving tactical surprise, he sank the German command-ship *Wilhelm Heidkamp* and one of her sisters and damaged three more; the British raiders also sank five merchantmen. The five undamaged German destroyers, which had been dispersed, now came together for a counter-attack, sinking Warburton-Lee's *Hardy* and one other and damaging a third. But the latter and two other British destroyers managed to escape, sinking an ammunition ship on their way out of the fjord. Warburton-Lee died in this gallant action but was awarded a posthumous VC. Whitworth on his own initiative had sent the light cruiser *Penelope* and his four remaining destroyers to support his embattled Captain (D), but too late. The Admiralty, urged on by Churchill, was also bombarding these ships with direct orders; Whitworth protested but was ordered to attack Narvik again on 12 April. It was called off on the 11th, when *Penelope* ran aground, and re-ordered when Forbes arrived on the 12th.

On 8 April the Admiralty had ordered the First Cruiser Squadron of four ships to disembark their troops at Rosyth and join the Home Fleet, which had left Scapa Flow on the 7th, northward bound. The cruiser and six destroyers waiting in the Clyde to escort the troop transports assembled there were also sent to sea to support Forbes, who was not consulted about these decisions, even though by taking them the First Sea Lord, Admiral Pound, scuppered Plan R4. Also on the 8th the minelaying destroyers were pulled back by the Admiralty from the waters off Narvik and sent to join the *Renown* – which meanwhile had been ordered by Forbes to cover the area they were abandoning. Forbes, well to the south of Trondheim, detached *Repulse* to join her sister ship off Narvik, keeping his two battleships, *Rodney* and *Valiant*. The understandably confused admiral further received, on the 8th, an aircraft report of a strong German naval force heading west on the approximate latitude of Trondheim (the *Hipper*, holed above the waterline by *Glowworm* but with power and armament intact, plus escorts, sailing to and fro while awaiting H-hour for taking the port).

The chaos on the British side contrasted sharply with the Germans' thorough preparations for an eleven-fold operation on 9 April; even the loss of their principal command-ship off Oslo did not put them off their stroke. The Admiralty seemed to wake up only slowly when it was realized that the Germans were ashore in several places in Norway and needed to be dislodged quickly before they could entrench themselves. But when Coastal Command wanted to bomb Stavanger airfield, seized by the Germans, it was frustrated by rules of engagement which forbade the bombing of towns because of the risk of civilian casualties. This forbearance gave the Luftwaffe air superiority over southern Norway, which they promptly put to use against Forbes as his ships moved in adjacent waters. He was even sent heavy reinforcements from the Clyde, including the battleship *Warspite* and the carrier *Furious* – the latter, however, was hurriedly sent to sea without her fighter squadron just as the Luftwaffe was preparing to attack. Forbes wanted to assault Bergen but was told by London to concentrate on Trondheim and Narvik to the north, leaving the southern port to the four troopless cruisers and seven destroyers. Then the Admiralty, again without consultation, dropped the idea of attacking Bergen on the grounds that the naval forces available were inadequate. Forbes, off Trondheim on the 10th, decided to send the torpedo-bombers from *Furious* against the *Hipper*, which nonetheless managed to slip out of the port that night, her task accomplished, with a single destroyer, also evading ninety-two RAF bombers. Lütjens brought his two battlecruisers down from the north to escort her home as Forbes sailed in the other direction for the second attack on Narvik on the 12th.

Appalling weather prevented his aircraft from attacking the Germans, who already had six army divisions in southern Norway. But Forbes sent Whitworth, his flag transferred to the *Warspite*, and nine destroyers into the Vestfjord. The old battleship's spotter aircraft sighted and sank *U64*, on picket duty, and also spotted a German destroyer lying in wait behind a headland. The latter was briskly dispatched as the strong British force entered the waterway. In a fierce action seven German destroyers were sunk while two British were badly damaged but saved. London now stepped in again to urge Whitworth to make an armed landing, but the vice-admiral wisely decided that his handfuls of Royal Marines and such sailors as he could spare were inadequate to dislodge some 2,000 first-class, well-dug-in German troops, and called for a suitable force of infantry from Britain. As the first phase of the struggle for Norway ended on this day, the Germans were left with a powerful and by now unshakable grip on southern Norway and a precarious but strategic foothold at Narvik in the north.

The Admiralty was cobbling together its Norwegian 'strategy' as it went along. It sent the first convoy of British troops to sea from the Clyde on 11 April, having on the previous day appointed as Flag Officer, Narvik (already in enemy hands), no less a figure than Admiral of the Fleet the Earl of Cork and Orrery, who was so senior that he outranked the First Sea Lord. The first British landing in Norway was made by 350 sailors and marines on the 13th at Namsos, north of Trondheim. They seized a beachhead for Operation 'Maurice', an attack by 12,000 troops on Trondheim from the north. The Germans immediately started bombing Namsos, and then Andalsnes, south of Trondheim, when another small, preparatory landing was made there. The British had no airfields, no fighters or shore-based anti-aircraft guns and were forced to expose invaluable anti-aircraft cruisers to the Luftwaffe's attentions without adequate defences. The carrier *Glorious* arrived with Gladiator fighters which were briefly able to fly from a frozen lake – until the Luftwaffe bombed them (and the ice).

Meanwhile the Germans were massively reinforcing Trondheim, determined to hold on to the strategic key to the entire Norwegian north, which Hitler intended to rebuild as his principal naval base outside Germany. Forbes, back in Scapa on the 14th, was told to attack it with the bulk of the Home Fleet, an order that was repeated the next day; the hapless (but far from toothless) admiral refused for lack of air cover. He could not contemplate an opposed landing without it, demanding at least a week to prepare and insisting on carrying the troops on warships rather than transports. This Operation 'Hammer' was cancelled on 19 April, by which time Britain had all but run out of anti-aircraft ammunition. Forbes probably saved the Home Fleet by his determined stand.

Major-General P. J. Mackesy, commanding the force to invade Narvik, first met Lord Cork on 15 April when troop convoy NP 1 arrived in the Lofoten Islands. The old admiral wanted to attack at once, but the general pointed out that the ships had not been 'combat-loaded' (the same mistake as at Gallipoli twenty-five years before) and would have to be unloaded to allow equipment and supplies to be reloaded in the reverse of the order in which they would be needed. Cork was appointed supreme commander on 20 April; Narvik fell to the counter-invaders, by then 30,000 strong and led by Major-General Claude Auchinleck, on 28 May – four days after the British and French governments had decided to give up the fight for Norway in the light of the German invasion of the Low Countries and northern France. British, French and Free Polish troops were withdrawn from Norway with minimal loss, the first of many miraculous evacuations which the Navy was forced to carry out in the early years of the war.

Unaware of the Allied withdrawal, Admiral Wilhelm Marschall, C-in-C of the German fleet, decided to attack the Allied base at Harstad in the Lofotens with his two battlecruisers, the temporarily patched-up *Hipper* and four destroyers. Marschall sank three British supply ships on the way and concluded by 8 June from radio traffic analysis that a withdrawal was in progress. He therefore took the *Scharnhorst* and *Gneisenau* on a sweep off central Norway, detaching his lesser ships to Trondheim to refuel. On the afternoon of the 8th the Germans sighted HMS *Glorious* (Captain G. D'Oyly Hughes, RN) and her escort of two destroyers. The old carrier had not only her own aircraft but also the last RAF fighters from Narvik aboard (the pilots had to make their maiden carrier-landing in order to escape) and was short of space. But that was no excuse for the failure by her captain, a submariner and no aviator, to fly scouts or even to launch any aircraft when the Germans attacked. Hughes showed the same lack of resolve as had dogged the entire sorry campaign, of which this was the last major incident. He had even left his commander (air) behind, after a dispute.

The carrier's defence was left to the two destroyers, which gallantly laid smokescreens and attempted suicidal torpedo attacks. *Ardent* (Lieutenant-Commander J. F. Barker, RN) was soon sunk; *Acasta* (Commander C. E. Glasfurd, RN) managed to hit the *Scharnhorst* in the stern with a torpedo before going under, obliging Marschall to send her into Trondheim for repair and thus indirectly preserving Cork's lightly escorted main evacuation convoy from serious attack. By this time the *Glorious* was ablaze and heeling over to starboard. The inexcusable loss of the inert carrier, her valuable aircraft and above all the trained aircrew aboard was the most melancholy naval setback of the irretrievably botched, British-led Norwegian campaign.

The fiasco had much in common with the Dardanelles debacle as a naval attack on a distant flank, hastily conceived, ill-considered and not pressed home with vigour against an enemy known to be thoroughly ruthless. Forbes and Whitworth and even the commanders of individual ships had been subjected to the same neurotic interference in their tactical and operational dispositions as Milne and Troubridge and their unfortunate successors in the Mediterranean during the earlier war.

On each occasion the man giving the orders as First Lord was Winston Churchill. Once again there had been 'bungling in high places' and heads had to roll. But this time Churchill became Prime Minister rather than scapegoat. On 9 May Neville Chamberlain only just survived a motion of no confidence in the House of Commons but resigned anyway because his majority had been slashed by 150. The abysmal leadership of the Norwegian episode, the long-standing underestimation of Hitler, the helplessness of Britain when faced with the Blitzkrieg that put an end to the passive inertia of the Phoney War, and memories of the appeasement which seemed to have left the country defenceless, combined to cause a crisis. On 10 May Churchill, who had almost alone cried warnings from the political wilderness, was suddenly the man of the hour and was called to Buckingham Palace by King George VI. The Admiralty had lost a bullying, demanding, impetuous, interfering and administratively incompetent chief; the country gained a defiant, irrepressible, energetic and inspiring leader. Both parties thus profited from his translation.

*

The German invasion of Norway led Britain to occupy the Danish Faroe Islands on 13 April and neutral Iceland on 6 May, to deny the Germans complete control of the north-east Atlantic. But the Irish Free State, independent of the UK since 1922, refused to allow the Royal Navy back into Lough Swilly on its north-west and Bear Haven on its south-west coast, given up as bases by Britain in 1938 as a goodwill gesture. This forced Atlantic convoy escorts to sail 200 miles further in each direction as the Irish adopted a policy of strict neutrality; had the Irish let the British return, the Germans would have felt (and been) entitled to bomb the two harbours. The loss of the two Atlantic outposts was felt with special keenness after the fall of France and the swift move by the German Navy to take over the ports and harbours of the French Atlantic coast for U-boats, fast surface craft and even their larger ships.

On the very day that Churchill kissed hands on his appointment, Hitler unleashed stage three of his Blitzkrieg programme after Poland and Norway/Denmark: he invaded the Netherlands, Belgium, Luxembourg and France, ignoring the declared neutrality of the first three named. The Low Countries held out for less than a week and the Germans soon gained the upper hand in northern France, driving a wedge between the French Army and the British Expeditionary Force on its left, which was soon involved in another of those famous fighting retreats. In a rare display of competence and determination, Vice-Admiral Ramsay sent four destroyers to his French colleague at Dunkirk to help guard the flank of the French 7th Army and another four to demolish harbour installations in the ports threatened by the German advance to the Channel coast.

Fortunately the C-in-C, Nore, Admiral Sir Reginald A. R. Plunkett-Ernle-Erle-Drax, had resisted a suggestion from Admiral Pound that Dover be reabsorbed by his command. Drax took charge of operations at sea in the Channel and southern North Sea while Ramsay looked after shore tasks. It fell to Drax to spirit away the Dutch royal family, government and gold reserves by destroyer and to Ramsay to use his two flotillas to demolish IJmuiden, the outer port of Amsterdam, the Hook of Holland, the gateway to Rotterdam, plus Dutch Flushing and Belgian Antwerp on the River Scheldt. Only at IJmuiden did the British receive cooperation from the authorities, but the substantial oil stocks at the other three ports were largely destroyed or at least adulterated. Merchant shipping and port vessels such as tugs and dredgers were removed by 14 May; submarines and destroyers of the Royal Netherlands Navy escaped in significant numbers.

The Germans caused maximum confusion by their parachute drop on Rotterdam, which outflanked the Dutch Army and sealed its fate. Ramsay's destroyers rescued a force of Irish and Welsh Guards and Royal Marines which had landed at the Hook of Holland but could not evacuate Dutch military units ahead of the ceasefire forced by the bombing of Rotterdam, where Dutch marines had been fiercely defending the Rhine bridges. The busy British destroyers also escorted French units which had landed on Walcheren to try to secure the Scheldt, but now had to be withdrawn across the river. German Stukas (dive-bombers) came into their own with howling attacks on retreating troops and the warships trying to help them. With the Low Countries defeated, the Germans on 18 May broke through French lines at Sédan, opening up the prospect of cutting off large French and British units.

General Gort, the BEF commander, decided to withdraw his divisions, and the War Office planned to lift 45,000 troops if all went well, barely a quarter. When the Germans broke through, Gort ordered two divisions to counter-attack at Arras on the 19th to delay them. On the 20th Ramsay chaired a conference under the White Cliffs of Dover, proposing his immortal plan to round up all available small boats for taking troops from shore out to ships off the French coast. Three days later British troops were ordered on to half rations with the Germans only nine miles short of Calais (Boulogne was cut off from the landward side). Ramsay sent demolition parties to both ports and covered a landing by two Guards battalions and Royal Marines for a last-ditch defence of Boulogne. Two destroyers which had been using their guns as artillery inside the harbour were taken out to sea in flames by junior officers and saved; two more went in to replace them, blasting away at the German positions on the hills outside the town while a third lay at the mouth of the harbour, joining in the fierce exchange of fire with the German field-guns. Faced with overwhelming force, the British destroyers took off 1,600 troops and marines; a last destroyer entered the harbour and lifted 1,400 more. Only 200 men were left behind, to surrender when they had used up their ammunition.

As Boulogne was falling, more troops were being landed to hold Calais as long as possible – a brigade of infantry, a rifle regiment and a tank regiment. Once again the burden of landing and covering them fell on the overworked destroyers, one of which was sunk and two crippled, though not sunk, by air attacks. Small craft were sent in to pick up as many troops as possible before Calais in its turn fell on 26 May; the last to leave was a yacht. Only just over 1,000 were saved from there compared with the 4,368 men brought out of Boulogne, where more destroyers had been available.

That left Dunkirk, to which on 25 May the Germany Army was closer than the British. As the Belgian Army collapsed on his left, Gort transferred troops to that side of his front and formed a perimeter round Dunkirk and an embarkation beachhead six to ten miles in radius covered by the French to the west and the British to the east. Troops withdrew to the fifteen miles of sand between Dunkirk and Nieuport; and the German advance paused, or at any rate did not send in armour or aircraft to finish off the BEF. Gort was therefore able to strengthen his western flank and pull all three British corps back in reasonable order to the beaches. Ramsay and his staff had been working on their evacuation plan for a week and the diminutive admiral was determined to save far more than 45,000 men, scouring the south of England and beyond for small boats. Fifty 200-ton Dutch schuyts, ideal shallow-water craft with their side-boards instead of keels, were among the heterogeneous flotillas mobilized for Operation 'Dynamo' along with motor boats of all kinds, yachts, pleasure craft and launches. Owners of boats between 30 and 100 feet long had responded overwhelmingly to Admiralty appeals in the press, creating the Small Vessels Pool. Naval officers toured ports and harbours all over southern England and helped to gather over 400 boats; the commands at the Nore and Western Approaches (Plymouth) joined in this instant legend.

The evacuation from Dunkirk began on Sunday 26 May, with the British government still hoping to recover only 45,000 men. An endless queue formed on the three-quarter-mile mole at Dunkirk to board the warships tied up on either side. The small boats took men directly off ten miles of beach to other warships, ferries and transports waiting offshore. Ramsay was unusual in his readiness to delegate to competent officers chosen by himself, such as Captain W. G. Tennant, RN, his Senior Naval Officer ashore at Dunkirk, who was left to get on with his work. Vice-Admiral Sir James Somerville smoothly relieved Ramsay, who had scarcely slept for a fortnight, in command for short periods. The gifted Somerville had been invalided out of the Navy before the war with tuberculosis but had been working unofficially on the installation of radar in ships and now volunteered his services, like Ramsay, from the retired list; he was on the last destroyer out of Calais and would play a major role in naval operations after Dunkirk.

Ashore near Dunkirk, Major-General Harold Alexander led the British rearguard action covering the last phase of the evacuation. Some 40,000 French troops were also still in action, thereby helping the British withdrawal; Ramsay decided they too should be evacuated. The deadline for completion was extended from 1 June to the 4th, by which time six of the forty-one destroyers engaged had been sunk, fourteen damaged by bombing and another twelve in collisions. They alone had rescued more than 96,000 troops, while forty-five transports (eight were sunk, three crippled) collected 88,000. As the last frantic efforts to rescue the beached troops began, Ramsay found the time to send a Nelsonian message: 'The nation looks to the Navy to see it through.' On the night of 1 to 2 June, Captain Tennant signalled to Ramsay: 'BEF evacuated.' The work continued for another forty-eight hours to rescue as many French soldiers as possible (26,000 on the last night). Expected to save 45,000, Ramsay brought off 308,888 men in British and 29,338 in Allied ships, a total of 338,226. Only about 2,000 troops had been lost at sea; 180,982 men were actually landed at Dover, the rest at four other Kent ports and Harwich in Essex. On 7 June 1940 Ramsay was made a Knight Commander of the Order of the Bath (KCB). He was still not on the active list. When a Dover cinema showed a newsreel featuring Ramsay, the audience erupted in applause, prompting the projectionist to repeat the item three times.

In the later days of June 1940 the naval commands at Plymouth and Portsmouth were responsible for the rescue of 200,000 more French and British soldiers from further west and south in France in Operation 'Ariel'. During this remarkable follow-up to 'Dynamo', however, there occurred the greatest single tragedy in the history of British seafaring, when the SS *Lancastria* was sunk in an air attack in the Bay of Biscay with some 4,500 rescued troops aboard. The disaster, in which four times as many were lost as went down with the *Lusitania*, was covered up for many years.

Ramsay managed a few days' leave but soon plunged into his next assignment, countering the universally expected German invasion. The Admiralty did not know just how badly damaged the German fleet had been by the Norwegian operation or how half-hearted Hitler was about invading a country with which he still vaguely hoped to conclude an early truce. The threat was seen as real and urgent if not immediate; the RAF had not yet been challenged for control of the air over the Dover Strait and south-east England, an issue the Germans would have to tackle before an assault. Ramsay was working closely with General Sir Alan Brooke, C-in-C Home Forces, and Lieutenant-General Bernard Montgomery of XII Corps, the local General Officer Commanding.

The victorious Germans meanwhile set up huge, long-range guns on the French coast which fired their first shells at Dover on 12 August 1940. The barrage went on intermittently for four years; the British retaliated in kind with two dismounted naval guns named Winnie and Pooh. The Luftwaffe began its attacks on RAF airfields and coastal radar stations the next day. British reconnaissance flights and spies ashore reported barges, small vessels and freighters assembling in French and Belgian ports. German convoys were passing up and down the Channel coast under the triple protection of shore batteries, fast escorts and fighters. Ramsay sent out his motor torpedo boats at night, forcing the enemy to stay in harbour after dark, but at this moment in the war the sailors under Ramsay's command spent much time looking up into the clear summer sky and watching the dogfights in progress, in anticipation of an enemy invasion in September. Yet by the middle of that month the Luftwaffe had switched the focus of its attack to bombing London and other cities. This saved Fighter Command just as that overstretched force was reeling under the pressure, threatened by a breakdown in the radar chain that enabled it to target its aircraft with maximum efficiency. The RAF kept control of the skies over the invasion area, including the Dover Strait, for the rest of the war; the Battle of Britain had been won. On the other side of the country, the real battle *for* Britain was only just beginning.

The fall of France had a terrible naval postscript. The effect on British naval operations was threefold. The French coastline from the Channel to the Spanish frontier came under German control (and Spain was friendly to the Axis). This gave Dönitz bases 400 miles further west and 600 miles further south than before on the Atlantic. The Luftwaffe profited similarly in its maritime operations. The French metropolitan and North African coasts in the Mediterranean were left to the puppet Vichy regime of Marshal Pétain just when Italy entered the war on Hitler's side on 10 June 1940. Thirdly, while it had to contend with this new, well-equipped naval enemy, the Royal Navy lost a powerful ally: the French fleet. A. V. Alexander, the new First Lord, and Admiral Pound, First Sea Lord, flew on 17 June to Bordeaux, to which the last government of the Third Republic had withdrawn under the German threat to Paris, for a meeting with Admiral Jean Darlan, the French naval C-in-C.

They begged this Janus in navy blue to disperse his ships to British, French overseas or American neutral ports, but all Darlan would do was promise that the Germans and the Italians 'would not be allowed' to have the fleet. This assurance inspired no more confidence than the sanctimonious promises of Hitler and Mussolini not to use French men of war against Britain if France surrendered. On the very same day as the abortive talks with the French naval staff, Pétain's government asked the Germans for an armistice, which was signed on the 21st. The British now acted with the iron resolution which had been generally absent from their prosecution of the war and which was born of their newly desperate and solitary plight after the fall of France.

His health fully restored, Vice-Admiral Somerville was given command of a new 'Force H' (not to be confused with one of the groups temporarily set up in 1939 to hunt Raeder's raiders). This 'detached squadron' of the Home Fleet functioned as an independent command, based at Gibraltar alongside the separate command of the Flag Officer, North Atlantic, and positioned to operate in the Atlantic or the Mediterranean as required. By the end of June, Somerville had the *Hood* (flag), the battleships *Resolution* and *Valiant*, the carrier *Ark Royal*, the light cruiser *Arethusa* and four destroyers under command. Their role was to replace the French fleet. Their first task was to destroy it.

On the collapse of the French Army, two old battleships, four destroyers, seven submarines and a few small vessels came over from France to Britain. The British C-in-C, Mediterranean, Admiral Sir Andrew Cunningham, persuaded Rear-Admiral Godfroy's East Mediterranean Squadron of four cruisers to join him at Alexandria. But the core of the French Navy, its strongest assets, were dispersed by Darlan. The incomplete battleship *Jean Bart* went to Casablanca in French Morocco; the battleship *Richelieu* was at Dakar in French Senegal. Vice-Admiral Gensoul controlled two modern battlecruisers, *Dunkerque* and *Strasbourg*, plus two battleships, a seaplane carrier and six fleet destroyers in the Algerian port of Mers-el-Kebir, together with seven destroyers and four submarines at nearby Oran. Many of these ships had worked with the British in Norway and in the heavy *Force de raid* which had helped to hunt the German marauders in the Atlantic.

On 3 July, Somerville, ordered to execute the grisly Operation 'Catapult', arrived off the Algerian coast and sent the erstwhile naval attaché at Paris, Captain C. S. Holland, RN, in a destroyer to call on Gensoul with a six-hour ultimatum: to join the British, go into internment, sail to the French West Indies and disarm, scuttle – or be destroyed. Gensoul thought the British were bluffing and played for time as his ships raised steam. The *Strasbourg*, despite at least one hit on her quarterdeck, and five destroyers broke out and managed to reach Toulon, the main French naval base. All other ships in the two ports were sunk or crippled inside a quarter of an hour, in a hail of shot from nine miles out. The battleship *Bretagne* exploded and sank in three minutes. Other French ships fired back, without effect. Some 1,250 Frenchmen were killed.

On 8 July the carrier *Hermes* (Captain R. F. J. Onslow, RN) and two heavy cruisers arrived off Dakar to attack the *Richelieu*. Depth charges dropped under her stern by a fast motorboat failed to explode, but torpedo-bombers caused enough damage to engender a year's repair work on the spot. Such was the untidy ending to the British elimination of the French fleet from the strategic board. It was almost as much of an ordeal for the Royal Navy as for its lost ally, and even French anti-Nazis were extremely embittered; but American opinion, outraged by the recent Nazi rape of Scandinavian and Low-Countries neutrality, was surprisingly sympathetic to this new British display of 'hardball'. There were those in Washington who wondered what America would do if the Nazis ever got control of the British fleet; and there were those in London who understood that this was a useful card to play in pressing the Americans for aid.

9

War on Two Fronts

Churchill chose Bastille Day, the French national day on 14 July, to spell out Britain's motivation and new resolve:

> During the last fortnight the British Navy ... has had imposed upon it the sad duty of putting effectually out of action for the duration of the war the capital ships of the French Navy ... The transference of these ships to Hitler would have endangered the security of both Great Britain *and the United States* [author's italics]. We therefore had no choice.

To continue to resist Hitler after the fall of France, isolated Britain depended once more on the transatlantic link with North America, which was in the most literal sense the nation's lifeline. Britain needed 55m tons of imports per year in peacetime and had by now completed its worldwide and coastal convoy systems. Perhaps the biggest flaw in these complex arrangements was the exclusion of merchant ships capable of a consistent speed higher than fifteen knots and (especially) those slower than nine. The impatient Churchill resented the time 'wasted' in convening convoys and then sailing them, necessarily, at the speed of the slowest member. The lower speed threshold was, however, a false economy which condemned many ships to death; it was surely better to arrive late than not at all, even if convoys caused massive congestion at the ports. Ships capable of sustaining a speed higher than that of a surfaced U-boat (upwards of fifteen knots), especially if they were fast liners or special cargo ships capable of twenty-eight knots or even more, could certainly be allowed out alone, as was the practice with the six 'monsters' (Cunard's *Queen Elizabeth* and *Queen Mary* were the largest) which sailed alone as troopships without loss throughout the war. As it was, of the 5,756 sailings in convoy by the end of 1939 just four ships had been lost to U-boats, or 0.07 per cent.

In May 1940, against the background of the Norwegian campaign, nearly 300,000 tons of shipping were sunk, the only month of the war in which sinkings by aircraft surpassed those by U-boat (by a factor of three to one). The total for June, much the worst month of the war so far, was 585,000 tons lost, nearly half to U-boats and the rest to surface raiders and mines, with only a small minority sunk by the Luftwaffe. From the start of the war to the isolation of Britain 2.25m tons were sunk, 48 per cent by U-boats (215 ships and two major warships, despite defective German torpedoes, a major crisis for Dönitz especially in Norway), 26 per cent by mines, 13 by air attack, 6 by surface raiders and the rest by other or unknown causes. This represented a loss of about 5 per cent of the total stock of shipping, domestic and foreign, available to Britain. The average loss touched 280,000 tons a month; new building capacity was 88,000. The U-boats lost twenty-four of their original fifty-seven and sank 195 independently routed ships (IRS); only twenty-two of their victims were in convoys, while eleven German submarines were lost in attacks on escorted shipping. Eighteen new submarines were commissioned by Germany in the period. One U-boat had been sunk for every two protected victims; the rate for IRS was one for fifteen. Small wonder that U-boat skippers preferred IRS.

The British government cut imports by about 20 per cent and rationing was brought in by stages, completed by the time France fell. The system was a model; inevitably a black market sprang up but just about everyone got just about enough to keep going. The spartan quantities of food accidentally proved to be a boon for the health of the nation, even though bread (always white) was never rationed and little was then known about a healthy diet. Half the country's food came from abroad, despite a vigorous import-substitution campaign; a quarter of all Britain's needs had to be carried in neutral shipping. The Merchant Navy bore the brunt, mustering 160,000 at the outset, including 4,500 masters, 13,000 mates and 20,000 engineers.

The movements of their ships were controlled by the Admiralty Trade Division and their individual protection was in the hands of the Defensively Equipped Merchant Ship (DEMS) organization. This was set up by the Navy in June 1939 to arm merchantmen with old naval guns whose crews were drawn either from the Royal or the Merchant Navy (and later from the 14,000 men of the Maritime Regiment, Royal Artillery, which operated anti-aircraft guns aboard ships); 24,000 naval and 150,000 merchant seamen worked in DEMS during the war. The main value of the old guns was probably psychological; they certainly encouraged the Germans to lift all restrictions on U-boat warfare by August 1940. But the principal defensive stratagem for commerce was the protected sailing, led by a convoy commodore (usually a retired senior naval officer) but under the overriding orders of the naval Senior Officer, Escort (SOE), who might be as junior as a lieutenant-commander, RNVR. Early friction between the two seafaring services eased very quickly under the pressure of the shared danger.

The first U-boat to move to France was Lemp's *U30*, which arrived at the Breton base of Lorient, chosen to replace Wilhelmshaven as U-boat headquarters and 450 miles closer to the main British sea lane, the Western Approaches, on 6 July. Dönitz's small staff, led by Captain (later Admiral) Eberhard Godt, a key man as chief of staff, soon moved into a requisitioned villa at nearby Kernevel. E-boats were stationed in the Dutch ports for raiding the North Sea. This forced the Royal Navy to shift as much shipping as possible from east to west coast ports and to abandon the Western Approaches for the North-Western (north rather than south of Ireland). Forbes moved southward from Scapa to the Firth of Forth to oppose a German invasion. Cruisers were placed round the eastern and southern coastlines for the same reason.

On 17 August Hitler declared a total blockade of British waters, in which any ship, even neutral, could be sunk without warning. From March 1940 the Germans had been sending disguised merchant raiders to sea as an additional hazard to British shipping. Much deadlier than AMCs, the half-dozen sent out by July were strong enough to sink anything less powerful than a cruiser with their six modern 5.9-inch guns concealed behind false upperworks, their seaplanes, mines and four torpedo tubes. They had a maximum speed of about eighteen knots, averaged 7,500 tons capacity and carried copious supplies of plywood, paint and flags to change their appearance. By the end of 1941 seven of these deadly ships sank 600,000 tons of shipping in most of the world's oceans, including an Australian cruiser (HMAS *Sydney*) and three AMCs. Their huge range and elusiveness was an extra and serious headache for an already overstretched Royal Navy, just when Italy's entry into the war effectively closed the Mediterranean to British shipping, forcing it to go the long way round the Cape of

Good Hope instead of via the Suez Canal – 10,000 miles or six more weeks at sea, a combined delay equivalent to 150 average-size merchantmen.

Britain's most important ally for the next eighteen months was Canada, whose role, especially at sea, has usually been underestimated. A demographically small, geographically vast country, it declared war one week after Britain and sent over an army division (later expanded to a corps). The Royal Canadian Navy in 1939 consisted of 2,000 men (plus 1,700 in the RCN Volunteer Reserve), seven first-class destroyers and a handful of smaller vessels, including four home-built minesweepers. The Prime Minister, W. L. Mackenzie-King, announced massive industrial and naval expansion: the RCN was to swell by a larger factor than any other navy, to 378 warships and 95,700 personnel at its 1944 peak. The growing pains would be severe, sometimes crippling, but Admiral Sir Percy Noble, C-in-C, Western Approaches in 1941 and 1942, said after victory was won: 'The Canadian Navy solved the problem of the Atlantic convoys.'

Canada's disproportionate maritime contribution lay in the future as the Dominion government turned its mind to what it could provide immediately: food and shelter. There was wheat from the prairies and safe haven for convoys and escorts, members of the British and other royal families, refugees, children, even prisoners-of-war – and if need be for the British Fleet itself. In the event of a successful German invasion, the Canadians planned to provide what they called a 'spare bedroom' for the fleet at Gaspé Bay, New Brunswick, on the Gulf of St Lawrence. Meanwhile all seven Canadian destroyers were generously dispatched to Britain, Canadian shipyards started a programme to build ninety 'off-the-peg' freighters, sixty-four corvettes of the standardized British type and twenty-four minesweepers. Two precious Canadian destroyers were soon lost in a tragic double catastrophe involving separate collisions with British ships in 1940, but by the end of the year the first Canadian corvettes were in service with the convoys.

Until displaced by New York later in the war, Halifax, Nova Scotia, became the principal convoy terminus in the western Atlantic, accommodating the British Third Battle Squadron under Rear-Admiral L. E. Holland. This consisted at first of two battleships and supporting vessels assigned to dealing with the threat posed by the major German surface units. Holland was no diplomat and caused some resentment among RCN officers junior to himself whom he felt to be entirely at his disposal. This was an early taste of the Canadian Navy's uncomfortable lot, caught between the vastly superior strength of the Royal and US navies, under whose overall command the RCN successively came until it acquired a supreme command of its own in 1943 – after the U-boats were defeated. The British were not always kind or fair to their hard-pressed sister-navy.

The Canadians had their own Naval Control Service in charge of convoys on their east coast, enabling the first sailing to be dispatched from Halifax within a week of Canada's entry into the war. Halifax became the terminal for fast convoys and St John's, Newfoundland (then still under direct British rule), for slow. Captain Eric Brand, RN, detached to Naval Service Headquarters in Ottawa in June 1939, set up an Operational Intelligence Centre mirroring its London namesake, with which it would work closely throughout the war, as well as with its US equivalent in time. Brand saw out the war as RCN Director of Naval Intelligence and head of the Convoy and Routeing Section for the Canadian Director of Mercantile Movements, who controlled all Canada's shipping from 26 August 1939. The Royal Canadian Air Force and its bases on the long east coast gained importance as the war went on; and the Canadian Army sent troops to relieve the Royal Marines occupying Iceland in May 1940.

Canadian generosity could not meet all of Britain's needs, many of which could now be assuaged only by the United States. Churchill's direct line to Roosevelt increased immeasurably in importance when the former became Prime Minister, but their talks were not always harmonious; far from it. Just five days after taking office Churchill, alarmed by the high losses and damage among British destroyers, asked Roosevelt for the 'loan' of fifty. The gladhanding American prevaricated, still worried by the isolationists who remained a power in the land, and angered Churchill by ruminating aloud about what would happen to the British Fleet in the event of a German occupation. 'Cash and carry' still ruled, but Britain had effectively run out of money for arms; orders placed from September 1940 would outstrip British reserves (orders outstanding in the US were worth £400m, and £600m was owed to Canada).

As ever, US lawyers did not let the law stand in their way, finding that the administration was entitled to dispose of surplus arms as it liked. From 3 June obsolete equipment such as First World War rifles started to pass across the Atlantic. The next providential discovery was that the neutrality laws did not debar America from bartering arms; Roosevelt therefore offered Churchill fifty World War I destroyers in exchange for bases in Newfoundland and the West Indies, a hard-nosed deal concluded at the end of August. The old, coal-burning destroyers with their four tall smokestacks, once modernized and rechristened with the names of towns found in both America and Britain, did sterling service, increasing British destroyer strength by more than a third in short order. By this time the first 'off-the-peg' freighters ordered by Britain early in 1940 were coming out of US yards; later named 'Liberty' ships, they had a capacity of 10,800 tons and became a major factor in the struggle to overcome the U-boat threat.

The British, seeking other means of getting round American neutrality, hit upon bartering technology for aid. A British Technical Mission met US Navy experts in Washington at the end of August 1940. At first the Americans were sceptical, wondering what 'a nation that has been so backward' in naval technology could offer in submarine detection and above all 'RDF' (radio direction-finding, as radar was originally called – not to be confused with location by intercepting signals). After sending observers to see British devices in action the US Navy concluded that they were indeed well ahead and had a great deal to offer. This proved a breakthrough for Britain in general and its Navy in particular, the gateway to unlimited US industrial capacity. Colonel Frank Knox, Secretary of the Navy, wrote this note to a senior US administration official in October 1940: 'It is agreed that all devices, instruments or systems in use, developed for use or under development by the War and Navy departments will be offered for release to the representatives of the British Government.' The only exceptions were a naval mine and the Norden bomb-sight.

Two months later Roosevelt came up with a solution to Britain's biggest problem in its dealings with the US: finance. The Lend-Lease Bill, to be introduced early in 1941 and foreshadowed in a Christmas 'fireside chat' on American radio, gave the President the right to 'sell, transfer title to exchange, lease, lend or otherwise dispose of' items to any foreign country deemed by the President to be vital to American security. The Bill was tabled in the House of Representatives under the unintentionally ironic number HR 1776, the year of the Declaration of Independence from Britain. The Bill passed both houses of Congress, comfortably but not without controversy, by 9 March. Roosevelt was openly committed to giving Britain 'all aid short of war', and the first Lend-Lease budget passed by Congress on 24 March ran to a cool $7bn, or almost 50 per cent more than Britain's entire prewar reserves. By the end of the war the programme cost $48bn, of which Britain as principal beneficiary received some 40 per cent, twice as much as the next biggest recipient, the Soviet Union. Only $9.4bn was repaid, in cash or in kind, mainly by the British Commonwealth; the rest, with unprecedented magnanimity (and realism) was written off. In the end the money came back to US industry, which produced vast quantities of ships, aircraft, munitions and weapons systems for Britain, its Commonwealth and free European allies, alongside a staggering output for the US Navy and Army and their respective air forces.

From the end of January to the end of March 1941 the British and American Chiefs of Staff held the groundbreaking 'American– British Conversations', known as ABC-1 and designed to develop joint strategy and bilateral cooperation in the event of US involvement in the war (against Japan and Italy as well as Germany). The paramount principle was 'Germany first', which did not prevent the US Navy from sending the majority of its resources to the Pacific when the time came but did ensure that the US Army and Army Air Force concentrated the bulk of theirs against Germany and Italy. Rear-Admiral Robert L. Ghormley, USN, was sent to London by the Chief of Naval Operations, Admiral Harold R. Stark, to liaise with the Admiralty. From 1 February 1941 the US Atlantic Squadron became the Atlantic Fleet, commanded by Admiral Ernest J. King; from its Neutrality Patrol a new Support Force, based at Norfolk, Virginia, but with its own subsidiary bases for ships and naval aircraft in Scotland and Northern Ireland was detached on 1 April to escort transatlantic convoys, an extraordinary step for a 'neutral' nation. The US Navy also established a base at Argentia, Newfoundland, in February 1941. Roosevelt was rightly confident that Hitler would not gratuitously take on the USA for its mounting support of Britain – confident enough to relieve the Anglo-Canadian garrison of Iceland with US Marines in July.

Meanwhile the German submarine service was enjoying what it

termed its 'happy time', thanks to the great leap forward provided by the acquisition of the French coastline and the British weakness in destroyers and escorts. In the second nine-month segment of the war from the collapse of France the Germans had an average of only six boats on patrol but achieved an unmatched record of efficiency per operational U-boat. In the worst month for Britain's shipping of the war thus far, October 1940, they accounted for 352,000 tons of shipping, or very nearly 60,000 tons per patrolling submarine; 18 and 19 October were the worst two days for shipping losses of the entire war. Delays in delivery of new submarines and a heavier training programme in anticipation of expansion accounted for the temporary but far from inhibiting reduction in numbers. In February 1941 Dönitz had an all-time low for the war of twenty-one submarines operational; but many of them were captained by 'aces' such as Prien, the first to qualify by sinking 50,000 tons. The most proficient submariner of the war was Otto Kretschmer, who accounted for 238,000 tons in *U99* before his capture. The aces achieved huge scores against weak escorts (even so they sank twice as many IRS as vessels in convoy). Dönitz was able virtually to dispense with the services of twenty-six Italian submarines stationed at Bordeaux; only ten remained there by November 1940 and they contributed little or nothing to the continuing slaughter.

Whenever enough boats were available Dönitz was combining them into groups, dubbed 'wolfpacks' by the press of both sides. A tactic developed by the Germans at the end of the First World War in response to the adoption of convoy, the pack was originally commanded like a small flotilla by a senior officer, but the difficulty of communicating between boats submerging and surfacing in action put paid to this. Instead packs were assembled and named on an ad hoc basis against shipping detected by direction-finding or decrypts of the convoy sailing-telegram and all boats were centrally directed from Lorient. This most intensive use of radio so far in the history of warfare became an Achilles' heel which the Admiralty learned to use against the U-boats. But their tactic of attacking on the surface at night, when they were least detectable by ASDIC and eyeball alike, was paying enormous dividends.

One of the most poignant tragedies of the increasingly harsh war at sea occurred in mid-September 1940, when *U48* sank the liner *City of Benares*, commodore's ship of a westbound convoy, 600 miles west of Ireland. Because only a few lifeboats could be launched, more than 300 of the 400 passengers were killed; but seventy-seven of the dead were children on their way to Canada under the Children's Overseas Resettlement Scheme. The survivors drifted for about a week before they were sighted by an air patrol and rescued by destroyers; thirteen children were among them. The scheme was abandoned, not before time, amid a wave of hostile public opinion. A month earlier the Dutch liner *Volendam* had been torpedoed with 321 such children aboard (fortunately they and their ship were all saved) – two weeks after Hitler publicly lifted the last restraint on the U-boats, which had laid off passenger ships until 17 August.

The British response to pack tactics was the escort *group*, no longer a collection of warships that happened to be sailing in company but a team, trained and kept together to apply freshly rethought tactics. The retired Rear-Admiral Gilbert Stephenson, who set up the Otranto Barrage in 1914–18, was recalled and appointed Commodore, Western Isles, in July 1940 to take charge of escort group training at Tobermory on the Scottish island of Mull. Other ASW training schools followed at Dunoon and Campbeltown on the Scottish mainland. In October Admiral Dunbar-Nasmith, C-in-C at Plymouth, formed eight escort groups and set up a tactical training school for escort officers in Liverpool. The command itself was separated from Plymouth and moved to Liverpool and the flag of a new C-in-C, Western Approaches, Admiral Sir Percy Noble, in February 1941, occupying an underground bunker beneath a central Liverpool office block – the forward command-post for the Battle of the Atlantic. Number 15 Group of RAF Coastal Command, led by Air Vice-Marshal J. M. Robb, was also relocated to Merseyside and run by the Area Combined Headquarters underneath Derby House, directly linked to the Admiralty's Operational Intelligence Centre with its Submarine Tracking Room, and the Air Ministry, by telephone and teleprinter. Complete operational control of Coastal Command in and around Britain was transferred to the Admiralty in April 1941, simplifying joint operations. The HQ also had a copy of the London Trade Plot showing all shipping.

As the U-boat campaign intensified, the opposed forces in the Atlantic played a deadly leapfrog. The submarines moved ever further westward, waiting to attack convoys after their escorts put about to cover an incoming group. The escorts sailed further out into the mid-Atlantic 'Gap' between the end of the cover from

Halifax and the beginning of that from Western Approaches as soon as they could, as and when more escorts became available. In the slowly shrinking Gap the only cover available was one of the forty-six AMCs, which soon proved helpless against contemporary U-boat tactics. Inevitably, full escort cover was extended all the way across, supplemented by local escort at each end of a voyage and, when resources allowed, support groups acting as tactical reinforcements for convoys under attack. Eventually the surface gap was superseded by the air gap, the area of ocean south-west of Iceland out of reach of land-based air patrols from there or from Britain or Canada, pending the deployment of Very Long Range (VLR) aircraft and of escort carriers. There was another air gap around the neutral Portuguese Azores.

Recovered from the ravages of the Norwegian campaign, the German surface fleet returned to the Atlantic in autumn 1940, once again causing major disruption to the convoy system and making it necessary for a battleship to sail with convoys whenever possible. The *Hipper* was first but, plagued with engine trouble, achieved little and was lucky to find a refuge in the French port of Brest at Christmas. She came out again undetected on 1 February 1941 and sank eight merchant ships in a fortnight; she left Brest again on 15 March and arrived, unseen by the Northern Patrol, in Bergen on the 23rd after sailing west about the British Isles. After refuelling the *Hipper* sailed round to Kiel for another refit.

Next was the pocket-battleship *Admiral Scheer* (Captain Theodor Krancke), which embarked on the most successful single surface-raiding voyage of the war at the end of October 1940. By the time she too sailed unscathed into Bergen on her captain's forty-eighth birthday on 30 March 1941 she had sunk fourteen merchantmen, taken two prizes and destroyed the AMC *Jervis Bay* (Captain E. S. F. Fegen, RN) in a fierce attack on a convoy on 5 November. Fegen was awarded a posthumous VC for interposing his weakly armed liner between the enemy and his charges, only five of which were destroyed thanks to his order to scatter. Krancke's haul came to almost 100,000 tons; strategically the upheaval he caused in British naval dispositions from the Indian Ocean to the Arctic just as the U-boats got into their stride was much more valuable to the enemy. Krancke, boldest of the German captains, seemed to have no difficulty in meeting his supply ships and other German predators at will and evading detection with ease as he sailed across the main convoy routes.

Admiral Lütjens took *Scharnhorst* and *Gneisenau* to maraud in the north Atlantic on 23 January, after a false start a month earlier when the latter's engines forced a return to port. The pair evaded the Home Fleet and Somerville's Force H between Greenland and Sierra Leone, sinking twenty-one merchant ships of 116,000 tons and sailing into Brest on 22 March 1941 – after escaping three times from heavy British ships that briefly sighted them. Grand-Admiral Raeder, the German naval C-in-C, thus made the most of his small surface fleet as well as his small U-boat arm in causing maximum strategic discomfort to the world's leading navy.

By this time the outspoken Admiral Forbes had been 'relieved' as Home Fleet commander, on 2 December 1940; he was moved to the Plymouth command, soon to be truncated. He had challenged the Admiralty over Norway, its interference in local operations and tactical decisions, its incomprehension of air power at sea and its overestimation of the risk of German invasion after the Battle of Britain. But, despite having knocked out the bulk of the German surface fleet for half a year in piecemeal actions by May 1940, he had been unable to deliver the kind of spectacular victory that might have silenced his critics. He was made scapegoat for a series of setbacks, including the loss of several major warships, which were at least as much the Admiralty's fault. His last suggestion, ignored as usual though taken up later, was to take the AMCs off convoy duty, for which they were not suited. Forbes was replaced by Vice-Admiral John Tovey, who was to prove no less outspoken when the crisis of the Battle of the Atlantic loomed in due course.

The British escorts in the stormy Atlantic painstakingly achieved an important psychological victory over the U-boats in March 1941, whose significance took time to become apparent. A prolonged battle raged round outward-bound convoy OB 293 southeast of Iceland from the 7th, when four submarines made a predawn attack. The escort group was led by the destroyer HMS *Wolverine* (Commander J. M. Rowland, RN, as SOE), with another, *Verity*, and two corvettes, *Arbutus* and *Camellia*. The Germans torpedoed four ships but two U-boats were sighted and attacked for five hours; Joachim Matz's *U70* briefly surfaced before sinking; the other, Otto Kretschmer's *U99*, managed to escape. But on the next day the *Wolverine* sighted *U47* and the destroyers took turns to drop patterns of five depth charges, set to go off at various depths. One escort used her ASDIC to direct the other on to the target, thus covering the device's blind spot directly beneath each ship's hull. Prien's boat, which had sunk 161,000 tons of shipping, eventually rose almost to the surface before sinking out of sight. A gigantic orange flash was seen deep in the sea, a Wagnerian dénouement for the most notorious enemy submariner of them all.

The Germans concealed Prien's death until 23 May. In the meantime another fierce fight had developed round fast convoy HX 122 from Halifax on 15 March, when five U-boats formed a pack against it. Commander Donald Macintyre, RN, one of the most successful escort group leaders of the war, was SOE in the destroyer *Walker*, accompanied by the destroyer *Vanoc* and the corvettes *Bluebell* and *Hydrangea* in the 5th Escort Group. Two extra destroyers were added to the cover of the fully laden and valuable convoy, which included several tankers. Joachim Schepke, one of the top aces in *U100*, hit a tanker on the night of the 15th but was driven off without sinking it; on the evening of the 16th Kretschmer's *U99* cut a fearsomely destructive swathe diagonally across the convoy, sinking six vessels in little more than an hour from within the rows of ships. Walker then sighted *U100* and damaged it with a pattern of ten depth charges. When it returned to the surface, it had the misfortune to become the first U-boat detected by the new Type 286 ASV (anti-surface vessel) radar just fitted to the *Vanoc* (Commander Denese, RN), which rammed it. The destroyer's keel crushed the boat, killing all but six men who happened to be in the conning tower as Schepke and *U100* vanished.

Walker now picked up *U99* on ASDIC and dropped five depth charges, sending the boat down to 700 feet (250 more than it was designed to withstand). Kretschmer used up all his reserves of compressed air to shoot back to the surface, where he came under a hail of fire. He signalled by lamp from his conning tower in English: 'Captain to captain. Please save my men drifting in your direction. I am sinking.' All but one of the crew of forty-six were rescued by Macintyre. On interviewing the cool and cultivated Kretschmer in captivity an Admiralty staff officer remembered: 'I sincerely hoped that there were not too many like him.' He had sunk nearly 240,000 tons in eighteen months, which remained a record for the war.

On 23 March an ASW trawler caught *U551* off guard between the Faroes and Iceland and sank it. the fifth British U-boat 'kill' in fifteen days, including the elimination of the three top German aces from the war. Prior to this, no U-boat had been sunk in four months. When the Germans announced the loss of Schepke and Kretschmer on 25 April, Churchill was jubilant and thought the Navy had gained the upper hand in the Atlantic; rumours spread in Germany that the British had developed a secret anti-submarine weapon.

But there was still the surface threat to contend with, and it was about to be formidably augmented by the biggest and strongest warship so far engaged in hostilities: the brand-new super-battleship *Bismarck*, commissioned in April 1941 and displacing 41,700 tons (50,900 fully loaded). The ship was 800 feet long and boasted eight 15-inch guns, a cruising range of 8,100 miles, six seaplanes and the world's most effective armour, and could make thirty-one knots; Captain Ernst Lindemann had a crew of 2,090 men. Lütjens moved his flag to her as he planned Operation *Rheinübung* ('Exercise Rhine') in Gotenhafen (now Gdynia in Poland) – a thrust against the north Atlantic convoys supported by the new heavy cruiser *Prinz Eugen* (14,050 tons but only eight 8.1-inch guns), third in the overrated 'Hipper' class. The German plan was conceived by Raeder and originally involved the two battlecruisers as well, but had been questioned by Lütjens and even Hitler ever since the pair had locked themselves up in Brest. The *Bismarck* was to draw the attention of the Home Fleet while the *Prinz Eugen* beat up some convoys.

The British naval attaché in Stockholm was able to report that the Germans had passed from the Baltic into the North Sea via the Kattegat channel on 20 May. Coastal Command found them in a fjord south of Bergen on the 21st and Admiral Tovey resolved to fight them. He detached Vice-Admiral L. E. Holland with the battlecruiser *Hood*, the new battleship *Prince of Wales* and six destroyers from Scapa Flow to Hvalfjord in Iceland, poised to move south-east against the Germans. On 22 May the Fleet Air Arm's Commander G. A. Rotherham carried out a perilous, low-level reconnaissance of the Bergen area in bad weather to establish that the two German heavies had left Norwegian waters. Tovey sent cruisers to watch the passages east and west of Iceland, keeping his main strength between Scapa and Iceland to await a sighting. On the 23rd the cruiser *Suffolk* spotted Lütjens from seven miles away, heading south-west off the west coast of Iceland. Her sister, HMS *Norfolk*, confirmed the sighting shortly afterwards from six miles, briefly coming under fire from the *Bismarck*.

Norfolk escaped behind her smokescreen and reported in detail to
Tovey, then some 600 miles to the south-east; aboard her, Rear-
Admiral W. F. Wake-Walker, commanding the 1st Cruiser
Squadron, ordered the two cruisers to keep in touch with the
Germans as they headed south.

Meanwhile Admiral Holland was racing south-westward from
Iceland on a converging course. On paper his force was somewhat
more than a match for the Germans: the 'mighty *Hood*', much-
venerated flagship of the fleet, displaced 48,000 tons unladen and
outpaced the *Bismarck* by a knot or two, matched her armament
with eight 15-inch guns in four double turrets (two forward, two
aft) but, as a battlecruiser conceived in the First World War, was
seriously inferior in armour (and design). Although launched in
August 1918, the *Hood* (Captain Ralph Kerr, RN) was as untried
in battle as her quarry. She was also in need of a refit after much
frustrating deployment in rough waters; long service 'showing the
flag' between the wars had prevented a much-needed modernization. Her companion, *Prince of Wales* (Captain J. C. Leach, RN),
conceived as a 'Washington Treaty' battleship, displaced 35,000
tons unladen and carried ten 14-inch guns in two quadruple turrets
(fore and aft) and one double turret forward. She had a design-
speed of twenty-nine knots but had not fully 'shaken down' or
overcome her teething troubles.

Admiral Holland sighted the Germans twenty-three miles to
starboard, still heading south-west on a course not quite parallel to
his own. In order to attack them he had to charge in line abreast
from an angle not far short of ninety degrees – which meant he
could bring only those heavy guns to bear that could fire over the
bow, ten in all, four 15-inch on *Hood* and six 14-inch on her
companion, whereas the Germans were broadside on, the cruiser
leading the battleship. Holland thus gratuitously sacrificed what
could have been an overwhelming advantage in firepower; his two
ships were close together, helping the German gunners, who
opened fire at thirteen miles, exposing the *Hood* with her poor
deck-armour to plunging shot. Holland, dictating every move by
his captains, confused the two German ships and ordered his own
to concentrate their fire on the *Prinz Eugen* instead of the *Bismarck*.
Fortunately Captain Leach did not make the same mistake and
engaged the *Bismarck* regardless, dividing the British fire; but one
of his six forward guns broke down. The Germans concentrated on
the *Hood*, and with their customary high-class rangefinding scored

an early hit, setting off a fire amidships. Holland now turned both his capital ships to port, broadside on, to bring all seventeen available big guns into play. As this move was in progress a heavy German broadside straddled the *Hood*. It was 6 a.m. on 24 May and the pride of the Royal Navy exploded, just as the British battlecruisers had done at Jutland twenty-five years before: 'flash' penetrated her magazines and the ship went down in four minutes. There were three survivors from a crew of 1,419; the destruction of the *Hood* had a more devastating effect on British public opinion than the loss of any other ship in the war.

The Germans turned their attention to the *Prince of Wales*, which took a direct hit on the bridge at 6.02 a.m. One of her quadruple turrets fell silent thanks to a mechanical failure as four 15-inch and three 8-inch German hits forced the battleship to make smoke and withdraw. But her armour had withstood the test very well, and Leach did score two 14-inch hits on the *Bismarck*, one causing leaks in some fuel tanks, which began slowly to let in seawater. A jubilant Lütjens now decided to make for Brest, shadowed by Wake-Walker, who had taken over command from Holland, lost with the *Hood*. Tovey was still racing north to join forces as the Admiralty mobilized every available ship, including Somerville's Force H, two battleships from Halifax and HMS *Rodney* from a convoy in mid-Atlantic: nineteen major ships (cruisers and upwards) plus over a dozen destroyers joined the hunt.

The first attack was led by Lieutenant-Commander Eugene Esmonde, RN, of HMS *Victorious*, which sent up nine Swordfish torpedo-bombers escorted by six Fulmar fighters from about a hundred miles away. One torpedo struck the *Bismarck* amidships, causing little damage; two fighters were shot down. Lütjens detached the *Prinz Eugen* on the evening of the 24th with orders to operate independently further south in the Atlantic, turning the *Bismarck* briefly as if to attack her pursuers. After the air attack he put on speed and shook off the slower British surface forces as he raced south-eastward towards France, hoping not to have to use his contaminated fuel-oil. A Coastal Command pilot sighted her 700 miles west of Brest at 10.30 a.m. on 26 May, when Force H lay across her path seventy miles to the east, consisting of *Ark Royal*, *Renown* and the light cruiser *Sheffield*. The carrier launched fourteen Swordfish in atrocious weather, which by 2.50 p.m. were heavily engaged in an attack – on HMS *Sheffield*, which managed to escape damage by violent manoeuvring. A second wave of Swordfish, led by Lieutenant-Commander T. P. Coode, RN, attacked the intended target just before 9 p.m., scoring two torpedo hits. One amidships bounced off; the other, under the stern, disabled the German battleship's steering-gear and damaged her propellers. A grim Captain Lindemann sent for a U-boat to collect the ship's papers.

The next British attack was by Captain Philip Vian's 4th Destroyer Flotilla. Ignoring his orders to act as extra escort for Tovey's capital ships, Vian launched a torpedo attack in the early hours of 27 May, scoring a few ineffectual hits but without damage to the five attackers. Admiral Tovey then sent in two battleships, the new *King George V* and the *Rodney*, which joined battle at 8.47 a.m., supported by cruisers *Dorsetshire* from Force H and HMS *Norfolk*. The *Bismarck* was subjected to 109 minutes of bombardment at ever-closer ranges; the *Dorsetshire* delivered the apparent coup de grace with three torpedoes into her sides. Even this may not have been enough to destroy the extraordinarily strong, blazing hulk: when the wreck was explored more than fifty years later, there were indications of scuttling. She sank at 10.36 a.m. on 27 May; only 110 of her crew were saved. The summoned U-boat arrived too late, rescuing just three men after the British had gone.

The Battle of the North Atlantic, as this biggest naval action after Jutland and before the great Pacific clashes is loosely styled, set the Home Fleet, Force H and many other units against just two German heavy ships, one of which got away to Brest after aborting its sortie against the convoys because of engine trouble. Each side lost its fleet flagship plus crew and a fighting admiral, but the ease with which the *Hood* was destroyed contrasted embarrassingly with the extraordinary effort required to avenge her by sinking the *Bismarck* – whose even mightier sister, the *Tirpitz*, was approaching completion. The action was more of a 'draw' than Jutland, because while the Germans won the first phase of the battle and the British the second, just as in 1916, the strategic situation was not changed at all as a result of the 1941 engagement. Major German surface units posed a threat to the plethora of targets presented by the convoys just as before, and constituted a 'fleet in being' which, because they might find targets anywhere in the Atlantic, had to be countered by much larger but scattered forces – at the same time as the U-boats were increasing their depredations. Indeed, the presence in Brest of the two battlecruisers and the *Prinz Eugen* meant that the Royal Navy had to divide its attention between them and the permanent threat in the north.

There was indeed a secret weapon against the U-boats. The greatest British secret of the war was tantalizingly exposed to alert readers of naval history as early as 1956, but did not become the subject of a sensational 'revelation' until 1974, since when it has never lost its fascination. British intelligence had cut its teeth against the revived German Navy in the context of the Spanish Civil War from 1936 to 1939; German naval intelligence, the *Beobachtungsdienst*, and its decryption section, known as the *xB-Dienst*, had not only reciprocated but achieved rather more on the same occasion. They gained at least partial entry to British naval codes and ciphers, knowledge which lasted well into the war, when they broke the main Royal Navy cipher number three, used not only for convoy control but also for communication with the Canadian and American navies until 1943. The Admiralty, unlike the RAF and the British Army, had set its face against encipherment machines such as the 'Enigma', originally a German commercial device whose details were on file at the British Patent Office. Recording the initial German lead in this vital area, Captain Stephen Roskill, RN, added, clearly but without emphasis, on page 208 of the second volume of his official British history of the war at sea: 'The reader should not, of course, assume that we British were meanwhile idle in achieving the opposite purpose.' This unusually inelegant sentence with its implicit double negative is nonetheless absolutely unmistakable.

There is no accompanying detail whatsoever, but Roskill managed to fire a torpedo through the Official Secrets Act by stating that Britain broke German naval cipher. The metaphorical missile did not detonate; it was only when a veteran of the Government Code and Cipher School at Bletchley Park wrote his memoirs in 1974 that the secrets of 'Station X' began to be disclosed. Roskill was patently frustrated by the conflict between his need to genuflect to British official secretiveness on the one hand and his duty as a historian on the other, because in 1959 he wrote a monograph called *The Secret Capture*. This brief book described the seizure and pillaging on 9 May 1941 of *U110*, the new command of Fritz-Julius Lemp. His boat was damaged by depth charges and forced to the surface during his attack on a westbound convoy; as its crew was taking to the water the 3rd Escort Group led by Commander A. J. Baker-Cresswell, RN, managed to put a boarding party on the submarine and seize its Enigma machine with that day's settings in place, together with all the current German codes and ciphers, which was just as well because the U-boat later sank while under tow. Lemp was killed, probably in an exchange of fire between his crew and the boarders, led by Sub-Lieutenant David Balme, RN. Baker-Cresswell's destroyer *Bulldog* raced to Scapa Flow to hand over the priceless material to intelligence officers who had flown up from London. According to Roskill, on examining the loot, they exclaimed: 'What? This . . . ? And this. . . ? We've waited a long time for one of these!' The great historian still did not feel free to reveal what 'one of these' was.

Bletchley Park, which eventually had 10,000 people on its staff, attacked all enemy ciphers, and had been working on Enigma from the beginning of the war. German naval ciphers proved to be the hardest to break, mainly because the service was more security-conscious than the rest of the Wehrmacht, though not totally so. Luftwaffe and German Army messages were penetrated in 1940. Enemy naval cipher material was gleaned from the belongings of careless prisoners of war and by boarding captured or wrecked enemy vessels in Norway and elsewhere in 1940 and 1941. Polish and French intelligence officers had provided invaluable information from their own early work against Enigma, enabling the British to develop the 'bombe' machines which laboriously went through the possible settings of the three ratcheted wheels at the core of the machine. From the end of May 1941, just too late to influence the *Hood-Bismarck* drama, the naval cryptanalysts at Bletchley were able to feed fresh and priceless operational information continuously to the Operational Intelligence Centre (OIC) at the Admiralty and its Submarine Tracking Room (STR), led by Commander (later Captain) Rodger Winn, RNVR, who now became a key man in the British war effort, and to Western Approaches. Its main value until ASW forces reached peak strength lay in the diversion of convoys away from U-boats, whose movements and orders could now be followed as never before. The breakthrough was as important as the delivery of the *Magdeburg*'s codebook in 1914.

All intelligence gathered by deciphering Enigma messages was codenamed 'Ultra' and Churchill insisted on reading it from a special dispatch box delivered nightly – as if the Prime Minister did not have enough to do. But he derived a special thrill from his 'golden eggs' and put an 'Action this day' tag on a letter from Alan Turing, the Bletchley mathematician who contributed more than anyone else to solving the Enigma problem, asking for more equipment and better facilities.

Rodger Winn had wanted to join the Navy as a boy but was debarred by poliomyelitis, which left him with a limp and a twisted back. He became an accomplished barrister and used his forensic skills to extract information from prisoners at the beginning of the war. But when Paymaster-Captain Thring proved unable to sustain the burden of running the STR, the job he had done at the end of the First World War, the Director of Naval Intelligence, the free-thinking Rear-Admiral John Godfrey, a veteran of Room 40, invited Winn to take over at the end of 1940. He ran it for the rest of the war from Room 39 in the Old Admiralty Building; the OIC was in a bunker underneath. Winn's talent lay not just in gleaning maximum information from intercepted and deciphered enemy radio traffic to form an overall picture of U-boat deployment and operations; he was able to build up a psychological profile of Dönitz and read the mind of Godt, his highly effective chief of staff.

They too had instinct: as early as 9 June 1941, when convoys were already becoming harder to find, the U-boat command ordered all submarines to reduce their garrulous radio traffic to a minimum. A new doubly encoded grid system was introduced for chart references, along with new transmission channels and frequently changed wavelengths. U-boats were addressed by their captain's surname rather than their number. All this forced Bletchley Park to strain harder to lay its golden eggs, but early profits from naval Ultra included a torpedo-bomber attack on the pocket-battleship *Lützow* between Germany and Norway on 13 June, putting her out of action for seven months; and fifteen supply ships sent out in April to replenish German surface raiders were picked off in under ten weeks from early in May. Eight were located by Enigma breaks in June. In the same month a large convoy from Halifax was identified as the target of a wolfpack and escorts from two other convoys were successfully diverted to its defence.

But something of even greater strategic significance, for the war at sea as much as on land, occurred on 22 June, when Hitler's Operation 'Barbarossa' unleashed 120 divisions against Russia. Exactly a year after the fall of France, Britain once more had a major fighting ally, albeit on the basis of the principle that my enemy's enemy is my friend. The said friend, however, showed every sign of an early collapse. It was now clear to the British, who had picked up hints of great events from Ultra, why the Luftwaffe had been winding down, though not abandoning, its operations over the Channel, North Sea and eastern Atlantic. The German Navy had no air arm at all; Göring in Germany had far surpassed Trenchard in Britain in asserting his claim to authority over anything that flew. The Germans planned two aircraft carriers before the war, one of which was hardly started and the other partly built in two stages before being totally abandoned. Two squadrons, a total of thirty aircraft, were earmarked for work with the Navy in April 1940. They flew a maritime version of the three-engined Focke-Wulf 200 bomber known as the Kondor. Its range of 1,000 miles was augmented after the success of the Blitzkrieg; a base at Mérignac in western France was supplemented by another at Stavanger in Norway, enabling them to take off at one and land at the other, flying 2,000 miles in one direction (provided the weather did not change at the terminal airfield). British east-coast ports, as we have seen, were subject to heavy attack after the fall of France, as was shipping in the Western Approaches and the Channel. All these factors eased in spring 1941 as German squadrons moved east for the planned offensive against Russia.

Another consideration which reduced the Luftwaffe's presence in Western Europe was the war on land and sea in the Mediterranean after the fall of France and the entry of Italy, anticipated from March 1940 by British intelligence and prompting reinforcement of sea, land and air forces in North Africa. Four battleships, the small carrier *Eagle* and half a dozen cruisers were under Admiral Cunningham's flag by June, as were Godfroy's French battleship and four cruisers. When France fell and Italy declared war on Britain, Admiral Pound had wanted to evacuate the Mediterranean altogether and concentrate on the transatlantic lifeline and the German threat to it. Churchill overruled him, regarding such a move as the death knell of the British Empire, whose main artery ran from Gibraltar via Suez to the Indian Ocean. The result of this decision was profound, making the Mediterranean theatre the focus of British land operations for the best part of four years, even though the imperial sea route could not be safely used for most of that time. Instead of following the Clausewitz dictum of concentrating against the main force of the main enemy, Britain in effect elected to open a second front. On the other hand the country, even if it had focused exclusively on Germany, was in no position to tackle Hitler's 'Fortress Europe', dominated by the world's best army. Thanks to the RAF victory in September, Britain did have one means of striking at Germany itself: by aerial bombardment. But that was the only strategic possibility, and it would take time to build up into a threat that the Nazis would have to take seriously. An invasion and a fight with the Wehrmacht on land in Europe was ruled out indefinitely.

Churchill remained confident that the Navy would be able to deter a Japanese threat to Britain's Asian interests by reinforcing Singapore and Ceylon from the Mediterranean in due course. Meanwhile Cunningham had to contend with the Italian fleet, superior to his in both numbers and tonnage in all types of vessel, from cruisers to submarines, and supported by Mussolini's large air force, which was able efficiently to track British naval movements all over the Mediterranean. Three of 'A.B.C.'s' battle-ships – all except his flagship *Warspite* – were unmodernized First World War veterans. And although the British were able to break into Italian prewar ciphers, these were replaced by October and proved highly resistant to penetration. Early in July the two fleets clashed off Calabria and the Italians were forced to withdraw with considerable damage; the British also intercepted ten Italian submarines, capturing those not sunk.

Cunningham's policy was simple: to miss no opportunity of hounding the enemy. He was a destroyer man and a bit of a gambler rather than a battleship bureaucrat, and retained all the dash of the former at the age of fifty-six. Unusually, and unlike his predecessor Pound, he could delegate authority to his captains, only making sure that they understood his thinking and his outlook. Salty in his language, intolerant of fools and a master of tactics, 'A.B.C.' was ready, willing and able to go on the offensive, a luxury denied to most of his colleagues further north for most of the first four years of the war. But he was not strong enough to dominate the enclosed ocean, especially when the Germans arrived to reinforce their Italian allies at sea, in the air and on land. Normal Allied mercantile shipping could not use the Mediterranean, even in convoy, and had to take the long route to India and the Far East, via the Cape of Good Hope. Only military convoys sailed the Mediterranean; and they were far from safe.

Nevertheless, much of the often fierce fighting in what Mussolini, echoing the Roman emperors he imitated, unjustifiably called

Mare nostrum – our sea – was focused on military convoys, whether British and sailing west–east between Gibraltar and Alexandria, or Axis shipping plying the much shorter, north–south route between Italy and North Africa. The key to this struggle was the British mid-ocean island colony of Malta, due south of Italy and well within range of enemy air attack. The island began the war almost defenceless, with forty-two anti-aircraft guns, three old biplane fighters nicknamed Faith, Hope and Charity, and one radar set. Guarding the entrance to the ocean was Vice-Admiral Somerville's Force H, strategically placed at Gibraltar to intervene in the Atlantic or the Mediterranean. Somerville, a little older than Cunningham, was no less proficient but rather more cautious. The two admirals made a good team in a series of joint operations.

One of the first was to deliver twelve Hurricane fighters to Malta, a massive operation to deceive, delay and deter the Italian fleet while bringing the old carrier *Argus* within reach of the island on 1 August. At the end of the month Cunningham was considerably reinforced by the new carrier *Illustrious*, a modernized battleship and two modern cruisers, delivered in Operation 'Hats' and escorted for most of the way by the bulk of Force H. Malta was reinforced en route, despite intermittent shadowing and attacks by Italian and German aircraft. The Italian fleet stayed clear. Meanwhile General Wavell's Middle East Command in Egypt had to be reinforced by military transports that delivered 76,000 troops from Britain and 50,000 from India, Australia and New Zealand via the Cape and the Red Sea to fight the Italians in the Western Desert. In September a hastily conceived and abysmally executed attempt to capture the French West African port of Dakar, sheltering the battleship *Richelieu*, with Royal Marines and Free French troops in the ill-named Operation 'Menace', collapsed in confusion, an irritating diversion for Force H. One old British battleship, *Resolution*, was put out of action for a year.

Six Vichy French cruisers and destroyers managed in the same month to leave Casablanca and pass the Straits of Gibraltar to reach Libreville in Gabon, a matter of considerable embarrassment to the force that had destroyed the bulk of the French fleet two months before. Somerville was not blamed for this but was made to answer to an Admiralty Board of Inquiry (on Churchill's order) for deciding not to chase the faster Italian fleet during Operation 'Collar', an abortive attempt to reinforce Malta by convoy in November. Most of another squadron of Hurricanes launched by the *Argus* ditched in the sea for lack of petrol, having taken off too far to the west. But by this time (28 October) the Italians had unwisely invaded Greece.

A fortnight later, as the Greek Army smartly repelled the Italian attack from Albania, Admiral Cunningham led Operation 'Judgment' against the bulk of the Italian fleet in its main base of Taranto, on the inside of Italy's 'heel'. The plan was focused on Cunningham's two carriers, the modern *Illustrious* (Captain Denis Boyd, RN) and the older *Eagle*, led by Rear-Admiral A. L. Lyster. The latter ship broke down but Cunningham, having missed one deadline three weeks earlier, decided to go ahead on 11 November with the one carrier – covered by all five of his battleships, two cruisers and thirteen destroyers. RAF reconnaissance flights from Malta supplied clear pictures of the port and its defences. Taranto was to be attacked by Swordfish biplane torpedo-bombers with their open cockpits (top speed when loaded of 100 knots) against six battleships, five cruisers, destroyers and many anti-aircraft guns. Five of *Eagle*'s aircraft had been added to those on *Illustrious*; each Swordfish could carry just the one torpedo or a bomb-load of 1,500lb.

The attack was launched after dark from about 170 miles to the south-east. The lead aircraft carried flares and bombs, to light a path for the others before attacking the port's oil tanks. The first strike included one dive-bombing Swordfish and five armed with torpedoes; several in the first wave of twelve lost contact in clouds. The torpedoes were launched from just thirty feet, well below mast-head height, at ranges as short as 400 yards. The second wave was guided to the objective by the fires caused by the first, as well as by its own flares – and a dense hail of tracer-rounds from the Italian anti-aircraft guns. Three battleships were badly damaged by tor-pedoes in this attack, the first carrier assault on a battlefleet in its defended base: one was beached in a sinking condition, never to go to sea again, while the other two victims needed up to six months in dock. A cruiser, destroyers and the oil tanks were all badly damaged by bombs. On the same night Rear-Admiral H. D. Pridham-Wippell led three cruisers plus destroyers in an attack on an Italian military convoy: all four ships in it were sunk in the mouth of the Adriatic. The spectacular raid on Taranto (Lyster's idea) proved to be of particular interest to the admirals of the Imperial Japanese Navy: its immediate result was a decisive shift in the naval balance of power in the Mediterranean towards the British.

Four weeks later XIII Corps of British, Indian and Australian troops under Lieutenant-General Richard O'Connor roundly defeated three Italian corps at Sidi Barrani in Egypt. As the Italians retreated along the coast into Libya they came under fire from the elderly but heavy guns of the Inshore Squadron of a monitor and three gunboats, led by Captain H. Hickling, RN. In the first week of 1941 O'Connor triumphed over the Italians again at Bardia and began his advance on Tobruk. O'Connor, having duly taken Tobruk on 22 January, completed the demolition of the Italian Tenth Army at Beda Fomm on 7 February, raising his tally of prisoners to 130,000 at a cost of just 2,000 casualties. The small British imperial land force, supported and supplied by the Royal Navy, was poised to expel the Italians from North Africa altogether.

Churchill's 'soft underbelly' stratagem of attacking the weaker Axis partner in his own backyard had produced, in short order, the kind of victory that had so agonizingly and expensively failed to materialize at the Dardanelles in 1915. There was understandable jubilation in Britain over the series of successes after all the bad news from the North Cape to the Pyrenees of half a year earlier. But it was a false dawn: the British had not had to face the enemy 'A-team' – the Wehrmacht – in the Mediterranean. This was about to change. German troops had been pouring into the Balkans from early winter, preparing to go to the rescue of the Italians in Greece, even though Mussolini had attacked it without consulting Hitler. The first Wehrmacht intrusion into the Mediterranean theatre, however, was by the Luftwaffe, which established its *Fliegerkorps X* – tactical air force – at bases in Sicily by the turn of the year. Some 120 aircraft, including dive-bombers, medium bombers, and fighters, and aircrew trained in maritime flying, were a formidable reinforcement for Italy's *Regia Aeronautica*.

Although Bletchley Park had gleaned a great deal about the new piece on the Mediterranean board, the information inexcusably did not reach Cunningham or Somerville. Their forces came under surprise attack on 10 January during a joint operation to cover a munitions and food convoy bound from Gibraltar to Malta and Athens as well as other shipping movements. Near Malta Cunningham's force – two battleships *Illustrious* and escorts – was attacked by forty-three German dive-bombers, inevitably concentrated on the carrier, which reeled from six 500kg bomb hits within a few minutes; the ship was hit once more as she limped into

Valletta harbour in Malta, and remained a target for the Germans as long as she lay helpless in port. Miraculously her engines were in surprisingly good condition; hastily patched up, she stole out of harbour after dark on 23 January and started her dash for Alexandria at twenty-four knots, arriving to a hero's welcome at noon on the 25th. Her escape was particularly fortunate because the Suez Canal was by now often blocked by ships wrecked by Luftwaffe mines: the weapons were acoustic and impossible to counter in narrow waters. Thus the 'back door' to Cunningham's main base was often jammed and the carrier could not be relieved for two months. Somerville, however, got away unscathed after Force H carried out a heavy bombardment of Genoa in north-west Italy at dawn on 9 February.

The next day Churchill made a blunder comparable with Gallipoli: in the teeth of opposition from his military advisers on the spot, including Wavell, the army C-in-C in the Middle East, Longmore, the RAF commander, and Cunningham, he decided to divert O'Connor's triumphant Western Desert Force, poised to drive the Italians out of Tripoli and North Africa altogether, to support Greece against the Germans. The order to risk the Libyan bird in the hand (including the prospect of RAF control of the skies over the southern Mediterranean) for the two in the Balkans was sent to Wavell on the 11th. On the 12th the German General Rommel and a small staff arrived in Tripoli, ahead of the new Afrika Korps that was to tie down massive British forces for two years. It is some measure of the relative performance of the land forces engaged in the fight for North Africa that the British Army, one corps of which had broken much larger Italian ground forces with ease, had to assemble its main strength to defeat 1 per cent of the German Army (three divisions out of 300) and its much more numerous but less effective Italian allies in what now became the principal land campaign of the British Empire forces until spring 1943.

Cunningham went out of his way to warn the Admiralty that the impending commitment to Greece against heavy Axis air superiority and German troops was a high-risk enterprise, not least for his ships. An attempt to dislodge the Italians from the Dodecanese Islands offered a bad omen in February, ending in complete failure. But the superb New Zealand Division, an Australian division and a British armoured brigade were landed at Athens during March. On the 26th a large Italian naval force set out from southern Italy to attack the trooping convoys running between North Africa and the Piraeus: Admiral Angelo Iachino had assembled the modern 30-knot battleship *Vittorio Veneto*, 41,000 tons, with six 8-inch and two 6-inch cruisers plus nine destroyers. The British convoys were being covered by Admiral Pridham-Wippell's Force B – four light cruisers and four destroyers.

Ultra intelligence and RAF reconnaissance from Crete alerted the Mediterranean Fleet to the Italian move. Part of Iachino's force was sighted between Sicily and Crete, bound for the latter. In the evening of the 27th Cunningham aboard HMS *Warspite* led the bulk of his fleet out of Alexandria: two more battleships, the carrier *Formidable* (replacement for *Illustrious*) and nine destroyers were with him. Scouting aircraft of each side sighted ships of the other just after dawn on the 28th. Then a group of three Italian 8-inch cruisers sighted Pridham-Wippell's four 6-inchers. The outgunned British admiral executed the classic manoeuvre in such a situation: he set out to draw the enemy on to the guns of the approaching British battleships, but soon found himself sailing between the first Italian group and a second, which included the Italian flagship with her nine 15-inch guns; Cunningham, limited to twenty-two knots by his old battleships, was nearly four hours' steaming away as Pridham-Wippell withdrew southward towards him behind a smokescreen. An abortive attack by six Albacore torpedo-bombers from *Formidable* on the Italian battleship was enough to prompt a reversal of course by Iachino as the two British forces joined up for an apparently hopeless north-westward chase of the retiring Italians. A second air strike by five British aircraft injected a torpedo under the stern of the *Veneto*, halving her speed as she shipped a mass of water. A third strike left the cruiser *Pola* dead in the water. Other Italian warships formed a protective cordon round their flagship as the British C-in-C ordered a night chase of the faster Italians – on the off-chance that he might catch up after all and ignoring standing orders not to risk torpedo attacks if enemy destroyers were present at night.

Unaware of Cunningham's determination to press home an attack, Iachino sent one light and two heavy cruisers plus three destroyers to fetch the *Pola*. This detached force was sighted by the British main body due south of the Greek mainland off Cape Matapan at about 10.30 p.m. and came under its crushing broadsides at a range of less than two miles. In under five minutes the two heavy cruisers *Fiume* and *Zara* were demolished and abandoned in flames. The former sank; the latter and the *Pola* were dispatched by British destroyers, which also sank two of their opposite numbers: the Italian Vice-Admiral Cattaneo was among the 2,400 enemy dead. The *Vittorio Veneto*, however, managed to escape to Taranto, eluding the destroyers sent after her. Such was the Royal Navy's most crushing victory since Trafalgar in 1805 – and its last battlefleet action.

From this martial high point the fortunes of the British in the Mediterranean ran rapidly downhill. Hitler invaded Yugoslavia and Greece on 6 April from north and east. The Commonwealth force which had just completed its landings immediately entered on yet another fighting retreat. Yugoslavia surrendered on 17 April; the Greek Army, exhausted by its earlier efforts against the Italians, crumbled on 21 April. London decided to extricate the two and a half divisions, starting on the 24th, just as Cunningham returned from a successful bombardment of faraway Tripoli. Pridham-Wippell, now a vice-admiral, was in charge of Operation 'Demon' at the British forward base at Suda Bay, Crete, with Rear-Admiral H. T. Baillie-Grohman working with the army command ashore, requisitioning small craft to lift troops from seven beaches on the eastern coast of Greece, on either side of the Saronic Gulf south of Athens. Thirty warships and twenty-one transports ferried the troops to Alexandria or Suda Bay in a reprise of the 1940 operations in Norway and France. The Luftwaffe was so overwhelmingly superior that it was able to sink a total of twenty-six ships including transports, five hospital ships and two destroyers. Some 51,000 troops were evacuated; 12,000 men were killed, wounded or left behind in the terrible fiasco of the intervention in Greece. A mass of equipment and stores was abandoned.

The next British mistake was to defend Crete, the long island south of mainland Greece, despite Ultra indications of a heavy German assault. The Germans struck in mid-May: after nearly a week of massive air attacks, virtually unopposed, the Luftwaffe sent in its 7th Parachute Division in 600 aircraft and gliders, backed by 700 combat aircraft, on the 20th. Once airfields had been secured, a mountain division was landed, raising the German invasion force to 22,000 frontline troops. Tanks and heavy guns followed by sea. German air superiority rendered Suda Bay useless as Cunningham sent four task forces, A, B, C and D, to attempt to disrupt the anticipated seaborne invasion. Force A had two battleships; the others were led by two cruisers each; all had destroyers. Cunningham stayed in Alexandria with his reserves, two battleships, the carrier and four cruisers plus sixteen destroyers. But the main enemy thrust against Crete was airborne; only relatively small numbers of German troops were coming by sea (none got there). The four task forces did destroy a convoy with 4,000 troops, forcing another to turn back, but had to endure prolonged air attacks, losing two cruisers (*Gloucester* and *Fiji*) plus two destroyers and suffering a great deal of damage, not least to HMS *Warspite*, which was reduced to a crawl, and the other battleship, *Valiant*, struck by two bombs. Two more destroyers were sunk in the withdrawal, including Captain Lord Louis Mountbatten's *Kelly*.

The last British reinforcements were landed at Suda Bay on the night of 26 May by three destroyers, covered by Pridham-Wippell with Cunningham's last two battleships and six destroyers. The battleship *Barham* was badly damaged by German bombers but got back to Alexandria with her companions by the evening of the 27th. The Germans were now unshakably established on Crete with General Student's paratroops and two mountain divisions. Another British evacuation was ordered, starting on the night of the 28 to 29th. In four nights of yet another well-nigh miraculous withdrawal some 18,000 troops were taken off, out of 22,000 landed, but at appalling cost to the Mediterranean Fleet: two battleships and the carrier out of action for many weeks, three cruisers sunk and five badly damaged, six destroyers lost and seven crippled, 50 per cent of Cunningham's ships. The victor of Taranto had very much had a taste of his own aeronautical medicine at the hands of the Luftwaffe and fully expected to be dismissed.

Rommel had been rolling back the British gains in North Africa from the end of March 1941, reaching the Egyptian border at the end of April. Cunningham was staggered on the 15th to be asked to sacrifice a battleship and a cruiser as blockships for Tripoli harbour to deny it to the Axis supply convoys. He successfully resisted and instead made a daring raid on the port from Alexandria, nearly 1,000 miles away, with three battleships, a cruiser and the carrier *Formidable* (whose air cover was not needed). The night bombardment went on for forty-five minutes, wrecking installations and sinking two freighters and one destroyer; the attackers got back unscathed and without enemy air attack, which was fortunate because the port carried on exactly as before. Cunningham was increasingly angered by the stream of interfering advice from London, based on ignorance of local conditions and apparent lack of confidence in himself as the commander on the spot. But he was not sacked.

Between the evacuations of Greece and Crete, Cunningham and Somerville successfully executed Operation 'Tiger' in the second week of May, taking 295 new tanks and fifty-seven crated Hurricane fighters to British forces in Egypt. One-fifth of the consignment was lost, with one of the five freighters involved, to a mine south of Sicily. Nearly a quarter of a million Commonwealth servicemen arrived in Egypt in the first half of 1941; the new Eighth Army stood at 100,000, perhaps twice as numerous as the Germans under Rommel, who were now the main enemy. Force H and the Mediterranean Fleet suffered more and more damage in their efforts to sustain the battered garrisons of Tobruk and Malta in defiance of the air superiority of the Axis. Supporting the island was extremely costly, yet no surface ships could safely be allowed to operate from there for most of 1941. Attacks from Malta on the north–south Axis convoys were left to the RAF and HM submarines such as *Upholder* (Lieutenant-Commander M. D. Wanklyn, VC, RN) until Force K, Captain W. G. Agnew's two cruisers and two destroyers detached from Force H, arrived in October 1941. Before then the British were stopping one ship in three bound for Tripoli; thereafter the rate rose to two in three, briefly touching 70 per cent. One Italian convoy of seven ships was wiped out by Force K in this campaign, mirroring the Battle of the Atlantic but with the British as the marauders. Wanklyn sank two 19,500-ton Italian liners in a three-ship convoy on 1 September, on his way to becoming the most successful British submarine ace of the war. The RAF sank 102,000 tons and HM submarines 75,000 in this successful onslaught.

But the attrition of the Royal Navy on the long east–west convoy route across the Mediterranean continued relentlessly at the same time. The Germans sent in another tactical air force, *Luftflotte II*, and a flotilla of ten U-boats to join the fight, for a total Mediterranean presence of twenty-four. The carrier *Ark Royal*, modern by British standards and attached to Force H, was on her way back to Gibraltar on the afternoon of Friday, 13 November after helping to fly off forty-four more aircraft to Malta, when she was sighted by *U81* (Fritz Guggenberger) and attacked at 1,200 metres, despite the presence of a battleship, a light carrier and a cruiser. Massively holed by one of four torpedoes, left dead in the water and on fire after the failure of all her power systems, the *Ark Royal* (Captain L. E. H. Maund, RN) rolled over and sank the next morning, despite every effort to get her into Gibraltar, just twenty-five miles to the west. Only one sailor died, but the loss of the poorly designed ship was a bitter blow to the British side, which could ill afford such a reduction in its maritime air strength after so many carrier losses earlier in the war. But modifications were made to other British carriers, considerably improving their 'survivability'.

Twelve days later *U331* (Lieutenant Hans Diedrich von Tiesenhausen), submerged off Alexandria, sighted and attacked one of a squadron of three British battleships from a position inside the escort screen. HMS *Barham* (Captain G. C. Cooke, RN) took three torpedoes in her starboard side and listed, sinking in minutes when her magazines exploded. The First World War veteran was the first dreadnought to be sunk in the war by submarine attack on the open sea, and the catastrophe was not admitted until early 1942. By December the Mediterranean Fleet was down to one light cruiser; and by Christmas it was without a serviceable battleship, following a uniquely brave attack by six Italian frogmen on three underwater 'chariots' inside the defences of Alexandria, launched from Commander Borghese's submarine *Scire* and led by Lieutenant-Commander Durand de la Penne. This staggering exploit, which left *Queen Elizabeth* and *Valiant* ignominiously sitting on the bottom of the harbour, forever gave the lie to the traditional British disparagement of Italian military prowess – altogether a most gallant riposte for Taranto.

It brought the Navy's Mediterranean casualty list at the end of 1941 to one battleship sunk and four damaged, one carrier sunk and two damaged, seven cruisers sunk and ten damaged, sixteen destroyers sunk and twelve damaged, five submarines sunk and three damaged. Just keeping Tobruk in the fight cost the Navy twenty-five warships sunk and nine damaged in 1941 – which began and ended with the British Army standing on the same spot, El Agheila in Libya, all of which, but for the disastrous diversion to Greece, would have been in British hands by Easter. The unfortunate General O'Connor was a prisoner, captured by the Germans while on a brief visit to North Africa.

Strategically the war had been transformed by Hitler's attack on the Soviet Union. His intervention in the Balkans, a disaster for the British, was also a setback for him because it delayed the eastern offensive by what turned out to be an absolutely vital couple of months. As the Wehrmacht followed the ghost of the *Grande armée* into the vastness of Russia, the Luftwaffe's effort in the Mediterranean reached and passed its peak at the turn of the year because of events much further north. An Anglo-Soviet mutual assistance pact was signed and sealed in Moscow on 12 July 1941 and the Red Army managed to fend off a German attempt to seize Murmansk, the main, ice-free Soviet naval harbour in the far north.

Britain's acquisition of a new ally, however, increased rather than decreased the burden on the Royal Navy, especially the Home Fleet, responsible for protecting the fraught Britain–Iceland–Murmansk route via which American munitions, brought to Britain or Iceland by convoy, would be forwarded to the Russians. Roosevelt and Churchill met in August for the first of many Anglo-American wartime summit meetings at Argentia, Newfoundland, where the US Navy had set up its base at the end of 1940, to discuss grand strategy in the post-'Barbarossa' climate. One of the main topics was how best to help Stalin, and a small trial convoy left Iceland on 21 August: the hard-worked old carrier *Argus* and a freighter, both carrying aircraft for Russia and escorted by a Home Fleet carrier, two cruisers and six destroyers, got through without incident. At the end of September the double convoy series QP (south-west bound) and PQ (to Murmansk) was set up, PQ 1 sailing from Hvalfjord, Iceland, on the 29th.

By this time the U-boats appeared to be losing their touch. The worst month for shipping of the war thus far had been April 1941, when 688,000 tons, 45 per cent in the Mediterranean, were lost to all causes; the tally dropped to 511,000 in May, 432,000 in June, a mere 121,000 in July and a vestigial 80,000 in August. The diversions, of the Luftwaffe to the eastern front and of shipping in response to Ultra intercepts, were complemented by improvements in convoy-escort tactics and deployment. Any relief was short-lived: the U-boats alone claimed 203,000 tons out of an overall total of 286,000 tons sunk in September 1941 as the packs returned to the north Atlantic from the Mediterranean and from guarding Norway; the neutral Americans announced that they would help escort some convoys from Halifax to Iceland. Their useful intervention was timely, as the Canadian Navy was cracking under the strains of forced growth and the hard grind of escorting the slow convoys of the SC series from Sydney, Cape Breton.

The Germans meanwhile, having moved their submarines around the north and central Atlantic in probing for the weaknesses in the convoy system, were focusing their efforts in the air gap south-east of Greenland, around longitude 30 degrees west and latitude 50 degrees north, from September. This area was out of reach of Allied aircraft then flying from Britain, Newfoundland or Iceland. The only plane with the range to close this gap and its smaller cousin south-west of the Azores (used by the Germans for refuelling and resupply at sea) was the American B24 Liberator bomber, whose potential had been spotted by the RAF and which was just coming into mass production to meet orders from Bomber Command, which all but monopolized it in Britain. The Admiralty's dilemma was that in order to enjoy air cover, which was proving extremely effective over convoys, shipping in the eastern Atlantic had to be sailed within reach of the German Kondor aircraft, which could not only find and attack convoys but also home U-boats on to them.

The ultimate solution to the problem of air cover was to sail aircraft carriers with the convoys. A stopgap to deal with Kondors was the CAM (catapult-aircraft merchant) ship, which could launch one Hurricane fighter from a ramp: the brave pilot could only hope to ditch in the sea and be rescued when his fuel ran out. Five merchantmen were adapted to launch several Hurricanes but they too were simply discarded after one flight. The British invented the escort carrier when they converted the captured German cargo liner *Hannover* into HMS *Audacity* in June 1941. Adapted in the same way as the first carriers of the 1914–18 war, *Audacity* (Commander D. W. McKendrick, RN) kept her six Swordfish torpedo-bombers and six US-made Martlet fighters on her deck, but could land them with arrester-wires as well as launch them by steam catapult, both British inventions, like the escort carrier concept itself. Her short career was spent entirely on the England–Gibraltar route and ended in spectacular fashion in December 1941, when she joined the 36th

Escort Group with homeward-bound convoy HG 46 of thirty-two ships, led by Commander (later Captain) F. J. 'Johnnie' Walker, RN, the best escort leader and tactician of the war, in the sloop *Stork*.

The voyage developed into one of the hardest convoy battles of the entire war: only two merchantmen were lost to attacks by half a dozen U-boats and a similar number of Kondors, whereas four U-boats and three Kondors were destroyed by the double-strength escort. But the submarines blew up the destroyer HMS *Stanley* – and Gerhard Bigalk in *U751* cut *Audacity* in half with three torpedoes on the evening of 21 December, the fifth day of the battle; each half sank separately. Bigalk got back to base in time to make a Christmas propaganda broadcast about his exploit. On the 22nd, however, still 700 miles from home, the convoy came under the eye of a single Liberator from England, enough to deter several more U-boats and a Kondor. More Liberators took turns to fly over the convoy, which arrived without further loss on the 27th.

To the north-west, convoy SC 42 had come under massive attack from the 'Markgraf' pack early in September, losing a quarter of its sixty-four ships, but the Canadians sank their very first U-boat, by ramming, during a chaotic battle. In this fraught period, one American destroyer was damaged and another sunk by U-boat torpedoes, to the amazement of American public opinion, which had no idea how deeply the US Navy was involved in convoy protection. The poorly trained, demoralized Canadians with their inferior equipment, unable to say no to the demands of their American and British mentors, were getting as little as four days' leave in every thirty (the British usually got twelve) and the Admiralty was becoming alarmed by adverse reports on their performance and condition as winter approached. SC 52 was the only convoy in the entire war to turn back to port, under the threat of a large wolfpack detected by Bletchley Park.

On 6 December the Red Army halted the Wehrmacht outside Moscow. The next day the Japanese Navy proved how well it had absorbed the lesson of Taranto by sending 370 carrier aircraft to attack, without declaring war, the US battlefleet in its Hawaiian base of Pearl Harbor. Six out of eight battleships were incapacitated; fortunately three American carriers and thirteen cruisers were away at the time, enough to render the devastating stroke a strategic failure. Congress promptly declared war on

Japan, which gave Churchill sleepless nights until Hitler foolishly declared war on the United States on the 11th. Britain now had the world's mightiest industrial power on her side. The immediate results were disastrous for the Allied cause.

10

War on Three Fronts

Admiral Sir Tom Phillips died on the bridge of his flagship on 10 December 1941 in a battle that still has no official name. Vice-Chief of Naval Staff from summer 1939, 'Tom Thumb', as the diminutive admiral was known to the lower deck, was delighted to be appointed C-in-C, Eastern Fleet, in October 1941. For both Britain and America, war with Japan had moved up the scale from very likely to inescapable as soon as Tokyo and Moscow concluded their non-aggression pact in April. The treaty startled the world as much as the Nazi–Soviet pact of August 1939 and was motivated by a similar mixture of cynicism and self-interest. Stalin feared a war between the Soviet Union and Germany while the military junta which had ruled Japan since 1928 feared there would not be one. That would have left Moscow free to oppose Japanese ambitions in China and south-east Asia.

The British government therefore decided it was high time to activate the policy of basing a force at the main imperial naval base of Singapore, expanded for this very purpose before the war, to protect its imperial interests in south and east Asia. But, hard-pressed in the Mediterranean, where the British fleet had endured massive losses, and in the Atlantic, where the major German surface units and U-boats posed an increasing threat to the North American and Russian convoy routes, Churchill's 'powerful squadron' consisted of one modern battleship, HMS *Prince of Wales* (flag), and one old battlecruiser, *Repulse* – to face what was then, ship for ship and by virtue of its strategic position, the strongest navy in the world. The carrier *Indomitable*, which was to have joined the pair by the time they reached Singapore on 2 December, ran aground on the way from the West Indies and thus lived to fight another day: she would have been of little use against the carriers and land-based squadrons of the world's mightiest and most advanced naval air force. She went to Norfolk, Virginia, for repairs under another 'friendly neutral' arrangement with the US, available since the fall of France.

Force Z, as the proposed nucleus of an Eastern Fleet was temporarily called, thus had no dedicated air cover, despite the terrible losses which weakness in the air had exacted in the Mediterranean and far northern waters. There were just four destroyers to protect the two capital ships as they set out to deter rampant Japanese expansionism. US embargoes on strategic exports precipitated the Japanese southward advance early in December 1941 that achieved total surprise across an 8,000-mile front, from Indo-China to Hawaii, and secured control of a great swathe of territory from Manchuria round to Dutch New Guinea, in just three months of fighting.

HMS *Repulse* (Captain W. G. Tennant, RN), completed in 1916 but modernized twice between the wars, had fired her guns in anger only once: in 1917, also the last time Admiral Phillips had seen action. As a lightly armoured, 36,000-ton, 30-knot battlecruiser she carried only six heavy 15-inch guns of 1916 design and fifteen 4-inch in five triple turrets. For specific defence against aircraft she had only four high-angle, 4-inch guns plus four eight-barrel 'pom-poms'. Her crew consisted of sixty-nine officers and 1,240 rates; her captain was nicknamed 'Dunkirk Joe' because he had been Ramsay's Senior Naval Officer there and was the last Briton to leave the port. *Prince of Wales* was a 35,000-ton, 28-knot 'Treaty' battleship, ordered in 1939 and regarded as unlucky: she was hit by a German bomb before her launch and ran aground just after commissioning in January 1941. On the other hand, she had escaped the fate of her companion, HMS *Hood*, seven months earlier. Repaired in haste, she carried 100 officers and 1,502 men; her Captain Leach was known as 'Trunky' for his prominent nose. Her main armament consisted of ten rapid-firing 14.2-inch guns with a range of eighteen miles, eight pairs of 5.25-inch heavy anti-aircraft guns, and six multiple pom-pom batteries as well as arrays of lighter Bofors and Oerlikon AA-guns.

In Singapore on 8 December, Tom Thumb conferred with Trunky, his flag captain, and Dunkirk Joe over lunch aboard his flagship, HMS *Prince of Wales*. They debated what to do in the light of the shocking news of the past twelve hours. The Japanese had not only bombed Pearl Harbor but also marched into the international quarter of Shanghai in China, landed troops at Kota Bharu in north-eastern Malaya, invaded southern Siam (modern Thailand), sunk a British gunboat in Chinese waters, bombed Singapore (ineffectually because of bad weather), overrun the US

Pacific island of Guam and stormed into the unfortified British colony of Hong Kong on the Chinese coast. All this was followed, not preceded, by Emperor Hirohito's declaration of war at 11.40 a.m., Tokyo time, on the 8th; and it was only the hors d'oeuvres. Phillips decided to take his squadron on a sweep up the eastern side of the Malayan peninsula to disrupt rumoured Japanese landings. He asked the local RAF command for fighter cover, and a Royal Australian Air Force squadron of twelve Brewster Buffalo fighters, indifferent American aircraft soon to be relegated to a training role by the US Navy, was put on standby.

The British ships went as far north as the Thai border on the 9th, found nothing and turned back. They picked up a wireless report of a landing at Kuantan, halfway along the Malayan east coast, during the night, and Phillips decided on a surprise attack at dawn. But just before midnight the Japanese submarine *I58* sighted his force and reported it to the 22nd Air Flotilla of the Japanese Naval Air Force, based near Saigon in Vietnam with the reluctant consent of Vichy France since late October 1941. Preceded by scouts trying to locate the British ships, seventy-six aircraft, fifty-two armed with torpedoes and the rest with bombs, took off to attack them. If they failed to find the ships they were to go on to raid Singapore harbour (beyond the return range of many of the aircraft). They had passed their 'point of no return' by 10.45 a.m. Singapore time on the 10th when a reconnaissance aircraft found Force Z. Sixty-seven Japanese aircraft reversed course, found the target and attacked at about noon.

The Japanese pilots were astonished to encounter no opposing aircraft and pressed home their attack on the larger ship, the *Repulse*, in wave after wave for half an hour until she turned turtle and sank. The *Prince of Wales* put up a much more intense barrage of anti-aircraft fire but could not hope, despite desperate manoeuvres, to escape such a swarm of attackers. The flagship too turned over and sank forty-eight minutes later, at 1.18 p.m. The report of the landing fifty miles to the west of the scene of this humiliating total defeat proved to be an unfounded rumour. Only after the Japanese aircraft had left to make emergency landings wherever they could did eleven of the RAAF Buffaloes drone over the wreckage. During the one-sided battle off Kuantan, Phillips had requested first destroyers and then tugs; he did not even ask for fighters. Three Japanese bombers were lost. The British destroyers rescued 2,081 survivors; 840 men were lost and three were captured later from their boat by the Japanese. One of them, James Milne, a pom-pom gunner from the *Prince of Wales* (rate unknown), told Japanese reporters:

> Admiral Sir Thomas Phillips stood on the bridge from the beginning to the end. A destroyer drew near just before his ship sank and signalled, 'Come aboard'. But he answered, 'No thank you'. Raising his arm in salute from the bridge, he went down with the ship. Captain Leach stayed with Admiral Phillips . . . They disappeared into the sea as if swallowed by it.

With them went not only Britain's naval strategy in the new theatre of war but also the last vestige of the long-since compromised supremacy at sea of the battleship. Their battlefleet in ruins at Pearl Harbor, the Americans had no choice but to use their initially outnumbered aircraft carriers (and their submarines) if they wished to counter-attack the Japanese, which they most certainly did. The British, already overstretched in the Atlantic and Mediterranean, had no such option: they now had no strategic presence in the Far East or the Pacific.

The shattered Allies were soon reeling from further Japanese strokes. A Japanese Army corps supported by an Army Air Force group advanced southward from the landing at Kota Bharu and bases in Thailand and French Indo-China towards the great fortress of Singapore, whose main coastal artillery faced out to sea because the British had never anticipated an overland attack. The advance, largely by bicycle through the conveniently spaced rubber trees of Malaya, surprised even the Japanese with its speed as numerically superior Commonwealth forces fell back in disarray, betrayed by their own side's propaganda about the 'inferiority' of the enemy, his small stature, his poor eyesight and bandy legs. The hastily formed ABDA (American-British-Dutch-Australian) command under the British General Sir Archibald Wavell, was defeated piecemeal, unable to concentrate against an enemy who seemed to be everywhere at once. The last Commonwealth troops crammed into Singapore from Malaya by the causeway, which was blown up on 31 January. Royal Navy demolition parties were already blasting the lavish installations of their base as the last merchant ships left – and the last reinforcing troops were still coming ashore. Lieutenant-General Arthur Percival surrendered Singapore to the Japanese Army on Sunday 15 February 1941, along with 138,708 Commonwealth service personnel, British, Australian and Indian.

It was the greatest single defeat in all British history; the Empire never recovered from this unprecedented blow to Britain's prestige. The Japanese invaded Burma in mid-January 1942, directly threatening India, the 'jewel in the crown' of the British Empire. The Japanese programme for Phase I of the 'Outline Plan for the Execution of the Empire's National Policy' was comfortably ahead of a schedule which envisaged a culmination in the capture of Java, heartland of the Dutch East Indies, in 150 days. Singapore was supposed to be taken in 100 days; only seventy-two were required.

The Japanese invested just 200,000 troops, including eleven divisions, in Phase I, backed by 700 frontline Army aircraft and 1,500 more in support, plus 1,600, supported by 3,300, from the Imperial Navy. The key to success was air superiority on all fronts, most importantly the Zero fighter, fast, well armed and capable of staying airborne for an astonishing three hours or more; it was deployed in large numbers by both imperial services on land and carriers in many roles: reconnaissance, ground-attack, strafing ships, pursuit of enemy fighters, bomber protection and combat air patrol over carriers. The Japanese also possessed large numbers of modern, long-range medium bombers. Their pilots had learned their deadly trade in thirteen years of fighting in Korea, Manchuria and China. The fact that the main American asset in east Asia, the Philippines, was 450–500 miles away from the nearest Japanese land-based aircraft in Formosa was not an obstacle for such long-legged aircraft – fighters capable of flying nearly 1,200 miles and 'Betty' land-based naval bombers that could manage 3,745. Their Western opponents, whether on land, at sea or in the air, simply had no answer to the readiness of Japanese airmen (and soldiers and sailors) to die in battle: the men who flew against Force Z simply did not care that they would be unable to get back to base and saw nothing odd in their admiral's order, superfluous as it turned out, to 'come back dead'. Surrender or even capture in battle was a disgrace whose only remedy was suicide. The contempt felt by contemporary Japanese for those who surrendered at Singapore and later in Java is beyond the reach of the Western imagination, with its assumptions about Geneva conventions and the rules, customs and practices of war.

The Japanese crippled American air power in the Philippines mostly while it was lined up on the ground: thirty-four B17 Flying Fortresses, which was the largest concentration anywhere of the latest and best US bombers, and eighty-seven fighters came under attack from Japanese naval bombers and fighters from Formosa on 8 December; some 100 US Army Air Force planes were destroyed or crippled. A few days later the Japanese found it all the easier to make various landings in the Philippines against General Douglas MacArthur's command of 140,000 ill-prepared Filipino and American troops and Admiral Thomas H. Hart's elderly US Asiatic Fleet, also based on Manila. American ships and submarines made as little impression on the many Japanese landings as their British counterparts to the west. Hart abandoned Manila by 31 December; Borneo and Hong Kong had fallen by Christmas, Sarawak on Christmas Eve.

General Wavell's ABDA command operated from Bandung, Java, from January 1942. The American Admiral Hart was his deputy and naval commander, his chief of staff and air chief were British, his fleet and army commanders Dutch. His strategy was to hold Singapore as the last redoubt of the East Indies, a forlorn hope as we have seen. The Japanese sent in Vice-Admiral Kondo's Second Fleet, divided into Eastern and Western Area forces and further subdivided into task groups. The Imperial Navy deployed flotillas of purpose-built landing craft and its Special Landing Forces (equivalent to marines) to make a series of coordinated invasions of American, British and Dutch-controlled islands. The Japanese Southern Army had its own fleet of transports and supply ships, symptomatic of inter-service rivalry of a level of ferocity unknown to any other belligerent (which is saying a lot): eventually the Japanese Army was the only one in the world to operate its own submarines. Field-Marshal Count Terauchi's eleven divisions and plethora of specialized units were divided among four corps, one for the Philippines, one for Burma, one for Java and Sumatra, the fourth for Malaya and Singapore.

ABDA abandoned its main naval base at Surabaya in north-east Java in the last week of January as its air space and that over the short route to northern Australia were now dominated by Japan. The alternative base at Tjilatjap on the south coast had to be abandoned in its turn. The Dutch Rear-Admiral Karel Doorman led the ABDA Combined Striking Force, at that stage consisting of two Dutch and two American cruisers and eight destroyers, in one of several ineffectual attempts to disrupt Japanese landings: three of the four cruisers were badly beaten up from the air. The Dutch East Indies Army crushed a paratroop assault on Palembang, the oil port in south-east Sumatra, on 14 February, while Doorman raided and disrupted Japanese shipping in the Sunda Strait between Sumatra and Java, but these moves only delayed the Japanese schedule for the area by one day. A Japanese division overwhelmed the defenders of Palembang the next day as Doorman's reduced force withdrew. Sensing all-round defeat as Singapore fell, the Americans withdrew Admiral Hart and allowed the Dutch Vice-Admiral Conrad Helfrich to relieve him on 16 February.

Three days later the apparently unstoppable Japanese heavily bombed Darwin in northern Australia, a shock to the Commonwealth: the population briefly evacuated the port, which ceased to be a naval base for the duration of the war. The Japanese Second Fleet's various task groups, backed by Vice-Admiral Nagumo's force of four carriers and escorts which had led the raid on Pearl Harbor, now joined forces for the attack on the main prize, Java. One light and four fleet carriers, four battleships, eight heavy cruisers and a swarm of destroyers and light vessels converged to cover ninety-seven transports and supply ships. ABDA fell apart. The Americans withdrew their remaining B17s and transport aircraft to India on 24 February, and Wavell himself flew to Colombo, Ceylon, on the 25th. ABDA's Western naval force of one Australian and two British light cruisers plus destroyers withdrew without a fight to the same refuge three days later, leaving the Dutch to defend their vanishing empire all but unaided.

The Battle of the Java Sea on 27 February proved to be the last sea fight for the East Indies. Admiral Doorman in light cruiser HNethMS *De Ruyter* (flag), with HMS *Exeter* (heavy cruiser hero of the River Plate), USS *Houston* (heavy cruiser), HMAS *Perth* (light) and HNethMS *Java* (light), plus Dutch, American and British destroyers, had no radar or air cover; even the spotter seaplanes normally aboard the heavy cruisers had been left behind in anticipation of a night action. Sailing into the sunset from an abortive move against Surabaya on the north coast of Java,. and halfway between that lengthy island and Borneo to the north, ABDA's naval Combined Striking Force came under fire from two Japanese heavy cruisers fourteen miles to the north: twenty 8-inch guns concentrated on the Allied heavies, *Exeter* (Captain O. L.

Gordon, RN) and *Houston*, while two Japanese light cruisers and destroyers approached to attack the smaller ships. As a running battle developed between the two opposed lines, the heavy cruiser *Haguro* landed a single 8-inch shell at extreme range on the deck of the *Exeter*, penetrating a magazine and causing a massive explosion. The Allied line crumpled in confusion, two destroyers were sunk but the shattered *Exeter* managed to keep on firing while moving at half-speed.

Doorman made frequent changes of course, from west to south to north and back to west, trying to elude the Japanese cruisers and search for the invasion fleet at the same time. The opposed forces lost touch for a while but as the Allies turned north-east they were sighted again by the westbound Japanese squadron. Battle was renewed after dark under Japanese starshells. Doorman turned south, only to run into a new Dutch minefield of which he had no knowledge, losing a British destroyer. The Allied cruisers were sailing apart from their remaining destroyers when the Japanese heavies found them again for a last duel. The issue was decided by the Japanese Long Lance torpedoes, the best in the world; enemy destroyers quickly sank *De Ruyter* and *Java*. Doorman chose to go down with his flagship after sending *Houston* and *Perth* and one Dutch destroyer to the Dutch East Indies capital of Batavia. The *Exeter* stole away to Surabaya with one British and one American destroyer.

But a desperate Admiral Helfrich sent the three battered cruisers straight back into action, to attack the main Japanese landing on Java from the Sunda Strait late on 28 February. They sank four transports out of fifty-six then gathered there, but were soon overwhelmed by the Japanese naval escort: HMAS *Perth* (Captain H. M. L. Waller, RAN) went down at five minutes past midnight, while USS *Houston* (Captain A. H. Rooks, USN) turned turtle and sank forty minutes later, having fired every last round aboard, whether 8-inch shells or rifle bullets: one-third of her crew of 368 survived to go into harsh captivity. Later in the morning of 1 March four Japanese heavy cruisers caught HMS *Exeter* limping down the Sunda Strait; abandoned, she rolled over and sank at 11.30 a.m. after Captain Gordon had told his two destroyers to run for it. But they too were caught and sunk.

The remnant of the ABDA naval strike force, six US destroyers, got away to Australia as the Governor-General of the Dutch East Indies officially dissolved ABDA on 1 March. Batavia fell on 6

March; the Dutch formally surrendered at Bandung on the 10th. What the Japanese were to call the Greater East Asia Co-Prosperity Sphere was complete. Only in Burma, on its western flank, did fighting continue, a threat to British India; and a doomed last-ditch stand by local and American troops was still going on at Bataan in the Philippines. Japan already had a whole string of islands and atolls in the western Pacific, mostly taken over from the Germans during or after the First World War, as forward outposts against the Americans. The eastern side of the huge Bay of Bengal was dominated by the Japanese, and the Royal Navy based itself at Ceylon (not out of reach, as will be seen).

On 24 March Admiral Sir James Somerville, formerly of Force H at Gibraltar, was appointed C-in-C of the British Eastern Fleet. Its nucleus consisted of the fleet carriers *Indomitable* and *Formidable* and the light carrier *Hermes*; but collectively these could deploy just fifty-seven obsolescent strike aircraft and thirty-six mediocre fighters. They were joined by five repaired battleships of First World War vintage, two heavy and five light cruisers, a dozen destroyers and five submarines. This force, though considerable on paper, could only be deployed defensively against the Japanese fleet, which heavily outnumbered and outclassed it, ship for ship, in every department except quality of submarines. The Eastern Fleet had three bases: Colombo and Trincomalee in Ceylon and at Addu Atoll (Gan), 700 miles to the south-west of Colombo – so secret that the Japanese never even discovered its role.

Australia became America's principal ally in the impending struggle for the Pacific. General MacArthur and his staff, and the residue of the US Asiatic Fleet, withdrew to Australia, the main base for MacArthur's future, US Army-dominated, Allied South-West Pacific Command (SOWESPAC), which would include the US Seventh Fleet, successor to the Asiatic Fleet. In Hawaii, Admiral Chester W. Nimitz was appointed Allied C-in-C of the Pacific (CINCPAC), the vast naval command charged with attacking the Japanese from the east.

The reorganization of the United States Navy prompted by its belated propulsion into a war on two ocean fronts propelled Admiral Ernest J. King from the Atlantic Fleet, soon stripped to the bone to reinforce the Pacific, to the command of the entire Navy. Understandably rejecting the acronym CINCUS, he became COMINCH and was the first to combine the post of naval C-in-C

with that of Chief of Naval Operations (CNO). A convinced and
dedicated Anglophobe of Scottish extraction, Admiral King was
described by one of his daughters as 'even-tempered – always in a
rage' but soon proved himself a brilliant administrator of a rapidly
expanding fleet. But his determination to concentrate on the Pacific
war and his inability to recognize that the Royal Navy might have
expensively acquired lessons to impart turned into a catastrophe
for Britain.

Ironically the arrival of the US as a belligerent doubled the
operational area available to Admiral Dönitz and his U-boats by
annulling the US-protected neutrality zone in the western half of
the Atlantic. At the same time the transfer of many destroyers and
other American ships to the Pacific via the Panama Canal reduced
the convoy escorts available. Thirdly, Admiral King, ignoring the
British credo that any escort was better than none, stuck for many
disastrous months to his view that a weak escort was worse than
none. The result was what the U-boat crews soon began to describe
as 'the second happy time', which lasted through the first half of
1942. Dönitz unleashed Operation *Paukenschlag* ('Drumbeat' or
'Thunderbolt') on 12 January with a mere half-dozen, long-range
Type IX U-boats strung out along the long east coast of the United
States, all he could spare at the time thanks to continuing Mediterranean commitments. Seven medium-range Type VII boats were
sent to the waters off Newfoundland and Nova Scotia.

The result, in the words of the official US naval historian, was 'a
merry massacre'. By the end of the month the Germans sank
200,000 tons of shipping off the coast between Newfoundland and
Bermuda, compared with 63,000 on the north Atlantic convoy
routes. In the first quarter of 1942 they sank a total of 1.25m tons,
216 vessels, the vast majority in the waters off the lengthy American
east coast, out of a worldwide total of 1.93m, 1.34m tons of which
were sunk by enemy submarines. More than half the tonnage lost
in waters for which the US Navy was responsible consisted of
tankers, the most valuable merchantmen afloat. Despite the hard-
won, eleventh-hour lesson of 1917 and the Royal Navy's two and a
half years' experience since 1939, Admiral King, having all but
denuded the Atlantic of American destroyers, set his face against
convoy until 'enough' escorts were available. General Eisenhower,
not the most vindictive of men, confided to his diary that the Allied
war effort would probably have gone rather better had King been
taken out and shot.

But the north Atlantic navies could at least agree on their escort requirements: the Anglo-Canadians needed 725 and the US 590 to add to their respective strengths of 383 and 122 in March 1942. Britain already had 300 destroyer-escorts or frigates on order, and it was agreed that new escorts would be allocated to the three fleets according to need. The American Chiefs of Staff, including King, were naively anxious to go on the offensive as soon as possible and slowed down the escort programme in order to accumulate material, labour and construction space for landing craft, over-looking the salient fact that in order to be able to attack Germany, the agreed 'main enemy', they needed to make the transatlantic convoy route as secure as possible. But so vast was the capacity of Roosevelt's 'arsenal of democracy' that the construction of 82,000 landing craft did not prevent the Americans from adding 1,265 warships to their own fleet and hundreds more to Allied navies, or from building 80,000 naval aircraft, all included in a naval spend-ing programme worth $105bn over the five years from 1 July 1940.

It was hugely ironic that Admiral Pound, chief of a one-ocean navy embroiled with three disparate enemies, felt moved after Pearl Harbor in December 1941 to offer the US Navy ten corvettes and two dozen armed ASW trawlers. Admiral King accepted. RAF Coastal Command was able to station an ASW squadron in Rhode Island in June 1942. Pound pressed for convoy in American waters in March while Churchill was making the same case to Roosevelt. British chagrin can be imagined when ships which had been escorted all the way across the Atlantic were picked off at leisure by U-boats whose hunting was generously simplified by the failure of American coastal communities to black out their lights at night; or, even worse, when loaded eastbound ships on their way to rendezvous with an ocean escort were sunk before they could join up. But Admiral King determinedly forced the US Navy to learn for itself, in six catastrophically expensive months of the Atlantic campaign, what the rival service had discovered in two and a half years.

In February the US Atlantic Fleet diverted one or two of its residual destroyers to coastal convoy duty on an ad hoc basis, usually on the way back from ocean escort duty, which meant they were short of supplies and their crews were tired. The British were eventually driven to slow down the entire north Atlantic convoy cycle so as to release two precious escort groups to work in US waters.

King was not opposed to the principle of convoy in the way the British admirals had been in the previous round. He merely adhered rigidly to his view that coastal escort could be provided only when US resources were adequate. His subordinate naval commanders were thus freed to make all the mistakes from which the British had learned and a few new ones of their own devising. The tactical errors included protecting marked sea lanes instead of the shipping using them; Q-ships (not much use in unrestricted submarine warfare as practised by the U-boats since August 1940); neglecting air cover; having ships sail alone as close to shore as possible, passing through dangerous waters by day (without even zigzagging, as this was held to slow ships down rather than making them harder to hit) and entering harbour at night – the 'bucket brigade' system, on the analogy of hand-to-hand firefighting; relying on amateur, untrained 'pickets'; and sending all possible ASW forces to the scene of an alleged U-boat sighting, a variation of Churchill's early 'hunting-group' error which merely denuded a huge area of such protection as was available. Underlying all this carelessness and wilful stupidity were the fundamental facts that the US was not dependent on the shipping that was being lost – and its Navy was focused on the war with Japan.

Essentially, as far as King and most other American admirals were concerned, the Atlantic was a British problem and the European theatre a matter for the US Army. Unfortunately that rapidly expanding body and its voracious supply requirements had to be transported across a U-boat-ridden Atlantic – even more strain on the escorts, which naturally gave priority to military convoys; and now the freight convoys were supplying Russia as well as Britain, the forward base for any invasion of Hitler's Fortress Europe, adding a uniquely harsh new route to the convoy system – a new burden for the British Home Fleet. So seriously was the crisis of the convoys in American waters taken in Britain that the Air Ministry allowed the diversion of seventy American-made maritime bombers meant for Coastal Command to the US Navy from March.

Admiral Dönitz, despite his commitments in the Mediterranean and Norwegian waters (Hitler constantly feared a second British attack on Norway to help Stalin), kept the three Allied Atlantic navies off balance by shifting the focus of his attack, within weeks of the start of *Paukenschlag*, southwards towards the Gulf of Mexico and the Caribbean, which also enabled his captains to pick off more oil tankers, their most valuable targets. Operation 'Neuland' started with spectacular devastation, when a U-boat shelled the big oil refinery at Aruba on the Dutch Caribbean island of Curaçao as early as the night of 16 to 17 February, setting it on fire as three others sank seven tankers in the area. The Americans believed hundreds of German submarines were operating off their east coast and introduced rationing of oil and petrol, even coffee. Any British inclination to divert escorts to the North American coast was discouraged by the occasional reversion to wolfpack attacks on convoys in mid-ocean: westbound ON 67 lost six ships on 24 February under attack from four boats.

In this black month of February 1942 Britain's fortunes after two and a half years of war reached their nadir. Unable to take the offensive in the Far East after the loss of Force Z, the destruction of the ABDA command and the ignominious fall of Singapore, much reduced and on the defensive in the Mediterranean and defenceless against American stupidity in the Atlantic, the Royal Navy on the 1st of the month was suddenly deprived of its precious flow of intercepted enemy naval intelligence material. German naval Enigma, though penetrated by Bletchley Park in May 1941, had been the hardest to crack and enemy naval intelligence was the least complacent of all seven German espionage and security agencies about ciphers. Some German naval officers had even wondered aloud whether the British were somehow intercepting signals. Without ever acquiring proof that this was so, Raeder's staff decided before the end of 1941 to introduce as a precaution a fourth wheel into their Enigma machines, an intention of which Bletchley Park got wind at that time – without being able to do much about it in advance. There were no four-wheel 'bombes' on which to try all the extra millions of possible setting combinations, and no time to develop one.

Thus on 1 February naval Ultra intelligence dried up when a new cipher, codenamed Triton by the Germans, Shark by the British and linked to the addition of the extra wheel, came into use specifically for communications between the U-boats and their headquarters. Fortunately other naval commands, the Luftwaffe (the most careless enemy arm) and the German Army did not follow suit, so the British cryptanalysts suffered a dim-out rather than a blackout. Further, by this time Rodger Winn and his staff in the Submarine Tracking Room had developed a sixth sense about the thinking of the U-boat command; and location of U-boats by their radio signals (High-Frequency Direction-Finding, HF/DF or 'Huff-Duff') – even if they were now impenetrable – had become much more sophisticated and accurate. It took six three-wheel bombes seventeen days in March 1942 to decipher a four-wheel message recording the promotion of Dönitz to full admiral, even though Bletchley Park had decrypted the same signal as sent via three-wheel Enigma. Such was one of only three Triton signals decrypted in the ten and a half months Bletchley Park took to break the new cipher.

The disappearance of U-boat Ultra was a serious blow but beyond the ken of all but the handful of innermost or uppermost officials who were in on the secret, including Churchill. But the great escape of the three major enemy warships from Brest up the 'English' Channel in broad daylight back to Germany was a shaming event which affected the morale of every sailor in the fleet and of the British public as a whole. It will be remembered that the battlecruisers *Scharnhorst* and *Gneisenau* and the heavy cruiser *Prinz Eugen* had been lying up in the great French naval base for the greater part of 1941 after sorties into the north Atlantic and the sinking of the *Bismarck*. This meant that the Home Fleet had two enemy 'fleets in being' to cater for, south and north of Britain: the Brest group and the other major enemy ships in Germany and Norway, now including the *Bismarck*'s even stronger sister, the new super-battleship *Tirpitz*. The RAF had been using the Brest trio for bombing practice, but this only proved over many months how ineffectual Bomber Command was at the time against this kind of target, best attacked by torpedo-bombers. It also failed to make more than a superficial impression on the massive U-boat pens at Brest with their thick carapaces of concrete and sand: by the time the RAF was ready to divert bombers from German cities to such targets, building was too far advanced. The pens are still used by today's French Navy for its nuclear submarines.

Perennially worried about a British initiative there, Hitler now took the view that 'every ship that is not in Norway is in the wrong place' and urged Grand-Admiral Raeder at the end of 1941 to send the Brest group north. In fact planning for the breakout was already advanced at Navy Group West headquarters in occupied Paris. It was to be a massive affair, codenamed Operation *Cerberus* and involving an intricate, interchanging escort made up of minesweepers, destroyers, E-boats and a special effort by 250 aircraft from three groups, the bulk of the Luftwaffe's fighter strength in France and the Low Countries. The British side was fully informed about Hitler's concern with Norway and anticipated a breakout; they correctly assumed that the Germans would make a run up the Channel where thick air cover was available rather than the four times longer route round the British Isles, which would give the British that much more opportunity – five days – of destroying the trio.

The British even drew up Operation 'Fuller', involving the Navy, the RAF and the Army's heavy guns at Dover in a scheme to frustrate Vice-Admiral Otto Ciliax, who was given seagoing command of the group and flew his flag on the *Scharnhorst*; three Luftwaffe officers joined his staff to direct the fighter cover from on board. The Admiralty's biggest mistake was to assume that Ciliax would time matters in such a way as to pass up the Channel, the most narrow and dangerous stretch, at night. The Germans however recognized that it was much more important to achieve tactical surprise by starting the voyage unobserved, which entailed leaving Brest in the dark and reaching the limit of British land-based radar at dawn, when the ships would be visible to the naked eye wherever they were. This meant they would be racing past the White Cliffs in broad daylight.

The main weapon against the German ships would be aerial bombardment, although Bomber Command had neither the training nor the specialized munitions for attacking ships at sea. Regular and special RAF reconnaissance flights by high-flying bombers and low-flying Spitfires kept watch for any sign of movement. The fourteen Coastal Command Beaufort torpedo-bombers stationed in Scotland against a *Tirpitz* sortie were on standby to fly south to Norfolk in support of their nineteen colleagues in southern England – effectively the whole of the thinly spread command's anti-ship striking power. Admiral Ramsay, still in charge at Dover, had the coordinating role, even though the Navy's operational participation would perforce be secondary. The Home Fleet was preoccupied with *Tirpitz*, the Russian route and Atlantic trooping or supply convoys from North America to the Middle East, while Force H was involved in supporting the Mediterranean Fleet.

The exhausted, sixty-five-year-old Admiral Pound, in a lacklustre response, specifically forbade any move by capital ships against the Brest group's run for home, accurately predicted by Coastal Command on 8 February. But three submarines kept a lookout off Brest, as did spies inside the port. Motor torpedo boats and gunboats were primed to make hit-and-run raids from the east Kent coast, but only six elderly destroyers, based at Harwich, could be spared for a seaborne torpedo attack; a similar number of the Fleet Air Arm's Swordfish torpedo-bombers were moved to Manston airfield in Kent. The fast minelayer HMS *Welshman* laid 1,000 mines off Boulogne; and Coastal Command far-sightedly dropped ninety-eight more to the north of the Dutch Friesian Islands, which the Germans would have to pass as they 'turned the corner' for their North Sea bases.

The British Navy seemed to have run out of luck on all fronts, from the Arctic to Bletchley. The Germans had not. RAF Wellingtons bombed Brest on the evening of the 11th, just as Ciliax was getting ready to leave 'on exercise' after ostentatiously having tropical kit loaded aboard his ships. As usual the raid did little real damage, but it did delay the group's departure by two hours, so that when the raiders flew back with their films, the pictures developed during the night prompted Bomber Command to report that the ships were 'still in port' – by which time they had gone for ever. Ciliax set sail only sixteen minutes before his safety margin of time ran out, which would have wrecked a complicated escort schedule and forced him to postpone the departure for twenty-four hours.

Another stroke of luck for the Germans was a series of technical failures on no fewer than three RAF night radar-patrol reconnaissance aircraft, all of which missed the runaway squadron. Ciliax meanwhile was making up time at twenty-seven knots, reaching the designated 'point of no return' off the Breton island of Ushant seventy-two minutes late. At this point the German admiral told the crews of the three big ships over their linked-up public address systems that they were on their way home. The rapidly deteriorating weather, inimical to aerial scouting, was also on the side of Hitler, who had forecast that the run for home would be Germany's 'most spectacular naval success of the war'. Thus the daytime Channel reconnaissance by Spitfire saw nothing like the full picture when it spotted E-boats coming out of Boulogne to join the escort – in themselves a common enough sight. A bank of cloud hid the powerful force just a few miles to the south. The pilot had not been alerted to the possibility of the breakout and was not even privy to the 'Fuller' arrangements.

The oncoming Germans were massively jamming British coastal

radar, but were unaware of the latest advances in that priceless British technology, which now used a wavelength of unprecedented brevity. The control room at Biggin Hill, epicentre of the Battle of Britain, was therefore able to pick up a swirling, swarmlike image of circling aircraft moving from south-west to north-east up the Channel at twenty-eight knots on the morning of the 12th. Squadron-Leader Bill Igoe alerted the headquarters of Number 11 Group, Fighter Command, at Uxbridge: 'I think it's "Fuller".' But nobody dared disturb Air Vice-Marshal Trafford Leigh-Mallory, the Air Officer Commanding the group, who was taking a parade at RAF Northolt, west of London. Yet Spitfires sent up by Igoe confirmed a sighting of the German ships to the Dover Command. Admiral Ramsay's staff, trained to exercise initiative, contacted Lieutenant-Commander Eugene Esmonde, RN, at Manston. He prepared his half-squadron of antiquated Swordfish for an attack as the German force approached the narrows of the Strait of Dover, led by a screen of ten destroyers, flanked and followed by forty-five smaller escorts with a heavy fighter umbrella circling overhead, the whole now advancing at thirty knots. The Germans had known for about an hour, thanks to efficient intercepts by their naval intelligence, that the RAF had spotted them and were mystified by the lack of response, due to a string of communications failures among British forces.

It was the British Army that fired the first shot, which exploded in the wake of the cruiser *Prinz Eugen*. The German guns on the other side of the Channel fired back, but neither side scored a hit as the fugitive formation entered a providential patch of mist. Next to try were Lieutenant-Commander Nigel Pumphrey's five motor torpedo boats and a pair of motor gunboats from Ramsgate, swept aside by the much more powerful enemy E-boats. Commander Esmonde had returned only the previous day from London, where he had been presented with the Distinguished Service Order by King George VI for his courageous and crucial part in the air attack on the *Bismarck*. Aware that the cloth-covered Swordfish were meant for a night attack whereas the Germans were making their run at high noon, Ramsay vainly interceded with the Admiralty and then left it to Esmonde to decide whether to risk what could only turn into a suicide attack. The admiral was not at all surprised by Esmonde's choice, though deeply saddened by its result: all six biplanes shot down without a hit, only five out of their total of eighteen aircrew, not including Esmonde, saved by

Pumphrey's MTBs. Five squadrons of Spitfires had been sent up to cover the torpedo-bombers; only ten fighters found them in the poor weather, and they were too late and too few. The attack had been so slow that the big enemy ships had been able to land heavy shells in their path, sending up blinding gouts of water as they made their agonizing, unwavering approach at thirty feet.

Now one shot was left in the Royal Navy's locker: Captain Mark Pizey, RN, and his half-dozen destroyers from Harwich, at that time on their way to Sheerness in Kent after a fruitless sweep of the southern North Sea the previous day. As the incompetence and delay ashore continued, Pizey had no time to sail round his own side's minefields in order to get in an attack. Bravely deciding to sail through them at top speed, he was rewarded by an unscathed passage. By this time the German flagship *Scharnhorst* was level with and a few miles west of the Dutch port of Flushing, where overall control of *Cerberus* passed from German Navy Group West to Navy Group North. At this juncture Admiral Ciliax's powerful warhorse hit a British mine and went dead in the water.

The bulk of his formation obeyed orders and raced on, only four torpedo boats standing by as the admiral transferred in a heavy sea to the destroyer he had summoned. But only the battlecruiser's outer skin had been pierced, and only the shock of the explosion had temporarily interrupted the electrical controls of her mighty engines. There was no other damage and Captain Kurt Hoffmann confidently took his ship back up to twenty-seven knots, leaving Ciliax looking a little foolish and the flagship half an hour behind the main body.

The RAF meanwhile was launching what ultimately totalled 675 mostly uncoordinated sorties by fighters, bombers and torpedo-bombers against the Germans. Some of them aimed at Pizey's destroyers; neither they nor the enemy were hit as Pizey sighted the *Gneisenau* and *Prinz Eugen* off the Hook of Holland and tried a torpedo attack under the German heavy guns while a massively confused air battle went on overhead. One destroyer, HMS *Worcester*, was badly damaged but escaped with the rest. No torpedo struck home. As its flagship closed the gap, the German formation was looking ragged when the leading big ship, *Gneisenau*, 'turned the corner' rounding the largest Dutch island of Texel.

As she passed the third island in the West Friesian chain, Terschelling, she hit one of the fresh RAF mines at 8 p.m., but managed to keep going at only slightly reduced speed. Two hours later the *Scharnhorst* rocked to her second mine explosion, which reduced her speed to twelve knots. Ciliax now caught up in his destroyer and together they limped towards the mouth of the Elbe at Cuxhaven. *Gneisenau* and *Prinz Eugen* got there first in the early hours of the 13th – only to find that nobody was expecting them, an extraordinary oversight after such a dashing escape. The *Gneisenau* was driven by wind on to a submerged wreck as she approached Brunsbüttel on the other side of the estuary from Cuxhaven, without benefit of tug, icebreaker or pilot. This seriously worsened the damage caused by the RAF mine. When the *Scharnhorst* reached Wilhelmshaven later in the morning there were no tugs for her either, but Hoffmann managed to berth without incident. The *Prinz Eugen*, junior member of the trio, was completely unharmed.

The 'Channel Dash' cost the Germans two dead, seventeen aircraft shot down, some damage to two torpedo boats and the moderately serious if conveniently invisible mine damage to the battlecruiser 'terrible twins', which needed six months in dock. All in all, this looked remarkably like a brilliant victory for the Germans and was seen as such, not only by the hyperactive propaganda machinery of Dr Goebbels but also by the British government, the Admiralty and public opinion. Vice-Admiral Ciliax, *The Times* thundered, had 'succeeded where the Duke of Medina-Sidonia failed. Nothing more mortifying to the pride of our seapower has happened since the seventeenth century.' The Duke had led the Spanish Armada to defeat in British waters in 1588; the Dutch Admiral M. A. de Ruyter had sailed up the River Medway in Kent in 1667, attacking the English fleet at anchor and hijacking its flagship. The whole sorry affair was 'symptomatic of the general feeling that there is something wrong with Britain's war direction, and this feeling is crystallised in an almost universal demand for removal from high places of the tired and incompetent', said an unusually critical editorial in the *Daily Mail* – on the very day that Singapore fell. Churchill was furious when Admiral Pound telephoned him with the bad news of the Germans' apparently unscathed evasion. The Prime Minister must have been reflecting on his plight in 1915 after the Dardanelles failure, when similar sentiments forced him and Fisher out of office: 'Why?' he barked as he slammed the receiver back into its cradle.

He appointed Mr Justice Bucknill, a High Court judge, supported by an admiral and an air marshal, to lead an official tribunal of inquiry into a lost battle in the middle of a war. The ensuing Whitehall whitewash blandly concluded that 'co-ordination was not entirely successful' and medals were handed out to many brave individuals whose best efforts had been expended to no avail, thanks to indecisive commanders (some of whom received higher decorations). The highest of all, the Victoria Cross posthumously awarded to Commander Esmonde, stood out as singularly well deserved amid this hollow harvest.

Admiral Ciliax and Captain Hoffmann each received the Knight's Cross of the Iron Cross. Ten days after reaching port without a scratch on her paintwork, the cruiser *Prinz Eugen* was sighted off the Norwegian port of Trondheim, then a major German naval base, by HM Submarine *Trident* (Commander G. M. Sladen, RN). Hit squarely in the stern by a single British torpedo, the cruiser managed to make harbour but took no further part in the war. At the end of February the RAF completed the immobilization of the *Gneisenau* in three nights of bombing: she was never seen on the open sea again. Only the *Scharnhorst* lived to fight another day after half a year under repair – and what a fight it was to be.

It was only after some months that the Admiralty was able to see that the ignominious 'Channel Dash' had resulted in more of a setback than a gain for the Germans. The one part of 'Fuller' that had worked was the thoughtful sowing of mines across the Brest squadron's unavoidable path; and the Home Fleet was permanently relieved of one of the two German 'fleets in being' it had been obliged to bear in mind whenever it committed its major units: Brest never again sheltered a German capital ship. Even Admiral Raeder conceded that the affair had been 'a tactical success but a strategic defeat'. Here at least, if in no other respect, was the Second World War's nearest parallel to the outcome of the Battle of Jutland in the First.

Admiral Dönitz enhanced his ability to cause havoc along the north American littoral by a new method of refuelling his U-boats at sea. One quietly useful harvest for the British from naval Ultra during the latter part of 1941 was the elimination of all German surface supply ships by penetrating radio rendezvous messages and sending a cruiser to the designated spot. This deprived enemy surface raiders, disguised cruisers and blockade runners of the extremely valuable services of *Altmark*-style mid-ocean replenishment. Submarines were another matter. At the end of 1941 work was in hand on a large, Type XIV U-boat, displacing 1,688 tons on the surface and capable of carrying a stock of 432 tons of diesel oil as well as four torpedoes for its own protection. The first 'U-tanker' was the *UA*, an experimental fighting submarine converted to carry 250 tons of fuel, which left Lorient on 14 March for the outer Western Approaches and successfully refuelled three Type VIIc boats (the workhorses of the German submarine service). These medium-sized vessels needed a good week to cross the Atlantic and a week to get back, leaving them barely a week of operational time if they husbanded their hundred or so tons of fuel capacity. With the underwater 'milch-cows' at their disposal, they could greatly increase their endurance. The purpose-built submarine tanker had made its debut in the Caribbean in February.

One example of how markedly the initiative still lay with the Germans in the unrestricted Atlantic was shown in March, when Dönitz sent just two of his boats into the central ocean off Sierra Leone. The sinking of eleven ships (64,000 tons) in a few days caused the British to divert large escort resources southward for several weeks, prolonging the agony further north, which is exactly what the Germans intended. In that month, very nearly the worst on record, 834,000 tons of Allied shipping were sunk, including 538,000 tons by submarines and 534,000 tons (ninety-five ships) in the north Atlantic, mainly off the US east coast. In the first four months of American belligerence 250 ships were lost in those waters to a new generation of German aces. On 14 April the US Navy sank its first U-boat.

Deeply depressed by the huge losses in the western Atlantic, the Admiralty sent the silver-tongued Commander Rodger Winn, RNVR, to use his forensic skills to persuade the Americans to set up an equivalent of the Operational Intelligence Centre (OIC). Winn worked his way up a sceptical, not to say hostile, US naval chain of command all the way to Admiral King's office. 'The trouble is, Admiral,' Winn told King's deputy chief of staff, 'it's not only your bloody ships you are losing; a lot of them are ours!' King himself amazed Winn by proving a pushover, immediately ordering the creation of a transatlantic OIC with its own submarine tracking room. The task was given to 'Op-20-G', led by Commander Kenneth A. Knowles, USN, who was to report directly to King – and to forge with Winn one of the most important Allied liaison channels of the war. Under pressure from Washington, King decided that the US Navy would have enough escorts by mid-May, whereupon coastal convoys would be introduced in both directions between Long Island, New York, and the Florida Keys. Since the Germans had penetrated the British cipher used by all three north Atlantic navies to communicate with each other, it need not be seen as a coincidence that Dönitz chose this moment to shift the focus of his operations to the Gulf of Mexico and the Caribbean as never before. Only fourteen ships (out of a monthly total of 123) were sunk in the western Atlantic north of the Gulf in May as the Americans laid on seven escort groups of seven ships each, including some British corvettes and trawlers. The two British groups culled from the Mid-Ocean Escort Force stayed on, and a separate pool of escorts was created for covering oil tankers, among which losses had reached crisis proportions in April.

Even so June 1942 turned out to be the very worst month of the Second World War for shipping losses, as 834,196 tons went down worldwide (submarines sank 700,000 tons; 624,000 were lost in the north Atlantic). General George C. Marshall, Chief of Staff of the US Army, now developed an opinion of King not altogether dissimilar from that of his colleague, Eisenhower, and directly challenged the fire-eating admiral in the middle of the most disastrous month: 'The losses by [sic] submarines off our Atlantic seaboard and in the Caribbean now threaten our entire war effort.' King coolly asserted that his military opposite number was preaching to the converted: 'Escort is not just one way of handling the submarine menace; it is the *only* way . . . We must get every ship that sails the seas under constant close protection' (King's emphasis).

The closure of the yawning gap in the worldwide Interlocking Convoy System heralded the great turning point in the Battle of the Atlantic, even if its significance was realized only after postwar statistical analysis. In July 1942 global shipping losses were still enormous at 618,000 tons – but that was a fall of over 25 per cent; and in the same month, Allied new construction for the first time exceeded total sinkings. It was Dönitz himself who had developed the concept of the 'tonnage war', whereby any merchantman in Allied service sunk anywhere in the world was part of the same equation. His was a refinement of Admiral Holtzendorff's calculation in 1917. Given a sinking rate of 700,000 tons a month, the target he set himself in May 1942, and an Allied shipbuilding rate calculated to be below that, there could be only one outcome from a war of attrition as more and more U-boats came off the stocks: final victory for Germany.

Britain's best efforts could not produce more than 1.25m tons of new shipping per year although the country was more dependent than ever on the transatlantic lifeline. But the U-boat arm's equation did not include such extraneous factors as the conversion of Admiral King, the awesome productive energy of the American shipbuilding industry, which managed to build three times as many ships in 1942 as the Germans thought possible, and the relentless, forced march of Allied technology, especially in electronic warfare but also in ASW weapons. Even the organization of individual convoys was constantly improved: oilers and rescue ships were added to enable the escorts to stay with their charges and attack or at least fend off U-boats.

But Churchill and the Air Ministry could not be moved on the question of long-range air protection for shipping. The new C-in-C of Coastal Command, Air Chief Marshal Sir Philip Joubert de la Ferté, calculated on his appointment in summer 1941 that he needed 818 aircraft and found himself some 250 short. Bomber Command, supported by the Prime Minister, repeatedly asked for such bombers as Coastal possessed to add to the mass air attacks on German cities, and complained in February 1942, just before the Channel Dash, of 'useless diversions' to the bombing of Brest, without acknowledging that they had begun as too little, too late: the German construction rate kept ahead of the escalating intensity of the raids so that even the heaviest Allied bombs could make no real impression later in the war.

The Admiralty reacted by demanding a dozen more squadrons for maritime patrols over the Bay of Biscay, as a 'choke-point' the best place for catching U-boats, and the Indian Ocean, in what was now known among the cognoscenti of Whitehall as the 'Battle of the Air'. The Navy grew all the more depressed as the catastrophic losses off the American eastern seaboard continued into summer 1942. Admiral Pound demanded a doubling of British maritime air strength worldwide to nearly 2,000 aircraft. To the chagrin of 'Bomber' Harris the British Chiefs of Staff agreed in April to the transfer of four squadrons to Coastal Command for ASW in the North-Western Approaches and Biscay; the C-in-C of Bomber Command reacted as if it was being disbanded. Dönitz, however, soon noticed this modest reinforcement, its effect compounded by the thinning out of the Luftwaffe in France, and complained bitterly about his skippers' mounting difficulties thanks to increased British air patrols over Biscay from May 1942 – round the clock, weather permitting. Merely by forcing U-boats to depart and return under water the aircraft significantly reduced their operational time; sinkings were rare, near misses less so, but all were a bonus for the British side.

In a withering letter on the 28th to the Admiralty Board, not his first on the subject, Admiral Tovey, C-in-C of the Home Fleet, urged his colleagues to resign en masse unless the Air Ministry came to the Navy's aid; he found it 'difficult to believe that the population of Cologne would notice much difference between a raid by 1,000 bombers and one by 750'. Yet Coastal Command still had only one squadron of sixteen Liberators, the adapted bomber which alone had the legs to reach all parts of the north and central Atlantic. With extra fuel tanks it was uniquely classed as Very Long Range (VLR) and could still carry an entirely adequate load of depth charges. But the US Navy's needs in the Pacific came first; and the RAF soon took half the squadron for special missions.

Coastal Command's reconnaissance failures against the Brest squadron were compounded by a similarly poor performance against Germany's other 'fleet in being', the heavy naval forces in the north, now led by the 52,600-ton *Tirpitz*. She was able to sail undetected from the Baltic via the Kiel Canal up the west coast of Jutland to an anchorage near Trondheim in Norway in the middle of January 1942. She was located there a week later by the overstretched patrols of Coastal Command but an attack at the end of the month by sixteen bombers was a total failure. In mid-February the pocket-battleship *Admiral Scheer* and the heavy cruiser *Prinz Eugen* set out to join the new monster. They reached Bergen undetected; but on the run north to Trondheim the cruiser was crippled by HM Submarine *Trident*, as we saw. The *Scheer* got away undamaged to join the *Tirpitz*, protected by a flotilla of large destroyers and a strong Luftwaffe presence. Vice-Admiral Ciliax was in command. The Home Fleet's three battleships were accompanying the carrier *Victorious* early in March as distant cover for the Russian convoys when *Tirpitz* and three destroyers were sighted by one of her aircraft. Twelve Albacore torpedo-bombers once again completely failed to scratch the battleship's paint, losing two of their number in a running battle off the Lofoten Islands. Tovey's main force did not sight the Germans as they withdrew to Narvik in the Norwegian north – where the heavy cruiser *Hipper* joined them undetected on 21 March. Tovey complained about the usual interference in tactical decisions by the Admiralty, which had ordered him to make the Russian convoys and not the principal surface threat to them his priority.

Losses on the appalling run to and from Murmansk and Archangel were steady and heavy, thanks to U-boat and Luftwaffe attacks. The cruiser HMS *Trinidad* suffered the ignominy of shooting herself with her own rogue torpedo during an engagement with German destroyers (she sank one) and had to limp away to Russia at the end of March; the cruiser *Edinburgh* was hit by two U-boat torpedoes in the same fraught area of the Arctic Ocean a month later. As she too limped north-eastward, she was hit by a third during a German destroyer attack (she sank one of her tormentors) and had to be dispatched by British destroyers when the Germans broke off to rescue their comrades. A large consignment of Soviet gold went down with her as British minesweepers plucked most of her freezing crew from the water and took them to Murmansk. When the patched-up *Trinidad* tried to limp home on 15 May she was attacked and further damaged by German aircraft and had to be sunk by her escorting destroyers. The Germans meanwhile had managed to add the other pocket-battleship, *Lützow*, to their formidable force in Narvik.

Six weeks after the Channel Dash humiliation, Admiral Tovey received a little strategic consolation, in the shape of the certain knowledge that the *Tirpitz* could only be operated in northern waters. Refuge in France ceased to be an option at the end of March 1942 when a joint Navy–Army operation destroyed the only dry dock in France large enough to take the *Tirpitz* – at the port of St Nazaire south-east of Brittany. The *Bismarck* was bound thither when she was caught and sunk in May 1941. The dock in question had been constructed to take the liner *Normandie*, one of the world's largest, and doubled as a canal lock. Commander R. E. D. Ryder, RN, led eighteen small coastal vessels and one old ex-American destroyer, HMS *Campbeltown* (Lieutenant-Commander S. H. Beattie, RN), from Falmouth in Cornwall to land 268 Army commandos under Lieutenant-Colonel A. C. Newman. The motley force was covered at sea by four destroyers.

The plan was for the troops to cause maximum damage ashore and engage local forces while the old destroyer, her bow packed with explosives timed to go off later, rammed the lock gates and embedded herself in the bottom. A tumultuous battle developed inside the harbour in the early hours of 28 March. Many of Ryder's launches were sunk and many British commandos and men of the destroyer's crew were taken prisoner. Only four motor launches escaped after an attack by five German torpedo boats. Ten hours after ramming the gates, and just as German officers were examining her, *Campbeltown* blew up and accomplished the mission. Faulty detonators on some delayed-action torpedoes fired by the naval party took thirty-six hours to work, but they completed the destruction of the lock-cum-dock. The whole bloody affair, which had cost the British 144 dead and 300 captured plus heavy casualties among the local population and the German defenders, was another Zeebrugge, on a smaller scale but with a much larger strategic return. Not only was the *Tirpitz* denied a repair facility and thus the possibility of operating in the broad Atlantic; the Germans thought the raid foreshadowed an invasion and diverted large resources in manpower and materiel to strengthen prematurely the defences of the long coastline of Fortress Europe. And on 29 March Hitler ordered Dönitz to move his headquarters away from Lorient on the Breton coast back to Paris, well out of reach of British 'pinprick' raids.

The move inland did not dampen the aggressive spirit of the U-boat arm; on the contrary. German submarines were still exacting a heavy toll in the Gulf and Caribbean area when their comrades in arms in northern waters, aided by the Luftwaffe and the surface 'fleet in being', inflicted a particularly poignant and painful defeat on the British Home Fleet. Operation *Rösselsprung* ('Chess-knight's Move') was conceived by Admiral Raeder in June 1942 as a massive surface raid on the Russian convoy traffic, to be led by *Tirpitz*. Vice-Admiral Otto Schniewind had relieved Ciliax as fleet C-in-C and Admiral Rolf Carls of Navy Group North based in Kiel was in operational control. Hitler insisted, however, that any British carrier in the area had to be knocked out before the big ships set out, a rather inhibiting proviso.

Bear Island, due south of Spitsbergen (the latter had been occupied by an Anglo-Norwegian force since May to deny it to the Germans), was a key reference point for both sides in the coming clash. The German surface units were to operate to the east of it while the Luftwaffe and the U-boats would work to the west. The British covering force of four cruisers, operating north of the convoy route under Rear-Admiral L. H. K. Hamilton (the Home Fleet acted as distant cover well to the south), was ordered not to sail east of Bear Island if the *Tirpitz* was out; to the west of it thirteen submarines would provide cover against German surface ships. The focus of these elaborate dispositions by both sides was the eastbound convoy PQ 17 and the westbound QP 13, both setting off on 27 June. The former, fully laden with 157,000 tons of mostly American munitions for the Soviet Union on American, British and Soviet freighters, was given a massive close escort of six destroyers, four corvettes, two submarines, three rescue ships, two anti-aircraft ships, an oiler, minesweepers and trawlers; Senior Officer, Escort, was Commander J. E. Broome, RN, in the destroyer *Keppel*. Eight RAF Catalina flying boats were temporarily stationed in northern Russia for reconnaissance purposes. Commodore J. C. K. Dowding, RNR, was in charge of the convoy of thirty-three ships.

PQ 17 was sighted independently by enemy aircraft and by U-boats at lunchtime on 1 July. The convoy shook off both as Hamilton's cruisers (two British, two American, plus three destroyers) sailed past the convoy to cover it from forty miles to the north. In the evening nine Heinkel 111 torpedo-bombers were driven off without loss to either side and a fog shrouded the convoy overnight. On the afternoon of the 2nd, the two convoys crossed over without sighting each other. On the 3rd, RAF reconnaissance discovered that *Tirpitz* and *Hipper* had left Trondheim, their most recent port of call, but not their present whereabouts. Unbeknown to the British also was the fact that the *Lützow* and three out of four destroyers in the surface group had run aground in fog off Narvik and were inoperable. But the *Scheer* joined the battleship and the heavy cruiser at the deep Altenfjord in the Norwegian far north. Narvik was closed in by weather which frustrated RAF searchers. On the night of the 3rd PQ 17 passed north of Bear Island undisturbed. There being no word of the German ships, Hamilton felt free to keep pace with them east of the island, planning to put about on the evening of the 4th. At that time twenty-four German torpedo-bombers damaged three ships in the convoy; two had to be sunk by the escort after their crews were rescued (one more had suffered a similar fate earlier in the day after a single enemy bomber torpedoed it through a gap in the cloud).

By the standards of the Murmansk run these losses were small change, and there had been no U-boat attack. But back in London a perennially exhausted Admiral Pound was desperately anxious about the *Tirpitz* and her companions, of which there was still no sign. He knew by the evening of the 4th that the Germans had joined up at Altenfjord, but not whether they were still there. The enemy surface fleet did not use the Triton cipher and Bletchley Park was intercepting its Enigma messages and breaking them – but with a few hours' delay. Pound calculated that the convoy and Hamilton's cruisers could come under surface attack at any time after dawn on the 5th and asked Captain Norman Denning, RN, in charge of the OIC, for an assurance that *Tirpitz* was still in Altenfjord. Unable to provide anything so definite, Denning yet cited the absence of sightings and signals alike as reasons for his confidence that this was the case. But Pound was deeply unhappy when he chaired a staff meeting at 8.30 p.m.

Convoy tactics decreed that in the event of air or submarine attack, ships should stay together to maximize the effectiveness of anti-aircraft and anti-submarine defences; but in the event of surface attack the merchant ships should scatter to minimize the number of victims. Which, Pound agonized, was the greater threat to PQ 17 that night? By 10 p.m. he had personally ordered the dispatch of three signals. The first told Hamilton to withdraw westward at once at top speed; since he was much further east than originally envisaged, this was not unreasonable. But the second signal was to Broome, the convoy SOE: 'Owing to threat from surface ships the convoy is to disperse and proceed to Russian ports.' Minutes later came the third, fateful message: 'Most immediate. Convoy is to scatter.' Dispersal was a measured procedure involving the orderly dissolution of the convoy with individual ships making for safety at their best speed. 'Scatter' implied dire emergency and required ships to flee at once on their own individual courses (predetermined in convoy orders to avoid collisions). Hamilton and Broome were stunned; Dowding twice asked for confirmation of the order as relayed by Broome. The latter decided on his own account to run northwards and join the retiring Hamilton so as to present the strongest possible resistance to German surface forces, which he expected to encounter at any minute.

But there was no sign of them; nor would there be. Instead the U-boats and the Luftwaffe on 5 July began a measured slaughter of the ships of PQ 17 as soon as they became aware of the disintegration of the convoy. By noon six freighters were sunk; then a U-boat sank Dowding's ship, of which he was one of very few survivors. The score for the day was twelve sunk, taking the total so far to fifteen. Broome wanted to return to his helpless charges but Hamilton decided that the close and intermediate escort should withdraw on to the Home Fleet to the south-west, once again so as to concentrate maximum force against the German surface ships. It was nearly a full day after the order to scatter when the Admiralty realized from one of Hamilton's messages that Broome was (still) with him, a fact for which Pound later criticized him severely, in an apparent attempt to displace his own awesome burden of responsibility for the PQ 17 disaster.

Ironically it was only on the morning of the 5th that Hitler, satisfied that the Home Fleet and its carrier were hundreds of miles out of range, sanctioned *Rösselsprung*. The *Tirpitz* force left Altenfjord at about 11 a.m. heading first north, then east about the North Cape, like a knight on a giant chessboard. Ten hours later, hearing of the massacre going on to the south-west and realizing that the operation's intended objective was already being handsomely achieved, Admiral Raeder aborted the sortie and ordered the ships into Narvik, some way south of Altenfjord. There can hardly have been a clearer demonstration of the validity of the 'fleet in being' concept: the mere existence of *Tirpitz* and her cohorts had set the scene for Pound's tragic miscalculation and the demolition of a vitally important convoy. The U-boats alone sank ten freighters but were outdone on this occasion by the Luftwaffe, which sank twelve and a rescue ship. One-third of the convoy, eleven ships plus two rescue vessels, reached Russia; 100,000 tons of precious munitions had been lost too. No Allied warship was even slightly damaged.

The Americans, having so recently learned the value of convoy, were as furious as only the converted can be. But their assertion that the Royal Navy had abandoned a priceless convoy for no good reason was not only shared by the British Merchant Navy but also entirely valid. It is simplistic, however, to condemn Admiral Pound from the omniscient advantage of hindsight. He had been right in anticipating a surface attack because the Germans actually embarked on one – before they learned that it was superfluous to requirements. The tragedy lay in Pound's premature command to scatter. As such it was one of the worst examples of the Admiralty's congenital inability to refrain from abusing the boon of wireless by bombarding the commander on the spot with tactical orders, a sure sign of lack of confidence. Broome and Hamilton, professional naval officers, knew exactly what to do in the event of an attack of any kind from their training and from standing orders; Hamilton had specific orders not to engage a German force that included *Tirpitz*. That was enough. Neither officer got over the disaster; but when Pound died of overwork in the following year nobody would have been surprised to find 'PQ 17' engraved on his heart.

The tragedy was the climax of the most devastating period of shipping losses of the entire war. The first seven months of 1942 saw 4,765,000 tons sunk worldwide, 3,319,000 in the north Atlantic and 3,556,000 lost to U-boats. The only new weapon on the British side was the Hedgehog, a forward-firing multiple launcher of small explosive charges, offsetting the disadvantage of depth charges, which had to be lobbed over the stern of an escort. Towards the end of the war the Squid, another British idea, appeared – enabling ships to hurl full-sized depth charges over the bow, an advantage which compensated for the 'blindness' of ASDIC in the last stage of an attacking run against a submerged submarine. Radar and HF/DF were spreading and improving constantly.

Admiral Karl Dönitz chose the very moment of climax of his most deadly onslaught so far to make a broadcast unmatched in the brief and violent history of the Third Reich. On 27 July 1942, to the astonishment of the eavesdropping British, he went on to German radio to warn the public that times were about to become harder and losses higher. The U-boat chief's motive was to restore a sense of proportion after German propaganda had so unremittingly extolled (and exaggerated) his submariners' successes. The effect in Germany was all the more marked for the rarity of such frankness in the Nazi media. In Britain and at the Admiralty in particular, the warning was read as heralding a return to the hard grind of mid-Atlantic operations now that the haemorrhage along the American coastline had been staunched. In the absence of such easy pickings, the Germans' best hope lay in the areas south-west of Greenland and around the Azores, which Allied air cover could not reach for lack of a handful of VLR bombers. U-boats operating in mid-ocean could patrol three or even five times as long without the lengthy extra mileage to and from the far side of the ocean. By summer 1942 the U-boats at last passed the total of 300 with which Dönitz would have liked to start a war against Britain: 331 on 1 July, 140 operational, against 170 Allied escorts available for mid-ocean work.

The escort system was at full stretch and in urgent need of reinforcement. Merchant Aircraft Carriers (MACs) supplanted CAMs (Catapult-Aircraft Merchantmen) to provide more stopgap air cover: six tankers and six bulk carriers, all with long uncluttered decks, were chosen for conversion to carry a flight of three or four Swordfish each, as well as their normal cargoes; but conversion took nine months. The British wanted escort carriers, American mercantile conversions capable of carrying as many as two dozen aircraft, but their order took second place, as ever, to the Pacific needs of the US Navy. The ultimate solution to the problem of air cover was thus recognized to be including it in the mid-ocean escort, even more effective than long-range, land-based patrols which could not always be called in quickly in an emergency. But the latter could have been assigned overnight whereas even the Americans needed time for carrier conversions. As things stood in 1942, the Germans persistently inflicted heavy losses in what they called 'the Devil's Gorge' and the Allied sailors christened 'Torpedo Junction', south of Greenland, and the subsidiary 'Black Gap' (the English phrase was used by both sides) at the Azores. As the occupied countries of Europe and Asia longed for liberators, so the British and Canadian navies longed for Liberators, still few and far between over the Atlantic.

The PQ 17 disaster prompted the Home Fleet to rethink its escort strategy for PQ 18 and QP 14 in September. Three dozen aircraft were positioned in north Russia and the entire, massive eastbound escort was to make a double journey, also covering the westbound convoy, which would not leave Murmansk until the loaded ships were almost there. Tovey stayed in Scapa Flow in overall command, sending his deputy, Vice-Admiral Sir Bruce Fraser, with two battleships, a cruiser and five destroyers to Akureyri in Iceland, ready to provide rather less distant cover against *Tirpitz* or other heavy enemy units. The immediate escort consisted of eighteen ships, including the new British escort carrier HMS *Avenger* with fifteen aircraft. Sixteen Home Fleet destroyers and three cruisers formed the intermediate escort; two more cruisers, five destroyers and seven submarines provided supplementary cover on their way to other tasks in northern waters. No convoy was more heavily protected, which no doubt helps to explain why PQ 18 lost 'only' one third of its thirty-nine merchantmen instead of the two-thirds lost by PQ 17; eight ships were sunk in eight minutes in a savage attack by forty German torpedo-bombers. In all, ten ships were lost to air attack and three to U-boats, while three of the latter were destroyed along with forty-one German planes. The U-boats were numerous enough to be engaged simultaneously in a major convoy battle in mid-Atlantic.

QP 14 consisted largely of the survivors of PQ 17: the doubly unfortunate Commodore Dowding lost the ship that was meant to bring him home and was once again plucked out of the icy water as four out of fifteen ships were sunk, along with two of the escort. German surface forces merely moved north from Narvik to Altenfjord, taking no part in the actions. The dreadful PQ/QP series was terminated at the end of the month with QP 15, mostly survivors of the previous double battle. Only two out of twenty-eight returnees were sunk, by U-boats in weather too bad for flying or even surface attacks. The massive northern escort forces were needed in warmer climes.

In April 1942 the battered island of Malta was awarded a collective George Cross for the bravery of its civilian population under unrelenting Axis air attacks. Even RN submarines had fled the island and no surface warship could stop there from April until August, so fierce was the struggle for control of the mid-ocean bastion. The British regarded it as a matter of honour to hold on to the rocky island at all costs: there would be no second Singapore in the Mediterranean. Thirteen warships and twenty merchantmen were lost in attempts to keep the island going; ten supply ships gave up and went back out of sixty dispatched to Malta in 1942. Many other ships were damaged. The ideal solution was for the British Eighth Army to capture the airfields of northern Libya which alone would enable the RAF to control the airspace between Malta and Alexandria. Unfortunately General Rommel wanted them too, and for most of 1942 his wish prevailed.

In mid-February a heavily escorted convoy of just three ships failed to get anything through to the island from Alexandria. Cunningham was ordered to try again five weeks later with an even heavier escort, effectively every ship at his disposal, once more commanded at sea by Rear-Admiral Philip Vian. He had to face not only German dive-bombers but also a strong Italian surface force led by a battleship, in rough weather. Even so he managed to drive the Italians off by aggressive deployment of a huge smokescreen, five light cruisers and sixteen destroyers. Just two of the latter were knocked out but saved in two and a half hours of seaborne brawling, led by a fighting junior admiral very much in the Cunningham mould. When Vian returned to Alexandria, having left the convoy and its close escort to finish the voyage to Malta in the moonless night, he and his ships were cheered from the quayside; Churchill sent congratulations and Vian was given a knighthood. But of the four ships in the convoy only two reached Malta: they were cheered too. A third ship sank twenty miles out and the fourth had to be taken in tow eight miles offshore (she sank later) after heavy Luftwaffe attacks in daylight on 23 March. The two that entered harbour were bombed again; one was flooded and the other had to be towed away and scuttled. Two destroyers of the close escort were also sunk. The Maltese salvaged just 5,000 tons of stores, less than a fifth of the total consignment.

On 1 April Cunningham gave up his command, to lead the British naval staff mission in Washington; his successor was the seriously over-promoted Acting Admiral Sir Henry Harwood of River Plate fame, who arrived nearly two months later. Meanwhile the struggle for Malta continued. The American carrier USS *Wasp* made two strongly escorted forays into the Mediterranean to fly off replacement fighters in April and May. The old British carrier *Eagle* made four similar if smaller deliveries, raising the island's Spitfire strength to well over 150 of the latest marks – a serious threat at last to the persistent Axis bombers and proper cover for approaching friendly ships. In June two convoys were dispatched, one of six freighters from Gibraltar, the other of eleven from Alexandria, to sail simultaneously under the strongest escort available – inadequate as usual. The former came under Italian air attack from 12 June but the two old carriers *Eagle* and *Argus*, with a combined fighter screen of just ten planes airborne at a time, managed to limit the damage to one freighter sunk, with one cruiser crippled and sent back to Gibraltar under tow. Six British fighters were lost in shooting down eleven enemy bombers from a veritable swarm of attackers. But on the 15th two Italian cruisers and five destroyers came down from Sicily to challenge the close escort, led by Captain G. C. Hardy, RN, in the flak cruiser HMS *Cairo* with five fleet and four escort destroyers plus four minesweepers. Once again determination and dash drove off the Italians, although two British destroyers were left dead in the water. But the five surviving merchantmen, which had been detached during the surface action, were battered by 200 enemy aircraft; one was sunk and two badly damaged freighters had to be scuttled so the remaining two could maintain speed. One of them hit a mine but managed to get into Valletta; four escorts also hit mines and one destroyer sank.

Harwood, a passed-over captain with the honorific rank of commodore until his admittedly gallant feat against the *Graf Spee*, had enough wit to question the wisdom of sending yet another convoy from Alexandria, his first operation in charge, when he had no carrier. Eight cruisers and twenty-six destroyers plus a miscellany of other vessels, including the pathetic stratagem of a dummy battleship made up to look like the *King George V*, formed the escort; Harwood asked for land-based air cover but only forty bombers could be spared from Malta and Egypt to fly over the convoy. Admiral Vian was once again in command at sea on the cruiser *Cleopatra*. A remarkably familiar story of attrition followed. One ship was sunk and one so damaged that she was detached; a third could not keep up, leaving eight.

The crucial difference was that Harwood subjected Vian to a stream of nervous and ill-informed orders, something Cunningham had never felt the need to do, especially when the man on the spot was so competent. Heavy Italian ships came out again, and the RAF disabled a cruiser while scoring a minor hit on a battleship. Once again the enemy turned back without joining battle, but the air attacks continued. Vian was running low in ammunition and Harwood recalled the convoy to Alexandria – two more cruisers were lost in this demoralizing Axis victory.

The British Army was at El Alamein, only sixty miles west of Alexandria, for the final round against the thrusting Rommel on the very doorstep of Egypt. Despite enemy air superiority and the enormous losses it above all inflicted on the Mediterranean Fleet in more than two years of hard fighting, the Royal Navy had safely delivered some 200,000 fresh troops and mountains of munitions to the hotly contested North African theatre to face the now heavily outgunned Rommel and his Italian Army allies. Meanwhile Harwood precipitately evacuated Alexandria, his ships withdrawing to Haifa and Port Said in just two days. But General Sir Claude Auchinleck at last halted Rommel, whose supply line was now cripplingly over-extended and underserved, at the first Battle of El Alamein in July.

The salvation of Malta was the objective of the following month's saga, Operation 'Pedestal'. A convoy of fourteen supply ships, trained like a corps de ballet in joint turns on the way from the Clyde, arrived at Gibraltar for a truly massive attempt to relieve the aeronautically besieged island. Three carriers, two battleships, seven cruisers, two dozen destroyers and four support ships from Force H and the Home Fleet would provide the heavy escort; a fourth carrier protected by eight more destroyers would accompany the convoy and fly off Spitfires to reinforce RAF Malta, commanded by Air Marshal Keith Park, hero of the Battle of Britain. Vice-Admiral E. N. Syfret in HMS *Nelson* gave the departure order on 10 August, when a convenient fog shrouded Gibraltar. But on the next day German aircraft found and resolutely shadowed the convoy, refusing to be shaken off as three dozen Spitfires were flown from HMS *Furious* over 500 miles west of Malta. The old carrier *Eagle* (Captain L. D. Mackintosh, RN), a 1923 conversion, succumbed at lunchtime to four torpedoes fired by *U73* from the middle of the vast formation, sinking in ten minutes with the loss of 260 men out of nearly 1,200. *Furious*, however, retired unscathed after completing her assignment in the late afternoon.

Syfret's heavy force beat off the first massed Luftwaffe attack by more than a hundred aircraft in the evening without loss; four Germans were shot down. The next wave came over from Sardinia at noon on the 12th: seventy bombers with a heavy fighter escort. One merchantman was sunk and the carrier *Victorious* slightly damaged. The convoy next had to smash its way through an Italian submarine ambush; one was sunk by a ramming British destroyer. The third air attack that evening was even heavier, with some 100 dive- and torpedo-bombers covered by a fighter group. A destroyer was crippled and had to be abandoned and scuttled as the enemy squadrons concentrated on the carrier *Indomitable* (Captain T. H. Troubridge, RN), which was put out of action by armour-piercing bombs but remained afloat. Between Sardinia and Tunisia, Syfret withdrew the heavy escort as planned, leaving Rear-Admiral H. M. Burrough in charge of the close escort of four cruisers (one anti-aircraft) and twelve destroyers to cover the last leg to Malta with the remaining twelve merchant ships. Park's fighters had an operational range of less than 200 miles, but four minesweepers were able to sail from Malta in support.

Unfortunately Lieutenant Renato Perrini of the Italian Navy chose this moment to make the most successful submarine attack in the history of his service. Commanding *Axum*, with a single torpedo salvo he destroyed the flak cruiser *Cairo*, damaged

Burrough's flagship, the cruiser *Nigeria*, which had to turn back for Gibraltar escorted by two destroyers, and badly holed the tanker *Ohio*, which miraculously limped onward without catching fire. Burrough transferred to the destroyer *Ashanti*, having lost his only two cruisers equipped to control the fighters from Malta. With the convoy in disarray the Luftwaffe sent twenty dive-bombers, soon sinking two more merchantmen and damaging a third, which kept going. HMS *Kenya* was holed in the bow by Lieutenant Sergio Puccini's submarine *Alagi*, which had also sunk a merchantman; the cruiser managed to stay with the shrunken convoy. German and Italian torpedo boats came next, so damaging the cruiser *Manchester* that Captain H. Drew, RN, had to scuttle. Four more merchantmen were destroyed and another was damaged but managed to sail on. More air attacks ensued the next day, resulting in the loss of one more freighter and further damage to the *Ohio* and two others, all of which struggled on. Now there were five, two of which were little better than hulks, the *Ohio* actually under tow.

But the ever-nervous Italian surface fleet was deterred from joining the slaughter by Lieutenant Alastair Mars, RN, in the submarine *Unbroken*, who caused serious damage to one heavy and one light cruiser in the waters north of Malta.

On the evening of 13 August 1942, three battered supply ships, one almost awash, sailed slowly into Valletta harbour. A fourth arrived the next day. The 15th was Malta's National Day, and delirious cheers greeted the scorched and shattered tanker *Ohio* (Captain D. W. Mason) as the destroyer *Penn* towed her into port with very little freeboard showing. Her master was awarded the George Cross. Her fuel, the 30,000 tons of supplies and the thirty-six Spitfires, which were all that Operation 'Pedestal' was able to deliver at such extraordinary cost after the most intense convoy battle of the war in the Mediterranean, proved to be just enough. The island fortress was able to hold out until the strategic situation in the Mediterranean was transformed at the beginning of November, when General Montgomery led the Eighth Army to a pivotal victory in the second Battle of El Alamein, saving Egypt and enabling the Western Allies to go on the offensive at last. The Wehrmacht was now in retreat in the west, while in the east it had been halted at Stalingrad. A sheepish Admiral Harwood returned to Alexandria shortly afterwards.

Montgomery's long overdue victory was about to be consolidated by the first major American intervention against

Germany on land. But the preparations for Operation 'Torch' so overstretched the transatlantic lifeline on which it relied that the convoy system came close to breakdown. At the end of autumn 1942 the war against Hitler was still in the balance. In the Far East Japan was already on the defensive.

11

The Defeat of the German Navy

The year 1943 saw the cause of the United Nations, as the grand coalition against the dictatorships was now called, gain the upper hand on all fronts. From the viewpoint of the Royal Navy, most of the Mediterranean would become a British lake; the U-boats were checkmated; and at the Anglo-American summit at Quebec in August 1943, codenamed 'Quadrant', Britain got its own supreme Allied command in the war against Japan, that of South-East Asia. Cynical Americans referred to Admiral Lord Louis Mountbatten's SEAC as 'Save England's Asian Colonies'; but Admiral King was not about to allow the Limeys he so heartily loathed to horn in on the US Navy's private war in the Pacific.

Instead of concentrating its Far Eastern efforts on the Indian Ocean, Britain made the strategic mistake of insisting on a place for a new British Pacific Fleet in the final stages of the war against Japan and was thoroughly humiliated for its pains. The Royal Navy had its nose rubbed in the fact that Britannia no longer ruled the waves (and never would again): Uncle Sam did. So vast were his resources that the President of the United States saw no need to decide between the US Navy's drive across the Pacific under Admiral Nimitz and General MacArthur's across the South-West Pacific with the Seventh Fleet: Roosevelt ducked the issue of Army–Navy rivalry to the very end by 'choosing' both, in the most wasteful and expensive example of strategic duplication on record. For this and Europe the Americans mobilized 100 munificently staffed and equipped divisions and expanded their Navy to such an extent that it dominated the oceans with ease for the rest of the century. During the Second World War the British practice of measuring the Royal Navy against the fleets of other leading powers quietly perished and a different, more modest and realistic, standard of power was adopted.

Early in May 1942 the Americans won their first strategic victory, at the Battle of the Coral Sea north-east of Australia. Two US fleet carriers and escorts took on a stronger Japanese force with one light and two fleet carriers plus covering ships. Although the weaker and less experienced Americans lost one carrier and the other was extensively damaged – a tactical defeat – the Japanese lost their light carrier and one large carrier was damaged; more important, they abandoned not only the scene of the first carrier clash in history but also their plan to attack south-east New Guinea, ending their advance for ever.

Only one month later the US Pacific Fleet, led by Vice-Admiral Raymond A. Spruance, won its most important action, the turning point in the Pacific campaign: the Battle of Midway. The patched-up survivor of the Coral Sea, USS *Yorktown*, and two other carriers, with the US island of Midway acting as an immovable fourth, annihilated Admiral Nagumo's Mobile Force of four big carriers, the kernel of the fleet that had attacked Pearl Harbor. The highly risky decision to confront the bulk of the Japanese fleet, led by the carriers, as it set out to extend and consolidate its Pacific conquests, was taken by Nimitz on the basis of a brilliant decipherment coup by US naval intelligence. The biggest concentration of naval tonnage since Jutland fought it out off the remote Hawaiian island; all four Japanese carriers, 225 planes and a heavy cruiser were destroyed, while the Americans lost the *Yorktown*, 146 aircraft and a destroyer. From now on the Japanese were on the defensive, only six months after starting the war in the Pacific. But a divided American command would need three more years to corner them. Meanwhile the US administration had decided in principle on the very eve of Pearl Harbor to develop the atomic bomb.

Roosevelt proposed to Churchill in March 1942 that the Americans should take charge in the Pacific while the British took on the Indian and Mediterranean oceans and the two powers cooperated in the Atlantic. In fact the latter ocean enjoyed only a token US naval presence from then on, while the Royal Canadian Navy took on the drudgery of playing second fiddle in the war of attrition around the convoys. The ratio of Allied surface strengths in the principal naval strategic theatre at this stage of the war was 50 per cent British, 48 per cent Canadian – and 2 per cent American.

Despite the manifest difficulty of keeping the transatlantic route open and capable of delivering enough munitions to sustain, let alone expand, the war against Germany and Italy, the Americans, even before their Navy had halted the Japanese, envisaged an invasion of north-west France as early as spring 1943, perhaps with the seizure of a bridgehead in autumn 1942. But the British, although they had already drafted plans for landings in France, would not agree until the Mediterranean and India were safe. The initial joint command set up to study and execute Operation 'Round-up', as it was originally styled, consisted of General Sir Bernard Paget, Air Chief Marshal Sir Sholto Douglas – and Admiral Sir Bertram Ramsay, mastermind of Dunkirk, who had justly escaped censure for the 'Channel Dash' fiasco and in July 1942 was appointed Naval C-in-C, Expeditionary Force, with the acting rank of full admiral (even though he was still on the retired list!). The general and the air marshal would eventually be replaced; but Ramsay would retain responsibility for the safe delivery and seaborne protection of the Normandy invasion when it finally began nearly two years later. The Americans joined them on a joint staff.

Ramsay's duties included not only the mustering and preparation of thousands of warships and transports but also the training of sailors and troops in amphibious operations, regardless of Vice-Admiral Mountbatten's Combined Operations command (before he became SACSEA), which in the end was superseded for the greatest joint operation ever. Ramsay wisely sought out Mountbatten to make sure there would be no clash between the two commands. Afterwards Mountbatten gracefully congratulated Ramsay on his appointment and promised that there would be 'no more friction'. This amounted to a clear admission that there had been some conflict between the staff of the aggressively competent Ramsay and the voraciously ambitious Mountbatten, determined to surpass his father, unjustly dismissed in the previous war. Ramsay made no secret of his view that training for amphibious operations was 'not anything like up to standard'; in his usual blunt manner, he urged Mountbatten to resolve 'the ambiguity of your position', a reference to the conflict between his command responsibilities and the duties imposed by his ex officio seat on the Chiefs of Staff Committee.

The royally connected, charismatic Mountbatten was only forty-two and was still in charge of 'Combined Ops' in August 1942 when the disastrous Operation 'Jubilee', better known as the Dieppe

Raid, was launched. Dieppe was a scaled-down adaptation of a draft Operation 'Sledgehammer', designed to establish a beach-head in Normandy. The Americans saw this as a prelude to a full-scale invasion, the British as a last-resort diversion to take pressure off the embattled Russians. The British talked the Americans out of it (they later conceded that it was a bad idea) but unwisely decided, against Ramsay's advice, on a large 'pinprick' attack on Normandy in any case, partly as a rehearsal, partly to dissimulate their own reluctance to tackle Fortress Europe. To the great relief and positive enthusiasm of the British, the Americans turned their attention to a large-scale landing in North Africa, to help swing the balance in the Mediterranean. It was provisionally scheduled for 26 October.

But on 19 August two Canadian infantry brigades, two British Army and one Royal Marine Commando units and small numbers of American and Free French troops, 6,100 men with thirty tanks, were taken across the Channel by a total of 252 naval vessels, including landing craft, troopships, minesweepers and eight destroyers. The strategic objective was vague: to mount a 'reconnaissance in force', take the port and hold it for a while, in the hope of persuading the Germans to reinforce their western front at the expense of the eastern. There was no plan for exploiting a success and there were no reinforcements to do so. Even before it started, the misbegotten enterprise must have looked like a suicide mission to some commanders: Dieppe housed a German divisional headquarters and the whole area, so close to Britain, was bristling with troops. Tactically, the attackers hoped to capture the HQ and a German naval direction-finding station and to knock out some coastal artillery.

The raid got off to a disastrous start when its eastern landing group was scattered in a clash with a German coastal convoy; the Germans lost two small escorts but the Allied force lost tactical surprise as the enemy alerted ground, sea and air forces. The encounter fatally disrupted the Allied chain of command and the landing took place piecemeal across an eleven-mile front. Air support was erratic and only one of the artillery batteries was knocked out, leaving the rest free to pound the invaders; the absence of heavy bombardment ships meant the Navy could do nothing to help. Once on the beaches the troops were pinned down by a combination of barbed wire and heavy German fire. All the tanks were destroyed or captured.

The bitter fighting lasted some nine hours, from before dawn to lunchtime, and almost two-thirds of the Allied troops were killed, wounded and/or taken prisoner, including all seven battalion commanders – an extremely high casualty rate. One destroyer was wrecked by air attack and had to be scuttled; three others were damaged, and thirty-three landing craft and other small vessels were sunk. The Allies also lost 106 aircraft to the Germans' 48; enemy casualties ran to 591, including 37 prisoners taken to England. The German defenders were not impressed by the invaders' tactics or equipment, especially the tanks. At least some lessons were learned by the Allied side: the need for heavy preparatory and supporting naval bombardment (noted by the US Navy in the Pacific), the impracticability of capturing a major port as a beachhead, the importance of diverting enemy attention and, above all, the absolute necessity of adequate preparation in both quantity and quality.

By then Ramsay had been temporarily detached from 'Round-up' to take charge of preparations for 'Torch', for which the US General Dwight D. Eisenhower had been chosen as supreme commander. The bulk of the maritime support was to be British; to Ramsay's chagrin, the naval command under Eisenhower was given to Admiral Sir Andrew Cunningham, specially detached from his duties with the Combined Chiefs of Staff in Washington. It was the right choice, not only because of Cunningham's prestige as a fighting admiral but also because he was well known to the Americans, who were providing the bulk of the troops and all the supplies. Nevertheless the better-qualified Ramsay did the planning and all the preparatory work at great intensity and high speed as Cunningham's deputy, pending the latter's return from Washington, and there can be no doubt that the naval credit for the efficiency of the landings belongs to the erstwhile gatekeeper at Dover.

Advance American opinion on the operation was divided. The US Navy predictably favoured the primacy of the Pacific over 'adventures' in the Atlantic while the US Army high command was keen to follow Clausewitz's dictum by attacking the main strength of the main enemy, the Germans in France. The American generals in London, including Eisenhower, supported the British Mediterranean-first strategy, a view not unrelated to the fact that they would be in charge. These multifarious tensions led to one change of plan after another as Ramsay fought to complete the naval operational plan and battle orders by the deadline of 30 October. Although the British Eighth Army had been massively strengthened in North Africa, thanks to the Royal Navy, and had already saved Egypt from Rommel, Montgomery had yet to deliver the great victory in the east that was to be immediately followed by the American stroke from the west. Delays to 'Torch' saw to it that the two events almost exactly coincided: Montgomery triumphed at El Alamein on 4 November and the landings in North Africa began four days later.

'Torch' was a three-pronged compromise. A wholly American convoy with nearly 25,000 troops sailed direct from the United States to land on the other side of the Atlantic, on the coast of Morocco, its main objective Casablanca. Another American force of 18,000 was aimed at Oran, Algeria, and an Anglo-American force of similar size at Algiers itself. All three landing forces enjoyed British heavy naval cover and the latter two also had close escort and support from the Royal Navy; all naval units involved, including American, came under Cunningham, reappointed C-in-C, Mediterranean.

The invasions themselves went well with only one transport sunk to mar Ramsay's logistical triumph, achieved in three days; but events ashore threatened to collapse in confusion as the Americans negotiated with the commanders of the 100,000 Vichy French troops in the region. The Germans acted with their customary ruthlessness, marching into unoccupied south-eastern France on 11 November, whereupon the devious Admiral Jean Darlan, the Vichy C-in-C, agreed a ceasefire, which, however, was only patchily observed.

The political problem of Darlan, who had played such a murky role in the fall of France, leading to the British attack on the French fleet, and whose endorsement as French regional commander by Eisenhower evoked angry incomprehension in Britain and America, was brutally solved on Christmas Eve by an assassin. The more amenable General Henri Giraud took his place. Sadly, the residual French fleet, having received no clear orders from the ineffable Darlan, had scuttled itself in Toulon on 27 November, the second time it missed an opportunity to rejoin the Allied cause (to which even now it could have been most useful) and the last tragic chapter in an ignominious story. But by the turn of the year the mainly American eastward thrust against the Axis forces assembled in Tunisia was well in hand, enabling Churchill and

Roosevelt and their key advisers to hold one of the most important Allied summit conferences of the war at Casablanca in January 1943.

This gathering, codenamed 'Symbol', was from the British viewpoint the high point of Anglo-American wartime collaboration. They had achieved their long-delayed strategic victory in North Africa and the US Army had been blooded in the Mediterranean/European theatre. American power, while growing exponentially in the Pacific, had successfully vaulted the Atlantic and would now rapidly increase, absolutely and relatively, while there was little more that Britain could add to its own all-out war effort. Stalin declined to attend the meeting, preoccupied as he was in defending the battered city named after himself. Ten days of sometimes fierce argument ensued, with Admiral King pressing for an all-out US naval effort in the Pacific unless US General Marshall got his way with an invasion of France later in 1943. The British side wanted to use the victorious Allied forces in North Africa for an invasion of Sicily (Operation 'Husky'), followed by an assault on mainland Italy. Churchill favoured the 'soft underbelly' approach, insisting that it was too early for an invasion of France. For the last time in strategic terms, he won his point.

In naval terms the most important result of Casablanca was to give renewed impetus to the campaign against the U-boats, now the most effective German threat to the Allied cause in the West. The priority given to this problem was not absolute: it was described in the official communiqué as 'a first charge . . . on the United Nations' (the choice of the indefinite article made it clear that other issues were regarded as equally important). It was obvious to the Allies that 'Torch' had set back this cause by several months, and that an invasion of France could not proceed unless the U-boat menace was brought under control. Here at least the American desire for the earliest possible invasion and the British for priority in defeating the U-boats complemented each other. The British side argued that the latter objective was most likely to be achieved soonest with the help of end-to-end air cover for convoys, whether by escort carriers or by land-based VLR Liberators or preferably both. The Americans seemed to accept the argument; but General Eisenhower hung on to his two squadrons of Liberators in Morocco and to the escort carriers working for him in the Mediterranean, well after Allied successes there made it possible for him to spare some if not all of each. It need hardly be said that

Admiral King did not feel moved to divert Liberators or escort carriers from the Pacific theatre, which had large quantities of both.

On 28 December 1942 a new convoy designation came into use, as TM 1 (Trinidad–Mediterranean) set sail for Gibraltar: nine oil tankers with fuel for the 'Torch' forces, escorted by Commander R. C. Boyle's weak British B5 escort group of a single destroyer (HMS *Havelock*) and just three corvettes – a sign of the pressure on escort forces caused by 'Torch'. Classed as a military convoy, TM 1 kept wireless silence and was therefore not detected, unlike most commercial convoys, by German eavesdroppers. Instead *U514*, on its way to maraud in the Caribbean, sighted it by chance and reported it. The Admiralty knew of a pack of six other boats (christened 'Delphin' – dolphin – by the U-boat command) lurking south of the Azores for 'Torch' traffic, and advised Boyle to divert southward after dark on 3 January. Bletchley Park had just broken the naval intelligence drought caused by the fourth Enigma wheel after ten months of intellectual struggle, but was still taking as much as two days to break into the U-boat traffic: the OIC could give no more help to Boyle, who decided to ignore its advice for the sake of the calmer water on his existing course, which would make the imminent refuelling of the escorts easier. *U514* sank one of the tankers, evaded counter-attack and kept in touch until the Delphin group and four other boats had positioned themselves across the path of the convoy. From 8 to 10 January the submariners sank six more of the tankers in repeated attacks, Dönitz urging his men on to what he hoped would be the first 'whitewash' – total destruction of a convoy – in the war.

But on the morning of 11 January a solitary RAF Sunderland flying boat from Gibraltar, at the limit of its range, appeared over the two surviving tankers, which reached Gibraltar undamaged on the 14th; once air cover was on hand, no U-boat attacked. The TM 1 disaster had brought the highest losses to a single convoy of the entire Atlantic campaign: 77 per cent of the total capacity or 55,000 tons of shipping, seven fully laden tankers lost with 100,000 tons of fuel. Boyle managed to damage one U-boat, which got away. None of the escorts was hit. Had their commander followed the OIC's advice, Delphin would have missed TM 1 by 100 miles.

The news of the catastrophe reached Casablanca as the conference was about to get into its stride and concentrated minds on the Greenland and Azores air gaps. Even King could not now pretend that this was a minor issue; he simply took the view that it was the US Army Air Force that would have to supply the necessary Liberators. Thus the 'first charge' on the Allied agenda remained for another three months an all too heavy, well-nigh disastrous, charge of another kind on the long-suffering merchant and fighting navies in the Atlantic. But, to King's chagrin, the American side agreed to reinforce the Atlantic in a limited but important manner: they would henceforward escort the military convoys involved in the build-up for the invasion of Europe, and also the special tanker convoys from the Caribbean to prevent a repetition of TM 1.

The Admiralty set about improving the efficiency of the convoy system pending the arrival of the promised air cover. The return, albeit at a slow pace, of naval Ultra also restored much of the value of the preventive stratagem, diversion of convoys out of danger (offset by the sheer increase in quantity of shipping). The strengths of escort groups were fine-tuned to the size of their convoys after it was established that the larger the convoy, the lower the ratio of warships needed to protect it efficiently, as indicated by the relationship between the area of a circle (the convoy) and its circumference (the escort). It took a British Nobel prizewinner in economics, Professor P. M. S. Blackett, to recognize this extremely helpful fact. But such adjustments were the merest tinkering against the imminent German 'big push' in the Atlantic for which the Allies were bracing themselves at the turn of the year. They knew that Dönitz had just reorganized his radio channels so that U-boat HQ could control two major convoy battles simultaneously and that record numbers of U-boats were being commissioned. The return of Ultra postponed the crunch, but there was no evading it.

As far as the Admiralty was concerned, the weakest link in the elaborate convoy-defence system was now the Royal Canadian Navy, thanks mostly to its phenomenal expansion to help Britain, a cruel irony. The Admiralty unfairly blamed the Canadians, providing 48 per cent of the escorts, for 80 per cent of convoy losses at the grim back-end of 1942. This was a statistical fact; but the Canadians were normally allotted the slow, and therefore most vulnerable, convoys; they had the least modern escorts and were at the back of the queue for the latest technical advances such as radar, HF/DF (none) and Liberators (also none). The Canadian naval command was at fault for concealing from its government the acute growing pains it was suffering, which meant that Canadian sailors were uniquely overworked, but their unsentimental British allies took no account of these special difficulties.

The dashingly abrasive Admiral Sir Max Horton, hitherto Flag Officer, Submarines, had relieved the conciliatory and conscientious Sir Percy Noble as C-in-C, Western Approaches, in Liverpool in November 1942 and resolved to tackle the Canadian problem with a ruthlessness commensurate with the importance to Britain of the Atlantic campaign. When Vice-Admiral Percy Nelles, Canadian naval Chief of Staff, appealed for help, Horton and the Admiralty seized the chance. The four Canadian mid-ocean escort groups were to be switched to the Gibraltar route, giving them a base in Londonderry, Northern Ireland, and milder weather to work in, plus end-to-end air cover and a less punishing schedule, leaving time for rigorous training. British groups previously on the route took their places.

The Canadians at first jibbed at the implied criticism, but a series of convoy disasters convinced them. When the Canadian government asked for more destroyers, the Admiralty supplied them – complete with Royal Navy crews, who were thus able to stiffen the Canadians. The British were not above ensuring that the captains of these destroyers happened to be senior to all Canadian commanders present, ensuring that the SOE was British. In the end Escort Group C3, the most competent formation, continued to work on the main north Atlantic route and was the only Canadian one there for the climax of the campaign in spring; C1, C2 and C4 stayed on the Gibraltar run until the beginning of April. Only at the end of May were all four groups back under Canadian control; and only at this stage did Canada acquire its first ever independent command, when the Canadian Admiral L. W. Murray was appointed C-in-C, Canadian North-west Atlantic.

The Royal Navy could hardly be blamed for taking no unnecessary chances with the campaign which, as no other, was a matter of life or death for the United Kingdom. The Canadians expanded their navy at breakneck speed, more on their own initiative than on British urging; and they did escort hundreds of convoys and many thousands of ships across the Atlantic in the first three years of the war without mishap. We have already noted the just verdict of Admiral Noble, who commanded Western Approaches in the darkest period of the campaign, that the Canadians 'solved the problem of the Atlantic convoys'.

The harsh winter of 1942–3 brought a considerable improvement in the success rate of the Russian convoys, suspended in February so that twenty-seven destroyers and frigates and an escort carrier could be transferred from the Home Fleet to Western Approaches for the anticipated renewal of the German onslaught further south. When the *Scharnhorst* joined the *Tirpitz* group in Altenfjord in March, the Americans moved their Task Force TF 22 from covering the North African route to the Gulf of Maine in their far north-east. The force's fleet carrier, battleship, cruisers and destroyers were to come under British Home Fleet command in the event of a German surface sortie in strength.

The gloom of 1942 was scarcely lifted for the British by December's comparatively low shipping loss of 349,000 tons; and even though the new-construction rate had picked up hearteningly from July, the year ended with a net loss of 750,000 tons. British non-military oil reserves had fallen to 300,000 tons, enough for three months' miserly use (after the TM 1 disaster, the petrol ration was cut by another 10 per cent). The debilitating Battle of the Air was still going on in Whitehall on a new front: the RAF obtained priority for the new 'centimetric', higher definition radar set, now being manufactured in the United States, for Bomber Command over both Coastal Command and the Navy's ASW forces, whose need was rather more urgent. The airborne was given priority over the shipboard version; but the Admiralty was at least able to insist that each of the trickle of Liberators now reaching Coastal Command was fitted with the maritime variant of the airborne version in the US. It was good enough to detect the conning tower of a surfaced submarine at five miles.

There was one other moment of good cheer for the British Navy in December to add to the penetration of the German Triton cipher on the 13th: the Battle of the Barents Sea at the end of the month, which had consequences out of all proportion to its strategic significance. Vice-Admiral Oskar Kummetz brought the heavy cruiser *Hipper* and the pocket-battleship *Lützow*, escorted by six destroyers, out of Altenfjord against convoy JW 51B (a new designation) of fourteen freighters bound for Murmansk. The close escort of ten ships included seven destroyers under Captain R. St V. Sherbrooke, RN; the covering force of two cruisers and destroyers was commanded by Rear-Admiral R. L. Burnett. In a chaotic engagement in a fierce storm, *Hipper* sank Sherbrooke's sole minesweeper and badly damaged two of his destroyers, one of which sank later. *Lützow* damaged but failed to sink one merchantman. When Burnett's cruisers arrived, they damaged *Hipper* and sank a German destroyer, driving Kummetz off despite his greater firepower. The German cruiser was never deployed on the high seas again. At moderate cost to themselves, the British escorts had repelled a superior enemy without losing one of their charges. Fortunately the Luftwaffe in Norway had been thinned out to reinforce the Mediterranean.

Hitler was furious and carpeted Grand-Admiral Raeder on 6 January, ordering him to scrap all Germany's heavy ships, even though his own strictures against risking them, and with them the defence of Norway, had prompted Kummetz's decision to break off the action. Raeder argued that this would hand the British a huge strategic victory on a plate, but Hitler was adamant and the humiliated C-in-C resigned on 30 January.

He was replaced by Karl Dönitz, the only possible candidate, now promoted to grand-admiral. As so often happens in such disputes, the sacked man's argument against scrapping the fleet was not only taken up but also won by his successor. Raeder had done a sound job with limited resources; his real difficulty was that his face no longer fitted at Hitler's court, whereas that of Dönitz, the Wehrmacht's only high commander still capable of a strategic victory, was very much in favour after a long run of successes as the war in general turned against the Nazis. The TM 1 victory only seemed to confirm the wisdom of Hitler's choice. The new C-in-C, aged fifty-one, retained personal command of the U-boats, his most important arm, leaving day-to-day control to Admiral Godt.

The suspension of the Murmansk run in February also brought deliverance until November 1943 from Soviet paranoia for British personnel stationed in northern Russia. But the difficult ally produced some splendid news when the German Army surrendered at Stalingrad on 2 February – a setback from which the Wehrmacht did not recover and one of the great turning-points of the war.

The return of Ultra and the bad weather reduced Allied worldwide shipping losses to 261,000 tons (203,000 to U-boats) in January 1943, the 'best' month since November 1941; but the losses from TM 1 were a particularly bad blow within a north Atlantic total of 173,000 tons. The Germans now had more than 100 submarines at a time on patrol in the north Atlantic, their peak operational strength as the total U-boat fleet rose to nearly 400.

Twenty of them from three lurking packs combined against eastbound slow convoy SC 118 just as naval Ultra suffered a temporary blackout. The British escort of three destroyers and six others was the 'scratch' group B2, not yet welded into a team, but it was reinforced by three rare American warships from Iceland. A prolonged engagement ensued across the Greenland air gap and even beyond, the Germans undeterred by the occasional long-range aircraft from pressing home their attacks in what Dönitz himself described as 'perhaps the hardest convoy battle of the war'. First blood went to the escort when Lieutenant-Commander Richard Stannard, VC, RNR, on the destroyer *Vimy*, sank *U187*, but thirteen freighters out of fifty-three were sunk, compared with three enemy submarines lost and two badly damaged. Commander Siegfried Freiherr von Forstner sank seven merchantmen in *U402*, becoming an instant 'ace' (a rare achievement at this stage of the war) and winning the Knight's Cross, despite being forced to submerge seven times by aircraft. The battle lasted four days in foul weather and the escort ran out of depth charges in repeated attacks on the tormentors.

Huge convoys with large escorts were now coming under attack from big packs spontaneously assembled against them by Godt. He placed seventeen boats in the path of westbound convoy ON 166 for a second massive melee in the bitter February of 1943. The escort was a hybrid group, classed as American because led by Captain Paul R. Heineman, USN, in the Coastguard cutter USS *Spencer*, supported by another such American vessel, and one British and four Canadian corvettes; but group A3 had experience of working together and styled itself, American fashion, 'Heineman's Harriers'. A Polish destroyer lent temporary support. On the 21st *Spencer* sank one of the marauders; but over the next five days, as the sixty-three freighters struggled across the air gap, the Germans sank fourteen. Only one other U-boat was sunk, rammed by the cutter USS *Campbell*, which had to be taken in tow. This enemy victory was a considerable contribution to the 289,000 tons lost in the north Atlantic out of a worldwide total of 403,000 tons for February. The Germans now reached their operational pinnacle of 120 boats at a time in the north Atlantic, ensuring that March would be rather worse.

'The Germans never came so near to disrupting communication between the New World and the Old as in the first twenty days of March 1943', an Admiralty staff review noted at the end of that year: 'It appeared possible that we should not be able to continue [to regard] convoy as an effective system of defence.' The crisis of the long and gruelling second attempt to isolate the United Kingdom by U-boat focused on four fully laden, eastbound convoys: SC 121, HX 228, SC 122 and HX 229. The first-named left New York on 23 February, escorted by Heineman's Harriers, still tired after their setback with ON 166. Detecting two packs totalling twenty-six submarines across its path, OIC ordered an initially effective diversion, but a pack of nine kept in touch. Western Approaches detached two American and two Canadian escorts from westbound shipping to help the convoy, in disarray because of storms. SC 121 was harassed for five days from 7 March, losing thirteen out of fifty-two ships, exactly one in four, 62,000 tons plus cargoes. No U-boat was damaged.

Separate but overlapping in time, another fierce battle developed over HX 228, a fast convoy of sixty escorted by Commander A. A. Tait's British B3 group of four destroyers and five corvettes. A successful diversion by OIC sidestepped one pack but placed the convoy in the path of another of thirteen. The new American 6th Support Group, including the escort carrier USS *Bogue*, the first to join the fray, was sent to help, but the opening attack by a single submarine sank two merchantmen and damaged a third. Another U-boat was damaged by the fallout of wreckage blown hundreds of feet into the air when it torpedoed an ammunition ship.

The fourth and last sinking from HX 228 was made by *U444*, the first in a unique chain. Tait's HMS *Harvester* rammed it as it dived, never to be seen again. But the destroyer was so badly damaged that it was unable to save itself from an attack by *U432*, and Tait went down with his ship. Next up was the Free French corvette *Aconit* (Lieutenant-Commander Levasseur), which forced *U432* to the surface with depth charges, then shelled it with its one 4-inch gun, then rammed the boat. It sank. The atrocious weather prevented the *Bogue* from helping HX 228, which got off relatively lightly in a battle that dragged on from 10 to 14 March.

Less than a week later, SC 122 and HX 229 were embroiled in the largest convoy battle of all time, the terrible climax of the Atlantic campaign after three and a half years of bitter conflict between the U-boats and the escorts. SC 122, fifty strong, left New York on the 5th, escorted by B5 (Commander Boyle, RN, in the destroyer *Havelock*, as he had been with TM 1) but which now included a US destroyer, a frigate, five corvettes and a trawler. Fast convoy HX 229 departed three days later under the weakened protection of B4, temporarily led by Lieutenant-Commander G. J. Luther, RNVR, of HMS *Volunteer*, in the absence of the regular SOE: he had four destroyers and two corvettes. The U-boat command gathered one pack of eight and another of eighteen ('Stürmer') to lie in wait in two parallel lines across the path of SC 122, located and tracked by the German eavesdroppers. A third pack of eleven was quickly assembled against HX 229. The first pack of eight was foiled by a gale, which blew SC 122 past the planned waiting line before it could assemble there; it was therefore diverted against HX 229, also being driven by a following gale, but only managed to sight its rearguard from astern. Had it not been for a sighting by a lone U-boat limping home with mechanical problems, HX 229 might have got away. As it was, the German command was able to exploit the lucky encounter and regroup its boats for a successful chase on 16 March.

Three ships from HX 229 were sunk that evening and another five at dawn. The Stürmer pack arrived on the 17th in the gap between the two convoys; after some confusion the Germans realized that their spreadeagled pack was engaged with two convoys, one at each end of its line. The original pack of eight was by now attacking HX 229 from the west and the third lurked to the south-east. One U-boat sank five SC 122 ships on the 17th; two more submarines sank one freighter apiece at lunchtime from HX 229, which now gained a respite as long-range aircraft made brief appearances overhead at the limit of their range. The aircrews surveyed a scene of unmatched complexity as two sprawling convoys, only minutes of flying time apart, zigzagged eastward across a turbulent sea. The first pack regrouped for another attack on SC 122 and the third targeted HX 229; Stürmer was divided into two and deployed against both from the evening of the 17th. Boyle lost the destroyer *Granville* to *U338* while another boat sank two merchantmen from SC 122. On the 18th two more HX 229 members were sunk, together with one straggler and one romper sailing behind and ahead of the convoy respectively. The last fatal casualty from HX 229 was sunk on the morning of the 19th; so was one nearby U-boat by a Coastal Command Sunderland – the only German loss in this vast maritime brawl.

The battle had involved ninety merchantmen, of which twenty-two were sent to the bottom; sixteen escorts, of which one was sunk and one (the trawler) foundered in heavy seas; and thirty-eight U-boats, of which only one was sunk. A total of 146,000 tons of shipping was destroyed, an all-time Atlantic record for a convoy battle. A deep depression fell upon the Admiralty, where many staff members were losing faith in the value of diversion (and, the ultimate heresy, in convoy itself). There was so much traffic at sea that space for evasion was limited; and there were so many enemy submarines that they had little difficulty in making a sighting. Particularly ominous to informed observers was the fact that so many convoyed ships were being sunk, apparently in the teeth of the trained escort groups: 72 ships out of 108 sunk in the black month of March 1943. Naval Ultra fell out again for nine days from 10 March, and the appalling weather also helped the enemy. The U-boats sank no fewer than twenty-two out of twenty-eight independently routed ships, a formidable 79 per cent, which should have been the clinching argument against letting any but the very fastest merchant ships out alone. But they were a tiny proportion of the ships that crossed the Atlantic in the month; to find targets the Germans were being forced to attack escorted shipping, always their last resort. An unprecedented number of U-boats was able to take on a plethora of targets in conditions which favoured the attackers and worked against the aircraft-starved escorts.

But numeracy was no more the Admiralty's strong suit in March 1943 than it had been at the previous U-boat crisis in April 1917. Only later was it noticed that just 4 per cent of ships were lost from the totality of attacked convoys – and that the great majority of convoys were not even attacked. The OIC was not at all down-hearted, detecting a new note of irresolution in mid-March in the garrulous radio traffic that was the Achilles' heel of the U-boat arm. Only hindsight enables us to appreciate the supreme irony in this climax of the Battle of the Atlantic. Each side, unbeknown to the other, was complaining about Allied maritime air power: the British that there was too little, the Germans that there was too much. The written reports of returning U-boat skippers, even those involved in the rout of the four attacked eastbound convoys in March 1943, complained, out of reach of British eavesdroppers, of the increasing reach of Allied aircraft (and the harassing patrols over the Bay of Biscay against departing and returning boats which had been going on for some time).

What those of little faith at the Admiralty could not know was that nearly every U-boat involved in the apparently one-sided massacre had been attacked by depth charges, and that more than half of them had been damaged, two seriously. The Germans also believed they had sunk thirty-two merchantmen, not a propaganda exaggeration but an understandable accumulation of the kind of error so common also among bomber pilots on both sides: not every spectacular explosion fleetingly sighted by a withdrawing attacker was fatal. Despite the best efforts of a special committee with standing orders to be sceptical, the Admiralty consistently overstated the numbers of U-boats destroyed for most of the war.

Even though it started very badly for the British, the most important of the long series of Anglo-American convoy conferences, begun in Washington on 1 March, at last opened the way to the elimination of the air gap. Admiral King, still seething about the PQ 17 disaster of July 1942, stunningly and stingingly announced the withdrawal of the US Navy from the main transatlantic route; in future the Americans would only cover military and tanker convoys south of the main route. As a sop, however, the Bogue support group would be added to the five being formed by the British as 'fire brigades' to help threatened convoys and their escorts (a sure sign that the overall total of escorts had risen handsomely); one of the British groups would be built around HMS *Biter*, the first US-built RN escort carrier. More responsibility would be given to the new Canadian command, the Northwest Atlantic, to be activated on 1 May. King had so far ignored the Casablanca decision to provide Liberators for the air gap; he blatantly sent all his to the Pacific. Coastal Command managed to scrape together fifty-two, but there was a constant shortage of spares (the Pacific again). Bomber Command had relinquished none. There were none stationed west of Iceland, even though the Canadians had crews available. Professor Blackett had calculated that a force of 200 VLR and LR aircraft would save at least 2m tons of shipping or 400 vessels in a full year.

The convoy conference at last agreed to allocate twenty Liberators to the RCAF to fly from Newfoundland; but in the end King had to be overruled by Roosevelt himself, on Churchill's urging. The President ordered the US Navy to divert sixty VLRs to the north Atlantic and the USAAF to detach seventy-five from bombing Germany; Bomber Command was told to hand over 120 from its hoard. 'Bomber' Harris reacted predictably, as if his right arm were being amputated. By the end of the month, twenty VLR Liberators were in service over the convoys, and the air gap was closed altogether when the first three American-built, British escort carriers joined Western Approaches Command.

Worldwide Allied shipping losses in the climactic month of

March 1943 came to 693,000 tons, 627,000 to submarines (their second-highest monthly score after November 1942). Ninety-five ships had been sunk by the 20th, forty-one in the first ten days, fifty-four in the second; in the last third of the month twenty-five were lost, a notable if not decisive decline. The U-boats sank 108 ships out of 120 lost, eighty-two in the north Atlantic. There was no air gap for the next pair of major eastbound convoys to sail through at the end of March. SC 123 and HX 230 between them lost just one straggler and enjoyed air cover from the *Bogue* throughout. In the pivotal month of April, worldwide Allied losses were almost halved, to 345,000 tons (235,000 in the north Atlantic, 328,000 to submarines). To sink thirty-nine freighters on the main route the Germans had to accept the loss of fifteen submarines. As he had done before when the going got harder, Dönitz sprang a surprise and shifted the focus of his attack, this time to the central Atlantic and the West African routes. On the night of 30 April to 1 May *U515* (Werner Henke) sank five ships in five minutes from a lightly escorted coastal convoy between Takoradi and Freetown, Sierra Leone. The unaccompanied ace's final score before three destroyers turned up from Freetown was seven, a remarkable day's work, if also unlikely to be repeated.

As we saw in the Introduction, the hard struggle for convoy ONS 5 ended with twelve merchantmen lost but also six U-boats sunk in the action and another three in peripheral incidents. The German attack on HX 237 and SC 129 cost them three more boats for three ships sunk, an even clearer victory for the escorts. Then came Commander Gretton's unscathed SC 130. Yet there would be much more hard work for the escorts to do in order to retain the upper hand gained by the Royal Navy and its seaborne and airborne comrades in the Atlantic in May 1943. An enemy hard at work on the world's first jet aircraft, cruise missile and ballistic missile, with plans for much deadlier submarines, could hardly be written off. But Admiral Dönitz once again surprised his opponents with a startlingly frank broadcast, this time addressed to each of his captains by name. Thirty-one did not reply because their boats had been sunk:

> The struggle for our victory, becoming ever harder and more bitter, prompts me to reveal to you in all clarity the seriousness of our situation at this moment and of our future . . . Only you can fight the enemy offensively and beat him . . . The German

nation has long felt that our arm is the sharpest and most decisive and that the outcome of the war depends on the success *or failure* of the Battle of the Atlantic [author's emphasis].

On 22 May, the very day of the dissemination of this portentous message, with its un-Nazi recognition of the possibility of defeat, Dönitz pulled his boats out of the north Atlantic to the secondary air gap south-west of the Azores, leaving a handful to generate disinformation by radio and tie down the escorts. Recalling this moment in his memoirs, the admiral wrote: 'We had lost the Battle of the Atlantic.' One of the most remarkable facts about this historic turning point is surely how soon it was clear and recognized by each side, as shown by the very different messages sent by Horton and his opponent at almost the same time.

Thus before summer 1943 the Royal Navy knew it had won the hardest and most important conflict in its entire history. The transatlantic lifeline was safe, guaranteeing not only the physical survival of the people of the United Kingdom but also the island's viability as the launching platform for the invasion of mainland Europe, for which hundreds of thousands of American, British, Canadian and other troops were already being gathered. So were mountains of supplies, thousands of landing craft, tanks and guns, nearly all escorted across the so recently perilous Atlantic Ocean. This British strategic victory was the result of no single 'magic ingredient', whether air power, Ultra, radar, US shipbuilding capacity or Allied support, but a combination of all these things and more – brought together by the doggedness of the nation and its Navy in a war of attrition – a finest hour that dragged on for the best part of four years.

But there was much unfinished business for the British fleet, and many threats still to face, despite the fact that the entire enemy submarine arm had been rendered obsolete at a stroke by the new universality of Allied airborne radar. The U-boats' endurance and speed underwater were far too weak and their vulnerability to detection on the surface far too great for them to operate as they had in the first forty-four months of hostilities. The Germans therefore worked on radar detectors, protection against ASDIC and also breathing tubes (adopting the Dutch invention of the snorkel) for existing types of U-boat while striving at breakneck speed to develop Professor Helmuth Walter's revolutionary new generation of submarines, shaped like sperm whales and capable of an underwater speed that would render most escorts obsolete. They very nearly succeeded. The Germans also introduced two new types of torpedo, one that homed on to the sound of the target's propeller, the other that travelled corkscrew fashion to make it harder to avoid.

Meanwhile the Americans thought of a new application of naval Ultra: against the ten 'milch-cow' submarines which had successfully refuelled some 400 U-boat patrols in the year up to May 1943. To avoid arousing German suspicion that their ciphers, as used in rendezvous messages, had been compromised, aircraft were used to pinpoint the supply submarines detected by sigint, to give the impression that they had been found by normal air patrols. Aircraft from USS *Bogue* destroyed the first on 12 June. A Coastal Command patrol guided Captain 'Johnnie' Walker in the sloop *Starling*, leader of the war's most successful U-boat hunting support group, to the destruction of the second, twelve days later. The Americans mobilized no fewer than four support groups against the third, sunk on 13 July. The fourth was destroyed by a Coastal Command Wellington which crash-landed on its deck in the Bay of Biscay on 24 July. The fifth and sixth were destroyed on the same day in the same area at the very end of the month, one by aircraft, the other by Captain Walker. The seventh was caught by a RCAF patrol west of the Faroes on 4 August: a British destroyer rescued the crews of the U-boat and the aircraft, which had been forced to ditch by German anti-aircraft fire. The remaining three were all sunk by June 1944; so were six out of seven Type XIV long-range fighting boats adapted to refuel their comrades in place of the milch-cows.

Allied technological ingenuity continued to flourish in the ASW field: the British brought in the Squid, a forward-firing triple depth-charge launcher, while the Americans invented the Magnetic Anomaly Detector (MAD), an airborne device which detected submerged submarines by their magnetic field. Another long-term US contribution to the art of ASW was the sonar buoy, a battery-powered detector which alerted aircraft to the presence of submarines. The Germans meanwhile were experimenting with anti-radar and anti-sonar coatings for U-boats; both sides developed air-to-surface rockets for use at sea as well as over land. We have noted how Allied (overwhelmingly American) shipbuilding passed the German sinking rate in July 1942; progress in this all-important field was so rapid that by October 1943 the Allies had made good all the tonnage lost to all enemy action in four years of war. 'Liberty' off-the-peg merchant ships were being launched at a phenomenal rate; the fastest feat of construction saw one of these remarkable steamers produced in eighty hours, an all-time record. Even had the Germans managed to field their revolutionary new U-boats early enough to affect the outcome of the war, it is difficult to imagine how these could have reversed the overwhelming advantage conferred on the Allied cause by American industrial production at full blast. The Azores ceased to be a mid-ocean haven for the U-boats when the Portuguese dictator, Dr Salazar, suddenly noticed that the Allies now dominated the Atlantic and acceded to a two-year-old request from his 'oldest ally', Britain, for an airbase there in October 1943.

There remained the strong residue of the German surface fleet in northern Norway, led by its most powerful component, the super-battleship *Tirpitz*, as the Russian convoys resumed in autumn. From May 1943 Britain had been developing the 'X-craft' miniature submarine (fifty-one feet long and displacing thirty-five tons) with a crew of four and armed with two detachable bombs. In September six of them were sent against *Tirpitz*, *Scharnhorst* and *Lützow* at their anchorages in or near the Altenfjord in Operation 'Source'. Four were lost to various mishaps before they could make their attacks, two disappearing with their crews and without trace. The surviving two, *X7* (Lieutenant B. C. G. Place, RN) and *X6* (Lieutenant D. Cameron, RNR), slipped into the Altenfjord on the 20th and lurked on the bottom before attacking the *Tirpitz* on the morning of the 22nd. Place led the pair through the booms and nets of the battleship's anchorage, which caused damage to both craft. *X6* hit bottom and bounced to the surface briefly, whereupon it came under heavy small-arms fire from alert sailors high above; none of the ship's guns could be sufficiently depressed against such a small target so close to the side.

Cameron dived, dumped his primed charges under the ship, surfaced to enable his crew to evacuate, and scuttled. All four went into captivity. *X7* was not sighted until she had laid her two bombs and managed to withdraw as far as the anti-torpedo nets, in which the craft was entangled – until blown clear by a huge explosion, which eye-witnesses said lifted the battleship bodily. The submarine was lost, but Place and one colleague survived to be taken prisoner. The great ship was immobilized for six months and never took part in a sea operation again. The two lieutenants collected their hard-earned VCs on their release after the war. The *Tirpitz* had fired her guns in anger at sea only once, at the beginning of the month, in a brief shelling of Allied-occupied Spitsbergen, which might just as well have been done by a destroyer or two.

Lützow left for home on 26 September; Admiral Sir Bruce Fraser, C-in-C of the Home Fleet since May, was keen to attack her but no carrier was available. In a small re-run of the Channel Dash, Coastal Command and Fleet Air Arm planes failed even to find the pocket-battleship on passage, let alone bomb it, and she reached Gotenhafen (now Polish Gdynia) unscathed on 1 October. She remained in the Baltic for the rest of the war, leaving the *Scharnhorst* as the only German capital ship in a position to intervene in the Arctic or north Atlantic. Only now did Coastal Command at last acquire three strike-wings of 120 aircraft in all; the Americans took back their Task Force 22, detailed to reinforce the Home Fleet against the German 'heavies' in November.

Dönitz and Hitler agreed on a stroke against the Russian convoys at Christmas 1943 by *Scharnhorst* and five fleet destroyers, under the flag of Rear-Admiral Erich Bey (Kummetz was ill). Fraser anticipated the move, prompted by Ultra, and took his flagship, the new battleship *Duke of York* with ten 14-inch guns, to Murmansk to cover the next pair of convoys. The Russians were startled, and inevitably suspicious, to see their first British battleship, complete with full admiral, call in for two days, but Fraser returned to Iceland, having surveyed the route and worked out his plans. He would act as distant cover, supported by the cruiser *Jamaica* and four destroyers; the newly promoted Vice-Admiral Burnett's squadron of three cruisers (*Belfast*, flag, *Sheffield* and *Norfolk*) gave intermediate protection and ten destroyers escorted northbound convoy JW 55B; the southbound, unladen convoy RA 55A, also had ten destroyers in company for the joint operation.

From Christmas Eve the attenuated Luftwaffe was managing to provide a continuous shadow over JW 55B, although no German attack yet materialized. Fraser raced north, boldly breaking his own wireless silence by ordering the Murmansk-bound convoy to reverse course towards him for a few hours (Ultra had told him *Scharnhorst* was on short notice to sail). The Germans came out of Altenfjord in the early evening of Christmas Day, sweeping first to the north and then to the south; Admiral Bey unaccountably allowed his destroyers to lose visual touch, which meant that the *Scharnhorst* was alone when sighted by the *Belfast* on the morning of 26 December. Burnett's three cruisers gave chase and opened fire, but *Scharnhorst* raced southward out of range at thirty-two knots, at least five more than Burnett could manage in the conditions. Bey then turned north for a pass against the convoy as Burnett stationed himself between the Germans and the merchantmen. Belfast picked up the *Scharnhorst* a second time on radar with Fraser still 150 miles or nearly six hours' sailing away.

In the exchange of fire HMS *Norfolk* lost a gun turret and *Sheffield* took superficial damage (dropping out later with engine trouble). The cruisers' fire and a destroyer torpedo attack were contemptuously shaken off by the Germans, now once again sailing southward – towards Fraser. Burnett followed, staying out of sight but keeping in touch by radar. Bey heard from his destroyers and decided they were now so far away that they might as well go back to port. HMS *Duke of York* detected the *Scharnhorst* on her radar from twenty-two miles away at 4.17 p.m. on the 26th.

What followed was to be the last 'all big-gun action' in the history of the Royal Navy: the opposing 'lines' each consisted of a single capital ship but no submarines or aircraft were involved in the finely balanced duel. The British battleship was assisted by several smaller ships and had the heavier guns, but the Germans were three knots faster and their armour and construction, though lighter, were of superior quality and endurance. The *Scharnhorst*, sailing unwittingly between Burnett's two battleworthy cruisers to the north and Fraser's force to the south, still had her 11-inch guns in fore-and-aft position when surprised by the closeness of the *Duke of York*'s first broadside from six miles at 4.50 p.m. *Scharnhorst* turned north. The two big ships began to score hits on each other in the waters between Norway and Spitsbergen, the British cruisers unable to reach the Germans, although their presence inhibited Bey's movements and ensured that the British flagship could stay in range until the *Scharnhorst* was slowed down by damage. British destroyers were able to score torpedo hits, which slowed the Germans down further. The final stage had the *Scharnhorst* (Captain Fritz Julius Hintze) limping along at five knots surrounded by Fraser's forces and taking an extraordinarily heavy battering from a battleship and three cruisers firing at will.

The German ship burned until her hull was red-hot without exploding; even a would-be coup de grace by several torpedoes seemed to have no effect. The German ship went down in her own time at 8 a.m. and only thirty-six men out of nearly 2,000 were saved by the British victors of the hard-fought, ultimately one-sided Battle of the North Cape. But once *Scharnhorst* had gone, for the first time in almost three years there was no 'fleet in being' in the far north for the Home Fleet to worry about.

Losses on the Russian convoy route were minimal in the sailing seasons from autumn to spring 1943–4 and again in 1944–5. In March 1944 Fraser sent two fleet carriers, *Victorious* and *Furious*, with a battleship and four escort carriers, four cruisers and fourteen destroyers under the flag of his deputy, Vice-Admiral Sir Henry Moore, to attack the *Tirpitz*, expected to be ready for sea again on 1 April. Forty-two Barracuda bombers covered by eighty fighters attacked in two waves on 3 April, achieving tactical surprise and scoring perhaps fifteen hits.

But the monster was too strongly built for the Fleet Air Arm's bombs and was put out of action for only three more months; 122 men were killed and 216 wounded. In the end Bomber Command was called in to use its new 'Tallboy' bombs, twenty-one feet long and weighing 12,000lb, against the *Tirpitz*. Even they only succeeded at the third attempt, in mid-November 1944, by which time the ship was in Tromsö, 200 miles south of Altenfjord, relegated to service as a coastal artillery and ack-ack battery. Some 900 men went down with her, while 600 were rescued from the water; a further 87 were saved via a hole cut through the overturned ship's bottom. Sixteen earlier air attacks had failed to sink a three-year grand obsession of the Royal Navy, as had the gallant X-craft. Torpedoes might well have sunk the ship that had caused so much havoc by merely existing; but she was too well protected in narrow anchorages and hardly ever appeared on the open sea where such an attack could have worked – had British ships or torpedo-bombers got near enough.

The man whose long career was blighted by his decision to scatter convoy PQ 17 for fear of the *Tirpitz* did not live to hear the news of her destruction. Admiral of the Fleet Sir Dudley Pound, First Sea Lord and Chief of Naval Staff from the beginning of the war, had a stroke in Canada in August 1943 during an Allied summit conference, and resigned. Soon after a second attack he died on Trafalgar Day, 21 October 1943, at the age of sixty-six. The underlying cause of the frail admiral's death was probably overwork and his inability to delegate. At least he lived long enough to savour the turn of the tide in the Atlantic campaign, the heaviest component of a crushing burden of responsibility which he elected to carry alone. But by the same token, a great deal of the credit for ultimate victory must go to him. He was succeeded by Andrew Cunningham.

The Germans tried to make a comeback in the north Atlantic in 1943, their disadvantages compounded by the scrapping of British Naval Cipher number three in June. This had been in use up to then for communication between the forces of all the north Atlantic navies, but it was only now that the GC & CS at Bletchley Park, in its other, somewhat neglected, role as defender of British ciphers, concluded that German Naval Intelligence had penetrated it (as it had done before the war, something the British should have picked up much sooner). The old-fashioned, ledger-based cipher had been used *faute de mieux* because the Royal Navy, unlike its allies or the other British services, had failed to adopt an electro-mechanical system. It was replaced by Cipher number five, which the Germans failed to break. They tried to make up for this loss of intelligence by using new long-range bombers to locate Allied shipping and report it to U-boat HQ. They countered the massive Allied air superiority over the Bay of Biscay by sailing their submarines submerged to and from Spanish waters at the beginning and end of patrols.

In February 1944 'Johnnie' Walker's 2nd Escort Group of four sloops completed a record patrol, during which it destroyed six U-boats in the waters west of Ireland, to which the enemy had returned with several packs for a slogging match against various convoys which went on for four weeks. Walker's last victim, *U264*, was a special achievement: the first snorkel-boat to go on operational service, it yielded prisoners to question when it was abandoned in a sinking condition on 19 February. On 22 March Dönitz ordered a final withdrawal from the north-west Atlantic; he had lost three dozen boats but sunk just three merchantmen out of 3,360 in convoy in the preceding quarter. Even for the Canadians, the north Atlantic route had now become the 'milk-run'.

But on 25 February 1945 *U2322* sank the 1,317-ton SS *Egholm*, which thus acquired the dubious distinction of being the first victim of one of Professor Walter's 'electro-boats': the escorts of the coastal convoy were amazed by the speed with which the attacker, a small coastal U-boat of Type XXIII, eluded them. Only two of the larger, ocean-going Type XXI made operational patrols in the last days of the war, without result. Allied bombers conclusively disrupted and delayed mass production of the deadly new boats by at least six months, preventing them from prolonging the war.

During the Second World War 2,452 ships of 12.8m tons were sunk in the Atlantic and 2,828 ships of 14,687,231 tons were lost to enemy submarines, overwhelmingly from Germany, which built 1,162 U-boats and sent 830 of them on operations; 696 were destroyed in battle. To achieve this level of destruction, two German submariners in three, more than 26,000 in all, were killed on duty, a loss rate unmatched by any other arm of any service of any belligerent. The British Merchant Marine lost 30,248 men and the Royal Navy 73,642, the majority of both totals in the defence of trade. The U-boats also sank 175 warships in the Atlantic, most of them British. RAF Coastal Command lost 5,866 men and 1,777 aircraft. The Royal Canadian Navy lost 1,965 men in the Atlantic, more than the US Navy.

12

A Pyrrhic Victory

At Casablanca in January 1943 Roosevelt had announced, apparently without prior consultation with the British delegation, that the war would continue until the 'unconditional surrender' of Italy, Germany and Japan. As we saw, however, Churchill got his wish that the victory in North Africa should be followed by an invasion not of France but of Sicily, which would both secure the Mediterranean, the main artery of the British Empire, and prepare the way for an assault on the Italian mainland. For these operations the naval command was once again given to 'A.B.C.', Admiral Cunningham. Eisenhower was supreme commander; the British General Alexander was his deputy; Air Chief Marshal Tedder was the air C-in-C. Montgomery led the Anglo-Canadian eastern and General Patton the American western task force, of five and three divisions respectively, in a two-pronged assault; Admiral H. K. Hewitt, USN, commanded American naval assault forces under Cunningham and Admiral 'Bertie' Ramsay was appointed Naval Commander of the British assault forces.

Ramsay managed to produce a coherent plan for the larger, British component of Operation 'Husky', despite several serious rows with Cunningham, Montgomery and the Americans. The influence of Admiral King could be detected in the chronic shortage of landing craft, which was not fully resolved even in the final planning stages. Mountbatten sent eighty officers to instruct 65,000 sailors and soldiers in amphibious warfare techniques at a new naval base on the Suez Canal. The Allies were able to pass convoys from one end of the Mediterranean to the other without interference once the Germans and Italians surrendered in Tunisia in the middle of May. The abandonment of the much longer route to the Far East via the Cape of Good Hope significantly boosted Allied shipping capacity at no cost. Malta was safe and the North African air bases could be freely used to dominate the airspace to their north. The invading armies would make capturing the Sicilian airfields their first priority. To land five divisions (four British in the Eighth Army, and the Canadian 1st Infantry, supported by three armoured brigades and two Royal Marine Commandos) on 10 July, Ramsay divided his force into three assault groups, each with its own rear-admiral, HQ ship, anti-aircraft cruisers, destroyers, escorts, minesweepers, bombarding monitors and armed landing craft, over 1,000 vessels in all. Only three transports were sunk by enemy aircraft in a remarkably smooth surprise landing and another triumph of orchestration by Ramsay, who was able to leave the scene as early as 19 July to return to his main task.

Sicily fell on 17 August, when both Allied armies entered Messina in the north-west corner of the island. Ramsay's reward was to be formally appointed Allied Naval C-in-C of the Expeditionary Force for the invasion of France in October, now codenamed Operation 'Overlord'; the naval side was christened 'Neptune'. Mussolini was toppled in July and his successor, Marshal Badoglio, looked for an armistice. But negotiations were slow, giving the Germans plenty of time to take a tight grip on the Italian peninsula, where fighting was to continue until the very last week of the war. American and British troops landed at Salerno in south-west Italy in September, while Montgomery's forces invaded Reggio di Calabria and British paratroops were landed at Taranto to the east. Italy capitulated on the 9th, but the Germans showed their customary ruthlessness and fighting skill by almost closing down the Salerno beachhead, scene of a bloody week's struggle. The Americans took a shattered Naples on 1 October. The Germans hastily threw up a heavily defended 'Gustav' line across southern Italy and halted the Allied advance in January 1944, when a titanic struggle for the massive strongpoint of Monte Cassino developed. An attempt to outflank the Germans by another landing at Anzio, behind their line, was little short of a disaster for the Allies, who were almost thrown back into the sea.

The Americans lost patience with the Italian campaign, bogged down not least because of poor American generalship, and pressed for a new landing in southern France to divert the Germans' attention, and their troops from Normandy, in advance of the main invasion there. A last attempt by Alexander to break through the Gustav line succeeded in spring, but the American General Mark Clark, against orders, threw away the chance to cut off the German 10th Army in favour of an advance on Rome, which fell on 4 June – two days before D-Day in Normandy. The Germans could thus retreat to the Gothic line in the northern Apennines, where they held out until their surrender on 2 May 1945, against Allied forces whose needs were now decidedly secondary to those of the armies on the main front in France. The underbelly of the Axis had proved anything but soft. The diversionary landing in southern France took place in August 1944, well after Normandy.

Having cut their teeth on 'Husky', Admiral Ramsay and General Montgomery, leaders of naval and ground forces for Normandy under Eisenhower's supreme command, worked as well together in planning operations 'Neptune' (naval) and 'Overlord' (land) as their strong personalities permitted: there seems to have been an amicable stand-off between the general's vertiginous self-regard and the admiral's unshakable certitude, and Ramsay was one of the very few people from whom Montgomery would take advice. The blunt and doctrinaire Air Chief Marshal Sir Trafford Leigh-Mallory as Air C-in-C was the third component of an unlikely but ultimately successful trio. But whereas the Sicilian operation had been comparatively short and sharp, Normandy entailed not only a larger and more complex landing by far but also a sustained and massive supply and reinforcement afterwards in support of armies confronting a Wehrmacht fighting closer to home than ever before. The unreliable weather and high tides in the Channel were among other factors absent in Sicily.

Admiral Ramsay commanded no fewer than 6,833 vessels, including 1,200 warships, over 4,000 landing craft and nearly 900 merchant ships, for landing five divisions across a fifty-mile front. Three-quarters of the warships were British and Canadian, one-sixth American. The need for safe and reliable supply ports from the very beginning was brilliantly solved by Ramsay's staff through the advance construction of two 'Mulberry' artificial harbours, to be towed into place. The insatiable demand for fuel for the invading armies was partly solved by PLUTO (pipeline under the ocean). Ramsay held out for his enormous fleet in the teeth of objections to its size from the Americans, the Admiralty in general and Cunningham.

Once again, as for 'Torch', the Atlantic convoy escorts were thinned out, as were the Home and Mediterranean fleets. British ambitions to intervene in the Far East had to be reined in for lack of reinforcements. Admiral King with unusual generosity provided three battleships, two cruisers and twenty destroyers for the

Preserving the translantic lifeline in the Second World War: Headquarters, Western Approaches Command, Liverpool; workhorse of the convoys, corvette HMS Pentstemon; *a north Atlantic convoy*

*All at sea in the Mediterranean: helicopters and landing-craft ferrying troops in the brilliantly organised but politically disastrous Suez landing in November 1956 (*ABOVE*); carrier HMS* Ark Royal *and the Royal Navy's first guided-missile ship, the destroyer HMS* Devonshire, *on exercise in 1963*

Into the modern age: a new HMS Dreadnought, *the Royal Navy's first nuclear-powered submarine* (ABOVE); *and a new HMS* Invincible, *launching a Harrier*

Falklands figures, 1982: Admiral Sir John Fieldhouse, Commander-in-Chief, Fleet (ABOVE, LEFT), *who controlled the Task Force; Mr Ian McDonald, Ministry of Defence spokesman* (ABOVE RIGHT), *whose mechanical delivery was almost as remarkable as the content of his announcements; and below, the two commanders 'on the spot', Major-General Jeremy Moore, Royal Marines* (LEFT), *and Rear-Admiral John 'Sandy' Woodward*

Modern warfare: HMS Sheffield (ABOVE), *ablaze and mortally wounded by an Argentine Exocet missile off the Falklands; the Royal Navy's contribution to the Gulf War, 1991, in the shape of a much-enlarged 'Armilla Patrol'*

Into the new millennium:
(TOP) *a 'Tomahawk' cruise missile being loaded aboard fleet submarine HMS Superb; A 'Vanguard'-class Trident-missile nuclear submarine* (RIGHT); *Admiral Sir Michael Boyce, the last First Sea Lord of the Twentieth Century*

covering forces, which was more than the British had asked for, but the US Chief of Naval Operations proved less understanding on landing craft, insisting that the British had more than enough. Ramsay was unwilling to load them to the limit as the Americans were wont to do in their series of great island invasions in the Pacific; allowance had to be made for the rougher weather. To ensure there were enough to meet Ramsay's requirements, 'Anvil' (southern France, later renamed 'Dragoon') was postponed indefinitely and 'Overlord' deferred to the very end of May 1944. Ramsay was obdurate and even the autocratic Cunningham bowed to his insistence on getting everything he needed, at the expense of British operations in all other areas. Ramsay was delighted in mid-February to be told by Churchill himself that he would be back on the Navy's active list from 1 April, an ironic event for the man who had probably worked harder than any other British admiral.

As in the Mediterranean, each army was landed by its own naval forces. The British Second Army (two British divisions and one Canadian plus two Army and one Royal Marine Commando units) was landed on three beaches by the eastern task force under Rear-Admiral Sir Philip Vian while the western, under the US Rear-Admiral Alan Kirk, put two divisions of the American First Army ashore on two beaches – after Eisenhower put his faith in the RAF weather forecast for 6 June 1944. One American and one British division would lead the reinforcement of the first wave; Ramsay planned to have twenty-one divisions ashore in twelve days and thirty-five after five weeks.

Preparations for the largest amphibious operation in all history went on in harbours from the River Humber all the way round the English coast to the Bristol Channel, with the main focus on the Solent, between Portsmouth and the Isle of Wight. An enormous effort was invested in disinformation, to deceive the Germans about the area chosen for invasion (Hitler put his money on the Pas de Calais, nearest to Britain, well after the beachhead in Normandy had been established). German E-boats caused immense disruption and heavy casualties among US troops rehearsing for the landings at Slapton Sands in Devon at the end of April, an embarrassment for the Royal Navy, which was responsible for protecting coastal waters.

Coastal Command, the Fleet Air Arm and escort and support groups from Western Approaches and the Home Fleet were on hand to preclude any significant U-boat intervention. A colossal bombardment by some 150 warships, and sweeps along the coast by twenty-two flotillas of minesweepers, nearly all British, were included in the last stage of preparation. Even the Americans were staggered by Ramsay's elaborate dispositions and attention to detail in the planning: he tried very hard to leave nothing to chance. Whatever the initial difficulties of the Allied armies in Normandy and beyond, which were considerable, his strategy was completely vindicated and continued to function even after such major setbacks as the loss of one of the 'Mulberry' harbours to the worst Channel storm in forty years.

Ramsay's organizational services were called upon once more for the Allied assault on 1 November upon the Dutch reclaimed island of Walcheren, to clear the Scheldt estuary and secure access to Antwerp, captured intact but seventy miles from the sea. The troops came from the 2nd Canadian Division, British, French and Dutch Commandos, the Scottish 52nd Lowland Division and the Royal Marines, and 200 vessels were assembled to deliver and protect them, with the battleship HMS *Warspite* leading the bombardment. The strong German defending division was hoist on its own petard when it partly flooded the 'island', a polder below sea-level protected by dykes, to inhibit Allied paratroops and ground movements. The RAF was called in to breach the sea defences in several places, deepening the flooding and marooning the powerful German batteries on the dykes while confining their infantry to such high ground as was left and providing convenient gaps for Allied amphibious craft to sail through. The assault began on 1 November and Walcheren was secured in four days of hard fighting. Minesweeping began in the Scheldt on the 4th, and the first supply convoy entered Antwerp on the 28th, enabling the surviving but battered Mulberry to be abandoned to the sea.

As headquarters for the Allied Naval C-in-C in the last phase of the war in Europe, Ramsay was allotted a chateau at St Germain-en-Laye, outside Paris. At the end of 1944 he supervised naval dispositions in support of the Allied armies after the German counter-offensive in the Ardennes which had so badly rattled them. The British 21st Army Group was about to move off towards Germany and Ramsay decided to visit Montgomery at the latter's headquarters near Brussels on the morning of 2 January 1945, in his new personal Hudson bomber. The aircraft crashed in flames just after take-off for reasons never discovered. All five aboard were killed. Among the mourners at the funeral at St Germain the next day were Eisenhower, Cunningham and senior French and Allied officers; Ramsay was also afforded the honour of a memorial service in Westminster Abbey on the same day. Nonetheless his accidental death before the final victory over Germany robbed him of the degree of recognition his unique contribution historically warrants. As much a master of improvisation as of detailed organization on a massive scale, Ramsay rescued the British Army from annihilation in France and four years later, almost to the day, took it back again in triumph. Had he lived, he would surely have been recognized as Britain's ablest admiral of the war. After Taranto and Matapan his chief, Admiral of the Fleet Viscount Cunningham of Hyndhope, is rightly regarded as the country's premier fighting admiral of the day, but he also presided, willy-nilly, over the loss of nearly 200 warships in the Mediterranean. Cunningham fought; Ramsay thought.

Sir James Somerville also has a claim to be regarded as one of Britain's best admirals in the war. But as C-in-C of the British Eastern Fleet he now had little chance to shine or affect the course of the war against the immensely superior Imperial Japanese Navy, which could only be checked by the phenomenal expansion of the US fleet. His principal ships were largely second- or third-rate and his overall strength depended on what the Admiralty felt could be spared from the Atlantic and the Mediterranean, which was little enough until 1943 and unimpressive even then. Woeful British neglect of naval aviation between the wars, from which the Royal Navy had never recovered, affected Somerville no less than his colleagues on Britain's primary naval front in the Atlantic and the secondary one in the Mediterranean. As the perennial third in line, the Eastern Fleet was in no position to take any serious initiative. It came under Mountbatten's supreme command when SEAC was created; the dividing line between his and MacArthur's South-West Pacific commands passed through the Sunda Strait between Sumatra and Java in the Dutch East Indies.

The main struggle in SEAC was against the Japanese threat to British India, as represented by their armies in Burma, the western extremity of the Japanese landward advance in 1941. The appalling conditions of jungles, mountains and swamps on this front were made no easier by overlapping and sometimes fiercely competitive Allied commands – American, British Indian, Chinese – and commanders, whether the Chinese Nationalist leader Chiang

Kai-shek (Supreme Allied Commander in China), Generals 'Vinegar Joe' Stilwell and Frank Merrill of the US Army, or Generals Sir William Slim and Orde Wingate (the one quietly brilliant, the other obsessive and bizarre) from Britain. The Burmese capital, Rangoon, had fallen to the Japanese on 8 March 1942. On the 23rd the Andaman Islands south-west of Burma fell to a small Japanese task force. On 20 May the Japanese Army took Mandalay in central Burma. The Allied supply route to China via the corkscrew Burma Road over the mountains was cut.

Four days later Somerville arrived in Ceylon, where he had two main bases at Colombo and Trincomalee. He also had a reserve harbour-cum-hideout 600 miles to the south-west at Addu Atoll. British land-based air power in Ceylon was negligible.

Thus when Allied decrypts revealed in the nick of time at the end of March that Vice-Admiral Kondo and the Japanese Western Force or Second Fleet (fresh from the conquest of the East Indies) were about to attack India and the Ceylonese bases, there was not much Somerville could do about it. Under orders to avoid a fleet engagement, he split his capital ships into a 'fast' division (battle-ship *Warspite* and the two fleet carriers) and a slow (four battle-ships and *Hermes*), dividing the light cruisers and destroyers among them – and sailed for Addu, where he still was on 4 April. On the same day a patrolling RAF Catalina sighted Nagumo's carrier group, which had supported first the Eastern and now the Western Force of the IJN, 360 miles south-east of Ceylon. Somerville was at least eighteen hours away and in the midst of refuelling; he decided to stay put, hoping to mount a night counter-attack by air later.

Japanese bombers attacked two towns on the east coast of India on the 4th, and on the morning of the 5th ninety-one bombers and thirty-six fighters subjected Colombo to a scaled-down Pearl Harbor assault. The RAF was able to put up forty-two fighters, of which it lost nineteen while shooting down seven enemy bombers. Shipping had been dispersed, but the Japanese sank a destroyer and an AMC in port, also damaging harbour facilities. But the scattered ships had not scattered far enough: among them were Somerville's two heavy cruisers, *Dorsetshire* and *Cornwall*, which were pinpointed by Japanese air patrols and subjected to their own Kuantan-style attack on the same morning, by more than fifty aircraft. They were sunk by air-launched Lance torpedoes within minutes, with the loss of 424 men; 1,122 were rescued. Nagumo moved at his leisure from the western to the eastern side of the great island for a raid on Trincomalee on the 9th. Attacking in similar strength, the Japanese were met by twenty-two RAF fighters and nine Blenheim medium bombers; seven of the latter and one British fighter were shot down. So were fifteen Japanese aircraft. The base was almost empty after another hurried dispersal, but one merchant ship, a corvette and two valuable tankers were caught and sunk and the harbour itself beaten up. By this time Somerville was approaching – which made it all the more convenient for Nagumo to deliver another, even deadlier afterthought blow: the light carrier *Hermes* was sunk with every one of her old planes aboard, together with an Australian destroyer, HMAS *Vampire*. All this took place out of range of the fighters based on Ceylon.

In a parallel operation, Vice-Admiral Ozawa's First Detachment Fleet made a highly damaging sweep off the west coast of India, sinking twenty-three Allied merchantmen (112,300 tons). In an almost unique display of aggression against commerce, Japanese submarines, which normally limited themselves to naval targets, sank five more freighters totalling 32,400 tons in the same area. Kondo's heavy ships stayed in the background to the south, leaving the destructive work to the two detached formations. Somerville withdrew ignominiously all the way to East Africa, ending two centuries of British naval supremacy in the Indian Ocean. He had no means of knowing that the Japanese Navy, having wrought havoc across an ocean front of 8,000 miles over four months, had gone as far as it ever would from Japan's Inland Sea, 4,000 miles in either direction. Nagumo's next engagements were in the Coral Sea and then off Midway Island, as mentioned above; boldly and aggressively handled, the American carriers proved strong (and lucky) enough to stem and reverse the tide.

The only Asian territory ruled by whites before 7 December 1941 that was still ruled by them after March 1942 was India, once General Slim had led the 900-mile fighting retreat from Burma to the Indian north-east, from which he would slowly fight his way back. The Casablanca conference at the beginning of 1943 committed the British to try harder to reconquer Burma, as part of their quid pro quo for deferring the invasion of France. Admiral King, even as he hung on to his Liberators for the Pacific, offered the British all the landing craft they could use for Burma – purely, it seems, to embarrass them for their weak effort against Japan. At the same time he won approval for doubling Allied resources for the Pacific from a notional 15 to a no less notional 30 per cent of the global, total Allied war effort. In fact the US Navy never devoted less than two-thirds of its strength to the Pacific.

Somerville's frustrated fleet of old battleships and slow, short-range aircraft found an East African hideout at Kilindini, Kenya, and was not called upon to supervise Operation 'Ironclad', the invasion of the huge Vichy-controlled Indian Ocean island of Madagascar. Three British brigades were landed at the northern end in May 1942, to deny its naval base to the Japanese. Ironically the naval covering force was provided by Somerville's old command, the slimmed-down Force H from Gibraltar (which had to be temporarily replaced by American ships), and the enterprise was commanded by its new chief, Rear-Admiral E. N. Syfret, who did borrow a carrier and the battleship *Ramillies* from Somerville: the latter ship was badly damaged by a Japanese submarine, which also sank a tanker in a remarkable attack at the end of May. The battleship limped to Durban, South Africa, for repairs. Two Vichy French submarines were sunk during vain attempts to disrupt the invasion, which was followed by four months of skirmishes. It took a second British landing in September, aimed at the capital, Tananarive, to secure the whole island. Those involved, including an excessively enthusiastic Churchill, had no means of knowing that the Japanese had no interest in the place; as it was, the invasion only served to embarrass General de Gaulle in his bid to win over French forces in North Africa on the eve of Operation 'Torch'. The Americans regarded the whole affair as another of Churchill's diversions from attacking north-west Europe.

The Prime Minister lost patience with Somerville's under-standable caution over taking on the Japanese. Churchill was as blind to the admiral's disadvantages as he had been to the fatal weakness of Force Z: two capital ships, one nearly a quarter of a century old, sent without air cover to deter the world's strongest fleet. In response to Churchill's forceful complaints, the Eastern Fleet was reduced to one carrier and two battleships in autumn 1942 in order to strengthen the covering forces for 'Torch'. The following spring, the other carrier and one more battleship were withdrawn, reflecting Japan's lack of further interest in the Indian Ocean. The enemy armies in Burma and Indo-China were sustained overland as they drove back the British 14th Army's advance by May 1943, despite support from Royal Navy coastal forces. Field Marshal Wavell was 'kicked upstairs' from C-in-C,

India, to Viceroy and was replaced by General Auchinleck, who proved no more able to provide an instant victory. The reorganization foreshadowed by the 'Quadrant' summit in Quebec took place in autumn 1943, resulting in the promotion of Acting Admiral Mountbatten over the head of substantive Admiral Somerville. Mountbatten was already behaving like the last Viceroy that he would become in succession to Wavell after the war, and Somerville took exception to being treated like a servant whose sole function was to obey orders without question or discussion.

For the later part of 1943 and early 1944, the Mediterranean enjoyed priority over Mountbatten's command; later in 1944 Normandy took precedence over everything as Mountbatten and a swollen court of staff officers continued to underachieve. German U-boats stiffened the normally conservative and cautious Japanese submarine arm in two months of attacks on Allied shipping in the Indian Ocean from February 1944, forcing Somerville to set up a convoy escort system without air cover. The British 8th Submarine Flotilla based itself alongside the US 7th Fleet's submarines in Fremantle, Western Australia, and patrolled the Indian Ocean against such targets as the Japanese provided, which were few indeed. The British boats, supported by Dutch submarines, operated on the eastern side, off the coasts of Burma, Malaya and Sumatra. HM Submarine *Tally Ho* lived up to its name by sinking the Japanese cruiser *Kuma* off Penang on 11 January 1944. Five weeks later, Lieutenant-Commander Bennington, RN, achieved a second success by sinking the German-crewed Italian submarine *It23* in the same area (Penang was the easternmost base of the German U-boat arm). British submarines reached their peak performance in the Far East in the autumn, when they sank sixty-eight Japanese merchant vessels and one ASW warship in just five days of November. Three weeks earlier, on 24 October, the American Pacific (3rd) and 7th Fleets had broken the residual strength of the Japanese Navy in the largest naval engagement ever fought, involving 282 warships and including the last action involving two lines of battleships as one of the three phases of a complex Battle of Leyte Gulf. The Americans lost six ships, but the Japanese forfeited twenty-eight, including four fleet carriers. But it was in this sprawling engagement that the kamikaze pilots made their first terrifying appearance.

*

It was another irony, a considerable one given Britain's sorry record in naval aviation and Admiral King's Anglophobia, for the Admiralty to receive an American request at the beginning of 1943 for the loan of an aircraft carrier for the Pacific, until US yards could deliver those on order or under repair. In the meantime the US Navy was temporarily short of 'flat-tops' after losses and damage suffered in the Solomon Islands campaign and elsewhere. HMS *Victorious*, completed in 1941 and now adapted to work with the US Pacific Fleet, reported for duty in May 1943 and served satisfactorily until she returned to the Home Fleet in time for the April 1944 carrier raid on *Tirpitz*.

The ship was the second in the '*Illustrious*' class of six, an important, well-nigh revolutionary, new departure in carrier design displacing 23,000 tons and capable of more than thirty knots. She differed from her American contemporaries in three important respects: she had an armoured deck and aircraft hangar; she bristled with scores of anti-aircraft guns (the largest, sixteen 4.5-inchers, were dual-purpose and could also be used against surface attackers); and thus she carried rather fewer aircraft, between thirty-six and fifty-four, depending on types. The Americans expected a carrier to defend itself with its own aircraft, supported by surface escorts, and neglected armour, and also the fire precautions to which the British attached so much importance (after losing escort carrier HMS *Dasher* to an internal explosion before she could be deployed) that they insisted on elaborately adapting US-built escort carriers before commissioning them, to American chagrin. The Americans changed their tune in the last stage of the war against Japan, when they saw how carriers in the British Pacific Fleet, including *Victorious*, were able almost to shrug off the kamikaze suicide air attacks that did so much more damage to American ships because they lacked armoured decks and sides and could not put up a hail of shot against enemy aircraft.

The British Eastern Fleet, having reached its nadir over the turn of the year, began to expand again towards the end of January 1944. The Admiralty had decided to send some 150 ships to the Far East, determined to be in at the death of the war against Japan as the first move to recover Britain's Asiatic empire. The old battlecruiser *Renown*, two battleships, the carrier *Illustrious* and supporting ships reached Ceylon from the Mediterranean from the end of January; *Victorious*, more cruisers and dozens of destroyers would follow. After nearly two years of enforced inactivity, Admiral Somerville was delighted to carry out Mountbatten's order to bombard Sabang, an island with oil installations, a harbour and an airfield, off the north-east of Sumatra on 16 April, not least as a diversion from MacArthur's attack on New Guinea. Somerville's force, assembled at Trincomalee, included the carrier USS *Saratoga* on loan from the 7th Fleet, the French battleship *Richelieu*, the Dutch cruiser *Tromp*, Australian and New Zealand ships as well as *Illustrious* and two British battleships. All this was rather like using a sledgehammer to crack a nut, but twenty-seven Japanese aircraft, most of the oil tanks and the port installations were duly battered, for the loss of one American aircraft. On her way home for a refit in May, *Saratoga* supported Somerville one last time in a raid on the oil refinery and port at Surabaya in Java, another destructive success in which ten Japanese merchant ships were sunk. In all Somerville carried out eight such carrier and battleship raids in the East Indies up to October 1944.

But these were no more than pinpricks compared with the spectacular gains of the hugely expanded US Navy on both American fronts in the Pacific. As the Normandy invasion went ahead, Nimitz's series of island invasions and MacArthur's leap-frogging drive across the south-west Pacific converged to point at the Japanese-occupied Philippines. Even then the President could not or would not settle the inter-service rivalry between the admirals and the generals; MacArthur won the argument about recovering the Philippines before the main thrust against Japan proper – and was duly photographed unnecessarily wading ashore and fulfilling his promise that he would return. Meanwhile there was a debate of a different sort, but no less fierce, going on in Whitehall. Churchill was in favour of focusing British naval and military efforts on the Indian Ocean, to recover and/or secure the main components of the British Empire in Asia, while leaving the Pacific in the obviously capable hands of the Americans. The Chiefs of Staff, however, wanted a hand in the final assault on Japan in and from the Pacific, and were bent on creating a British Pacific Fleet to fight alongside the Americans. Admiral Sir Bruce Fraser was appointed C-in-C, Pacific Fleet, at the end of July 1944.

Admiral King was not amused. Here were the British, who had been objecting for three years to the scale of the American effort in the Pacific, insisting on sending a fleet there which was patently superfluous. The idea had provisionally been agreed at the

'Sextant' summit in Cairo in November 1943 by the Combined (Anglo-American) Chiefs of Staff, Roosevelt and Churchill. But by January 1944 Churchill had formulated his preference for Operation 'Culverin', his proposal for invading Sumatra, which lay within Mountbatten's SEAC area. In February the British Chiefs of Staff argued against this and against Mountbatten's plans for naval operations in the eastern Indian Ocean and in favour of a maximum maritime effort in the Pacific; they wanted to re-establish imperial military links with Australia while at the same time displacing it, if possible, as America's principal Pacific ally for the last push against Japan. The idea of a new Anglo-Australian command in the Pacific was stillborn, as the Australians were too deeply involved in tasks set them by MacArthur (who treated them with even more disdain than Britain often showed to Canada, that other huge dominion with a small but hugely loyal population exploited by the two major Western Allies in turn). Operations inside SEAC would concentrate on the landward campaign in Burma.

And not before time. The Japanese might have been on the defensive in the Pacific, but they still had the energy and will to press on from Burma into north-east India in March 1944, advancing towards Imphal and Kohima in the province of Assam. The Battle of Imphal halted their advance on 6 April, but it was not until 22 June that General Slim broke the siege and could draw up plans to roll up the Japanese in Burma from the north. Mandalay was captured in March 1945 and Rangoon, the capital, fell to the 'forgotten army' on 3 May, in the very last week of the war in Europe.

Having been brought round to the idea of a British Pacific Fleet, Churchill had a blazing row about it with King at the 'Octagon' summit conference, once again held in Quebec, in September 1944. The American CNO pointed out that the British had no naval bases in the Pacific other than Australia, and had no fleet train, a logistical device of great brilliance and complexity which was enabling the US Navy to fight at enormous distances from its island bases. Curiously enough, King asked his British opposite number, Admiral Cunningham, in July 1944 for the loan of six 'landing ships, infantry' for MacArthur's 7th Fleet in August (the general was otherwise excluding all Australian, British and Allied forces from the planned recovery of his old fiefdom). Even though they were short of such vessels in Europe (thanks not least to Admiral

King) the British rushed to comply, a decision that led to one of the most shameful episodes in modern British naval history.

'Force X' of six LSI, led by Rear-Admiral A. G. Talbot's command ship, left for the Panama Canal before the end of July. The force had been assembled in such a rush that it had no air conditioning, no tropical kit and none of the comforts American servicemen were used to. The ratings staged a mutiny at Balboa as the force, belatedly, was about to exit from the Canal into the Pacific. Seventeen men were court-martialled when the bedraggled force reached the French Society Islands in mid-September. When the sorry seven reached Admiral Kinkaid in Australia, the 7th Fleet commander rejected them as unfit for use in the combat zone, consigning them to duty in the rearmost area. They were reassigned to the hundred ships of the new British fleet train assembling at the fiendishly humid and inhospitable island of Manus in the Admiralty Islands; Force X took no further part in the war because Japan surrendered before it sailed.

Challenged by the Prime Minister at Quebec to reject His Majesty's fleet, King coolly said the offer would be considered. Churchill's reaction can be imagined. Roosevelt had to step in, accepting the British intervention in the Pacific for political reasons. But King soon made it clear that they would have to fend for themselves. He even questioned Admiral Fraser's title of C-in-C, Pacific Fleet, in a signal to Cunningham, pointing out that it was already spoken for (twice over; Admirals William F. Halsey and Raymond Spruance took it in turns, with their respective staffs, to lead the US Pacific Fleet, styled 3rd Fleet under the former and 5th Fleet under the latter, in Nimitz's supreme command). As a full admiral, Fraser would outrank almost all US naval commanders, several of whom, such as Vice-Admirals Thomas Kinkaid, commander of MacArthur's 7th Fleet, and Marc A. Mitscher, commander of Task Force 58, which alone disposed of ten fleet and six light carriers, seven battleships, eighteen cruisers and fifty-eight destroyers, led rather larger formations than the entire British strength. For the invasion of the Philippines Kinkaid alone commanded 157 combat ships and 581 other vessels to deliver 160,000 American troops, while Halsey provided another 106 warships for extra protection of the landings in October 1944. Such was the most powerful armada ever assembled before the nuclear age, the victor in the world's largest naval battle at Leyte Gulf.

Eventually the strongest concentration of striking power

assembled at sea thus far by the Royal Navy – four fleet carriers, two modern battleships, five cruisers and fifteen destroyers – was attached by Nimitz to the US Pacific Fleet as Task Force 57; the hurriedly assembled fleet train became TF 37. Thanks to King's objections, Fraser, C-in-C, Eastern Fleet, from August 1944, hoisted his flag as C-in-C, Pacific Fleet, in Colombo three months later, but had to base himself at Sydney, where the BPF assembled over the turn of the year, leaving command at sea to Vice-Admiral Sir Bernard Rawlings, with Rear-Admiral Vian in charge of the carriers. Their first notable contribution was to bombard the Sakishima Islands between Okinawa and Formosa on 26 March; they were also ordered to assist in the distant cover of Operation 'Iceberg', the invasion of Okinawa at Easter 1945, when 175,000 US marines and troops in seven divisions, plus 115,000 technical and logistical personnel, were put ashore. The carrier HMS *Indomitable* was damaged, but not knocked out, by kamikaze pilots during this last major landing before the planned invasion of Japan proper, for which Okinawa was to be the jumping-off point (she was similarly damaged on 9 May, as was her sister, *Victorious*; four days earlier, *Formidable* suffered likewise in another raid on Sakishima, but all three ships were saved by their armour). In June the British carriers bombarded the Caroline Islands, north of New Guinea, where the Japanese garrison had been isolated by MacArthur's advance.

For their vast effort at Okinawa the supreme commands of Nimitz and MacArthur combined their resources on land and sea and in the air for the first time, the Navy commanding until the landing was secure, whereupon the Army took over. The British Pacific Fleet also took part in the mopping-up operations of the last days of the war, bombing and shelling airfields, ships and port installations until Admiral Nimitz ordered a ceasefire across the Pacific on 15 August. The two atomic bombs dropped on Hiroshima and Nagasaki in August prompted Japan to surrender, making what would undoubtedly have been a terribly bloody invasion of the Home Islands unnecessary. Only then did General MacArthur, at sixty-five, become generalissimo in the Pacific as Supreme Commander, Allied Powers, for the occupation. Japan's 'unconditional' surrender was made on one condition: that Emperor Hirohito would remain on his throne (as indeed he did under MacArthur's remarkably benign authority until and after the latter retired in 1951). MacArthur ordered that no Japanese surrender should be taken anywhere before the vast ceremony he supervised aboard the battleship *Missouri* in Tokyo Bay on the morning of 2 September 1945; a token British squadron of a carrier and two battleships was present.

On the creation of the Pacific Fleet, the Admiralty renamed the reduced Eastern Fleet the East Indies Fleet, under Vice-Admiral Sir Arthur Power, previously second-in-command of the BEF. Somerville was sent to Washington, as Cunningham once had been, to head the British Naval Mission; senior enough not to have to call Admiral King sir, Somerville nevertheless told Fraser he would have preferred to command a trawler. The East Indies command concentrated on supporting General Slim's offensive in Burma from December 1944. Light coastal forces staged hit-and-run raids along a waterlogged shoreline while larger warships landed troops to outflank or surprise the retreating Japanese. The last major naval operation was another amphibious landing on 2 May, to complete the capture of Rangoon and end the campaign. Two weeks later five destroyers cornered the Japanese heavy cruiser *Haguro*, already damaged by British escort carrier aircraft, in the Malacca Strait and sent her to the bottom. In June the submarine HMS *Trenchant* sank a similar ship, the *Ashigawa*, off the coast of Sumatra. At the end of July four midget submarines, *XE1*, *XE3*, *XE4* and *XE5*, were involved in operations against Japanese cruisers in the Johore Strait between Malaya and Singapore, and also against undersea cables in the area. Lieutenant I. E. Fraser, RNR, captain of the *XE3*, and Leading Seaman J. J. Magennis, his diver, were each awarded the VC for sinking the cruiser *Takao*.

Mountbatten's next major assignment was to liberate Malaya and Singapore, which were reoccupied by British forces at the end of August; a detached squadron from the Pacific Fleet reoccupied Hong Kong on 29 August, when the Japanese in Singapore surrendered to Mountbatten (in deference to MacArthur, the formal ceremony was deferred until 12 September). His command also terminated the Japanese occupations of the Dutch East Indies, where a vicious war of liberation began at once, and of French Indo-China, where decolonization took rather longer.

In another Asian development of serious significance for the postwar world, Stalin kept his promise to declare war on Japan three months after Germany had been defeated, just in time to profit from the overwhelming American victory. This resulted in the Soviet seizure of some previously Japanese island territory – and in the partition of Korea.

But such matters belong to the following chapters. For Britain the Second World War had been just as Churchill described it in June 1940: 'Let us . . . so bear ourselves that, if the British Commonwealth and its Empire last for a thousand years, men will still say, "This was their finest hour."' From the fall of France in that month until Germany attacked Russia exactly one year later, Britain and the faraway Commonwealth stood alone against Hitler and Mussolini, *pace* the small Free Forces of occupied Europe and the decidedly benevolent neutrality of the United States, propelled into combat another half-year after the Soviet Union. As in the First World War, it was the Royal Navy that saved Britain's bacon, literally as well as metaphorically, by winning the strategic confrontation that mattered most, the struggle for domination of the north Atlantic. The lifeline from North America brought the food, fuel and fighting equipment that Britain needed to survive so that, when the time came, she would serve as the launching platform for the liberation of Europe from the west. As in the First World War, Germany nowhere came closer to victory and to defeating Britain than in the U-boat campaign against the convoys. The Royal Navy had saved the nation for the second time in a quarter of a century by winning the Atlantic campaign, which came to a head after three and a half gruelling years.

From June 1940 the Navy was also fighting in the Mediterranean against Italy, strongly supported, especially in the air, by Germany. Taranto, Matapan, the submarines of the 1st and 10th Flotillas plus a few Allied boats and the destruction of much Axis shipping apart, the Mediterranean Fleet was on the defensive almost all the time until the end of 1942, just managing to 'save' Malta, which was almost destroyed in the process and was useless as a base most of the time. Meanwhile in December 1941 war broke out on a third front in the Far East, where the Royal Navy was all but swept from the board by the Japanese, made a modest comeback in the Indian Ocean when the Mediterranean permitted, and reappeared in the Pacific purely by the grudging courtesy of the Americans, and then to no strategic effect.

Only a massive investment in maritime air power between the wars might have eased the Navy's position in the Mediterranean and given it a chance to hold up (but surely not defeat) the Japanese southward advance. The cynical adage that the creation of the Royal Air Force was the greatest defeat in the history of the Royal Navy is now a cliché, but the whole point of such a cliché is that it is also a truism. The other supreme wartime achievement of the Navy lay in evacuating and later landing large numbers of troops, both British and foreign. Dunkirk and Normandy were the largest, most complex, important and successful operations of their kind in all history. While nothing can detract from the skill and panache of the US Navy's many Pacific landings, they were usually against much weaker opposition, however fanatically determined and well entrenched. The Royal Navy discharged its fundamental duties by protecting shipping and the Army and by helping to deter an invasion of Britain.

The fleet went to war in 1939 with fifteen mostly elderly dreadnoughts, but there was to be no Trafalgar this time either, any more than there had been in 1914–18. There was not even a Jutland, and such gun actions as there were in the Atlantic tended to involve a single enemy capital ship – *Graf Spee, Bismarck, Scharnhorst* – against several, or very many, British ships. The Royal Navy was unable to finish off the strongest of them all, the *Tirpitz*, even with its new carriers; the RAF had to do it. In the Mediterranean British battleships achieved little more strategically than their underused Italian rivals. The biggest fleet actions of the war were fought by the US Navy in the Pacific and were led by carriers.

Having struggled mightily to preserve numerical parity with the United States in capital ships before the war, the British Navy not only lost the plot in relation to maritime aviation but also made the mistake of underestimating the submarine, for the second time in twenty-five years, and found itself desperately short of small warships, especially those invaluable workhorses, destroyers. Despite a long series of priceless British initiatives such as ASDIC, radar and the cavity magnetron, HF/DF, Bletchley Park, Hedgehog and Squid, British warships were generally technologically backward compared with those of Germany, America and Japan – and remained so throughout. Admiral Fraser, having had the chance to compare the British with the American Navy in some detail, concluded that the latter was more adventurous and progressive while the former was more cautious and conservative – but sound. As in previous wars, the salient fact about the Royal Navy in the Second World War was how the morale of the lower deck generally remained remarkably high, often in the most appalling conditions and after many serious setbacks. This was especially true on smaller warships. The average quality of admirals was markedly higher than it had been in the First World War and the captains of individual ships were generally as good as ever.

British submarines made much of their limited opportunities, mainly in the Mediterranean, sinking an average 9.3 ships for every boat lost (seventy-five British submarines were destroyed). This represents a 'rate of exchange' second only to that of the US Navy (23:1) with its unique combination of opportunities presented by the Pacific theatre and Japanese neglect of convoy and ASW (the Germans achieved a ratio of 20.5:1 before August 1942 but only 3.6:1 for the war as a whole). But the Royal Navy undoubtedly emerged from its most important conflict as the world leader in anti-submarine warfare.

The price was heavy enough. The Navy, swollen to more than twice the numbers of personnel it had in the previous war, lost 73,642 killed and the British Merchant Navy 30,248, as we saw. Forty-one submarines and 175 surface warships went down in the Mediterranean alone; 175 warships of all types were lost in the Atlantic campaign, the vast majority British. Some fifty more British warships were sunk by the Japanese. Such was the price of the victory in the Atlantic, the maritime draw in the Mediterranean and the defeat at sea in the Far East. An exhausted Britain emerged on the winning side of the second worldwide war of the century – but bankrupt, its debts surpassing its assets by a factor of well over twelve to one. The war cost the United Kingdom the last vestige of its status as a world power of the first rank and any claim to mastery of the seas. If Britons thought on VJ Day in August 1945 that the nation would get the rest it had undoubtedly earned, they were sadly deceiving themselves. Britain faced many more years of austerity, some of it harsher than in wartime.

As part of the nation, so did its Navy.

PART III

The Warsaw Pact (and After)

13

Losing an Empire

The Royal Navy had already passed its historical maximum strength of some 880,000 men and women before the end of the conflict. A war-weary Britain and her Navy experienced a manpower crisis in 1944, and the war ended with 865,000 in the service, the vast majority 'hostilities only'. Although demobilization could not happen fast enough for most of the millions in the King's various uniforms, it was running at a rate of 30,000 per month in the Navy alone soon after VJ Day in August 1945, when the Navy consisted of 790,000 men, 74,000 women, 8,940 ships of all types and 1,336 front-line aircraft. Total personnel fell to 503,000 in 1946 and 195,000 in 1947, bottoming out (for the time being) at 140,000 in 1951. Meanwhile 840 warships were paid off by autumn 1946, and 727 which had been ordered were cancelled; 4,500 merchant ships and more than 1,200 fishing vessels were released by the Admiralty and 450 foreign-owned merchant ships returned to their proprietors. This still left the fleet with more than 800 warships and major auxiliaries plus large numbers of small coastal craft. Eleven aircraft carriers, four cruisers and more than twenty destroyers were nearing completion; among the cancelled orders were nine fleet and four light carriers (three of the former would have displaced over 50,000 tons), and swarms of destroyers, submarines, sloops and ocean minesweepers. The further a vessel was from completion the more likely it was to be cancelled. At a time when a fleet destroyer cost about £1m, the 1946 naval estimates showed commercial shipyards holding naval contracts worth more than £33m.

Despite the vast numbers to be demobilized, the Navy all too soon sank into a manpower and recruitment crisis which to a greater or lesser degree outlasted the century. Viscount Hall, the postwar First Lord of the Admiralty, set a target of the end of 1948 for the discharge of all 'hostilities only' ratings. The Labour government, which had won the general election of July 1945 with

319

a massive majority for its commitments to the welfare state and widespread nationalization, was anxious to save money by reducing the forces as soon as possible. But Britain retained obligations all over the world and Labour, never as radical as advertised, was not about to abandon the 'responsibility of empire' overnight, despite a commitment to Indian independence. In the Navy in particular demobilization had to be selective (an obvious problem for morale) as the service was short of regular able and leading seamen. The last regular sailors to join up for a twelve-year berth in 1939 were inevitably concentrated in the higher rates by war's end. Petty officers then earned 9s a day, compared with the ordinary seaman's 4s, a lieutenant's 17s and a captain's £3 5s.

To regard the history of the Royal Navy for the fifty-five years from its greatest triumph to the end of the century as a story of unremitting decline is not just an oversimplification but a distortion, of which not a few politicians and observers, officers and ratings were often guilty. It would also be tedious and depressing. Certainly the service entered a new millennium with its smallest fleet since the dawn of the steam age and lowest manpower since 1850; but it possessed in its four '*Vanguard*'-class boats, armed with Trident ballistic missiles, not only far more potential firepower than it ever had, more than that of any other Navy except the American and the Russian, but also the world's most modern strategic nuclear-missile submarines. The 1998 Strategic Defence Review promised two new 50,000-tonne carriers and a successor for the Harrier aircraft as well as increased amphibious capability. The numerical decline of the British fleet and its personnel was an understandable source of constant anxiety within the service and among those concerned and interested in its welfare, but did not prevent a shrinking fleet from staying abreast of astounding developments in technology most of the time, albeit with crucial American help in some cases. On the contrary, the Royal Navy's very shortage of funds, unremitting and perennial as it was from 1914, seemed to inspire the service to acquire a world lead in many important areas. We need only mention three disparate examples here: silent running, systems integration and – ironically in view of Britain's notoriously late start and persistent neglect of naval aviation – a whole string of improvements to aircraft carriers, all eagerly adopted by the US Navy (as was the Sea Harrier aircraft).

So what follows is not a story of decline (except in the relative and numerical senses) but of adaptation, of learning to cut one's coat according to one's cloth, of adjustment to changing (and sometimes misread) threats and challenges. There were plenty of cuts, many of them false economies, a British besetting sin, but the Navy was not found wanting in such varied crises as Korea, the Falklands, the Gulf and the Balkans, to name but four.

The period from 1946 to 1999 brought much pain and even some humiliation to the Royal Navy, twice saviour of the nation in its greatest wars, because those involved often saw only cuts and more cuts, and found it hard to live with the postwar fact that as a fleet it was by a large margin 'only' third in the world, with the French Navy hot on its heels, and often could not even function independently of the United States. Nor was it only politicians, civil servants and military leaders who found it hard to adjust to Britain's reduced influence in the world (which at its peak had derived from the subjugation of one third of the earth's surface). This decline was relative, not absolute; Britain remained a member of the 'G7' group of the world's leading economics and at the very end of the century seemed to be faring better than most of the others. The US meanwhile had become not only the world's sole superpower but also its largest debtor nation. The remaining chapters of our story are also a tale of remarkable success, often against unnecessary odds such as political error and 'short-termism' as well as financial stringency. Yet having focused its efforts, quite rationally, on countering the very real Soviet submarine threat in the north Atlantic, the resulting ASW-oriented surface fleet successfully transformed itself overnight into a punitive expeditionary force to recapture territory 8,000 miles away. It was almost as if the turbulent century between the Royal Navy's bombardment of Alexandria (and subsequent British seizure of Egypt) in 1882 and Operation 'Corporate' to retake the Falkland Islands in 1982 had never happened. This extraordinary 'last hurrah' was the third time in a century that the Royal Navy had played the main part in the defeat of a dictatorship threatening national interests. No other fleet in the world could say the same.

Nevertheless the extraordinarily rapid rundown of the fleet from 1945 surpassed in intensity the reductions of 1815 after the final defeat of Napoleon and of 1919 after the first defeat of Germany. More than 300,000 left the service in each of the first two complete years of peace. But even as the fleet shrank so drastically there seemed to be no end of tasks for the Navy, whether bringing home prisoners of war or taking Commonwealth troops (and their British brides) to such far-flung places as Australia. The Mediterranean Fleet remained in being, once again based on Malta (Alexandria was abandoned and only a handful of patrol boats and harbour vessels in the Suez Canal Zone remained in Egypt), and had to work very hard for its living.

Inevitably, it seems, local conflicts erupted in the Balkans even before the war ended. Rivalry between royalist and Communist partisans in Greece developed into a full-scale and thoroughly nasty civil war as early as 1944. The British backed the former and the Soviet Union the latter, foreshadowing the Cold War which dominated most of the rest of the century. American money funded intervention by British troops, delivered, supplied and supported by the Navy. The war ended with the defeat of the Communists in October 1949.

In neighbouring Albania a similar struggle between liberal nationalist and Communist resistance groups ended with the opposite result, ushering in what was probably the harshest Communist regime ever known. One of the issues in a conflict that began in 1942, was suppressed by the Allies in 1943 and broke out in earnest in 1944 would return to haunt the world, drawing in the Royal Navy once more, at the end of the century: Kosovo. The Yugoslav province with its high concentration of ethnic Albanians was attached to Albania by the conquering Italians in 1941 and the nationalists wanted to keep it (what a deal of trouble that might have saved). But the Communists, like their Greek counterparts supported by Tito's Yugoslav Communist regime, were bent on returning it to Yugoslavia, which duly made it an autonomous region of Serbia. The Albanian upheaval led to an extraordinary and melancholy incident for the British Navy in October 1946. In May the Communists shelled British warships (on patrol for reasons connected with the Greek civil war in the Corfu Channel, between that Greek island and Albania), causing no damage. But five months later two destroyers, HMSs *Saumarez* and *Volage*, ran on to German-made mines in the same waterway and suffered serious damage, with the loss of forty-three sailors. Although the mines were probably laid by the Yugoslavs, Britain unsuccessfully sued Albania in the International Court of Justice at The Hague, which awarded damages of £844,000. The odious Enver Hoxha regime ignored the judgement, whereupon the British government seized Albanian gold reserves, worth £5m, which happened to be on deposit for wartime safekeeping in the vaults of the Bank of England! The dispute was only cleared up after the general collapse of Communism in Europe from 1989.

Further east in the Mediterranean the Navy was required to perform a task it probably relished less than any other in the century. On the break-up of the Ottoman Empire after 1918, the British had acquired a poisoned chalice: the League of Nations mandate for Palestine, renewed by the successor-organization, the United Nations, at the end of the Second World War. Palestine thus became a temporary member of the British Empire, as did the other formerly Turkish fiefs of Jordan and Iraq, while Syria and Lebanon came under French administration. Even under Turkish rule, before the end of the nineteenth century, Zionists settled in Palestine in significant numbers, hoping to establish a Jewish state; Nazi persecution boosted the Jewish population in the 1930s and migration by survivors of the Holocaust compounded this trend. Nascent Arab nationalism, fomented by the British from 1916 as a weapon against Germany's then ally, Turkey, was naturally offended by the Anglo-French 'carve-up' of the Levant; and both the long-standing antipathy between Arab and Jew as well as Arab anti-British sentiment had been compounded by the 'Balfour Declaration' of 1917, in which the British Foreign Secretary promised a Jewish national home in Palestine. Such was the origin of Britain's self-imposed and insoluble dilemma in what was called Palestine until the nascent Israel defeated the Arabs in 1948.

The mass migration of Jewish survivors of the Nazi concentration and death camps, funded by the very large, wealthy and powerful Jewish population of the United States, whence many volunteers for the Zionist cause also came, led to a series of highly embarrassing confrontations when British naval patrols stopped immigrant ships. The oil-rich Arab states, with which Britain had once again curried favour before and during the Second World War as it had in the First, persuaded Britain in 1939 to promise to limit the Jewish population of Palestine to one third (10 per cent in 1919 had risen to 30 in two decades). In cold figures, this meant that the British could admit just 75,000 more Jews and felt obliged, during and after the war, to turn away Jewish refugees, something which Holocaust survivors and American Jews alike could neither understand nor accept. The 1939 decision led the Zionists to give up on the British and switch very effectively to the US, finding their strongest sympathizers in successive presidents (Roosevelt and Truman). This thorny issue did nothing for the 'special relationship' between America and Britain. The Americans backed the appeal in August 1945 by the Zionist leader, David Ben-Gurion, for entry permits for 100,000 Jews who had survived the Holocaust. As Zionist terrorism (and British countermeasures) mounted in Palestine, Arabs, Jews, Americans and British could not agree, and in February 1947 Britain asked the United Nations to take over. Meanwhile the Navy, to the distress of ships' crews, intercepted some seventy-eight vessels with about 70,000 migrants aboard, escorting them to the British colony of Cyprus; twenty-one ships are known to have evaded the patrols. When refugees pelted them with tins of food, British sailors pragmatically rigged up nets and collected welcome extra rations.

The culminating incident in this awful early stage of the long retreat from empire and global police work came in May 1947, when the rusting hulk emotively restyled *Exodus 1947* arrived off Haifa from the south of France with more than 4,500 migrants aboard. The British turned it away, harvesting a massive crop of bad publicity, especially in the US, and the floating wreck went back to the south of France, where the refugees were denied permission to land. The French authorities, unbelievably, sent it on to Germany. In July the British government unilaterally announced its intention to withdraw from Palestine. In December London said it would ditch its mandate on 15 May 1948. The state of Israel was proclaimed immediately, Jewish fighters having gained control of the bulk of the land of Palestine, denying the Arabs the share they had been promised and entrenching a dispute which outlasted the century. The perennial Arab−Israeli quarrel became America's headache and came close to causing a Third World War on several occasions; but it would embroil Britain and its armed forces again more than once during the Cold War period. The main strength of the Navy even as it shrank was concentrated in and around the eastern Mediterranean in the late 1940s: two destroyers helped put down an Arab pogrom against Jewish businesses in Aden, and in the Red Sea British warships mounted anti-slavery patrols in 1947 and 1948 to inhibit the 'export' of east African forced labour to Saudi and other Arab destinations, as if the twentieth century had never arrived.

Admiral Mountbatten seemed to come into his own on his brief appointment as Viceroy of India, to oversee the British withdrawal from empire in 1947. His royal connections and pretensions were well suited to the ceremonial side of the post, but he presided over what closely resembled a high-speed scuttle. Imperial authority having been undermined by Japanese victories over the British in the Far East and the knowledge that freedom was coming, the subcontinent succumbed to religious and ethnic violence in the months preceding independence at midnight on 14 August 1947. At that moment British India was partitioned into a Hindu India and an Islamic Pakistan, the latter in two parts, West and East, the East becoming a third state, Bangladesh, within a generation. Six million Moslems fled to Pakistan and 4.5m Hindus to India, a chaotic double mass migration estimated to have led to at least 1m deaths, although the official figure was 180,000. The Royal Navy was not called upon to play any strategic part in this largest of all imperial evacuations, but the successor states each acquired a navy on British lines with British-built ships and British-trained officers. Some twenty-five ships were handed over to Commonwealth navies between 1945 and 1948, and 300 to other navies. Ceylon (now Sri Lanka) and Burma were granted independence around the same time. A substantial residual British Empire, however, lived on, for the time being, mainly in the East Indies and Africa, but Indian independence took the heart out of it. The Far East Fleet, derived from the short-lived British Pacific Fleet, was reduced to a squadron in 1948, when the Royal Navy also removed its vestigial presence in Japan.

For reasons of geography and naval strength, and as the occupiers of the north-west zone of Germany, the British had the primary responsibility for the huge and formidable postwar task of mine-clearance in the North Sea and Channel. The main effort lasted for one and a half years, drawing in the Royal Navy as the leading agency, with Merchant Navy volunteers; all available German minesweepers were kept in service by the Allied Control Commission with their crews, and the navies of formerly occupied countries such as France, the Netherlands and Belgium joined in. Nearly 2,000 minesweeping craft, more than a quarter of them British, were engaged in sweeping 125,000 square miles of sea clear of Allied and enemy mines. Three British vessels were lost to them. The British Navy was also simultaneously involved in smaller sweeps off Greenland, the Faroe Islands and Hong Kong and in the Mediterranean and South China seas. Sixty-five minesweepers were still at work in the North Sea early in 1947, by which time restored fishery protection patrols were able to guide shipping away from remaining patches of mined water. The odd mine continued to appear on the surface or turn up in a fishing boat's net for the rest of the century.

Occupied Germany was 'demilitarized' in the immediate aftermath of the war. More than 115 U-boats were towed away from German North Sea and western Baltic bases and sunk off Northern Ireland while German surface warships were parcelled out among the navies of the former Nazi-occupied countries; Britain kept two destroyers, a few E-boats, minesweepers and smaller vessels. Mountains of naval munitions were removed from port dumps to the German fortress of Heligoland, where they were conveniently destroyed in blowing up the massive fortifications in 1948. Some wartime concrete structures, such as the submarine pens at Kiel, were too strong to demolish and were left to rot. The British also commandeered *U3017*, the experimental submarine developed by Professor Walter to run on hydrogen peroxide fuel, the use of which produced oxygen for the crew while propelling the boat at high speed underwater. The Germans had failed to make the system work properly by war's end, but the British renamed the boat HMS *Meteorite* for further experiments. For a few years British submarine research was concentrated on this apparently promising but ultimately unworkable idea while the Americans focused their much more lavish efforts on developing a nuclear reactor for submarine use. But the hydrodynamic shape of the intermediate Walter 'electro-boats' with their unprecedented underwater speeds was adopted by both navies for postwar submarines. The first British boat built, as distinct from converted, on these lines was HMS *Porpoise*, leader of a 1950s class.

Meanwhile existing RN boats were pressed into service as electricity generators in Britain's shattered shipyards, which completed most surviving wartime orders by early 1947. The largest of these, HMS *Vanguard*, proved the least useful. Ordered in 1941 as the last of six wartime capital ships and launched in 1944, the 42,500-ton ship (50,000 fully laden) was the last battleship ever commissioned into the Royal Navy or indeed any fleet. Her hull cost £9m but there must have been a saving on her eight antique 15-inch guns, made in 1917 for two super-cruisers but removed when they were converted into the ill-fated carriers *Courageous* and *Glorious*. With her advanced radars, strong armour, speed of about thirty knots and sophisticated damage control, this majestic dinosaur never fired a shot in anger and spent most of her life 'on parade', taking the Royal Family to South Africa in 1947, after a £170,000 refurbishment for their comfort, and leading the Coronation Review in 1953, whereupon she went into reserve, until scrapped in 1960. She was the ninth of her name to serve in the fleet; the tenth was the class-leader of Britain's four Trident nuclear-missile submarines. The principal function of the five battleships that briefly remained in the fleet was to train new recruits in harbour – two remained in service at Portland for this purpose by 1948, when the naval estimates were cut by nearly a quarter to £153m and personnel by a similar proportion to 152,000.

The uneven effect of demobilization, still incomplete, continued to burden the shrinking service. Out of a total of eighty-six warships in commission, the Home Fleet had an effective strength of a single cruiser and four destroyers, while a total of seventy-four warships covered the rest of the world, including four carriers (two for training). Within a month in 1948, when five capital ships were scrapped, ships in commission fell to sixty-six. Ninety ships suffered the indignity of being used as targets for weapons trials.

Rather more useful among the wartime overhang was the light fleet aircraft carrier *Triumph*, as well as sixteen destroyers, four sloops, one frigate and six submarines completed at this time. The fleet carrier *Eagle*, laid down in 1944, was also completed, though not commissioned until 1951. The naval estimates for 1947 included just two destroyers. Hundreds of ships were expensively refitted over five years and placed in reserve, 'mothballed' by being covered in nets which were sealed with sprayed-on plastic, hulls being protected by electrolysis against marine growths and kept at a constant temperature and humidity level. Unfortunately many of the ships thus cocooned had been built of cheap wartime steel and rotted from within. Financial stringency notwithstanding, research into new technologies and weapons continued, albeit on a small scale, in the long postwar austerity period: the research which was to lead to the highly successful conversion of the surface fleet to gas-turbine propulsion from the 1960s began in 1946; two years later the Navy's first anti-aircraft missile, the Seaslug, was on the drawing board, although it did not come into service for another fourteen years. The Navy founded its Electrical Branch in 1947, a prudent step into the electronic age. As 'hostilities only' ratings had the most experience of radar and other modern technologies, continuing demobilization left the service seriously weak in this crucial area.

But the true revolution in seapower, the only one comparable with the change from sail to steam a century earlier, had been anticipated as early as 1939, when the US Navy was urged to consider the practical application of nuclear fission. Once war came, priority was given to developing the atomic bomb, the other application of nuclear energy that was to have an even more radical effect on naval strategy. Alongside this double development, awesome in its implications for the very survival of the human race, there would soon be spectacular, parallel advances in ballistics and electronics, including computers. All in all, these and associated technological advances outclassed even the helter-skelter technical changes from the later nineteenth century to 1914. They were also fearsomely expensive, leading before the end of the century to bills for a single vessel, such as a nuclear ballistic-missile submarine or a carrier, running to hundreds of millions of pounds; even a frigate cost a nine-figure sum. Small wonder that the British fleet did nothing but shrink in numbers after 1945. The potential effect of nuclear weapons on warships was closely studied at Bikini Atoll in the Pacific in 1946, when the Americans conducted their first postwar atomic test, in which several seized enemy hulks were vaporized. The British were already working on their own atom bomb as the Americans started developing the reactor for the first nuclear submarine in 1946.

The running sore of the manpower crisis led the Admiralty into a series of reforms, several of which had to be reversed; the Fleet Air Arm, for example, became Naval Aviation in 1946 and reverted to the title Fleet Air Arm in 1953; the rank of warrant officer was abolished in 1948, its holders transmogrified into 'commissioned branch officers' with access to the wardroom. But in 1970 the rank was brought back under the new name of fleet chief petty officer. The age of entry to Dartmouth Naval College was raised from thirteen and a half to sixteen and a quarter (later eighteen) in 1948, the same year as the Women's Royal Naval Service became a permanent part of the Navy – and corporal punishment, unused for decades, was officially abolished! Sons of parents with an annual income of under £300 paid no fees at the College, to encourage more entrants from state grammar schools. National service was temporarily reduced from eighteen months to one year in 1947, making it virtually useless as a source of naval manpower. When it went up to two years in 1948–9, only 2,000 conscripts joined a Navy which found such a period inadequate for training most of the specialists the service needed. National servicemen were required to remain in the Royal Naval 'Volunteer' Reserve for two years after their full-time conscription ended. The 10,000 recruits who joined voluntarily in 1949 included boys as young as sixteen and a quarter. Of the 145,000 males in the service, 33,000 were instructors. A sign of the gravity of the manpower problem was the fact that the Admiralty raised pay twice in five years, in 1946 and again in 1950 (when pensions also rose), an unprecedented development.

There was if anything even more for a straitened fleet to do in the late 1940s. The Far East command was already operating anti-terrorist patrols off the coast of Malaya in 1948, a task which grew in complexity after the Communists won power in China (a whole Royal Marine Commando brigade was engaged alongside British Army units by 1951). In 1949 on the other side of the world the cruiser *Sheffield* landed troops in British Honduras to deter a threatened takeover by Guatemala, the start of a commitment which lasted for most of the rest of the century, even after the territory became independent Belize in 1981.

But the most important and eventually spectacular British naval involvement in 1949 was in the civil war, begun in 1946, in China, where the Communists were overcoming the Nationalists, who had ruled during the war. The Far East command was on standby to evacuate British diplomats and business people from Nanjing, about 200 miles up the great Yangtse River. A lone destroyer or frigate was on hand in the river, between the Communists on the north bank and the Nationalists on the south. The 'Reds' were expected to make the crossing on 21 April, causing the destroyer *Consort* to delay her departure; the frigate HMS *Amethyst* was sent west from Shanghai on the 19th to relieve her, the White Ensign at the stern augmented by a large, painted Union flag on either side. Still sixty miles short of Nanjing, the vessel (Lieutenant-Commander B. M. Skinner, RN) came under Communist artillery fire from starboard. The frigate ran aground in her attempts to evade the shelling, which killed seventeen men and wounded ten, including the captain, who died shortly afterwards. The First Lieutenant, G. L. Weston, took over.

Coming to the rescue, the *Consort* made six attempts to refloat the stricken frigate but had to withdraw under continued bombardment, losing nine of her crew with three wounded (one died later). The Far East command raised the stakes by sending the cruiser *London* and the frigate *Black Swan* to assist, but they too were driven back by the shelling, with fifteen fatal casualties and twenty-two injured. Meanwhile the *Amethyst* managed to refloat herself and put sixty-three sailors on the southern shore, reducing the crew to the operable minimum. One surgeon from the RAF and another from the US Navy were flown in from Nanjing by Sunderland flying boat and boarded the *Amethyst* from the Nationalist shore; the Communists refused to release the ship unless it helped to ferry their troops across the river. The British assistant naval attaché from Beijing, Lieutenant-Commander J. S. Kerans, RN, boarded *Amethyst* with the two surgeons and the British military attaché, by which time the wounded Lieutenant Weston had been on duty for more than two days without a break. Kerans assumed command. Negotiations with the Communists under flag of truce lasted for months without result as the ship, also besieged by insects, sweltered in the humid heat, the fans unused to save fuel. The Reds interfered with ration deliveries to step up the pressure.

Having destroyed the ship's secret books and papers, Kerans was unable to signal the C-in-C, Far East, Admiral Sir Patrick Brind, in cipher. So early in July 1949, he asked in plain language what action he should take in the event of a typhoon. The admiral cautiously replied that he should take plenty of sea room. On the 30th the anchor chain was muffled and stealthily hauled in while canvas screens were used to alter the frigate's outline. As the ship put about to sail east the Communist guns opened fire once more under flares. But *Amethyst*, with full steam up, kept going, in the wake of a river steamer to inhibit the Red artillery. Her own gunners had the satisfaction of sinking a Chinese gunboat as it came in to attack. The frigate ran the gauntlet of hostile artillery batteries for three hours, smashing through a boom. Then, after two hours of blessed silence, *Amethyst* was 100 miles downstream; completing the last forty miles without further incident, Kerans reached Shanghai and signalled: 'Have rejoined the fleet. No damage or casualties. God save the King.' Kerans was awarded the DSO as the story of the fabulous escape went round the world; the ship and her crew got a rapturous reception on their return to England.

The situation in China prompted heavy reinforcement of the Far East from the Mediterranean, including the latter fleet's only carrier, *Triumph* (eventually replaced by the *Glory*). HMS *Ocean*, the light carrier that had helped cover the British evacuation of Palestine, came out without her air group, having instead loaded masses of stores in England for the Far East command: a depot ship followed with 100 crated planes. The cruiser *Kenya* relieved the *London*, which went home to be scrapped. Two new frigates replaced *Amethyst*. At the same time the East Indies Squadron, based on Singapore, was covering the burgeoning emergency in Malaya. Back home, as the 1949 naval estimates went up by a quarter over 1948 to £189m, only three battleships remained on active duty, including *Vanguard*, in the Training Squadron of the Home Fleet, whose flagship was now the fleet carrier *Implacable*; her predecessor, the battleship *Duke of York*, became flagship of the Reserve Fleet in 1949. The new flagship flew Sea Vampires, maritime variant of a RAF fighter; the Navy's first purpose-built jet fighter, the Attacker, had been tried out on *Illustrious*. A prudent move by the Admiralty, in the light of events described immediately below, was the conversion of twenty-three wartime fleet destroyers into Type 15, and another ten to Type 16, ASW frigates which could seal themselves off against nuclear fallout. Historically the Russians had always taken a special interest in submarines, even though their boats were serious underachievers in the Second World War; after it, the Soviet Union sustained this interest, which soon became the Navy's main cause for concern in the waters close to home.

The most important political development for the Royal Navy and British defence policy, in 1949 and in the entire postwar era alike, was the conclusion of the North Atlantic Treaty. It was presaged in March 1948 by the Treaty of Brussels, where Britain, France and the three Benelux countries signed a general cooperation agreement which included collective defence. These powers joined the United States and Canada in Washington in July, when a broader North Atlantic security organization was agreed in principle; negotiations began at the end of the year and in spring 1949 five more Western European nations were invited to join. The Treaty was signed on 4 April; several other Western European states joined later, and the alliance spread to much of Eastern Europe in the 1990s, after the collapse of the Soviet Union and its Communist bloc. The Soviet response was to create the Warsaw Pact, led by Moscow and embracing its six Communist 'satellites' in Eastern Europe, including East Germany (but not Yugoslavia, where Tito had broken with Stalin in 1948).

Such were the two massive alliances that faced each other across the Iron Curtain dividing Europe for forty years, their land and air forces concentrated and focused on the inter-German border. In maritime terms, the Nato area included the whole of the north Atlantic from the North Pole to the Tropic of Cancer and also covered all of the Mediterranean. In the event of a war in Europe, the basic Nato strategy was to hold the line in Germany as massive North American reinforcements and supplies were convoyed across the Atlantic. The Warsaw Pact planned to neutralize the standing Nato armies while fending off their reinforcements by massed submarine attack. As deadly defence technologies advanced each side assembled nuclear stockpiles: atomic and then hydrogen bombs, long-range bombers, short-, medium- and long-range nuclear missiles, shells, torpedoes and mines were added to the apocalyptic mixture, the final ingredient of which was to be the ballistic nuclear-missile submarine.

But it was the Far East rather than the deepening East–West freeze in Europe that now threw up the first great, world-scale crisis since 1945. The Communists completed their takeover in China in 1949, the Nationalists retreating to the large offshore island of Formosa where, with American support and encouragement, they established a rump-state later known as Taiwan. The regime led by Mao Zhedong had enjoyed Soviet support and the two vast powers now constituted a political alliance. The United States was determined with missionary zeal to contain, frustrate and confront 'international Communism' across the world with a view to undermining it. America's allies were not always as enthusiastic but knew which side their bread was buttered in the postwar era of austerity – and of reconstruction, massively funded by the dollars of the Marshall Plan, the most generous example of enlightened self-interest on record.

Korea resembles Poland in one unfortunate respect: it is a relatively weak nation sandwiched between two larger ones, in this case China and Japan. As the former crumbled in the century prior to the Communist revolution, Russia and Japan intervened in China and Korea suffered at the hands of both. In the dying days of the Second World War Stalin invaded Manchuria and neighbouring Korea, where Japanese forces surrendered to the Russians in the north and the Americans in the south. The two victorious armies made an ad hoc decision to divide the Korean peninsula along the 38th parallel, a division which outlasted the century. Called in by the US in 1947, the United Nations failed to engender a united, independent Korea as promised by the Americans, British and Chinese at the wartime Cairo Conference in 1943 (Stalin was absent). Russian and American forces evacuated the peninsula in 1949 but in June 1950 the North Korean Communists, encouraged by apparent American indifference to the fate of the peninsula, invaded the South, quickly occupying its capital, Seoul, just over the de facto border. Shocked, the Americans changed their tune, embracing South Korea (and Taiwan) in their declared sphere of interest. The nine-month-old Chinese Peoples' Republic could have done without this sudden crisis on its eastern border but felt bound to support the North.

With United Nations backing (the Russians did not appear at the Security Council and the Chinese permanent seat was occupied by the Taiwanese Nationalists, so there was no veto) President Truman ordered General MacArthur, still Allied supremo in Japan, to go to the help of the South, and cordoned off Taiwan with the US Seventh Fleet. The UN and South Korean forces however were pushed into a small enclave at the southern extremity of the peninsula with a single port, Pusan. At sea, the American and Commonwealth navies formed a carrier-led task force (TF 95) in June 1950, which rapidly made its presence felt by sinking five out of six attacking North Korean torpedo boats off the UN enclave. The British Far East Fleet made a total of twenty-nine warships available, including a carrier (*Triumph*), three cruisers, eleven destroyers and eleven frigates; seven of these came from Australia and other Commonwealth countries. The Commonwealth contribution, Task Group 95.1, was commanded by the British Rear-Admiral W. G. Andrewes. When he was promoted vice-admiral in January 1951, he outranked the American commander of TF 95, Rear-Admiral Allan Smith, who gallantly agreed to serve under Andrewes instead of over him for a few weeks in order to foster the very good working relationship of the two task groups. The Navy's nagging manpower crisis meant that most of the British ships were as much as 20 per cent undermanned; the '*Hermes*'-class light carrier *Theseus* was detailed to relieve *Triumph* but was delayed by sabotage, apparently by men overdue for their discharge from the service (a problem which recurred more than once).

As early as July 1950 the cruiser HMS *Jamaica* was hit in an exchange with North Korean coastal artillery, losing five killed and seven wounded. By September the Commonwealth had 7,000 men engaged off Korea, but could have done with more sailors, frigates and minesweepers to augment hectic activity, including coastal bombardments and air attacks. Food for thought was provided when the Americans flew helicopters from the British *Theseus* when she finally arrived; they were used for several purposes, including ASW, in which sonobuoys were also deployed. Britain bought forty-five US Skyraiders for the Airborne Early Warning (AEW) role on carriers (replaced by the excellent British Gannets in 1960). National service was extended for 3,600 ratings by six months to two years in 1950, and a planned cut of one fifth in the Royal Marines to 10,000 was put off as the Malayan emergency continued. To attract more regulars (20,000 recruits a year were needed to sustain extant manning levels) living allowances and conditions ashore were improved and attempts were made to ease the spartan conditions of service at sea, especially on the smaller ships. Hammocks were still in use, and the quality of rations was generally regarded as abysmal, with few or no recreational facilities. The long, short-sighted historical tradition of neglect of the lower deck was obviously still flourishing at the Admiralty and in Parliament. But in 1951 pensions and discharge gratuities were improved in a bid to attract long-term recruits.

Some 6,600 extra officers and men had to be recalled for eighteen months' duty from the Royal Fleet Reserve in 1951 because of Korea and Malaya. The naval estimates shot up again by 47 per cent to £278m as the Labour government, narrowly re-elected in 1950, promised a construction programme of no fewer than 300 new warships, including six carriers, thirty-two destroyers and frigates and 200 minesweepers and patrol craft. Forty-five destroyers were to be converted into fast frigates and sixty ships to be taken out of reserve or mothballs and modernized. But the shipbuilding industry was far from fully recovered from the world war and could not cope with such an expansion of naval work. Huge delays and deferments resulted, often doubling the already long lead time for new ships to ten years. It was even more difficult to find adequate engine-building capacity. Somehow Britain managed to produce a more or less steady stream of reliable frigates and minesweepers, often best in the world in their classes and also sold to other navies.

The strength of the Navy fell to 140,000 men in 1951, but 50,000 reservists had been called up to help cope with the Far East emergencies. The US Navy at this time mustered over 850,000, equivalent to the peak wartime strength of the Royal Navy, and had more than three times as many ships, of a distinctly larger average tonnage. Even so it came as a shock in Britain when Nato appointed an American admiral as the first SACLANT (Supreme Allied Commander, Atlantic), even though the British C-in-C, Channel, was supposed to enjoy equal standing. In the same year (1952) Nato conducted an elaborate exercise in the far northern Atlantic, 'Mainbrace', whose purpose was to rehearse the Alliance's maritime strategy of bottling up the Soviet submarine fleet in time of war or high tension, preventing the boats from passing through the Norwegian Sea or the Denmark Strait into the broad Atlantic.

The British fleet had been stretched even further in 1951 and there was no sign of relief a year later: to Korea and Malaya was now added the Persian Gulf and the Anglo-Iranian dispute over control of the British-built oil refinery at Abadan, then the world's largest, and Iran's oil output. One carrier and accompanying cruisers, destroyers and frigates were operating constantly off Korea. They had provided invaluable support to MacArthur's tide-turning counter-attack in September 1950, the UN landing at Inchon 160 miles north-west of Pusan and just a few miles due west of Seoul. The UN forces pressed on over the 38th parallel and penetrated as far north as the Manchurian border on the Yalu River by the end of December. This apparent easy victory was a false dawn. China, concerned not only by the impending defeat of its North Korean client but also by the prospect of an American anti-Communist crusade on its soil, intervened massively on the ground and in the air, forcing the UN out of Seoul early in 1951. But the Chinese became bogged down and by spring the capital had been recovered. The dismissal of MacArthur by Truman in April for seeking to promote all-out war against China (with atomic weapons if necessary) encouraged a stalemate in Korea, reflected in the long-drawn-out truce negotiations from July 1951 at Panmunjom, on the 38th parallel north-west of Seoul. As sporadic fighting continued alongside agonizingly slow diplomatic moves, Commonwealth Task Group 95.1 remained in being and on active duty for two more years, when an armistice was at last signed. HMS *Ocean*'s four Sea Fury fighters distinguished themselves by seeing off an attack by eight MiG 15s, probably the best fighters of their day. The result of the war was the permanent division of the peninsula into two states, one fanatically totalitarian and Communist, the other no less enthusiastically capitalist but a less than shining example of democracy.

To pre-empt the Germans, the British and the Russians had between them occupied the whole of Iran, the successor state of the historic Persian Empire, in 1942, driving out the Shah, who died in exile in 1944. The British Army left as agreed in March 1946, the Russians only a few weeks later. The Anglo-Iranian Oil Company, in which the British government had a major shareholding, continued to dominate the country's oil industry, from which the Royal Navy was able to buy fuel at advantageous rates. At this time Iran, under the second (and last) Shah of the Pahlavi dynasty, was the largest oil producer in the Middle East and was also at odds with its Arab neighbours for political, ethnic and religious reasons. Iranian nationalism and economic ambitions led to a successful demand for a 50 per cent increase in royalties paid by the company and other extra payments. But the nationalists still wanted to take over the company altogether; the Majlis (parliament) requisitioned it in 1951, when Dr Muhammad Musaddiq became premier for two years.

Britain, anxious about the implications elsewhere in the Middle East of the seizure for its oil supply and its prestige alike, demanded compensation plus damages, winning reluctant American support thanks to Musaddiq's flirtation with homegrown and Soviet Communism. Unwilling to intervene militarily, Britain blocked Iranian oil sales on the international market, which hastened the economic downfall of Musaddiq's government. He was finally unseated by the Army and dismissed by the Shah, with the backing of British and American intelligence. But the nationalization survived, although a group of British, American and French oil companies set up a consortium to market the output from Abadan for twenty-five years; Britain owned 40 per cent (and received modest compensation for its losses) while Iran got half its profits Iran joined the Baghdad Pact in 1955, a short-lived regional anti-Soviet alliance later renamed the Central Treaty Organisation, with Turkey, Iraq, Pakistan – and Britain, for which this was another burdensome commitment far from home. Throughout the Abadan crisis British warships and marines stood by in the Gulf, not so much a threat to invade as an insurance for British citizens. The ships came from the Mediterranean Fleet, reinforced by the East Indies Squadron.

The troublesome early 1950s brought yet another problem for the Navy – in Egypt, where the King was ousted by an army coup. When Britain refused to heed nationalist demands to evacuate its troops from the Suez Canal Zone, the Egyptians abrogated the 1936 Anglo-Egyptian treaty. After Port Said at the northern end was paralysed by a political strike, the Royal Navy was called in to operate and maintain the Canal, an international waterway purportedly open to all. With remarkable versatility the Mediterranean Fleet kept the British Army garrison supplied, put armed parties on ships to deter attacks on them, patrolled the Canal itself against saboteurs, looked after the water supply and patched up broken-down merchant ships. By the end of 1951 the Navy had seen 2,600 ships pass safely through without interruption in three months. A sign of the pressure the fleet was under was the 1952 Navy estimates, which rose by a startling 28 per cent to £357m regardless of austerity; and for the first time since the war manpower rose from the 1951 low of 140,000 (by 8,000). Another thirteen destroyers were converted into fast ASW frigates, but there was to be no new construction in this first full year of the first postwar Conservative government, led by a visibly ageing Winston Churchill, seventy-seven when he returned to power in 1951. Had Labour won, defence production costs would apparently have risen to £850m by 1953–4; the Conservatives pegged them at £600m a year in 1952.

Nevertheless under Churchill Britain became the world's third atomic power in October 1952, when a device was set off at Montebello Island, north-west of Australia, aboard the old frigate HMS *Plymouth*, which evaporated. Preparations had of course begun under Labour, which in opposition succumbed to a damaging split over nuclear weapons, helping it to lose the next two general elections. Otherwise there was a solid consensus across the mainstream political spectrum that Britain should acquire and retain nuclear weapons. Labour left-wingers had to channel their opposition into a vigorous Campaign for Nuclear Disarmament, which enjoyed massive public support for at least a decade and revived in the late 1970s; by the end of the century CND seemed to be a spent force and the British nuclear deterrent had become an accepted fact of life for all but a few diehards – even though the collapse of the Soviet Union in 1989–90 left it with nobody immediately obvious to deter. Arrangements for the first British test were in the hands of a specially formed naval squadron.

The United States raised the stakes immeasurably by exploding the world's first hydrogen bomb in the same year, to be followed remarkably quickly by the Soviet Union (which had let off its first atom bomb in 1949) within nine months. Britain's debut in this ultimate-weapon arena would come in 1957. France and then China joined the 'nuclear club', whose five-strong membership coincided exactly with the permanent members of the UN Security Council (and the owners of ballistic-missile nuclear submarines). The spread of nuclear arms transformed the world strategic situation and the Cold War; towards the end of the century the technology spread beyond the Big Five to such volatile states as Israel, India and Pakistan (not to mention apartheid South Africa, Libya, Iraq, and North Korea, all of which tried hard to acquire the technology with various degrees of success). This proliferation raised the spectre of an unspeakable 'accident' arising from the conflicts in which any of those countries were, or might become, engaged. In the meantime a veritable procession of countries would unaccountably fail to be deterred by the West's 'deterrent' capabilities, including Vietnam, Iraq and Argentina (to name but three).

Impressed by the many uses the Americans made of helicopters in the Korean War, including 'guest appearances' on British carriers, the Royal Navy acquired its first squadron of American Sikorsky Whirlwind machines for Malayan operations early in 1953, a period when the Navy was also operating small patrol craft on rivers deep in the jungle of the peninsula. If the British followed the Americans in adopting helicopters, it was the other way about when it came to some of the most important improvements in the history of the aircraft carrier, such as the steam catapult and the angled flight deck.

The catapult, announced in 1952, was the idea of Commander Colin Campbell, RNVR, an engineer who exploited the principle used by the Germans to launch the V1 flying bomb (the first cruise missile). The aircraft was attached to a hook protruding from a slit in a cylinder flush with the deck. High steam pressure was built up behind the piston to which the hook was attached and instantaneously released, propelling the aircraft, its engines already racing, into the air. Cordite was used in early experiments, started in 1948, but steam was found to give a more reliable and sustained thrust. The arrester wire, to halt incoming aircraft on the deck, was already in general use.

In 1953 Captain D. R. F. Cambell, RN, unveiled his idea for the angled flight deck. This enabled carriers to launch and land aircraft at the same time, to use their aircraft lifts while operating aircraft on deck and to 'park' aircraft at the forward end of the main deck (used for launching) without exposing them to the risk of being struck by a landing aircraft (which used the angled deck). As the British had no immediate plan to refit one of their bigger fleet carriers, the only vessels large enough to exploit the idea, the first ship to adopt it was the American carrier *Antietam*. But the conflicts of the early 1950s had persuaded the Admiralty to give priority to carrier construction: five were on the stocks in 1953, the future *Ark Royal*, *Albion*, *Bulwark*, *Centaur* and *Hermes*. As ever, the British were way behind the Americans in carrier aircraft: the unimpressive British Attacker maritime fighter was more than sixty miles per hour slower than the Soviet MiG 15 encountered over Korea. The least happy development in the British carrier forces, however, occurred on *Indomitable*, which was extensively damaged by arson during a particularly severe bout of incendiary and other sabotage in the fleet. Such damage was usually a protest against extended service overseas; but the Egyptians lifted the last restrictions they had imposed on the Suez Canal in April 1953, whereupon extended conscription in the Navy was cancelled in anticipation of reduced deployment and therefore less need for manpower. The restoration of the Fleet Air Arm in place of Naval Aviation was also good for morale.

The official emergence in 1953 of the Soviet Navy as number two in the world, even though it had no battleships or carriers, was another shock to Britain. The Russians had 750,000 men, 350 submarines, over 100 destroyers and twenty modern cruisers. At the same time the First Lord of the Admiralty, the Navy's political chief, lost his right to a Cabinet seat. This was just one of several symptoms of reduction in status for the Navy as a whole, also reflected in its share of the defence budget compared with the Army, which received 60 per cent more, and in its continuing inability to obtain the best aircraft against RAF competition. A combination of disdain and ineptitude seemed to leave the 'silent service' lagging most of the time in the twentieth-century skills of self-promotion, marketing, political in-fighting and public relations. The aristocratic assumption of superiority by the admirals before 1914, Beatty's revealing signal to the fleet on the German naval surrender in 1918, the loss of the Royal Naval Air Service to the RAF in that year, failure to contain the Air Ministry between the world wars and to obtain adequate RAF support during the Second all indicated a certain lack of clout in Cabinet; now the Navy had no voice there, and the British public evinced no sign of the special interest in the service which it had traditionally shown before 1939. The little boy in his sailor-suit was now an antiquated figure, confined to old-fashioned story books. Yet none of the postwar shows of force, foreign interventions and evacuations would have been possible without the Navy, which was increasingly hard put to meet all the demands upon it.

Nonetheless the service managed a turnout of 197 warships for the Queen's Coronation Review at Spithead in summer 1953 (forty-two more than had gathered to mark her father's accession in 1937) – even if some had to be towed into place and others were unarmed. *Vanguard* led the parade, the last public display of the obsession with the battleship that had distracted the attention of the Navy, to its own serious disadvantage, before two world wars. But five fleet carriers were on view, in British terms an unprecedented and unrepeatable display of naval air power.

The long overdue Korean armistice in July 1953 was a welcome relief for the overstretched British fleet. Four RN carriers and HMAS *Sydney* had led a commitment involving thirty-four major warships, many auxiliaries and 25,000 aircraft sorties. Casualties were remarkably light at fifty-nine dead, eighty-five wounded and twenty-eight captured. Submarine involvement was virtually nil and hostile warships were seldom seen and even less often engaged. The main naval activities included air strikes, bombardment and support of landings. The British Navy could now devote more time and resources to the Malayan counter-insurgency operation. The new helicopters were kept very busy shifting munitions and supplies, lifting casualties and making low-level reconnaissance flights. They were also used for the first time anywhere to airlift troops into action, a tactical development soon copied by the US and forces round the world.

There were many other tasks in Coronation Year. Nato staged another northern-waters exercise, 'Mariner', in which its fleets deployed against a postulated 'Redforce' southward breakout. British warships were called in to give humanitarian aid in the great floods of early 1953, whether in East Anglia or in the desperately affected Netherlands. The Mediterranean Fleet provided the first foreign aid when Greece was hit by severe earthquakes in August. The America and West Indies Squadron landed troops in British Guiana (now Guyana) when rioters demanded independence. Three Mediterranean frigates had to be sent to Trieste at the northern end of the Adriatic, postwar bone of contention between Yugoslavia and Italy eventually awarded to the latter.

A small peak on the downward graph of naval manpower occurred in busy 1953, when the strength of the service touched 153,000. One year later the total fell to 137,500 but the Fleet Air Arm was beginning to remedy its technical deficit, acquiring both the Hawker Sea Hawk jet aircraft and the De Havilland Sea Venom all-weather turbojet fighter in 1953 and 1954 respectively. That recruitment of both officers and ratings remained a problem was shown by the restructuring of the officer corps on the introduction of the general service commission in 1954 and the allocation of the first married quarters, as promised five years earlier, in 1955. The stoker left the Navy, to be instantaneously replaced by the 'engineering mechanic', as Admiral Mountbatten, C-in-C in the Mediterranean from 1952, was appointed First Sea Lord and Chief of Naval Staff in 1955, when manpower fell again to 132,000. The British Empire enjoyed its final extension in the same year, when the survey ship HMS *Vidal* with its experimental helicopter formally took possession of the well-named islet of Rockall, 400 miles west of the Outer Hebrides.

Winston Churchill retired in April 1955, making way for his long-serving lieutenant and Foreign Secretary, Anthony Eden. By this time the charismatic former colonel, Gamal Abd al-Nasser, had become President of Egypt. The Anglo-Egyptian Treaty of 1954 provided for a British military withdrawal from the Suez Canal Zone by June 1956, already in progress by the time Eden took over. The British imperial star was still dominant, but on the wane, in the Middle East while the Americans were hoping to establish their post-colonial influence via a general defence pact in the region, lubricated by dollars. Nasser on the other hand was a prominent figure in the new 'Non-Aligned' movement established by the Bandung Conference in April 1955 and supported by such emergent powers as China and India as well as the host country, Indonesia. Egypt had since 1951 been obstructing ships bound to or from Israel from using the Canal, despite a British protest at the United Nations, and tension between Israel and the Arab states was rising. When the pro-Israeli Americans refused to supply Nasser with arms, he turned to the Soviet Union. France supplied arms to Israel; Nasser supported the anti-French revolutionaries in Algeria, scene of one of the bloodiest colonial liberation wars of them all. His designs on the Canal and his flirtation with the Russians, whose offer of financial aid for the colossal Aswan Dam project on the Nile was accepted by Egypt in July over that of the American-controlled World Bank, convinced Eden that Nasser was Britain's public enemy number one in the world. Britain too sold some arms to Israel.

At the end of July, four weeks after the last of 80,000 British troops left the Zone, Nasser nationalized the Canal, purportedly as a means of financing the Aswan project. He offered £70m compensation to shareholders, which included above all Britain (45 per cent), one-quarter of whose imports passed through the Canal, as did some 60,000 of her troops each year, on their way to and from the Far East. Eden's decision to 'stand firm' was the stubborn posture of a man weakened by stones in his bile duct and subject to bouts of fever and liverishness, for which he was constantly taking tablets. Despite a long and distinguished career in diplomacy, Churchill's 'eternal lieutenant' could not delegate, take criticism or shrug off the insults which were the daily small change of domestic politics. Anxious, temperamental and arrogant, Eden was also personally courageous and honest, disdaining political intrigue. Diplomatic intrigue was another matter.

The British Cabinet set up a Suez Committee on July 27. The Chiefs of Staff, including Mountbatten, threatened to resign if ministers ordered an immediate strike such as a paratroop assault. British forces were in no position to mount such a venture without some months' notice, being geared either for all-out war with the Warsaw Pact or small-scale colonial 'brushfire' operations. In addition to Malaya, British troops were increasingly involved in fighting EOKA, the ethnic Greek, pro-independence revolt in Cyprus. French forces were even less ready as the British and French governments secretly colluded in a plot to topple Nasser. The Americans saw the straws in the wind and set their faces against force. President Eisenhower sent his Secretary of State, John Foster Dulles, to dissuade London and Paris, where he became a hate-figure in political circles. At a joint Chiefs of Staff meeting in London the French offered two crack divisions. The British Cabinet decided to use force on 2 August unless negotiations produced a 'reasonable' result reasonably soon. Two dozen maritime powers were invited to a conference about the future of the Canal in mid-August; neither Israel nor Egypt was represented.

The Labour opposition was sympathetic but wanted United Nations approval for the use of force, successfully demanding the recall of the House of Commons from its inordinately lengthy summer recess in September. Unlike the French, the British public was deeply divided as over no other postwar issue except the country's role in a uniting Europe. A prolonged period of sabre-rattling ensued. (The author recalls watching an Army convoy in sand-coloured livery from a flat overlooking the South Circular Road in London. As schoolboys will, he noted vehicle numbers; when the next procession came past, he saw that the numbers were the same, in a different order.) Three carriers, *Bulwark*, *Theseus* and *Ocean*, were specially sent to the eastern Mediterranean, as were landing craft. French ships also moved east as a joint Anglo-French military staff got to work on 5 August. The British as main contributor took the lead; the military supremo, the chiefs of sea, land and air forces were all British with a French deputy. The naval commander was Vice-Admiral Maxwell Richmond. Britain mobilized 50,000 men, half of them reservists, and over 100 ships, including six carriers; France put up 30,000 men and thirty ships, including two carriers.

The nearest practicable assembly point for the swollen British invasion force, its fleet and its 20,000 vehicles was Malta, 1,000 miles away. Cyprus, otherwise the obvious choice, was ruled out as the main British base by the unrest there. The intervention plan, comparable in scale with the Anzio landing, was a remarkable effort in the time available; military observers said it was more complicated in some respects than 'Overlord'. The fleets were to sail from Malta and Algiers on the night of 9 to 10 September. Paratroops were to be dropped as an infantry division approached by sea from Southampton, Royal Marines were to be ferried ashore by helicopters from two carriers and RAF bombers would destroy the Egyptian squadrons, which included more than 100 MiG 15s, on the ground. There would be a march on Cairo on 15 and 16 September but the city would not be occupied. The political aim seemed to be to provoke the Egyptians themselves into deposing Nasser. The plan for Operation 'Musketeer' was ready on 8 August and accepted by the two premiers, Eden and Guy Mollet, two days later. Eden broke with precedent by failing to inform the Labour opposition of these massive preparations, a fact which unsettled the Minister of Defence, Walter Monckton, and the First Sea Lord, Mountbatten. A furious Hugh Gaitskell, the Labour leader, therefore broke with Eden, exacerbating the deep division in the country.

D-day was repeatedly postponed until 26 September, which was also cancelled. The Russians publicly warned against the use of force; privately the Americans did the same, until Dulles made it public at a press conference, an inept slap in the face for Eden. A cynical French summary of the crisis said: '*Il faut coloniser le canal ou canaliser le colonel* [Nasser].' The United Nations Security Council decided to debate the matter on 5 October, the latest D-day. As the British hesitated, the French became more bullish, secretly coordinating the Anglo-French invasion plan with General Moshe Dayan of Israel. This collusion led Monckton to resign as Minister of Defence, a rare example of probity (but not unique: Anthony Nutting, the Foreign Office minister, soon followed, as did Eden's press secretary, William Clark). The basic strategy now was to have Israel attack Egypt across the Sinai Desert in the direction of the Canal, giving the Anglo-French forces the excuse to invade in order to separate the Israelis and the Egyptians!

Finally, after abortive diplomatic moves at the UN and elsewhere, Eden and his Foreign Secretary, Selwyn Lloyd, flew to Paris to meet their French counterparts on 16 October – three days after Eden's rousing, gung-ho, oratorical swansong at the Conservative Party Conference. In naval terms, it was perilously late in the year for amphibious operations in the Mediterranean. Stage one of the repeatedly revised Anglo-French plan was now to have the RAF's bombers, the only force available and up to the job, destroy the Egyptian Air Force on the ground. This would happen thirty-six hours after the Israelis attacked, on 29 October. And so it came to pass.

The Anglo-French carriers sailed from Malta on the 27th. The 'ultimatum' to both sides to withdraw ten miles from either side of the Canal to allow a 'temporary' intervention by the British and

French was well received by the Israelis, who had to advance in places in order to comply! Some 130 warships and 100 landing craft and merchantmen were poised for action in the south-east corner of the Mediterranean when the go-ahead was given by General Sir Charles Keightley at 5 a.m. on the 31st. Another fleet of 100 ships would follow from Malta. After radio and leaflet warnings to Egyptian civilians to keep clear of the targeted airfields, 200 RAF and forty French bombers delivered a remarkably accurate series of annihilating raids on a dozen Egyptian airbases. In the Gulf of Suez the cruiser HMS *Newfoundland* sank an Egyptian frigate. The carriers *Albion*, *Ark Royal*, *Bulwark* and *Eagle* carried out air strikes while *Theseus* and *Ocean* deployed twenty Whirlwind and Sycamore helicopters to ferry marines into the Canal Zone, as had already been tried on a smaller scale in Malaya, one of the only aspects of the whole operation admired (and inevitably imitated) by the Americans, and its sole tactical novelty.

President Nasser pulled his troops out of Sinai and concentrated them round Cairo, anticipating an Anglo-French landing at Alexandria. Nearly fifty blockships were sunk in the Canal by the Egyptians. Israel achieved all its objectives by 5 November, by which time it had conquered the Sinai peninsula and taken many thousands of Egyptian prisoners – and vitiated the thin excuse for Anglo-French landings to separate the combatants. Israel said it would accept the UN Security Council's ceasefire proposal if Egypt did. Despite the unsubtle arrival of the US 6th Fleet under Vice-Admiral Brown in the middle of the very area chosen by Vice-Admiral Durnford-Slater for his carrier operations, the latter calmly provided air cover for the landings by one British and one French parachute battalion near Port Said on the 5th, as well as landing 45 Commando of 415 Royal Marines by helicopter. Destroyers bombarded the port, which soon fell to the Marines.

The follow-up convoy arrived from Malta on time, shadowed by two American submarines. But under intense pressure from the Americans and international opinion, the British and French agreed to a ceasefire at midnight on 6 November, by which time an armoured column was well on its way from Port Said to its objective, the port of Suez at the southern end. Israel had what it wanted; Eden was ill, fearful of unrest at home and bloodcurdling threats from Moscow; and a run on sterling began when the US blocked Britain's plan to withdraw capital from the International Monetary Fund.

Having used the stick without subtlety, the Americans now saw fit to offer a carrot: a £300m IMF loan to ease the balance of payments crisis if Britain declared a ceasefire by midnight on the eve of the US presidential election. Harold Macmillan, Chancellor of the Exchequer, threatened to resign if Eden did not accept. He did so, only informing Mollet afterwards. The British and French handed over to a United Nations force as the Israelis withdrew behind their borders. Eden resigned on health grounds, to be succeeded by Macmillan. The humiliating fiasco was the last gasp of the 1904 Entente Cordiale and of Anglo-French hegemony in the Middle East: Britain, dependent on the United States for oil, support for the pound and protection from the Soviet Union, never again pursued a foreign policy unacceptable to Washington. The Commonwealth, not consulted, was undermined and became a talking shop. France decided to became a law unto herself, eventually withdrawing from the military infrastructure of Nato, which had to move from Paris to Brussels, while building her future with a resurgent West Germany at the heart of the new European Community. When Selwyn Lloyd soon afterwards visited Dulles, in hospital with terminal cancer, the humourless American disingenuously asked: 'Why did you stop?' The three-month-long Suez crisis was a tragicomic political disaster for Britain; in the global context it also left the Russians with a free hand to crush the simultaneous Hungarian uprising, which a preoccupied Washington all but ignored at the time.

For the British Navy, the massive mobilization for just thirty-six operational hours had been an organizational triumph, despite damaging political vacillation in the week beforehand: tactical surprise was complete. The use of naval air power, including the spectacular, five-at-a-time helicopter 'train service' delivering marines exactly where they needed to be and taking just one minute to reload, had been exemplary; the entire amphibious side of the operation had gone off without a hitch in a masterpiece of improvisation. For this Mountbatten deserved much credit, especially as he was among those military leaders who foresaw the political and economic consequences and had commendably democratic doubts about Eden's failure to consult the opposition. But much of the blame attached to the politicians for the Suez shambles unfairly rubbed off on the armed forces.

The Navy's 'reward' for this loyally and efficiently wasted effort was the most radical retrenchment since 1945, as foreshadowed in the White Paper presented by the Minister of Defence, Duncan Sandys, in April 1957. It marked Britain's wholehearted adoption of a nuclear deterrent strategy predicated on a short war between Nato and the Warsaw Pact; otherwise there would be limited, brushfire conflicts in far-flung places, to which a carrier or destroyer might have to be sent. The underlying motive was financial rather than philosophical, to save money on the defence budget, which was dominated by personnel costs. The Navy was ultimately to be reduced to 75,000 and was allotted no role in delivering the nuclear deterrent, such as by carrier aircraft. ASW ships and aircraft in the north Atlantic were to be reduced, despite warnings about the ever-expanding Soviet submarine fleet. A short-war strategy was seized upon as making deep cuts in all the armed services possible: there could be no effective defence against nuclear attack, apparently – an updated version of the inter-war doctrine that 'the bomber will always get through'. National service was to be abolished in 1961.

'Natural wastage' and voluntary redundancy reduced the Navy by 5,500 to 120,000 as the Reserve Fleet, including four battleships and twenty-one cruisers, was scrapped wholesale and almost 100 shore bases and facilities at home and abroad were closed. The 827 warships on the books in 1957 were reduced to 228 in 1958, when the service lost a net total of another 10,000 personnel; but pay was raised in the hope of stabilizing numbers for the future: an able seaman got a basic £5 19s per week and a lieutenant-commander started on £1,022 a year. The Volunteer Reserve was absorbed into the Royal Naval Reserve. A Flag Officer, Sea Training, was appointed and a school of seamanship set up at Portland.

Midshipmen had left the 'gunroom' for the schoolroom: the rank was abolished at sea as part of the 1954 reform of the officer corps. Even the uniform had changed: white caps were worn all year round from 1956 as part of a general modernization. But morale and recruitment continued to cause concern. Sabotage, especially on carriers, flourished whenever a long overseas commission was in prospect, and the government borrowed more money to hasten construction of married quarters. Complaints about harsh discipline and poor food often surfaced in the press in the mid-1950s. *Vanguard* was placed in reserve rather than refitted to save on manpower, and a brand-new destroyer had to go straight into mothballs for the same reason. The practice of buying out, last in force in 1939, was brought back fifteen years later as a safety valve for the seriously discontented; free of charge after sixteen years' service, it was permitted after only three (at a price that fell for each further year served). Overseas commissions were reduced from two and a half years to one, except on carriers (two) and in places where men could take their families with them. Some pay rates were raised and better conditions were introduced both at sea and ashore, although irritating petty restrictions remained: the Admiralty solemnly took the bold decision to allow junior ratings to go ashore on leave in civilian clothes. The distinctions between Seaman officers and others were abolished; Engineer, Electrical and Supply officers all joined them on a General List. Commanders and upwards were divided into 'post' and 'general' (informally, 'wet' and 'dry') categories; all were equally eligible for flags.

By the time of Suez, British carriers had adopted another home-grown innovation, the gyroscopically stabilized mirror invented by Commander H. C. N. Goodhart, RN, in 1954, which made landing on a heaving deck much safer. Once again the Americans copied as mirrors and angled decks cut crashes by 80 per cent. But the Navy, as ever, was laggardly in marketing the flexibility of carriers as a means of projecting air power anywhere on the seven seas, not merely for offshore and amphibious operations. This reflected not only the customary public relations weakness of the naval high command but also a lack of penetrating strategic thought. The latest aircraft were being introduced agonizingly slowly thanks to financial constraints, teething troubles and poor choices, such as the Attacker and the De Havilland DH 110 Sea Vixen. Helicopters were in use for ASW purposes (845 Squadron was the first British unit to use the Sikorsky S55 in this important role).

The Sandys White Paper bore the title *Outline of Future Policy*, and lived up to its name in many ways, not least in foreshadowing Britain's first nuclear submarine (eventually christened HMS *Dreadnought*). The many and varied developments, not forgetting frequent failures, in and around Britain's submarine arm in the crucial decade of the 1950s deserve a special mention. There were three disasters. The war had prevented a proper investigation of the *Thetis* tragedy which immediately preceded it, but in 1946 the Admiralty set up a committee under Captain Philip Ruck-Keene, RN, to look into thirty-two submarine accidents and also to examine escape methods. The committee's work was exhaustive, starting with interviews with twenty-eight survivors from five navies and ending with recommendations still followed aboard the latest nuclear submarines more than half a century later. But even the most far-sighted proposals could not be adopted overnight, or in some cases for years, as the Navy, like the rest of the nation, passed through the long grey austerity zone.

On 12 January 1950 the submarine *Truculent* was on the surface of the Thames estuary on her way upstream to Sheerness after a day's trials. She had just undergone a long refit at nearby Chatham and was due to set off for Scotland the next day. Downstream amid the heavy shipping traffic came the little coastal tanker SS *Divina*, at 643 tons rather less substantial than the submarine. Loaded with petrol, she sported a bright red hazard-warning light at the top of her foremast as required by the Port of London Authority (the only red light normally seen on a vessel is the navigation light on the port side). The submarine could not turn to starboard to avoid her, as navigational 'rules of the road' required, because of the shallow coastal water and therefore turned to port, those on the conning tower mystified by the strange lighting display on the approaching vessel – which struck amidships with her bow. The height of the red light may have persuaded the submariners that the small ship was more distant than she was. The boat went down in one minute in just forty feet of water, taking sixty-seven sailors and dockyard workers with her; the five on the bridge were swept overboard and rescued by a Dutch ship. All sixty-seven managed a superbly disciplined exodus from the sunken submarine. But the fast-running tidal water was icy and only ten were picked up alive, turning what should have been a brilliant escape into a tragedy. Had the thermal escape suits, recommended by Ruck-Keene four years earlier and slowly being introduced, been issued to *Truculent*, only a few non-swimmers might have died.

Just fifteen months later, on 16 April 1951, the new submarine HMS *Affray* left Portsmouth submerged for the waters off Falmouth on the Cornish coast, where she was due to surface the next morning at 8.30. As per Ruck-Keene, when she was one hour overdue the signal 'Submiss' went out to all ships in the area, followed one hour later by 'Subsunk'. The largest search operation ever mounted by the Royal Navy involved more than twenty ships, including American, Dutch and French warships and dozens of aircraft. The missing boat could have been anywhere in thousands of square miles of ocean and the massive search was called off after three days. Seventy-five men, more than on *Thetis*, made this the worst British submarine disaster numerically. The Navy's deep-diving vessel *Reclaim* eventually found the wreck north of the Channel Islands and well outside the main search area six weeks later, in 300 feet of water. Divers established that the boat's snort-mast (breathing tube) had broken off – because it had been made of inferior metal to save money, despite a warning from the steel supplier. There may also have been a gas explosion, but no full explanation of the boat's loss was ever obtained. The last reported words of Admiral Sir Max Horton, the wartime submarine chief, as he lay dying at the end of July 1951 were: 'Any news of the *Affray*?' As he had been told long since that she had been found, the sad mystery must have been preying on his mind.

We noted above how Britain decided after the war to pursue the advanced German technology of hydrogen peroxide propulsion, which Professor Walter believed could deliver phenomenal underwater speeds, leaving nuclear energy to the Americans for the time being. Two experimental boats, *Explorer* and *Excalibur*, were built in the 1950s to join the converted HMS *Meteorite* in trials, but were eventually scrapped because the system was unstable, volatile and lethally dangerous; yet the former did deliver a contemporary underwater speed record of over twenty-five knots. A series of in-board explosions miraculously failed to lead to a tragedy. But in tandem with the experiments on 'High Test' hydrogen peroxide engines for submarines, trials were undertaken of a torpedo powered by the same method. On 16 June 1955 one of these blew up spontaneously in its tube aboard the submarine *Sidon* as she lay alongside in Portsmouth; thirteen men died. This marked the end of experimentation with hydrogen peroxide: the Navy now turned its attention to nuclear propulsion, in which the Americans were rapidly establishing a world lead (USS *Nautilus* was launched as early as 1954). Vickers Shipbuilding and Engineering Ltd, whose yard at Barrow-in-Furness pioneered British submarine construction and dominated it throughout the century, formed a new subsidiary to develop nuclear submarines in 1956. Sandys set his face against nuclear-powered surface ships on grounds of cost, a saving which for once happily coincided with safety and environmental considerations. A nuclear reactor was much more appropriate for underwater use, where it could produce unlimited quantities of desalinated water and oxygen along with the steam to propel the first true submarines (as distinct from submersibles, which is what their predecessors really were), at phenomenal speed underwater for months on end.

The British Navy's postwar efforts to produce reliable, modern torpedoes were dogged with failures and disappointments well into the 1980s (the GEC-Marconi Spearfish, ordered in 1982, was delivered only in 1994, having reportedly exceeded its development budget by a cool £186m). A more profitable area of research concerned the thermal layers in the sea and how submarines could use them to evade detection by sonar. Depth charge technology reached its limit in 1953 with the Limbo mortar, which had a range of 2,000 yards and could be fired forward or to either side at various elevations; it replaced the wartime Squid, which could fire 1,200 yards over the bow. The main ASW development in this period was the helicopter, deployed exclusively by carriers until 1960, when frigates and destroyers began to acquire them.

The sensitivity and accuracy of both active and passive sonar (previously ASDIC and hydrophones respectively) developed rapidly after the Second World War, with Britain often in the lead. Passive sonar was preferred aboard submarines because active, with its notorious 'ping', gave away the user's position.

It was probably par for the course that Commander Lionel 'Buster' Crabbe, RN, the Navy's leading diver, went down to inspect the bottom of the cruiser *Ordzhonikidze* in Portsmouth after she had brought the Soviet leaders, Bulganin and Khrushchev, on an official visit in April 1956; but he disappeared without trace. Britain possessed sixty submarines at this time, three more than she had in 1939, but Russia was reportedly adding more than this to her fleet every year. Spying on the expanding Russian fleet was a dangerous business, one of the principal tasks of Nato submarines, in which British boats played an important role throughout the Cold War period, sometimes only narrowly evading disaster. Retired submariners made clear to the author the well-nigh unbearable tension of this long-running exercise in brinkmanship, so secret that anodyne awards such as the OBE were made to commanders who would otherwise have received a gallantry award, such as the DSO or DSC. The risks, apart from detection and the ensuing diplomatic furore, included collision, breakdown and running aground in perilous, ice-strewn waters without the option of calling for help. The Soviets for their part blatantly deployed huge numbers of 'trawlers' whose main catch was electronic, via their top-heavy array of antennae, as they shadowed any Nato surface warships on the move.

The Navy's 103 flag posts were cut by a quarter in 1958; even so the time was not so far off when the number of admirals would exceed the number of major warships in the fleet. Some 2,000 officers less senior, including 100 marines, were made redundant. The Navy remained busy. Four British carriers were involved in operations off Lebanon alongside the US 6th Fleet in another crisis in 1958. In the same year the first of three bizarre conflicts, known as the Cod Wars, broke out over Iceland's determination to control fishing rights in the waters round the huge volcanic island, a member of Nato. It went on in desultory fashion for two years as Icelandic gunboats confronted frigates guarding British trawlers – until they withdrew from the twelve-mile limit. In 1959 the light fleet carrier *Hermes*, last of the wartime programme, was completed; so was HMS *Oberon*, first of the most successful British postwar diesel-electric submarine class.

Having softened many, and averted not a few, of the naval cuts in the Sandys programme with a mixture of charm and hard politicking, Admiral of the Fleet Earl Mountbatten of Burma finally achieved his ambition of surpassing his father when he became the first Chief of Defence Staff (CDS) in 1959, after four years (a double term) as First Sea Lord. This final appointment, which he held for six years, was a highly visible manifestation of the impending convergence of the command and administration of the three services under a single Ministry of Defence (MoD), which was to supersede Admiralty, War Office and Air Ministry from 1964. Its minister (later secretary of state) was their sole voice in Cabinet, with junior ministers looking after the individual services under him. Although the MoD produced no startling reductions in the civil service 'tail' administering the forces (on the contrary!) there were gains in standardization and inter-service collaboration and less rivalry of the kind at which the Navy so often seemed to lose. It is no exaggeration to say that as First Sea Lord under Sandys, Mountbatten was the right man in the right place at the right time and saved the Royal Navy as a versatile fighting force. The price was the adoption of a strategically defensive posture in which the Navy concentrated on anti-submarine warfare in the north-east Atlantic, leaving the strategic maritime strike role to the much stronger American Navy with its huge, nuclear-armed, carrier task groups. As the British Empire rapidly wound down in the 1950s and early 1960s, the writing went up on the wall for the Royal Navy's carriers.

As the first CDS, Mountbatten went on to make a crucial contribution to armed forces integration, the value of which was enhanced by the fact that he was still in place for the first year of Harold Wilson's Labour government, which ousted the Conservatives after thirteen years in 1964. In 1960 he oversaw another radical departure when the headquarters of the C-in-C Home Fleet (who was also Nato C-in-C, Eastern Atlantic) moved inland, to HMS *Warrior* at Northwood, Middlesex, in reality a bunker (the Royal Navy always treated shore establishments as ships). By this time nearly three-quarters of naval officers and three-fifths of ratings were based ashore in a service which now mustered just over 100,000. Three vessels made their bow in 1960 as if to underline the pace of change. *Dreadnought*, the first British nuclear-powered submarine, and the destroyer HMS *Devonshire*, the Navy's first guided-missile ship, were launched; and the *Bulwark* was recommissioned as the first Commando carrier, specifically for service outside the Nato area. *Albion* would soon follow.

The Navy and Vickers had to admit defeat with the *Dreadnought*; Britain was not yet capable of producing a viable underwater reactor and was obliged to buy one from the Americans, making her in effect the seventh member of a class of six (the US '*Skipjack*' class), although her hull design differed considerably. There were also problems in producing the high-grade steel needed to enable the boat to operate at unheard-of depths.

The vast expense of the nuclear programme inevitably hastened cuts elsewhere as the Navy shed foreign commitments such as the East Indies Squadron, the Hong Kong, Trincomalee, Malta and Singapore dockyards, the Simonstown base in South Africa and more and more facilities at home, including the historic Nore command on the Thames estuary and six naval air stations. Vice-Admiral Hyman G. Rickover, the organizational genius behind the American nuclear submarine programme, and his staff gave invaluable advice to his British opposite number, Rear-Admiral G. A. M. Wilson, throughout the project, but *Dreadnought* still took four years to build, amid industrial relations problems, never long absent from British yards in peace or war. The second British nuclear boat, *Valiant*, would, however, be fitted with an all-British reactor. The naval argot for this was 'the kettle' and the radiation threat it represented to the crews of the earliest nuclear boats was clearly underestimated all round. Veteran sailors and dockyard workers developed startling cancers and told horror stories of how hot water from the 'kettle' was used to brew tea and safety precautions were routinely ignored. The MoD joined the Nuclear Industry Compensation Scheme only in 1994; safety standards were sharply raised when naval yards were privatized.

The US Navy meanwhile, in November 1960, was allowed to establish a forward base for its ballistic-missile nuclear submarines at Holy Loch in Strathclyde, Scotland. British boats would operate from Faslane nearby and be maintained at Rosyth. It is a safe bet that this region of Scotland was heavily targeted by Soviet missiles.

British defence policy in the final years of Conservative rule, and beyond 1964, was chaotic. The country's last three cruisers, *Tiger*, *Lion* and *Blake*, part of the wartime overhang, were repeatedly delayed as their role and design were chopped and changed. The hybrid trio never made much of a mark in the fleet, and *Blake* went straight into mothballs to free her crew of 700 for other duties. Problems with their guns and their engines seemed endless as hold-ups mounted in naval and civil dockyards generally. But among the better decisions taken at the start of the 1960s were orders for the amphibious assault ships *Fearless* and *Intrepid*, with their helicopter decks and docks for landing craft, and the highly successful 'Leander' frigate. Poor old *Vanguard* ran aground – off Portsmouth – on her way to the scrapyard in August 1960, an ignominious end to the Navy's association with the line-of-battle ship.

Costly aircraft and missile projects were commissioned and then abandoned, notably the Blue Streak air-launched nuclear-tipped missile, intended to extend the life of the RAF V-bombers, custodians of Britain's strategic deterrent; when it was cancelled, the government opted for the American Skybolt missile instead – which was itself cancelled when ballistic missiles in land silos and on submarines became available. Prime Minister Macmillan met President John F. Kennedy at Nassau, Bahamas, in December 1962 and all but begged him to allow Britain to buy the Polaris nuclear-tipped, submarine-launched ballistic missile, which was coming into service with the US Navy and initially had a range of 1,200 miles. What this meant for the British Navy is considered in the next chapter.

Regardless of high politics, incompetence and vacillation at home, the fleet was still being kept busy in far-flung places. The

Malayan emergency, a dragging commitment for the Navy, was officially declared at an end on 31 July 1960 after twelve years, although it had been contained by the mid-1950s. The result was a costly but definitive British victory over Communist insurrection, even though it had been strongly supported by the ethnic Chinese population and China itself. British success against jungle insurgents and guerrillas helped to persuade the Americans, and may have deluded the French before their defeat in 1954, that the same could be achieved in Vietnam. The way was clear for Malayan independence; but British military involvement in the region was far from over. Malaya, British North Borneo (Sarawak, Brunei and Sabah) and Singapore (which later broke away) formed the independent Malaysian Federation in 1963, in the teeth of strong political opposition from the Philippines and threats (including active insurgency) from Indonesia. By the end of 1962 two carriers, two Royal Marine Commandos on *Albion* and *Bulwark*, two helicopter squadrons plus destroyer, frigate, minesweeper and submarine formations were involved in the burgeoning 'Confrontation' with an expansionist Indonesia, whose territory shared a long border with British North Borneo. Admiral Sir David Luce was appointed the first combined C-in-C, Far East, with Vice-Admiral Desmond Dreyer under him as Flag Officer, Far East Fleet, which was expanded again, mainly at the expense of the Mediterranean.

The Middle East continued to draw in British forces. In June 1961 the Sheik of Kuwait asked for British protection against Iraq. The ever-busy *Bulwark* with 42 Commando was hastily dispatched from Karachi, backed by: three frigates and a landing-ship with Centurion tanks, 45 Commando flown in from Aden, the carriers *Victorious* and *Centaur*, four more destroyers, four frigates, plus supporting ships – all diverted to the sweltering Persian Gulf so that Britain had 5,700 marines and troops ashore within nine days. The RAF sent fighters from Aden to work under carrier control. Iraq backed down – for the time being – and the impromptu armada could disperse.

The British fleet was unable to make its allotted contribution to Nato's autumn exercise because of the Kuwait crisis. But the first frigate to carry a helicopter, HMS *Ashanti*, was commissioned in November, and the gas-turbine engine made its first appearance, though in combination at first with steam turbines. The Americans were impressed and bought two Rolls Royce gas-turbine engines for experiments. The Seaslug anti-aircraft missile, after many vicissitudes and delays (and runaway expenditure), was proving itself at both high and low levels. The Buccaneer bomber and the Westland Wessex ASW helicopter were about to join the fleet, though not without teething troubles. The first all-British nuclear submarine, *Valiant*, was launched at last in 1963, when an experimental Vertical Take-Off and Landing aircraft was flown from *Ark Royal*. At a more mundane level, cafeterias became universal throughout the fleet, ousting the last traces of the old messing system.

It was not only the Americans who respected British naval inventiveness. The Russians did too, and showed it by elaborate espionage operations against such establishments as the new one at Portland for underwater weapons, where crucial work was done on 'dipping sonar' (the Canadian variable-depth sonar for helicopters) and silent running, a field in which Britain led the world. The 'Portland spy ring', Britons led by a KGB agent styled 'Gordon Lonsdale', went on trial at the Central Criminal Court (the Old Bailey in London) early in 1961. At the end of the following year William Vassall, an Admiralty clerk, was convicted of spying, having been ensnared by a homosexual 'honey-trap' while serving at the British Embassy in Moscow; he spied for the Russians for six years on his return to London.

These and other cases led to near-panic in Whitehall, complaints from the Americans and a drastic tightening of security in the armed forces, especially the Navy. The greatest scandal of them all broke in 1963, when the Secretary of State for War, John Profumo, was found to be sharing a prostitute with the junior Soviet naval attaché, Captain Ivanov, who had been making a special study of British nuclear submarine plans for the KGB. A tired Macmillan resigned and Sir Alec Douglas-Home took over as Prime Minister, leading the Conservatives to a surprisingly narrow defeat in the general election of October 1964. As his successor, Harold Wilson, was wont to say, it was 'time for a change'. In this regard there was to be no relief for the Royal Navy: far from it.

14

Finding a Role

Still reeling from the effects of the Conservative defence review by Duncan Sandys, the Navy and the new Ministry of Defence braced themselves for another, promised by Denis Healey, Labour's Defence Secretary, as 1964 drew to a close – duly begun in 1965. The last meeting of the historic Board of Admiralty before it was subsumed into the all-services Defence Council had taken place; the office of Lord High Admiral previously exercised collectively by the Board reverted nominally to the Sovereign. Business at sea was as brisk as ever. Royal Marines delivered by HMS *Centaur* suppressed an army mutiny in the former colony of Tanganyika in east Africa, and the 'Confrontation' with Indonesia got into its stride, with the Far East Fleet protecting the new Federation of Malaysia. But in 1965 the strength of the Navy fell below 100,000 to 97,000. The service made a rare ceremonial appearance in the heart of London early in the year when 156 sailors drew the gun-carriage carrying the body of Sir Winston Churchill, First Lord of the Admiralty at the start of both world wars, to his state funeral at St Paul's Cathedral with a solemn precision to challenge the Brigade of Guards.

The first major casualty of Labour's new defence broom, by far the most important in terms of equipment, was the cancellation of 'CVA.01', a projected 50,000-ton fleet carrier announced by the Conservatives in July 1963 (when no mention was made of a second or a third as originally envisaged). The ship was to have operated conventional and VTOL aircraft. Britain's carriers were ageing; *Victorious* and *Ark Royal* were to be scrapped in the early 1970s but *Eagle* and *Hermes* were provisionally expected to serve until 1980. *Centaur* was not even mentioned. This projection implied the scrapping of American-style task forces built round a carrier because, given normal maintenance requirements, there would soon be only one British fleet carrier at sea at a time, which meant either no carrier for Nato deployment or none for East of Suez. The

357

RAF breezily argued that there was no need for any carriers at all because, outside Nato, British forces would only intervene when invited, which meant that the RAF could provide the air cover from local landward bases. The two services were also locked in dispute about future aircraft orders, on which they could not agree. The RAF wanted the proposed British TSR2 long-range strike aircraft (which Labour soon cancelled) while the Navy preferred the Buccaneer and the US Phantom (with Rolls Royce Spey engines), even though it was too heavy for British carriers.

A new and faintly ridiculous assignment for the Royal Navy followed the entirely ridiculous 'Unilateral Declaration of Independence' (UDI) by the white minority regime in Rhodesia, led by Ian Smith, at eleven minutes past eleven o'clock on 11 November 1965 (the forty-seventh anniversary of the 1918 Armistice, to the minute). Early in 1966 the 'Beira Patrol' was inaugurated by HMS *Eagle*, soon to be relieved by *Lowestoft* and a succession of frigates over the next nine years. The Mozambique port of Beira was the oil terminal to which landlocked Rhodesia's oil supplies had been delivered, now banned under UN sanctions, which had been proposed by Britain as an alternative to military action. Thanks to the vigilant British naval presence, not a drop of oil was delivered by this route; unfortunately, South Africa's white minority regime allowed petroleum products, thoughtfully supplied by local subsidiaries of British oil companies among others, to flow by road tanker over the border at Beit Bridge. Prime Minister Harold Wilson, unusually for such a consummate politician, publicly excluded the use of military force against the Smith regime in advance, effectively encouraging the Rhodesians and South Africans to drive a procession of tankers through sanctions for a decade and a half. The Navy's other role in the long drawn-out impasse of UDI was to provide floating hotels for fruitless negotiations, at sea in every sense, between Wilson and Smith: first the cruiser *Tiger* (1966) and then the amphibious assault ship *Fearless* (1968).

Indonesia's will to sustain its Confrontation with Malaysia collapsed under the strain of internal problems and disorder, which led to the downfall of President Sukarno and the rise of General Suharto in his place in 1966 – but not before Royal Marines had carried out an assault, the first of its kind in the crisis, on Limbang in Brunei. One of the more dramatic last retreats from empire occurred in 1967, when the Navy's aircraft and marines covered the British Army's fraught withdrawal from Aden after a long period of tension, terrorism and riots by nationalists. The blistering port of Aden at the mouth of the Red Sea had been an important staging post on the route from Britain via the Mediterranean and the Suez Canal to India, but rather lost its point in 1947 when the latter became independent. Aden and its south Yemeni hinterland became the short-lived People's Democratic Republic of Yemen until it united with the Yemen Arab Republic (north Yemen) in 1990. Closer to home, and not without embarrassment, Fleet Air Arm Buccaneers joined the RAF in vainly trying to destroy the giant tanker *Torrey Canyon* by bombing after she ran aground off Cornwall and leaked masses of crude oil in spring 1967.

The contraction and streamlining of the Navy continued, even as it was acquiring the most powerful weapons system the fleet (and the nation) had ever possessed: four nuclear-powered submarines armed with the Polaris ballistic nuclear missile. The forces in general and the Navy in particular had often come under attack from politicians and parliamentary committees for overspending on abortive or inordinately delayed and uncontrollable projects, duplication, quarrelling with the RAF, maladministration and general waste or inefficiency. If there was ever an outstanding exception, it was surely the Polaris programme, which was placed in the hands of Rear-Admiral Hugh Mackenzie only days after Harold Macmillan talked President Kennedy into selling Britain the system.

The diminutive Highlander Mackenzie, nicknamed Rufus for his red hair and previously Flag Officer, Submarines, was appointed Chief Executive for the Polaris programme, which probably made him the most important submariner in British history. From 1946 to 1948 he had run the notorious 'perisher' course for would-be submarine skippers. His last service to the Navy was uniquely intricate, involving not only supervising the construction of four boats with all their complex command and control and navigation equipment but also the acquisition of British-made warheads for the A3 version of the missile with its improved, 1,500-mile range. The first to be launched was HMS *Resolution* in 1966; she set off from HMS *Neptune* at Faslane on her first armed patrol, on time, in June 1968, when Wilson dedicated the force to Nato. The British hull was fitted with an American-designed mid-section containing the sixteen missile silos. *Renown*, *Repulse* and *Revenge* followed (Labour cancelled the fifth), also on time and on budget, and on 1 July 1969, to the ill concealed chagrin of the RAF, the Royal Navy took over, for the foreseeable future, responsibility for Britain's strategic deterrent from the V-bomber force.

For maximum efficiency of use, each boat had two captains and two crews, 'port' and 'starboard', one of which sailed the boat on its two-month cruise to undisclosed parts of the deep Atlantic while the other underwent training, lived with family and took leave. With four submarines, at least one would always be on patrol, its whereabouts unknown to anybody, even if one was in dock, a third on the way out and the fourth on the way home. Mackenzie retired as a vice-admiral with the KCB but lived to attend the ceremony at Faslane in August 1996 marking the final paying off of the Polaris force after twenty-eight years, just two months before his death. The 'Chevaline' programme extended the life of the system by updating the weapons during the premiership of James Callaghan (1976–9).

But the Navy, inevitably, had to pay a high price for this awesome if invisible new power, in the form of further reductions in its visibly dwindling surface fleet. There would be no more carriers, apparently, a decision which not only hurt morale but also prompted a spectacular political crisis when the Navy Minister, Christopher Mayhew, and the First Sea Lord, Admiral Sir David Luce, resigned in protest in February 1966. The Defence Secretary, Denis Healey, also announced that Britain would refrain from armed intervention anywhere unless with an ally (i.e. usually the United States). But Luce's successor, Admiral Sir Varyl Begg, almost immediately set up a Future Fleet Working Party to look into the types of ship a slimmed-down Navy should choose for its increasingly circumscribed role. Begg, who commanded in the Far East for most of the 'Confrontation', was no enthusiast for big, expensive carriers but saw no reason to sacrifice the Navy's ability to project air power by sea altogether. The result in 1967 was the concept of the 'through-deck cruiser', a small carrier by any other name (the word was forbidden in high naval circles: Begg actually sacked an officer for breaking the taboo). Such was the genesis of the 'Invincible' class that became the pride of the surface fleet for the rest of the century. One is reminded of the 'protected milling' of the First World War and how one could not call them convoys, or the 1939 'escorts' that could not be called destroyers.

The Home Fleet became the Western Fleet in 1967, when out-lying formations were subsumed into the renamed command, based at Northwood; the Mediterranean Fleet was now abolished, as foreshadowed by the Tories (part of the price for Polaris), after a long and glorious history as the Navy's senior command outside home waters. All these changes and reductions in the surface fleet pointed to one conclusion, duly announced by Healey in January 1968 with three years' notice: Britain's withdrawal from 'East of Suez'. The remaining carriers would be paid off also in 1971. Only as recently as 1967 had the government been talking of sustaining such a capability; but a deepening economic crisis forced the second Wilson administration to slash expenditure wherever it could. The dockyards at Bahrain and Singapore would be handed over to the governments of those states; and the planned purchase of the American F111 'swing-wing' bomber was cancelled – the very aircraft with which the RAF had planned to fly maritime air cover from the friendly airbases nearest to any battles Britain was likely to fight in future.

Healey's most important announcement by far, however, was that the future role of the British surface fleet would be entirely within Nato and focused on ASW. This fundamental change of policy was even more drastic than the Sandys review of the previous decade: the Royal Navy would withdraw from 'blue water' to the grey seas of the north-east Atlantic. Shortly after the announcement, Nato set up STANAVFORLANT (Standing Naval Force, Atlantic), in which the Royal Navy would play its new role with seven other regional navies. At the same time an unhappy, American-inspired experiment aimed at establishing a Multilateral Nuclear Force with ships from the North Sea navies, including multinational crews and intended to deploy Polaris missiles on surface vessels, went the same way as Wilson's abortive proposal for an 'Atlantic Nuclear Force', made to appease his anti-nuclear left wing. Britain kept its 'independent' nuclear deterrent (which had depended on American know-how and consent for its construction); France kept hers, built round land-based rockets at first and then extending to ballistic-missile nuclear submarines (the Americans turned out to have given the French considerable technological help also, but this was not revealed until well after the death of President Charles de Gaulle).

Even now, however, the story of the changing Navy was by no means all retrenchment except for Polaris. The historic title of

C-in-C, Portsmouth, was abolished (C-in-C, Naval Home Command, absorbed the role); and naval dockyards at Plymouth and even Portsmouth completed their last ships. But the fleet was the first in the world to deploy vessels wholly powered by the revolutionary British gas-turbine engines in 1968. In the following year the Navy had to intervene about as close to home as it was possible to get, when the first Royal Marines were deployed in Northern Ireland alongside the Army, as the age-old hatred between Protestants and Catholics, 'loyalists' and republicans, flared up again and Wilson decided to send in troops to try to keep them apart. Naval patrols were also used to watch for arms smugglers. But in the same year the Fleet Air Arm got its first squadron of (land-based) Phantoms; the first excellent Type 21 frigate, the future HMS *Amazon*, was laid down; the first Westland Wessex helicopter was taken into service; and of course the Navy once again became the guardian of the nation's chief strategic armament, as it had been until the heyday of the battleship passed a generation earlier.

The costly nuclear hunter-killer (later known as fleet) submarine became the new capital ship in the 1960s; the Polaris boats surpassed them in technological complexity and firepower if not in speed, but could not be used except in a crisis the world preferred to regard as unthinkable. All in all, therefore, the cost-driven strategic rethink of 1968 stands as the most far-reaching shift in British naval policy since the Second World War. But, as we shall see, nothing lasts for ever, not even a 'final' withdrawal from East of Suez or abandonment of the aircraft carrier (Washington tried various inducements to persuade Wilson to keep the carriers beyond 1971, to no avail). The irresistible logic of events from the beginning of 1968 and what they meant for the Royal Navy led to another rationalization after Labour lost the 1970 general election to the Tories: in 1971 the Far East command and the Western Fleet were wound up and Britain was left with a single fleet, run from Northwood and led by an admiral junior only to the First Sea Lord and the Chief of the Defence Staff: the Commander-in-Chief, Fleet.

The said fleet had been constructed in the main to provide ASW (frigates) and anti-aircraft (destroyers) protection to the carriers that were now about to be scrapped. The '*Tiger*'-class cruisers were hybridized by flattening the after section so that they could operate helicopters; this lent legitimacy to the Future Fleet Working Party's proposal for a purpose-built successor with a through-deck.

Meanwhile Churchill's ten-year-rule, adopted when he was Chancellor of the Exchequer in the 1920s, was back in favour: it was assumed year on year that there would be no major war for ten years. The abandonment of carriers also meant that maritime AEW would have to be provided by land-based aircraft instead of the Gannets on carriers, or else by shipboard helicopters, which lacked height and endurance. Healey announced in 1966 that the Gannet would not be replaced by a fixed-wing aircraft. This particular chicken would come home to roost in 1982.

Nuclear submarines and the Polaris boats in particular brought great advances in electronics. Ballistic missiles needed to be targeted with maximum precision from a firing position that was always shifting as the submarine patrolled. The boats also needed to be able to communicate without revealing themselves, despite the inability of radio transmissions to penetrate deep water. But very low frequency signals could reach below the surface as far as an aerial in a buoy or inside the 'sail' (as the conning tower was now known) or eventually a boat's long 'towed array' of sensors. The Satellite Inertial Navigation System (SINS) was introduced in the 1960s: satellites locked in geosynchronous orbits, which kept them in precisely the same position above the rotating earth, enabled submarines, other ships and aircraft to work out instantaneously where they were within a few metres. The original SIN came to Britain as part of the Polaris package bought from the US. Satellites also came into use to spy on ship or other military movements or to relay information: Britain was dependent on US goodwill in this field for many years until she could assemble her own network. Within a few years the unprecedented accuracy of navigation by satellite became available to soldiers on the ground and even, in deliberately less accurate form, ramblers and motorists as GPS (global positioning system).

Britain's reputation as a source of ideas and inventions taken up or commercially exploited by other countries was in no sense diminished by the atmosphere of constant cutbacks which prevailed for all but a few precious years in the latter part of the century; on the contrary. The Navy experimented with the hovercraft from 1970, a British-designed conveyance that travelled at speed over water (or flat land) on a cushion of air; so did the Americans. But what seemed at first to be an ideal landing-cum-assault craft for coastal or river operations never came into general military or naval use, though larger versions proved themselves on the cross-Channel and other short sea routes. The hovercraft was sensitive to rough weather and was probably too vulnerable in other respects for military use, although the Americans tried them out thoroughly in Vietnam. Experiments had been going on at Vosper Thornycroft since 1966 with fibreglass hulls for a new generation of mine-countermeasure vessels that began to come into service in 1972: HMS *Wilton* was the world's first such ship. Westland Helicopters built the excellent and versatile American Sea King machine under licence. The first Fleet Air Arm Sea King squadron was formed in 1970 for ASW; eventually they also performed the AEW function last done by the Gannet fixed-wing aircraft. The Type 42 anti-aircraft destroyer made its bow in the shape of HMS *Sheffield* in 1971, and the P1127 VTOL aircraft, the embryo Harrier, was coming along nicely, as trials on the Commando carrier *Bulwark* showed in 1966 and after. The long-delayed amphibious assault ships *Fearless* and *Intrepid*, still on the books more than thirty years later, proved invaluable in such contexts as Aden from that time onward.

Several joint projects were undertaken with European Nato partners such as the Netherlands (the Sea Dart anti-aircraft missile and its three-dimensional radar; the Dutch later pulled out on grounds of expense) and West Germany (the Seawolf close-range anti-aircraft and anti-missile missile). Finding a modern and reliable torpedo for the fleet submarines seemed to be an insuperable problem for decades: the Mark VIII, developed before the Second World War, had to remain in service for use against surface ships into the 1980s, and was the only weapon known to have been fired in anger by a British fleet boat until 1999. In June 1967 *Dreadnought* was unable to dispatch a crippled tanker off the Azores with her Mark 20 homing torpedoes; the frigate *Salisbury* had to do it by old-fashioned gunfire. The Mark 31 anti-submarine torpedo was cancelled, after years of work, in 1971.

Modern navies the world over were taken aback when two small Egyptian fast patrol boats sank the Israeli destroyer *Eilat* in a hit-and-run attack with Soviet Styx heat-seeking surface-to-surface missiles in October 1967. The type II Seaslug short-range anti-aircraft/missile missile was intended to be Britain's answer to such threats, but Rear-Admiral John Adams, a promising Assistant Chief of Naval Staff (Policy), resigned over the lack of a sense of urgency on this requirement. The spectre of the *Eilat* was only laid to rest – by the British Navy – in the Gulf in 1991.

Embarrassingly for a government intent on phasing out aircraft carriers, those in service were kept very busy in their twilight. Despite the abolition of the 300-year-old Mediterranean Fleet in 1967, the British presence in the ocean actually increased (*Victorious*, *Hermes* and two extra frigates) thanks to the unrest in Aden and the build-up of tension ahead of the Six-Day War between Israel and Egypt in June 1967, won by the former. The Commando carriers *Bulwark* and *Albion* respectively deployed Royal Marines in Hong Kong as the 'Cultural Revolution' caused major unrest in China and patrolled off Nigeria during the civil war there in 1967.

One long overdue concession to modernity was the abolition of the daily tot of rum from 31 July 1970. The Navy had stubbornly refused to recognize that this old tradition, rooted in the need for stiffening before battle but also for something to counter scurvy as well as to neutralize the taste of the appalling rations of times not so distantly past, had led to all manner of problems aboard ship, including drunkenness and alcoholism, violence, corruption and impaired ability to operate increasingly sophisticated equipment. A single tot of one gill, though diluted by water, was enough to put a sailor over the legal blood-alcohol limit being enforced ashore by the new breathalyser. The money saved went into a new sailors' fund for social purposes. But unlike the American, the British Navy did not go 'dry'; wet canteens were available on all ships. These customs died hard; it was only in 1963, long after the need for it had gone, that the notorious ship's biscuit or 'hard tack' vanished from HM ships. The ancient title of coxswain for the senior helmsman also disappeared except on submarines. Messdecks were reorganized, in consultation, praise be, with their occupants, who got folding bunks to maximize usage of confined space; the hammock, which had lingered on in the fleet for a surprisingly long time after 1945, was a rapidly receding memory.

Although Navy personnel fell from 100,000 in 1966 to 87,500 in 1970, 79,000 in 1975 and 72,000 in 1980, there were chronic shortages of skills and recruits over the entire period, despite pay and pension awards and the creation in 1966 of a Royal Naval Presentation Team to tour the country preaching the need for the Navy and the Navy's needs. But everything that potential recruits heard or read about the service seemed to be about cuts and more cuts. The old lure to 'Join the Navy and see the world' had clearly lost its relevance. One straw in the wind was the Navy's first female air-traffic controller, a Wren third officer, at Lossiemouth, Scotland, in 1967. Two years later the base was, coincidentally, handed over to the RAF.

But in London the Navy's political representation declined again in 1967 when the MoD superstructure was reorganized. The political team headed by the Secretary of State, the solitary defence representative in Cabinet, now consisted of two centralized ministers of state for administration and for equipment (later changed to armed forces and procurement) and just one under-secretary of state (third-rate junior minister) for each service. So much for the old First Lord, Civil Lord, Parliamentary Secretary and Financial Secretary that used to speak for the Navy in government. But such developments were all of a piece with contraction and quite logical. The Royal Navy was still number two in Nato and number three in the world in 1968, but the cuts envisaged for the following three years threatened to allow the French Navy to overtake: France was planning to retain at least two carriers, wanted nuclear power for them and was working on nuclear submarines and a deadly anti-ship missile, the Exocet. Britain's uneconomic and unhappy naval dockyards, with their poor management, productivity and industrial relations, were being run down, unable to compete with commercial British yards, which themselves were finding it harder and harder to survive against competition from places as diverse as Japan, South Korea, West Germany, Scandinavia and Poland.

As the carrier *Ark Royal* was the only one in the fleet that could fly Phantoms, fifty interceptor versions of that aircraft, the only supersonic plane in the Navy, were transferred to the RAF in 1968, leaving the Navy with twenty-eight and a morale problem in the Fleet Air Arm, which had been obliged to obtain pilots from the RAF. All four amphibious ships (*Fearless*, *Intrepid*, *Albion* and *Bulwark*), each of which carried a Royal Marine Commando, were dedicated to Nato; the latter ship pioneered a new commitment in 1968 when she went to Norway for the first annual 'Polar Express' exercise, to reinforce Nato's northern flank and honour a wartime pledge to Norway. Dutch marines joined in; their cooperation in the Maritime Contingency Force to support Norway before American reinforcements could get there was one of many uniquely close links between the two corps, which also trained together.

Anti-tank missiles were borrowed from the Army and

successfully adapted for use against small fast patrol boats by Wessex helicopters. The Warsaw Pact invasion of Czechoslovakia in summer 1968 indirectly led to an order for twenty more Harriers for the RAF, but there was still no official indication that the Navy would get any; despite many successful trials on carriers, the aircraft had not yet been adapted for maritime service. In 1969 the government said that the RAF would fly Harriers from carriers. Twenty-six more Buccaneers were ordered for the RAF as consolation for the cancellation of the fifty F111s. But the Fleet Air Arm was offered hope: the government did say in 1969 that upgraded Harriers would be flown from naval flight decks if this proved operationally and financially justifiable, and when the design for the through-deck cruiser reached Vickers at Barrow, it was clear that the ship was meant to operate them. But it was to be four years before the first was laid down. More money was saved by extending the interval between starts of fleet submarines from one year to eighteen months. HMS *Conqueror*, launched in 1969, was the last in this category to come out of the Cammell Laird yard in Birkenhead on Merseyside; all future nuclear submarines were to be built at Barrow. A promising Anglo-French project for a surface-to-surface anti-ship missile, the Martel, languished when the British pulled out and opted for the American Harpoon; but the latter did not become available until 1982, leaving a serious gap in the Navy's armoury.

Deployments of dwindling resources in far-flung places continued to the end of a tumultuous decade. Unrest on several West Indian islands led to an embarrassing over-reaction as Royal Marines, paratroops and British police officers were landed on Anguilla to keep order after that island chose to secede from a mini-federation with St Kitts and Nevis. St Vincent and Montserrat, both then still under British tutelage, also experienced political unrest, earning visits from the Royal Navy which had once appropriated them for the British Crown. A much more serious and massive deployment took place at Gibraltar, British since 1713 but the subject of constant Spanish demands for its return, in 1969. A United Nations resolution called for this by the end of September, when the carrier *Eagle*, the helicopter-carrying cruiser *Blake*, two missile destroyers and other ships pointedly occupied the harbour as *Bulwark* staged a spectacular 'invasion' of the Rock by sending her marines up the cliffs, with six Spanish warships among the spectators. The Franco regime cut Gibraltar off by land

and air on 1 October. By insisting on staying 'British' the population of Gibraltar managed, like the Falkland islanders and the Ulster Protestants, to remain a political, financial and military liability for post-imperial Britain beyond the end of the century.

The change of government to Conservative in 1970 brought promises of a greater commitment to defence that evaporated in difficult economic conditions. An exercise to show that Britain could still deploy forces to protect Malaysia began under Labour and ended in chaos under the Tories. Although air cover was supposed to be provided from friendly airfields, the only functioning cover available came from half a dozen aircraft on Australia's sole carrier, HMAS *Melbourne*. The RAF proved unable to supply the promised Phantoms. The helicopter cruiser HMS *Blake* broke down and had to withdraw. Ten per cent of the 16,000 British personnel were taken ill in the stifling heat and humidity.

Ark Royal was recommissioned in February 1970, able to fly Phantoms at last; *Hermes* was withdrawn for conversion to a Commando carrier; *Eagle* came home for a last refit. All this was decided by Labour; would the Conservatives under Edward Heath reverse the decision to abandon carriers? In his first major statement, the new Defence Secretary, Lord Carrington, said at the end of October 1970 that five frigates and/or destroyers would stay East of Suez, including one off Hong Kong and one in the Gulf. Exocets would be acquired as anti-ship defence in partial compensation for the wind-down of carriers. *Ark Royal* would definitely stay on until the 'Invincibles' were commissioned in the mid-1970s. The cruiser *Lion* would not be converted to a helicopter carrier as her two underachieving sisters had been. *Eagle* would be scrapped as planned in 1972. Pre-election pledges to keep two carriers and shorten the intervals between fleet-submarine starts were ditched. The first RAF Nimrod aircraft for maritime patrols came into service in August after many delays. The plane, based on the first civilian jet airliner design, the Comet, was to replace the RAF Shackletons which had done sterling service for a quarter of a century but now had patches on their patches; an attempt to produce a more sophisticated, AWACS (Airborne Warning and Control System) version of the Nimrod failed amid insuperable British problems with the technology after many years. The design of the *Invincible*, described as a command cruiser, was completed in

October, after many adjustments, but to 'save' money the ship was not ordered until April 1973, when the cost was put at £96m (it would have been £60m in 1971; it reached an inflated £180m in 1980 for the third, a new *Ark Royal*).

Meanwhile the new government reinforced the Mediterranean amid more tension in the Middle East. *Ark Royal* and *Albion*, the Commando carrier, a missile destroyer and several frigates went there; 42 Commando was shifted from Singapore to Malta. British and American forces had been obliged to leave Libya when Colonel Muammar Gaddafi took power there; six Royal Fleet Auxiliary landing ships (logistics) ferried stores from there to Malta. Britain's 'Skynet' satellite communications system, covering half the globe from British waters to Australia, came on stream in the second half of the year. The satellites were positioned by US rockets from November 1969.

As the first refit of a Polaris submarine, *Resolution*, began at Rosyth, the Conservatives decided that they would not after all order the fifth cancelled by Labour. Work on the British 'Chevaline' upgrade of Polaris, giving the missile a triple instead of a single warhead and turning it into a MIRV (multi-targeted independent re-entry vehicle), begun under Labour, continued. The consensus across the political establishment on nuclear weapons clearly survived. So did the function of the Chief Polaris Executive, restyled the Chief Strategic Systems Executive at the end of 1970. He was responsible for supervising the Chevaline conversion, which also involved new electronics, and then for the successor programme for 'Trident' missiles and their associated submarines.

The number of operational ships fell by thirty-eight to 143 in 1970; personnel numbered 87,500. New helicopters such as the Lynx were on trial by the end of the year; Harriers were still being tried on the remaining carriers but the Fleet Air Arm almost died as the Navy was reduced to one fleet carrier, the *Ark Royal*. Labour returned to power under Harold Wilson in 1974 and the *Invincible* was launched in the following year as the first in her class of three, while the Sea Harrier was at last approved to fly with her. It was discovered that a short 'ski-jump' ramp over the bow significantly increased the aircraft's endurance by saving the extra fuel needed to power a vertical take-off; the Sea Harrier therefore became a STOVL (short take-off/vertical landing) aircraft, able to carry 2,000lb more fuel or weapons. Its stated role was to protect its ship, whose main purpose was ASW with its Sea King helicopters, from Soviet air attack and to attack Soviet surface forces, all impeccably Nato-oriented. So were the fleet submarines, undoubtedly the most effective counter to Soviet nuclear submarines, whether hunter-killer or ballistic. Nevertheless the British Navy, almost wholly committed to Nato though it was, somehow managed to retain a considerable ability to deploy a long way from the north Atlantic and Mediterranean. It was supported by the Royal Fleet Auxiliary, crewed by the Merchant Navy under RN officers, with its tankers, supply ships and landing ships (logistics), the latter all built in the mid-1960s just when distant operations were said to be going off the agenda – a large 'fleet train' for a small fleet, larger than that of any other navy except the American. Nato set up a STANAVFORCHAN (Standing Naval Force, Channel) in 1972, based at Ostend in Belgium but led by Britain.

Another Cod War broke out in 1973, when Iceland decided to extend its hard-won twelve-mile fishing limit to fifty miles; it ended in the usual manner, after a few fraught confrontations, with the Icelanders getting their way. It happened again and for the last time in 1976, when Iceland extended its limit to 200 miles. Britain meanwhile, having joined the European Community on 1 January 1973, faced the prospect of sharing its own fishing waters with its European partners. In the same year the Navy received its last steam-powered (turbine) ship, the frigate *Ariadne*, which was also the last to be armed with the Limbo depth charge mortar and with guns fore and aft (which meant she was the last British ship to be able to fire a broadside); she was to serve until 1992. Three British ships led by the restored *Hermes* evacuated British citizens from Kyrenia in Cyprus when Britain's Nato ally, Turkey, invaded and occupied the northern 40 per cent of that island for the rest of the century. British mine-countermeasures vessels, at the invitation of Egypt, also completed the clearance of the Suez Canal, blocked ever since the Six-Day War of 1967.

The introduction aboard ship of the post of principal warfare officer (PWO) in 1972 reflected progress in both thinking and practice in the field of systems integration. Various weapons and electronics systems had been introduced piecemeal for at least fifteen years, and initially each was operated in virtual isolation until all were controlled from the ship's operations room. From there it was a short and logical step to conceive of a warship as a single weapons system. Eventually detection and observation radars would converge with weapon targeting and guidance and other systems to form an integrated 'nerve system' controlled by computer. The PWO's job was to oversee this fighting 'brain' under the captain. Such traditional specialisms as gunnery and torpedoes disappeared; the new operations specialism of 1975 was divided between Above Water for surface ships and Under Water for submarines. Reflecting the importance of communication in all its forms, ratings were reorganized into two main groups, seamen and communications specialists.

The officers' General List included Seamen, Engineers (marine and weapons) and Supply and Secretariat, covering administration and regulation. (There was also the new shibboleth of reform in the public sector, 'man-management'. Echoing the earlier despair of the mid-century naval officer who observed that 'if Nelson had had a telex machine there would have been no Trafalgar', Desmond Wettern, author of *The Decline of British Seapower*, wrote: 'So a future Nelson would be a "manager". He would not provide leadership but a "programme". His "band of brothers" would pre sumably become a group of "man-managers" or even "pro- grammers".' These changes were mild compared with those brought in by the Thatcher government of 1979 onwards, when the curse of the MBA, the master's degree in business administration, flooded the land with gobbledygook about free market forces, turning leading public servants such as armed forces and police officers, ward sisters or senior teachers into line managers, team leaders and budget holders.)

The Instructor branch was added to the officers' General List in 1978. Meanwhile the WRNS sent officer candidates to Dartmouth from 1976 and the corps came under the Naval Discipline Act in 1977: could integration be far behind? More concern for naval wives, and through them for their husbands' peace of mind, was shown by the establishment of the Naval Personnel and Family Service in 1977.

Operationally in that year, Royal Marines in rigid inflatables powered by outboard motors captured five IRA terrorists in a coastal raid at Warrenpoint in the south-east of Northern Ireland; HMS *Vigilant* which delivered them also engaged shore positions, surely the first time that the Royal Navy fired in anger on the coast of the United Kingdom.

*

One of the post-1967 cuts led to the withdrawal of the single frigate that made regular visits to the South Atlantic region round the Falklands, and the Falkland Islands Dependencies far to the south-east, to back up the naval survey ship that had patrolled the area from 1957. HMS *Endurance*, a red-hulled ice-patrol ship leased from Denmark in 1968, then became the only ship to fly the Union flag in waters acquisitively eyed by Argentina, which constantly laid claim to '*las Malvinas*'. An Argentine destroyer fired on the visiting British survey ship *Shackleton* in February 1976, some eighty miles to the south of the Falklands, without hitting her, although the unarmed vessel had to zigzag to avoid being boarded, in the worst of a series of Argentine 'pinpricks'. As a result the *Endurance* was not withdrawn as planned. After a military junta took over power in Buenos Aires later in 1976, the Callaghan government sent a task force made up of the nuclear submarine *Dreadnought* and two frigates to the Falklands in 1977, an unpublicized fact of which Argentina could hardly have been ignorant for long. At the same time *Ark Royal* was sent to Belize in Central America, not just to impress the Guatamalans with their long-standing claim on the colony. Tension in the south Atlantic was high because of a territorial dispute between Argentina and Chile over islands in the Beagle Channel at the extreme south of the continent. The rapidly expanding Argentine fleet put to sea in January 1978 as the junta told Britain and Chile it would not accept the pro-Chilean verdict of the International Court. Argentina's victory in the soccer World Cup on its own soil seemed to ease the tension – for the time being.

In the following year the Phantoms were withdrawn from the *Ark Royal*, prior to her decommissioning in 1979 as the Royal Navy's last fleet aircraft carrier. After unprecedented inflation in Britain, naval and other armed forces pay was raised by 32 per cent, not quite enough, inevitably, to restore its buying power of only a few years earlier. *Invincible* was commissioned at last in 1980, while her sister *Illustrious* was completing; the third and last in the class was named *Ark Royal* and would be launched in 1981, when the elderly *Hermes* was recommissioned as a light aircraft carrier rather than Commando carrier, complete with ski-jump for Sea Harriers, in a stopgap measure. The Fleet Air Arm was not about to be amputated after all.

But on 25 June 1981, in the person of the Defence Secretary,

John Nott, the Conservative government elected in 1979 introduced a White Paper entitled *The Way Forward*. For the Royal Navy it looked like the Way Down. The *Invincible* was to be sold to Australia and the *Hermes* to India. Destroyers and frigates would be slashed to fifty, including eight in reserve. *Fearless* and *Intrepid* would be scrapped; so would Chatham dockyard, while Portsmouth was downgraded to an anchorage (only Devonport and Rosyth dockyards would remain); total strength of 74,500 in 1981 would be cut by up to 19,000 in five years. The Royal Marines, having already lost one of four Commandos, survived; and the Type 23 light frigate was promised – but not for years. Bravely the Parliamentary Under-Secretary for the Navy, Keith Speed, protested publicly and was promptly sacked. He was the last minister with specific responsibility for the Royal Navy; the Minister of State for the Armed Forces now represented all three services in government.

On 19 March 1982 forty-one 'scrap dealers' landed from the Argentine Navy transport *Bahia Buen Suceso* at Leith on the Falk-lands Dependency island of South Georgia. What followed saved the Royal Navy – but only after the Royal Navy had saved the government.

15

An 'Invincible' Returns to the Falklands

Lord Falkland was Treasurer of the Navy when the English privateer John Strong set off for the small archipelago 350 nautical miles north-east of Cape Horn in 1690 – hence the name. The islands were in the Spanish sector of the New World as allotted by the Pope two centuries earlier. A French expedition from St Malo (hence *les Malouines – las Malvinas* in Spanish) attempted a settlement at Port Louis in 1764 but Britain claimed them in 1765 and garrisoned them in 1766. A Spanish expedition arrived in 1770. The British retired peacefully but landed a new garrison on East Falkland in 1771 (and withdrew it to save money in 1774) without ousting the Spanish. The South American provinces revolted against Spain while it was occupied by Napoleon but the Spanish garrison remained loyal to Madrid and eventually sailed home. Argentina claimed the Falklands and leased them to a private entrepreneur for twenty-five years in 1823. The Royal Navy formally reclaimed sovereignty in 1833, a year after a US Navy warship had called to support American seal-hunters in a dispute with the lessee. Argentina protested when Britain founded a colony in 1843, but the Falkland Islands Company was incorporated by royal charter soon afterwards. Sheep, staple of the economy, were introduced in 1852 and the first British settlement on West Falkland took place in 1867. Port Stanley on East Falkland displaced Port Louis as the capital. The archipelago lost its strategic importance when Britain failed to set up a commercial coaling station for steamships, which called at Punta Arenas in Chile instead.

In one of many territorial disputes with Chile, Argentina moved closer to the islands when she was awarded eastern Patagonia, the nearest part of the South American continent, in 1881. In the very same year they became self-sufficient without the burden of the

Royal Marine garrison, withdrawn to save money two years earlier (the South America Squadron, based at Montevideo, Uruguay, now provided the only protection). Argentina based its claim on 'contiguity' (we are nearest, therefore they are ours) rather than as the successor of imperial Spain; but in comparison with either argument, Britain's claim looks no stronger than 'squatter's rights' backed by force. Yet the 2,500 islanders were of British stock and wanted nothing to do with Argentina, especially after 1982: the direct air connection was restored only in 1999.

The islands were of strategic significance in both world wars; without them the British victories in the battles of the Falkland Islands in 1914 and the River Plate in 1939 would have been impossible. The likelihood of oil deposits within the 200-mile territorial waters round the islands conferred a new significance; meanwhile the rich fish stocks attracted foreign poachers, against whom Argentina and Britain agreed in 1999 to cooperate. But Argentina laid claim to the islands throughout the century and her defeat by Britain in 1982 failed to settle the issue of sovereignty. Spain sympathized, not only because of the Hispanic connection but also because of Gibraltar, that other post-imperial millstone. Various unofficial Argentine landings on parts of the Falkland Islands Dependencies and even on the Falklands proper, with or without government knowledge, took place after the wartime naval base closed in 1948 (the Labour government of the day threatened to use force). As in 1981, when the British government announced, as part of John Nott's drastic naval cuts, that it was paying off the *Endurance*, the last official maritime link, Buenos Aires read a cheeseparing action as a sign of declining British interest in the islands.

On the latter occasion Argentine hopes seemed well founded: in a meeting of the two foreign ministers at the United Nations in New York, the British side said it would do its best to convince the islanders of the benefit of an accommodation with Argentina (taken as readiness to compromise on sovereignty); and the Nationality Act of 1981 denied full British citizenship to the islanders (and many others round the world, principally the population of Hong Kong, the real target). Lord Carrington, by then Foreign Secretary, and the Foreign Office favoured surrendering sovereignty and leasing the islands back in February 1981 but could not sell this to the Falklanders.

The junta led by General Jorge Videla, which had taken power in

1976 in the latest military intervention in Argentina's explosive politics, restored order (at a price of 6,000 prisoners and 2,000 'disappearances', causing President Jimmy Carter to slash aid and arms supplies) and stabilized the economy. But by 1981 the junta, now led by General Roberto Viola, had plunged Argentina into a deep economic crisis fuelled by huge debts. Viola resigned over this in December, making way for General Leopoldo Galtieri, C-in-C of the Army. At talks in New York in February 1982 Argentina and Britain agreed to set up a joint commission for one year to try for an accord on the Falklands and also agreed to make a short, flat announcement to this effect on 1 March. But the Argentine Foreign Ministry under Dr Nicanor Costa Mendez embellished this with an emotive claim that the transfer of sovereignty of *las Malvinas* was on the agenda – and implying the use of force if it was not granted. To London's surprise and incredulity, the ensuing crisis got out of hand as the junta, like many another dictatorship in trouble, seized on a foreign quarrel as a diversion from troubles at home.

The scrap-dealers having raised the Argentine flag there on 19 March, HMS *Endurance* (Captain Nicholas Barker, RN) set sail for South Georgia from Port Stanley the next day, her marine contingent of thirteen reinforced by nine men borrowed from the detachment based in the Falklands capital. Arriving off Grytviken harbour on the 23rd, the ice-patrol ship, armed with just two 20mm anti-aircraft guns, sent her two Wasp helicopters to overfly the occupiers of Leith, marooned by the departure of their transport, but took no further action. The bulk of the Argentine fleet went on manoeuvres with marine commandos in the latter part of March, practising amphibious landings as well as anti-submarine warfare. The latter was wise; Mrs Thatcher and Lord Carrington decided on 29 March to send to the south Atlantic three nuclear fleet submarines plus two RFA support ships, to reinforce and resupply *Endurance* and to be on hand. HMS *Spartan* sailed from Gibraltar and *Splendid* from Faslane, from where *Conqueror* followed shortly afterwards.

Captain Barker left Lieutenant Keith Mills, RM, and all his twenty-one marines on South Georgia to protect members of the British Antarctic Survey there and keep watch on Leith, while he headed back to Stanley. Barker's warnings to London of Argentine aggressiveness, picked up when the ship had called briefly at

Argentine ports earlier in March, had been dismissed as an attempt to preserve his ship and his job from the cuts.

Major M. J. Norman, RM, arrived on 30 March on a research ship with forty-two marines to relieve the Falklands detachment, which the Governor, Rex Hunt, asked to remain. A Navy officer and nine ratings from *Endurance*, left behind for survey work when she went to South Georgia, reinforced the major's tiny garrison to a total of eighty-five men. They set up observation posts overlooking the approaches to Stanley and blocked the airport road, and its runway, with vehicles, while a Falkland Islands Company coaster was used as a radar picket.

The Argentine Navy was in general rather old, with notable exceptions such as two British-made Type 42 destroyers, two West German submarines and three French corvettes. Its principal advantage in the coming conflict was its short lines of communication, close to home and 8,000 miles from Britain, seventeen days away at twenty knots. Fleet flagship *Veintecinco de Mayo* ('Twenty-fifth of May') was a 20,000-ton aircraft carrier, the erstwhile *Karel Doorman* of the Dutch Navy from 1948 to 1969; she had started life, appropriately enough, as HMS *Venerable* in 1945. She carried twelve obsolete aircraft and three Sea King helicopters and was probably capable of twenty knots. Around the time of the invasion on 2 April 1982 the carrier plus the two Exocet-armed Type 42s (Task Group 1) and two ex-American wartime destroyers with an oiler (Task Group 2) provided a distant covering force, commanded by Rear-Admiral Gualter Allara, some 500 to 400 miles north of the Falklands and due east of the Comodoro Rivadavia naval base. Task Group 4 of three corvettes armed with Exocet anti-ship missiles was to the north of the other two. Task Group 3, consisting of the cruiser *General Belgrano* and two ex-American wartime destroyers, was commanded by her skipper, Captain Hector Bonzo. The cruiser, capable of twenty-five knots, displaced 13,500 tons fully loaded and had fifteen 6-inch and eight 5-inch guns, but had first sailed as USS *Phoenix* in 1938 and may have seemed, forty-four years later, to be held together by her countless coats of paint. Her sole sister ship, of similar origin, vintage and specifications, was laid up. TG 4 was on patrol about 300 miles south of Stanley and due east of the base of Ushuaia, in the Argentine part of the island of Tierra del Fuego.

The invasion was originally planned for the turn of the year (with the 150th anniversary of the British naval annexation in January 1833 in mind) but was brought forward, partly in response to riots in Buenos Aires and partly because the junta got wind of the dispatch of the British submarines. Nonetheless its execution was efficient enough under the command of Rear-Admiral Carlos Busser of the Argentine Marines, of whom one battalion of 700 men sailed aboard the country's sole landing ship (tank); this vessel carried four landing craft and about twenty amphibious armoured landing vehicles. The submarine *Santa Fe*, another veteran of the Second World War acquired from the US Navy, landed frogmen to scout the landing beaches. Three destroyers and two corvettes were detached from the other task groups to provide close support; one of the former, a Type 42, carried a naval special-forces group of seventy men who made two preliminary landings in rigid inflatables five miles south of Stanley. Four naval transports and three ships taken up from trade (STUFT) brought some 300 army troops, artillery, ammunition and stores to support a first wave of over 1,000 men in Operation 'Rosario'.

In a three-hour battle with the bulk of Major Norman's marines and sailors, one Argentine marine officer was killed – the first fatality in an outlandish war. Helicopters from the invasion flotilla landed troops to clear the airfield, whereupon Hercules transport aircraft began landing more infantry. Governor Hunt asked Admiral Busser for terms and surrendered at 9.15 a.m. local time (four hours behind GMT), whereupon Port Stanley radio fell silent. The defenders were rounded up and flown to Montevideo, Uruguay, as were the Governor and his officials: all were repatriated to Britain by 5 April, together with the flag from Government House, preserved by the marines. Argentine losses amounted to three dead and seventeen wounded; there was no British or Falklands casualty. The Argentine occupation force was rapidly built up to divisional strength, some 13,000 men, commanded by General Mario Menendez, who was also appointed Governor of *las Malvinas* by a jubilant junta. Vehicles, artillery, radars, helicopters and light ground-attack aircraft were among the weaponry brought to the islands; a sophisticated anti-aircraft defence of seventy radar-controlled automatic guns plus British and French-made missiles was in place within four days. The Argentine Air Force possessed some fifty Mirage 5 and Dagger fighter-bombers bought from France and Israel respectively, while the Navy boasted fourteen French Super-Etendard fighter-bombers, armed with Exocets and intended to replace the old aircraft on the carrier. Both types could have flown from Stanley airport had the runway been extended by steel netting; fortunately for the British Navy, this was not regarded as worth the effort. Troops were placed at various strongpoints in West as well as East Falkland. The weather was wet and windy, typical of autumn in the bleak archipelago.

News of the invasion reached London at noon BST. British Intelligence had failed to anticipate it, having underestimated Argentine sentiment and the rashness of the junta, which decided on 26 March, amid a diplomatic impasse over South Georgia, to invade on 1 April (deferred for a day because of bad weather). Only on 31 March did US intelligence sources indicate that the invasion would start on 2 April. The Americans were embarrassed by the looming conflict between two allies (President Ronald Reagan had decided in 1981 to lift Carter's arms embargo against Argentina). As at the time of Suez, American intelligence officials kept their British counterparts informed of what they knew without too much regard for policy in Washington. Former White House Chief of Staff General Alexander Haig was appointed to mediate between the Argentines and the British as the United Nations and other Latin American countries tried to resolve the crisis resulting from the invasion of territory recognized by the United Nations as British. The junta was confident that it would be left in possession of *las Malvinas*, and that the British lacked the means and the will to take them back.

The British government had been caught well and truly napping; by the time it took the rising tension in Buenos Aires seriously enough to send three nuclear submarines (even they needed some ten days to reach the area) it was too late. On the same day as this decision, 29 March, the Commander-in-Chief, Fleet, Admiral Sir John Fieldhouse, contacted the Flag Officer, 1st Flotilla, Rear-Admiral J. F. 'Sandy' Woodward, exercising off Gibraltar with a total of sixteen destroyers and frigates, to prepare to detach a substantial force to the south Atlantic. Fortunately there had been a recent theoretical exercise on rapid mobilization of the fleet which saved much grief as Northwood got to work. The Chief of Defence Staff, Admiral of the Fleet Sir Terence Lewin, was on an official visit to New Zealand. Admiral Sir Henry Leach, aged fifty-nine, the First Sea Lord and Chief of Naval Staff, stood in for him.

Leach's role in the Falklands saga was full of irony. Not one of nature's diplomats, he was at daggers drawn with John Nott over his drastic plans for cutting the Navy by a third. The hapless Defence Secretary believed that an Argentine invasion once made was irreversible and the only hope was to limit the damage by diplomacy. Leach arrived in London by helicopter from a ceremony at Portsmouth on 31 March and went in full uniform straight to Parliament, where ministers and officials were wringing their hands while Mrs Thatcher fumed with frustration. 'I had an immediate and acute feeling: what the hell's the point of having a navy if you're not going to use it? So I rushed along to get in on the act quickly,' he told Channel 4 Television on the tenth anniversary in 1992. On reaching the Prime Minister the admiral insisted that the Navy was entirely capable of delivering a successful counter-invasion and that a task force could be mobilized by the weekend. Even Nott admitted that Leach's 'Nelsonian gung-ho' had 'helped our self-confidence in a very difficult situation'. Mrs Thatcher told a special session of Parliament on Saturday 3 April, that the task force would sail. The live transmission was one of the most electrifying radio broadcasts since the Second World War: it was obvious that she was taking an immense gamble on the Navy and on her own political future and reputation.

Northwood brought Britain's two remaining carriers, ear-marked for sale to India and Australia, up to forty-eight hours' notice. *Hermes* had 40 Commando, twenty-nine helicopters and five Sea Harriers, while *Invincible* had five and five. *Hermes* was to be the flagship when the task force came together and would cram an extra ten Sea Harriers and six RAF Harriers aboard while reducing her Sea Kings to six; *Invincible* kept all hers but managed to find space for five more Sea Harriers. As so often in the century, the Royal Navy's weak point in Operation 'Corporate' was air cover, which could only come from the two little carriers – and they lacked fixed-wing AEW (helicopters had to serve, supplemented by ships acting as radar pickets). The two elderly amphibious-assault ships *Fearless* and *Intrepid* were also at Portsmouth, the latter just paid off and placed in reserve. All four swiftly had their crews and stores brought up to war strength.

The first wave to leave was to be destroyers *Antrim*, *Glamorgan*, *Coventry*, *Glasgow* and *Sheffield* and frigates *Arrow*, *Brilliant* (Prince Andrew was aboard, serving as a helicopter pilot) and *Plymouth*, from the group that had now abandoned the exercise off Gibraltar, where the dockyard had been run down preparatory to closure. Admiral Woodward was in the first-named; each ship acquired its war loading by 'plundering' a sister ship. The RFA *Engadine*, a helicopter-support ship with extra Sea Kings aboard, was also present and joined the run south. Other ships and auxiliaries came or would come from as far afield as the Gulf, Belize and Vancouver. The invasion force included all three Royal Marine Commandos (40, 42 and 45) in 3 Commando Brigade, complete with its Logistics Regiment and Royal Artillery Commando Regiment (Brigadier Julian Thompson, RM); two battalions of the Parachute Regiment, one each of Gurkhas and Welsh Guards plus supporting units from the Army formed the other brigade, whose equipment included a dozen Rapier anti-aircraft missile-launchers. Admiral Woodward was in charge at sea under the direct command of Fieldhouse at Northwood; once troops were ashore, Major-General Jeremy Moore of the Royal Marines would take charge. Forty-five STUFT included the pride of the rapidly dwindling British Merchant Navy, Cunard's *QE2*, and P&O liners *Canberra* (troopship) and *Uganda* (hospital ship), several roll-on, roll-off (ro-ro) ferries and container ships such as Cunard's *Atlantic Conveyor*, converted in days to carry troops, aircraft, vehicles, guns and/or stores. The first surface vessel to leave Britain for the South Atlantic was the humble *Typhoon*, an 800-ton tug of the Royal Maritime Auxiliary Service (provider of harbour and coastal vessels to the Navy).

In the end the extraordinary Falklands campaign would draw in from the Royal Navy itself twenty-seven major surface warships (carriers, assault ships, destroyers, frigates), one diesel-electric and five nuclear submarines, and a swarm of smaller ships, including patrol craft, landing craft, minesweeping trawlers and survey vessels. The RFA would send ten oilers, five fleet replenishment ships, a helicopter-support ship and six landing ships (logistic) such as *Sir Galahad*. It was by no means the largest invasion fleet ever assembled by Britain but it was undoubtedly the most costly – and the most imaginatively improvised.

The only maritime staging post for this rapidly cobbled-together armada was the halfway house of Ascension Island, a little south of the Equator and midway between Brazil and Angola, a tiny imperial leftover whose main activity was to support a US military airfield with a 10,000-foot runway. The airfield was central to the campaign, coping with RAF tanker aircraft, Hercules transports and other heavy-lift planes carrying special equipment, spares and personnel. Naval facilities were limited and ships had to anchor without protection offshore, under constant surveillance from Soviet long-range reconnaissance aircraft based in Angola. Others flew over southbound British ships from European bases. Hitherto best known for its BBC relay transmitter, Ascension had never been so important: accommodation had to be found for 1,000 extra naval, military and RAF technicians.

It was from there that the first British strike on the occupied Falklands, a single Vulcan which attacked Stanley airport, was mounted: the thirsty delta-wing bomber was fuelled by airborne tankers which were themselves fuelled by others of their kind and so on. The result was one hole in the runway, soon repaired – and a boost for morale. Special forces were flown to Ascension for collection by ship or submarine for clandestine operations: small groups of men from the Special Boat Squadron, Royal Marines, and the Army's Special Air Service Regiment were landed behind enemy lines on the Falklands and also undertook spy missions on the Argentine mainland. Several unfounded submarine scares, probably caused by sonar detection of large whales, disrupted dispositions on and around Ascension, sometimes for days.

The guided-missile destroyer *Antrim* (Captain B. G. Young, RN) supported by the frigate *Plymouth* and RFA *Tidespring*, an oiler with two Wessex helicopters to add to the destroyer's three, was sent by Woodward to recapture South Georgia and was given the go-ahead by Mrs Thatcher's 'War Cabinet' on 20 April. Weather conditions made it all but impossible to fly helicopters. Twenty SAS troopers were landed on the second attempt, on the 21st, but had to be lifted off again, which cost two helicopters. *Endurance* was back, sending SBS parties ashore on the 23rd but forced by the freezing wind and weather to take them off again the next day. Captain Young temporarily withdrew all ships except *Endurance* when he learned on the 24th that the submarine *Santa Fe* (Lieutenant-Commander Hugo Bicain) was on hand: she landed twenty marines and supplies to reinforce the garrison but was sighted on the surface by a Wessex from *Antrim*, which promptly delivered the first British air attack on a submarine in thirty-seven years by dropping two old-fashioned depth charges. Bicain, fearing a homing torpedo, had stayed on the surface and suffered damage to his oil tanks and diving gear. Helicopters from *Plymouth* and *Endurance* did further damage with air-to-surface missiles; the

Santa Fe finished the engagement in flames and listing against a jetty at Grytviken. Reinforced by the frigate *Brilliant*, some seventy-five Royal Marines and SAS troopers were ferried ashore by helicopters. The defending 'scrap dealers' ran up the white flag at 5 p.m. on 25 April. Lieutenant-Commander Alfredo Astiz, wanted by the French and Swedish governments for torturing citizens of theirs during the Argentine 'dirty war' against opponents of the junta, surrendered last and was placed under close arrest on *Antrim*. The marines were left in charge of the recaptured island with *Endurance* standing by. *Tidespring* took the scrap dealers and Argentine marines away. But the recapture of South Georgia, warmly received in Britain, was the merest hors d'oeuvre.

The amphibious force, led by Commodore Michael Clapp on *Fearless*, began to assemble at Ascension on 17 April, when the Commander, Task Force 317, Admiral Fieldhouse, paid a brief visit for a staff meeting on *Hermes*. As there were no AEW aircraft on the carriers, Nimrod patrols were flown as far south as possible from Ascension while the carriers and their escorts (three destroyers and a frigate, reinforced later), Task Group 317.8, sailed for the Falklands the next day. Sea Kings with sonar buoys hanging from them flew constant ASW patrols while Sea Harriers looked out for surface intruders and drove off the occasional high-flying Argentine reconnaissance aircraft, usually an unarmed Boeing 707 airliner with only civilian radar – good enough, however, for the purpose. The rest of the amphibious group, led by *Intrepid*, left England on 25 and 26 April, distantly escorted by Soviet Bear bombers; a Russian trawler yawing under the weight of its antennae was off Ascension on 2 May; an Argentine merchantman which had passed within four miles of the island on 25 April was politely but firmly escorted to a distance of 100 miles. The extra Sea and RAF Harriers flew out non-stop from Britain to Ascension, repeatedly refuelling from tanker aircraft as they came. The *Atlantic Conveyor* (15,000 tons, Captain Ian North, master) was converted in three weeks to carry and maintain Harriers and helicopters; she also brought five huge RAF Chinook helicopters for heavy lifts, plus a large quantity of stores for 3 Commando Brigade. She was the most important STUFT and sailed from Devonport via Freetown to arrive at Ascension on 7 May, when the amphibious group, TG 317.0, finally set off.

Britain declared a circular 200-mile exclusion zone round the

Falklands from dawn on 28 April; any Argentine ship or aircraft, military or not, found within it was liable to attack. By the evening of the next day the carrier group, now including four destroyers and four frigates plus three RFA tankers, was refuelling 500 miles east of Port Stanley. On the 30th TG 317.8 was complete, consisting of two carriers and ten escorts plus two oilers, and ready to start its overnight run to the exclusion zone.

Had it been left to the Navy with its usually tenuous grasp of public relations, there would have been no media presence with the Task Force that was about to spend hundreds of millions of pounds of taxpayers' money (to say nothing of likely losses of men and *matériel*) in an undeclared war. Downing Street overruled Northwood and the MoD, on the urging of the editor of *The Times*, Charles Douglas-Home, a former defence correspondent with all the right contacts. Twenty-one reporters from the press, television and radio, two photographers and four TV technicians sailed with the Task Force – eleven with the carriers and sixteen with the amphibious group. Relations between the Task Force and the MoD on the one hand and the media on the other were fraught throughout the campaign. Task Force members were particularly infuriated by the BBC World Service radio, which seemed to be broadcasting well-informed speculation about the next moves in the campaign that might well have been of considerable value to the enemy. There were also official complaints about what British reporters were relaying from Argentina, as if it were unpatriotic to know thine enemy.

What the objectors could not have known at the time was that much of the sensitive information emanated from unattributable MoD briefings in London. The media for their part were frustrated by such factors as delays in transmitting their reports and films to London via naval facilities and the extraordinary briefings given by the chief MoD spokesman who, apparently for the convenience of reporters who had forgotten or never learned shorthand or else suffered from low intelligence, unforgettably made his press-conference statements in the tones of a constipated speak-your-weight machine. But then Whitehall in general and the military in particular had never fully accepted the public's right to know, a foible which was only accentuated in wartime.

The lone Vulcan should have been two but one had to turn back. Twelve Victor tankers flew with it, refuelling each other as well as the raider with its twenty-one 1,000lb bombs. Flight Lieutenant M.

Withers, RAF, set up a world record for a bombing mission (7,860 miles), eluding anti-aircraft fire and radar. Also on 30 April, two Sea Harriers from HMS *Invincible* in the role of Combat Air Patrol (CAP) overflew Stanley at 8,000 feet, drawing anti-aircraft fire and taking photographs. *Hermes* then sent up twelve Sea Harriers in three flights, two to bombard Stanley airfield and anti-aircraft positions nearby and one to attack the grass airfield at Goose Green, well to the west of Port Stanley on the 'waist' of East Falkland, where the Argentines had stationed Pucará ground-attack aircraft. One of the latter was destroyed and a number of bombs with delayed-action timers were dropped; one Harrier was hit by a single 20mm round. Two Argentine Mirages flew over briefly from the mainland at the limit of their range and fired missiles at the *Invincible*'s patrolling pair but missed, thanks to 'chaff' decoys and the high manoeuvrability of the slower British aircraft. In a similar incident later in the day one Mirage was destroyed by an American Sidewinder missile fired by a RAF pilot while the other was shot down by Argentine anti-aircraft fire.

Three Daggers (Israeli-made Mirage 'clones' without the sophisticated electronics of the French original) attacked a group of three of Woodward's escorts led by the guided-missile destroyer *Glamorgan*, which was slightly damaged. One of two covering Daggers was shot down by another RAF pilot from *Hermes*. Two frigates hunting a rumoured submarine north-west of the islands came under attack by some of half a dozen elderly British-made Canberras on their way to the Falklands: one was shot down by a CAP sent to protect the ASW ships. Woodward's escorts also shelled Stanley airport from a distance to delay repairs to the runway, which, however, was soon restored. On the opening day of hostilities over the Falklands, the Argentines had lost four aircraft out of twenty-five that had managed to fly as far as the islands.

British submarines were shadowing the two main elements of the Argentine Navy, the larger led by the carrier some 400 miles to the north-west of the Falklands, the other led by the *General Belgrano* about 300 miles to the south-east. Woodward's carriers were just outside the Total Exclusion Zone (TEZ) and to the north of the islands on the night of 1 to 2 May when a CAP from *Invincible* located the enemy carrier, regarded as the main threat to the British task force, which now withdrew into the TEZ. The anticipated Argentine dawn attack, however, did not materialize; unbeknown to the British, an attack on the carriers by the dangerous Super-

Etendards from the mainland was aborted when the Argentines experienced problems with their airborne tankers.

Woodward regarded the two Argentine groups to north and south as a potential pincer. He asked Northwood for a change in his rules of engagement so that he could destroy its weaker arm, the *Belgrano*, constantly shadowed as she was outside the TEZ by the submarine HMS *Conqueror* (Commander C. L. Wreford-Brown, RN). The fleet submarine *Valiant* had followed but then lost contact with the carrier group when it passed into the shallow waters of the continental shelf. Mrs Thatcher's War Cabinet sanctioned the attack; the message reached the submarine at 1.30 p.m. GMT (9.30 a.m. Falklands time): her captain asked for clarification, which took another four hours to achieve. The *Belgrano* with her two old ex-USN destroyers in attendance was in a position to enter the TEZ or to make a diversionary run at more than twenty knots towards South Georgia; her 6-inch guns outweighed and outranged any British gun while her four inches of good old-fashioned side-armour should have stopped a shell or even an Exocet.

At 6.57 p.m. on 2 May the *General Belgrano* was sailing westward, i.e. away from the Falklands, at a leisurely ten knots, well outside the TEZ and 240 miles from the Argentine base at Ushuaia on the Beagle Channel. She was not at action stations or even mounting defence watches, the next-highest state of alert. Wreford-Brown ordered a salvo of three Mark VIII 21-inch torpedoes to be fired from his position 1,400 yards off the port bow and to the south-west of the ancient cruiser. All three struck home, although one of the missiles, of a design more than fifty years old, did not detonate. No lookout gave a warning or even saw the tracks. One torpedo went off close to the bow, the other aft of amidships at the engine room. The ship went dead in the water as a fireball raced through the hull, unimpeded by the open watertight doors, killing more than 350 men; 879, including Captain Bonzo, abandoned ship in half an hour. The cruiser rolled over to port and sank by the bow forty-five minutes after the attack, by which time *Conqueror* was well clear of the scene. The destroyers hunted her for some hours and dropped depth charges, which she distantly detected, but did not stop to pick up survivors (the correct course of action with an enemy submarine in the vicinity). Despite not being found for at least twenty-four hours, all those who managed to get off the lost ship survived and were picked up.

It was the horrific sinking of the *Belgrano* that finally brought home to people – in Argentina and Britain, their shared ally the United States, at the United Nations and elsewhere – that the imbroglio in the south Atlantic had passed well beyond the posturing phase. The Argentine invasion of the Falklands had passed off with virtually no casualties and the initial assumption on all sides was that diplomacy would come up with some kind of face-saving compromise, such as the leaseback idea favoured by the British Foreign Office before the war. President Belaunde Terry of Peru had just begun his attempt to broker such a compromise when *Conqueror* torpedoed it along with the cruiser, on which more Argentines died than the eventual total of British fatalities in the entire conflict. In London the unabashedly jingoistic *Sun* news-paper printed its infamous celebratory headline, 'GOTCHA'. When the submarine eventually came home she was flying a skull-and-crossbones testimonial to her successful attack, in the tradition invented by Max Horton in the First World War. Her commander was awarded the DSO. It was the first time a nuclear submarine had fired a shot in anger, the first time a Royal Navy submarine had torpedoed a cruiser since June 1945 (in the last weeks of the war against Japan) and the first time a submarine had sunk a cruiser since a Japanese boat destroyed USS *Indianapolis* in the following month.

But the most interesting and revealing aspect of this one-sided action was the political aftermath in Britain. A series of conflicting statements which began by claiming that the *Belgrano* was inside the TEZ, then near it, then sailing east (towards the Falklands and the British task force), then west, seemed to show profound govern-ment unease, not to say guilt, under a barrage of parliamentary questions from the indefatigable Labour MP Tam Dalyell and others. It was another manifestation of the appalling public relations prevalent in government and at the MoD at the time, partly based on assumptions that nobody would have the temerity to question military actions during a conflict, and that even if some did they had no right to do so and would soon be seen off by a public opinion that strongly supported the war (a common error brought on by attaching too much importance to the views of a mostly right-wing press). A competent government mouthpiece would have said firmly that the cruiser was a major unit of a fleet that had just landed an invasion force five times larger than the local population to occupy territory internationally recognized as British, that it was in a holding position closer to the Falklands than to Argentina, that its intentions were unknown, that it could have reversed course at any time to make a hostile move, and that in conjunction with the northern carrier group it constituted a standing 'fleet in being' threat – so it was, with regret, sunk. The strategic consequence was also of great advantage to the task force with its attenuated air power: the rest of the Argentine fleet went home and took no further part in the war. But Her Majesty's government appeared badly rattled by its belated discovery that war means death.

The Argentines soon got their revenge through the agency of their bravest and most skilled fighting men – the pilots of their Air Force and Navy. Two naval Super-Etendards, each equipped with one Exocet anti-ship missile, came roaring in at deck level, popping up quickly for a radar sweep before dropping down again and launching their missiles at the Type 42 anti-aircraft destroyer HMS *Sheffield* (Captain J. F. T. G. 'Sam' Salt, RN). She and two sister ships were between forty and seventy miles south of Port Stanley at the time, acting as a screen for Woodward's carriers forty miles further out. One missile hit the ship square amidships, the other missed. There was no warning, despite the presence of a double CAP overhead, and the missile was only sighted when one mile off, too late for any counter. The warhead did not explode, but the rest of the Exocet's fuel was enough to cause a fire that could not be extinguished. Twenty men were killed and twenty-four wounded; 266 survived as the destroyer was abandoned afloat (a lure for further attackers until she sank in rough weather) five hours later, despite a Herculean firefighting effort by several other ships. Her funeral pyre made horrific viewing when the film finally reached Britain. Her loss, despite a light casualty list thanks to an efficient state of alert aboard, caused severe irresolution at Westminster; Admiral Lewin, Chief of Defence Staff, had returned from New Zealand to carry out his role as the government's chief military adviser, and had to extend a steadying hand as the War Cabinet learned that war meant not only death but also losses to one's own side. Frantic efforts were made in Britain to find an ad hoc defence against Exocets as HMS *Exeter* was ordered to replace the lost ship, one of eight reinforcements sent in May. More losses would follow.

The first was a Sea Harrier, shot down in an attack on Goose Green airfield the same day, 4 May. The pilot, Lieutenant Nick

Taylor, RN, was buried with military honours by the Argentines. Another disappeared without trace from a CAP on 5 May, leaving Woodward with just seventeen invaluable fixed-wing strike aircraft. Two of them on the 8th bombed the *Narwal*, an Argentine trawler in use as a spy ship, which was then boarded and seized by an SBS raiding party fifty miles south of Stanley. The Type 21 frigate *Alacrity* passed northwards up the Falkland Sound between the two main islands, West and East Falkland, to look for mines and other Argentine measures on the night of 10 to 11 May. She found none but sank the transport *Isla de los Estados*, which blew up with the loss of all but two aboard. The frigate was fired on by the submarine *San Luis*, whose torpedoes were temperamental: the controlling wire of the one fired broke and it hit a decoy towed by HMS *Arrow*, which by this time was with her sister. The boat had been off the north of the Sound for four weeks but now went home on 11 May, never to return: her West German sister had engine trouble, which meant that Argentine submarines took no further part in the conflict, leaving the northern end of the Sound unwatched.

The next major British casualty was the Type 42 destroyer *Glasgow*, attacked by Skyhawks on 12 May. Her Sea Dart anti-aircraft missiles and her 4.5-inch gun both failed; the frigate *Brilliant* nearby had the close-range missile Sea Wolf, which destroyed two of the three attackers and drove the third to miss with his bomb. Less than half an hour later four more came in, one of which struck the *Glasgow* amidships with a 1,000lb bomb that passed right through the ship without exploding, holing each side above the waterline and causing damage to one engine, the steering gear and other equipment. The two ships gave up their shore-bombardment work for the time being. Some of the Type 21 frigates worryingly developed metal fatigue in the rough weather, showing cracks in at least two cases. But an SAS party got ashore in northern East Falkland to destroy eleven aircraft at Pebble Island airstrip, damaging ground facilities without loss to themselves.

TG 317.0, the amphibious group led by Commodore Clapp on *Fearless* with *Intrepid* and a flotilla of RFAs and merchant ships in company, was ready from 16 May to land 3 Commando Brigade, while the Army contribution, the four battalions of 5 Infantry Brigade, approached on *QE2*, *Canberra* and other ships. The Cabinet sanctioned a landing on East Falkland in the early hours of the 20th as TG 317.8 (the carriers) came to the northern end of Falkland Sound in support. *Hermes* now mustered twenty-one Harricrs, including six RAF models, shedding her Sea Kings; one of the latter crashed, killing twenty-two SAS men being transferred to *Intrepid*. First to land at San Carlos, north-west of Stanley and on the other side of East Falkland, just after midnight on 21 May, was 2 Para, the 2nd Battalion, the Parachute Regiment, followed by 40 Commando, Royal Marines; the second wave included 45 Commando and 3 Para; 42 Commando (minus the company left to guard South Georgia) was brigade reserve on Canberra. SAS and SBS detachments were landed well away from the beachhead to tackle lookouts and strongpoints and to provide distractions. Complete tactical surprise was achieved and there were only handfuls of Argentine troops in the area chosen for the landing.

Once again it was the Argentine pilots who did the most harm in a series of fierce raids. Daggers and Skyhawks came in, sometimes six at a time, doing much damage to the destroyer *Antrim* and frigates *Ardent* and *Argonaut* with their bombs. *Ardent* succumbed to repeated bomb hits, losing twenty-two killed and thirty-seven wounded. *Argonaut* was towed away. An unexploded 1,000lb bomb was removed from *Antrim* in a ten-hour drama. Only two out of seven escorts on hand for the San Carlos landing escaped damage from the dashing Argentine pilots, whose very bravery sometimes blunted their striking power: in many cases they came in so close to their targets that their bomb detonators did not have time to work. Some three dozen aircraft had come over in the first wave, of which just two were shot down; another two dozen came over later, of which seven were claimed as destroyed. The amphibious force the escorts were covering, however, suffered no damage at all and the Argentine Army did not attack the landing, preferring to dig trenches at Goose Green some fifteen miles to the south.

After a day too bad for flying, the air attacks from Argentina resumed, badly damaging the frigate *Antelope* and leaving an unexploded bomb in her vitals. This blew up when British Army bomb-disposal men tackled it, setting the ship ablaze on 23 May, whereupon she broke in two and sank; only two men died and four were injured. Using the terrain for cover against radar with consummate skill, the Argentine flyers came back on the sixth day and attacked the landing ships, starting fires on *Sir Galahad*, *Sir Lancelot* and *Sir Bedivere*. The first named was hit by several attackers and was beached in flames, though she was saved from sinking and was sent to the rear to be patched up. The British expected something special on D-day plus four, 25 May, Argentina's national day (hence the name of their carrier). Instead, the number of air sorties was markedly lower. Yet three bombs penetrated the hull of the destroyer *Coventry* and tore her heart out; despite the fact that she rolled over and sank in little more than fifteen minutes, only nineteen men were killed and twenty wounded while 263 men were saved in a superbly organized rescue.

Insofar as the San Carlos landing by 3 Commando Brigade was in no way hampered by the Argentine naval and air force pilots, it was a British victory; but the fact that three modern warships had been sunk, in addition to HMS *Sheffield*, and half a dozen sufficiently damaged to reduce their effectiveness while two landing ships had been burned out, made it an expensive victory. Had many Argentine planes not been at the end of their tether on arrival over the target area, the 'butcher's bill' would have been rather higher. Pilots had to attack the first target they saw and did remarkably well. Defence systems on several British ships failed or performed unreliably, including radars and missiles. Nor was the account closed yet.

The Super-Etendards had apparently been kept in reserve for attacking the British carriers close to the Falklands. Two of them, refuelling out to sea before their attack, flew over unexpectedly from the north rather than the west, each launching its Exocet, on sighting Task Group 317.8, at the same target: the frigate *Ambuscade*, which managed to deflect completely only one with its chaff screen. The other missile homed in on a rather larger target, the 15,000-ton transport *Atlantic Conveyor*, which had arrived to join the carriers at lunchtime on the 25th and was the last in the line of ships. The errant missile proved much more effective than even the pilot could have hoped; once again the warhead did not explode but the remaining fuel caused a fire on the container ship, which was soon blazing from end to end; when the flames reached the ammunition stored in the bow, that section was blown off. In another remarkable instantaneous rescue operation, 150 of her crew were saved but twelve, including her master, Captain North, were killed: he was decorated posthumously with the DSC. The wreck remained afloat but everything she had been carrying, including four out of five irreplaceable Chinook heavy-lift helicopters, was lost (one Chinook managed to escape). The

Atlantic Conveyor was the most serious British loss in material terms of the entire campaign, forcing the marines to 'yomp' (march over rough terrain; the Paras called it 'tabbing') eastwards towards their objectives in inferior boots and bad weather, as they began to do on Brigadier Thompson's orders on the 26th, four days before the land commander, Major-General Moore, arrived on the *QE2*. Thus Argentina's national day had been a most successful one for her gallant pilots, who suffered no losses on 25 May: they had certainly avenged the *Belgrano*. Fortunately for the British, only one Exocet remained in mainland Argentina, which was unable to acquire replacements.

The British were rapidly using up their highly effective, updated Sidewinder air-to-air missiles but were able to get more from the United States, along with Shrike anti-radar missiles. Apart from such weaponry, the Americans supplied not only intelligence to the British but also communications facilities and equipment, such as the Submarine Satellite Information Exchange System, needed because the British satellite network did not yet cover large parts of the southern hemisphere.

The first major British land victory was the capture on 29 May of Goose Green by 2 Para, in which the commander, Lieutenant-Colonel H. Jones, won one of only two VCs of the campaign (both posthumous) in an attack on a machine-gun position. The next day a coordinated attack by the Argentine Air Force tried to hit the *Invincible* with the last Exocet, launched by a Super-Etendard, but failed.

After one month of operations around the Falklands, preceded in the case of many ships by another month at sea, the Royal Navy was in auxiliary mode, as seaborne support for the two reinforced brigades. Harriers were now able to operate from recaptured territory on East Falkland, while the carriers continued to act as floating airfields. The Argentine pilots had not given up; far from it. On 8 June they attacked the landing ships bringing units of 5 Infantry Brigade ashore to a second beachhead at Bluff Cove, south-west of Stanley: *Sir Galahad*, already scorched from her previous experiences at San Carlos, was set on fire a second time, with many Welsh Guards aboard waiting for landing craft to take them ashore. Forty-three soldiers and seven sailors died or were reported missing, fifty-seven men were wounded, many with serious burns. *Sir Tristram* was also hit at least twice, but her damage was less drastic, with two sailors killed. Both ships were abandoned amid some of the worst filmed scenes of the war. The frigate *Plymouth* was damaged in the same raid but was able to put out her flames and stay on.

The advance on Stanley began on 11 June, with the marines and paratroops of 3 Commando Brigade taking one objective after another at such temporarily famous places as Mount Harriet and Mount Longdon, where tough resistance was encountered and Sergeant Ian McKay of 3 Para won the other posthumous VC. Otherwise casualties among British troops were very light. British air raids, including the occasional Vulcan from Ascension and carrier strikes, continued. So did the naval bombardments. An Exocet fired from land hit the destroyer *Glamorgan*, causing a major fire in her helicopter hangar and a marked list; even so she managed to control her damage and remain on duty after losing nine men killed, four missing and fourteen wounded. The ro-ro ferry *Norland* took more than 1,000 Argentine prisoners of war to Montevideo on 12 June. The last Argentine daylight air raid by three Daggers took place on the 13th, causing no damage. Occasional night raids by Canberras and Skyhawks followed, to little or no effect.

The 6,000 fighting men of the two British brigades advanced on the last major obstacles on the way to Stanley, Wireless Ridge to the north-west and Mount Tumbledown and Mount William to the south-west, on the night of 13 to 14 June; General Menendez had about 9,000 men in and around the capital, but most of them were conscripts whose low morale was not alleviated by poor-quality officers. The best Argentine troops on hand were the regulars of the Marine Corps. 2 Para attacked Wireless Ridge supported by the light armour of the Blues and Royals; the Scots Guards attacked Tumbledown; the Welsh Guards and 40 Commando, and later the Gurkhas, Mount William. Half a dozen escorts bombarded in support, as did 105mm artillery pieces on land. The Argentine Marines and artillery fought hard, holding up British attacks by as much as three hours, until the only vantage point on high ground left to the Argentines was Sapper Hill, a little to the west of Stanley. Royal Marines of 40 Commando were lifted into position by helicopters to attack it.

The Argentine troops then retreated into the town and General Menendez decided to ask for terms, seventy-five days after the invasion, forty-five days after the first British counter-strike. General Moore arrived under flag of truce at Government House at 6 p.m. and Menendez signed the surrender at 8 p.m., midnight in Britain. Juliet Company of 42 Commando Royal Marines, which included the men who had surrendered Government House after the invasion, re-hoisted the Union flag they had taken to Britain and brought back to the Falklands.

When the 2,000 Argentines on West Falkland surrendered, the tally of prisoners of war rose to 10,250. Many young conscripts were in poor condition, neglected by their officers, indifferent in every sense. Galtieri resigned on 18 June, paving the way for Argentina's early return to democracy. The junta endorsed the surrender on 21 June. The Task Force rapidly dispersed; the hulk of *Sir Galahad* was dispatched by the submarine *Onyx*. After a slap-up wardroom dinner in Berkeley Sound, north of Port Stanley, where her namesake had celebrated in December 1914, *Invincible* went home, relieved by *Illustrious*. The returning ships received delirious welcomes, the *Hermes* and *Canberra* in mid-July, *Invincible* on 17 September.

The story goes that some of the returning Task Force members received a salute at sea from a Soviet naval unit for a job well done. And so it was: an extraordinary projection of seapower across 8,000 miles, in which 255 British men died and 777 were wounded; Argentine casualties were more than twice as high. A hugely relieved Mrs Thatcher said, 'Rejoice!' Just how grateful, the Navy wondered, would she be? As a strong garrison of all three British services closed the stable door on the Falklands, it seemed clear that it would have been cheaper to give each Falkland islander a million pounds as a bribe to go away – enough for half a dozen 'Invincibles' and more.

16

'Modern Forces for the Modern World'

The Falklands War saved the Royal Navy. It remained capable of delivering limited but effective British military force anywhere in reach of the sea – eight years before the collapse of Soviet Communism made this the only justification for a flexible fleet. It kept its carriers and its Harriers, its amphibious assault ships and its marines; and it acquired new AEW helicopters, better defences against anti-ship missiles, new torpedoes and missiles of several kinds, better fire precautions, more integrated electronics, better communications, stronger hulls and replacements for all its lost ships and auxiliaries. Its role as guardian of the nuclear deterrent was hugely enhanced by the substitution of the Trident missile with four new submarines for the Polaris system, even though the disappearance of the Warsaw Pact removed the only obvious justification for it. John Nott's proposals in *The Way Forward* were scrapped and their author, pausing only to collect the usual knighthood at the exit, soon left politics for richer pickings in the City of London.

By twentieth-century standards it had been a small war, fought in quasi-laboratory conditions and blessedly free of 'collateral damage' (in plain English, civilian casualties). A few thousand professional soldiers and marines had attacked an occupation force of 13,000 to liberate the 1,800 people then living in the Falklands. But the 8,000 miles of ocean between Britain and the islands, the overnight conversion of an expensive ASW fleet into a colonial expeditionary force and the necessary reliance on largely untested technologies made it an extremely intricate and dangerous undertaking for a service which had more often than not felt slighted by an ungrateful nation since its supreme victories in two world wars.

Only days before the Argentine invasion Keith Speed, the Navy

Minister whose protest against cuts had got him sacked, became a founder of the British Maritime League, set up to campaign against the precipitous decline of the Royal Navy, the Merchant Navy and Britain's shipyards alike. All this looked like a perilously insouciant attitude for an island nation still heavily dependent on seaborne trade. Forty-five merchant ships taken up from trade made an indispensable contribution to the Falklands campaign in supporting forty warships, twenty Royal Fleet Auxiliaries, ten Fleet Air Arm squadrons, all three Royal Marine Commandos and the troops. The Navy derived an advantage unique in the world from having fought such a campaign, gathering unparalleled experience in the age of missiles and electronics.

But the merchant fleet under the Red Ensign went on declining, to such an extent that within a year it would have been impossible to repeat the exploit (for most people, however, an outcome devoutly to be wished). The practice of 'flagging out' by British shipping companies – registering ships in less demanding countries which did not impose British standards of safety, salary or seamanship – continued unabated. The RFA meanwhile became Britain's largest employer of merchant seamen, with twenty-three ships displacing up to 38,000 tonnes in service in 1999. Their mercantile crews received naval training in such fields as armed self-defence.

The long lead-time between deciding on a warship's design and its arrival in the fleet – up to fourteen years – worked to the Navy's advantage after the Falklands. The Type 23 frigate, commissioned from 1989 and a mainstay of the fleet ten years later, was in development and could be modified in the light of hard-won experience. Its hull was adjusted to include five rather than three smoke-containment zones in view of the effect of fire on the four lost warships. The new type got improved air-defence radar and passive early-warning, also retro-fitted to other ships such as the Type 42 destroyers (sisters of *Sheffield* and *Coventry*), which served on to the end of the century. The Sea Wolf missile was given a second tracking radar to improve its air-defence capability.

The American Phalanx short-range anti-missile system, a 'Gatling gun' that fired a dense, high-speed, rotating pattern of 20mm rounds at an incoming missile, was to be fitted to major ships. From 1980 the Dutch Goalkeeper system, which worked on the same lines, was preferred for its heavier projectiles. The two destroyers and two Type 21 frigates lost were replaced from 1985 by four modified Type 22 frigates (4,100 tons); two extant members of this '*Boxer*' class were renamed *Sheffield* and *Coventry* in the meantime. Although the original design was for ASW, the new batch was multi-purpose. The 4.5-inch, rapid-firing gun on the foredeck proved invaluable in the south Atlantic and was fitted to the replacements, as were eight American 'Harpoon' anti-ship missiles instead of four Exocets. More robust than the Type 21, soon to be scrapped, the new 22s had good anti-aircraft and missile defences, highly sensitive, long-range ASW sonar in their towed array and a new, larger EH 101 helicopter in a bigger hangar aft. The Type 23 that followed was at 3,500 tons slightly smaller, thanks to advances which tended to reduce the size of electronic and weapons systems, but was probably the most advanced frigate in the world when it made its bow in the shape of HMS *Norfolk* in 1989. A new coating reduced its radar profile, its towed array, redesigned to maximize silent running, was even more sensitive and its Sea Wolf short-range anti-aircraft/anti-missile missiles could be fired vertically as well as horizontally. It too sported a 4.5-inch, general-purpose gun.

A third 'Invincible' was commissioned as *Ark Royal* in 1985, with improvements, such as a longer ski-jump, more storage capacity for ASW torpedoes and sonobuoys, plus three Goal-keepers, all thanks to Falklands experience. The Sea King helicopter used faute de mieux for AEW in the Falklands was enhanced by the addition of American Searchwater radar. Two machines were able to try it out there before the end of the operation, though too late for the invasion period. The two earlier 'Invincibles' were upgraded to the new standard from 1986. On the correct assumption that one of the trio would always be refitting or in reserve, the Fleet Air Arm deployed only two squadrons of Sea Harriers, of eight aircraft each, to fly from them in rotation, which saved money by imposing a heavy strain on both units. The Sea King helicopter squadrons which formed the other element of each deployed carrier's air group were similarly stretched. But all aircraft lost in the south Atlantic were replaced, with improved radars and air-to-air missiles.

The 1981 decision to scrap the amphibious assault ships *Fearless* and *Intrepid* was formally rescinded in 1986; both were refitted at Swan Hunter on Tyneside. The latter was paid off in 1991 but kept in reserve at Portsmouth; replacements, to be called *Albion* and *Bulwark*, were ordered in 1996–7 with a view to scrapping the veterans by 2002. Meanwhile a new helicopter carrier, the 20,000-ton HMS *Ocean*, was launched in 1995 and entered service in 1999. While on hot-weather trials in the Caribbean in 1998, she was able to land British and Dutch marines to help alleviate a flood disaster in Central America.

The fibreglass mine-countermeasures vessel was already the best in the world; more of this '*Hunt*' class were built, to a simpler design, after the Falklands, where adapted trawlers stood in very effectively, reminding commanders of the importance of minesweeping in time for later events in the Gulf.

The under-reported work of the five nuclear fleet submarines deployed in the south Atlantic proved their value sufficiently to prompt annual additions to the latest '*Trafalgar*' class from 1983 (three more were added after a three-year gap, again at a rate of one per year, until 1991). Of earlier classes, five '*Valiants*', five '*Churchills*' and six '*Swiftsures*' remained in service along with the four '*Resolutions*' (the Polaris boats). Twelve fleet boats remained on active service in 1999, with seven (plus four Polaris boats) laid up, awaiting a solution to the problem of safely dismantling their reactors. Three more '*Trafalgars*' were ordered in 1997. The latest fleet boats, along with the '*Vanguard*' class of Trident-missile boats, were equipped with the second-generation, British-designed PWR 2 reactor, rather quieter than its predecessor, with a longer life and greater output of power.

The fleet boats were from 1981 armed with the submarine version of the US Harpoon ('sub-Harpoon') anti-ship missile and from 1986 with the home-made Tigerfish wire-guided, Mark 24, 21-inch torpedo, which was at last proving reliable (it will be remembered that *Conqueror* preferred the old Mark VIII for sinking the *Belgrano*). The British Spearfish torpedo, also 21-inch and wire-guided, began to enter service at the end of the century after an inordinately long development period and was said to be the world's fastest at over seventy knots. Unlike the electrically powered Tigerfish, the Spearfish was given a turbine motor. The ultimate conventional weapon for the fleet submarines was acquired in 1998: the American Tomahawk cruise missile, of which the Royal Navy, uniquely among America's allies, was allowed to buy sixty-five, at a cost, including electronics, guidance and firing systems, of £180m. This extraordinarily accurate descendant of Hitler's V1 flying bomb, with its 1,000lb warhead, was designed for launch from the standard 21-inch torpedo tube and had a range of about 1,000 miles at a cruising speed of 550 miles per hour, about the same as a passenger jet. To put Britain's purchase in context, it is worth pointing out here that the United States fired about 300 at Afghanistan and Sudan in a strike against alleged terrorist bases in 1998; and on the first night alone of the Nato bombardment of Kosovo in March 1999 the Americans launched about 100, whereas Britain's HMS *Splendid* fired six. For the Americans Tomahawk was no more than a tactical weapon; for Britain it was expensive enough to qualify as strategic.

The conventional diesel-electric submarine was phased out well before the end of the century, although the first of a new class, *Upholder*, was ordered in 1983. Completed in 1989 and followed by three more in 1991–3, her class was never commissioned. All four were paid off in 1994 and laid up at Barrow with a view to being leased to Canada from 2000. This decision of 1993 to abandon conventional boats altogether may yet prove to be a false economy. In the Gulf, for example, of which we have surely not heard the last as a focus of international tension, the sea is too shallow for the nuclear boats, twice as large, to operate safely; whereas in the Gulf War of 1991 British conventional submarines were able to land special forces teams for clandestine operations in Kuwait and Iraq. The Americans, having gone 'all-nuclear' in submarines rather earlier, noted this application and 'de-mothballed' one of their own diesel-electrics for experiments.

The last major reinforcement of Task Force 317 in the south Atlantic had consisted of eight destroyers and frigates, seven of which sailed from Portsmouth and Devonport on 10 May 1982. The eighth was HMS *Cardiff*, a Type 42 destroyer completed in 1979, which after loading extra stores at Gibraltar joined the rest in mid-ocean on 12 May. The *Cardiff* had been on her way home from the Straits of Hormuz at the mouth of the (Persian) Gulf.

In 1979 a revolution had brought the Ayatollah Khomeini to power in Iran and a palace plot did the same for Saddam Hussein in Iraq on the other side of the Gulf. The two countries shared a long land border and boasted vast oil reserves but were bitterly divided ethnically (Persians and Arabs) and religiously (Shi'ite Moslems in Iran versus Sunni), and therefore politically and diplomatically. They fell out in 1980 over the Shatt al-Arab waterway straddling their frontier at the northern end of the Gulf. This was particularly important to Iraq as its only direct access to the sea, via the port of Basra north of independent Kuwait (Iran's territory extended along the entire northern coastline of the Gulf down to Hormuz and beyond). The Iran–Iraq frontier ran down the middle of the 125-mile Shatt al-Arab, as agreed by treaty in 1937 and again in 1975 amid many disputes about it between the two countries under various regimes.

Seeing the chaos in Iran following the ousting of the Shah and the return of the turbulent Ayatollah, Saddam Hussein thought he saw his opportunity to redraw the map and invaded Iran in 1980. But, like Hitler in Russia in 1941, he was taking on a nation which however prostrate internally outnumbered his own by three to one. This meant that the best he could reasonably hope for was a quick victory and a limited gain which would then have to be consolidated. But half-trained masses of Iranian conscripts fell in their hundreds of thousands on the promise from the mullahs of eternal bliss for dying in a holy war. The Iraqi blitzkrieg ran into the sand after Saddam took a breather in the belief that he had won. The Iranians even took back some captured ground at enormous cost in blood, and Saddam, subsidized by his fellow Arabs including Kuwait (fearful of trouble from its 33 per cent Shi'ite minority stirred up by Iran), changed the focus of his attack to the oil industry, which the Iranians needed even more than the Iraqis to finance the war. Clandestinely the Americans supported Iraq because of their blind hatred of the Khomeini regime, which in 1979 had humiliated the United States by toppling its client, the Shah, and seizing its embassy in Teheran; the staff were taken hostage and a catastrophically bungled American rescue attempt helped Ronald Reagan to defeat President Jimmy Carter in November.

The West in general and the United States in particular feared for its oil supply, and Western navies, the Americans to the fore, sent ships to the Gulf to lay down their markers and try to protect their interests in the ever-volatile region. In October 1980, therefore, the British government established a naval squadron of two destroyers and two frigates for the Gulf of Oman, supported at sea by a tanker and a stores ship from the RFA and using Mombasa, Kenya, as a base for maintenance and shore leave. Two ships would be on hand at any one time in the Gulf of Oman, the continuation of the Persian Gulf outside the Straits of Hormuz: the origin of the Navy's 'Armilla Patrol', from which HMS *Cardiff* came in 1982. Its purpose was to protect international shipping sailing into or out of the Persian Gulf. In one form or another it remained there for the rest of the century, along with an ever-changing cast of ships of the American and other navies from as far afield as Australia and Belgium.

Fighting between Iraq and Iran continued in a desultory fashion until 1985, when Iraq tried another major offensive, again without a breakthrough. Saddam hoped to provoke international intervention in the Gulf to the disadvantage of isolated Iran, which was producing far in excess of the quota of oil allotted to it by the Organization of Petroleum-Exporting Countries to pay for its war. In 1987 Iraq effectively opened a second front, at sea in the Gulf. The American frigate *Stark* was damaged by an Iraqi Exocet missile, losing twenty-eight sailors, and Iran was reported to have installed Chinese surface-to-surface missiles at the Straits of Hormuz. Kuwait therefore asked the United States for permission for its tankers to fly the Stars and Stripes (in fact a breach of Geneva Convention flagging rules) so as to be entitled to the protection of the US Navy and its allies. To encourage Washington's agreement, Kuwait approached Moscow with a similar request. Soon it was possible to see televised pictures of vast tankers escorted by tiny-looking Western warships, including British.

Unlike the Royal Navy, the Americans had neglected mine-sweeping; their only serious capability was in mothballs. US Navy embarrassment knew no bounds when more than one of its charges suffered damage from indiscriminately sown Iranian contact mines of First World War design. Helicopters were used as a stopgap until Britain's mine-countermeasures vessels, still the best in the world and made of fibreglass, led a European sweeping force into the Gulf. That modern naval electronics were not infallible was tragically shown by the US cruiser *Vincennes* when it shot down an Iranian airliner, killing 290 passengers, in the belief that it was a fighter capable of more than three times the speed. Fortunately Iran and Iraq accepted the ceasefire called for by the United Nations Security Council shortly afterwards, in July 1988. Saddam blithely gave up all his territorial demands. Khomeini died at last in 1989; Saddam lived on, his expansionist aims undiminished.

He revived Iraq's claim to Kuwait, last deterred by the British naval and military intervention after the emirate became independent in 1961. Saddam simply sent his Republican Guard, the elite of his army, over the border on 2 August 1990 and seized the little state, which had oil reserves out of all proportion to its small size and a population of which half was made up of foreign workers. A large part of the oil was soon on fire as the Iraqis deliberately set wells ablaze, in a catastrophe for the local region's environment. The Emir, who had abolished his parliament in 1986, fled and Kuwait was declared a province of Iraq. But one UN member had driven its tanks through the Charter by invading another. More important, one Arab state had invaded another Arab state and there was no reason to believe that Saddam would stop there: Kuwait's southern border adjoined Saudi Arabia with its vast oil wealth. Worried that its pro-Western king might go the same way as the Shah, President George Bush found it surprisingly easy to gather a large coalition of regional and Western powers ready to intervene militarily to help expel the invaders from Kuwait, with the UN's blessing.

Exports, especially oil, from Iraq were subjected to a worldwide embargo, to enforce which a naval blockade was established by Allied warships. Britain sent an armoured division as well as building up the Armilla Patrol into Task Force 321.1, under Commodore P. K. Haddacks, RN, until 3 December, when Commodore C. J. S. Craig, RN, took over for what the Navy called Operation 'Granby' (the overall Allied maritime effort was Operation 'Desert Shield'; the eventual invasion of Kuwait was 'Desert Storm'). The commodore hoisted his pennant on the destroyer HMS *London*.

The Americans mustered 250,000 troops for a counter-invasion of Kuwait from Saudi well before the end of 1990. If this appeared to be an over-reaction, likely to make other members of a strictly temporary and uneasy coalition suspicious as well as impatient, President Bush nevertheless sent 200,000 more by year's end; with British, French and other troops, 500,000 soldiers and marines were present at the beginning of 1991. Much opinion in the United States and the Arab world alike took the view that the embargo and blockade might have been enough on their own, although hindsight suggests that Saddam Hussein was quite capable of staying put until forced to move. But such countries as Egypt, Syria, Morocco, Pakistan and Bangladesh continued to support the coalition with troops. Its sole aim was to liberate Kuwait; the American-British desire to unseat Saddam, disarm Iraq, exact reparations and try those responsible for the invasion as war criminals, the real reason why the Americans sent so many troops, was suppressed. The result was an army more than large enough to recapture Kuwait and large enough to defend Saudi Arabia, but not large enough to conquer and occupy Iraq.

Headquarters of the swollen British forces in the Gulf were in Riyadh, the Saudi capital, under Lieutenant-General Sir Peter de la Billière. The first British ships to arrive were the destroyers *Gloucester* and *Cardiff* with the frigate *Brazen*, which duly relieved the Armilla Patrol warships as planned while the oiler RFA *Orangeleaf* stayed on. *London* was rapidly fitted with the extra communications needed for the Senior Naval Officer, Middle East, to be able to exercise command. The heavy repair ship RFA *Diligence* (the former MV *Stena Inspector* acquired in haste for the Falklands), the maintenance and supply ship RFA *Fort Grange* and the oiler *Olna* arrived with extra technicians and Sea King helicopters. '*Hunt*'-class mine-countermeasures vessels came with their command ship, HMS *Herald*; so did the new *Sir Galahad* to support them. Three more LSLs joined her to carry supplies and ammunition, as did RFA *Resource*. The *Argus*, the former MV *Contender Bezant* chartered for the Falklands and bought for the RFA in 1984, came out to handle casualties. The main role of this versatile RFA with her long helicopter deck behind a forward-sited superstructure was as an aviation training ship, but she was hurriedly converted for hospital work in October 1990 – a capability which was mothballed in case of future need after she reverted to peacetime duty.

In the end four frigates, seven destroyers, eight mine-counter-measures vessels, two depot ships and eleven RFAs, plus elements of six Fleet Air Arm helicopter squadrons from the Royal Navy, took part in the biggest British naval deployment since the Falklands War. Hostilities began on the night of 15 to 16 January 1991 with air raids, mostly American but also involving RAF Tornados and other allied aircraft. The Royal Navy formed part of a multinational Maritime Interdiction Force which had already challenged 2,000 vessels, boarded twenty-five and diverted one by the end of 1990.

British destroyers were in the forefront of anti-aircraft and anti-missile defence, screening American battle groups in the Gulf. Royal Marine and Royal Artillery missile detachments were also deployed for this purpose on the relevant RFAs. All ships took precautions against nuclear, biological or chemical attack and reported themselves 'ready in all respects' on 14 January. Fifteen days later HMS *Gloucester*'s Lynx helicopter raised the alarm on sighting seventeen small, fast attack craft making for the anti-aircraft screen; helicopters from *Gloucester*, *Cardiff* and *Brazen* destroyed every one of them with their Sea Skua missiles, laying to rest the spectre of the Israeli destroyer sunk by Egyptian missile boats decades earlier. Seven more hits were scored on such craft in the next two days.

The Americans had brought minesweepers to work with those of Britain and other allies in clearing a 'box' for two US battleships, updated World War II veterans, to use for long-range bombardment of the Iraqi naval base on Faylaka Island with their 16-inch guns; even so, on 18 February two American escorts hit mines and the few casualties were lifted to RFA *Argus* for treatment. A week later *Gloucester* detected two large incoming missiles heading for the battleship *Missouri* and launched her Sea Dart (medium-range anti-aircraft) missiles against them. One was destroyed at a safe distance, the other failed (but may also have been hit). American liaison officers on British ships were impressed by the degree of integration of the electronic systems aboard. The US Navy, being much larger, still had highly specialized, less versatile ships, whereas the Royal Navy had been obliged to opt for almost interchangeable destroyers and frigates. The Americans were also surprised, on offering the British access to data from their satellites, to find that they had already deciphered the signals . . .

No submarine is listed among the British naval contribution to the Gulf War, but it emerged later that at least one British diesel-electric boat was involved in landing SAS men at the north-western end of the Gulf. So secret was this that US ships almost attacked it. Such enterprises could not be repeated, at least in that perennially unstable region, where British ships remained on patrol for the rest of the century, because Britain no longer operated conventional submarines and her nuclear boats were too large for such shallow waters.

In the last week of February the American General Norman Schwarzkopf unleashed 'Desert Storm', defeating the Iraqi Army in less than a week with minimal loss to the coalition; British technical superiority over Argentina in 1982 was as nothing compared with the American advantage over Iraq. That hapless nation lost between 30,000 and 100,000 killed, together with the bulk of its air and naval assets; the capital, Baghdad, was badly damaged by cruise missiles and bombs. Kuwait City was also severely damaged by the Iraqis, who set many fires before they retired over the border. For the allied navies there was much work after the war, clearing mines and harbours; the mine-countermeasures craft HMS *Cattistock* headed a relief convoy into Kuwait harbour and was the first to tie up alongside after the liberation.

The Americans wanted to 'finish the job' by marching on Baghdad and deposing Saddam, but were deterred by escalating costs and unease about US intentions among their temporary allies and at the United Nations. Saddam's intransigence therefore remained a problem for the world's sole superpower for the rest of the century. Aerial bombardment of Iraq continued for years on a fitful basis as American, British and allied aircraft imposed no-fly zones over the north and south of the country in a bid to hinder Saddam's persecution of ethnic minorities such as Kurds and 'marsh Arabs' in those regions. After years of grudging co-operation with UN inspection teams looking for weapons of mass destruction, Saddam chanced his arm and expelled them in 1998. The British carriers *Invincible* and *Illustrious* took turns in joining the Armilla Patrol for brief tours of duty in the Gulf throughout the later 1990s.

In spring 1999 HMS *Invincible* was on her way home from one of these when the de facto flagship of the British fleet was diverted, not for the first time, to another zone of longstanding international tension – the Balkans, where another authoritarian ruler was engaged in persecution of ethnic minorities. As an indirect consequence of the collapse of Soviet Communism and the Warsaw Pact after 1989, Balkan nationalism reared its extremely ugly head once again, as so often before in the bloodstained history of south-east Europe. The unrest emanated from Serbia, the dominant republic in the federation of Yugoslavia, where Slobodan Milosevic had been elected president in 1989. One of his first moves was to assert Serb domination over the hitherto autonomous province of Kosovo, where 90 per cent of the population was of Albanian origin (Albania lies on the other side of Kosovo from Serbia).

Earlier, as Yugoslavia imploded, Slovenia, then Croatia and later Macedonia all broke away to become independent states, recognized (sometimes prematurely) by the international community. Bosnia-Herzegovina achieved an extremely uneasy independence after a singularly vicious and complicated civil war involving Moslem and Croatian minorities and local and imported Serbs – and the long and bloody siege of unfortunate Sarajevo, already notorious as the flashpoint of the First World War. Under United Nations auspices, troops from Britain and several other Nato nations finally arrived in 1994, three years late, to try to keep the warring groups apart. American and allied aircraft were deployed to the same end, including Sea Harriers from *Invincible*.

But the war in Kosovo was worse in many respects. The Serbs were already persecuting the Albanian majority in their well-tried manner, sending in paramilitary police and troops to terrorize the targeted ethnic group into leaving its houses and then setting them on fire while making able-bodied men disappear, whether into prisons, detention camps or mass graves. Talks aimed at an internationally monitored settlement at Rambouillet outside Paris broke down and Nato, this time without United Nations backing, issued an ultimatum to President Milosevic. Perhaps he believed it was a bluff; or perhaps he welcomed the foreign threat as a boost to the power he was determined to retain above all other considerations. At any rate, for the first time since 1945, a sovereign European country was attacked by other European countries in alliance with the United States, without a suggestion of a United Nations blessing. Nato air forces began bombing Serbia in the fourth week of March 1999, from heights that ensured the safety of the pilots but also led to a series of appalling incidents of 'collateral damage', such as the Chinese Embassy and refugee columns.

The American and British navies provided flanking support in the Adriatic. The US Navy deployed a carrier task force including ships armed with cruise missiles. HMS *Splendid* (Commander Richard Barker, RN), the submarine that fired a live test missile off California in the previous year on delivery of the system to Britain, was diverted from the Mediterranean to launch the first six British Tomahawks to be fired in anger, on Wednesday 24 March. It was reported that she fired another ten later in the eleven-week bombing campaign, compared with about 400 fired by the Americans. In a classic Whitehall seizure of bombastic secretiveness, combined with the ministerial pomposity and braggadocio that was such a feature of the Kosovo campaign, the British government refused to reveal exactly how many missiles the Navy had fired – on grounds of national security! As the Americans ran down their Tomahawk stocks Britain probably had to wait before being able to buy replacements for the unconfirmed sixteen expended out of sixty-five. Almost in the same breath the MoD announced that British aircraft had dropped 1,005 bombs on Serbia.

Invincible's 'guest appearance' with seven Sea Harriers and ten Sea Kings was to help protect Nato bombers flying from Italian airfields; air reinforcements from the United States and other Nato countries enabled the carrier to complete her journey home after four weeks and give replenishment leave. She was replaced by RFA *Argus* with her three Sea Kings and hospital facilities, ready to support military movements into Kosovo on land and humanitarian aid requirements. Her deployment was another demonstration of the ever-increasing importance of the RFA fleet to the Royal Navy's operations.

Falklands victory or not, British governments of both colours never ceased in the century's last decade to look for economies in the defence budget, false or not – their bounden duty, indeed, as guardians of the taxpayers' money. The fall of the Berlin Wall in November 1989 and the ensuing unification of Germany and collapse of Soviet Communism, the results of chronic economic mismanagement and the unsustainable East–West arms race that had underpinned the Cold War, prompted the Conservative government to produce a defence review entitled *Options for Change* in 1990. Presented as a considered programme designed to take advantage of the 'peace dividend' yielded by the collapse of the Warsaw Pact (which left Nato without a potential enemy), it lacked strategic depth and was no more than the usual financially motivated cost-cutting exercise, though less drastic for the Navy than it might have been. The British Army of the Rhine and RAF Germany were the obvious focus for serious reductions. The Navy's aircraft and flying facilities ashore and at sea came under a single Flag Officer, Naval Aviation, a wholly rational reform. The Women's Royal Naval Service adopted male ranks in preparation for complete integration into the Navy. Another handful of older destroyers, frigates and submarines was paid off. The decision to upgrade the deterrent from Polaris to Trident, which cost £12.5bn at 1999 prices, was not affected: the first 15,000-ton submarine to carry them, HMS *Vanguard*, was completed in 1992, the second in 1994 and the third in 1997. The Polaris force was scrapped in 1996. Faslane had to be massively expanded from 1987 to 1991 to handle the huge new boats – the biggest European construction project after the Channel Tunnel.

In 1993 John Major's government carried out a 'Defence Costs Study' foreshadowing reductions in destroyers, frigates and submarines, henceforth nuclear only. Personnel, 73,000 in 1982 and 67,000 in 1987, fell to 59,000 in 1993, when the Royal Naval Reserve was cut by a third and the Royal Naval Engineering College was closed. The Wrens were fully absorbed into the Navy. In 1998, by which time 850 women were serving at sea, two female lieutenants were given command of coastal patrol vessels. No bets were being taken on the first female submarine commander as, after an unsuccessful experiment, no woman had been allowed to serve underwater by 2000. But the European Court of Justice unexpectedly ruled in a discrimination case in October 1999 that the Royal Marines could exclude women. In November, however, the court decreed that British forces must no longer exclude homosexuals, a ban which had much support from senior commanders (notably Admiral Sir Jock Slater on his retirement as First Sea Lord in 1998). As most such men had attended boarding schools and as the services had since time immemorial had at least their fair share of homosexuals, the posture of the 'antis' was absurd and hypocritical. But the government outlawed homophobia in a new code of conduct for the forces, as it was obliged to do under the European Convention on Human Rights. In May 2000 the last homosexual man to be dismissed was the first to be reinstated: last out, first in . . .

Although the Navy still possessed more than seventy warships and submarines in 1996, the Merchant Navy had dwindled to such an extent that eleven foreign freighters (but no British) were chartered from ex-Soviet bloc countries such as Poland and the Ukraine to carry supplies for a joint exercise with the US Navy. There was deep embarrassment when one of these ships was declared unseaworthy by US authorities and impounded for eleven days on its arrival in American waters. At the same time it was revealed that the Navy had spent £40m keeping *Fearless* and *Intrepid* on the books, although the latter was unusable and the former could only limp across the Atlantic for exercise 'Purple Heart' – even though the amphibious capability was meant to be one of Britain's main naval contributions to Nato.

Yet in January 1997 more than thirty Royal Navy and RFA vessels, led by *Illustrious*, took part in exercise 'Ocean Wave', the largest British 'blue water' deployment since the Falklands, a marketing exercise which took the formation, among many other ports of call, to Hong Kong as it was about to be handed back to China in July. The eight-month voyage began with the Conservatives in power and finished three months after the Labour landslide in the May general election, ending eighteen years in opposition.

Inevitably and as usual, one of the first moves of Tony Blair's government was to order a Strategic Defence Review. 'New Labour' prided itself on its presentational skills, and the review, subtitled *Modern Forces for the Modern World*, published after only fourteen months in July 1998, was a glossy production which also showed signs of deeper thought than usual on such occasions. The Tories had cut the defence budget by a quarter in real terms from 1990 to their defeat in 1997 – their 'peace dividend', which reduced British submarine strength by more than half and escorts by a third. Would there now be more of the same, given an austere Chancellor of the Exchequer and Labour's reputation for being 'unsound' on defence?

The review looked ahead as far as 2015 and took a worldwide view, conceding that there was no immediate military threat to Britain or its foreign interests as vested in the double framework of the Nato alliance and the European Union. The government cautiously favoured a 'European Security and Defence Identity' within Nato, built on the hitherto moribund Western European Union. The reduced threat made it possible to deploy smaller forces for a broader range of tasks.

Labour had been widely expected to cancel the fourth '*Vanguard*' but the review kept it. On launching HMS *Vengeance* in September 1999, Defence Secretary George Robertson said in all solemnity that Britain was working with 'great urgency' towards global nuclear disarmament. After the withdrawal of the last RAF free-fall nuclear bombs in March 1998, Trident was Britain's only deployed nuclear weapon. Nevertheless it was so accurate that Labour would reduce by one third the stockpile of British-made warheads to fewer than 200 for the fifty-eight American-built missiles held, taking the total reduction of Britain's nuclear destructive capacity since the end of the Cold War to 70 per cent. Only one submarine would be on patrol at a time, carrying a reduced load of forty-eight warheads, three per missile, each independently targetable, but half the originally intended ninety-six. Boats would thus become available for a limited range of other tasks, such as joint exercises and oceanographic surveys. The adjustments (reversible) reduced the firepower of a Trident submarine to two-thirds of the Polaris boats. A lower level of alert would prevail on deterrent patrols, though it could be raised at any time. The nuclear warhead programme cost £400m per year (including decommissioning of previous weapons) and the annual running costs of the strategic submarines were £280m in 1999. The deterrent accounted for little more than 3 per cent of the defence budget, according to the review.

More inter-service integration was promised, with joint intelligence, logistics and combat forces, variable according to task. The electronic information explosion created both problems and opportunities for the forces; and precautions against nuclear, chemical and biological weapons that might be used by a smaller power against a larger one had to be maintained and intensified as such technologies proliferated.

'At sea, the emphasis is continuing to move away from large-scale maritime warfare and open-ocean operations in the north Atlantic. In future, littoral operations and force projection, for which maritime forces are well suited, will be our primary focus,' the review said. 'Air power will be a crucial factor in maritime warfare, on most battlefields and as part of the most demanding peace-support operations as in Bosnia.'

The existing Nato Joint Rapid Deployment Force led by the British Army in Germany would be surpassed in flexibility by Britain's Joint Rapid Reaction Forces, which would from 2001 be able to deliver the appropriate combination of personnel and equipment from all three services to a crisis area, or to Nato's Allied Command Europe. Four more ro-ro transport ships would be acquired, as well as an additional casualty-receiving ship with 200 beds (this requirement was raised to two in 1999).

The most important single proposal for the Navy was two new carriers of 40,000 tons each, to be called *Albion* and *Bulwark* and to replace the three 'Invincibles' by 2012. Meanwhile HMS *Ocean*, the new helicopter carrier, would be deployable from 1999. By 2012–15 there would be a replacement for the Harrier also. Meanwhile naval and RAF Harriers would be combined into a 'Joint Force 2000' with joint RN/RAF training under the Chief of Joint Operations. This amounted to a rationalization of previous operation of RAF as well as RN Harriers from the carriers. The naval version, the FA 2, was mainly for maritime air defence but with a bombing capability; the RAF version, the GR 7, was mainly used as a ground-attack fighter-bomber. The successor would be multi-role, intended for both services.

There would be a price, as ever, to be paid by the Navy: escorts would be reduced from thirty-five to thirty-two, fleet submarines from twelve to ten and mine-countermeasures vessels by three to twenty-two. The '*Swiftsure*' submarines would be paid off and replaced by a new '*Astute*' class (all would be capable of firing Tomahawks) and the Type 23 frigate programme would be completed, pending the development of a replacement. The planned total of the latest Merlin ASW helicopters would be held at forty-four. These cuts would release enough personnel to fill gaps elsewhere (the Navy was 2,000 short in 1998). A concerted attempt would be made to improve career structures and con-solidate recruiting, including among ethnic minorities (markedly under-represented in all services) and women; and to reduce early departures among expensively trained specialists.

All this – and a promised reduction in real terms of the defence budget too, from 2.7 to 2.4 per cent of Gross Domestic Product! Labour's defence review looked forward to a net reduction of £685m a year between 1999–2000 and 2001–2. The review confidently predicted an efficiency saving of 3 per cent a year and promised a further saving of some £2bn over ten years by 'smart procurement', i.e. eliminating most of the sheer waste in past defence spending. Old hands in this area of expertise regarded these undertakings as the hardest part of the review to fulfil and the most likely to fail. Early vindication for the sceptics came in a govern-ment admission in the dying days of the century that the Kosovo intervention had revealed serious inadequacy and ageing in a wide range of equipment, from boots to destroyers – a classic British example of false economy: after spending tens of billions of pounds per year on defence it seemed positively criminal to 'save' a few tens of millions by failing to ensure that the equipment worked on the rare occasions when it was really needed. Shades of the dud shells of 1914, the old naval biplanes of 1939, the lack of early-warning planes on the Falklands carriers. The sceptics were given more ammunition in April 2000, when forty-four of the Navy's fifty-nine Lynx helicopters were grounded with faulty rotors.

And – as ever was – the Navy at the turn of the century was 1,500 short of its notional strength of 40,000, the lowest since 1850. The overstretch caused by a wide variety of commitments prompted the Navy to cancel the annual amphibious exercise to reinforce Norway with British and Dutch marines. As if there were not already enough to do, the MoD sent the destroyer HMS *Glasgow*, visiting Darwin, Australia, to help pacify East Timor as that ravaged territory gained independence from a reluctant Indonesia. Commander John King, RN, placed his ship, its helicopter and Royal Marine detachment at the disposal of the UN intervention force led by Australia. An SBS team was the first British contingent to land, in September 1999. Eight months later, in May 2000, a Royal Navy task force went to Sierra Leone to back up a battalion group from the Parachute Regiment in stiffening local and UN attempts to quash a rebellion. Helicopter-carrier *Ocean* and HMS *Illustrious* plus 700 Royal Marines took part.

The service suffered from personnel problems throughout the century, even when at inflated wartime strength, as has been made clear. But at the end of the period the underlying problems looked intractable. The small, all-volunteer, highly technical armed forces in general and the Navy in particular were more than ever worlds apart. Even their admittedly rather hackneyed annual showcase, the Royal Tournament at Earl's Court, died with the century for lack of public interest. Deference was emphatically out of fashion, a challenge to the kind of discipline and obedience traditionally demanded by the forces. Unemployment, that old recruiting sergeant, was in retreat. The monarchy, to which service-people swore loyalty, was no longer the unchallenged cynosure of national pride; and the nation appeared to have turned its back on all things maritime. In November 1999 the government duly announced naval expenditure of £12bn – from 2004 – in line with its defence review, including the two carriers and the Type 45 destroyers, derived from an abortive, tri-national combined project. But the forces themselves had no real answer to a growing existential crisis. 'Join the Navy and see the Balkans' seemed an unlikely draw for a young generation more concerned with virtual reality. The forces, including the Navy, remained among 'the best of British', publicly envied by such unlikely admirers as President Jacques Chirac of France, but enfeebled by declining interest and respect for national institutions all the way up to Whitehall, Westminster and Buckingham Palace. And the Navy's public relations ineptitude was shown once again in May 2000 when trainees were ordered to shout 'bang' instead of firing practice-rounds – for a saving of £5m over three years at the gunnery school near Plymouth. How Sir Francis Drake would have laughed!

The finest defences in the world are open to undermining by espionage, the historic 'equalizer' which ensures that no power retains an edge over its rivals for very long. Britain had been profoundly embarrassed by the scandals of the early 1960s, not least because many of the secrets compromised were American, which naturally worried Washington and impaired US willingness to share with Britain. But the exchange of ideas, begun in earnest in 1939, continued for the rest of the century – and 'exchange' is the correct word, as Britain persistently came up with ideas that were eagerly adopted by the US Navy.

Yet as the century drew to a close it was the Americans' turn to be embarrassed by spy scandals, in two specific cases of a catastrophic order of magnitude which also affected the security of Britain and her Navy. In the mid-1980s it was revealed that John Anthony Walker, Jr, a chief warrant officer in the US Navy, and other members of his family, supplied an enormous collection of naval secrets to the Soviet Union for money from 1968 to 1985. The information concerned surface ships, submarines, ciphers, electronics, weapons systems, silent running (a British speciality) and even construction methods. This enabled the Russians to catch up with the US technologically and also to counter its naval deployments in periods of tension. As a result the Americans had to spend billions to regain their lead (which was good news for their defence industry at least). Insofar as the British Navy relied on US equipment and systems, it too was affected by the Walker ring's treachery.

Then in 1999 it was revealed that China had been milking American technology to update its nuclear armoury, including submarine-launched strategic missiles, for more than twenty years. An ethnic Chinese scientist working at the nuclear research laboratory at Los Alamos, Wen-Ho Lee, had allegedly downloaded thousands of files into his laptop computer. Britain was directly affected as Trident technology was among the stolen information. China also received details in 1997 of a long-standing Anglo-American research programme into a new kind of satellite-based detector for locating submerged submarines. The latter leak was allegedly the work of another Chinese-American, Peter Lee (no relation), employed by the Pentagon at a Californian weapons laboratory.

*

With an assertive China inexorably advancing towards superpower status, and with India and Pakistan openly testing nuclear devices in 1998, the world remained a no less dangerous place than it was in the Cold War between the Western and Soviet blocs; indeed it was even more dangerous because less predictable. Israel had nuclear weapons and would undoubtedly use them if threatened by such as Saddam Hussein's Iraq, whose weaponry was of unknown potency. Other small countries could develop ambitions beyond their station and exploit readily available, inexpensive technologies to make weapons of mass destruction with which to terrorize neighbours or rivals. How much damage they could do depended on the level of sophistication of their delivery systems. Russia was desperately impoverished yet still possessed a vast, crumbling nuclear stockpile – along with underpaid, demoralized armed forces. It would be more than merely astonishing if the other four 'official' nuclear powers, America, Britain, China and France, did not retain deterrent insurance against a despairing Russian backlash, especially as the rebellion in Chechnya refused to die down. Certainly in Britain's case there was an unshakable, cross-party consensus in favour of Trident, even though no politician would be specific about what it was for, or would admit that nuclear weapons had notably failed to deter the likes of Galtieri, Saddam or Milosevic.

Meanwhile the nation's ultimate weapon was in the same hands at the end of the century as it had been at the beginning. The White Ensign remained the standard of ultimate British power as the nuclear submarine filled the vacancy left by the dreadnought and the Royal Navy once again deployed the nation's strategic armament.

Epilogue

The Legacy

The most turbulent century in the history of the Royal Navy, the nation it twice saved and the world they once bestrode began with a British fleet as strong as those of the next two powers combined, and to spare. The 'two-power standard' gave way by 1914 to 'Germany plus 60 per cent' and after 1918 to the 'one-power standard' – parity with the largest foreign fleet, the United States Navy, which was already more modern, if less experienced. Wartime expansion and the crippling of the American battlefleet at Pearl Harbor in 1941 temporarily restored the British Navy's primacy but the disastrous events of 1942 and the vast American naval construction programme, carriers to the fore, relegated the British fleet to a second place which was ceded in turn to the Soviet Navy in the 1960s. Meanwhile the Royal Navy usually held its own, if not more, with the French Navy, the fleet of the neighbouring second-rank power with a roughly equivalent economy. But from the 1960s, as its visible presence shrank, the Royal Navy's underwater strength attained a degree of firepower unimaginable in the days of the grand obsession with battleships.

I had the good fortune to win the 'Best Book of the Sea' prize, awarded by King George's Fund for Sailors, for 1982, the year of the Falklands War, for a work which had nothing to do with that reprise of past glory. The cheque was presented by Admiral of the Fleet Sir John (later Lord) Fieldhouse, the man who had commanded the Task Force, in full uniform. Asked by a photographer to stand chatting, the admiral turned to me and said, 'More ships; more ships; what the Navy needs is more ships; we need more ships . . . ' and so on. Before I could summon assistance, he explained that this was his message on all public occasions, and since standing on a chipboard island in an indoor 'lake' a few inches deep at the Boat Show in London's Earls Court could hardly be more public, he would stick to this principle: 'More ships, more ships . . . ' Sad to say he died at sixty-four, shortly after his retirement from the post of Chief of Defence Staff.

In his day, at least until 1982, the Navy seemed to have a split personality, with a dwindling collection of rusting and worn-out surface ships (the classic example being *Fearless*, the greatest exception the 'Invincibles') sailing over an expanding fleet of nuclear-powered submarines, the new capital vessels. But the true heir and successor of the battleship was the nuclear submarine armed with sixteen nuclear-tipped ballistic missiles, capable of hitting a corner shop at 5,000 miles without coming to the surface. The Navy's acquisition of the nuclear deterrent in 1969 put an end to more than half a century of counter-productive 'competition' from the RAF, whose separate existence from 1918, combined with the Treasury's demands for savings, crippled naval aviation. This left the fleet severely exposed to air attack and, until 1943, without the airborne support that was the key to the final defeat of the U-boats. When the Falklands crisis erupted the Royal Navy was down to two carriers, the one very old, the other very small, both up for sale. The War of Mrs Thatcher's Face would not have been won but for the sheer professionalism of a handful of naval pilots, and their RAF colleagues, enabling the Task Force narrowly to wrest air supremacy from Argentina's deadly airmen.

The history of the Royal Navy in the twentieth century is full of ironies. Twice within thirty years a majestic fleet built round battleships was almost reduced to impotence by small submersible torpedo boats, which necessitated the deployment of many hundreds of escorts while the battleships seldom got within range of the enemy. The submarine, introduced at the very beginning of the century, to widespread disparagement from 'regular' sailors, dominated naval thinking and expenditure at its end. Britain's surface fleet was on the verge of becoming a small, localized anti-submarine force in 1982 when the tocsin sounded in the south Atlantic. But from then on, even as the cuts continued, it gradually became a versatile fleet again, preserving its ability to go anywhere on the seven seas until a New Labour government promised it two carriers for a new millennium – thirty-two years after an old Labour government announced the end of carrier construction in Britain.

Throughout the century hope seemed to triumph over experience as British shipwrights and naval officers, scientists and engineers, technicians and inventors produced a stream of new ideas in war and peace that somehow kept the Royal Navy in the forefront of technological progress and often in the lead, even in the straitened circumstances of the postwar years. This was still going on as the century drew to a close. Two British firms unveiled designs for 'stealth' surface warships at a Paris exhibition in 1996, applying the American radar-invisibility technology of the stealth aircraft to the much larger challenge of the ship. Three firms were invited by the MoD to tender for a trial version of a revolutionary trimaran 'frigate'. Vosper Thornycroft of Southampton won the £13m contract to build a reduced-scale experimental vessel in 1998, a development of much interest to the US Navy and other allies. RV *Triton* was to be ninety metres long and displace 1,100 tonnes; it would have diesel-electric propulsion (as would the two new carriers and two oilers for the RFA), much quieter and more environmentally friendly than the propulsion systems of earlier vessels. If successful the trials could lead to triple-hulled frigates as early as 2010. More conventionally, GEC-Marconi was awarded the British contract for supervising the production of the first 'Horizon' tri-national Type 45 anti-aircraft warfare frigates, to be produced jointly by Britain, France and Italy as replacements for AAW destroyers (the programme envisages twelve for Britain at a daunting £500m each, but not for several years; an earlier project of this nature collapsed, as we saw).

It remains to describe the composition of the Royal Navy in 2000 – the product not only of cuts and erratic defence reviews but also of centuries of tradition, of history and experience which have engendered a fleet making up in quality what it has lost in quantity, restoring the Senior Service to pride of place in the armed services.

At its head from 8 October 1998 was Admiral Sir Michael Boyce, GCB, OBE, ADC, who joined in 1961, qualifying as a submariner in 1965 and passing the 'perisher' course in 1973, whereupon he commanded two 'O'-class diesel boats and, after staff training and attachments, the nuclear fleet submarine *Superb*. A captain in 1982, he briefly commanded a frigate before taking charge of submarine sea training. He led the Armilla Patrol as a commodore and raised his rear-admiral's flag in 1991 at Portland as commander of the base and of sea training. Then he led the Surface Flotilla as Nato's Commander, Anti-Submarine Warfare Striking Force. His rapid rise continued in 1994, when he was made vice-admiral; knighted and promoted full admiral in 1995, he became Second Sea Lord and C-in-C, Naval Home Command. Two years later he rose again to C-in-C, Fleet, along with the Nato appointments of C-in-C,

Eastern Atlantic, and Commander Allied Naval Forces, North-western Europe.

Of 210,000 British men and women in military uniform, the Navy retained 44,500, the lowest figure since 1850 (39,000), including 6,000 Royal Marines. A sub-lieutenant was paid about £14,500 and a freshly appointed captain over £50,000 (more than £62,000 after six years in the rank). Able seamen received upwards of £1,000 per month, petty officers £1,600 and warrant officers £2,100. Allowances were added, inter alia, for submariners, divers and service abroad; subsistence ashore was deducted. Marines and medical assistants were on similar scales; technicians and nurses did about 10 per cent better.

The Navy had twenty-one shore establishments in Britain. Its strategic force consisted of three 'Vanguard' submarines (15,000 tons) with a fourth fitting out, each armed with sixteen Trident II D5 nuclear ballistic missiles and capable of twenty knots. There were twelve fleet or 'tactical' nuclear-powered submarines, all of at least 4,500 tons, five 'Swiftsures' and seven 'Trafalgars', armed with some of a variable range of weaponry for their five 21-inch torpedo tubes: Tomahawk cruise missiles (range 600 miles), Sub-Harpoon anti-ship missiles (seventy miles), Mark 24 Tigerfish wire-guided (ten miles) and Mark 8 anti-ship torpedoes (up to fifty mines could be carried instead of some or all of these). They could receive extra-low frequency radio messages at depths down to 330 feet, dive to 2,000 feet and travel at twenty knots surfaced or thirty-two submerged. Each boat was about 275 feet long with a beam of thirty feet and had twelve officers and eighty-five ratings. All these submarines could go round the world without surfacing. The next generation of (eventually) five 'Astutes' would displace at least 6,000 tons and their reactors would not need refuelling throughout their anticipated lifetime of up to thirty years; they were to be armed with Spearfish torpedoes and Tomahawks. The 'Vanguards' and 'Swiftsures' (First Squadron) were based at Faslane, the 'Trafalgars' (Second Squadron) at Devonport.

The three 'Invincibles' based at Portsmouth displaced 19,000 tons unladen and had a maximum speed of twenty-eight knots. Measuring 650 by 90 feet, with a flight deck of 520 feet, these vessels, originally intended as command ships for ASW but also capable of aviation command and control, carried 131 officers and 870 ratings, plus 320 in the air group. Depending on task, each ship could carry up to eight Sea Harriers and eight ASW plus 3 AEW

Sea Kings or other combinations. Heavy Chinook helicopters were also flown from them. On-board defences included Goalkeeper anti-missile guns and Sea Dart for anti-aircraft and anti-ship defence. The helicopter carrier *Ocean* with a crew of 258 and 180 air personnel could carry twelve Sea King transport and six Lynx attack helicopters plus a Royal Marine Commando with support (800 men) at nineteen knots.

The two old '*Fearless*' assault ships based at Portsmouth displaced 12,500 tons and had crews of fifty officers and fifty ratings plus three officers and eighty-five air crew: each could carry hundreds of troops and/or armoured vehicles, four landing craft, four helicopters and a command staff for an amphibious operation at a notional twenty-one knots. Having proved themselves in the Falklands after years of neglect, they were to be replaced by larger successors at a cost of £450m by 2003; the order was placed in 1996.

All the Navy's destroyers in service in 1999 were of Type 42, the oldest being HMS *Birmingham* (1976), and all named after cities. They had two pairs of engines, both gas-turbine: 'Tyne' for speeds of up to eighteen knots (range 3,700 miles) and 'Olympus' for up to twenty-nine knots. They displaced between 4,350 and 5,350 tons, depending on age. They carried the Lynx helicopter and their main role was as area anti-aircraft defence ships for task-group operations, although they could also attack submarines by helicopter with Sea Skua missiles and surface ships with the dual-role Sea Dart. Other weapons included a 4.5-inch gun, anti-submarine torpedo tubes, Stingray torpedoes and the Phalanx close-range anti missile system. All these ships were based at Portsmouth.

Anti-submarine warfare was the prime role of ten Type 22 frigates, which had the same dual-engine propulsion as the destroyers and displaced 4,600 tons all up. Their crews were about the same size as those of destroyers – two dozen officers and about 300 ratings. Post-Falklands versatility enabled these frigates and the next generation (from 1990), the fourteen '*Duke*'-class Type 23s in service in 1999 (when two more were building), to put up stout defences against aircraft and surface attack. Weaponry included various combinations of the 4.5-inch gun, Exocets, Harpoons, Sea Dart medium-range and Sea Wolf close-range air-defence missiles, Lynx helicopters and Stingray torpedoes. Each ship towed a sonar array one third of a mile long. The '*Dukes*' could switch to diesel-electric propulsion for quiet running while hunting submarines. The frigates had a top speed of twenty-eight to thirty knots. All the escorts were assigned to six squadrons, four of frigates and two of destroyers, the latter plus one frigate squadron at Portsmouth, the other three at Devonport.

Britain's minesweeping force of twenty-five led the world and consisted of twelve '*Hunt*'-class fibreglass mine-countermeasures vessels (625 tons) and thirteen smaller single-role minehunters (378 tons). The fleet also included eight fishery and oilfield protection vessels, a squadron of four minesweepers patrolling off Northern Ireland, six survey ships, one ice-patrol ship (the replacement *Endurance*) and fourteen 44-ton patrol and training vessels.

The Fleet Air Arm consisted of three Harrier squadrons with a total of twenty-four aircraft, capable variously of reconnaissance, defence and strikes, four squadrons of Sea King ASW helicopters with forty-one aircraft distributed among various ships, two squadrons of Lynx ASW/anti-ship totalling fifty machines, and three commando air-assault squadrons with twenty-nine Sea Kings. Four further helicopter squadrons (twenty-six aircraft) fulfilled various support roles and one fixed-wing squadron of thirteen Jetstreams was used for training. Forty-four Merlin ASW helicopters were on order and coming into service in 2000, to replace Sea Kings and some Lynx.

The ever more important Royal Fleet Auxiliary included five fleet tankers, four support tankers, three fleet replenishment ships, an aviation training/hospital ship (*Argus*), one forward repair ship (*Diligence*), five landing ships (logistic) with a capacity of 3,440 tons of supplies and 400 troops, and one ro-ro general purpose freighter. The Royal Maritime Auxiliary Service, concentrated on the three main naval bases at Portsmouth, Devonport and the Clyde (Faslane), had about a hundred vessels in service – tugs, launches, recovery vessels, landing craft and salvage boats. Most of these were painted in the black and gold livery of the old wooden fleet, as worn by the official flagship of Her Majesty's Navy: HMS *Victory*, still in commission at Portsmouth as a memorial to the guiding spirit of the service for two centuries: Horatio Nelson, of 'immortal memory'.

Select Bibliography

AGAWA, Hiroyuki: *The Reluctant Admiral: Yamamoto and the Imperial Navy* (Kodansha International, Tokyo, 1979)

BARNETT, Correlli: *Engage the Enemy More Closely: the Royal Navy in the Second World War* (Hodder & Stoughton, London, 1991)

BEASLEY, W. G: *The Modern History of Japan* (Weidenfeld & Nicholson, London, 3rd edn, 1981)

BEESLY, Patrick: *Room 40 – British Naval Intelligence 1914–18* (Hamish Hamilton, London, 1982)

—— *Very Special Intelligence – the Story of the Admiralty's Operational Intelligence Centre 1939–1945* (Hamish Hamilton, London, 1977)

BEHR, Edward: *Hirohito: Behind the Myth* (Villard Books, New York, 1989)

BENNETT, Geoffrey: *Coronel and the Falkland Islands* (Batsford, London, 1962)

BÖDDEKER, Günter: *Die Boote im Netz* (Bastei-Lubbe, Bergisch-Gladbach, 1983)

BREEMER, Jan: *Soviet Submarines: Design, Development and Tactics* (Jane's Information Group, Coulsdon, Surrey, 1989)

BROGAN, Patrick: *World Conflicts* (3rd edn, Bloomsbury, London, 1998)

BROWN, David: *The Royal Navy and the Falklands War* (Leo Cooper, London, 1987)

CALVOCORESSI, Peter: *World Politics since 1945* (6th edn, Longman, London, 1993)

—— and WINT, Guy and PRITCHARD, John: *Total War: the Causes and Courses of the Second World War* (revised edn, Viking, London, 1989)

CHALMERS, Rear-Admiral W. S: *Full Cycle: the Biography of Admiral Sir Bertram Ramsay* (Hodder & Stoughton, London, 1959)

CHILDERS, Erskine: *The Riddle of the Sands* (Smith Elder, London, 1903)

COMPTON-HALL, Richard: *Submarines and the War at Sea 1914–18* (Macmillan, London, 1991)

CORBETT, Julian: *History of the Great War: Naval Operations* (5 vols, Longman, London, 1920–1931)

COSTELLO, John: *The Pacific War* (Collins, London, 1981)

CRANE, Jonathan: *Submarine* (BBC, London, 1983)

DIXON, Norman F: *On the Psychology of Military Incompetence* (Jonathan Cape, London, 1976)

DÖNITZ, Gr-Adm Karl: *10 Jahre und 20 Tage* (Athenäum, Bonn, 1958)

ELLIS, John: *Brute Force: Allied Strategy and Tactics in the Second World War* (André Deutsch, London, 1990)

FITZSIMONS, Bernard (ed.): *Warships and Sea Battles of World War I* (Phoebus, London, 1973)

FORESTER, C. S: *Hunting the Bismarck* (Panther, London, 1963)

FRIEDMAN, Norman: *Submarine Design and Development* (Conway Maritime Press, London, 1984)

GARDINER, Robert (ed.): *Navies in the Nuclear Age: Warships since 1945* (Conway Maritime Press, London, 1993)

GILBERT, Martin: *First World War Atlas* (Weidenfeld & Nicholson, London, 1970)

—— *First World War* (Weidenfeld & Nicolson, London, 1994)

GLENTON, Bill: *Mutiny in Force X* (Hodder & Stoughton, London, 1986)

GRAY, Edwyn: *Few Survived – a Comprehensive Survey of Submarine Accidents and Disasters* (Leo Cooper/Secker & Warburg, London, 1986)

GRAY, Randal and ARGYLE, Christopher: *Chronicle of the First World War* (2 vols, Facts on File Ltd, Oxford, 1990–91)

HACKMANN, Willem: *Seek and Strike: Sonar, Anti-Submarine Warfare and the Royal Navy, 1914–54* (HMSO, London, 1984)

HALPERN, Paul G: *The Royal Navy in the Mediterranean 1915–1918* (Navy Records Society, London, 1987)

HASTINGS, Max, and JENKINS, Simon: *The Battle for the Falklands* (Michael Joseph, London, 1983)

HERRICK, Robert Waring: *Soviet Naval Theory and Policy: Gorschkov's Inheritance* (US Naval Institute Press, Annapolis, MD, 1988)

HESSLER, Günter: *The U-boat War in the Atlantic 1939–1945* (HMSO, London, 1989)

HILL, J. R. and RANFT, Bryan (edd.): *The Oxford Illustrated History of the Royal Navy* (Oxford University Press, Oxford, 1995)

HILL-NORTON, Adm of the Flt Lord, and DEKKER, John: *Sea Power* (Faber and Faber, London, 1982)

HINSLEY, F. H et al.: *British Intelligence in the Second World War* (3/4 vols, HMSO, 1979–1983)

HOUGH, Richard: *The Great War at Sea 1914–1918* (Oxford University Press, Oxford, 1983)

—— *The Longest Battle: the War at Sea 1939–45* (Weidenfeld & Nicholson, London, 1986)

HOWARTH, Stephen (ed.): *Men of War – Great Naval Leaders of World War II* (Weidenfeld & Nicholson, London, 1992)

HUGHES, Terry, and COSTELLO, John: *The Battle of the Atlantic* (Collins, London, 1977)

HUMBLE, Richard: *The Rise and Fall of the British Navy* (Queen Anne Press, London, 1986)

JANE'S *Fighting Ships* (London, various editions, especially *World War I, 1919*, and *World War II, 1946–7*)

JONES, Tristan: *Heart of Oak* (Triad Grafton, London, 1986)

KEEGAN, John: *The Price of Admiralty* (Hutchinson, London, 1988)

—— *The First World War* (Hutchinson, London, 1998)

—— (ed.): *The Times Atlas of the Second World War* (Times Books, London, 1989)

KEMP, Peter: *The Oxford Companion to Ships and the Sea* (Oxford University Press, Oxford, 1988)

KENNEDY, Ludovic: *The Life and Death of the Tirpitz* (Sidgwick & Jackson, London, 1979)

KENNEDY, Paul: *The Rise and Fall of the Great Powers* (Unwin Hyman, London, 1988)

KERR, J. Lennox (ed.): *Touching the Adventures of Merchantmen in the Second World War* (Harrap, London, 1953)

KIMBALL, Warren F. (ed.): *Churchill and Roosevelt: the Complete Correspondence* (3 vols, Princeton University Press, 1984)

LENTON, H. T. and COLLEDGE, J. J: *Warships of World War II* (Ian Allan, London, 2nd edn, 1973)

LEWIN, Ronald: *Ultra Goes to War* (Hutchinson, London, 1978)

LIDDELL HART, B. H: *History of the First World War* (Cassell, London, 1970)

—— *History of the Second World War* (Cassell, London, 1970)

LLOYD GEORGE, David: *War Memoirs*, Vol III (Ivor Nicolson and Watson, London, 1933)

LOVE, Robert W. and MAJOR, John (eds.): *The Year of D-Day – the 1944 Diary of Admiral Sir Bertram Ramsay* (University of Hull Press, 1994)

LUMBY, E. W. R. (ed.): *Policy and Operations in the Mediterranean 1912–1914* (Navy Records Society, London, 1970)

MACINTYRE, Donald: *Jutland* (Evans Brothers, London, 1957)

—— *The Battle of the Atlantic* (Pan, London, 1983)

MARDER, A. J: *From the Dreadnought to Scapa Flow: the Royal Navy in the Fisher Era* (5 vols, Oxford University Press, Oxford, 1961–1970)

—— and JACOBSEN, Mark, and HORSFIELD, John: *Old Friends, New Enemies: the Royal Navy and the Imperial Japanese Navy*, vol. II, *The Pacific War 1942–1945* (Oxford University Press, Oxford, 1990)

MASSIE, Robert K: *Dreadnought* (Jonathan Cape, London, 1991)

MERCER, Derek (ed.): *Chronicle of the Second World War* (Longman, London, 1990)

—— *Chronicle of the Twentieth Century* (Doring Kindersley, London, 1995, plus annual additions)

MIDDLEBROOK, Martin: *The Battle for Convoys SC 122 and HX 229* (Penguin, London, 1978)

—— and MAHONEY, Patrick: *Battleship: the Loss of the Prince of Wales and the Repulse* (Allen Lane, London, 1977)

MILLER, David: *Modern Sub-Hunters* (Salamander Books, London, 1992)

—— *Submarines of the World* (Salamander Books, London, 1991)

MILNER, Marc: *North Atlantic Run* (University of Toronto, 1985)

MONSARRAT, Nicholas: *The Cruel Sea* (Penguin, London, 1956)

—— *Three Corvettes* (Cassell, London, 1945)

MORISON, R-Adm Samuel Eliot: *History of the US Naval Operations in World War II* (Little, Brown, Boston (MA), 10 vols, 1947–1956)

PADFIELD, Peter: *The Battleship Era* (Rupert Hart-Davis, London, 1972)

PAINE, Lincoln: *Ships of the World: an Historical Encyclopedia* (Conway Maritime Press, London, 1998)

POTTER, John Deane: *Fiasco: the Breakout of the German Battleships* (Heinemann, London, 1970)

PRESTON, Anthony (ed.): *History of the Royal Navy in the 20th Century* (Bison/Hamlyn, London, 1987)

RAYNER, Cdr D. A: *Escort: the Battle of the Atlantic* (William Kimber, London, 1955)

ROBERTSON, Terence: *Night Raider of the Atlantic* (Evans Brothers, London, 1981)

ROHWER, Jürgen: *Axis Submarine Successes 1939–1945* (Patrick Stephens, Cambridge, 1983)

—— *The Critical Convoy Battles of March 1943* (Ian Allan, London, 1977)

—— and HUMMELCHEN, Gerhard: *Chronology of the War at Sea 1939–1945* (revised edn, Greenhill Books, London, 1992)

—— and JÄCKEL, Eberhard (eds.): *Die Funkaufklärung und ihre Rolle im 2. Weltkrieg* (symposium; Motorbuch Verlag, Stuttgart, 1979)

ROSKILL, Capt. S. W: *The War at Sea 1939–1945* (3/4 vols, HMSO, London, 1954–1961)

—— *Naval Policy between the Wars* (2 vols, Collins, London, 1968)

—— *The Secret Capture* (Collins, London, 1959)

ROWLAND, Peter: *Lloyd George* (Barrie and Jenkins, London, 1975)

RYDER, A. J: *Twentieth-Century Germany: from Bismarck to Brandt* (Macmillan, London, 1973)

SCHOFIELD, V-Adm B. B: *The Russian Convoys* (Pan, London, 1984)

SERVICE HISTORIQUE de la marine: *Les marines de guerre du dreadnought au nucléaire* (symposium; Vincennes, 1990)

SHIRER, William L: *The Rise and Fall of the Third Reich* (Secker & Warburg, London, 1960)

SPECTOR, Ronald H: *Eagle Against the Sun: The American War with Japan* (Free Press/Macmillan, New York, 1984)

TAYLOR, A. J. P: *English History 1914–1945* (Oxford University Press, Oxford, 1976)

—— *The Origins of the Second World War* (Penguin, London, 1964)

TERRAINE, John: *Business in Great Waters: the U-Boat Wars 1916–1945* (Leo Cooper, London, 1989)

THOMAS, Hugh: *The Suez Affair* (Pelican, London, 1970)

THORNE, Christopher: *Allies of a Kind: the United States, Britain and the War Against Japan* (Hamish Hamilton, London, 1978)

TREVOR-ROPER, H. R. (ed.): *Hitler's War Directives* (Pan, London, 1976)

TUCHMAN, Barbara W.: *August 1914* (Macmillan, London, 1980)

VAN DER VAT, Dan: *The Grand Scuttle: the Sinking of the German Fleet at Scapa Flow in 1919* (Hodder & Stoughton, London, 1982)

—— *The Ship that Changed the World: the Escape of the Goeben to the Dardanelles in 1914* (Hodder & Stoughton, London, 1985)

—— *The Atlantic Campaign: The Great Struggle at Sea 1939–1945* (Hodder & Stoughton, London, 1988)

—— *The Pacific Campaign: the US–Japanese Naval War 1941–1945* (Hodder & Stoughton, London, 1991)

—— *Stealth at Sea: the History of the Submarine* (Weidenfeld & Nicholson, London, 1994)

WALTON, Francis: *Miracle of World War II: How American Industry Made Victory Possible* (Macmillan, New York, 1956)

WELLS, Captain John: *The Royal Navy – an Illustrated Social History 1870–1982* (Sutton, Stroud/Royal Naval Museum, Portsmouth, 1994)

WETTERN, Desmond: *The Decline of British Seapower* (Jane's, London, 1982)

WINTON, John: *Convoy* (Michael Joseph, 1983)

—— *The Death of the Scharnhorst* (Panther, London, 1984)

WOODWARD, E. L: *Great Britain and the German Navy* (Frank Cass & Co, London, 1964)

WOODWARD, R-Adm Sandy, and ROBINSON, Patrick: *One Hundred Days* (HarperCollins, London, 1992)

Maps

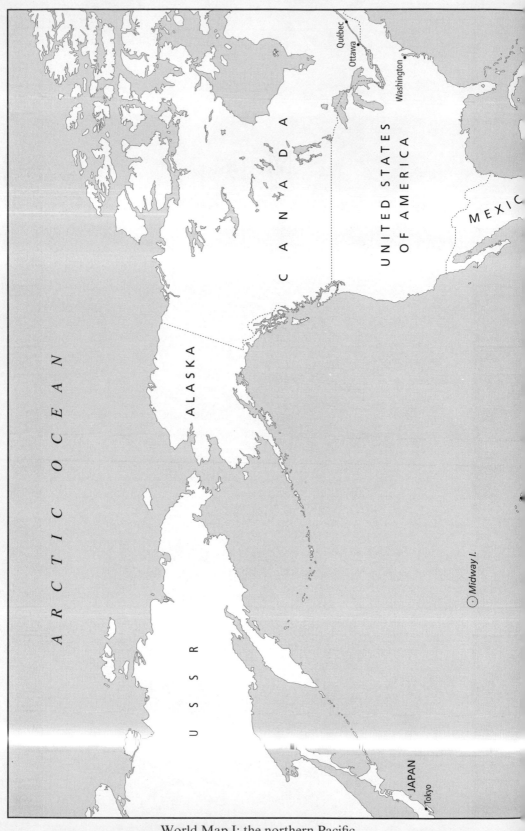

World Map I: the northern Pacific

World Map II: the southern Pacific

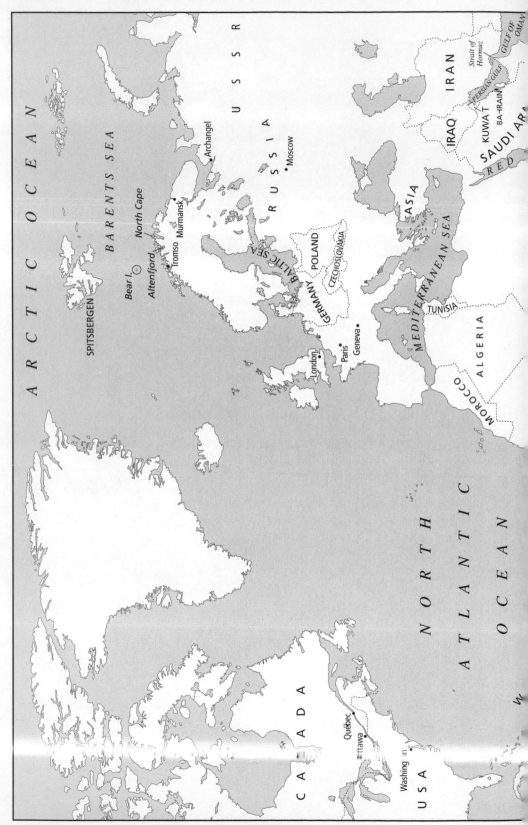

World Map III: The Arctic and north Atlantic

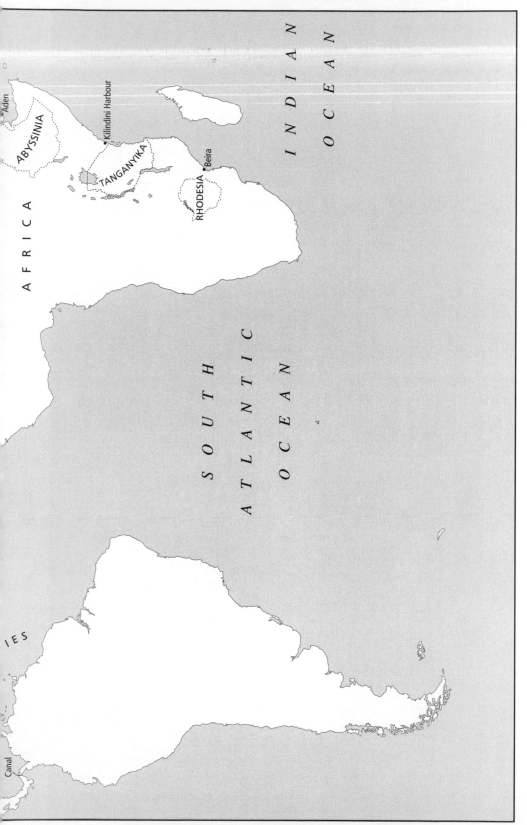

World Map IV: the south Atlantic and east Africa

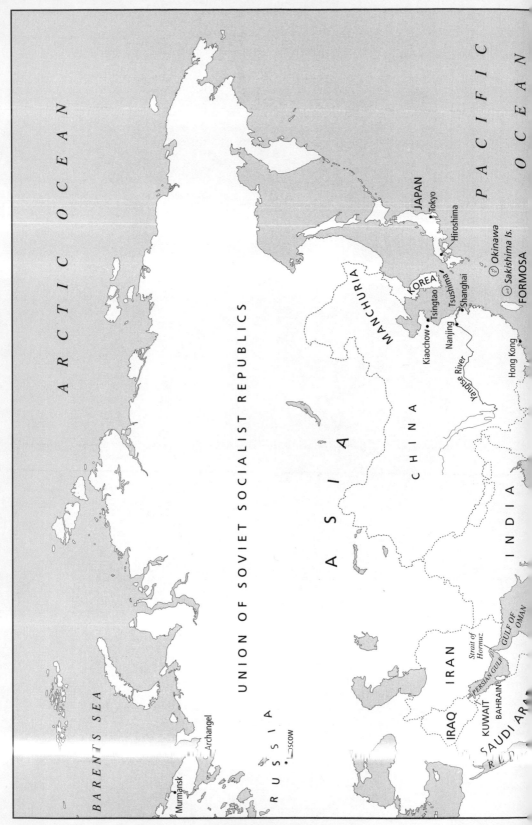

World Map V: Asia

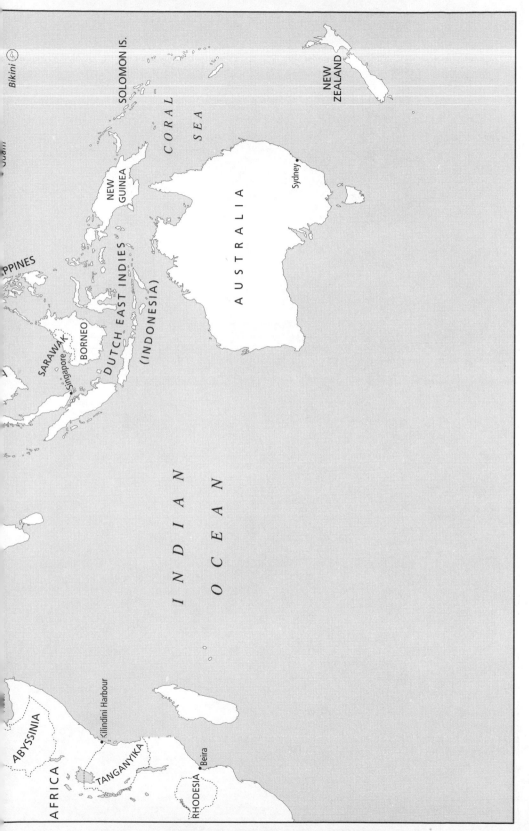

World Map VI: The Indian Ocean

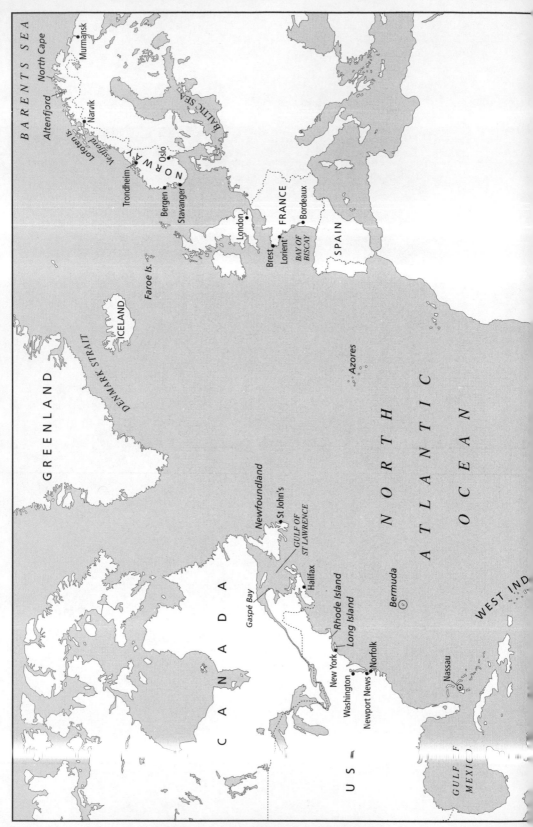

The all-important North Atlantic Theatre

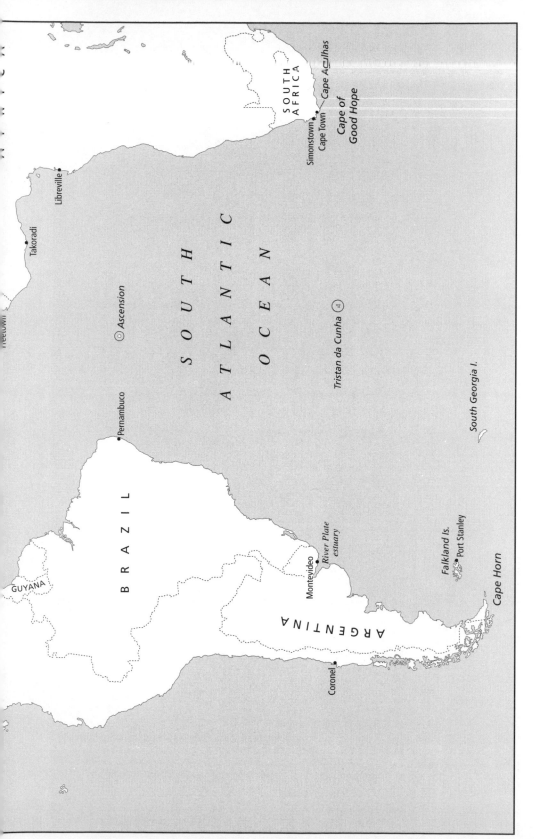

The south Atlantic

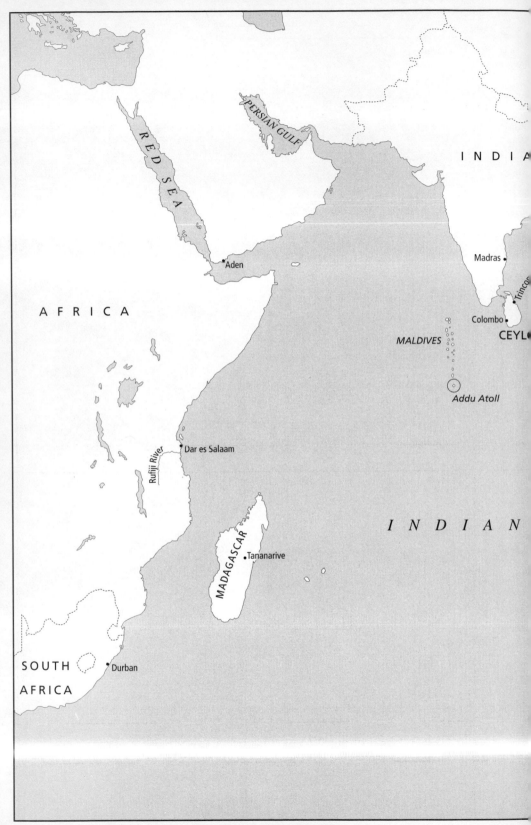

The western Indian Ocean

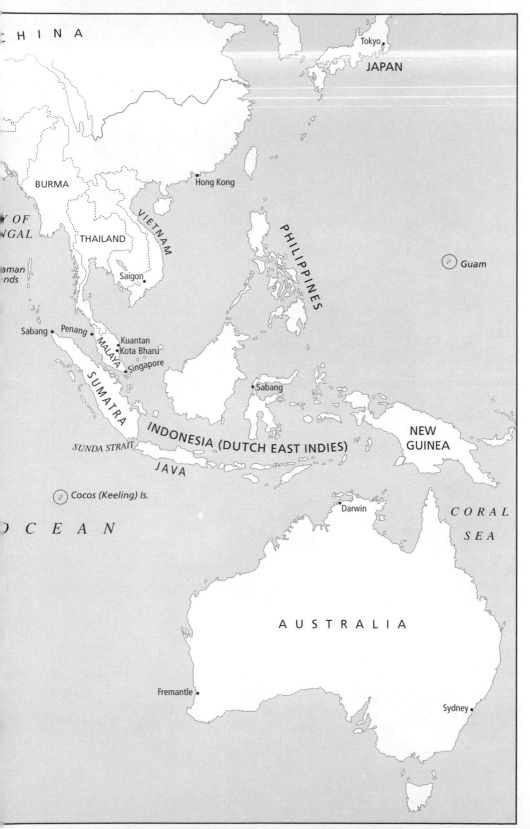

The eastern Indian Ocean and South-West Pacific

The British Isles and British Home Waters

The eastern North Sea and western Baltic

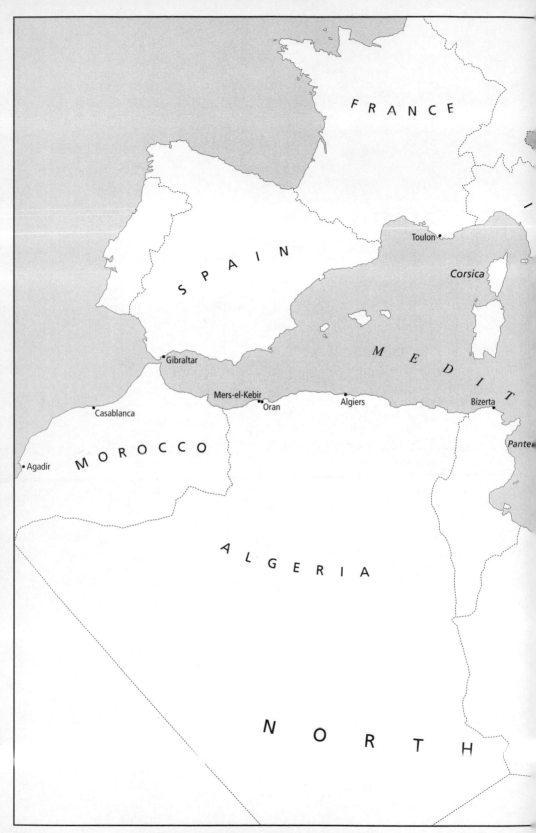

The western Mediterranean and north Africa

The eastern Mediterranean, Balkans and north Africa

Index